Innovation and Entrepreneurship

Second Edition

John Bessant and Joe Tidd

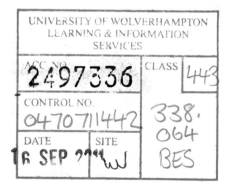

John Wiley & Sons, Ltd

This edition first published 2011
© 2011 John Bessant and Joe Tidd
Published in 2011 by John Wiley & Sons Ltd

Last edition published in 2007
© 2007 John Bessant and Joe Tidd
Published in 2007 by John Wiley & Sons Ltd

Registered office
John Wiley & Sons Ltd, The Atrium, Southern Gate, Chichester, West Sussex, PO19 8SQ, United Kingdom

For details of our global editorial offices, for customer services and for information about how to apply for permission to reuse the copyright material in this book please see our website at www.wiley.com.

Library of Congress Cataloging-in-Publication Data

Bessant, J. R.
 Innovation and entrepreneurship / John Bessant and Joe Tidd. — 2nd ed.
     p. cm.
   Includes bibliographical references and index.
  ISBN 978-0-470-71144-6 (pbk.)
 1. Creative ability in business. 2. Entrepreneurship. I. Tidd, Joseph, 1960- II. Title.
  HD53.B476 2011
  658.4'21—dc22

                                                    2010054182

A catalogue record for this book is available from the British Library.

Set in 10/12 Sabon by Thomson Digital, India
Printed in Italy by Printer Trento

Bessant and Tidd's *Innovation and Entrepreneurship* 2nd Edition is an ideal undergraduate textbook. It successfully synthesises relevant frameworks from previously segmented fields of inquiry and presents them within a practical and logical process model which is packed with illustrative material and useful aids to learning.

John Storey, Professor of Management, The Open
University Business School

This is a comprehensive and authoritative text prepared by an authoritative team—professors John Bessant and Joe Tidd. They both have an excellent grounding and credible presence in innovation studies and have been at the forefront of research in the field for many years.

The text is an extremely timely melding of insights about innovation and about entrepreneurship. Around the world today it is being increasingly recognised that innovation—the commercial exploitation of new ideas—is a crucial driver for improving economic and social wellbeing across both public and private sectors. At the same time, recognition is also growing that effective and successful innovation requires the ingenious involvement of individuals with the energy and commitment to build appropriate organisational arrangements to deliver the potential of innovation. This text explains and illustrates in a very accessible manner just how this can be done. It will prove to be an extremely effective anchor text for any undergraduate courses in the area, and indeed is worthwhile reading for researchers and practitioners who would like authoritative confirmation that what they are doing makes sense.

Professor James Fleck, Dean of the Open University Business
School and Professor of innovation Dynamics

Innovation and Entrepreneurship is positioned well for the undergraduate level and also draws in new key areas such as innovation systems and socio-technical aspects of innovation. Students can be shown that innovation is not just about technology development. The provision of integrated modern examples for illustrative and case study use is also helpful.

Dr Paul Harborne, Senior Research Fellow,
Cass Business School, UK

An excellent primer in entrepreneurial innovation. From principles to application, this book aggregates best practices for practical application; building a solid foundation from their own vast expertise, Bessant and Tidd educate the reader with action oriented, practical approaches to bringing innovation and entrepreneurship together in the real world.

Charlie Nagel Schmidt, Associate Professor, Business
and Graduate Faculty, Champlain College, USA

This book is very well balanced, with chapters on both manufacturing and service sectors. The chapters on sustainability and economic development are timely. Most books on innovation are excessively concerned with the 'how' of innovation. There is always a need to provoke thought on the 'why?' – what economic, social and environmental goals does innovation serve?

Ken Green, Professor of Environmental Innovation
Management, Manchester Business School, UK

The inclusion of chapters on entrepreneurship and individual innovation fills an important gap in the market for undergraduate textbooks that combine theories of innovation management. It also differentiates from other textbooks by adding contemporary issues on innovation as sustainability and a greater focus on service innovation.

Dr Dolores Anon Higon, Lecturer in Economics,
Aston Business School, UK

Contents

Preface   xi

Acknowledgements   xiv

Part I Entrepreneurial Goals and Context   **1**
Chapter 1   **The Innovation Imperative**   3

Innovation Matters   4
Innovation and Entrepreneurship   10
Innovation Isn't Easy!   12
Managing Innovation and Entrepreneurship   15
What Do We Know about Managing Innovation and Entrepreneurship?   17
Understanding the Innovation Process   19
What Has to be Managed?   23
A Model for Innovation and Entrepreneurship   24
What, Why and When – The Challenge of Innovation Strategy   30
Chapter Summary   38
Key Terms Defined   40
Further Reading and Resources   40
References   42
Discussion Questions   42
Team Exercises   43
Assignment Questions   44
Reflection Questions/Assignments Linked to the Case   49
Summary of Web Resources   51

Chapter 2   **Social Entrepreneurship and Innovation**   53

Thinking about Innovation   54
Uncommon Heroes   58
The Challenge of Social Entrepreneurship   59
Big Can be Beautiful Too   60
The Potential of the 'Bottom of the Pyramid'   65
Challenges in Managing Social Entrepreneurship and Innovation   68
Chapter Summary   73
Key Terms Defined   73

Further Reading and Resources   74
References   74
Discussion Questions   75
Team Exercise   75
Assignment Question   75
Summary of Web Resources   82

Chapter 3   Globalisation, Development and Sustainability   83

Globalisation and Development   84
Globalisation of Innovation   84
National Systems of Innovation   94
Building Capabilities and Creating Value   107
Limits of the Core Competence Approach   110
New Socio-technical Systems   125
Open Systems of Innovation   130
Chapter Summary   136
Discussion Questions   136
Team Exercise   137
Assignment   137
Key Terms Defined   137
Further Reading and Resources   138
References   139
Team Exercise: Identifying Capabilities   150
Summary of Web Resources   151

Part II   Recognising the Opportunity   153

Chapter 4   Individual and Organisational Characteristics   155

Linking Creativity, Entrepreneurship
   and Innovation   156
Personality: Promoting Individual Creativity   158
Processes: Strategies and Stages of Creativity   164
Environment: Creating a Climate for Innovation   172
Developing Personal Capabilities   187
Chapter Summary   191
Discussion Questions   191
Team Exercise: Brainstorming and Spider Diagrams   191
Assignment   193
Key Terms Defined   193
Further Reading and Resources   194
References   194
Summary of Web Resources   201

Chapter 5	**Sources of Innovation**	**203**
	Introduction	204
	Where Do Innovations Come From?	204
	A Framework for Looking at Innovation Sources	231
	How to Search	234
	Chapter Summary	237
	Key Terms Defined	237
	Discussion Questions	238
	Team Exercises	239
	Further Reading and Resources	239
	References	240
	Reflection Questions/Assignments Linked to the Case	244
	Summary of Web Resources	245
Chapter 6	**Searching for Opportunities**	**247**
	The Innovation Treasure Hunt	248
	A Map of Innovation Search Space	252
	Innovation Search Strategies	253
	Implementing Search Strategies	264
	Tools, Structures and Mechanisms to Enable Search	269
	Searching the Innovation Space	283
	Absorptive Capacity – Developing the Capability to Search and Use Knowledge	284
	Chapter Summary	286
	Key Terms Defined	286
	Further Reading and Resources	289
	References	290
	Discussion Questions	290
	Team Exercises	291
	Summary of Web Resources	296
Part III	**Finding the Resources**	**297**
Chapter 7	**Building the Case**	**299**
	Developing the Business Plan	300
	Forecasting Innovation	306
	Assessing Risk, Recognising Uncertainty	315
	Anticipating the Resources	320
	Chapter Summary	326
	Discussion Questions	326
	Key Terms Defined	326
	Further Reading and Resources	327

References 328
Summary of Web Resources 336

Chapter 8 **Exploiting Networks** 337
No Man is an Island . . . 338
The Spaghetti Model of Innovation 340
Types of Innovation Networks 341
Networks at the Start-Up 346
Networks on the Inside . . . 347
Networks on the Outside 348
Using Networks to Help Learning 352
Using Networks for Exploration 354
Making Networks Happen – Networks by Design 356
Learning to Manage Innovation Networks 358
Chapter Summary 360
Key Terms Defined 360
Further Reading and Resources 361
References 361
Discussion Questions 362
Team Exercises 362
Assignment Questions 362
Summary of Web Resources 367

Part IV **Developing the Venture** 369

Chapter 9 **Developing New Products and Services** 371
Service versus Product Development 372
Products and Service Development Strategies: Success Factors 377
Organisation for Development and Delivery of New Products
and Services 385
Processes for New Product and Service Development 390
Tools and Technology to Support Service Innovation 393
Chapter Summary 403
Discussion Questions 403
Team Exercise 404
Assignment 404
Key Terms Defined 405
Further Reading and Resources 405
References 406
Summary of Web Resources 412

Chapter 10 Creating New Ventures   **413**

   Types of New Venture   414
   Context for Entrepreneurship   419
   Process and Stages for Creating a New Venture   429
   Assessing the Opportunity   430
   Developing the Business Plan   433
   Acquiring the Resources and Funding   434
   Harvesting the Venture: Growth and Exit
      Strategies   442
   Developing Personal Capabilities   447
   Chapter Summary   450
   Discussion Questions   450
   Team Exercise   450
   Assignment   451
   Key Terms Defined   451
   Further Reading and Resources   452
   References   453
   Summary of Web Resources   458

Part V   Creating Value   **459**

Chapter 11 Exploiting Knowledge and Intellectual Property   **461**

   Generating and Acquiring Knowledge   462
   Identifying and Codifying Knowledge   464
   Storing and Retrieving Knowledge   468
   Sharing and Distributing Knowledge   470
   Translating Knowledge into Innovation   475
   Exploiting Intellectual Property   481
   Copyright   486
   Design Rights   486
   Licensing IPR   488
   Chapter Summary   496
   Discussion Questions   496
   Team Exercise   497
   Assignment   497
   Key Terms Defined   497
   Further Reading and Resources   498
   References   499
   Summary of Web Resources   502

Chapter 12 Creating Value and Growing Ventures 503

Creating Economic and Social Value 504
Innovation and Firm Performance 507
Choosing a Business Model 511
Growing the Venture 519
Chapter Summary 527
Discussion Questions 527
Key Terms Defined 527
Further Reading and Resources 528
References 529
Summary of Web Resources 538

Chapter 13 Learning to Manage Innovation 539

Introduction 540
Entrepreneurship as the Engine for Innovation 541
Making Innovation Happen 542
Recognising the Opportunity 544
Finding the Resources 546
Developing the Venture 548
Innovation Strategy – Having a Clear Sense of Direction 551
Building an Innovative Organisation 554
Networking for Innovation 557
Learning to Manage Innovation 558
Innovation Auditing in Practice 559
Managing Innovation and Entrepreneurship 561
Chapter Summary 562
Key Terms Defined 563
Further Reading and Resources 564
Discussion Questions 565
Team Exercise 565
Assignment Questions 565
Summary of Web Resources 571

Index 573

Preface

This book has been developed specifically for undergraduate students of Business and Management Studies, and Science and Engineering students studying courses on these subjects. It is designed to complement our best-selling text *Managing Innovation: Integrating technological, market and organizational change* (Wiley, fourth edition, 2009), which is focused more on the needs of post-graduate and post-experience audiences.

In this second edition we were inspired by the pioneering scholars of entrepreneurship and innovation, such as Joseph Schumpeter and Peter Drucker, to attempt to re-integrate these two fields. For too long the two subjects have diverged into narrow disciplines, each suffering as a result: entrepreneurship has become preoccupied with small business creation, and innovation dominated by new product development. In this text we aim to re-unite the study and practice of entrepreneurship and innovation.

There are a few good existing texts on innovation management, and many more on entrepreneurship in various guises. However, most texts tend to be too theoretical, whereas innovation and entrepreneurship are inherently about management practice and creating change. Much of this theory of innovation has been derived from studies of large manufacturing firms in developed economies, and is very much concerned with the successful development of products, whereas theories of entrepreneurship focus too much on small business creation, rather than the broader issue of creating new ventures and managing change in the corporate, public and third sectors. Moreover, too much emphasis is typically placed on the (important) roles of national systems and institutions, which are difficult for managers to influence in any significant way.

We believe that this text is unique in two significant respects. Firstly, how it treats and applies the key theories and research on innovation and entrepreneurship. Secondly, the pedagogy and approach to learning. In this text we review and synthesise the theory and research, where relevant, but put far greater emphasis on the practice of innovation and entrepreneurship applied in a much broader context, including the corporate and public services, emerging technologies and economies, and for sustainability and development. In this second edition we have adopted a more explicit process model to help organise the material:

- Entrepreneurial Goals and Context
- Recognising the Opportunity
- Finding the Resources
- Developing the Venture
- Creating Value

In the first section, Entrepreneurial Goals and Context, we review the key theories and recent research relevant to understanding the dynamics and practice of innovation and entrepreneurship. In the first chapter we begin with mapping out different definitions and types of innovation, and identify the relationships between innovation, entrepreneurship and the performance of organisations in the private and public sectors. We develop a process for innovation and entrepreneurship that consists of four phases: Recognising the Opportunity; Finding the Resources; Developing the Venture; and Creating Value. In Chapter Two we explore the context and goals of social entrepreneurship and innovation, including public organisations and other third-sector bodies such as non-governmental organisations (NGOs) which includes charities and the voluntary sectors. In many advanced economies the service sector, broadly defined, accounts for 60–75% of employment, and more than half of this is in public and third-sector services. Chapter Three examines the contributions of innovation and entrepreneurship in emerging and developing economies, and for sustainability in the more advanced nations.

The rest of the text is organised by the process model. Part II, Recognising the Opportunity, includes chapters on the sources of and searching for opportunities, with a focus on the respective roles of individuals, groups and organisations in innovation and entrepreneurship, and identifies the key characteristics of creative people, and the factors which contribute to an innovative organisation, including trust, challenge, support, conflict and debate, risk-taking and freedom. In Finding the Resources we discuss how to develop a business plan and how to use this to identify and manage uncertainty, and the critical contributions of personal and organisational networks. Developing the Venture focuses on how to develop new, innovative products, services and businesses, including corporate entrepreneurship and ventures. Finally, in Part V, Creating Value, we identify paths to create and capture value, in the broadest sense. This includes creating and sharing knowledge and intellectual property, novel business models and factors which influence the success and growth of new ventures. The final chapter reviews the steps and resources necessary to make innovation and entrepreneurship happen and provides an action plan for translating ideas into practice.

Throughout the book, the pedagogy and approach to learning we adopt is a combination of the tried and tested and the more novel. Like any good text, each chapter includes clear learning objectives, key terms, a guide to further resources and individual reflective questions and suggested group assignments. However, in addition to these, each chapter has four key elements:

- *Exploring Innovation in Action* – contemporary anchor case studies.
- *Developing Personal Capabilities* – to help students reflect and develop skills.
- *Advice for Entrepreneurs* – practical implications and advice.
- *Strategic and Social Impact* – broader strategic and social relevance.

The text is also fully integrated with our interactive Web resources, available at **www.iande.info**, which feature:

- additional, full-length case studies;
- tools to support innovation and entrepreneurship;

- video and audio media;
- flash interactive exercises;
- a self-test bank of questions and answers.

We welcome your feedback and invite you to share your experiences.

John Bessant and Joe Tidd
January 2011

Acknowledgements

We would like to thank all those colleagues and students at SPRU, CENTRIM, Exeter, Imperial College, and elsewhere, who have provided feedback on our work. We are also grateful for the more formal reviews by various anonymous reviewers whose comments and suggestions helped develop this new edition.

Thanks are also due to Dave Francis, Stefan Kohn, Girish Prabhu, Richard Philpott, David Simoes-Brown, Alastair Ross, Suzana Moreira, Michael Bartl, Roy Sandbach, Lynne Maher, Helen King, Patrick McLaughlin, David Overton, Michelle Lowe, Gerard Harkin, Dorothea Seebode, John Thesmer, Tim Craft, Bettina von Stamm and Kathrin Moeslein for their help in creating case studies and podcast/video material for the text and website. Particular thanks are due to Anna Trifilova for her help in background research and assembling many of the web-based cases.

As always we're really grateful for the help and support of the extended team at Wiley, who have practised what we preach with their seamless cross-functional working, especially Steve Hardman, Deb Egleton, Mark Styles, Nicole Burnett, Sarah Booth and Peter Hudson.

PART I

ENTREPRENEURIAL GOALS AND CONTEXT

Part I Entrepreneurial Goals and Context

The national, regional and sectoral contexts can have a significant influence on the rate and direction of innovation and entrepreneurship through the availability or scarcity of resources, talent, opportunities, infrastructure and support. However, whilst context influences the rate and direction, it does not determine outcomes. The education, training, experience and aptitude of individuals also has a profound effect on the goals and outcomes of innovation and entrepreneurship.

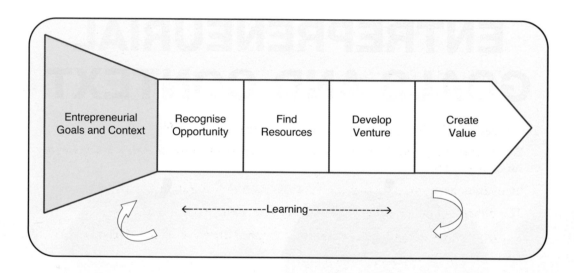

Chapter 1

The Innovation Imperative

LEARNING OBJECTIVES

By the end of this chapter you will develop an understanding of:

- What 'innovation' and 'entrepreneurship' mean – and how they are essential for survival and growth.
- Innovation as a process rather than a single flash of inspiration.
- The difficulties in managing what is an uncertain and risky process.
- The key themes in thinking about how to manage this process effectively:
  - identifying the opportunities for change;
  - finding the resources to take that idea forward;
  - developing the new idea;
  - capturing value from innovation.

Go online to find additional . . .

Cases

Tools

Media

www.iande.info

Innovation Matters

INNOVATION IN ACTION

Innovation – Everybody's Talking about It

- 'We have the strongest innovation program that I can remember in my 30-year career at P&G, and we are investing behind it to drive growth across our business,' *Bob McDonald, **Procter & Gamble's** Chairman of the Board, President and Chief Executive Officer*
- 'We believe in making a difference. Virgin stands for value for money, quality, innovation, fun and a sense of competitive challenge. We deliver a quality service by empowering our employees and we facilitate and monitor customer feedback to continually improve the customer's experience through innovation' (*Virgin website*).
- 'Adi Dassler had a clear, simple, and unwavering passion for sport. Which is why with the benefit of 50 years of relentless innovation created in his spirit, we continue to stay at the forefront of technology,' **Adidas** about its future (*www.adidas.com*).
- 'Innovation is our lifeblood,' Siemens about innovation (*www.siemens.com*).
- 'We're measuring GE's top leaders on how imaginative they are. Imaginative leaders are the ones who have the courage to fund new ideas, lead teams to discover better ideas, and lead people to take more educated risks,' *J. Immelt, Chairman & CEO, General Electric.*
- 'We are always saying to yourself . . . we have to innovate. We've got to come up with that breakthrough,' *Bill Gates, Microsoft.*
- 'Innovation distinguishes between a leader and a follower,' *Steve Jobs, Apple.*
- 'John Deere's ability to keep inventing new products that are useful to customers is still the key to the company's growth,' *Robert Lane, CEO, John Deere.*

You don't have to look far before you bump into the innovation imperative. It leaps out at you from a thousand mission statements and strategy documents, each stressing how important innovation is to 'our customers/our shareholders/our business/our future and, most often, our survival and growth'. Innovation shouts at you from advertisements for products ranging from hairspray to hospital care. It nestles deep in the heart of our history books, pointing out how far and for how long it has shaped our lives. And it is on the lips of every politician, recognising that our lifestyles are constantly shaped and reshaped by the process of innovation.

INNOVATION IN ACTION

. . . and It's a Big Issue

- OECD countries spend $700 billion/yr on R&D.   (*continued*)

- More than 16,000 firms in the USA currently operate their own industrial research labs, and there are at least 20 firms that have annual R&D budgets in excess of US$1 billion.
- In 2008 16.8% of all firms' turnover in Germany was earned with newly introduced products and in the research-intensive sector this figure was 38%. During the same year the German economy was able to save costs of 3.9% per piece by means of process innovations.

This isn't just hype or advertising babble. Innovation does make a huge difference to organisations of all shapes and sizes. The logic is simple – if we don't change what we offer the world (products and services) and how we create and deliver them, we risk being overtaken by others who do. At the limit it's about survival – and history is very clear on this point; survival is not compulsory! Those enterprises which survive do so because they are capable of regular and focused change. It's worth noting that Microsoft – currently one of the biggest and most successful companies in the world – takes the view that it is always only two years away from extinction! Or, as Andy Grove, one of the founders of Intel, points out 'only the paranoid survive!'.

INNOVATION IN ACTION

It's a Top National Priority . . .

'Companies that do not invest in innovation put their future at risk. Their business is unlikely to prosper, and they are unlikely to be able to compete if they do not seek innovative solutions to emerging problems' (Australian government website, 2006).

'Innovation is the motor of the modern economy, turning ideas and knowledge into products and services' (UK Office of Science and Technology, 2000).

In Canada, the success of many high-growth, small and medium-sized enterprises (SMEs) is significantly connected to innovation. According to Statistics Canada, the following factors characterise successful small and medium-sized enterprises:

- Innovation is consistently found to be the most important characteristic associated with success.
- Innovative enterprises typically achieve stronger growth or are more successful than those that do not innovate.
- Enterprises that gain market share and increasing profitability are those that are innovative.

(Government of Manitoba, Canada, 2006)

- '. . . our corporate strategy is designed to improve our innovative capacity and our human-capital profile', Naledi Pandor MP, Minister of Science and Technology, *Republic of South Africa*.

(continued)

- 'To promote innovation among entrepreneurs, a new golden jubilee initiative called "Technopreneur Promotion Programme (TePP)" has been initiated and implemented . . . (its) main thrust . . . is to tap the vast untapped innovative potential of the Indian innovators . . . support is provided to projects of individual innovators towards scaling up the idea/invention/know-how/designs to working models/prototypes/pilot plants' (Indian Government report).

On the plus side innovation is also strongly associated with **growth**. New business is created by new ideas, by the process of creating competitive advantage in what a firm can offer. Economists have argued for decades over the exact nature of the relationship but they are generally agreed that innovation accounts for a sizeable proportion of economic growth. In a recent book William Baumol pointed out that 'virtually all of the economic growth that has occurred since the eighteenth century is ultimately attributable to innovation'.

The survival/growth question poses a problem for established players but a huge opportunity for newcomers to rewrite the rules of the game. One person's problem is another's opportunity and the nature of innovation is that it is fundamentally about **entrepreneurship**. The skill to spot opportunities and create new ways to exploit them is at the heart of the innovation process. Entrepreneurs are risk-takers – but they calculate the costs of taking a bright idea forward against the potential gains if they succeed in doing something different – especially if that involves upstaging the players already in the game.

Of course not all games are about win/lose outcomes. Public services like healthcare, education and social security may not generate profits but they do affect the quality of life for millions of people. Bright ideas well-implemented can lead to valued new services and the efficient delivery of existing ones – at a time when pressure on national purse strings is becoming ever tighter. New ideas – whether wind-up radios in Tanzania or micro-credit financing schemes in Bangladesh – have the potential to change the quality of life and the availability of opportunity for people in some of the poorest regions of the world. There's plenty of scope for innovation and entrepreneurship – and at the limit we are talking here about real matters of life and death.

INNOVATION IN ACTION

When the Tasman Bridge collapsed in Hobart, Tasmania, in 1975, Robert Clifford was running a small ferry company and saw an opportunity to capitalise on the increased demand for ferries – and to differentiate his by selling drinks to thirsty cross-city commuters. The same entrepreneurial flair later helped him build a company – Incat – which pioneered the wave-piercing design which helped them capture over half the world market for fast catamaran ferries. Continuing investment in innovation has helped this company from a relatively isolated island build a key niche in highly competitive international military and civilian markets.

INNOVATION IN ACTION

'We always eat elephants . . .' is a surprising claim made by Carlos Broens, founder and head of a successful tool-making and precision engineering firm in Australia with an enviable growth record. Broens Industries is a small/medium-sized company of 130 employees which survives in a highly competitive world by exporting over 70% of its products and services to technologically demanding firms in aerospace, medical and other advanced markets. The quote doesn't refer to strange dietary habits but to their confidence in 'taking on the challenges normally seen as impossible for firms of our size' – a capability which is grounded in a culture of innovation in products and the processes which go to produce them.

INNOVATION IN ACTION

People have always needed artificial limbs and the demand has, sadly, significantly increased as a result of high technology weaponry such as mines. The problem is compounded by the fact that many of those requiring new limbs are also in the poorest regions of the world and unable to afford expensive prosthetics. The chance meeting of a young surgeon, Dr Pramod Karan Sethi, and a sculptor Ram Chandra in the hospital in Jaipur , India, has led to the development of a solution to this problem – the Jaipur foot. This artificial limb was developed using Chandra's skill as a sculptor and Sethi's expertise and is so effective that those who wear it can run, climb trees and pedal bicycles. It was designed to make use of low tech materials and be simple to assemble – for example, in Afghanistan craftsmen hammer the foot together out of spent artillery shells whilst in Cambodia part of the foot's rubber components are scavenged from truck tyres. Perhaps the greatest achievement has been to do all of this for a low cost – the Jaipur foot costs only $28 in India. Since 1975, nearly 1 million people worldwide have been fitted for the Jaipur limb and the design is being developed and refined – for example, using advanced new materials.

 Go online to find some case studies of public sector innovation on the website.

www.iande.info

Innovation is driven by the ability to see connections, to spot opportunities and to take advantage of them. Sometimes this is about completely new possibilities – for example, by exploiting radical breakthroughs in technology. New drugs based on genetic manipulation have opened a major new front in the war against disease. Mobile phones, iPads and other devices have revolutionised where and when we communicate. Even the humble window pane is the result of radical technological innovation – almost all the window glass in the world is made these days by the Pilkington float glass process which moved the industry away from the time consuming process of grinding and polishing to get a flat surface.

INNOVATION IN ACTION

Innovation in the Glass Industry

It's particularly important to understand that change doesn't come in standard sized jumps. For much of the time it is essentially incremental, a process of gradual improvement over time on dimensions like price, quality, choice, etc. For long periods of time nothing much shifts in either product offering or the way in which this is delivered (product and process innovation is incremental). But sooner or later someone somewhere will come up with a radical change which upsets the apple cart.

For example, the glass window business has been around for at least 600 years and is – since most houses, offices, hotels and shops have plenty of windows – a very profitable business to be in. But for most of those 600 years the basic process for making window glass hadn't changed. Glass was made in approximately flat sheets which were then ground down to a state where they were flat enough for people to see through them. The ways in which the grinding took place improved – what used to be a labour-intensive process became increasingly mechanised and even automated, and the tools and abrasives became progressively more sophisticated and effective. But underneath the same core process of grinding down to flatness was going on.

Then in 1952 Alastair Pilkington, working in the UK firm of the same name, began working on a process which revolutionised glass making for the next 50 years. He got the idea whilst washing up when he noticed that the fat and grease from the plates floated on the top of the water – and he began thinking about producing glass in such a way that it could be cast to float on the surface of some other liquid and then allowed to set. If this could be accomplished it might be possible to create a perfectly flat surface without the need for grinding and polishing.

Five years, millions of pounds and over 100,000 tonnes of scrapped glass later the company achieved a working pilot plant and a further two years on began selling glass made by the float glass process. The process advantages included around 80% labour and 50% energy savings plus those which came because of the lack of need for abrasives, grinding equipment, etc. Factories could be made smaller and the overall time to produce glass dramatically cut. So successful was the process that it became – and still is – the dominant method for making flat glass around the world.

Equally important is the ability to spot where and how new markets can be created and grown. Alexander Bell's invention of the telephone didn't lead to an overnight revolution in communications – that depended on developing the market for person-to-person communications. Henry Ford may not have invented the motor car but in making the Model T – 'a car for Everyman' at a price most people could afford – he grew the mass market for personal transportation. And eBay justifies its multi-billion dollar price tag not because of the technology behind its on-line auction idea but because it created and grew the market.

Innovation isn't just about opening up new markets – it can also offer new ways of serving established and mature ones. Low cost airlines are still about transportation – but the innovations which firms like Southwest Airlines, Easyjet and Ryanair have introduced have revolutionised air travel and grown the market in the process.

INNOVATION IN ACTION

Despite a global shift in textile and clothing manufacture towards developing countries, the Spanish company Inditex (through its retail outlets under various names including Zara) have pioneered a highly flexible, fast turnaround clothing operation with over 2000 outlets in 52 countries. It was founded by Ajaccio Ortega Goanna who set up a small operation in the west of Spain in La Coruna – a region not previously noted for textile production, and the first store opened there in 1975. Central to the Inditex philosophy is close linkage between design, manufacture and retailing and their network of stores constantly feeds back information about trends which are used to generate new designs. They also experiment with new ideas on the public directly, trying samples of cloth or design and quickly getting back indications of what is going to catch on. Despite their global orientation, most manufacturing is still done in Spain, and they have managed to reduce the turn-round time between a trigger signal for an innovation and responding to it to around 15 days. There is a more detailed description of the Zara case on the website (www.iande.info).

And it isn't just about manufactured products; plenty of examples of turnaround through innovation can be found in services. In most economies the service sector accounts for the vast majority of activity so there is likely to be plenty of scope. And the lower capital costs often mean that the opportunities for new entrants and radical change are greatest in the service sector. Online banking and insurance have become commonplace but they have radically transformed the efficiencies with which those sectors work and the range of services they can provide. New entrants riding the Internet wave have rewritten the rule book for a wide range of industrial games – for example, Amazon in retailing, eBay in market trading and auctions, Google in advertising, Skype in telephony. Others have used the Web to help them transform business models around things like low-cost airlines, online shopping and the music business.

The challenge which the Internet poses is not only one for the major banks and retail companies, although those are the stories which hit the headlines. It is also an issue – and quite possibly a survival one – for thousands of small businesses. Think about your local travel agent and the cosy way in which it used to operate. Racks full of glossy brochures through which people can browse, desks at which helpful sales assistants sort out the details of selecting and booking a holiday, procuring the tickets, arranging insurance and so on. And then think about how all of this can be accomplished at the click of a mouse from the comfort of home – and that it can be done with more choice and at lower cost.

Innovation offers huge challenges – and opportunities – for the public sector. Pressure to deliver more and better services without increasing the tax burden is a puzzle likely to keep many civil servants awake at night. But it's not an impossible dream – right across the spectrum there are examples of innovation changing the way the sector works. For example, in healthcare there have been major improvements in efficiencies around key targets such as waiting times. Hospitals like the Leicester Royal Infirmary in the UK or the Karolinska Hospital in Stockholm, Sweden, have managed to make radical improvements in the speed, quality and effectiveness of their care services – such as cutting waiting lists for elective surgery by 75% and cancellations by 80% – through innovation.

Go online to find the Karolinska Hospital case.

www.iande.info

Innovation and Entrepreneurship

Innovation matters – but it doesn't happen automatically. It is driven by **entrepreneurship** – a potent mixture of vision, passion, energy, enthusiasm, insight, judgement and plain hard work which enables good ideas to become a reality. The power behind changing products, processes and services comes from individuals – whether acting alone or embedded within organisations – who make innovation happen. As the famous management writer Peter Drucker put it:

> Innovation is the specific tool of entrepreneurs, the means by which they exploit change as an opportunity for a different business or service. It is capable of being presented as a discipline, capable of being learned, capable of being practised.
> —Peter Drucker (1985) *Innovation and Entrepreneurship*.

INNOVATION IN ACTION

One of the most significant figures in this area of economic theory was Joseph Schumpeter who wrote extensively on the subject. He had a distinguished career as an economist and served as Minister for Finance in the Austrian government. His argument was simple; entrepreneurs will seek to use technological innovation – a new product/service or a new process for making it – to get strategic advantage. For a while this may be the only example of the innovation so the entrepreneur can expect to make a lot of money – what Schumpeter calls 'monopoly profits'. But of

(continued)

course other entrepreneurs will see what he has done and try to imitate it – with the result that other innovations emerge, and the resulting 'swarm' of new ideas chips away at the monopoly profits until an equilibrium is reached. At this point the cycle repeats itself – our original entrepreneur or someone else looks for the next innovation which will rewrite the rules of the game, and off we go again. Schumpeter talks of a process of 'creative destruction' where there is a constant search to create something new which simultaneously destroys the old rules and establishes new ones – all driven by the search for new sources of profits.

In his view '[What counts is] competition from the new commodity, the new technology, the new source of supply, the new type of organization . . . competition which . . . strikes not at the margins of the profits and the outputs of the existing firms but at their foundations and their very lives.'

Entrepreneurship is a human characteristic which mixes structure with passion, planning with vision, tools with the wisdom to use them, strategy with the energy to execute it and judgement with the propensity to take risks. It's possible to create structures within organisations – departments, teams, specialist groups, etc. – with the resources and responsibility for taking innovation forward, but effective change won't happen without the 'animal spirits' of the entrepreneur.

Of course entrepreneurship plays out on different stages in practice. One obvious example is the new start-up venture in which the lone entrepreneur takes a calculated risk to bring something new into the world. But entrepreneurship matters just as much to the established organisation which needs to renew itself in what it offers and how it creates and delivers that offering. Internal entrepreneurs – often labelled as '**intrapreneurs**' or working in '**corporate entrepreneurship**' or '**corporate venture**' departments – provide the drive, energy and vision to take risky new ideas forward inside that context. And of course the passion to change things may not be around creating commercial value but rather in improving conditions or enabling change in the wider social sphere or in the direction of environmental sustainability – a field which has become known as '**social entrepreneurship**'.

Whatever the label and wherever the context, the underlying model is simple and the same – entrepreneurship drives innovation.

This idea of entrepreneurship driving innovation to create value – social and commercial – across the life cycle of organisations is central to this book. Table 1.1 gives some examples.

In the rest of the book we'll be using this lens to look at the what, why, when and how of managing innovation and entrepreneurship. We'll use three core concepts:

- '**innovation**' as a process which can be organised and managed, whether in a start-up venture or in renewing a 100-year-old business;
- '**entrepreneurship**' as the motive power to drive this process through the efforts of passionate individuals, engaged teams and focused networks;
- '**creating value**' as the purpose for innovation, whether expressed in financial terms, employment or growth, sustainability or improvement of social welfare.

TABLE 1.1   Entrepreneurship and innovation

Stage in life cycle	Start-up	Growth	Sustain/scale	Renew
Creating wealth	Individual entrepreneur exploiting new technology or market opportunity	Growing the business through adding new products/ services or moving into new markets	Building a portfolio of incremental and radical innova- tion to sustain the business and/or spread its influence into new markets	Returning to the radical frame- breaking kind of innovation which began the business and enables it to move forward as something very different
Creating social value	Social entrepreneur, passionately concerned to improve or change some- thing in their immediate environment	Developing the ideas and engaging others in a network for change – perhaps in a region or around a key issue	Spreading the idea widely, diffusing it to other communi- ties of social entrepreneurs, engaging links with mainstream players like public sector agencies	Changing the system – and then acting as agent for next wave of change

Innovation Isn't Easy!

Coming up with good ideas is what human beings are good at – we come with this facility already fitted as standard equipment in our brains! But taking those ideas forward is not quite so simple – and the evidence is clear. Most new ideas – and most entrepreneurs carrying them – fail. It takes a particular mix of energy, insight, belief and determination to push against these odds – and even more judgement to know when to stop banging against the brick wall and move on to something else!

It's very important in considering this to remember a key point – new ventures often fail, but it is the ventures rather than the people, which do. Successful entrepreneurs are very often those who have recognised that failure is an intrinsic part of the process – they learn from mis- takes, understanding where and when timing, market conditions, technological uncertainties, etc. mean that even a great idea isn't going to work. But they also recognise that the idea may have had its weaknesses, but that they have not failed themselves but rather learned some useful insights to carry over to their next venture.

Whilst the road for an individual entrepreneur may be very rocky with a high risk of hitting potholes, running into roadblocks or careering off the edge, it doesn't get any easier if you are a large established company. It's a disturbing thought but the majority of companies have a life span significantly less than that of a human being. Even the largest firms can show worrying signs of vulnerability and for the smaller firm, the mortality statistics are bleak. Sometimes it's individual firms which face the problem – sometimes it is whole sectors. We only have to consider the sad fate of European and US industries like motorcycles, machine tools, coal mining and toys, to realise how shaky the foundation of most of our industrial base really is. What goes up can come down just as fast.

Many small and medium-sized enterprises (SMEs) fail because they don't see or recognise the need for change. They are inward looking, too busy fighting fires and dealing with today's crises to worry about emerging storm clouds on the horizon. Even if they do talk to others about the wider issues it is very often to people in the same network and with the same perspectives – for example, the people who supply them with goods and services or their immediate customers. The trouble is that by the time they realise there is a need to change it may be too late.

And it isn't just a small firm problem – there is no guaranteed security in size or in previous technological success. Take the case of IBM – a giant firm which can justly claim to have laid the foundations of the IT industry and one which came to dominate the architecture of hardware and software and the ways in which computers were marketed. But such core strength can sometimes become an obstacle to seeing the need for change – as proved to be the case when, in the early 1990s, the company moved slowly to counter the threat of networking technologies – and nearly lost the business in the process. Thousands of jobs and billions of dollars were lost and it took years of hard work to bring the share price back to the high levels which investors had come to expect.

A common problem for successful companies occurs when the very things which helped them achieve success – their 'core competence' – become the things which make it hard to see or accept the need for change. Sometimes the response is what is sometimes called 'not invented here' – the new idea is recognised as good but in some way not suited to the business.

(A famous example of this was the case of Western Union who, in the nineteenth century, were probably the biggest communications company in the world. They were approached by one Alexander Graham Bell who wanted them to consider helping him commercialise his new invention. After mounting a demonstration to senior executives they received a written reply which said that '. . . *after careful consideration of your invention, which is a very interesting novelty, we have come to the conclusion that it has no commercial possibilities. . . . We see no future for an electrical toy.*' Within four years of the invention there were 50,000 telephones in the USA and within 20 years 5 million. Over the next 20 years the company which Bell formed grew to become the largest corporation in the USA.)

Sometimes the pace of change appears slow and the old responses seem to work well. It appears, to those within the industry, that they understand the rules of the game and that they have a good grasp of the relevant technological developments likely to change things. But what can sometimes happen here is that change comes along from *outside* the industry – and by the time the main players inside have reacted it is often too late.

For example, in the late nineteenth century there was a thriving industry in New England based upon the harvesting and distribution of ice. In its heyday it was possible for ice harvesters to ship hundreds of tons of ice around the world on voyages that lasted as long as six months – and still have over half the cargo available for sale. By the late 1870s the 14 major firms in the Boston area of the USA were cutting around 700,000 tons per year and employing several thousand people. But the industry was completely overthrown by the new developments which followed from the invention of refrigeration and the growth of the modern cold storage industry. The problem is that the existing players often fail to respond fast enough to the new signals coming from outside their industry – as was the case for many of the old ice industry players.

Of course for others these conditions provide an opportunity for moving ahead of the game and writing a new set of rules. Think about what has happened in online banking, call-centre linked insurance or low-cost airlines – in each case the existing stable pattern has been overthrown, disrupted by new entrants coming in with new and challenging business models. For many managers business model innovation is seen as the biggest threat to their competitive position, precisely because they need to learn to let go of their old models as well as learn new ones. By the time they do so they may well have been overtaken by newcomers for whom this is the only business model and one they are well-placed to exploit.

It's not all doom and gloom though – there are also plenty of stories of new firms and new industries emerging to replace those which die. And in many cases the individual enterprise can renew itself, adapting to its environment and moving into new things. Consider a firm like Nokia – once a humble timber company and now a major player in the global business of mobile telephones. Or the example of the Stora company in Sweden which was founded in the twelfth century as a timber cutting and processing operation but which is still thriving today – albeit in the very different areas of food processing and electronics.

Go online to find the case study of Marshalls, which gives an example of a company over 100 years old and the ways in which innovation has helped it develop and grow.

www.iande.info

The challenge is one of dealing with an uncertain world by constantly trying new things. At first sight this seems obvious – firms which don't recognise the need for change simply disappear whilst those which recognise that 'we must change' can use this to build new and growing businesses. But sometimes that 'change' is pretty dramatic, challenging the roots of where the company began and overturning a lot in the process. TUI is the largest European travel and tourism services company, owning, amongst others, Thomson Holidays, Britannia Airways and Lunn Poly travel agents. Its origins however go back to 1917 where it began as the Prussian state-owned lead mining and smelting company! Nokia's key role as a leader in mobile telephony hides its origins as a diverse timber products conglomerate with interests as wide as rubber boots and toilet paper!

ADVICE FOR FUTURE ENTREPRENEURS

'Only the paranoid survive!' These words – the title of Andy Grove's autobiography (one of the founders of Intel) – stress the need for managers to be constantly searching not just for innovation opportunities but for the early warning signals that someone else's innovation may pose a threat. But rather than just running around in a blind panic, smart managers use tools and techniques to research their environment – carrying out R&D to keep ahead on the shifting technological frontier, using market research and competitor analysis to keep track of the context in which they are playing, and futures tools (forecasting, scenarios, etc.) – to avoid being caught out or blindsided by unpleasant surprises when the world doesn't turn out quite as they had expected.

Can we do it? One indicator of the possibility of doing this comes from the experiences of organisations which have survived for an extended period of time. Whilst most organisations have comparatively modest life-spans there are some which have survived at least one and sometimes multiple centuries. Looking at the experience of these '100 club' members – firms like 3M, Corning, Procter & Gamble, Reuters, Siemens, Philips and Rolls-Royce – we can see that much of their longevity is down to having developed a capacity to innovate on a continuing basis. They have learned – often the hard way – how to manage the process and, importantly, how to repeat the trick. Any organisation gets lucky once but sustaining it for a century or more suggests there's a bit more to it than just luck.

It's the same with individuals – 'serial entrepreneurs' may start many different businesses and what they bring to the party is an accumulated understanding of how to do it better – they have learned and built long-term capability into a robust set of skills.

Managing Innovation and Entrepreneurship

If you asked most people about innovation they would readily sign up to its importance and the need for them to do it in order to survive and grow. But it is also clear from the many failure stories and experiences highlighted in the previous section that recognising the imperative is only the beginning of the story. What these and many other examples show is that simply wishing it to happen may not be enough – we need to actively *manage* the process. So how do we do this?

At its heart innovation is about four core themes:

- recognising the opportunity;
- finding the resources;

- developing the venture;
- creating value.

Looked at in this way we can see a parallel with biology and Darwin's theory of evolution. Organisms survive and grow through generating variation, selecting those new elements which help with adapting to a particular environment and propagating these across the species. Those that do it right survive, those that don't, disappear. Survival of the fittest, pure and simple.

But there's an important difference. In the case of the organisations we build and work in we have – unlike natural evolution – the chance to intervene in the process. Instead of random mutations and lucky accidents we can be a bit more strategic and purposive, searching and generating our own variety, making choices about which innovations to pursue and managing the process of implementation and diffusion to make sure they succeed.

Of course we shouldn't underestimate the task – for example:

- **Recognising the opportunity** – innovative ideas could come from inspiration, from transferring from another context, from listening to user needs, from frontier research or by combining existing ideas into something new. And they could come through building alternative models of the future and exploring options opened up within these alternative worlds. But if we're going to succeed we need to build rich and varied ways of picking up on all the potential trigger signals which offer us interesting variation opportunities. What marks out successful individual entrepreneurs is often this ability to spot the key opportunity from a forest of possibilities.
- **Finding the resources** – making it happen is critical and will need time, money, different knowledge sets, etc. But before we even begin to assemble the resources we need a plan. What will we need and when? And before that we need to be clear about which opportunity we will develop and why. Out of all the things we could do, what are we going to do – and why? Selecting the best of these sounds simple enough – except that we don't know which of them is best until we try. Innovation is fraught with uncertainty and guesswork and the only way to find out whether or not something is a good bet is to start developing it. So the process of strategic choice – which of the many possibilities should we back, given that we only have limited resources – is a big challenge. And if we get it wrong we could end up out of the game – especially if there is only us and our enthusiasm at the outset. How do we convince others to support us, contribute their time, energy – or as key investors, their money?
- **Developing the venture** – how do we go about taking it from a gleam in the eye into a fully fledged product or service or a process people use? That's a long haul and a journey where Murphy's Law dominates – if something is going to go wrong there's a good chance that it will! It's not just a matter of project management – balancing resources against time and budget – but doing so against this background of uncertainty. Even if we can steer a project through the rocks of making it real in terms of a new product, service or process proposition there's no guarantee that people will adopt it and it will diffuse widely.
- **Creating value** – even when we have managed to create something new, how can we capture value from it? How do we make sure there is a stream of income from its widespread use? How do we ensure the social gains are there if we are trying to change the world. How do we recover our – and other people's – investment of time and energy and money? How

do we protect ourselves from people copying our idea and capitalising on all our pioneering? And even if we fail, how do we capture the learning about how the innovation process works so that next time we try something we can increase our chances of success?

This book is about what we've learned – and what we still need to understand – around these questions. How do we manage innovation and entrepreneurship?

What Do We Know about Managing Innovation and Entrepreneurship?

An innovative business is one which lives and breathes 'outside the box'. It is not just good ideas, it is a combination of good ideas, motivated staff and an instinctive understanding of what your customer wants.

—Richard Branson – DTI Innovation lecture, 1998

Success in innovation – whether an individual first timer or a global corporation – is not just about having a good idea and assembling the resources (people, equipment, knowledge, money, etc.) to make it happen. It's also about having the capabilities to manage them – and these are the hardest to get a handle on; they can make or break the process. So what is involved – and how do we know?

Over the past hundred years there have been many attempts to answer the question – drawing on a wide range of studies. Researchers have looked at case examples, at sectors, at entrepreneurs, at big firms and small firms, at success and failure. Practising entrepreneurs and innovation managers in large businesses have tried to reflect on the 'how' of what they do. The key messages come from the world of *experience*. What we've learned comes from the laboratory of practice rather than some deeply rooted theory.

Although these studies give us a wealth of other insights, four core themes emerge which are critical. They may seem obvious – but if we want to succeed in managing innovation we need to:

- Understand *what* we are trying to manage – the better our mental models of what the innovation process involves, the more likely it is that the structures we create to make innovation happen will actually work!
- Understand the key messages about what makes for successful management of the innovation process – and how we can go about creating these conditions.
- Have a clear sense of purpose and direction – a *strategy* shaping the innovation work that we do.
- Recognise that it is a moving target – managing innovation is about building a *dynamic* capability.

What happens if we ignore these? Put simply, we run the risk of our good ideas running into the ground. For example, if we believe that innovation is simply about having the initial idea – some version of the cartoon characters, with a light bulb flashing on above their heads – then we shouldn't be too surprised when we find we can't turn that idea into a technical reality. Or when we do, that people won't necessarily see it as the best thing since sliced bread. We need richer mental models than if we are to design and run an innovation process.

Or if we simply innovate in any direction that takes our fancy – in other words, we have no idea of where or why we want to innovate – then we shouldn't be surprised to find a large hole in our bank balance where the money used to be. Innovation consumes resources – time, energy, ideas and money – and no organisation has infinite resources. So we need to think about being *strategic* in innovation activities.

Or if we believe that innovation is simply about letting it all hang out, creating a wacky space where people play basketball, lie around on sofas and have random conversations over endless cups of coffee, then we shouldn't be surprised if we have a bunch of people with some interesting ideas which never actually go anywhere. Innovation is about organising different pieces of a knowledge jigsaw puzzle and particularly about balancing creativity with the discipline of making something happen.

ADVICE FOR FUTURE ENTREPRENEURS

'You can't make an omelette without breaking eggs' – and you can't innovate without taking risks. But what separates good innovation managers from the gamblers is the recognition that there is a core process involved which can be organised and managed. Anyone can get lucky once with innovation – just by being in the right place at the right time. But repeating the trick requires skills and understanding – and in particular smart innovation managers:

- Understand what we are trying to manage – the better our mental models the more likely what we do with them in the way of building and running organisations and processes will work.
- Understand the how – creating the conditions (and adapting/configuring them) to make it happen.
- Understand the what, why and when of innovation activity – strategy shaping the innovation work that we do.
- Understand that it is a moving target – managing innovation is about building a dynamic capability.

And if we don't reflect and learn from the process – even if we get it wrong – then we risk being condemned to keep on making the same mistakes into the future. We operate in a world of massive complexity – where the sheer number of important elements is increasing and where their interactions make life extremely hard to predict. So we need to innovate – but we also need to innovate in our thinking about how to organise and manage the process. Not for nothing do we talk about the ability to organise and manage the process as a *dynamic capability*!

Whether we are thinking about starting our own business based on a bright idea or we are working in a giant public or private sector organisation concerned with renewing itself the challenges remain the same. These themes matter – so we'll take a closer look at them in the following sections.

Understanding the Innovation Process

Innovation is the successful exploitation of new ideas. *UK Government White Paper 'Innovation nation', 2007.*

Innovation is a change in the thought process for doing something, or the useful application of new inventions or discoveries. It may refer to an incremental emergent or radical and revolutionary change in thinking, products, processes, or organizations. Wikipedia, 2010.

Industrial innovation includes the technical, design, manufacturing, management and commercial activities involved in the marketing of a new (or improved) product or the first commercial use of a new (or improved) process or equipment. Chris Freeman (1982) *The Economics of Industrial Innovation* (2nd edition, Frances Pinter, London).

Innovation does not necessarily imply the commercialization of only a major advance in the technological state of the art (a radical innovation) but it includes also the utilization of even small-scale changes in technological know-how (an improvement or incremental innovation) . . . Roy Rothwell and Paul Gardiner (1985) 'Invention, innovation, re-innovation and the role of the user. *Technovation*, 3, 168.

So what is this innovation thing – and how can we use a better understanding of it to help us manage it better? The dictionary defines it as change – it comes from Latin *in* and *novare* – to make something new, to change. Helpful but a bit vague if we're trying to manage it. The definitions above get a bit closer to its meaning for us – in particular the simple one about it being the successful exploitation of ideas.

One important point about innovation is that it is a word that represents both a thing and an action. It's worth thinking about both of these – what we're going to change and the process of change itself.

What Can We Change in Innovation?

Innovation can take many forms but they can be reduced to four dimensions of change:

- 'product innovation' – changes in the things (products/services) which an organisation offers;
- 'process innovation' – changes in the ways in which they are created and delivered;
- 'position innovation' – changes in the context in which the products/services are introduced;
- 'paradigm innovation' – changes in the underlying mental models which frame what the organisation does.

For example, a new design of car, a new insurance package for accident-prone babies and a new home entertainment system would all be examples of product innovation. And change in the manufacturing methods and equipment used to produce the car or the home entertainment system, or in the office procedures and sequencing in the insurance case, would be examples of process innovation.

Sometimes the dividing line is somewhat blurred – for example, a new jet-powered sea ferry is both a product and a process innovation. Services represent a particular case of this where the product and process aspects often merge – for example, is a new holiday package a product or process change?

Innovation can also take place by repositioning the perception of an established product or process in a particular user context. For example, an old-established product in the UK is Lucozade – originally developed as a glucose-based drink to help children and invalids in convalescence. These associations with sickness were abandoned by the brand owners, Beechams (now part of GlaxoSmithKline), when they relaunched the product as a health drink aimed at the growing fitness market where it is now presented as a performance-enhancing aid to healthy exercise. In 2009 it made £376m in sales. This shift is a good example of 'position' innovation. In similar fashion Haagen Dazs created a new market for ice cream , essentially targeted at adults, through position innovation rather than changing the product or core manufacturing process.

Sometimes opportunities for innovation emerge when we reframe the way we look at something. Henry Ford fundamentally changed the face of transportation, not because he invented the motor car (he was a comparative latecomer to the new industry), nor because he developed the manufacturing process to put one together (as a craft-based specialist industry, car-making had been established for around 20 years). His contribution was to change the underlying model from one which offered a hand-made specialist product to a few wealthy customers to one which offered a car for 'Everyman' at a price he/she could afford. The ensuing shift from craft to mass production was nothing short of a revolution in the way cars (and later countless other products and services) were created and delivered. Of course making the new approach work in practice also required extensive product and process innovation – for example, in component design, in machinery building, in factory layout and particularly in the social system around which work was organised.

   Go online to find the case study of the Model T Ford.

www.iande.info

Recent examples of 'paradigm' innovation – changes in mental models – include the shift to low-cost airlines, the provision of online insurance and other financial services, and the repositioning of drinks like coffee and fruit juice as premium 'designer' products. Although in its later days Enron became infamous for financial malpractice, it originally came to prominence as a small gas pipeline contractor which realised the potential in paradigm innovation in the utilities business. In a climate of deregulation and with global interconnection through grid distribution systems, energy and other utilities like telecommunications bandwidth increasingly became commodities which could be traded much as sugar or cocoa futures.

Paradigm innovation can be triggered by many different things – such as new technologies, the emergence of new markets with different value expectations, new legal rules of the game, new environmental conditions (climate change, energy crises), etc. For example, the emergence of Internet technologies made possible a complete reframing of how we carry out many businesses. In the past similar revolutions in thinking were triggered by technologies like steam power, electricity, mass transportation (via railways and, with motor cars, roads) and microelectronics. And it seems very likely that similar reframing will happen as we get to grips with new technologies like nanotechnology or genetic engineering.

Go online to find a video of 'Finnegan's Fish Bar', which provides an example of applying the 4Ps approach.

www.iande.info

Go online to find the 4Ps exercise.

www.iande.info

From Incremental to Radical Innovation

Another thing to think about is the degree of novelty involved. Clearly, updating the styling on our car is not the same as coming up with a completely new concept car which has an electric engine and is made of new composite materials as opposed to steel and glass. Similarly, increasing the speed and accuracy of a lathe is not the same thing as replacing it with a computer-controlled laser forming process. There are degrees of novelty in these, running from minor, incremental improvements right through to radical changes which transform the way we think about and use them. Sometimes these changes are common to a particular sector or activity, but sometimes they are so radical and far-reaching that they change the basis of society – for example, the role played by steam power in the Industrial Revolution or the ubiquitous changes resulting from today's communications and computing technologies.

. . . and Components and Systems

We also need to think about innovation often being like those Russian dolls – we can change things at the level of components or we can change a whole system. For example, we can put a faster transistor on a microchip on a circuit board for the graphics display in a computer. Or we can change the way several boards are put together into the computer to give it particular capabilities – a games box, an e-book, a media PC. Or we can link the computers into a network to drive a small business or office. Or we can link the networks to others into the Internet. There's scope for innovation at each level – but changes in the higher level systems often have implications for lower down. For example, if cars – as a complex assembly – were suddenly designed to be made out of plastic instead of metal it would still leave scope for car assemblers – but would pose some sleepless nights for producers of metal components!

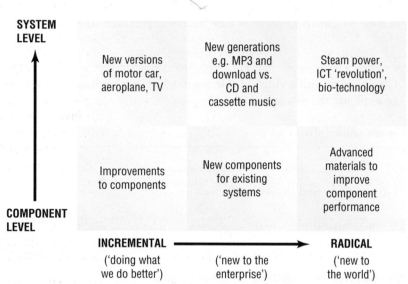

FIGURE 1.1   Types of innovation.

ADVICE FOR FUTURE ENTREPRENEURS

Innovation is often thought of as radical or breakthrough stuff – because that's what makes good headlines and sound bites. But the reality is that most innovation is about incremental changes, doing what we do but better. And most of it involves working within established rules of the game, improving on our particular pieces of the overall jigsaw puzzle. But sometimes radical change is needed – or happens because someone else has introduced it. And sometimes the underlying architecture of a system changes and the old rules no longer apply. (See the case study on the music industry later in this chapter for an example of this.) Smart managers don't wait for this to happen but explore a portfolio of innovation possibilities, from incremental through to radical and from component through to architecture.

What Has to be Managed?

Let's switch our attention to understanding innovation in the sense of it being a 'doing word'. What are the actions involved in innovation and how can we use this understanding to help us manage the process better? What comes into our minds when we think of innovation taking place?

If someone asked you 'when did you last use your Spengler?' they might well be greeted by a quizzical look. But if they asked you when you last used your 'Hoover', the answer would be fairly easy. Yet it was not Mr Hoover who invented the vacuum cleaner in the late nineteenth century but one J. Murray Spengler. Hoover's genius lay in taking that idea and making it into a commercial reality. In similar vein the father of the modern sewing machine was not Mr Singer, whose name jumps to mind and is emblazoned on millions of machines all round the world. It was Elias Howe who invented the machine in 1846 and Singer who brought it to technical and commercial fruition. Perhaps the godfather of them all in terms of turning ideas into reality was Thomas Edison who during his life registered over 1000 patents. Products for which his organisation was responsible include the light bulb, 35mm cinema film and even the electric chair. Many of the inventions for which he is famous weren't in fact invented by him – the electric light bulb for example – but were developed and polished technically and their markets opened up by Edison and his team. More than anyone else Edison understood that invention is not enough – simply having a good idea is not going to lead to its widespread adoption and use.

ADVICE FOR FUTURE ENTREPRENEURS

Unlike Messrs Spengler, Howe and the many others who tried and failed to get their inventions across, smart managers realise that innovation is an extended process with a number of key stages. More important, they avoid thinking in partial or simplistic terms about the process and instead develop rich and integrated models of how it works – which they can then use to organise and manage the process. Take a look at Table 1.2 and think about how you would design a system for innovation which avoids some of the traps on the right-hand side.

One of the problems we have in managing anything is that how we think about it shapes what we do about it. So if we have a simplistic model of how innovation works – for example, that it's just about invention – then that's what we will organise and manage. We might end up with the best invention department in the world – but there is no guarantee that people would ever actually want any of our wonderful inventions! If we are serious about managing innovation, then we need to check on our mental models and make sure we're working with as complete a picture as possible. Otherwise we run risks like those in Table 1.2 below.

TABLE 1.2   The problem with partial models

If innovation is only seen as . . .	. . . the result can be
Strong R&D capability	Technology which fails to meet user needs and may not be accepted – 'the better mousetrap which nobody wants'
The province of specialists in white coats in the R&D laboratory	Lack of involvement of others, and a lack of key knowledge and experience input from other perspectives
Meeting customer needs	Lack of technical progression, leading to inability to gain competitive edge
Technology advances	Producing products which the market does not want or designing processes which do not meet the needs of the user and which are opposed
The province only of large firms	Weak small firms with too high a dependence on large customers
Only about 'breakthrough' changes	Neglect of the potential of incremental innovation. Also an inability to secure and reinforce the gains from radical change because the incremental performance ratchet is not working well
Only associated with key individuals	Failure to utilise the creativity of the remainder of employees, and to secure their inputs and perspectives to improve innovation
Only internally generated	The 'not invented here' effect, where good ideas from outside are resisted or rejected
Only externally generated	Innovation becomes simply a matter of filling a shopping list of needs from outside and there is little internal learning or development of technological competence

A Model for Innovation and Entrepreneurship

Rather than the cartoon image of a light bulb flashing on above someone's head, we need to think about innovation as an extended sequence of activities – a *process*. Whether we are looking at an individual entrepreneur bringing their idea into action or a multi-million dollar corporation launching the latest in a stream of new products the same basic framework applies.

We can break it down into the four key steps we mentioned earlier:

- recognising the opportunity;
- finding the resources;
- developing the venture;
- creating value.

(i) *Recognising the opportunity*

Innovation triggers come in all shapes and sizes and from all sorts of directions. They could take the form of new technological opportunities, or changing requirements on the part of markets; they could be the result of legislative pressure or competitor action. They could be a bright idea occurring to someone as they sit, Archimedes like, in their bathtub. Or they could come as a result of buying in a good idea from someone outside the organisation. And they could arise out of dissatisfaction with social conditions or a desire to make the world a better place in some way.

The message here is clear – if we are going to pick up these trigger signals then we need to develop some pretty extensive antennae for searching and scanning around us – and that includes some capability for looking into the future.

(ii) *Finding the resources*

The trouble with innovation is that it is by its nature a risky business. You don't know at the outset whether what you decide to do is going to work out or even that it will run at all. Yet you have to commit some resources to begin the process – so how do you build a portfolio of projects which balance the risks and the potential rewards? (Of course this decision is even more tough for the first-time entrepreneur trying to launch a business based on his or her great new idea – the choice there is whether or not to go forward and commit what may be a huge investment of personal time, the mortgage,

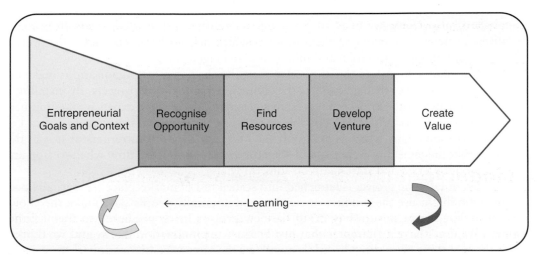

FIGURE 1.2   Illustration of this model for innovation and entrepreneurship.

family life, etc. Even if they succeed there is then the problem when they try and grow the business and need to develop more good ideas to follow the first.)

So this stage is very much about *strategic* choices – does the idea fit a business strategy, does it build on something we know about (or where we can get access to that knowledge easily) and do we have the skills and resources to take it forward? And if we don't have those resources – which is often the case with the lone entrepreneur at start-up – then how will we find and mobilise them?

(iii) Developing the venture

Having picked up relevant trigger signals, made a strategic decision to pursue some of them, found and mobilised the resources we need, the next key phase is actually turning those potential ideas into some kind of reality! In some ways this implementation phase is a bit like weaving a kind of 'knowledge tapestry' – gradually pulling together different threads of knowledge – about technologies, markets, competitor behaviour – and weaving them into a picture which gradually emerges as a successful innovation.

Early on it is full of uncertainty but gradually the picture becomes clearer – but at a cost. We have to invest time, money, people to find out via research and development, market studies, competitor analysis, prototyping, testing, etc. in order to gradually improve our understanding of the innovation and whether or not it will work. Eventually it is in a form which can be launched into its intended context – internal or external market – and then further knowledge about its adoption (or otherwise) can be used to refine the innovation. Developing a robust business plan which takes all of this into consideration at the outset is one of the key elements in entrepreneurial success.

Throughout this implementation phase we have to balance creativity – finding bright ideas and new ways to get around the thousand and one problems which emerge and get the bugs out of the system – with control – making sure we keep to some kind of budget on time, money, resources. This balancing act means that skills in project management around innovation – with all its inherent uncertainties – are always in high demand! This phase is also where we need to bring together different knowledge sets from many different people – combining them in ways which help rather than hinder the process raises big questions around teambuilding and management.

It would be foolish to throw good money after bad so most organisations make use of some kind of risk management as they implement innovation projects. By installing a series of 'gates' as the project moves from a gleam in the eye to an expensive commitment of time and money it becomes possible to review progress – and if necessary redirect or even stop something which is going off the rails. For the solo entrepreneur it is at this stage that judgement is needed – and sometimes the courage to know when to stop and move on, to let go and start again on something else.

Eventually the project is launched into some kind of marketplace – externally people who might use the product or service, and internally people who make the choice about whether or not to 'buy in' to the new process being presented to them. Either way we don't have a guarantee that just because the innovation works and we think it is the best thing since sliced bread they will feel the same way. Innovations diffuse across user populations over time – usually the process follows some kind of S-curve shape.

A few brave souls take on the new idea and then gradually, assuming it works for them, others get on the bandwagon until finally there are just a few diehards – laggards – who resist the temptation to change. Managing this stage well means that we need to think ahead about how people are likely to react and build these insights into our project before we reach the launch stage – or else work hard at persuading them after we have launched it!

(iv) Create value

Despite all our efforts in recognising opportunities, finding resources and developing the venture there is no guarantee that we will be able to capture the value from all our hard work. We also need to think about – and manage – the process to maximise our chances – through protecting our intellectual property and the financial returns if we are engaged in commercial innovation, or in scaling and spreading our ideas for social change so that they are sustainable and really do make a difference. We also have an opportunity at the end of an innovation project to look back and reflect on what we have learned – and how that knowledge might help us do things better next time. In other words we could capture valuable learning about how to build our innovation capability.

Configuring the Innovation Process

This core process runs through any successful innovation – from a lone entrepreneur right up to IBM or GSK. Of course making the model work in practice requires configuring it for different situations – for example, in a large company 'recognising the opportunity' might involve a large R&D department, a market research team, a design studio, etc., whereas all of this could go on in a lone entrepreneur's head. Finding the resources may involve bringing different departments together in a large organisation but a lone innovator will have to create networks. Attracting support may involve a lone entrepreneur in making a 'pitch' to venture capitalists, whereas in a large organisation the business case might be put to a monthly project portfolio meeting.

Allowing for the fact that we will organise and manage in different ways depending on different kinds of organisations, it is still possible to identify some generic recipes or conditions that help the innovation process to happen effectively. As we mentioned earlier, there has been plenty of research around this question and at the end of the chapter there are some links to good examples of these studies. But one of the most important points to make at the outset is that organisations and individuals aren't born with the capability to organise and manage this process – they learn and develop it over time, and mainly through a process of trial and error. They hang on to what works and develop their capabilities in that – and they try to drop those things which don't work.

For example, successful innovation correlates strongly with how a firm selects and manages projects, how it co-ordinates the inputs of different functions, how it links up with its customers, etc. Successful innovators acquire and accumulate technical resources and managerial capabilities over time; there are plenty of opportunities for learning – through doing, using, working with other firms, asking the customers, etc. – but they all depend upon the readiness of the organisation to see innovation less as a lottery than as a process which can be continuously improved.

Another critical point to emerge from research is that innovation needs managing in an *integrated* way; it is not enough just to be good at one thing. It's less like running the 100 metres sprint but more like developing the range of skills needed to compete effectively in a range of events in the pentathlon.

The Context of Success

It's all very well putting a basic process for turning ideas into reality in place. But it doesn't take place in a vacuum – it is subject to a range of internal and external influences which shape what is possible and what actually emerges. In particular innovation needs:

- Clear strategic leadership and direction, plus the commitment of resources to make this happen. Innovation is about taking risks; about going into new and sometimes completely unexplored spaces. We don't want to gamble by simply changing things for their own sake or because the fancy takes us. No organisation has resources to waste in that scattergun fashion – innovation needs a strategy. But equally we need to have a degree of courage and leadership, steering the organisation away from what everyone else is doing or what we've always done and into new spaces.

  In the case of the individual entrepreneur this challenge translates to one in which a clear personal vision can be shared in ways which engage and motivate others to 'buy-in' to it and to contribute their time, energy, money, etc.; to helping make it happen. Without a compelling vision it is unlikely that the venture will get off the ground.

- An innovative organisation in which the structure and climate enables people to deploy their creativity and share their knowledge to bring about change. It's easy to find pre-scriptions for innovative organisations which highlight the need to eliminate stifling bu-reaucracy, unhelpful structures, brick walls blocking communication and other factors stopping good ideas getting through. But we must be careful not to fall into the chaos trap – not all innovation works in organic, loose, informal environments or 'skunk works' – and these types of organisation can sometimes act against the interests of suc-cessful innovation. We need to determine appropriate organisation – that is, the most suitable organisation given the operating contingencies. Too little order and structure may be as bad as too much.

  This is one area where start-ups often have a major advantage – by definition they are small organisations (often one-person ventures) with a high degree of communication and cohesion. They are bound together by a shared vision and they have high levels of co-operation and trust, giving them enormous flexibility. But the downside of being small is a lack of resources – and so successful start-ups are very often those which can build a network around them through which they can tap into the key resources they need. Building and managing such networks is a key factor in creating an extended form of organisation.

- Pro-active links across boundaries inside the organisation and to the many external agen-cies who can play a part in the innovation process – suppliers, customers, sources of finance, skilled resources and of knowledge, etc. Twenty-first century innovation is most certainly not a solo act but a multi-player game across boundaries inside the

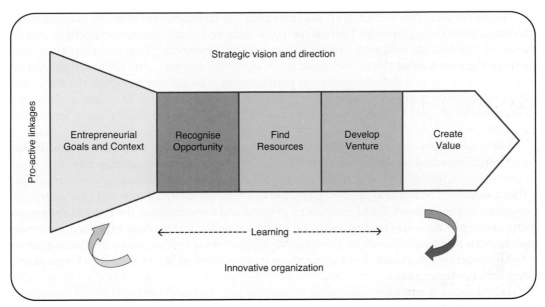

FIGURE 1.3 The resulting model – what we need to pay attention to if we are going to manage innovation well.

organisation and to the many external agencies who can play a part in the innovation process. These days it's about a global game and one where connections and the ability to find, form and deploy creative relationships is of the essence. Once again this idea of successful lone entrepreneurs and small-scale start-ups as network builders is critical. It's not necessary to know or have everything to hand – as long as you know where and how to get it!

Building Innovation Capability

ADVICE FOR FUTURE ENTREPRENEURS

If we want to manage innovation we ought to ask ourselves the following check questions:

- Do we have effective enabling mechanisms for the core process?
- Do we have strategic direction and commitment for innovation?
- Do we have an innovative organisation?
- Do we build rich pro-active links?
- Do we learn and develop our innovation capability?

There's a simple audit questionnaire on the website to help with this process.

Whatever their size or sector, all organisations are trying to find ways of managing this process of growth and renewal. There is no 'right' answer, every organisation needs to aim for the most appropriate solution for its particular circumstances. They develop their own particular ways of doing things and some work better than others. Any organisation can get lucky once but the real skill in innovation management is being able to repeat the trick. And whilst there are no guarantees there is plenty of evidence to suggest that firms can and do learn to manage the process for success – by consciously building and developing their 'innovation capability'.

These questions apply across the board – though the answers may take us in different directions depending on where we start from. A new start-up business may not need much in the way of a formal and structured process for organising and managing innovation. But a firm the size of Nokia will need to pay careful attention to structures and procedures for building a strategic portfolio of projects to explore and for managing the risks as they move from ideas into technical and commercial reality. Equally a large firm may have extensive resources to build a global set of networks to support its activities, whereas a new start-up may be vulnerable to threats from elements in its environment it simply didn't know about, never mind connect to.

Throughout the book we'll look at how these play out in different types of innovative organisations and how an understanding of them can help improve the chances of long-term innovation success. But for now let's turn our attention to the question of innovation *strategy*.

What, Why and When – The Challenge of Innovation Strategy

Building a capability to organise and manage innovation is a great achievement – but unless that capability is pointed in a suitable direction the organisation risks being all dressed up with nowhere to go! And for entrepreneurs starting a new venture the challenge is even greater – without a clear sense of direction, a vision which you can share with others to excite and focus them, the whole thing may never take off.

So the last theme we need to consider is where and how innovation can be used to strategic advantage. Table 1.3 gives some examples of the different ways in which this can be achieved – you might like to add your own ideas to the list.

Go online to find the Strategic advantage tool.

www.iande.info

TABLE 1.3   Strategic advantages through innovation

Mechanism	Strategic advantage	Examples
Novelty in product or service offering	Offering something no one else can	Introducing the first . . . Walkman, fountain pen, camera, dishwasher, telephone bank, online retailer, etc. . . . to the world
Novelty in process	Offering it in ways others cannot Match – faster, lower cost, more customised, etc.	Pilkington's float glass process, Bessemer's steel process, Internet banking, online bookselling, etc.
Complexity	Offering something which others find it difficult to master	Rolls-Royce and aircraft engines – only a handful of competitors can master the complex machining and metallurgy involved
Legal protection of intellectual property	Offering something which others cannot do unless they pay a licence or other fee	Blockbuster drugs like Zantac, Prozac, Viagra, etc.
Add/extend range of competitive factors	Move basis of competition – e.g. from price of product to price and quality, or price, quality, choice, etc.	Japanese car manufacturing, which systematically moved the competitive agenda from price to quality, to flexibility and choice, to shorter times between launch of new models, and so on – each time not trading these off against each other but offering them all
Timing	First-mover advantage – being first can be worth significant market share in new product fields	Amazon.com, Yahoo! – others can follow, but the advantage 'sticks' to the early movers
	Fast follower advantage – sometimes being first means you encounter many unexpected teething problems, and it makes better sense to watch someone else make the early mistakes and move fast into a follow-up product	Personal digital assistants (PDAs) and smart phones which have captured a huge and growing share of the market. In fact the concept and design was articulated in Apple's ill-fated Newton product some five years before Palm launched its successful Pilot range – but problems with software and especially handwriting recognition meant it flopped. By contrast Apple's success with iPod as an MP3 player came because they were quite late into the market and could learn and include key features into their dominant design

(continued)

TABLE 1.3 (*Continued*)

Mechanism	Strategic advantage	Examples
Robust platform design	Offering something which provides the platform on which other variations and generations can be built	Sony's original 'Walkman' architecture, which has spawned several generations of personal audio equipment – through minidisk, CD, DVD, MP3, iPod
		Boeing 737 – over 30 years old, the design is still being adapted and configured to suit different users – one of the most successful aircraft in the world in terms of sales
		Intel and AMD with different variants of their microprocessor families
Rewriting the rules	Offering something which represents a completely new product or process concept – a different way of doing things – and makes the old ones redundant	Typewriters vs. computer word processing, ice vs. refrigerators, electric vs. gas or oil lamps
Reconfiguring the parts of the process	Rethinking the way in which bits of the system work together – e.g. building more effective networks, outsourcing and co-ordination of a virtual company, etc.	Zara and Benetton in clothing, Dell in computers, Toyota in its supply chain management
Transferring across different application contexts	Recombining established elements for different markets	Polycarbonate wheels transferred from application market like rolling luggage into children's toys – lightweight micro-scooters
Others?	Innovation is all about finding new ways to do things and to obtain strategic advantage – so there will be room for new ways of gaining and retaining advantage	Napster. This firm began by writing software which would enable music fans to swap their favourite pieces via the Internet – the Napster program essentially connected person to person (P2P) by providing a fast link. Its potential to change the architecture and mode of operation of the Internet was much greater, and although Napster suffered from legal issues followers developed a huge industry based on downloading and file sharing

The problem isn't the shortage of ways of gaining competitive advantage through innovation but rather which ones will we choose and why? It's a decision which any organisation has to take – whether a start-up deciding the (relatively) simple question of go/no go in terms of trying to enter a hostile marketplace with their new idea, or a giant firm trying to open up new market space through innovation. And it's not just about commercial competition – the same idea of 'strategic advantage' plays out in public services and social innovation. For example, police forces need to think strategically about how they will deploy their scarce resources to contain crime and stabilise law and order, whilst hospital managements are concerned to balance limited resources against the increasing demands of healthcare expectations.

We can think about strategy as a process of exploring the space defined by our four innovation types – the 4Ps mentioned earlier. Each of our 4Ps of innovation can take place along an axis running from incremental through to radical change; the area indicated by the circle in Figure 1.4 is the potential innovation space within which an organisation can operate.

Where it actually explores and why – and which areas it leaves alone – are all questions for innovation strategy. And for new entrant entrepreneurs this can provide a map of explored and unexplored territory, showing where there is open opportunity, where and how to

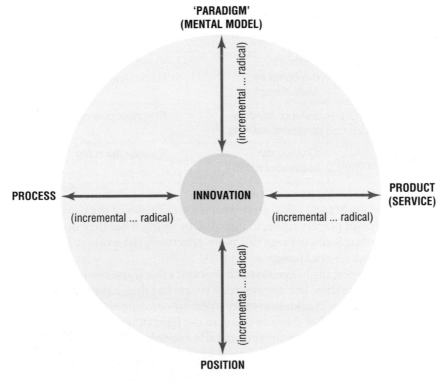

FIGURE 1.4 Exploring innovation space.

tackle existing players, etc. It also provides a useful map for social innovation – where we create new social value, where there is unexplored territory, where and how we might do things differently?

The challenge is for individuals and organisations to be aware of the extensive space within which innovation possibilities exist and to try and develop a strategic portfolio which covers this territory effectively, balancing risks and resources. So how can we choose which options might make sense for us? It's helpful to consider two complementary themes in answering this question:

- What's our overall 'business strategy' (where are we trying to go as an organisation) and how will innovation help us get there?
- Do we *know* anything about the direction we want to go in – does it build on something we have some competence in (or have access to)?

These form the basis for the strategic discussion which needs to go on.

Beyond the Steady State – The Challenge of Discontinuous Change

	Do it better	Do it differently
Product (service)	Product improvement	. . . and now for something completely different
Process	Getting lean, the quest for 'excellence'	Radical process change
Position	Extend, deepen, segment markets	Find new playing fields
Paradigm (business concept)	Change the business model	Rewrite the rules

Most of the time innovation takes place within a set of rules of the game which are clearly understood, and involves players trying to innovate by doing what they do (product, process, position, etc.) but better. Some manage this more effectively than others but the 'rules of the game' are accepted and do not change.

But occasionally something happens which dislocates this framework and changes the rules of the game. By definition these are not everyday events but they have the capacity to redefine the space and the boundary conditions – they open up new opportunities but also challenge existing players to reframe what they are doing in the light of new conditions. Taking advantage of the opportunities – or seeing the threats early enough and doing something different to help deal with them – requires an entrepreneurial approach which new entrants have but which may be difficult to revive in an established organisation. So under these conditions we often see *disruption* of the old market and technological order and new rules of the game.

The important message is that under such conditions (which don't emerge every day) we need different approaches to organising and managing innovation. If they try to use established models which work under steady state conditions, organisations are likely to find that they are increasingly out of their depth and risk being upstaged by new and more agile players.

Go online to find a more extended discussion of this theme of 'discontinuous innovation'.

www.iande.info

ADVICE FOR FUTURE ENTREPRENEURS

Most of the time managing innovation is about the 'steady state' – doing what we do but better under a set of rules which everybody plays by. But we know that the carpet does get pulled out from under us on occasions, triggered by violent shifts in the technological, political or market context. So smart managers in established organisations work to build not only the capability to manage innovation under stable conditions but also to create at least some capacity to pick up on, and do something about discontinuous conditions. They create resources for 'blue sky' project research, they send out scouts to pick up on early warning about radical developments, they fund internal entrepreneurs and venture capital. And at the limit they find ways to ask uncomfortable questions like 'how would we destroy this business?' – and use that to seek out potential areas of vulnerability.

Of course the reverse is true for start-up entrepreneurs seeking to break into new market space – the message here is to look for potential ways of disrupting the existing rules of the game. Can we use new technologies, new market entrants, new political or social conditions to create a new innovation game?

STRATEGIC AND SOCIAL IMPACT

Much of the innovation that we hear about is around commercial products and services – more gadgets added to our mobile phones, faster or more fuel-efficient cars, increasing customisation of our retail experience or lower cost flying, insurance, banking or bookselling. But apart from its role as an engine for economic growth, innovation has wider social implications which make understanding and managing the process a key challenge for all of our futures. For example:

- Innovation in micro-credit in poor countries like Bangladesh or Tanzania has revolutionised parts of the financial sector and opened up access to start-up capital for thousands of people who go on to grow their businesses, create employment opportunities and develop the wider local economy.

(continued)

- Innovation in sustainable energy systems offers a way out of the trap being sprung by spiralling fossil fuel prices and declining availability.
- Growing desire for 'green' products and services is fuelling demand for innovation across a range of sectors – to the point where a major consulting firm, Arthur D. Little, describe sustainability as *the new high ground* for innovation.
- Massively increased life expectancies coupled with static or declining birth rates and inadequate pension provision means a time bomb is ticking away under many 'developed' economies. Meeting expectations in fields like healthcare and social welfare on the back of limited resources is going to require radical innovation across the broad, not only in products and services but also in the underlying models of how such care is organised and delivered, and paid for.
- Law and order tops the list of concerns in many inner cities and is sometimes painted as a losing battle. But the experience of the New York Police Department in the 1990s suggests that innovation can play a decisive role here too. When William Bratton was appointed as police commissioner in 1994 murders were at an all-time high and muggings, thefts and armed robberies had reached the point where many felt the city was in irreversible decline. The 36,000 staff felt demoralised and unable to cope and the organisation was prone to in-fighting and blame swapping. Yet in less than two years he introduced innovations which turned the tide – murder rates fell by 50%, felonies by 39% and thefts by 35%, whilst public confidence grew from 37% to 73%. And after his departure in 1996 the figures continued in this positive direction.

These – and many other examples – point to the importance of innovation as a social shaper and driver. But getting the benefits and minimising the negative consequences depends critically on how we approach the challenge of understanding and *managing* the innovation process itself.

DEVELOPING PERSONAL CAPABILITIES

Innovation doesn't happen by accident as we've seen in this chapter. It results from a systematic and organised process of managed change, taking new ideas forward to successful reality. Entrepreneurial skills lie at the heart of this process – whether in terms of starting a new business, renewing or reinventing an established firm or opening up new possibilities for community development through social entrepreneurship. But entrepreneurship isn't just another name for gambling – instead it involves motivated and focused energy and commitment, and a core skill set which includes:

- A well-developed understanding of the process and its different elements.
- Project planning and management – against a background of uncertainty.
- Project team working – the ability to work with others under uncertain conditions.
- Strategic leadership – having a vision and being able to share it.
- Learning skills – the ability to analyse what works and why and to feed this back into the system to improve capability for next time.

Finally it's worth remembering some useful advice from an old but wise source. In his famous book *The Prince*, Niccolo Machiavelli gave a warning to would-be innovators:

It must be remembered that there is nothing more difficult to plan, more doubtful of success, nor more dangerous to management than the creation of a new system. For the initiator has the enmity of all who would profit by the preservation of the old institution and merely luke-warm defenders in those who gain by the new ones.

Chapter Summary

1   Innovation is about growth – about recognising opportunities for doing something new and implementing those ideas to create some kind of value. It could be business growth, it could be social change. But at its heart is the creative human spirit, the urge to make change in our environment.

   Innovation is also a survival imperative. If an organisation doesn't change what it offers the world and the ways in which it creates and delivers its offerings it could well be in trouble. And innovation contributes to competitive success in many different ways – it's a *strategic* resource to getting the organisation where it is trying to go, whether it is delivering shareholder value for private sector firms, or providing better public services, or enabling the start-up and growth of new enterprises.

2   Innovation doesn't just happen – it is driven by *entrepreneurship*. This powerful mixture of energy, vision, passion, commitment, judgement and risk-taking provides the motive power behind the innovation process. It's the same whether we are talking about a solo start-up venture or a key group within an established organisation trying to renew its products or services.

3   Innovation doesn't happen simply because we hope it will – it's a complex process which carries risks and needs careful and systematic *management*. Innovation isn't a single event, like the light bulb going off above a cartoon character's head. It's an extended process of picking up on ideas for change and turning them into effective reality. The core process involves four steps – recognising opportunities, finding resources, developing the venture and capturing value. The challenge comes in doing this in an organised fashion and in being able to repeat the trick.

4   Research repeatedly suggests that if we want to succeed in managing innovation we need to:
   - Understand *what* we are trying to manage – the better our mental models the more likely what we do with them in the way of building and running organisations and processes will work.
   - Understand the *how* – creating the conditions (and adapting/configuring them) to make it happen.
   - Understand the what, why and when of innovation activity – strategy shaping the innovation work that we do.
   - Understand that it is a moving target – managing innovation is about building a *dynamic* capability.

5   Innovation can take many forms but they can be reduced to four directions of change:
   - 'Product innovation' – changes in the things (products/services) which an organisation offers.
   - 'Process innovation' – changes in the ways in which they are created and delivered.
   - 'Position innovation' – changes in the context in which the products/services are introduced.

- 'Paradigm innovation' – changes in the underlying mental models which frame what the organisation does.

6 Within any of these dimensions innovations can be positioned on a spectrum from 'incremental' – doing what we do but better – through to 'radical' – doing something completely different. And they can be stand-alone 'component' innovations or they can form part of a linked 'architecture' or system which brings many different components together in a particular way.

7 The core process of recognising opportunities, finding resources, developing the venture and capturing value doesn't take place in a vacuum – we know it is strongly influenced by many factors. In particular innovation needs:
- Clear strategic leadership and direction, plus the commitment of resources to make this happen.
- An innovative organisation in which the structure and climate enables people to deploy their creativity and share their knowledge to bring about change.
- Pro-active links across boundaries inside the organisation and to the many external agencies who can play a part in the innovation process – suppliers, customers, sources of finance, skilled resources and of knowledge, etc.

8 Any organisation can get lucky once but the real skill in innovation management is being able to repeat the trick. So if we want to manage innovation we ought to ask ourselves the following check questions:
- Do we have effective enabling mechanisms for the core process?
- Do we have strategic direction and commitment for innovation?
- Do we have an innovative organisation?
- Do we build rich pro-active links?
- Do we learn and develop our innovation capability?

9 Building a capability to organise and manage innovation is a great achievement – but we also need to consider where and how innovation can be used to strategic advantage. Two key themes are important here – first, what is our overall 'business strategy' and how will innovation help us get there? And second, do we know anything about the direction we want to go in – does it build on something we have some competence in (or have access to)?

10 Most of the time innovation takes place within a set of rules of the game which are clearly understood, and involves players trying to innovate by doing what they do (product, process, position, etc.) but better. But occasionally something happens which changes the rules of the game – for example, when radical change takes place along the technological frontier or when completely new markets emerge. When this happens we need different approaches to organising and managing innovation. If we try to use established models which work under steady state conditions we find we are increasingly out of our depth and risk being upstaged by new and more agile players.

Key Terms Defined

Architecture innovation   changes in the whole system – e.g. moving from that computer design to a completely different way of processing information.

Component innovation   changes at the level of components in a bigger system – for example, a faster transistor in a microchip in a computer.

Discontinuous innovation   radical innovations which change the 'rules of the game' and open up a new game in which new players are often at an advantage.

Entrepreneurship   powerful mixture of energy, vision, passion, commitment, judgement and risk-taking – provides the motive power behind the innovation process.

Incremental innovation   small improvements to existing products, services or processes – 'doing what we do but better'.

Innovation   the process of translating ideas into useful – and used – new products, processes or services.

Invention   coming up with a new idea.

Product innovation   changes in the things (products/services) which an organisation offers.

Process innovation   changes in the ways in which products/services are created and delivered.

Position innovation   changes in the context in which the products/services are introduced.

Paradigm innovation   changes in the underlying mental models which frame what the organisation does.

Radical innovation   significantly different changes to products, services or processes – 'do what we do differently'.

Further Reading and Resources

1 The importance of innovation as a strategic imperative comes through in many case examples – some good ones can be found in the following.

Christensen, C. (1997). *The Innovator's Dilemma*. Cambridge, Mass., Harvard Business School Press.
Dell, M. (1999). *Direct from Dell*. New York, HarperCollins.
Dyson, J. (1997). *Against the Odds*. London, Orion.
Garr, D. (2000). *IBM Redux: Lou Gerstner and the business turnaround of the decade*. New York, HarperCollins.
Hamel, G. (2000). *Leading the Revolution*. Boston. Mass., Harvard Business School Press.

Kim, W. and R. Mauborgne (2005). *Blue Ocean Strategy: How to create uncontested market space and make the competition irrelevant.* Boston, Mass., Harvard Business School Press.

Tidd, J. and F. Hull, Eds. (2003). *Service Innovation: Organizational responses to technological opportunities and market imperatives.* London, Imperial College Press.

Utterback, J. (1994). *Mastering the Dynamics of Innovation.* Boston, MA., Harvard Business School Press.

Von Stamm, B. (2003). *The Innovation Wave.* Chichester, John Wiley & Sons Ltd.

Womack, J., D. Jones, et al. (1991). *The Machine that Changed the World.* New York, Rawson Associates.

2   More detailed discussion of the 4Ps approach is in Francis, D. and J. Bessant (2005). 'Targeting innovation and implications for capability development.' *Technovation* **25**(3): 171–183.

3   Incremental and radical innovation themes are covered well in sources like: Benner, M. J. and M. L. Tushman (2003). 'Exploitation, exploration, and process management: The productivity dilemma revisited.' *Academy of Management. The Academy of Management Review* **28**(2): 238; Imai, K. (1987). *Kaizen.* New York, Random House; Leifer, R., C. McDermott, et al. (2000). *Radical Innovation.* Boston, Mass., Harvard Business School Press.

4   The idea of component and architectural innovation was originally discussed in Henderson, R. and K. Clark (1990). 'Architectural innovation: The reconfiguration of existing product technologies and the failure of established firms.' *Administrative Science Quarterly* **35**: 9–30.

5   Seeing innovation as a process and the ways in which we think about how that process works are discussed in Rothwell, R. (1992). 'Successful industrial innovation: Critical success factors for the 1990s.' *R&D Management* **22**(3): 221–239 and Van de Ven, A. (1999). *The Innovation Journey.* Oxford, Oxford University Press. A good view of some of the twenty-first century challenges can be found in Chesborough, H. (2003). *Open innovation: The new imperative for creating and profiting from technology.* Boston, Mass., Harvard Business School Press.

6   Innovation strategy is discussed later in this book but for more background, see Burgelman, R., C. Christensen, et al., Eds. (2004). *Strategic management of technology and innovation.* Boston, McGraw-Hill Irwin.

7   The theme of 'discontinuous' innovation is explored, for example, in Foster, R. and S. Kaplan (2002). *Creative Destruction.* Cambridge, Harvard University Press. Bessant, J., R. Lamming, et al. (2005). 'Managing innovation beyond the steady state.' *Technovation* **25**(12): 1366–1376 and Day, G. and P. Schoemaker (2000). *Wharton on Managing Emerging Technologies.* New York, Wiley.

8   There are some useful websites covering innovation management and the challenges posed to future entrepreneurs. www.thefutureofinnovation.org offers the views of nearly

400 researchers in the area on future challenges whilst www.innovation-futures.org presents a number of different scenarios for the future, each with significant innovation and entrepreneurship challenges.

References

Baumol, W.J. (2004) *The Free-Market Innovation Machine: Analyzing the growth miracle of capitalism*. Princeton University Press.

Drucker, P. (1985). *Innovation and Entrepreneurship*. New York, Harper and Row.

Rothwell, R. and P. Gardiner (1985). 'Invention, innovation, re-innovation and the role of the user.' *Technovation* 3: 167–186.

Discussion Questions

1. Is innovation manageable or just a random gambling activity where you sometimes get lucky? If it is manageable, how can firms organise and manage it – what general principles might they use?

2. 'Build a better mousetrap and the world will beat a path to your door!' Will it? What are the limitations of seeing innovation simply as coming up with bright ideas? Illustrate your answer with examples drawn from manufacturing and services.

3. What are the key stages involved in an innovation process? And what are the characteristic sets of activities which take place at each stage? How might such an innovation process look for:
   a. A fast food restaurant chain?
   b. An electronic test equipment maker?
   c. A hospital?
   d. An insurance company?
   e. A new entrant biotechnology firm?

4. Fred Bloggs was a bright young PhD scientist with a patent on a new algorithm for monitoring brainwave activity and predicting the early onset of a stroke. He was convinced of the value of his idea and took it to market having sold his car, borrowed money from family and friends and taken out a large loan. He went bankrupt despite having a demonstration version which impressed those doctors he showed it to. Why might his failure be linked to having a partial model of how innovation works – and how could he avoid making the same mistake in the future?

5. How does innovation operate as a knowledge creation and transfer process? Illustrate your answer with relevant case examples.

6. If innovation is increasingly a matter of knowledge management, what sorts of challenges does this approach pose for managing the process?

7. How can knowledge be used to provide competitive advantage in a competitive marketplace – and how might this advantage be protected and preserved?

8. How does innovation contribute to competitive advantage? Support your answer with illustrations from both manufacturing and services.

9. Does innovation matter for public services? Using examples indicate how and where it can be an important strategic issue.

10. You are a newly appointed director for a small charity which supports homeless people. How could innovation improve the ways in which your charity operates?

11. Innovation can take many forms. Give examples of product/service, process, position and paradigm (mental model) innovations.

12. The low-cost airline approach has massively changed the way people choose and use air travel – and has been both a source of growth for new players and a life-threatening challenge for some existing players. What types of innovation have been involved in this?

13. You have been called in as a consultant to a medium-sized toy manufacturer whose range of construction toys (building bricks, etc.) has been losing market share to other types of toys. What innovation directions would you recommend to this company to restore their competitive position? (Use the 4Ps framework to think about possibilities.)

14. Innovation is about big leaps forward, 'eureka' moments and radical breakthroughs – or is it? Using examples from manufacturing and services make a case for the importance of incremental innovation.

15. Describe, with examples, the concept of platforms in product and process innovation and suggest how such an approach might help spread the high costs of innovation across a longer time period.

16. What are the challenges which managers might face in trying to organise for a long-term steady stream of incremental innovation?

Team Exercises

1. **Strategic advantage through innovation**

    Think about an organisation with which you are familiar and about the other firms or players in its sector. How do they choose to try to position themselves for strategic advantage – and how do they use technology to help them do so? They may try to offer the lowest prices – and have heavy investments in clever machines which help them achieve this. Or they may try to offer the best designs – and back this up with a commitment to design and R&D.

Try to research the strategies not only of one firm but of several within the sector and build up a picture of how the sector is shaped by firms using technology to try to gain competitive advantage. You might like to use Table 1.2 to help you think about how they are doing so – and to record your thoughts.

2. **Forces for strategic innovation**

Thinking about an organisation with which you are familiar, try to list the 'driving forces' for strategic technological innovation. What are the main sources of demand and how are they pulling particular responses from competing firms? What are the main trends in technology and how are these shaping new opportunities which firms can exploit to advantage? Jot your ideas down under the headings shown below. Then add a future dimension – thinking 5, 10, 20 years ahead what can you see on the horizon? Is it more of the same or might there be possible points where new demand issues or new technology opportunities change the rules of the game?

Timescale	Demand forces pulling innovation	Technology push creating opportunities
Now		
5 years ahead		
10 years ahead		
20 years ahead		

3. Following the chart below, try to list as many ways as possible in which a firm might be able to exploit knowledge for strategic advantage. What would be needed to create and sustain such advantage?

Source of competitive advantage	Examples	What has to be managed to build and sustain such advantage?
e.g. having a design no one else has thought of	Dyson's vacuum cleaner	How to protect it legally – patents, copyright, etc.

Assignment Questions

1. **Sector innovation patterns**

Imagine you work for a firm involved in children's toy manufacturing. Now try to list the major changes in that sector over the past 25 years in terms of what contributes to competitiveness. Who (which firms) have been the winners and losers and why? You are trying to get a feel in this for how technological change can shape the competitive dynamics of an industry so think about questions like these:

- How has the industry changed – and how has technology helped (or could it help) deal with these changes?
- What new technologies have emerged – and how have they been used?
- What are the main market demands (e.g. price, quality, design, customisation, speed of response, etc.) and how has technology affected the ability of firms to offer these?
- If a new entrant came into the industry what would he/she have to offer to become a market leader – and how might technology help them do so?

You may need to spend some time researching the wider sector to build up this picture. Try to summarise your research in the form of short 'bullet points' which highlight the strategic role which technology plays. You might like to use the framework below which is partially filled in.

Major changes in the industry	Major new technologies	Main market demands and how technology affects them	How to become a market leader
Big influence of TV and films – increasing tie-ins *Price pressures push actual manufacturing to the Far East* *Fashion industry with high risks – and benefits for the right products.* *Costs of new technologies mean fewer players can stay in the game of new product development – so consolidation of the industry*	Electronics and programmability TV/video and computer games – as competitors to traditional toys but also as complements which can extend their range – e.g. Lego bricks plus computer = programmable toys	Strong price pressure – pushes manufacturing to low cost locations – technology relevant in keeping costs low whilst enabling consistent quality Major emphasis on design technologies	Close market understanding and the ability to communicate this deep into the organisation and configure products to meet these demands Broad knowledge base – especially in newer technologies like computers and software but also in design of parts Access to distribution networks Strong design and marketing capability

2. **Innovation success and failure**

    Innovations don't happen by accident – and they don't always succeed. They are influenced by a variety of factors – organisational structures, project team dynamics, strategic decision-making, technological and market events, etc. Using any case examples and/or your own experience, list the key management/organisational factors which appear to affect the outcome of innovation in products or processes.

CASE STUDY 1

Exploring Innovation in Action: The Changing Nature of the Music Industry

1st April 2006. Apart from being a traditional day for playing practical jokes, this was the day on which another landmark in the rapidly changing world of music was reached. 'Crazy' – a track by Gnarls Barkley – made pop history as the UK's first song to top the charts based on download sales alone. Commenting on the fact that the song had been downloaded more than 31,000 times but was only released for sale in the shops on 3rd April, Gennaro Castaldo, spokesman for retailer HMV, said: 'This not only represents a watershed in how the charts are compiled, but shows that legal downloads have come of age . . . if physical copies fly off the shelves at the same rate it could vie for a place as the year's biggest seller'.

One of the less visible but highly challenging aspects of the Internet is the impact it has had – and is having – on the entertainment business. This is particularly the case with music. At one level its impacts could be assumed to be confined to providing new 'e-tailing' channels through which you can obtain the latest CD of your preference – for example, from Amazon.com or CD-Now or 100 other websites. These innovations increase the choice and tailoring of the music purchasing service and demonstrate some of the 'richness/reach' economic shifts of the new Internet game.

But beneath this updating of essentially the same transaction lies a more fundamental shift – in the ways in which music is created and distributed and in the business model on which the whole music industry is currently predicated. In essence the old model involved a complex network in which songwriters and artists depended on A&R (artists and repertoire) to select a few acts, production staff who would record in complex and expensive studios, other production staff who would oversee the manufacture of physical discs, tapes and CDs and marketing and distribution staff who would ensure the product was publicised and disseminated to an increasingly global market.

Several key changes have undermined this structure and brought with it significant disruption to the industry. Old competencies may no longer be relevant whilst acquiring new ones becomes a matter of urgency. Even well-established names like Sony find it difficult to stay ahead whilst new entrants are able to exploit the economics of the Internet. At the heart of the change is the potential for creating, storing and distributing music in digital format – a problem which many researchers have worked on for some time. One solution, developed by one of the Fraunhofer Institutes in Germany, is a standard based on the Motion Picture Experts Group (MPEG) level 3 protocol – MP3. MP3 offers a powerful algorithm for managing one of the big problems in transmitting music files – that of compression. Normal audio files cover a wide range of frequencies and are thus very large and not suitable for fast transfer across the Internet – especially with a population who may only be using relatively slow modems. With MP3 effective compression is achieved by cutting out those frequencies which the human ear cannot detect – with the result that the files to be transferred are much smaller.

As a result MP3 files can be moved across the Internet quickly and shared widely. Various programs exist for transferring normal audio files and inputs – such as CDs – into MP3 and back again.

What does this mean for the music business? In the first instance aspiring musicians no longer need to depend on being picked up by A&R staff from major companies who can bear the costs of recording and production of a physical CD. Instead they can use home recording software and either produce a CD themselves or else go straight to MP3 – and then distribute the product globally via newsgroups, chatrooms, etc. In the process they effectively create a parallel and much more direct music industry which leaves existing players and artists on the sidelines.

Such changes are not necessarily threatening. For many people the lowering of entry barriers has opened up the possibility of participating in the music business – for example, by making and sharing music without the complexities and costs of a formal recording contract and the resources of a major record company. There is also scope for innovation around the periphery – for example in the music publishing sector where sheet music and lyrics are also susceptible to lowering of barriers through the application of digital technology. Journalism and related activities become increasingly open – now music reviews and other forms of commentary become possible via specialist user groups and channels on the Web whereas before they were the province of a few magazine titles. Compiling popularity charts – and the related advertising – is also opened up as the medium switches from physical CDs and tapes distributed and sold via established channels to new media such as MP3 distributed via the Internet.

As if this were not enough the industry is also challenged from another source – the sharing of music between different people connected via the Internet. Although technically illegal this practice of sharing between people's record collections has always taken place – but not on the scale which the Internet threatens to facilitate. Much of the established music industry is concerned with legal issues – how to protect copyright and how to ensure that royalties are paid in the right proportions to those who participate in production and distribution. But when people can share music in MP3 format and distribute it globally the potential for policing the system and collecting royalties becomes extremely difficult to sustain.

It has been made much more so by another technological development – that of person-to-person or P2P networking. Sean Fanning, an 18-year-old student with the nickname 'the Napster', was intrigued by the challenge of being able to enable his friends to 'see' and share between their own personal record collections. He argued that if they held these in MP3 format then it should be possible to set up some kind of central exchange program which facilitated their sharing.

The result – the Napster.com site – offered sophisticated software which enabled P2P transactions. The Napster server did not actually hold any music on its files – but every day millions of swaps were made by people around the world exchanging their music collections. Needless to say this posed a huge threat to the established music business since it involved no payment of royalties. A number of high-profile lawsuits followed but whilst Napster's activities have been curbed the problem did not go away. There are now many other sites emulating and extending what Napster started – sites such as Gnutella, Kazaa, Limewire took the P2P idea further and enabled exchange of many different file formats – text, video, etc. In Napster's own case the phenomenally successful site concluded a deal with entertainment giant Bertelsman which paved the way for subscription-based services which provide some revenue stream to deal with the royalty issue.

Expectations that legal protection would limit the impact of this revolution have been dampened by a US Court of Appeal ruling which rejected claims that P2P violated copyright law. Their judgement said, 'History has shown that time and market forces often provide equilibrium in balancing interests, whether the new technology be a player piano, a copier, a tape recorder, a video recorder, a PC, a karaoke machine or an MP3 player' (*Personal Computer World*, November 2004, p. 32).

Significantly the new opportunities opened up by this were seized not by music industry firms but by computer companies, especially Apple. In parallel with the launch of their successful iPod personal MP3 player they opened a site called iTunes which offered users a choice of thousands of tracks for download at 99c each. In its first weeks of operation it recorded 1 million hits and in February 2006 the billionth song, 'Speed of Sound', was purchased as part of Coldplay's *X&Y* album by Alex Ostrovsky from West Bloomfield, Michigan. 'I hope that every customer, artist, and music company executive takes a moment today to reflect on what we've achieved together during the past three years,' said Steve Jobs, Apple's CEO. 'Over 1 billion songs have now been legally purchased and downloaded around the globe, representing a major force against music piracy and the future of music distribution as we move from CDs to the Internet.'

This has been a dramatic shift, reaching the point where more singles were bought as downloads in 2005 than as CDs, and where the overall shift to a majority of purchases being by download was expected to take place during 2006. New players are coming to dominate the game – for example, Tesco and Microsoft. And the changes don't stop there. In February 2006 the Arctic Monkeys topped the UK album charts and walked off with a fistful of awards from the music business – yet their rise to prominence had been entirely via 'viral marketing' across the Internet rather than by conventional advertising and promotion. Playing gigs around the northern English town of Sheffield, the band simply gave away CDs of their early songs to their fans, who then obligingly spread them around on the Internet. 'They came to the attention of the public via the Internet, and you had chatrooms, everyone talking about them,' said a slightly worried Gennaro Castaldo of HMV Records. David Sinclair, a rock journalist suggested that 'It's a big wakeup call to all the record companies, the establishment, if you like. . . . This lot caught them all napping . . . We are living in a completely different era, which the Arctic Monkeys have done an awful lot to bring about.'

The writing may be on the wall for the music industry in the same way as the low-cost airline business has transformed the travel business. And behind the music business the next target may be the movie and entertainment industry where there are already worrying similarities; or the growing computer games sector, with shifts towards more small-scale developers emulating the Arctic Monkeys and using viral marketing to build a sales base.

Reflection Questions/Assignments Linked to the Case

1. In this chapter we looked at the idea that innovations can be 'architectural' – changes in the ways different things are put together into a whole system. Examples might be a motor car, a mobile phone business, a hospital. And innovations can also be at the 'component' level – the parts which go into those systems – for example, the engine, brakes, fuel tank, electrics, etc. which go into a car. Changes at the component level may take place independently but when the whole architecture changes there are often major winners and losers.

   Looking at the case study, try to identify which of the changes are architectural and which are component. What are the implications for different players in terms of the likely threat to them and the ways in which they could respond?

Use the following framework to capture your answers.

	Architectural innovation	Component innovation
Likely threat/opportunity for player 1 – and why		
Likely threat/opportunity for player 2 – and why		
Etc.		

2. **Competence destroying and competence enhancing innovation**
    Try to review the case in terms of the following questions.

   - To what extent do the changes involve competence-enhancing (i.e. building on what a player in the industry already knows so they can strengthen their position) or competence-destroying (i.e. something completely new which requires learning some new tricks) innovations?
   - And for whom? (Think about the different players in the music industry – who are the likely winners and losers.)
   - What strategies might a firm use to exploit the opportunities? (Again think about the different players in the industry and how they might defend their positions or open up new opportunities.)

   Use the following framework to capture your answers.

	An established record company	A newcomer wanting to offer entertainment on the Web	A music publishing company (responsible for copyrights on sheet music, etc.)	Other examples . . .
Is the change competence enhancing? Why?				
Is it competence destroying? Why?				
What might you do about this to secure and improve your position?				

3. Can you map the different kinds of innovation in the case study? Which were incremental and which radical/discontinuous? Why? Give examples to support your answer.

4. Strategic advantage in innovation can come through combinations of four basic types of innovation – product/offering, process, position and paradigm (mental model). (Look at page 19 to remind yourself about this.) Giving examples to illustrate your answer, how has the pattern of strategic advantage changed in the music industry?

5. Is the 'revolution' in the music industry a result of the development of new technologies? Or is it happening because of changes on the demand side – shifts in what people want and are prepared to pay for? Or is it a mixture of both? What lessons might that offer to some-one wanting to enter the industry as a new player? And what might an established player do to preserve their position? Illustrate your answer with examples.

Summary of Web Resources

Cases

- Public sector innovation
- Karolinska
- Marshalls
- Model T Ford
- Discontinuous innovation
- Zara

Media

- Finnegan's Fish Bar video

Tools

- 4Ps
- Strategic advantage
- Innovation audit tool

Chapter 2

Social Entrepreneurship and Innovation

Go online to find additional . . .

Cases

Tools

Media

www.iande.info

Thinking about Innovation

INNOVATION IN ACTION

The Aravind Eye Care System has become the largest eye care facility in the world with its headquarters in Madurai, India. Its doctors perform over 200,000 cataract operations every year – and with such experience they have developed state-of-the-art techniques to match their excellent facilities. The cost of these operations runs from $50 to $300, with over 60% of patients being treated free. Despite only 40% of customers paying, the company is highly profitable and the average cost per operation (across free and paying patients) at $25 is the envy of most hospitals around the world.

Aravind was founded by Dr G. Venkataswamy back in 1976 on his retirement from the Government Medical College and represents the result of a passionate concern to eradicate needless blindness in the population. Within India there are an estimated 9 million (and worldwide 45 million) people who suffer from needless blindness which could be cured via corrective glasses and simple cataract or other surgery. Building on his experience in organising rural eye camps to deal with diagnosis and treatment he set about developing a low-cost high quality solution to the problem, originally aiming at its treatment in his home state of Tamil Nadu.

One of the key building blocks in developing the Aravind system has been transferring the ideas of another industry concerned with low cost, high and consistent quality provision – the hamburger business pioneered by Ray Croc and underpinning McDonald's. By applying the same process innovation approaches to standardisation, workflow and tailoring tasks to skills, he created a system which not only delivered high quality but was also reproducible. The model has now diffused widely – there are now five hospitals within Tamil Nadu offering nearly 4000 beds, the majority of which are free. It has moved beyond cataract surgery to education, lens manufacturing, research and development and other linked activities around the theme of improving sight and access to treatment.

In making this vision come alive Dr V has not only demonstrated considerable entrepreneurial flair – he has created a template which others, including health providers in the advanced industrial economies, are now looking at very closely.

Go online to see the full study of the Aravind Eye Care System.

www.iande.info

In this book we will be looking at the challenge of *change* – and how individuals and groups of entrepreneurs, working alone or inside organisations, try to bring this about. We've seen that innovation is not a simple flash of inspiration but an extended and organised process of turning bright ideas into successful realities – changing the offering (product/service), the ways in which it is created and delivered (process innovation), the context and the ways in which it is introduced to that context (position innovation) and the overall mental models for thinking about what we are doing (business model or 'paradigm' innovation).

Above all we've seen that getting innovation to happen depends on a focused and determined drive – a passion to change things which we call 'entrepreneurship'. Essentially this is about being prepared to challenge and change, to take (calculated) risks and put energy and enthusiasm into the venture, picking up and enthusing other supporters along the way.

> 'Social entrepreneurs are not content just to give a fish or teach how to fish. They will not rest until they have revolutionized the fishing industry'.
>
> —Bill Drayton, CEO, chair and founder of Ashoka,
> a global non-profit organisation devoted to developing
> the profession of social entrepreneurship.

If we think about successful entrepreneurs they are typically ambitious, mission driven, passionate, strategic (not just impulsive), resourceful, results oriented. And we can think of plenty of names to fit this frame – Bill Gates (Microsoft), Richard Branson (Virgin), James Dyson, Larry Page and Sergey Brin (Google) or Jeff Bezos (Amazon).

But we could also apply these terms to describe people like Florence Nightingale, Elizabeth Fry or Albert Schweizer. And whilst less famous than Gates or Bezos, there are some impressive individuals around today who have made a significant mark on the world through getting their ideas into action. As the Ashoka Foundation comments, 'Unlike traditional business entrepreneurs, social entrepreneurs primarily seek to generate "social value" rather than profits. And unlike the majority of non-profit organizations, their work is targeted not only towards immediate, small-scale effects, but sweeping, long-term change.'

For example Muhammad Yunus revolutionised economics by founding the Grameen Bank, or 'village bank', in Bangladesh in 1976 to offer 'micro-loans' to help impoverished people attain economic self-sufficiency through self-employment – a model that has now been replicated in 58 countries around the world. Or there's Dr Venkataswamy, founder of the Aravind clinics, whose passion for finding ways of giving eyesight back to people with cataracts in his home state of Tamil Nadu eventually led to the development of an eye care system which has helped thousands of people around the country.

These are people who undoubtedly fit our entrepreneur mould – as Table 2.1 shows – but target their efforts in a different, socially valuable direction. Wikipedia defines a social entrepreneur as 'someone who recognizes a social problem and uses traditional entrepreneurial principles to organize, create, and manage a venture to make social change. Whereas business entrepreneurs typically measure performance in profit and return, social entrepreneurs often start nonprofits and citizen groups.'

TABLE 2.1   Characteristics of social entrepreneurs

- *Ambitious:* Social entrepreneurs tackle major social issues – poverty, healthcare, equal opportunities, etc. – with the underlying desire – passion even – to make a change. They may work alone or from within a wide range of existing organisations including those which mix elements of non-profit and for-profit activity

- *Mission driven:* Their primary concern is generating social value rather than wealth – wealth creation may be part of the process but it is not an end in itself. Just like business entrepreneurs, social entrepreneurs are intensely focused and hard-driving – even relentless – in their pursuit of a social vision.

- *Strategic:* Like business entrepreneurs, social entrepreneurs see and act upon what others miss: opportunities to improve systems, create solutions and invent new approaches that create social value.

- *Resourceful:* Social entrepreneurs often work in contexts where they have limited access to capital and traditional market support systems. As a result, they must be exceptionally skilled at mustering and mobilising human, financial and political resources.

- *Results oriented:* Again, like business entrepreneurs, social entrepreneurs are motivated by a desire to see things change and to produce measurable returns. The results they seek are essentially linked to 'making the world a better place' – for example, through improving quality of life, access to basic resources, supporting disadvantaged groups, etc.

Importantly this is not just philanthropy or good works but rather the mobilisation of sound entrepreneurial principles – of the kind we've been looking at in this book – in pursuit of a different or parallel end. It's more than the basic human concern to give to others less fortunate – it is targeted at making long-term sustainable change rather than short-term alleviation of problems. And it is delivered in a much more systematic fashion – less 'good works' and more creating enabling structures which provide viable alternative models.

A key challenge in this is scaling up and spreading what may be good local ideas but which have much broader potential. As ex-US President Bill Clinton commented, 'nearly every problem has been solved by someone, somewhere. The challenge of the twenty-first century is to find out what works and scale it up!'

In many cases social innovation is an individual-driven thing, where a passion for change leads to remarkable and sustainable results. They include people like:

- Amitabha Sadangi of International Development Enterprises – India, who develops low-cost irrigation technologies to help subsistence farmers survive dry seasons.
- Anshu Gupta who has formed a channel for recycling clothes and fabric to meet the needs of rural poor in India. He initiated Goonj in 1998 with just 67 items; today, his organisation sends out over 40 tonnes of material every month, in 23 states.
- Mitch Besser, founder and medical director of the Cape Town-based programme mothers2mothers (m2m), which aims to reduce mother-to-child transmission of HIV and

provide care to women living with HIV. He founded mothers2mothers with one site in South Africa in 2001. It has grown to more than 645 sites in South Africa, Kenya, Lesotho, Malawi, Rwanda, Swaziland and Zambia.

- Tri Mumpuni, executive director of Indonesian NGO IBEKA (People Centred Economic and Business Institute), strives to bring light and energy into the lives of rural populations through the introduction of micro-hydropower (MHP) plants to more than 50 villages.

(These and other examples can be found on the www.ashoka.org website which links a global community of social entrepreneurs).

INNOVATION IN ACTION

Veronica Khosa was frustrated with the system of healthcare in South Africa. A nurse by trade, she saw sick people getting sicker, elderly people unable to get to a doctor and hospitals with empty beds that would not admit patients with HIV. So Veronica started Tateni Home Care Nursing Services and instituted the concept of 'home care' in her country. Beginning with practically nothing, her team took to the streets providing care to people in a way they had never received it – in the comfort and security of their homes. Just years later, the government had adopted her plan and through the recognition of leading health organisations the idea is spreading beyond South Africa.

(Asoka Foundation website)

But social entrepreneurship of this kind is also an increasingly important component of 'big business', as large organisations realise that they only secure a licence to operate if they can demonstrate some concern for the wider communities in which they are located. (The recent backlash against the pharmaceutical firms as a result of their perceived policies in relation to drug provision in Africa is an example of what can happen if firms don't pay attention to this agenda.) 'Corporate social responsibility' (CSR) is becoming a major function in many businesses and many make use of formal measures – such as the 'Triple Bottom Line' – to monitor and communicate their focus on more than simple profit-making.

Another increasingly significant development is the setting up by established organisations and successful business entrepreneurs of charitable foundations whose aim is explicitly to enable social entrepreneurship and the scaling of ideas with potential benefits. Examples include the Nike Foundation, Schwab Foundation, Skoll Foundation (established by Jeffrey Skoll, founder of eBay) and the Gates Foundation (established by Microsoft founder Bill Gates and which increasingly receives support from financier Warren Buffett). Other organisations – such as the Young Foundation in the UK – aim to develop connections and linkages across communities and enable social entrepreneurs to scale and extend their reach.

This chapter looks at how we might approach this challenge – how to mobilise the principles and practices of successful entrepreneurship and innovation to create social as well as economic value.

Uncommon Heroes

So far in this book we've assumed a profit-driven version of innovation – which is understandable, since it represents a powerful force for economic growth. As Karl Marx argued, innovation is 'the flywheel of capitalism' and many economists – notably Joseph Schumpeter[1] – have helped us understand the powerful links between innovation and the pursuit of profits. Of course these profits are not simply about making entrepreneurs and shareholders richer – they are also the fuel for future growth. It's the argument for spending on research and development (R&D) and on its relatives in market research – without it there may simply be no long-term future for the business. For example, in the pharmaceutical industry future growth depends on re-investing up to 25% of the sales in order to create the next wave of possibilities.

INNOVATION IN ACTION

Grameen Bank and the Development of 'Micro-finance'

One of the biggest problems facing people living below the poverty line is the difficulty of getting access to banking and financial services. As a result they are often dependent on moneylenders and other unofficial sources – and are often charged at exorbitant rates if they do borrow. This makes it hard to save and invest – and puts a major barrier in the way of breaking out of this spiral through starting new entrepreneurial ventures. Awareness of this problem led Muhammad Yunus, Head of the Rural Economics Program at the University of Chittagong, to launch a project to examine the possibility of designing a credit delivery system to provide banking services targeted at the rural poor. In 1976 the Grameen Bank Project (Grameen means 'rural' or 'village' in Bangla language) was established, aiming to

– extend banking facilities to the poor;
– eliminate the exploitation of the poor by money lenders;
– create opportunities for self-employment for unemployed people in rural Bangladesh;
– offer the disadvantaged an organisational format which they can understand and manage by themselves;
– reverse the age-old vicious circle of 'low income, low saving and low investment', into virtuous circle of 'low income, injection of credit, investment, more income, more savings, more investment, more income'.

The original project was set up in Jobra (a village adjacent to Chittagong University) and some neighbouring villages, and ran during 1976–1979. The core concept was of 'micro-finance' – enabling people (and a major success was with women) to take tiny loans to start to grow tiny businesses. With the sponsorship of the central bank of the country and support of the nationalized commercial banks, the project was extended to Tangail district (a district north of Dhaka, the capital

(continued)

city of Bangladesh) in 1979. Its further success there led to the model being extended to several other districts in the country and in 1983 it became an independent bank as a result of government legislation. Today Grameen Bank is owned by the rural poor whom it serves. Borrowers of the bank own 90% of its shares, while the remaining 10% is owned by the government. It now serves over 5 million clients, and has enabled 10,000 families to escape the poverty trap every month.

Grameen Bank has moved into other areas where the same model applies – for example, Grameen Phone is one of the largest mobile telephone operators in Asia but bases its model on providing communication access to the poorest members of society through innovative pricing models.

But the same core principles of innovation and entrepreneurship apply if we switch the motivating driver to something else. Just as mountaineers climb peaks simply *'because they are there'*, sometimes the motivation for innovating comes because of a desire to make a difference. Psychological studies of entrepreneurs (see Chapter 4) suggest they often have a high need for achievement – n-Ach, a technical term which is a measure of how far they want to make their mark on the world. High n-Ach requires some evidence that a mark has been made – but this doesn't have to be in terms of profit or loss on a balance sheet. As we saw earlier, many people find entrepreneurial satisfaction through social value creation – and even those with a long track record of building successful businesses may find themselves drawn into this territory. For example Bill Gates withdrawal from running Microsoft to concentrate on the Gates Foundation and other activities is the latest in a long line going back at least to the great industrial barons like Carnegie and Rockefeller.

The Challenge of Social Entrepreneurship

There are many heart-warming stories about individuals who have had the vision, creativity and drive to make something exceptional happen which creates social value. But we should be careful – just because there is no direct profit motive doesn't take the commercial challenges out of the equation. If anything it becomes harder to be an entrepreneur when the challenge is not only to convince people that it can be done (and use all the tricks of the entrepreneur's trade to do so) but also to do so in a form that makes it commercially sustainable. Bringing a radio within reach of rural poor across Africa is a great idea – but someone still has to pay for raw materials, build and run a factory, arrange for distribution, and collect the small money from the sales. None of this comes cheap – and setting up such a venture faces

 Go online to find a podcast interview with Suzana Moreira, a social entrepreneur who has been using mobile phones to distribute food and other goods across Africa.

www.iande.info

economic, political and business obstacles every bit as hard as a bright start-up company in medical devices or computer software working in a developed country environment. (For an illustration of this see the extended case study at the end of this chapter.)

Big Can be Beautiful Too

Of course it is not simply a matter of individuals and start-up ventures. As we will see throughout the book, entrepreneurial behaviour can be found in any organisation and is central to their ability to develop and reinvent themselves. In the field of social entrepreneurship a growing number of businesses are recognising the possibilities of pursuing parallel and complementary trajectories, targeting both conventional profits and also social value creation.

INNOVATION IN ACTION

BT, the UK telecommunications firm, has – under strong pressure from the regulator – a responsibility to provide services for all elements of society but it has used the connections in this 'stakeholder network' to move early into understanding and creation of services for what will be a major expansion in the future with an ageing population. By 2026, 30% of the UK population will be more than 60 years old. The pilot innovation is based on placing sensors in the home to monitor movement and the use of power and water – if something goes wrong it triggers an alarm. It has already begun to generate significant revenues for BT but has also opened up the possibility of relieving pressure on the NHS for beds and services – estimates suggest savings of around £700m of this kind if fully deployed. Most significantly the initial project can be seen as a stepping-stone, a transitional object to help BT learn about what will be a huge and very different market in the future.

By engaging stakeholders directly, companies are also better able to avoid conflicts, or to resolve them when they arise. In some cases, this involves directly engaging activists who are leading campaigns or protests against a company. For example, Starbucks responded to customers' concerns and activist protests about the impact of coffee growing on songbirds by partnering with leading activist groups to improve organic, bird-friendly coffee production methods, setting up a pilot sourcing program, and further increasing public awareness. The conflict was resolved, and Starbucks established itself as a leader on this issue

INNOVATION IN ACTION

The UK 'do-it-yourself' home and garden retailer B&Q has been honoured for its work on disability where it has used corporate social responsibility to drive improvements in customer services.

(*continued*)

What in retrospect looks like a successful business strategy has in fact evolved through real-time learning from partnerships between individual stores and local disability organisations. Following on from its pioneering experiments in having stores entirely staffed by older people, B&Q wanted to ensure that disabled people are able to shop in confidence and that they will be able to access goods and services easily. In the UK alone there are 8 million disabled people; it is estimated that the 'disabled pound' is worth £30 billion and is growing. However B&Q also saw this initiative as a way to improve wider customer care competencies: 'If we can get it right for disabled people we can get it right for most people.' To begin the process of understanding what it was like to shop and work in B&Q as a disabled person they started by talking to disabled people in a single store. They have now established 300 partnerships between store 'disability champions' and local disability groups to understand local needs and develop training on disability awareness and service provision. They see these partnerships as a way for B&Q to access 'the incredible amount of knowledge, commitment and enthusiasm which exists in this wide variety of organisations'. As a result all B&Q staff now take part in disability awareness training, they are improving store design and provide printed material in Braille, audio type, large print and CD-ROM. They are also developing their 'Daily Living Made Easier' range of products, from grab rails and bath chairs through to visual smoke alarms and lightweight garden tools.

Ahold, the largest retailer in the Netherlands, has also used stakeholder engagement to enable it to expand its operations into under-served urban areas. The company realised that on its own it would not be able to operate successfully and would need to work with government and other companies to create a 'sound investment climate' locally. With the local government and nine other retailers it developed a comprehensive development plan for the Dutch town of Enschede.

Sometimes there is scope for social entrepreneurship to spin out of mainstream innovative activity. Procter & Gamble's PUR water purification system offers radical improvements to point-of-use drinking water delivery. Estimates are that it has reduced intestinal infections by 30–50%. The product grew out of research in the mainstream detergents business but the initial conclusion was that the market potential of the product was not high enough to justify investment; by reframing it as a development aid, the company has improved its image but also opened up a radical new area for working.

In some cases the process begins with an individual but gradually a trend is established which other players see as relevant to follow, in the process bringing their resources and experience to the game. Examples here might include 'Fair Trade' products, which were originally a minority idea but have now become a mainstream item in any supermarket, or the wind-up radio, which provided a model that highlighted the needs – but also the opportunities – for communications in developing countries.

There is also increasing pressure on established businesses to work to a more socially responsible agenda – with many now operating a key function around corporate social responsibility. The concept is simple – firms need to secure a 'licence to operate' from the stakeholders in the various constituencies in which they work. Unless they take notice of the concerns and values of those communities, they risk passive – and increasingly active – resistance and their operations can be severely affected. CSR goes beyond public relations in many cases, with genuine efforts to ensure social value is created alongside economic value, and that stakeholders benefit as widely as possible and not simply as consumers. CSR thinking has led to the development of formal measures and frameworks like the 'triple bottom line' which many firms use as a way of expanding the traditional company reporting framework to take into account not just financial outcomes but also environmental and social performance.

It is easy to become cynical about CSR activity, seeing it as a cosmetic overlay on what are basically the same old business practices. But there is a growing recognition that pursuing social entrepreneurship-linked goals may not be incompatible with developing a viable and commercially successful business. For example, a survey by the consultants Arthur D. Little of around 40 technology firms in Europe, Japan and the USA suggested that a focus on the sustainability question was beginning to be recognised as a key way of creating new market space, products and processes. In particular 95% felt that it had potential to bring business value and almost a quarter felt it definitely would deliver such value. This value is in both intangible domains like brand and reputation but increasingly in bottom-line benefits like market share and product/service innovation. Significantly there has been considerable acceleration in these trends compared to the first time the survey was conducted, in 1999. When asked where they saw the benefits coming in five years' time, 90% believed they would come through new products and services and 75% in new markets and new business models.

The A.D. Little survey suggests that an increasing number of firms are looking to develop new opportunities via stakeholder innovation. They use the metaphor of a journey which begins with simple compliance innovation – the 'licence to operate' argument. Many companies have now moved into the 'foothills' of the 'beyond compliance' area where they are realising that they have to deal with key stakeholders and that in the process some interesting innovation opportunities can emerge. But the real challenge is to move on to the innovation high ground of full-scale stakeholder innovation, 'creating new products and services, processes and markets which will respond to the needs of future as well as current customers'.

INNOVATION IN ACTION

Mobilising Stakeholder Innovation

The Danish pharmaceutical firm Novo Nordisk is deploying stakeholder innovation through expansion and reframing of the role of its Corporate Stakeholder Relations activities. It has been consistently highly rated on this, not least because it is a board-level strategic responsibility (specified in the company's articles of association) with significant resources committed to projects to sustain and enhance good practice. It was one of the first companies to introduce the concept of the Triple Bottom Line performance measurement, recognising the need to take into account wider social and societal concerns and to be clear about its values.

(continued)

But there is now growing recognition that this investment is also a powerful innovation resource. It offers a way of complementing the compound pipeline R&D with special relevance to the right-hand side of our map. As we've seen, the questions here are:

- How does the organisation pick up on emergent phenomena?
- How do they get in the game early?
- And if they do manage that, how might they position themselves to shape the emergent new game?

Investing in stakeholder relations represents a powerful way of doing this by involving the company closely in learning from a wide range of actors. Three examples will help highlight this process.

(i) The DAWN (Diabetes Attitudes, Wishes and Needs) programme

The objective of DAWN, initiated in 2001, was to explore attitudes, wishes and needs of both diabetes sufferers and healthcare professionals to identify critical gaps in the overall care offering. Its findings showed in quantitative fashion how people with diabetes suffered from different types of emotional distress and poor psychological wellbeing, and that such factors were a major contributing factor to impaired health outcomes. Insights from the programme opened up new areas for innovation across the system. For example, a key focus was on the ways in which healthcare professionals presented therapeutic options involving a combination of insulin treatment and lifestyle elements – and on developing new approaches to this.

A DAWN Summit in 2003 brought together representatives from 31 countries and key agencies such as the World Health Organisation; it was widely publicised in specialist and non-specialist journals and via the International Diabetes Federation (IDF). The result has been to establish a common framework within which an understanding of the issues is combined with relationships with key players who could become involved in the design and delivery of relevant innovations. DAWN's value is as an independent, evidence-based platform on which extended discussion and exploration can take place around the future of diabetes management as a holistic system – not simply the treatment via insulin or other specific therapies. It has helped mobilise a global community of practice across which there is significant sharing of learning and interactive changing of perspectives.

Søren Skovlund, senior adviser, Corporate Health Partnerships, sees the key element as '. . . the use of the DAWN study as a vehicle to get all the different people round the same table . . . to bring patients, health professionals, politicians, payers, the media together to find new ways to work more effectively together on the same task . . . You can't avoid getting some innovation because you're bringing together different baskets of knowledge in the room!'

Why do it? One reason is a growing sense that the rules of the game around chronic disease management are shifting. For example the WHO estimates that diabetes is a bigger killer than AIDS with around 3.2 million deaths attributable to the disease – and its complications – every year. In developing countries the figures are particularly alarming where one in ten deaths of adults aged 35 to 64 are due to diabetes (in some countries the figure is as high as one in five).

(continued)

Chronic diseases like diabetes represent a time bomb around which major activity is likely to happen in the near future. Healthcare systems are increasingly focusing their efforts on reducing the socio-economic burden of disease through reorganisation of the care process and structure. These major shifts pose the risk that the product-focused pharmaceutical industry is falling behind.

DAWN is a learning investment for Novo Nordisk about the whole system of diabetes care, not just the drug side. It opens up possibilities around emergent models – for example, in integrated service solutions provision around chronic healthcare management.

(ii) National Diabetes Programmes

DAWN provides an input to a set of activities operated by Novo Nordisk under the banner of National Diabetes Programmes (NDPs). These programmes bring the company into close and continuing proximity with key and diverse players in that field. Beyond the PR value of showing the company's commitment to improving diabetes care it creates presence/positioning for emergence.

This initiative began in 2001 when the company set about building a network of relationships in key geographical areas helping devise and configure relevant holistic care programmes. Rather than a product focus, NDPs offer a range of inputs – for example, supporting education of healthcare professionals or establishing clinics for care of diabetic ulcers. CEO, Lars Rebien Sørensen argues that 'only by offering and advocating the right solutions for diabetes care will we be seen as a responsible company. If we just say "drugs, drugs, drugs", they will say "give us a break!"' This is clearly good CSR practice – but the potential learning about new approaches to care, especially under resource-constrained conditions, also represents an important 'hidden R&D' investment.

Typically the NDP process involves identifying needs with key partners and developing a National Diabetes Healthcare Plan – with Novo Nordisk providing resources to help with implementation. The NDPs are closely linked to another initiative, the World Diabetes Foundation, established in 2003 with an initial pledge of $100 m over a ten year period. It operates in over 40 countries trying to raise awareness and improve care especially in areas – such as India and China – where diabetes is seriously under-diagnosed.

The core underlying principle is one of developing and testing generic prototype plans which can then be 'customised' for a variety of other countries. For example, Tanzania was an early pilot. It was initially difficult to convince authorities to take chronic diseases like diabetes into account since they had no budget for them and were already fighting hard with infectious diseases. With little likelihood of new investment Novo Nordisk began working with local diabetes associations to establish demonstration projects. It set up clinics in hospitals and villages, trained staff and provided relevant equipment and materials. This gave visibility to the possibilities in a chronic disease management approach – for example, before the programme someone with diabetes might have had to travel 200 th km to the major hospital in Dar-es-Salaam whereas now they can be dealt with locally. The value to the national health system is significant in terms of savings on the costs of treating complications such as blindness and amputations which are tragic and expensive results of poor and delayed treatment. As a result the Ministry of Health is able to deal with diabetes management without

(continued)

the need for new investment in hospital capacity or recruitment of new doctors and nurses. Novo Nordisk is essentially a facilitator here – but in the process is very much centrally involved in an emerging and shifting healthcare system.

NDPs represent an experience-sharing network across over 40 countries. Much of the learning is about the context of different national healthcare systems and how to work within them to bring about significant change – essentially positioning the company for co-evolution. One of the big lessons has been the recognition of the problem of under-diagnosis. Typically around 80% of diabetes sufferers in developing countries remain undiagnosed, and as a result most attention (of the healthcare system and the pharmaceutical companies working with them) goes on the 20% who are identified. The move is now towards finding the undiagnosed and developing ways to manage their diabetes in such a way that they don't get complications which is where the major costs arise. This has implications not only for expanding the potential market for insulin treatment but also moving the company into much broader areas of healthcare management and delivery.

The Potential of the 'Bottom of the Pyramid'

In his powerful book *The Fortune at the Bottom of the Pyramid* C. K. Prahalad[2] points out that most of the world's population – around 4 billion people – live close to or below the poverty line, with an average income of less than $2 per day. It is easy to make assumptions about this group along the lines of 'they can't afford it so why innovate?' In fact the challenge of meeting their basic needs for food, water, shelter and healthcare require high levels of creativity – but beyond this social agenda lies a considerable innovation opportunity. But it requires a reframing of the 'normal' rules of the market game and a challenging of core assumptions. Table 2.2 gives some examples.

TABLE 2.2 Challenging assumptions about the bottom of the pyramid	
Assumption	**Reality – and opportunity**
The poor have no purchasing power and do not represent a viable market	Although low income the sheer scale of this market makes it interesting. Additionally the poor often pay a premium for access to many goods and services – e.g. borrowing money, clean water, telecommunications and basic medicines – because they cannot address 'mainstream' channels like shops and banks. The innovation challenge is to offer low-cost, low-margin but high-quality goods and services across a potential market of 4 billion people.
	(continued)

TABLE 2.2 (*Continued*)	
Assumption	**Reality – and opportunity**
The poor are not brand-conscious	Evidence suggests a high degree of brand and value consciousness – so if an entrepreneur can come up with a high-quality, low-cost solution it will be subject to hard testing in this market. Learning to deal with this can hep migrate to other markets – essentially the classic pattern of 'disruptive innovation'.
The poor are hard to reach	By 2015 there are likely to be nearly 400 cities in the developing world with populations over 1 million and 23 with over 10 million. 30–40% of these will be poor – so the potential market access is considerable. Innovative thinking around distribution – via new networks or agents (such as the women village entrepreneurs used by Hindustan Lever in India or the 'Avon ladies' in rural Brazil) – can open up untapped markets.
The poor are unable to use and not interested in advanced technology	Experience with PC kiosks, low-cost mobile phone sharing and access to the Internet suggests that rates of take-up and sophistication of use are extremely fast amongst this group. In India the e-choupal (e-meeting place) set up by software company ITC enabled farmers to check prices for their products at the local markets and auction houses. Very shortly after that the same farmers were using the Web to access prices of their soybeans at the Chicago Board of Trade and strengthen their negotiating hand!

Meeting the needs of people at the bottom of the pyramid is not about charity but rather about a fundamental rethink of the business model – *'paradigm innovation'* in the 4Ps model we looked at in Chapter 1 – to create sustainable alternative systems

INNOVATION IN ACTION

Changing the Game at the Bottom of the Pyramid

Pretty high on anyone's list of wants is a quality home – but financing more than basic shelter is often beyond the means of most of the world's population. But CEMEX, the Mexican

(continued)

cement and building materials producer has pioneered an innovative approach to changing this. Triggered by a domestic financial crisis in the mid-1990s, CEMEX saw a big drop in sales in Mexico. But closer inspection revealed that the market segment of do-it-yourself, especially amongst the less wealthy had sustained demand levels. In fact the market was worth a great deal – nearly a billion dollars per year – but it was made up of many small purchases rather than large construction projects. Since over 60% of the Mexican population earn less than $5 per day the challenge was to find ways to work with this market in the future.

The response was a novel financing approach, built on the fact that many communities operate a 'savings club' type of scheme to help finance major purchases – the tanda network. CEMEX set up Patrimonio Hoy – a version of the tanda system which allowed poor people to save and access credit for building projects. It relies on social networks, replacing traditional distributors with 'promoters' who work on a commission but who also help set up and run the tandas; significantly, 98% of these promoters are women. The scheme allows access not just to materials but to architects and other support services; it has effectively changed the way a large segment of society can manage its own construction projects. Success with the home improvements area has led to its extension to village infrastructure projects linked to drainage, lighting and other community facilities.

ITC is one of India's largest private sector firms, with a turnover of around $4bn. It operates in a variety of markets including agri-trading, dealing with a variety of Indian commodities including pepper, edible nuts and fruits and grains. It has been active in trying to improve its relationships with local farmers and pioneered the 'e-choupal' – village information centre – as a route for doing so. (Choupal is a Hindi word meaning traditional gathering place.) Some 2000 computer kiosks have been located in villages and linked to a wider network across the country, allowing access to information about weather, prices, agricultural advice, etc. It helps ITC plan its logistics more effectively but also brings benefits to the farmers – e-choupals allow them to find out about prices at local markets and reduces the high transaction costs which the traditional (and often corrupt) manual system of intermediaries and auctions carried. Uptake has been rapid and the farmers soon learn to use the system to strengthen their position – indeed one group began not only looking at local markets but at the Chicago Stock Exchange to monitor soya bean prices and futures!

In addition to direct benefits e-choupals also provide villages with access to educational and information resources.

Go online to find a case study of some examples written by Girish Prabhu, a director of Srishti Labs in Bangalore, specialists in developing 'bottom of the pyramid' solutions.

www.iande.info

Challenges in Managing Social Entrepreneurship and Innovation

We'll see throughout the book how innovation doesn't simply happen – it is a process which can be organised and managed. The model we introduced in Chapter 1 looks like this:

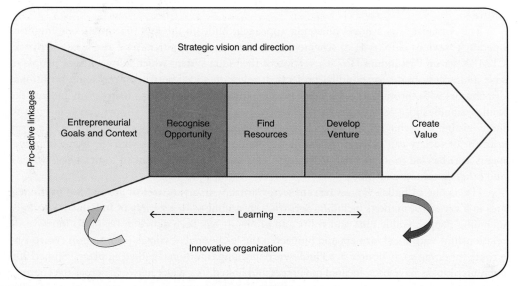

FIGURE 2.1   Model for innovation and entrepreneurship.

The process begins with seeking out opportunities – often new or different combinations which no one else has seen, and working them up into viable concepts which could be taken forward. It's then a matter of persuading various people – venture capitalists, senior management, etc. – to choose to put resources behind the idea rather than backing off or backing something else. If we get past this hurdle the next step is beginning to transform the idea into reality, weaving together a variety of different knowledge and resource streams before finally launching the new thing – product, process or service – onto a market. Whether they choose to adopt and use it, and spread the word to others so the innovation diffuses depends a lot on how we manage using other knowledge and resource streams to understand, shape and develop the market. We also know that the whole process is influenced and shaped by having clear strategic direction and support, an underlying innovative and enthusiastic organisation willing to commit its creativity and energy, and extensive and rich links to other players who can help with the knowledge and resource flows we need. Fuelling the whole is the underlying creativity, drive, foresight and intuition to make it happen – entrepreneurship – and take the risks.

So how does this play out in the case of social entrepreneurship? Table 2.3 gives some examples of the challenges

TABLE 2.3   Challenges in social entrepreneurship

What has to be managed	Challenges in social entrepreneurship
Recognising opportunities	Many potential social entrepreneurs (SEs) have the passion to change something in the world – and there are plenty of targets to choose from, like poverty, access to education, healthcare and so on. But passion isn't enough – they also need the classic entrepreneur's skill of spotting an opportunity, a connection, a possibility which could develop. It's about searching for new ideas which might bring a different solution to an existing problem – for example, the micro-finance alternative to conventional banking or street-level money-lending.
	As we've seen elsewhere in the book the skill is often not so much discovery – finding something completely new – as connection – making links between disparate things. In the SE field the gaps may be very wide – for example, connecting rural farmers to high-tech international stock markets requires considerably more vision to bridge the gap than spotting the need for a new variant of futures trading software. So SEs need both passion and vision, plus considerable broking and connecting skills.
Finding resources	Spotting an opportunity is one thing – but getting others to believe in it and, more importantly, back it is something else. Whether it's an inventor approaching a venture capitalist or an internal team pitching a new product idea to the strategic management in a large organisation the story of successful entrepreneurship is about convincing other people.
	In the case of SE the problem is compounded by the fact that the targets for such a pitch may not be immediately apparent. Even if you can make a strong business case and have thought through the likely concerns and questions, who do you approach to try to get backing? There are some foundations and no-profit organisations but in many cases one of the important skill sets of a SE is networking, the ability to chase down potential funders and backers and engage them in their project.
	Even within an established organisation the presence of a structure may not be sufficient. For many SE projects the challenge is that they take the firm in very different directions, some of which fundamentally challenge its core business. For

(continued)

TABLE 2.3 (*Continued*)

What has to be managed	Challenges in social entrepreneurship
	example, a proposal to make drugs cheaply available in the developing world might sound a wonderful idea from an SE perspective – but it poses huge challenges to the structure and operations of a large pharmaceutical firm with complex economics around R&D funding, distribution and so on.
	Important to build coalitions of support – securing support for social innovation is very often a distributed process but power and resources are often not concentrated in the hands of single decision-maker. There may also not be a 'Board' or venture capitalist to pitch the ideas to – instead it is a case of building momentum and groundswell.
	Very important to provide practical demonstrations of what otherwise might be seen as idealistic 'pipedreams'. The role of pilots which then get taken up and gather support is well-proven – for example, the Fair Trade model or micro-finance.
Developing the venture	Social innovation requires extensive creativity in getting hold of the diverse resources to make things happen – especially since the funding base may be limited. Networking skills become critical here – engaging different players and aligning them with the core vision.
	One of the most important elements in much social innovation is scaling up – taking what might be a good idea implemented by one person or in a local community and amplifying it so that it has widespread social impact. For example, Anshu Gupta's original idea was to recycle old clothes found on rubbish dumps or cast away to help poor people in his local community. Beginning with 67 items of clothing the idea has now been scaled so that he and his organisation collect and recycle 40 tonnes of cloth every month across 23 states in India. The principle has been applied to other materials – for example, recycling old cassettes to make mats and soft furnishings. (See http://www.goonj.org/)
Innovation strategy	Here the overall vision is critical – the passionate commitment to a clear vision can engage others – but social entrepreneurs can also be accused of idealism and '*having their head in the clouds*'. Consequently there is a need for a clear plan to translate the vision step-by-step into reality.

(*continued*)

TABLE 2.3 (*Continued*)	
What has to be managed	**Challenges in social entrepreneurship**
Innovative organisation/ rich networking	Social innovation depends on loose and organic structures where the main linkages are through a sense of shared purpose. At the same time there is a need to ensure some degree of structure to allow for effective implementation. The history of many successful social innovations is essentially one of networking, mobilising support and accessing diverse resources through rich networks. This places a premium on networking and broking skills.

STRATEGIC AND SOCIAL IMPACT

Innovation is about change – the word comes from the Latin and means changing, making new. One way in which change becomes a part of everyday life is through entrepreneurs finding and making available new products or services and new ways of creating and delivering them. They don't do this out of the goodness of their hearts – they do so because there is a strong economic imperative. If they can offer something which no one else can they will have a monopoly and be able to make a lot of money selling something which is scarce and desirable. Of course others will see the attractions of this and jump in with their imitations – and gradually the advantages will get competed away. At this point our entrepreneur will get fed up and go and look for the next opportunity to get ahead in the economic race.

So far, so obvious – and as an explanation for what drives the capitalist system it has been well developed by writers like Joseph Schumpeter. But not all entrepreneurs want to create wealth, either for themselves or the companies they work for. Social entrepreneurship is about using the same set of skills and following the same core innovation process to bring about change – the difference is that this is socially valuable, 'concerned in some way with making the world a better place'.

The two are not necessarily incompatible – increasingly we are seeing 'win-win' combinations of innovative projects which both improve social well-being and also deliver profits. There may well be a 'fortune at the bottom of the pyramid' as C.K. Prahalad suggests – and smart firms would do well to look at how they might open up this 4 billion person market. But there may also be no option – large firms won't continue to hold a 'licence to operate' unless they address wider social concerns amongst their stakeholders – as major pharmaceutical, food and other firms have been finding out. Innovating only along economically attractive pathways may well be profitable – but in the face of energy shortages, climate change, waste accumulation and depletion of natural resources we may find that the current models for doing business simply

(*continued*)

become unsustainable, as we will see in the next chapter. Social entrepreneurship isn't simply a 'feel good' aspect of the innovation puzzle to occupy the more idealistic players in the game – it is increasingly becoming a central component of successful and sustainable business. But making it happen will require learning and absorbing a new set of skills to sit alongside our current ways of thinking about and managing innovation. How do we find opportunities which deliver social as well as economic benefits? How do we identify and engage a wide range of stakeholders – and understand and meet their very diverse expectations? How do we mobilise resources across networks, how do we build coalitions of support for socially valuable ideas? One thing is already clear from studies of successful social entrepreneurship – it needs organising and managing in an even more professional fashion than 'conventional' business innovation.

DEVELOPING PERSONAL CAPABILITIES

Social entrepreneurs (SEs) need to possess – or develop – the same set of capabilities as commercial entrepreneurs. That means being prepared to take risks, spot and seize opportunities and build networks. Some of the key 'tips' for SEs offered by experienced players are:

- spot a gap in the market and try to fill it – for example, gaps exist where the private and public sectors fail to provide a service or product;
- be clear why you want to do it – many social entrepreneurs have the passion but lack enough patience in researching for constructive or feasible ideas;
- be able to network with a variety of people and communities;
- be good at spotting and re-using resources that are underused or abandoned, such as buildings and open spaces;
- don't be afraid to make mistakes – but do be prepared to learn from them;
- manage the cash flow – the commonest cause of any business failure is simply running out of cash (interestingly women are often key players in SE stories – perhaps because in most households they manage the family finances);
- use 'viral marketing' – unlike well-resourced businesses with access to marketing and advertising budgets SEs often need to mobilise low-cost options – and word of mouth is often powerful, especially via the Internet;
- identify your skill needs – and map your existing and required network (What do you need in the way of management, financial, sales and marketing, production, distribution, service? Can you link to specialist organisations like the Ashoka Foundation or Skoll Centre?);
- get someone expert to review your plan – business plans don't need to be long but they do need to contain critical components, and to pass scrutiny by people who know what will work and what won't in the business world;
- have an exit strategy – deciding ahead of time how you will react when/if things get tough. It may be a good idea to share your ideas with other social organisations – to spread the risks and costs and also because your idea may be a big catalyst in getting another organisation off the ground.

Chapter Summary

1 Innovation is not a simple flash of inspiration but an extended and organised process of turning bright ideas into successful realities. Getting innovation to happen depends on a focused and determined drive – a passion to change things which we call 'entrepreneurship'. Essentially this is about being prepared to challenge and change, to take (calculated) risks and put energy and enthusiasm into the venture, picking up and enthusing other supporters along the way.

2 These are people who undoubtedly fit this entrepreneur mould but target their efforts in a different, socially valuable direction. 'Social entrepreneurs' recognise a social problem and use traditional entrepreneurial principles to organise, create, and manage a venture to make social change.

3 Just because there is no direct profit motive doesn't take the commercial challenges out of the equation. If anything it becomes harder to be an entrepreneur when the challenge is not only to convince people that it can be done (and use all the tricks of the entrepreneur's trade to do so) but also to do so in a form that makes it commercially sustainable.

4 Social entrepreneurship of this kind is also an increasingly important component of 'big business', as large organisations realise that they only secure a licence to operate if they can demonstrate some concern for the wider communities in which they are located.

5 Increasingly we are seeing 'win-win' combinations of innovative projects which both improve social well-being and also deliver profits. There may well be a 'fortune at the bottom of the pyramid' – the estimated 4 billion people on less than $2/day income.

6 Making social entrepreneurship happen will require learning and absorbing a new set of skills to sit alongside our current ways of thinking about and managing innovation. How do we find opportunities which deliver social as well as economic benefits? How do we identify and engage a wide range of stakeholders – and understand and meet their very diverse expectations? How do we mobilise resources across networks, how do we build coalitions of support for socially valuable ideas?

Key Terms Defined

Double bottom line   assessing an organisation's performance against financial and social goals.

Social enterprise   an organisation that tries to pursue a double bottom line or a triple bottom line.

Social entrepreneurship   applying entrepreneurship to achieve social goals rather than (but not excluding) financial reward.

Triple bottom line   simultaneous assessment of a company's performance against its financial and shareholder performance, its internal and external stakeholder expectations and responsibilities and its environmental responsibilities.

Further Reading and Resources

There is a wealth of information about social entrepreneurship including useful websites for the Ashoka Foundation (www.ashoka.org) , the Skoll Foundation (www.skollfoundation.com), and the Institute for Social Entrepreneurs http://www.socialent.org/. Chapter 8 has a case example of the UK organisation UnLtd and weblinks to their site. Stanford University's Entrepreneurs website has a number of resources including videos of social entrepreneurs explaining their projects http://edcorner.stanford.edu

The Ashoka Foundation represents a global community of social entrepreneurs and Ashoka Fellows are recognised as having made a significant contribution in some area of social enterprise.

Video links can be found relating to many of these – for example the Goonj organisation set up by Anshu Gupta. Resource link – videos about goonj http://ibnlive.in.com/videos/88328/03_2009/realhero_award5a/real-heroes-honourçing-the-extraordinary-indian.html

A number of books describing approaches and tools include Bornstein, David, *How to Change the World: Social Entrepreneurs and the Power of New Ideas* (Oxford, 2004); Brinckerhoff, Peter, *Social Entrepreneurship: The Art of Mission-Based Venture Development* (Wiley, 2000); Dees, Gregory, Jed Emerson, and Peter Economy, *Enterprising Nonprofits: A Tool-kit for Social Entrepreneurs* (Wiley, 2001); Murray, Robin, Caulier-Grice, Julia and Mulgan, Geoff, *The Open Book of Social Innovation* (The Young Foundation, London, 2010). A good description of the shifting balance in innovation thinking towards emerging economies is provided by Forbes, Naushad, and Wield, David, in *From Followers to Leaders* (Routledge, 2002).

Case studies of projects like Grameen bank (www.grameen-info.org) and the wind-up radio (www.freeplayenergy.com) also give insights into the process and the difficulties confronting social entrepreneurs. A useful website here is http://www.howtochangetheworld.org/, as is the Ashoka Foundation. Prahalad's book *The Fortune at the Bottom of the Pyramid* is a useful collection of cases in this direction.

References

1. Schumpeter, J. (1950). *Capitalism, Socialism and Democracy*. New York, Harper and Row.
2. Prahalad, C. K. (2006). *The Fortune at the Bottom of the Pyramid*. New Jersey, Wharton School Publishing.

Discussion Questions

1. Give a man a fish, and you feed him for a day. Teach a man to fish and he can feed himself for life. How might you put this principle into practice through a social entrepreneurship venture – and what might stop you making a success of this?

2. 'Some problems have no solution' – a somewhat pessimistic Japanese saying. How might a social entrepreneur challenge this?

3. Jasmine Chang has approached you – as an innovation adviser – with a novel treatment for childhood diarrhoea. How would you advise her to take this idea forward to make a difference.

4. In many ways taking a socially valuable concept to market has much in common with 'conventional' new product development. Where do you see the similarities and differences?

Team Exercise

Dragon's Den is a popular BBC TV programme in which successful entrepreneurs and venture capitalists listen to would-be entrepreneurs pitch for money to fund their business ideas. Appoint several team members to be the tough, hard-nosed and business-minded 'dragons' and the remainder of the group should prepare 'pitches' setting out how they would carry through a social innovation. Groups should spend a few minutes brainstorming around key areas of social need – and at the same time the dragons should think of the key questions to ask of any entrepreneur to assess whether and how far they have thought through their business idea.

Assignment Question

1. Identify an area of social need and develop some ideas for possible innovative solutions which might help deal with this challenge. Then think about how you would turn this into a business plan and convince other people to back your idea or help you take it forward. Think about the likely questions they would ask and how you would make a strong case to convince the more sceptical members of your audience. Write your ideas up as an outline business plan.

CASE STUDY 2

Exploring Innovation in Action:
Power to the People – Lifeline Energy

Trevor Baylis was quite a swimmer in his youth, representing Britain at the age of 15. So it wasn't entirely surprising that he ended up working for a swimming pool firm in Surrey before setting up his own company. He continued his swimming passion – working as a part-time TV stuntman doing underwater feats – but also followed an interest in inventing things. One of the projects he began work on in 1991 was to have widespread impact despite – or rather because of – being a 'low-tech' solution to a massive problem.

Having seen a documentary about AIDS in Africa he began to see the underlying need for something which could help communication. Much of the AIDS problem lies in the lack of awareness and knowledge across often isolated rural communities – people don't know about causes or prevention of this devastating disease. And this reflects a deeper problem – of *communication*. Experts estimate that less than 20% of the world's population have access to a telephone, while even fewer have a regular supply of electricity, much less television or Internet access. Very low literacy levels exclude most people from reading newspapers and other print media.

Radio is an obvious solution to the problem – but how can radio work when the receivers need power and in many places mains electricity is simply non-existent. An alternative is battery power – but batteries are equally problematic – even if they were of good quality and freely available via village stores people couldn't afford to buy them regularly. In countries where $1 a day is the standard wage, batteries can cost from a day's to a week's salary. The HIV/AIDS pandemic also means that household incomes are under increased pressure as earners become too ill to work while greater expenditure goes towards healthcare, leaving nothing for batteries.

What was needed was a radio which ran on some different source of electricity. In thinking about the problem Baylis remembered the old-fashioned telephones of pre-war days which had wind-up handles to generate power. He began experimenting, linking together odd items such as a hand brace, an electric motor and a small radio. He found that the brace turning the motor would act as a generator that would supply sufficient electricity to power the radio. By adding a clockwork mechanism he found that a spring could be wound up – and as it unwound the radio would play. This first working prototype ran for 14 minutes on a two minute wind. Trevor had invented a clockwork (wind-up) radio! As a potential solution to the communication problem the idea had real merit. The trouble was that, like thousands of entrepreneurs before him, Trevor couldn't

convince others of this. He spent nearly four years approaching major radio manufacturers like Philips and Marconi but to no avail. But luck often plays a significant part in the innovation story – and this was no exception. The idea came to
the attention of some TV researchers and the product was featured in 1994 on
the BBC TV programme *Tomorrow's World,* which showcased interesting and
exciting new inventions.

Amongst those who saw it and whose interest was taken by the wind-up radio
were a corporate finance expert, Christopher Staines, and a South African entrepreneur, Rory Stear. They bought the rights from Baylis and received a UK government grant to help develop the product further, including the addition of solar
panel options. In South Africa, the details of the invention were featured in a new
broadcast and heard by Hylton Appelbaum, head of an organisation called the
Liberty Life Foundation, who saw the potential. Even in relatively rich South
Africa, half the homes have no electricity, and elsewhere in Africa the problem is
even more severe.

Liberty Life is a body set up by a major South African insurance company and
Anita and Gordon Roddick, the socially conscious owners of the Body Shop. Part of
the work of the Foundation is in providing access to employment for the disabled and
a third of the company's factory workers are blind, deaf, in wheelchairs, or mentally
ill. Through Applebaum, Liberty Life provided the $1.5 million in venture capital that
founded the company. Baygen Power Industries (from Baylis Generator) was set up
by Staines and Stear in 1995, in Cape Town. Sixty per cent of the shares were held
by a group of organisations for the disabled, a condition of Liberty's support.
Technical development was provided by the Bristol University Electronics Engineering Department. Shortly thereafter production of the radio began in Cape Town by
BayGen Products PTY South Africa.

It came on the market at the beginning of 1996 and one year later around
160,000 units had been sold. Much of the early production was purchased by aid
charities working in Rwanda and other African countries where relief efforts were
underway.

This was not a glamorous product – as a *New York Times* article described it,
'It is no threat to a Sony Walkman. It weighs six pounds, it's built like an over-
stuffed lunch box, and it has a tinny speaker. But its wholesale price is only $40 and
it gets AM, FM, and shortwave, meaning it can pick up the British Broadcasting
Corporation or the Voice of America, so a circle of mud huts can zip back into the
Information Age with a twist of the wrist.'

(Source(s): Donald G. McNeil Jr.,
New York Times News Service, 1996)

The impact was significant. In 1996 another BBC TV programme, *QED,*
featured the radio and at one point showed footage of Baylis, Staines and Stear

together with Nelson Mandela who commented that this was a 'fantastic product that can provide an opportunity for those people who have been despised by society'.

Although appearing basic and low-tech there is a surprising amount of invention in the product. Baylis filed no less than 13 patents covering the mainspring and gears that drive a little dynamo. The spring mechanism is not a simple clockwork type but is more closely related to the kind used in rewinding auto seat belts. A double-spool mechanism keeps its tension constant, which is crucial, and the gearing is sophisticated.

Baygen continued to develop products around the energy needs of developing countries including wind-up torches and small generators. The company renamed itself in 1999 as the Freeplay Energy Group and have taken the original concepts into a wide range of new product areas.

Although founded on strong social entrepreneurship principles the business has grown through expanding markets in both developing and advanced economies. At an early stage in their life they realised that dependence on government, international and charitable aid providers posed problems in terms of business sustainability and in 1997, following investment by the US General Electric Company, they began diversifying into commercial markets, modifying the product designs to suit this shift. One of the casualties in this shift has been the Cape Town factory – after five years manufacturing was outsourced to plants in China where labour costs are lower.

The company became commercially successful, and sold over 3 million units of their basic radio models, raising an additional $45m in capital on the way. Product development began to embrace a wider range of power options including solar cells, and an increasing range of applications including torches and lighting, small-scale generators and mobile phone chargers. Emphasis remains on replacing battery and fixed-line power applications with rechargeable or self-generating approaches – an approach which, given increasing concerns about sustainability in the advanced industrial economies, is opening new possibilities for market growth.

Typical of their current products is the Lifeline radio, a multi-band, self-powered radio 'designed specifically for providing dependable access to information across a broad range of humanitarian projects. The radio does not require batteries or mains electricity and can be used practically anywhere. Engineered to operate in the harshest of rural conditions, it is rugged, robust and easy to operate. It offers excellent FM/AM/SW reception and runs on wind-up energy and solar power. Fully charged, it can play for up to 24 hours. The Lifeline radio was field tested in various developing countries as part of an extensive research and development programme to identify and create a radio that truly meets the requirements of these unique and diverse applications.'

Since its launch in 2003 over 8 million people have received Lifeline radios and the product has had a marked impact on the lives of many others – neighbours, friends and families, etc.

Using the Products

The scope for application is wide since it meets the basic human need for communication and enables a wide range of information, education and community-building activities. Some examples from the radio side of the business include:

- A project (funded by various development agencies) using communication satellites and FM radio technology to communicate weather, agricultural and health information to nomadic communities and villages across Africa. The pilot is built on a model in the village of Bankilare, outside Niger's capital, Niamey, and combines a WorldSpace satellite receiver, a laptop, Freeplay radios, a transmitter, solar panels and other equipment. Information is downloaded from the Internet via a satellite connection. It is then rebroadcast via a community FM radio station powered by solar energy. Villagers, nomads and farmers living in remote and poorly served areas receive broadcasts on Freeplay radios. The aim of this project is to provide timely information on the weather, with implications for crop planting and livestock care, availability of water, market prices for crops, associated diseases, health and disaster mitigation. This is just as important for the nomad as for the farmer. As stated by a nomad: 'I do not depend on the rain that falls on my head, but on streams running from the hills when they flood. So just tell me when it will rain in that distant land and I will know what to do'.
- In Madagascar the Ministries of Communication and Health, working with various aid agencies, developed a radio drama series for women's listening clubs. Wind-up radios, funded by Rotary, were distributed to clubs who provided regular feedback on the programmes. The series is aimed at improving health education, family planning and AIDS prevention. Similarly in Ethiopia people living in remote communities in Ethiopia's Harar Province are tuning in twice weekly to a radio serial drama aimed at creating awareness and prevention of HIV/AIDS – a project funded by the Centers for Disease Control and Prevention.
- According to the Zambian Ministry of Education (MOE) 800,000 Zambian children are unable to attend school. They either cannot afford it, are orphans, live too far to walk to school or are girls who are kept at home. The attrition rate of teachers poses another problem – two teachers are dying of AIDS for every one who is trained. The MOE, together with the Educational Broadcasting Services, is using Interactive Radio Instruction to help fill the educational void. Each morning thousands of primary school learners listen to the lively English and maths programme

Learning at Taonga Market on the radio. To assist with the lesson, adult mentors from the community are trained to use radio as a teaching aid. The Peace Corps in Zambia purchased Freeplay radios for their volunteers to distribute. These volunteers are trained in the mentoring process and then train community mentors, enabling the programme to reach deep rural areas. In addition, Rotary UK is helping to raise funds to bring more radios to community schools.

- In early 2000, hundreds of thousands of Mozambicans were displaced by catastrophic flooding. One of the items that people lost were radios – often the only access to information. Various donor agencies including the Freeplay Foundation distributed over 7000 radios and a daily programme called *Ndhambi* was created in the local language, Shangani. *Ndhambi* covered information on health, sanitation, hygiene, the location of landmines, obtaining lost ID documents and title deeds, governance, tracing and contacting lost family members, as well as agricultural assistance, all of which were of great importance during the post-flood period.

- During the crisis in Kosovo in 1999, DFID and the ICRC purchased over 40,000 Freeplay radios to distribute to refugees on the move and in camps in Albania and Montenegro. Here the radio played a part in helping to find missing relatives and to inform of the location of landmines, contaminated water supplies and booby-trapped villages.

Broadening the Base – The Freeplay Foundation

In 1998 the Freeplay Foundation was established as an extension of the group's commitment to empowerment and development. The Foundation operates as an independent organisation with its own Board of Trustees but it still receives an annual grant from the Freeplay Energy Group with which it shares some managerial and administration resources. The balance of funding is raised from various donors and used to support a wide range of development and implementation projects. Working primarily in Africa, the Freeplay Foundation promotes access to radio broadcasting in rural and remote areas through alternative energy solutions. It seeks 'to advance economic progress, promote community development and help eradicate disease, famine and conflict'. It does this by continuing the original wind-up radio mission – supporting or initiating projects that harness appropriate and alternative energy solutions that deliver information and education through radio broadcasting.

The Foundation facilitates access to specialists who can provide the four components vital to the sustainable success of any radio communication initiative:

- **Software** – quality radio programming directed at a targeted audience;
- **Hardware** – radios that allow sustainable listening access to all groups;

- **Structured distribution** – a planned and coordinated distribution of radios, in consultation with communities;
- **Project monitoring and evaluation** – measuring effectiveness against set objectives.

The Future – Lifeline Energy

Building on their extensive experience and recognising the potential was much wider than the core radio and related products associated with the original business the company changed its name in 2010 to Lifeline Energy. Their vision is 'to develop a range of practical, fit-for-purpose products using innovative and appropriate technologies and distribution approaches that the poor can apply to their daily lives.' As they point out, fewer than 5% of the 500 million people living in rural sub-Saharan Africa have access to any form of electricity, so this is an urgent imperative.

A key new product development in this direction has been the Lifelight – an innovation developed in response to an urgent need. Poor families rarely have access to electric lighting and many – especially children and women – suffer because they use firewood, kerosene and candles. This raises major issues around health, fire risk and wider environmental consequences; as the company puts it, ' it is tragic that in 2010, well over 100 years after the invention of the light bulb, millions of people in the developing world are still in the dark at night'.

The concept underpinning the Lifelight is the use of bright, highly fuel efficient LEDs, which can last for thousands of hours and are relatively non-toxic compared to fluorescent lighting. At the same time there is scope for bringing in the same wind-up and solar technology in which the company has extensive experience.

Significantly they recognise the need for a sustainable business model and their vision now incorporates many of the lessons they have learned about scaling and spread. They are trying to work with a virtuous cycle – 'researching and assessing what the extremely poor want and need; creating fit-for-purpose products that people can afford; and then ensuring their distribution through various channels including the ability for women to earn income and create jobs by selling or renting lights and providing charging services to those without electricity'.

An important dimension of this is opening up the possibility of reverse transfer of technology – from the lessons learned under these extreme conditions creating alternative solutions to the energy needs of the advanced industrial nations – for example, rechargeable power supplies for computers and mobile phones.

Despite the change of name the underlying commitment to social entrepreneurship goals remains the same:

Lifeline Energy improves the quality of the lives of vulnerable populations through dependable and environmentally friendly technologies. We are committed to providing renewable energy alternatives to those most in need

Questions

1 How could you reconcile the social agenda – make radios freely available – with the commercial challenges of running a business? What problems do you think Freeplay/Lifeline Energy face in trying to sustain the business?
2 Jennifer Peters has an idea for water treatment which could help provide clean drinking water to millions of people in Africa. Using ideas from the Freeplay story, what advice would you give her to help her take this forward? And what should she watch out for?
3 Do you think it's easier – or harder – to create a sustainable business venture with a social entrepreneurship idea? Why?

Summary of Web Resources

Cases

- Aravind Eye Care System
- Bottom of the Pyramid solutions

Media

- Suzana Moreira podcast

Chapter 3

Globalisation, Development and Sustainability

Go online to find additional . . .

Cases

Tools

Media

www.iande.info

Globalisation and Development

Innovation and enterprise are central to the development and growth of emerging economies, and yet their contribution is usually considered in terms of the most appropriate national policy and institutions, or the regulation of international trade. Macro-economic issues are important and national systems of innovation, including formal policy, institutions and governance, can have a profound influence on the degree and direction of innovation and enterprise in a country or region, but it is also critical to consider a more micro perspective, in particular innovation by firms and the entrepreneurship of individuals. Therefore in this chapter we examine the respective roles of national systems and policy, the capabilities of firms, and initiative of individual entrepreneurs, and the interactions between these three perspectives.

Four factors have a major influence on the ability of a firm to develop and create value through innovation:

- The *national system of innovation* in which the firm is embedded, and which in part defines its range of choices in dealing with opportunities and threats.
- Its power and *market position* within the international value chain, which in part defines the innovation-based opportunities and threats that it faces.
- The *capability and processes* of the firm, including research, design, development, production, marketing and distribution.
- Its ability to identify and exploit *external sources of innovation*, especially international networks.

Globalisation of Innovation

In his best-selling book, *The World is Flat: The globalized world in the 21st century* (Penguin, 2007), Thomas Friedman argues that developments in technology and trade, in particular information and communications technologies (ICTs), are spreading the benefits of globalisation to the emerging economies, promoting their development and growth. This optimistic thesis is appealing, but the evidence suggests the picture is rather more complex.

Firstly, technology and innovation are not evenly distributed globally, and are not easily packaged and transferred across regions or firms. For example, only about a quarter of the innovative activities of the world's largest 500, technologically active firms are located outside their home countries.[1] Secondly, different national contexts influence significantly the ability of firms to absorb and exploit such technology and innovation. For example, state-ownership and availability of venture capital both influence entrepreneurship.[2] Thirdly, the position of firms in international value chains can constrain profoundly their ability to capture the benefits of their innovation and entrepreneurship. Many firms in emerging economies have become trapped in dependent relationships as low-cost providers of low-technology, low-value manufactured goods or services, and have failed to develop their own design or new products.[3]

Since the 1980s, some analysts and practitioners have argued that, following the 'globalisation' of product markets, financial transactions and direct investment, large firms' R&D activities should also become globalised – not only in their traditional role of supporting local production, but also in order to create interfaces with specialised skills and innovative opportunities at a world level. However, although striking examples of the internationalisation of R&D can be found (e.g. the large Dutch firms, particularly Philips, and some more progressive German firms, such as Siemens), more comprehensive evidence casts doubt on the strength of such a trend. Using the evidence from patent files and R&D data suggests that innovation remains unevenly distributed across the world:

- The world's largest firms perform about only 25% of their innovative activities outside their home country. Overall, the proportion of R&D expenditure made outside the home nation is growing, albeit slowly, from less than 15% in 1995 to 22% by 2001.
- The most important factor explaining each firm's share of foreign innovative activities is its share of foreign production. Firms from smaller countries in general have higher shares of foreign innovative activities. On average, foreign production is less innovation-intensive than home production.
- Most of the foreign innovative activities are performed in the USA and Europe (in fact, Germany). They are *not* 'globalised'.
- Since the late 1990s, European firms – and especially those from France, Germany and Switzerland – have been performing an increasing share of their innovative activities in the USA, in large part in order to tap into local skills and knowledge in such fields as biotechnology and IT.

Controversy remains both in the interpretation of this general picture, and in the identification of implications for the future. Our own views are as follows:[4]

1. There are major efficiency advantages in the geographic concentration in one place of strategic R&D for *launching major new products and processes* (first model and production line). These include dealing with unforeseen problems, since proximity allows quick, adaptive decisions; and integrating R&D, production and marketing, since proximity allows integration of tacit knowledge through close personal contacts.
2. The nature and degree of international dispersion of R&D will also depend on the company's major technological trajectory, and the strategically important points for integration and learning that relate to it. Thus, whereas automobile firms find it difficult to separate their R&D geographically from production when launching a major new product, drug firms can do so and instead locate their R&D close to strategically important basic research and testing procedures.
3. In deciding about the internationalization of their R&D, managers must distinguish between becoming part of global *knowledge networks* – in other words, being aware of, and able to absorb, the results of R&D being carried out globally. Practising scientists and engineers have always done this, and it is now easier with modern IT. However, business firms are finding it increasingly useful to establish relatively small laboratories in foreign countries in order to become strong members of local research networks and thereby

benefit from the person-embodied knowledge behind the published papers; and the *launching of major innovations*, which remains complex, costly, and depends crucially on the integration of tacit knowledge. This remains difficult to achieve across national boundaries. Firms therefore still tend to concentrate major product or process developments in one country. They will sometimes choose a foreign country when it offers identifiable advantages in the skills and resources required for such developments, and/or access to a lead market.

4. Matching global knowledge networks with the localised launching of major innovations will require increasing international mobility amongst technical personnel, and the increasing use of multinational teams in launching innovations.

5. Advances in IT will enable spectacular increases in the international flow of codified knowledge in the form of operating instructions, manuals and software. They may also have some positive impact on international exchanges of tacit knowledge through teleconferencing, but not anywhere near to the same extent. The main impact will therefore be at the second stage of the 'product cycle', when product design has stabilised, and production methods are standardised and documented, thereby facilitating the internationalisation of production. Product development and the first stage of the product cycle will still require frequent and intense personal exchanges, and be facilitated by physical proximity. Advances in IT are therefore more likely to favour the internationalisation of production than of the process of innovation.

Until recently, a useful rule of thumb for deciding where R&D should be performed was the following:

- *R&D supporting existing businesses* (i.e. products, processes, divisions) should be located in established divisions;
- *R&D supporting new businesses* (i.e. products, processes, divisions) should initially be located in central laboratories, then transferred to divisions (established or newly created) for exploitation;
- *R&D supporting foreign production* should be located close to that foreign production, and concerned mainly with adapting products and processes to local conditions.

The main factors influencing the decision where to locate R&D globally are, in order of importance:

1. The availability of critical competencies for the project.
2. The international credibility (within the organisation) of the R&D manager responsible for the project.
3. The importance of external sources of technical and market knowledge, e.g. sources of technology, suppliers, and customers.
4. The importance and costs of internal transactions, e.g. between engineering and production.
5. Cost and disruption of relocating key personnel to the chosen site.

There are two broad logics of organising innovation globally, *specialisation-based* and *integration-based*, or network structure. In the specialisation-based structure the firm develops global centres of excellence in different fields, which are responsible globally for the development of a specific technology or product or process capability. The advantage of such global specialisation is that it helps to achieve a critical mass of resources and makes co-ordination easier. As one R&D director told us '. . . the centre of excellence structure is the most preferable. Competencies related to a certain field are concentrated, co-ordination is easier, and economies of scale can be achieved. Any R&D director has the dream to structure R&D in such a way. However, the appropriate conditions seldom occur.' In addition, it may allow location close to a global innovation cluster. The main disadvantages of global special-isation are the potential isolation of the centre of excellence from global needs, and the subsequent transfer of technologies to subsidiaries worldwide.

In contrast, in the integration-based structure different units around the world each con-tribute to the development of technology projects. The advantage of this approach is that it draws upon a more diverse range of capabilities and international perspectives. In addition, it can encourage competition amongst different units. However, the integrated approach suf-fers from very high costs of co-ordination, and commonly suffers from duplication of efforts and inefficient use of scarce resources. In practice, hybrids of these two extreme structures are common, often as a result of practical compromises and trade-offs necessary to accommodate history, acquisitions and politics. For example, specialisation by centre of excellence may in-clude contributions from other units, and integrated structures may include the contribution of specialised units.

The histories of major firms in technology-based industries suggest there is no right answer, and that finding and maintaining the proper balance is not easy. Nonetheless, we can identify four sets of factors that will influence the proper balance:

1. *The firm's main technological trajectory*. This gives strong guidance on the appropriate balance. At one extreme, the corporate initiatives are very important in the chemically based – and particularly the pharmaceutical – industry, where fundamental discoveries at the molecular level are often directly applicable in technological development. At the other extreme, corporate-level laboratories are less important in sectors – like aircraft and auto-mobiles – that are based on complex products and production systems, where the benefits of basic advances are more indirect (e.g. the use of simulation technologies), and the crit-ical interface is between R&D and design, on the one hand, and production, on the other.
2. *The degree of maturity of the technology*. The examples of opto-electronics and biotech-nology show that, after the emergence of a fundamental technological breakthrough, extended periods of trial, error and learning are necessary before specific technological opportunities begin to emerge. During the early 'incubation' stage, there are advantages in isolating such learning processes from immediate commercial pressure by locating them in the corporate laboratory, before transfer to a more market-oriented framework in an established division or internal venture group.
3. *Corporate strategic style*. The corporate R&D laboratory will have low importance in firms whose strategies are entirely driven by short-term financial performance in existing products. Such 'market-led' strategies will concentrate on the division-level funding, but miss the op-portunities emerging from the development and exploitation of radical new technologies.
4. *Links to 'new science'-based technologies*. New forms of corporate linkages with basic and academic research are emerging in the 'new sciences' that have grown out of recent advances

in molecular biology, nanotechnology and IT. Advances in these fields are the basis of the growth of firms spun off from universities, since they have reduced the costs of technical experimentation to a level where university-type laboratories and research methods can make significant technical advances. This has also had the effect of increasing both the range of technological opportunities that large firms can exploit, and the uncertainties surrounding their eventual usefulness. Large firms therefore prefer to explore these opportunities through collaborations until the uncertainties are reduced.

INNOVATION IN ACTION

Frugal Innovation from Emerging Economies

An *Economist* Special Report argues that emerging economies are fast becoming sources of innovation, rather than simply relying on low-cost labour, and appears to support the popular belief that innovation is increasingly a global phenomenom.

They estimate that there are more than 20,000 multinationals originating from the emerging economies, and that the firms in the *Financial Times* 500 list from the BRIC economies – Brazil, Russia, India, and China – more than quadrupled in 2006–08, from 15 to 62. The focus of innovation is not confined to technological breakthroughs, but typically incremental process and product innovations, aimed at the middle or the bottom of the income pyramid, such as the US$3,000 car, $300 computer and $30 mobile phone, so-called 'frugal innovation'.

For example, in India Tata Consultancy Services (TCS) has developed a water filter which uses rice husks. It is simple, portable and relatively cheap, giving a large family an abundant supply of bacteria-free water for an initial investment of about $24 and around $4 every few months for a new filter. Similarly, General Electric's Bangalore R&D facility has developed a hand-held electrocardiogram (ECG) called the Mac 400. Through simplification the Mac 400 can run on batteries and fit in a rucksack, and sells for $800, instead of $2,000 for a conventional ECG, which reduces the cost of an ECG test to just $1 per patient. These innovations target two of India's most common health problems: contaminated water and heart disease, which cause millions of deaths each year.

Source: Derived from Adrian Wooldridge (2010) 'The World Turned Upside Down', *The Economist*, April 15, Special Report.

Go online to find Prahalad's video discussion of the potential for innovation at the 'Bottom of the Pyramid' of market demand.

www.iande.info

Learning from Foreign Systems of Innovation

Whilst information on competitors' innovations is relatively cheap and easy to obtain, corporate experience shows that knowledge of how to replicate competitors' product and process innovations is much more costly and time-consuming to acquire. Useful and usable knowledge does not come cheap. Such imitation typically costs between 60 and 70% of the original, and typically takes three years to achieve. These conclusions are illustrated by the examples of Japanese and Korean firms, where very effective imitation has been sustained by heavy and firm-specific investments in education, training and R&D.

Firms have at least three reasons for monitoring and learning from the development of technological, production and organisational competencies of national systems of innovation other than those in which they are embedded themselves, and especially from those that are growing and strong:

1. They will be the sources of firms with a strong capacity to compete through innovation. For example, beyond Japan, other East Asian countries are developing strong innovation systems. In particular, business firms in South Korea and Taiwan now spend more than 2% of GDP on R&D, which puts them up with the advanced OECD countries. By the early 1990s, Taiwan was granted more patents in the USA than Sweden, and together with South Korea, is catching up fast with Italy, the Netherlands and Switzerland. Other Asian countries like Malaysia are also developing strong technological competencies. Following the collapse of the Soviet Bloc, we can also anticipate the re-emergence of strong systems of innovation in the Czech Republic and Hungary.

2. They are also potential sources of improvement in the corporate management of innovation, and in national systems of innovation. However, as we shall see below, understanding, interpreting and learning general lessons from foreign systems of innovation is a difficult task. Effectiveness in innovation has become bound up with wider national and ideological interests, which makes it more difficult to separate fact from belief. Both the business press and business education are dominated by the English language and Anglo-Saxon examples: very little is available in English on the management of innovation in Germany; and much of the information about the management of innovation in Japan has been via interpretations of researchers from North America.

3. Finally, firms can benefit more specifically from the technology generated in foreign systems of innovation. A high proportion of large European firms attach great importance to foreign sources of technical knowledge, whether obtained through affiliated firms (i.e. direct foreign investment) and joint ventures, links with suppliers and customers, or reverse engineering. In general, they find it is more difficult to learn from Japan than from North America and elsewhere in Europe, probably because of greater distances – physical, linguistic and cultural. Perhaps more surprising, European firms find it most difficult to learn from foreign publicly funded research. This is because effective learning involves more subtle linkages than straightforward market transactions: for example, the membership of informal professional networks. This public knowledge is often seen as a source of potential world innovative advantage, and as we discussed earlier, firms are increasingly active

in trying to access foreign sources. In contrast, knowledge obtained through market transactions and reverse engineering enables firms to catch up, and keep up, with competitors. East Asian firms have been very effective over the past 25 years in making these channels an essential feature of their rapid technological learning.

INNOVATION IN ACTION

Technology Strategies of Latecomer Firms in East Asia

The spectacular modernisation in the past 25 years of the East Asian 'dragon' countries – Hong Kong, South Korea, Singapore and Taiwan – has led to lively debate about its causes. Michael Hobday has provided important new insights into how business firms in these countries succeeded in rapid learning and technological catch-up, in spite of underdeveloped domestic systems of science and technology, and of lack of technologically sophisticated domestic customers.

Government policies provided the favourable general economic climate: export orientation; basic and vocational education, with strong emphasis on industrial needs; and a stable economy, with low inflation and high savings. However, of major importance were the strategies and policies of specific business firms for the effective assimilation of foreign technology.

The main mechanism for catching up was the same in electronics, footwear, bicycles, sewing machines and automobiles, namely the 'OEM' (original equipment manufacture) system. OEM is a specific form of subcontracting, where firms in catching-up countries produce goods to the exact specification of a foreign transnational company (TNC) normally based in a richer and technologically more advanced country. For the TNC, the purpose is to cut costs, and to this end offers assistance to the latecomer firms in quality control, choice of equipment, and engineering and management training. OEM began in the 1960s, and became more sophisticated in the 1970s. The next stage in the mid-1980s was ODM (own design and manufacture), where the latecomer firms learned to design products for the buyer. The last stage was OBM (own brand manufacture) when latecomer firms market their own products under their own brand name (e.g. Samsung, Acer) and compete head-on with the leaders.

For each stage of catching up, the company's technology position must be matched with a corresponding market position, as is shown below.

Stage	Technology position	Market position
1.	Assembly skills Basic production Mature products	Passive importer pull Cheap labour Distribution by buyers
2.	Incremental process change Reverse engineering	Active sales to foreign buyer Quality and cost-based *(continued)*

Stage	Technology position	Market position
3.	Full production skills Process innovation Product design	Advanced production sales International marketing department Markets own design
4.	R&D Product innovation	Product marketing push Own brand product range and sales
5.	Frontier R&D R&D linked to market needs Advanced innovation	Own brand push In-house market research Independent distribution

Source: Mike Hobday (1995) *Innovation in East Asia: The challenge to Japan.* Edward Elgar, Guildford.

The slow but significant internationalisation of R&D is also a means of firms learning from foreign systems of innovation. There are many reasons why multinational companies choose to locate R&D outside their home country, including regulatory regime and incentives, lower cost or more specialised human resources, proximity to lead suppliers or customers, but in many cases a significant motive is to gain access to national or regional innovation networks. However, some countries are more advanced in internationalising their R&D than others. In this respect European firms are the most internationalised, and the Japanese the least.

Managers report that the most important methods of learning about competitors' innovations were independent R&D, reverse engineering and licensing, all of which are expensive compared to reading publications and the patent literature. More formal approaches to technology intelligence gathering are less widespread, and the use of different approaches varies by company and sector (Figure 3.1). For example, in the pharmaceutical sector, where much of the knowledge is highly codified in publications and patents, these sources of information are scanned routinely, and the proximity to the science base is reflected in the widespread use of expert panels. In electronics, product technology roadmaps are commonly used, along with the lead users. Surprisingly long-established and proven methods such as Delphi-studies, S-curve analysis and patent citations are not in widespread use.

INNOVATION IN ACTION

Building BRICs – Capabilities in India

India has a population of around 1.1 billion, a large proportion of which is English-speaking, a relatively stable political and legal regime, and a good national system of education, especially in science and engineering. It has some 250 universities and listed 1500 R&D centres (although care

(continued)

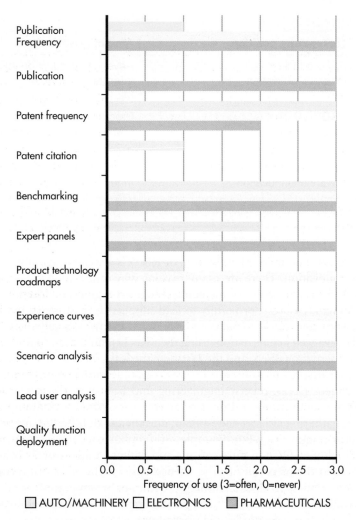

FIGURE 3.1   Use of methods of technology intelligence by sector.
Source: Derived from Lichtenthaler, E. (2004) Technology intelligence processes in leading European and North American multinationals', *R&D Management*, **34**(2), 121–134.

needs to be taken in the definitions used in both cases), and this has translated into international strengths in the fields of biotechnology, pharmaceuticals and software. As a result Indian firms have benefited greatly by the increasing international division of labour in some services and the support and development of software and services. India is now a global centre for outsourcing and offshoring. Until the mid-1980s the software industry was dominated by government and public research organisations, but the introduction of export processing zones provided tax breaks and

(continued)

allowed the import of foreign computer technology for the first time. The market liberalisation of 1991 accelerated development and inward investment, and in 2005 India attracted inward investment of $6 billion (significant, but still only around a tenth of that attracted by China). Since then the software and services industry in India grew by around 50% each year to reach US$8.3 billion by 2000, and employed 400,000, second only to the USA. The industry was forecast to grow to $50 billion by 2008. Unusually for India, which has historically pursued a policy of national self-reliance, the industry is very export-oriented, with around 70% of output being traded internationally.

There are three broad types of software firms in India. First, those that specialise in a specific sector or domain, for example accounting, gaming or film production, and these develop capabilities and relationships specific to those users. Second, those that develop methods and tools to provide low-cost and timely software support and solutions. The majority of the industry is in this lower-value-added part of the supply chain, and are involved in low-level coding, maintenance and design, and relies on a large pool of English-speaking talent which costs around 10% of that in the USA or EU. However, a third segment of firms is emerging that is more involved with new product and service development.

India's version of Silicon valley is around the southern city of Bangalore. This is home to a large number of firms from the USA, as well as indigenous Indian firms. Large employers include Infosys, and call and service centres here employ 250,000 operatives, including support services for firms such as Cisco, Microsoft and Dell. IBM, Intel, Motorola, Oracle, Sun Microsystems, Texas Instruments and GE all now have technology centres there. Texas Instruments was one of the few major foreign firms to start up a development unit, in 1985, prior to the opening up of the India economy in 1991. GE Medical Systems followed in the late 1980s, and established a development centre in Bangalore in 1990, which later resulted in a joint venture with the India firm Wipro Technologies. GE now employs 20,000 people in India, who generate sales of $500 million. IBM was one of the first investors in India, but later withdrew because of the onerous government policy and restrictions in the 1980s. It returned after the government liberalised the economy, and its Indian operations contributed $510 million in sales in 2005, employing 43,000 in India following the acquisition of the Indian outsourcing company Daksh in 2004. In 2006 IBM announced that it would triple its investment from $2 billion to $6 billion by 2009, including further service delivery centres to support computer networks worldwide and a new telecommunications research centre. Similarly, Adobe planned to invest $50 million in India over the late 2000s, and to recruit 300 software developers. Each year Adobe India contributes 10 of the 60 patents which Adobe files each year.

One of the challenges of the software and services industry in India is to increase value-added through product and service development. To date the impressive growth has been based on winning more outsourcing business from overseas and employing more staff, rather than by increasing the value-added by new services and products. For example, the Indian software and service firm Tata plans to increase the proportion of its revenue from new products from around 5% to 40%, to make it less reliant on low-cost human capital, which is likely to become more expensive, and more mobile. Ramco Systems developed an ERP system in the 1990s, which cost a billion rupees to develop and involved 400 developers. By 2000 the company was profitable, with 150 customers, half overseas. It has established sales and support offices in the USA, Europe and Singapore. In 2006 the Indian outsourcing

(*continued*)

company Genpact (40% owned by GE of the USA) launched a joint venture with New Delhi Television (NDTV) to offer digital video editing, post-production and archiving services to media firms. The industry is worth $1 trillion, and 70% of all media work is now digital.

Based on patent citations, Indian firms rely much more on linkages with the science base and technology from the developed countries, whereas China has a broader reliance which includes its Asian neighbours in other emerging economies, and specialises on more applied fields of technology. Indian firms rely on technologies from USA firms most – about 60% of all patent citations, followed by (in order of importance), Japan, Germany, France, and the UK. In many cases these linkages have been reinforced by inward investment by MNCs, but in other cases they are the result of Indians trained or employed overseas who have returned to India to create new ventures.

Infosys was one of the first and now one of the largest software and IT services firms in India. It was created by entrepreneur N.R. Narayana Murthy with six colleagues in 1981 with only US$250, but by 2006 it was worth $13.7 billion, with annual profits of $345 million. Murthy believes that 'entrepreneurship is the only instrument for countries like India to solve the problem of its poverty . . . it is our responsibility to ensure that those who have not made that kind of money have an opportunity to do so.'

Sources: N. Forbes and D. Wield (2002) *From Followers to Leaders: Managing technology and innovation.* Routledge, London; IEEE (2006) International Conference on Management of Innovation and Technology, Singapore; T. L. Friedman (2007) *The World is Flat: The Globalized World in the Twenty-First Century.* Penguin, London.

National Systems of Innovation

In this section we examine how the national and market environment of a firm shapes its innovation strategy. We first show that the *home country* positions of even global firms have a strong influence on their innovation strategies. The national influences can be grouped into three categories: *competencies* (workforce education, research), *economic inducement mechanisms* (local demand and input prices, competitive rivalry) and *institutions* (methods of funding, controlling and managing business firms). For example, the largest numbers of European firms amongst the technical leaders were to be found in the technological fields of industrial and fine chemicals, and defence-related technologies (i.e. aerospace), which are fields of national technological strength, whilst the reverse is the case in electronics, capital equipment and consumer goods. Japanese firms predominate in consumer electronics and motor vehicle technologies, and US firms in fine chemicals and in raw materials-based (i.e. oil, gas and food) and defence-related technologies, again reflecting the technological strengths of their home countries.

The strategic importance to corporations of home countries' technological competencies would matter little if they were all more or less the same, but they are not. Patterns of sectoral specialisation differ greatly: for example, the Japanese pattern of strengths and weaknesses is almost the opposite of that in the USA. In addition, countries differ in both the level and the rate of increase in the resources devoted by business firms to innovative activities. This captures corporate innovative activities only imperfectly, but remains one of the best available indicators of aggregate innovative investments, and international differences significantly influence national economic growth and trade performance. Importantly, the rate of increase in corporate commitment to R&D in a country is not closely related to its industrial structure. Compare Finland and Canada, both of whose economies rely heavily on natural resources; Finland's R&D expenditures have increased even more rapidly than Japan's as a share of GDP, whilst Canada's increased only slightly.

Contrary to what many observers continue to assume, Europe and Japan did not progressively and smoothly catch up with the USA, which was the technological leader in the period after the Second World War. Switzerland has always been amongst the leaders and remains so. As early as 1971, Germany and Japan overtook the USA and progressively increased their lead until the late 1980s. This was reflected in the relative performance in R&D and sales growth of the large firms based in these countries. Since then, the trend has changed, with the shares of business-funded R&D in GDP stabilising in Japan, declining in Germany, and increasing in the USA. At the same time, the three Scandinavian countries have continued to increase their shares, with the growth of major firms in pharmaceuticals and telecommunications. The other early leaders of the late 1960s – the UK and the Netherlands – have not reacted to the growing competition like the USA in the 1990s. The share of business-funded R&D in GDP in both countries declined considerably in the 1970s, and has not recovered to earlier levels.

A recent study of the innovation capabilities of European countries based on two Community Innovation Surveys (which are conducted every four years by all nation-states within the EU) and other data estimated the effects of different macro and micro factors on innovation. Table 3.1 provides a summary of the results. Using patents as an indicator of innovation, innovation at the national level is positively influenced by the size of the economy, foreign competition in the domestic market, public expenditure on R&D and the availability of venture capital; it is negatively influenced by the presence of a relatively large number of small and medium-sized firms, high company tax and a high level of economic prosperity. Using relative sales of innovative products as an indicator of innovation, firm- level effects

TABLE 3.1 European national systems of innovation and innovation capability

NIS variable	Regression coefficient on	
	Patents granted	**Sales of new products**
Public R&D expenditure	+ 0.839	
Firm expenditure on R&D		+ 0.421
Gross Domestic Product (GDP)	+ 0.691	+ 0.310
Openness of national economy	+ 0.319	− 0.454
Availability of venture capital	+ 0.200	
Presence of SMEs	− 0.146	+ 0.621
External sources of innovation		+ 0.688
Presence of innovative firms		+ 0.591

Source: Derived from J. Faber and A.B. Hesen (2004) 'Innovation capabilities of European nations: Cross sectional analyses of patents and sales of product innovations', *Research Policy*, 33, 193–207.

become more evident: national innovation is positively influenced by the size of the economy, R&D expenditure of firms, use of external sources of innovation and the presence of small and medium-sized firms, but negatively influenced by economic prosperity and foreign competition in the home market. Put another way, macro-economic conditions in a country and the structure of the national economy have significant effects on innovation, measured by patenting and sales of innovative products. At the national level, the innovative activities of firms appear to have a stronger influence on sales of innovative products than patenting.

In conclusion, the national system of innovation in which a firm is embedded matters greatly, since it strongly influences both the direction and the vigour of its own innovative activities. However, managements still have ample influence over their firms' innovation strategies, and firms can benefit from foreign systems of innovation through a variety of mechanisms. Next we will identify and discuss the main national factors that influence the rate and direction of technological innovation in a country: more specifically, the national market *incentives and pressures* to which firms have to respond, and the *institutions of corporate governance*.

Incentives and Pressures: National Demand and Competitive Rivalry

Patterns of National Demands

Those concerned to explain international patterns of innovative activities have long recognised the important influence of local demand and price conditions on patterns of innovation in local firms. Strong local 'demand pull' for certain types of product generates innovation opportunities for local firms, especially when the demand depends on face-to-face interactions with customers. In Table 3.2 we identify the main factors that influence local demands for innovation, and give some examples. In addition to the obvious examples of local buyers' tastes, we identify:

- Local (private and public) investment activities, which create innovative opportunities for local suppliers of machinery and production inputs, where competence is accumulated mainly through experience in designing, building and operating machinery.
- Local production input prices, where international differences can help generate very different pressures for innovation (e.g. the effects of different petrol prices on the design and related competencies in automobiles in the USA and Europe). High prices can also generate pressure for substitute products, like synthetic fertilisers in Germany at the beginning of the twentieth century.
- Local natural resources, which create opportunities for innovation in both upstream extraction and downstream processing.

A more subtle, but increasingly significant influence is the role of social concerns and pressure about the environment, safety and governance. For example, nuclear power as a technological innovation has evolved in very different ways in countries like the USA, UK, France and Japan. Similarly, innovation in genetically modified crops and foods has taken radically different paths in the USA and Europe, mainly due to public concerns and pressure.

TABLE 3.2   Local factors that influence the rate and direction of innovation

Factors in	Examples
Local buyers' tastes	• Quality food and clothing in France and Italy • Reliable machinery in Germany
Private investment activities	• Automobile and other downstream investments stimulating innovation in computer-aided design and robots in Japan, Italy, Sweden and Germany
Public investment activities	• Railways in France • Medical instruments in Sweden • Coal-mining machinery in the UK (<1979)
Input prices	• Labour-saving innovations in the USA • Europe–USA differences in automobile technology • Environmental technology in Scandinavia • Synthetic fertilisers in Germany
Local natural resources	• Innovations in oil and gas, mineral ores, and food and agriculture in North America, Scandinavia and Australia

Competitive Rivalry

Innovation is always difficult and often upsetting to established interests and habits, so that local demands by themselves do not create the necessary conditions for innovation. Both case studies and statistical analysis show that competitive rivalry stimulates firms to invest in innovation and change, since their very existence will be threatened if they do not. For example, comparison of public policies towards the pharmaceutical industries in Britain and France show that the former was more successful in creating a demanding local competitive environment conducive to the emergence of British firms amongst the world leaders. German strength in chemicals is based on three large and technologically dynamic firms, BASF, Bayer and Hoechst, rather than on one super-large national champion. Similarly, the Japanese strengths in consumer electronics and automobiles is based on numerous technologically active firms rather than a few giants (despite the early efforts of the Ministry of International Trade and Industry (MITI) to promote national champions and mergers – however, neither Sony nor Honda were members of the Japanese industrial groups, or *zaibatsu*). Relatively smaller size also reduces the severity of the task of management to maintain corporate entrepreneurship. This is because managers can spend more time familiarising themselves with the innovative potentialities of the various businesses, and can thereby avoid the dangers of managing divisions purely through financial indicators.

Thus although corporate policy-makers in large firms might often be tempted in the short term to avoid strong competition – and to reap extra monopoly profits – by merging with their competitors, the long-term costs could be considerable. Public policy-makers should be persuaded by the evidence that creating gigantic national champions does not increase innovation, quite the contrary, and therefore take countervailing measures. Lack of competitive rivalry makes firms less fit to compete on global markets through innovation.

In many countries, national advantages in natural resources and traditional industries have been fused with related competencies in broad technological fields that then become the basis for technological advantage in new product fields (Figure 3.2). For example, in Denmark, Sweden and Switzerland linkages with established fields of strength were the basis of local technological accumulation. This accumulation reinforced corporate and national competencies and created the potential for entry and competitiveness in new product fields. Firm-specific investments in technology and related basic research and training in universities led to the mastery of broad technological fields with multiple potential applications: metallurgy and materials in Sweden, machinery in Switzerland and Sweden, and chemistry and (more recently) biology in Switzerland and Denmark. Another example is the development of chemical engineering in the USA in response to the challenges and opportunities of refining petrol.

These differences in national endowments of research and education influence managers in their search to identify technological fields and related product markets where specific national systems of innovation are likely to be most supportive to corporate innovative activities. For example, firms in the UK and USA are particularly strong in software and pharmaceuticals, both of which require strong basic research and graduate skills, but few production skills; they are therefore particularly well matched to local skill structures. Similarly, Japanese strength in consumer electronics and automobiles is particularly well matched to its local strength in production skills, as are the German strengths in mechanical engineering.

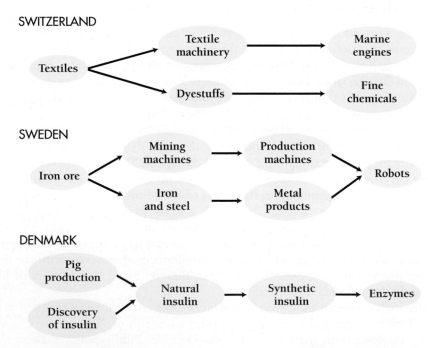

FIGURE 3.2 Evolution from natural endowment to national specialisation of innovation.

Institutions: Finance, Management and Corporate Governance

Firms' innovative behaviours are strongly influenced by the competencies of their managers and the ways in which their performance is judged and rewarded (and punished). Methods of judgement and reward vary considerably amongst countries, according to their national systems of *corporate governance*: in other words, the systems for exercising and changing corporate ownership and control. In broad terms, we can distinguish two systems: one practised in the USA and UK, and the other in Japan, Germany and its neighbours, such as Sweden and Switzerland. In his book *Capitalism against Capitalism*, Michel Albert calls the first the 'Anglo-Saxon' and the second the 'Nippon–Rhineland' variety. A lively debate continues about the essential characteristics and performance of the two systems, in terms of innovation and other performance variables. Table 3.3 is based on a variety of sources, and tries to identify the main differences that affect innovative performance.

In the UK and the USA, corporate ownership (shareholders) is separated from corporate control (managers), and the two are mediated through an active stock market. Investors can be persuaded to hold shares only if there is an expectation of increasing profits and share values. They can shift their investments relatively easily. On the other hand, in countries with governance structures like those of Germany or Japan, banks, suppliers and customers are more heavily locked into the firms in which they invest. Until the 1990s, countries strongly influenced

TABLE 3.3 National governance structures and innovation

Characteristics	Anglo-Saxon	Nippon–Rhineland
Ownership	Individuals, pension funds, insurers	Companies, individuals, banks
Control	Dispersed, arm's length	Concentrated, close and direct
Management	Business schools (USA), accountants (UK)	Engineers with business training
Evaluation of R&D investments	Published information	Insider knowledge
Strengths	• Responsive to radically new technological opportunities • Efficient use of capital	• Higher priority to R&D than to dividends for shareholders • Remedial investment in failing firms
Weaknesses	• Short-termism • Inability to evaluate firm-specific intangible assets	• Slow to deal with poor investment choices • Slow to exploit radically new technologies

by German and Japanese traditions persisted in investing heavily in R&D in established firms and technologies, whilst the US system has since been more effective in generating resources to exploit radically new opportunities in IT and biotechnology.

During the 1980s, the Nippon–Rhineland model seemed to be performing better. R&D expenditures were on a healthy upward trend, and so were indicators of aggregate economic performance. Since then, there have been growing doubts. The technological and economic indicators have been performing less well. Japanese firms have proved unable to repeat in telecommunications, software, microprocessors and computing their technological and competitive successes in consumer electronics. German firms have been slow to exploit radically new possibilities in IT and biotechnology, and there have been criticisms of expensive and unrewarding choices in corporate strategy, like the entry of Daimler Benz into aerospace. At the same time, US firms appear to have learned important lessons, especially from the Japanese in manufacturing technology, and to have reasserted their eminence in IT and biotechnology. The 1990s also saw sustained increases in productivity in US industry. According to *The Economist* in 1995, in a report entitled 'Back on top?', one professor at the Harvard Business School believed that people will look back at this period as 'a golden age of entrepreneurial management in the USA'.

However, some observers have concluded that the strong US performance in innovation cannot be satisfactorily explained simply by the combination of entrepreneurial management, a flexible labour force, and a well-developed stock exchange. They argue that the groundwork for US corporate success in exploiting IT and biotechnology was laid initially by the US Federal Government, with the large-scale investments by the Defense Department in California in electronics, and by the National Institutes of Health in the scientific fields underlying biotechnology. In addition, we should not write off Germany and Japan too soon. The former is now dealing with the dirt and inefficiency of the former East Germany, and Japanese firms like Sony are world leaders in exploiting in-home electronics and the opportunities opened up by advances in digital technology. And Scandinavian countries are now well ahead of the rest of the world (including the USA) in mobile telephony, as well as in more general indicators of skills and knowledge[5]. The influences institutions, incentives and competition have on innovation and entrepreneurship are complex, as illustrated by the case of Russia.

INNOVATION IN ACTION

Building BRICs – Capabilities in Russia

Industry in Russia is still dominated by heavy industry, including oil, gas, defence and aerospace. Consumer and service sectors are relatively poorly developed, reflecting national endowments and the legacy of the communist, centrally-planned era. For example, in 2001 oil and energy accounted for about 70% of all industrial output, and 40% of total GDP. Similarly, hydrocarbons account for more than half of exports, followed by metals which make up about a quarter of overseas sales. Some higher technology sectors have emerged from the earlier specialisation of the

(continued)

Soviet economy, such as space-launches, aviation and lasers, but these remain relatively small niches. This absence of significant innovations is an interesting paradox, given the strong national emphasis given to investment and training in science and technology.

In the year 2000, Russia had more than 4000 formal organisations dedicated to science and technology, including 2600 public R&D centres employing almost a million qualified scientists and engineers. However, historically the focus of these numerous organisations has been on basic scientific research, rather than technological or commercial innovation. The focus has been on 'big science' and science-push model of innovation and growth, rather than a market or demand coupled model. On the supply side, the prestigious Russian Academy of Sciences dominates this system, and emphasises disciplines traditional Soviet strengths in the theoretical and physical such as mathematics, chemistry and physics. The Academy has never had the responsibility or role to commercialise scientific research, or to support the development of new processes or products. Whilst overall investment in science and technology has declined in Russia, the investment in basic sciences has proportionally declined far less than investment in the applied sciences and technologies. On the demand side, the traditional centrally planned, target-based structure did not provide incentives or resources for firms to develop or seek such innovations. Given this industrial structure and political legacy, the industrial research and design centres have failed to flourish: in 2000 there were less than 300 industrial R&D enterprises, and around 400 design organisations.

Russia also has an unusual industrial structure by the size of enterprise. Compared to other industrial economies, very large firms and very small enterprises are relatively under-represented, and instead in Russia medium-sized firms are the most common and economically significant. In most advanced economies the very large firms are the main investors in formal R&D and development of commercially significant innovations, whereas the micro-businesses provide a continuous outlet for more entrepreneurial behaviour. Typically medium-sized enterprises are less important as they lack sufficient resources, but suffer from most of the disadvantages of size. They are also less likely to participate in international joint ventures and alliances, or to receive Foreign Direct Investment (FDI).

Unlike the case of many other emerging economies, FDI and international joint ventures have played only a minor part in the development of the Russian economy. It accounts for only around 5% of total investment in Russia, compared to more than 20% in other former Soviet economies of Hungary, Poland and Romania. The main foreign investments and associated transfers of technological and managerial know-how have been in the oil industry, because of its significance to the Russian economy, and the food industry, which historically has been a low national priority and has performed poorly. However, in most manufacturing and service sectors there has been little foreign investment or influence, and little improvement or innovation. There are many reasons for this relative isolation from international investment and innovation, including problems of governance, including legal restrictions on ownership and the dominance of dynastic insiders in the main industries. Therefore the institutional structure of Russia continues to constrain domestic and international innovation and entrepreneurship.

There are many cases of transfer of hard technologies in the oil and aerospace industries, both into and out of Russia, but these are usually rather conventional licensing agreements, with very

(*continued*)

little transfer or upgrading of critical managerial or commercial know-how. However, there are examples of successful innovation, often as a result of individual technical entrepreneurs or spin-offs from public research organisations working with firms overseas. For example, the Moscow Centre for SPARC Technology, founded by Boris Babayan, is funded by Sun Microsystems and is active in the workstation market, but is based on supercomputer technology used in the Soviet space and nuclear industries. Similarly, ParaGraph, a Russian software company, is based on technology used by the military for pattern recognition, but worked with Apple to commercialise the technology.

Sources: Derived from David A. Dyker (2006) *Closing the EU East–West Productivity Gap*. Imperial College Press; and (2004) *Catching Up and Falling Behind: Post-Communist Transformation in Historical Perspective*. Imperial College Press.

ENTREPRENEURSHIP IN ACTION

Russian SPIRIT

SPIRIT DSP is a world leading provider of embedded voice and communication software products. More than 200 million embedded voice channels in over 80 countries are based on SPIRIT's technology (http://www.spiritdsp.com). SPIRIT's award-winning multi-point full-duplex voice conferencing engine is now inside collaboration solutions lately rolled out by Oracle and Macromedia. During the past 10 years SPIRIT served over 200 global telecom OEMs and software vendors, including Agere, Atmel, Ericsson, Furuno, HTC, Hyundai, Iwatsu, JRC, Kyocera, LG, Macromedia, Marconi, Namco, NEC, Nortel Networks, Oracle, Panasonic, Philips, Samsung, Siemens, Tadiran, Texas Instruments, and Toshiba, among many other SPIRIT customers. Global top 7 semiconductor vendors have installed SPIRIT voice and communication software right on their processors. This example might certainly be an exception for emerging R&D sources but the fact is that the R&D centre is located in Moscow and the founder and chairman of SPIRIT is Andrew Sviridenko.

Go online to find the full case, written by Anna Trifilova.

www.iande.info

Positions in International Value Chains

Development of firms from emerging economies is much more than simply 'catching-up' with those in the more advanced economies, and is not (only) the challenge of moving from 'followers' to 'leaders'. Global standards and position in international value chains can constrain the ability of firms based in emerging economies to upgrade their capabilities and appropriate greater value, but they also present ways in which these firms can innovate to overcome these hurdles, for example, by using international standards as a catalyst for change, or by repositioning themselves in local clusters or global networks. By position, we refer to the current endowment of technology and intellectual property of a firm, as well as its relations with customers and suppliers.

According to Porter, firms must also decide between two broad innovation strategies:[6]

1. Innovation 'leadership'– where firms aim at being first to market, based on technological leadership. This requires a strong corporate commitment to creativity and risk-taking, with close linkages both to major sources of relevant new knowledge, and to the needs and responses of customers.
2. Innovation 'followership' – where firms aim at being late to market, based on imitating (learning) from the experience of technological leaders. This requires a strong commitment to competitor analysis and intelligence, to reverse engineering (i.e. testing, evaluating and taking to pieces competitors' products, in order to understand how they work, how they are made and why they appeal to customers), and to cost cutting and learning in manufacturing.

However, in practice the distinction between 'innovator' and 'follower' is much less clear. For example, market pioneers often continue to have high expenditures on R&D, but this is most likely to be aimed at minor, incremental innovations. A pattern emerges where pioneer firms do not maintain their historical strategy of innovation leadership, but instead focus on leveraging their competencies in minor incremental innovations. Conversely, late entrant firms appear to pursue one of two very different strategies. The first is based on competencies other than R&D and new product development, for example, superior distribution or greater promotion or support. The second, more interesting, strategy is to focus on major new product development projects in an effort to compete with the pioneer firm.

It is not necessarily a great advantage to be a technological leader in the early stages of the development of radically new products, when the product performance characteristics, and features valued by users are not always clear, either to the producers or to the users themselves. Especially for consumer products, valued features emerge only gradually through a process of dynamic competition that involves a considerable amount of trial, error and learning by both producers and users. New features valued by users in one product can easily be recognised by competitors and incorporated in subsequent products. This is why market leadership in the early stages of the development of personal computers was so volatile, and why pioneers are often displaced by new entrants. In such circumstances, product development must be closely coupled with the ability to monitor competitors' products and to learn from customers. In fact, pioneers in radical consumer innovations rarely succeed in establishing long-term market positions. Success goes to so-called 'early entrants' with the vision, patience and flexibility to establish a mass consumer market. For example, studies of the PIMS (Profit Impact of Market Strategy) database indicate that (surviving) product pioneers tend to have higher quality and a broader product line than followers, whereas followers tend to compete on price, despite having a cost disadvantage. A pioneer strategy appears more successful in markets where the purchasing frequency is high, or distribution is important (e.g. fast-moving consumer goods), but confer no advantage where there are frequent product changes or high advertising expenditure (e.g. consumer durables).

Therefore technological leadership in firms does not necessarily translate itself into economic benefits. The capacity of the firm to appropriate the benefits of its investment in technology depends on: its ability to translate its technological advantage into commercially viable products or processes, for example, through complementary assets or capabilities in marketing and distribution; and its capacity to defend its advantage against imitators, for example, through secrecy, standards or intellectual property. Some of the factors that enable a firm to benefit commercially from its own technological lead can be strongly shaped by its management: for example, the provision of complementary assets to exploit the lead. Other factors can be influenced only slightly by the firm's management, and depend much more on the general nature of the technology, the product market and the regime of intellectual property rights: for example, the strength of patent protection. We identify below some of the key factors which influence the firm's capacity to benefit commercially from its technology:

INNOVATION IN ACTION

Globetronics – Evolution of Global Supply Chains

Globetronics Bhd. was formed in 1990 by two Malaysians formerly employed by Intel. The Malaysian Technology Development Corporation (MTDC) provided 30% of the venture capital, and the company was subsequently floated in 1997 to raise additional capital for growth. The company's primary activities are similar to the majority of transnational semiconductor firms based in Malaysia, and involve post-fabrication manufacture of semiconductors, including assembly and packaging. Indeed, the company's main customers are American and Japanese transnationals. The significant difference is that domestic ownership and management have allowed Globetronics to more easily capture value-added activities such as development and marketing.

The company now has seven business divisions and a new plant in the Philippines. Two of the businesses are joint ventures with the Japanese firm Sumitomo. The relationship with Sumitomo began as a simple subcontracting agreement, but over the years a high level of trust has been achieved and two joint ventures have been established. The first, SGT, was created in 1994, and is 49% owned by Globetronics. It is the largest manufacturer in the world and the only company outside of Japan to produce ceramic substrate semiconductor packages. The second joint venture, SGTI, was created in 1996, and is 30% owned by Globetronics. In both cases the Japanese partner has maintained majority ownership, but it is clear that the Malaysian partner has made some progress in assimilating the technological and design capabilities. This provides a promising model for companies in developing countries, to escape dependent subcontracting relationships by using joint ventures to upgrade their technological and market competencies.

Source: Tidd, J. and M. Brocklehurst (1999) 'Routes to technological learning and development: an assessment of Malaysia's innovation policy and performance', *Technological Forecasting and Social Change*, **63** (2).

Translating Technology into Innovations

The following are important mechanisms for capturing value by translating technology into innovations:

- *Complementary assets*. The effective commercialization of an innovation very often depends on assets (or competencies) in production, marketing and after-sales to complement those in technology.
- *Accumulated tacit knowledge* can be long and difficult to imitate, especially when it is closely integrated in specific firms and regions. Examples include product design skills, ranging from those of Benetton and similar Italian firms in clothing design, to those of Rolls-Royce in aircraft engines.
- *The learning curve* in production generates both lower costs, and a particular and powerful form of accumulated and largely tacit knowledge that is well recognised by practitioners. In certain industries and technologies (e.g. semiconductors, continuous processes), the first-comer advantages are potentially large, given the major possibilities for reducing unit costs with increasing cumulative production. However, such 'experience curves' are not automatic, and require continuous investment in training, and learning.
- *Lead times and after-sales service* are considered by practitioners as major sources of protection against imitation, especially for product innovations. Taken together with a strong commitment to product development, they can establish brand loyalty and credibility, accelerate the feedback from customer use to product improvement, generate learning curve cost advantages (see below) and therefore increase the costs of entry for imitators.

 Go online to find the case study of Aravind Eye Care for an example of the importance of accumulated tacit knowledge and learning.

www.iande.info

Protecting Innovations Against Imitators

We will discuss intellectual property rights (IPR) in more detail in Chapter 11. Here we begin with those over which management has some degree of discretion for action, and move on to those where its range of choices is more limited.

- *Secrecy* is considered an effective form of protection by industrial managers, especially for process innovations. However, it is unlikely to provide absolute protection, because some process characteristics can be identified from an analysis of the final product, and because process engineers are a professional community, who talk to each other and move from one firm to another, information and knowledge inevitably leak out. Moreover, there is evidence that in some sectors firms that share their knowledge with their national system of innovation out-perform those that do not, and that those that interact most with global innovation systems have the highest innovative performance. Specifically, firms that regularly have their research (publications and patents) cited by foreign competitors are rated more innovative than others, after controlling for the level of R&D. In some cases this is because sharing knowledge with the global system of innovation may influence standards and dominant designs (see below), and can help attract and maintain research staff, alliance partners, and other critical resources.

- *Product complexity.* Product complexity is recognised by managers as an effective barrier to imitation. For example, IBM could rely on the size and complexity of their mainframe computers as an effective barrier against imitation, given the long lead times required to design and build copy products. With the advent of the microprocessor and standard software, these technological barriers to imitation disappeared and IBM was faced in the late 1980s with strong competition from IBM 'clones', made in the USA and in East Asia. Boeing and Airbus have faced no such threat to their positions in large civilian aircraft, since the costs and lead times for imitation remain very high.

- *Standards.* The widespread acceptance of a company's product standard widens its own market and raises barriers against competitors. Amongst other things the market leader normally has the advantage in a standards war, but this can be overturned through radical technological change, or a superior response to customers' needs. Competing firms can adopt either 'evolutionary' strategies minimising switching costs for customers (e.g. backward compatibility with earlier generations of the product), or 'revolutionary' strategies based on greatly superior performance–price characteristics, such that customers are willing to accept higher switching costs. Standards wars are made less bitter and dramatic when the costs to the losers of adapting to the winning standard are relatively small. Different factors will have an influence at different phases of the standards process. In the early phases, aimed at demonstrating technical feasibility, factors such as the technological superiority, complementary assets and credibility of the firm are most important, combined with the number and nature of other firms and appropriability regime. In the next phase, creating a market, strategic manoeuvring and regulation are most important. In the decisive phase, the most significant factors are the installed base, complementary assets, credibility and influence of switching costs and network effects. Where strong appropriability regimes exist, compatibility standards may be less important than customer interface standards, which help to 'lock-in' customers. Apple's graphic user interface is a good example of this trade-off.

- *Strength of intellectual property.* As we have already seen in the examples described above, this can be a strong determinant of the relative commercial benefits to innovators and imitators. On the whole, European firms value patent protection more than their US counterparts. However, with one exception (cosmetics), the variations across industry in the strength of patent protection are very similar in Europe and the USA. Patents are judged to be more effective in protecting product innovations than process innovations in all sectors except petroleum refining, probably reflecting the importance of improvements in chemical catalysts for increasing process efficiency. It also shows that patent protection is rated more highly in chemical-related sectors (especially drugs) than in other sectors. This is because it is more difficult in general to 'invent round' a clearly specified chemical formula than round other forms of invention. Radically new technologies are now posing new problems for the protection of intellectual property, including the patenting system. The number of patents granted to protect software technology is growing in the USA, and so are the numbers of financial institutions getting involved in patenting for the first time. Debate and controversy surround important issues, such as the possible effects of digital technology on copyright protection, the validity of patents to protect living organisms, and the appropriate breadth of patent protection in biotechnology.

Finally, we should note that firms can use more than one of the above factors to defend their innovative lead. For example, in the pharmaceutical industry secrecy is paramount during the early phases of research, but in the later stages of research patents become critical. Complementary assets such as global sales and distribution become more important at the later stages. Despite all the merger and acquisitions in this sector, these factors, combined with the need for a significant critical mass of R&D, have resulted in relatively stable international positions of countries in pharmaceutical innovation over a period of some 70 years. By any measure, firms in the USA have dominated the industry since the 1940s, followed by a second division consisting of Switzerland, Germany, France and the UK. Some of the methods are mutually exclusive: for example, secrecy precludes patenting, which requires disclosure of information, although it can precede patenting. However, firms typically deploy all the useful means available to them to defend their innovations against imitation.

INNOVATION IN ACTION

Chip Design in Asia

In the case of complex innovations, physical proximity is normally an advantage in the organisation and location of design and development. However, a study of 60 electronics firms and 15 research organisations found that in the design and development of electronic chips there has been a growing geographic dispersion of organisation and location. Over a decade, Asia's share of world chip design grew from almost nothing to around a third. It was forecast to reach a 50% world share by 2008, led by Japan, South Korea, Taiwan and Singapore, with Malaysia, India and China following fast.

The study concludes that two of the drivers of this trend are specific to the technology: changes in design methodology, which allow the de-coupling of design stages and the design of related components and sub-systems; and greater outsourcing and vertical specialisation within global innovation systems. Therefore any generalisations regarding the globalisation of innovation are unwise.

Source: derived from Ernst, D. (2005) 'Complexity and Internationalisation of Innovation – Why is Chip Design Moving to Asia?', *International Journal of Innovation Management*, 9(1), 47–74.

Building Capabilities and Creating Value

In this section we discuss the importance of developing firm-level capabilities. Firms in emerging economies may pursue different routes to upgrading through innovation:[7]

- *Process upgrading* – incremental process improvements to adapt to local inputs, reduce costs or to improve quality.

- *Product upgrading* – through adaptation, differentiation, design and product development.
- *Capability upgrading* – improving the range of functions undertaken, or changing the mix of functions, for example, production versus development or marketing.
- *Inter-sectoral upgrading* – moving to different sectors, for example, to those with higher value-added.

To some extent firms in emerging economies face a 'reverse product–process innovation life cycle'. We saw in Chapter 1 that the most common pattern of evolution of technological innovation in the industrialised world has been from product to process innovation on the one hand, and from radical to incremental innovation on the other. Initially a series of different radical product innovations emerge and compete in the market, but as the innovations and markets evolve together a 'dominant design' begins to emerge, and the locus of innovation shifts from product to process, and from radical to more incremental improvements in cost and quality. However, in emerging economies, the path of evolution is often reversed, and begins with incremental process innovations, to produce an existing product at a lower cost or at a lower quality for different market needs. As firms improve their capabilities they may then begin to make product adaptations and changes in design, and eventually move towards more radical product innovation. This has important implications for the type of capabilities firms needs to develop. For example, at first, the emphasis should be on incremental process improvement and development, which suggests innovation in production and organisation, rather than technological development or formal R&D. This suggests a hierarchy of capabilities or learning, each adding greater value.

C. K. Prahalad and Gary Hamel have had a major influence on management thinking by showing that the capacity to open up new product markets requires distinctive core competencies, coupled with methods of corporate organisation and evaluation that explicitly recognise the importance of these competencies, and top management visions that identify future opportunities.[8] Experience shows that, along some technological trajectories, the opportunities for product diversification are abundant but uncertain, whilst along others they hardly exist at all. It also shows that companies also need background competencies to co-ordinate and integrate changes coming from outside the firm, and that corporate visions can be wrong. Their basic ideas can be summarised as follows:

1. The sustainable competitive advantage of firms resides not in their products but in their *core competencies*: 'The real sources of advantage are to be found in management's ability to consolidate corporate-wide technologies and production skills into competencies that empower individual businesses to adapt quickly to changing opportunities' (Prahalad and Hamel, 1990, p. 81).
2. Core competencies feed into more than one core product, which in turn feed into more than one business unit. They use the metaphor of the tree:

End products = Leaves, flowers and fruit
Business units = Smaller branches
Core products = Trunk and major limbs
Core competencies = Root systems

Examples of core competencies include Sony in miniaturisation, Philips in optical media, 3M in coatings and adhesives and Canon in the combination of the precision mechanics, fine optics and microelectronics technologies that underlie all their products. Examples of core products include Honda in lightweight, high-compression engines, and Apple in product design and user-interfaces.

3. The importance of associated organisational competencies is also recognised: 'Core competence is communication, involvement, and a deep commitment to working across organisational boundaries' (Prahalad and Hamel, 1990, p. 82).

4. Core competencies require focus: 'Few companies are likely to build world leadership in more than five or six fundamental competencies. A company that compiles a list of 20 to 30 capabilities has probably not produced a list of core competencies' (Prahalad and Hamel, 1990, p. 84). The notion of core competencies suggests that large and multidivisional firms should be viewed not only as a collection of strategic business units, but as bundles of competencies that do not necessarily fit tidily in one business unit.

According to Hamel and Prahalad, the concept of the corporation based on core competencies should not replace the traditional one, but a commitment to it will inevitably influence patterns of diversification, skill deployment, resources allocation priorities, and approaches to alliances and outsourcing. David Teece and Gary Pisano integrate the various dimensions of innovation strategy into what they call the 'dynamic capabilities' approach, which underlines the importance of dynamic change and corporate learning.[9] This emphasises the key role of strategic management in appropriately adapting, integrating and reconfiguring internal and external organisational skills, resources and functional competencies towards a changing environment. To be strategic, a capability must be honed to a user need (so that there are customers), unique (so that the products/services can be priced without too much regard for the competition), and difficult to replicate (so that profits will not be competed away).

Technological development does have its own internal logic, which helps define where firms will find innovative opportunities. Thus, we can marvel at the rapid rate of improvement in the performance–price ratio of the electronic chip and at the economic and social changes it has made possible. But we can also be frustrated that our laptop computers can rarely be made to run independently for more than a few hours, or that battery-driven cars are so heavy, limited in range and slow to recharge: in spite of extensive private investments, existing knowledge of battery technology has not enabled us to do much better. The energy density of gasoline fuel (i.e. energy generated per unit weight) remains 100 times higher than electric batteries. Similarly, we can speculate that a set of technologies that could convert deep-mined coal into oil and gas at the same price, and with lesser adverse environmental consequences than existing supplies, would have economic, social and political effects at least equal to those of the microchip. But it will remain speculation, since the present state of knowledge does not enable it to be done.

In addition to the constraints of knowledge, there are those of competence: in other words, of what specific firms are capable of learning and exploiting. Innovation requires improvements and changes in the operation of complex technical and organisational systems. This involves trial, error and learning. Learning tends to be incremental, since major step changes in too many parameters both increases uncertainty and reduce the capacity to learn. As a consequence, firms' learning processes are path-dependent, with the directions of search strongly conditioned by the competencies accumulated for the development and exploitation of their existing product base. Moving from one path of learning to another can be costly, even impossible, given cognitive limits – think of the problems of learning a foreign language from scratch.

Furthermore, firms cannot easily jump from one major path to another through hiring individuals with the required competencies. Corporate competencies are rarely those of an individual, and most often those of specialised, interdependent and co-ordinated groups, where tacit technical and organisational knowledge accumulated through experience are of central importance. This is why firms perform most of their innovative activities in-house. And even when competencies come from outside the firm as part of a corporate acquisition, different practices and cognitive structures may make their assimilation costly or impossible. For example, it is no accident that electrical firms find it much easier to master and exploit semiconductor technology than chemical firms: the fields of technological competencies required are much closer.

The ability of firms to track and exploit technological trajectories depends on their specific technological and organisational competencies, and on the difficulties that competitors have in imitating them. The notion of firm-specific competencies has become increasingly influential amongst economists, trying to explain why firms are different, and how they change over time, and also amongst business practitioners and consultants, trying to identify the causes of competitive success. In the 1990s, management began to shift interest from improvements in short-term operational efficiency and flexibility (through 'de-layering', 'downsizing', 'outsourcing' and 'business process re-engineering', etc.), to a concern that – if taken too far – the 'lean corporation' could become the 'anorexic corporation', without any capacity for longer-term change and survival.

This has led to much confusion about the characteristics and implications of the 'new' or 'knowledge' economy. The more traditional notion of the knowledge economy included the broad opportunities created by developments in science and technology, and the role of intellectual capital and innovation for competitive advantage. The more recent and more narrow perspective focuses exclusively on the potential of information and communications technologies. However, these two views are based on contradictory assumptions and suggest different implications. The latter ICT perspective emphasises the low marginal costs of reproduction and near instantaneous transmission of such technologies, but too often assumes that the exchange and transfer of knowledge is almost effortless and unrestricted. The former, broader view highlights the difficulties of capturing and transferring knowledge due to its tacit nature and context-specificity.

Limits of the Core Competence Approach

The notions of core competence and dynamic capabilities are useful as they emphasise the importance of developing firm-level resources. However, there are a number of limitations to these approaches:

> *Differing potentials for technology-based diversification* It is not clear whether the corporate core competencies in all industries offer a basis for product diversification. Compare the recent historical experience of most large chemical and electronics firms,

where product diversification based on technology has been the norm, with that of most steel and textile firms, where technology-related product diversification has proved very difficult (see, for example, the unsuccessful attempts to diversify by the Japanese steel industry in the 1980s).

Multi-technology firms Recommendations that firms should concentrate resources on a few fundamental (or 'distinctive') world-beating technological competencies are potentially misleading. Large firms are typically active in a wide range of technologies, in only a few of which do they achieve a 'distinctive' world-beating position. In other technological fields, a *background* technological competence is necessary to enable the firm to coordinate and benefit from outside linkages, especially with suppliers of components, subsystems, materials and production machinery. In industries with complex products or production processes, a high proportion of a firm's technological competencies are deployed in such background competencies. In addition, firms are constrained to develop competencies in an increasing range of technological fields (e.g. IT, new materials, biotechnology) in order to remain competitive as products become even more 'multi-technological'.

In-house competencies in background (enabling) technologies are necessary for the effective co-ordination of changes in production and distribution systems, and in supply chains. In industries with complex product systems (like automobiles), background technologies can account for a sizeable proportion of corporate innovative activities. Background technologies can also be the sources of revolutionary and disruptive change. For example, given the major opportunities for improved performance that they offer, all businesses today have no choice but to adopt advances in IT technology, just as all factories in the past had no choice but to convert to electricity as a power source. However, in terms of innovation strategy, it is important to distinguish firms where IT is a core technology and a source of distinctive competitive advantage (e.g. CISCO, the supplier of Internet equipment) from firms where it is a background technology, requiring major changes but available to all competitors from specialised suppliers, and therefore unlikely to be a source of distinctive and sustainable competitive advantage (e.g. Tesco, the UK supermarket chain).

In all industries, emerging (key) technologies can end up having pervasive and major impacts on firms' strategies and operations (e.g. software). A good example of how an emerging/key technology can transform a company is provided by the Swedish telecommunications firm Ericsson. The accumulation of technological competencies, with successive generations of mobile cellular phones and telecommunication cables. In both cases, each new generation required competencies in a wider range of technological fields, and very few established competencies were made obsolete. The process of accumulation involved both increasing links with outside sources of knowledge, and greater expenditures on R&D, given greater product complexity. This was certainly not a process of concentration, but of diversification in both technology and product. For these reasons, the notion of 'core competencies' should perhaps be replaced for technology by the notion of '*distributed* competencies'.

Core rigidities As Dorothy Leonard has pointed out, 'core competencies' can also become 'core rigidities' in the firm, when established competencies become too dominant. In addition to sheer habit, this can happen because established competencies are central to today's products, and because large numbers of top managers may be trained in them. As a consequence, important new competencies may be neglected or underestimated (e.g. the threat to mainframes from mini- and microcomputers by management in mainframe companies). In addition, established innovation strengths may overshoot the target. Many examples show that, when 'core rigidities' become firmly entrenched, their removal often requires changes in top management.

Developing and Sustaining Competencies

The final question about the notion of core competencies is very practical: how can management identify and develop them?

There is no widely accepted definition or method of measurement of competencies, whether technological or otherwise. One possible measure is the level of *functional performance* in a generic product, component or subsystem: in, for example, performance in the design, development, manufacture and performance of compact, high-performance combustion engines. As a strategic technological *target* for a firm like Honda, this obviously makes sense. But its achievement requires the combination of technological competencies from a wide variety of *fields* of knowledge, the composition of which changes (and increases) over time. Twenty years ago, they included mechanics (statics and dynamics), materials, heat transfer, combustion, fluid flow. Today they also include ceramics, electronics, computer-aided design, simulation techniques and software.

Thus, the functional definition of competencies bypasses two central tasks of corporate strategy: first, to identify and develop the range of disciplines or fields that must be combined into a functioning technology; second (and perhaps more important) to identify and explore the new competencies that must be added if the functional capability is not to become obsolete. This is why a definition based on the measurement of the combination of competencies in different fields is more useful for formulating innovation strategy, and is in fact widely practised in business.

Richard Hall goes some way towards identifying and measuring core competencies. He distinguishes between intangible assets and intangible competencies. Assets include intellectual property rights and reputation. Competencies include the skills and know-how of employees, suppliers and distributors, and the collective attributes which constitute organisational culture. His empirical work, based on a survey and case studies, indicates that managers believe that the most significant of these intangible resources are company reputation and employee know-how, both of which may be a function of organisational culture. Thus organisational culture, defined as the shared values and beliefs of members of an organisational unit, and the associated artefacts, becomes central to organisational learning.

However, dynamic capabilities typically involve long-term commitments to specialised resources, and consist of patterned activity to relatively specific objectives. Therefore dynamic capabilities involve both the exploitation of existing competencies and the development of new ones. For example, leveraging existing competencies through new product development can consist of de-linking existing technological or commercial competencies from one set of current products, and linking them in a different way to create new products. However, new product development can also help to develop new competencies. For example, an existing technological competence may demand new commercial competencies to reach a new market, or conversely a new technological competence might be necessary to service an existing customer.

The trick is to get the right balance between exploitation of existing competencies and the exploitation and development of new competencies. Research suggests that over time some firms are more successful at this than others, and that a significant reason for this variation in performance is due to difference in the ability of managers to build, integrate and reconfigure organisational competencies and resources. These 'dynamic' managerial capabilities are influenced by managerial cognition, human capital and social capital (see Chapter 4). Cognition refers to the beliefs and mental models which influence decision-making. These affect the knowledge and assumptions about future events, available alternatives and association between cause and effect. This will restrict a manger's field of vision, and influence perceptions and interpretations. Human capital refers to the learned skills that require some investment in education, training experience and socialisation, and these can be generic, industry- or firm-specific. It is the firm-specific factors that appear to be the most significant in dynamic managerial capability, which can lead to different decisions when faced with the same environment. Social capital refers to the internal and external relationships which affect a managers' access to information, their influence, control and power.

INNOVATION IN ACTION

Building BRICs – Capabilities in Brazil

In his research, Fernando Perini examined the structure and dynamics of the knowledge networks in the IT and telecommunications sectors in Brazil. The Brazilian government promoted the development of the industry between 1997 and 2003 by the 'ICT Law' which provided tax incentives for collaborative R&D, following the liberalisation of the economy in the early 1990s and the unsuccessful period of import substitution. This policy promoted an overall private investment of more than US$2 billion in innovation supporting partnerships in innovation projects inside a network of 216 companies and 235 universities and research institutes, but the lasting effects on firm and national capabilities are more mixed. While the policy of tax incentives promoted a higher level of investments in innovation, it did not determine the direction or organisation of innovation in the sector.

The study concludes that the effect of the tax incentives depends on the nature of the technology and industry structure. They were important in helping to create knowledge networks in system and software technologies where multinational companies were key

(continued)

players, but much less successful in equipment, semiconductors, production process and hardware, where MNCs relied most on internal R&D and their own international networks. However, the MNCs did develop new partnerships in product development in IT systems and software, mainly with new private research institutes, rather than with established universities and research centres. Many of these private research institutes have become network integrators in the Brazilian ICT sector, and act as technological partners in activities such as training, technological services and research.

However, a small number of multinational companies still dominate the Brazilian market. More than 70% of the total investments under the ICT Law were conducted by the top 15 MNC subsidiaries.

For example, Lucent entered Brazil through the acquisition of two main national telecom companies, Zetax and Batik. It benefited from the ICT Law incentives between 2000 and 2002, but now invests more than three times the amount required by the original legislation, and the laboratory in Brazil had around 105 employees in 2005. The lab has competencies in both hardware and software, but there has been a shift toward software because it is less influenced by the regulation of international trade. The lab includes a new group of 50 engineers created in 2004 to develop competences in optical access, specifically, an optical concentrator for public commutation networks. The interaction with the global R&D community is very strong, in particular through the exchange of personnel. For example, the new optical unit involved the exchange of 35 people for two months. In addition, Lucent has developed local supply and research networks, and approximately 85% of its external activities are outsourced to FITEC. FITEC has facilities throughout Brazil, including Campinas, Belo Horizonte, and Recife.

Siemens Mercosur has the longest and largest MNC presence in Brazil. The subsidiary has developed technological capabilities mainly in telecommunications, and since the ICT Law still invests more than twice that required by legislation. R&D at the subsidiary is divided into six groups; the largest in Manaus, has 300 technical staff and specialises in Mobile Handsets that supply global markets. In addition, the Networks development group in Curitiba has around 120 engineers, and the Enterprise group 100 engineers. In relation to local technological partners, Siemens has focused on the upgrading of partnerships in the South, including two local universities (UTF-PR and PUC-PR) and one private institute (CITS), but the removal of public incentives and shifts in the technology have increased the importance of the partnership with the private research institute, CITS. However, the subsidiary has also invested in enabling institutes and postgraduate courses: for example, it helped to create a new postgraduate degree in Computer Science in Manaus. One recent development was the announcement in 2006 of a new 4 million euro development centre in Brazil, to develop digital TV technologies for the Brazilian market. Another initiative is the creation of an Innovation Portal to register and process innovative ideas from Brazilian companies and researchers.

Source: Fernando Perini (2010) 'The Structure and Dynamics of the Knowledge Networks: Incentives to Innovation and R&D Spillovers In the Brazilian ICT Sector', DPhil dissertation, SPRU, University of Sussex, UK.

Innovation and Sustainability

The most conventional approach to innovation and sustainability focuses on how to influence the development and application of innovations through regulation and control. In this approach, formal policies are used in an attempt to direct innovation by using systems of regulation, targets, incentives, and usually punishments for non-compliance. This can be effective, but is a rather blunt instrument to encourage change, and can be slow and incremental.

A more balanced and effective approach tries to understand how technology, markets and society co-evolve through a process of negotiation, consultation and experimentation with new ways of doing things. This perspective demands a better appreciation of how firms and innovation work, and highlights the need to better understand all the organisations involved – the policy-makers, consumers, firms, institutions, and other stakeholders that can influence the rate and direction of innovation.[10] By focusing on policy and regulation the innovation-environment debate and research has not really fully understood or engaged with the motivations and actions of individual entrepreneurs or innovative organisations.

INNOVATION IN ACTION

Managing Innovation for Sustainability

In their review of the field, Frans Berkhout and Ken Green argue that 'technological and organisational innovation stands at the heart of the most popular and policy discourses about sustainability. Innovation is regarded as both a cause and solution . . . yet, very little attempt has been made in the business and environment, environmental management and environmental policy literatures to systematically draw on the concepts, theories and empirical evidence developed over the past three decades of innovation studies.' They identify a number of limitations in the innovation literature, and suggest potential ways to link innovation and sustainability research, policy and management:

1. A focus on managers, the firm, or the supply chain is too narrow. Innovation is a distributed process across many actors, firms and other organisations, and is influenced by regulation, policy and social pressure.
2. A focus on a specific technology or product is inappropriate. Instead the unit of analysis must be on technological systems or regimes, and their evolution rather than management.
3. The assumption that innovation is the consequence of coupling technological opportunity and market demand is too limited. It needs to include the less obvious social concerns, expectations and pressures. These may appear to contradict stronger but misleading market signals.

They present empirical studies of industrial production, air transportation and energy to illustrate their arguments, and conclude that 'greater awareness and interaction between research and management of innovation, environmental management, corporate social responsibility and innovation and the environment will prove fruitful'.

Source: From *International Journal of Innovation Management*, 2002, 6(3), Special Issue on Managing Innovation for Sustainability, edited by Frans Berkhout and Ken Green.

Innovation is often presented as a major contribution to the degradation of the environment, through its association with increased economic growth and consumption.[11] However, innovation must also be a large part of any potential solution to a range of environmental issues, including:

- *cleaner products* – with a lower environmental impact over their life cycle;
- *more efficient processes* – to minimise or treat waste, to reuse or recycle;
- *alternative technologies* – to reduce emissions, provide renewable energy;
- *new services* – to replace or reduce consumption of products;
- *systems innovation* – to measure and monitor environmental impact, new socio-technical systems.

Figure 3.3 presents a typology of the different ways in which innovation can contribute to sustainability. One dimension is the novelty of the knowledge, and the other dimension is the novelty of the application of that knowledge. In the bottom left quadrant the innovation focuses on the improvement of existing technologies, products and services. This is not necessarily incremental, and may at times involve radical innovation, but the goals and performance criteria remain the same, for example, increasing the fuel efficiency of a power station or car engine. This is the most common type of innovation, and we have discussed this throughout the book. The top left hand quadrant represents the development of new knowledge, but its application to existing problems. This includes alternative materials, processes or technologies used in existing products. For example, in energy production and packaging of goods there are often many alternative competing technologies, with very different properties and benefits. In food packaging, glass, different plastics, aluminum and steel are all viable alternatives, but each has different energy requirements over their life cycle in their production and reuse or recycling.

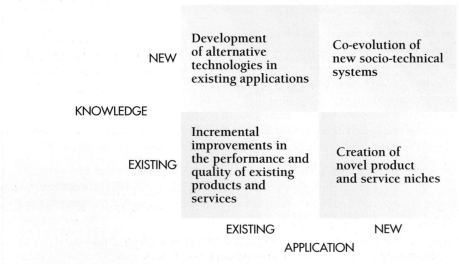

FIGURE 3.3   A typology of sustainable innovations.

Moving to the right-hand column, the bottom quadrant represents the application of existing knowledge to create new market niches. These are sometimes called *architectural* innovations because they reuse different components and subsystems in new configurations. These are very important for sustainable innovation, as typically such innovations emerge and are developed in niches which initially co-exist with the existing mass market, but these niches can mature and grow to influence demand and development in the dominant market. For example, in the car industry safety was not a significant feature until the early 1980s. Up until that point the assumption was that 'safety did not sell', and manufacturers were reluctant to develop such features. Corning was initially unable to convince any US manufacturer to adopt laminated windscreens (windshields). However, local demand for improved safety in Scandinavia, especially Sweden, encouraged local manufacturers such as Volvo and Saab to develop and incorporate new safety technologies. These slowly became popular in overseas markets, and competing manufacturers had to respond with similar features. As a result today almost all cars have a range of active and passive safety technologies, such as airbags, side-impact protection, crumple zones, anti-lock brakes, electronic stability systems.

The top-right quadrant is probably the most fundamental contribution of innovation to sustainability. It is here that new socio-technical systems co-evolve. Developers and users of innovation interact more closely, and many more actors are involved in the process of innovation. In this case firms are not the only, or even the most important, actor, and the successful development and adoption of such systems innovation demand a range of 'externalities', such as supporting infrastructure, complementary products and services, finance and new training and skills. For example, the micro-generation of energy requires much more than technological innovation and product development. It requires changes in energy pricing and regulation, an infrastructure to allow the sale of energy back to the grid, and new skills and services in the installation and service of generators. Such innovations typically evolve by a combination of top-down policy change and co-ordination, and bottom-up social change and firm behaviour.

Go online to find Richard Smith and Anna Trifilova discussing the development of sustainable buildings in the Middle East in their case study *Green building: Case study of Atkins' engineering sustainable design in Dubai*.

www.iande.info

Alternative Technologies

Alternative innovations are characterised by the application of new technologies to existing needs or applications. In this case the key issue is to identify existing applications where an alternative may have a performance advantage.

The first and most critical distinction to make is between a technology and a product. Technologists are typically concerned with developing devices, whereas potential customers buy products, which marketing must create from the devices. Developing a product is much more costly and difficult than developing a device. Devices that do not function or are difficult to manufacture are relatively easy to identify and correct compared to an incomplete product offering. A product may fail or be difficult to sell due to poor logistics and branding, or difficult to use because insufficient attention has been paid to customer training or support. Therefore attempting to differentiate a product on the basis of its functionality or the performance of component devices can be expensive and futile.

For example, a personal computer (PC) is a product consisting of a large number of devices or subsystems, including the basic hardware and accessories, operating system, application programs, languages, documentation, customer training, maintenance and support, advertising and brand development. Therefore a development in microprocessor technology, such as RISC (reduced instruction set computing) may improve product performance in certain circumstances, but may be undermined by more significant factors such as lack of support for developers of software and therefore a shortage of suitable application software.

The traditional literature on industrial marketing has a bias towards relatively low-technology products, and has failed largely to take into account the nature of high-technology products and their markets. In the case of alternative technologies it is not sufficient to carry out a simple technical comparison of the performance of technological alternatives, and conventional market segmentation is unlikely to reveal opportunities for substituting a new technology in existing applications. It is necessary to identify why a potential customer might look for an alternative to the existing solution. It may be because of lower costs, superior performance, greater reliability, or simply fashion. In such cases there are two stages to identify potential applications and target customers: technical and behavioural.

Statistical analysis of existing customers is unlikely to be of much use because of the level of detail required. Typically technical segmentation begins with a small group of potential users being interviewed to identify differences and similarities in their requirements. The aim is to identify a range of specific potential uses or applications. Next, a behavioural segmentation is carried out to find three or four groups of customers with similar situations and behaviour. Finally, the technical and behavioural segments are combined to define specific groups of target customers and markets that can then be evaluated commercially.

Several features are unique to the promotion of alternative technologies, and affect buying behaviour:

- *Buyers' perceptions of differences in technology affect buying behaviour.* In general, where buyers believe technologies to be similar, they are likely to search for longer than when they believe there to be significant differences between technologies.
- *Buyers' perceptions of the rate of change of the technology affect buying behaviour.* In general, where buyers believe the rate of technological change is high, they put a lot of effort into the search for alternatives, but search for a shorter time. In non-critical areas a buyer may postpone a purchase.
- *Organisational buyers may have strong relationships with their suppliers, which increases switching costs.* In general, the higher the supplier-related switching costs, the lower the search effort, but the higher the compatibility-related switching costs, the greater the search effort.

Novel Niches

Novel niches or architectural innovations consist of novel configurations of existing knowledge that serve new needs or applications. In such cases the critical issue is to identify or create new market segments. A fundamental issue in novel niches is the need to identify the need to change the architecture or configuration, rather than just the components within an existing system.[12]

Clayton Christensen distinguishes between two fundamental types of innovation.[13] The first, *sustaining* innovation, which continues to improve existing product functionality for existing customers and markets. The term is unfortunate, as it refers to sustaining in the sense of sustaining existing markets and performance characteristics, rather than sustaining the environment. The second, *disruptive* innovation, provides a different set of functions which are likely to appeal to a very different segment of the market. As a result, existing firms and their customers are likely to undervalue or ignore disruptive innovations, as these are likely to underperform existing technologies in terms of existing functions in established markets. This illustrates the danger of simplistic advice such as 'listening to customers', and the limitations of traditional management and marketing approaches. Therefore established firms tend to be blind to the potential of disruptive innovation, which is more likely to be exploited by new entrants. Segmentation of current markets and close relations with existing customers will tend to reinforce sustaining innovation, but will fail to identify or wrongly reject potential disruptive innovations. Instead firms must develop and maintain a detailed understanding of potential applications and changing users' needs.

Critical to this process is how to identify or help to create new market segments. Market or buyer segmentation is simply the process of identifying groups of customers with sufficiently similar purchasing behaviour so that they can be targeted and treated in a similar way. This is important because different groups are likely to have different needs. By definition the needs of customers in the same segment will be highly homogeneous. In formal statistical terms the objective of segmentation is to maximise across-group variance and to minimise within-group variance.

In such cases many of the standard marketing tools and techniques are of limited utility for the development and commercialisation of truly novel niches. A number of weaknesses can be identified:

- *Identifying and evaluating novel product characteristics.* Marketing tools such as conjoint analysis have been developed for variations of existing products or product extensions, and therefore are of little use for identifying and developing novel products or applications.
- *Identifying and evaluating new markets or businesses.* Marketing techniques such as segmentation are most applicable to relatively mature, well-understood products and markets, and are of limited use in emerging, ill-defined markets.
- *Promoting the purchase and use of novel products and services.* The traditional distinction between consumer and business marketing is based on the characteristics of the customers or users, but the characteristics of the innovation and the relationship between developers and users is more important in the case of novel and complex products and services.

Go online to find the Freeplay case study, an example of architectural innovation in a developing country context.

www.iande.info

In many cases potential users may have latent needs or unarticulated requirements. In such cases three types of user need can be identified:

> *Must haves, or pre-qualifiers* – those features which must exist before a potential customer will consider a product or service. For example, in the case of an executive car it must be relatively large and expensive.
>
> *One-dimensionals* – the more quantifiable features which allow direct comparison between competing products. For example, in the case of an executive car, the acceleration and braking performance.
>
> *Delighters, or order-winners* – the most subtle means of differentiation. The inclusion of such features delights the target customers, even if they do not explicitly demand them. For example, delighters in the case of an executive car include ultrasonic parking aids, rain-sensitive windscreen wipers and photochromatic mirrors. Such features are rarely demanded by customers or identified by regular market research. However, indirect questioning can be used to help identify latent requirements.

In practice segmentation is conducted by analysing customers' buying behaviour and then using factor analysis to identify the most significant variables influencing behaviour – descriptive segmentation – and then using cluster analysis to create distinct segments which help identify unmet customer needs – prescriptive segmentation. The principle of segmentation applies to both consumer and business markets, but the process and basis of segmentation is different in each case.

Segmenting Consumer Markets

Much of the research on the buying behaviour of consumers is based on theories adapted from the social and behavioural sciences. Utilitarian theories assume that consumers are rational and make purchasing decisions by comparing product utility with their requirements. This model suggests a sequence of phases in the purchasing decision: problem recognition, information search, evaluation of alternatives and finally the purchase. However, such rational processes do not appear to have much influence on actual buying behaviour. For example, in the UK the Consumers' Association routinely tests a wide range of competing products, and makes buying recommendations based on largely objective criteria. If the majority of buyers were rational, and the Consumers' Association successfully identified all relevant criteria, these recommendations would become best-sellers, but this is not the case.

Behavioural approaches have greater explanatory power. These emphasise the effect of attitude, and argue that the buying decision follows a sequence of changing attitudes to a product – awareness, interest, desire and finally action. The goal of advertising is to stimulate this sequence of events. However, research suggests that attitude alone explains only 10% of decisions, and can rarely predict buyer behaviour.

In practice the balance between rational and behavioural influences will depend on the level of customer involvement. Clearly, the decision-making process for buying an aircraft or machine tool is different from the process of buying a toothpaste or shampoo. Many purchasing decisions involve little cost or risk, and therefore low involvement. In such cases consumers try to minimise the financial, mental and physical effort involved in purchasing. Advertising is most effective in such cases. In contrast, in high-involvement situations, in which there is a high cost or potential risk to customers, buyers are willing to search for information and make a more informed decision. Advertising is less effective in such circumstances, and is typically confined to presenting comparative information between rival products. Assessing the level of involvement is absolutely critical in the case of developing and promoting novel niches for sustainable innovations. For example, surveys routinely suggest that consumers would be willing to pay a premium price for organic produce, but actual sales fall far short of expectations.

There are many bases of segmenting consumer markets, including by socioeconomic class, life-cycle groupings and by lifestyle or psychographic (psychological–demographic) factors. An example of psychographic segmentation is the Taylor–Nelson classification that consists of self-explorers, social registers, experimentalists, achievers, belongers, survivors and the aimless. Better-known examples include the *Yuppy* (young upwardly mobile professional) and *Dinky* (dual income, no kids), and the more recent *Yappy* (young affluent parent), *Sitcoms* (single income, two children, oppressive mortgage), and *Skiers* (spending the kid's inheritance). There is often a strong association between a segment and preferences for particular attributes, products and services.

Segmenting Business Markets

Business customers tend to be better informed than consumers and, in theory at least, make more rational purchasing decisions. Business customers can be segmented on the basis of common buying factors or purchasing processes. The basis of segmentation should have clear operational implications, such as differences in preferences, pricing, distribution or sales strategy. For example, customers could be segmented on the basis of how experienced, sophisticated or price-sensitive they are. However, the process is complicated by the number of people involved in the buying process:

- The actual customer or buyer, who typically has the formal authority to choose a supplier and agree terms of purchase.
- The ultimate users of the product or service, who are normally, but not always, involved in the initiation and specification of the purchase.
- Gatekeepers, who control the flow of information to the buyers and users.
- Influencers, who may provide some technical support to the specification and comparison of products.

Therefore it is critical to identify all relevant parties in an organisation, and determine the main influences on each. For example, technical personnel used to determine the specification may favour performance, whereas the actual buyer may stress value for money.

The most common basis of business segmentation is by the benefits customers derive from the product, process or service. Customers may buy the same product for very different reasons, and attach different weightings to different product features. For example, in the case of a new numerically controlled machine tool, one group of customers may place the greatest value on the reduction in unit costs it provides, whereas another group may place greater emphasis on potential improvements in precision or quality of the output.

It is difficult in practice to identify distinct segments by benefit because these are not strongly related to more traditional and easily identifiable characteristics such as firm size or industry classification. Therefore benefit segmentation is only practical where such preferences can be related to more easily observable and measurable customer characteristics. For example, in the case of the machine tool, analysis of production volumes, batch sizes, operating margins and value-added might help differentiate between those firms which value higher efficiency from those which seek improvements in quality. This suggests a three-stage segmentation process for identifying new business markets:

1. First, a segmentation based on the functionality of the technology, mapping functions against potential applications.
2. Next, a behavioural segmentation to identify potential customers with similar buying behaviour, for example regarding price or service.
3. Finally, combine the functional and behavioural segmentations in a single matrix to help identify potential customers with relevant applications and buying behaviour.

In addition, analysis of competitors' products and customers may reveal segments not adequately served, or alternatively an opportunity to redefine the basis of segmentation. For example, existing customers may be segmented on the basis of size of company, rather than the needs of specific sectors or particular applications. However, in the final analysis segmentation only provides a guide to behaviour as each customer will have unique characteristics.

There is likely to be a continuum of customer requirements, ranging from existing needs, to emerging requirements and latent expectations, and these must be mapped on to existing and emerging technologies. Whereas much of conventional market research is concerned with identifying the existing needs of customers and matching these to existing technological solutions, in this case the search has to be extended to include emerging and new customer requirements. There are three distinct phases of analysis:

1. Cross-functional teams including customers are used to generate new product concepts by means of brainstorming, morphology and other structured techniques.
2. These concepts are refined and evaluated, using techniques such as QFD.
3. Parallel prototype development and market research activities are conducted. Prototypes are used not as 'master models' for production, but as experiments for internal and external customers to evaluate.

Where potential customers are unable to define or evaluate product design features, in-depth interview clinics must be carried out with target focus groups or via antenna shops. In antenna shops market researchers and engineers conduct interactive customer interviews, and use marketing research tools and techniques to identify and quantify perceptions about product attributes. Product mapping can be used to expose the technological and market drivers of product development, and allows managers to explore the implications of product extensions. It helps to focus development efforts and limit the scope of projects by identifying target markets and technologies. This helps to generate more detailed functional maps for design, production and marketing.

New product introduction is, up to a point, associated with higher sales and profitability, but very high rates of product introduction become counter-productive as increases in development costs exceed additional sales revenue. This was the case in the car industry, when Japanese manufacturers reduced the life cycle to just four years in the 1990s, but then had to extend it again. Alternatively, expectations of new product introductions can result in users skipping a generation of products in anticipation of the next generation. This has happened in both the PC and cellphone markets, which has had knock-on effects in the chip industry. Put another way, there is often a trade-off between high rates of new product introduction and product life. The development of common product platforms and increased modularity is one way to try to tackle this trade-off in new product development. Incremental product innovation within an existing platform can either introduce benefits to *existing* customers, such as lower price or improved performance, or additionally attract *new* users and enter new market niches. A critical issue in managing architectural innovation is the precise balance between the frequency of radical change of product platform, and incremental innovation within these platforms. This suggests that a strategy of ever-faster new product development and introduction is not sustainable, but rather the aim should be to achieve an optimum balance between platform change and new product based on existing platforms. This logic appears to apply to both manufactured products and services.

INNOVATION IN ACTION

The Evolution of Electric and Hybrid cars

The car industry is an excellent example of a large complex socio-technical system which has evolved over many years, such that the current system of firms, products, consumers and infra-structure interact to restrict the degree and direction of innovation. Since the 1930s the dominant design has been based around a gasoline (petrol)- or diesel-fuelled reciprocating combustion engine/Otto-cycle, mass-produced in a wide variety of relatively minimally differentiated designs. This is no industrial conspiracy, but rather the almost inevitable industrial trajectory, given the historical and economic context. This has resulted in car companies spending more on marketing than on research and development. However, growing social and political concerns over

(continued)

vehicle emissions and their regulation have forced the industry to reconsider this dominant design, and in some cases to develop new capabilities to help to develop new products and systems. For example, zero and low emissions targets and legislation has encouraged experimentation with alternatives to the combustion engine, whilst retaining the core concept of personal, rather than collective or mass travel.

For example, the zero-emission law passed in California in 1990 required manufacturers selling more than 35,000 vehicles a year in the state to have 2% of all vehicle sales zero-emission by 1998, 5% by 2001 and 10% by 2003. This most affected GM, Ford, Chrysler, Toyota, Honda and Nissan, and potentially BMW and VW, if their sales increased sufficiently over that period. However, the US automobile industry subsequently appealed, and had the quota reduced to a maximum of 4%. As fuel cells were still very much a longer-term solution, the main focus was on developing electric vehicles. At first sight this would appear to represent a rather 'autonomous' innovation: that is, the simple substitution of one technology (combustion engine) for another (electric). However, the shift has implications for related systems such as power storage, drive-train, controls, weight of materials used and the infrastructure for refuellling/recharging and servicing. Therefore it is much more of a 'systemic' innovation than it first seems. Moreover, it challenges the core capabilities and technologies of many of the existing car manufacturers. The US manufacturers struggled to adapt, and early vehicles from GM and Ford were not successful. However, the Japanese were rather more successful in developing the new capabilities and technologies, and new products from Toyota and Honda have been particularly successful.

However, zero-emissions legislation was not adopted elsewhere, and more modest emission reduction targets were set. Since then, hybrid petrol-electric cars have been developed to help to reduce emissions. These are clearly not long-term solutions to the problem, but do represent valuable technical and social prototypes for future systems such as fuel cells. In 1993, Eiji Toyoda, Toyota's chairman, and his team embarked on the project code named G21. G stands for global and 21, the twenty-first century. The purpose of the project was to develop a small hybrid car that could be sold at a competitive price in order to respond to the growing needs and eco awareness of many consumers worldwide. A year later a concept vehicle was developed called the 'Prius', taken from the Latin for 'before'. The goal was to reduce fuel consumption by 50%, and emissions by more than that. To find the right hybrid system for the G21, Toyota considered 80 alternatives before narrowing the list to four. Development of the Prius required the integration of different technical capabilities, including, for example, a joint venture with Matsushita Battery.

The prototype was revealed at the Tokyo Motor Show in October 1995. It is estimated that the project cost Toyota US$1 billion in R&D. The first commercial version was launched in Japan in December 1997, and after further improvements such as battery performance and power source management, introduced to the USA market in August 2000. For urban driving the economy is 60 mpg, and 50 for motorways – the opposite consumption profile of a conventional vehicle, but roughly twice as fuel efficient as an equivalent Corolla. From the materials used in production, through driving, maintenance, and finally its disposal, the Prius reduced CO_2 emissions by more than a third, and has a recyclability potential of approximately 90%. The Prius was launched in the USA at a price of $19,995, and sales in 2001 were 15,556 and 20,119 in 2002.

(continued)

However, industry experts estimate that Toyota was losing some $16,000 for every Prius it sold because it costs between $35,000 and $40,000 to produce. Toyota did make a profit on its second generation Prius launched in 2003, and other hybrid cars such as the Lexus range in 2005, because of improved technologies and lower production costs.

The Hollywood celebrities soon discovered the Prius: Leonardo DiCaprio bought one of the first in 2001, followed by Cameron Diaz, Harrison Ford and Calista Flockhart at the 2003 Academy Awards. British politicians took rather longer to jump on the hybrid bandwagon, with the leader of the opposition David Cameron driving a hybrid Lexus in 2006. In 2005, 107,897 cars were sold in the USA, about 60% of global Prius sales, and four times more than the sales in 2000, and twice as many in 2004. Toyota planned to sell a million hybrids by 2010.

In addition to the direct income and indirect prestige the Prius and other hybrid cars has created for Toyota, the company has also licensed some of its 650 patents on hybrid technology to Nissan and Ford, which were expected to develop hybrid vehicles for 2007, and Ford planned to sell 250,000 hybrids by 2010. Mercedes-Benz showed a diesel-electric S-class at the Frankfurt auto show in autumn 2005, and Honda has developed its own technology and range of hybrid cars, and is also probably the world leader in fuel cell technology for vehicles.

Sources: Alan Pilkington and Romano Dyerson (2004) 'Incumbency and the disruptive regulator: the case of the electric vehicles in California', *International Journal of Innovation Management*, 8(4), 339–354; 'Why the future is hybrid', *The Economist*, 4 December, 2004; 'Too soon to write off the dinosaurs', *Financial Times*, 18 November, 2005; *Fortune*, 21 Feb 2006; 'Toyota: the birth of the Prius', *Wall Street Journal*, 13 February, 2006.

New Socio-technical Systems

New socio-technical systems are a special case of innovation because neither the technology nor applications are well-defined or understood. Therefore technology and markets co-evolve over time, as developers, potential users and other stakeholders interact. The main differences between systems innovation and novel niches are the scale and scope of the innovation. Systems innovation involves more actors than novel niches do, and typically requires greater co-ordination of these different actors, by some institutional or policy intervention, rather than relying only on market mechanisms.[14]

In such cases the process of development, implementation and diffusion of innovations has certain unique characteristics:

- Systems are likely to consist of a complex configuration of new technologies, products, services, institutions and infrastructure, interacting at various levels and interfaces, which complicate development and implementation.
- The role and knowledge of users is likely to be much more significant, but there is a burden on developers to educate potential users. This requires close links between developers and users.

- Adoption is likely to involve a long-term commitment, involving many different actors, and therefore the cost of failure to perform is likely to be high.
- The development and diffusion process is often lengthy and uncertain, and adoption may lag years behind availability and receipt of the initial information.

Systems innovations will consist of a number of components, or subsystems. Depending on how open the standards are for interfaces between the various components, products may be offered as bundled systems, or as subsystems or components. For bundled systems, customers evaluate purchases at the system level, rather than at the component level. For example, many pharmaceutical firms are now operating managed healthcare services, rather than simply developing and selling specific drugs. Similarly, robot manufacturers offer 'manufacturing solutions', rather than stand-alone robot manipulators. Bundled systems can offer customers enhanced performance by allowing a package of optimised components using proprietary interfaces of 'firmware', and in addition may provide the convenience of a single point of purchase and after-sales support. For example, many utility companies now offer services for domestic customers which include an environmental assessment, advice on insulation and appliances, as well as more traditional energy provision.

The growth of general service providers and systems integrators and 'turn-key' solutions suggests that there is additional value to be gained by developing and marketing systems rather than components: typically, the value added at the system level is greater than the sum of the value added by the components. There is, however, an important exception to this rule. In cases where a particular component or subsystem is significantly superior to competing offerings, unbundling is likely to result in a larger market. The increased market is due to additional customers who would not be willing to purchase the bundled system, but would like to incorporate one of the components or subsystems into their own systems. Moreover, bundled systems may not appeal to customers with idiosyncratic needs, or knowledgeable customers able to configure their own systems. In such cases the trick is to identify the specific needs of such users. For example, in the case of micro-generation discussed earlier, it is very unlikely to become a dominant energy system because of the particular characteristics of the technologies and potential users.

Links between Developers and Users

The development and adoption process for systems innovations is particularly difficult. The benefits to potential users may be difficult to identify and value, and because there are likely to be few direct substitutes available, the market may not be able to provide any benchmarks. The choice of suppliers is likely to be limited, more an oligopolistic market than a truly competitive one. In the absence of direct competition, price becomes less important than other factors such as reputation, performance and service and support.

Innovation research has long emphasised the importance of 'understanding user needs' when developing new products, but in the special case of complex products and services potential users may not be aware of, or may be unable to articulate, their needs. In such cases it is not sufficient simply to understand or even to satisfy existing customers, but rather it is necessary to lead existing customers and identify potential new customers. Conventional market research techniques are of little use, and there will be a greater burden on developers to work with potential users, in what has been called *expeditionary* or *agnostic* marketing, to reflect the emergent nature of the development and diffusion process. The main issue is how to learn as quickly as possible through experimentation with real products and users, and thereby anticipate future requirements and pre-empt future trends and demand.

The relationship between developers and users will change throughout the development and adoption process. Three distinct processes need to be managed, each demanding different linkages: development, adoption and interfacing. The processes of development and adoption are relatively well-understood, but managing the critical interface between developers and potential users is more problematic.

Two dimensions help determine the most appropriate relationship between developers and users: the range of different applications for an innovation; and the number of potential users of each application:[15]

- *Few applications and few users.* In this case direct face-to-face negotiation regarding the technology design and use is possible.
- *Few applications, but many users.* This is the classic marketing case, which demands careful segmentation, but little interaction with users.
- *Many applications, but few users.* In this case there are multiple stakeholders amongst the user groups, with separate and possibly conflicting needs. This requires skills to avoid optimisation of the technology for one group at the expense of others. The core functionality of the technology must be separated and protected, and custom interfaces developed for the different user groups.
- *Many applications and different users.* In this case developers must work with multiple archetypes of users and therefore aim for the most generic market possible, customised for no one group.

The interface between developers and users can be thought of as consisting of two flows, information flows and resource flows. Developers and adopters will negotiate the inflows and outflows of both information and resources. Therefore developers should recognise that resources committed to development and resources committed to aiding adoption should not be viewed as independent or 'ring-fenced'. Both contribute to the successful commercialisation of complex products, processes and services. Developers should also identify and manage the balance and direction of information and resource flows at different stages of the process of development and adoption. For example, at early stages managing information inflows may be most important, but at later stages managing outflows of information and resources may be critical. In addition, learning will require the management of knowledge flows, involving the exchange or secondment of appropriate staff.

In *Democratizing Innovation* Eric von Hippel builds on his concept of 'lead users' in innovation, and argues that innovation is becoming more democratic, with users increasingly being capable of developing their own new products and services.[16] He believes that such user innovation can have a positive impact on social welfare as innovating users – both individuals and firms – often freely share their innovations with others, creating user-innovation communities and a rich intellectual commons. Examples range from surgical equipment to surfboards to software security.

Role of Lead Users

Lead users are critical to the development and adoption of novel niches and systems innovations. As the title suggests, lead users demand new requirements ahead of the general market of other users, but are also positioned in the market to significantly benefit from the meeting of those requirements. Where potential users have high levels of sophistication, for example in business-to-business markets such as scientific instruments, capital equipment and IT systems, lead users can help to co-develop innovations, and are therefore often early adopters of such innovations. The initial research by von Hippel suggests lead users adopt an average of seven years before typical users, but the precise lead time will depend on a number of factors, including the technology life cycle. Characteristics of lead users include:[17]

- *Recognise requirements early* – are ahead of the market in identifying and planning for new requirements.
- *Expect high level of benefits* – due to their market position and complementary assets.
- *Develop their own innovations and applications* – have sufficient sophistication to identify and capabilities to contribute to development of the innovation.
- *Perceived to be pioneering and innovative* – by themselves and their peer group.

This has two important implications. First, those seeking to develop novel niches or system innovations should identify potential lead users with such characteristics to contribute to the co-development and early adoption of the innovation. Second, that lead users, as early adopters, can provide insights to forecasting the diffusion of innovations. Clayton Christensen and Michael Raynor make a similar point in their book *The Innovator's Solution*, and argue that conventional segmentation of markets by product attributes or user types cannot identify potentially disruptive innovations.

INNOVATION IN ACTION

Identifying Potentially Disruptive Innovations

In their book *The Innovator's Solution: Creating and sustaining successful growth* (Harvard Business School Press, 2003), Clayton Christensen and Michael Raynor argue that segmentation of markets by product attributes or type of customer will fail to identify potentially disruptive innovations. Building on the seminal marketing work of Theodore Levitt, they recommend *circumstance*-based segmentation, which focuses on the 'job to be done' by an innovation, rather than product attributes or type of users. This perspective is likely to result in very different new products and services than traditional ways of segmenting markets. One of the insights this approach provides is the idea of innovations from *non-consumption*. So instead of comparing product attributes with competing products, identify target customers who are trying to get a

(continued)

job done, but due to circumstances – wealth, skill, location etc. – do not have access to existing solutions. These potential customers are more likely to compare the disruptive innovation with the alternative of having nothing at all, rather than existing offerings. This can lead to the creation of whole new markets, for example, the low-cost airlines in the USA and UK, such as Southwest and Ryanair, or Intuit's QuickBooks. Similarly, in the MBA market, distance learning programmes were once considered inferior to conventional programmes, and instead leading business schools competed (and many still do) for funds for larger and ever more expensive buildings in prestigious locations. However, improvements to technology, combined with other forms of learning to create 'blended' learning environments, have created whole new markets for MBA programmes, for those who are unable or unwilling to pursue more conventional programmes.

The adoption process for systems innovation is likely to be lengthy due to the difficulty of evaluating risk and subsequent implementation. Perceived risk is a function of a buyer's level of uncertainty and the seriousness of the consequences of the decision to purchase. There are two types of risk: the performance risk, that is the extent to which the purchase meets expectations, and the psychological risk associated with how other people in the organisation react to the decision. Low-risk decisions are likely to be made autonomously, and therefore it is easier to target decision-makers and identify buying criteria. For complex products there is greater uncertainty, and the consequences of the investment are more significant, and therefore some form of joint or collective decision-making and responsibility is more likely.

In the case of organisational decision-making and investment, the expectations, perceptions, roles and perception of risk of the main decision-makers may vary. Therefore we should expect and identify the different buying criteria used by various decision-makers in an organisation. For example, a production engineer may favour the reliability or performance of a piece of equipment, whereas the finance manager is likely to focus on life cycle costs and value for money. Three factors are likely to affect the purchase decision in an organisation:

1. *Political and legal environment.* This may affect the availability of, and information concerning, competing products. For example, government legislation might specify the tender process for the development and purchase of new equipment.
2. *Organisational structure and tasks.* Structure includes the degree of centralisation of decision-making and purchasing; tasks include the organisational purpose served by the purchase, the nature of demand derived from the purchaser's own business, and how routine the purchase is.
3. *Personal roles and responsibilities.* Different roles need to be identified and satisfied. Gatekeepers control the flow of information to the organisation, influencers add information or change buying criteria, deciders choose the specific supplier or brand, and the buyers are responsible for the actual purchase. Therefore the ultimate users may not be the primary target.

Open Systems of Innovation

In this section we begin our discussion of open innovation and networks which we will discuss more fully in Chapter 8. Here we are concerned with the enabling routines for building effective linkages outside the organisation in order to identify, resource and implement innovations for sustainability. This is a good example of what has been called networked or 'open' innovation, in contrast to 'closed innovation', which primarily takes place within the firm.[18]

Increasingly, networks of relationships are the most appropriate unit of analysis for understanding the innovation process. A network is as much a process as a structure, which both constrains firms, and in turn is shaped by firms. In these terms collaboration can be understood as an attempt to cope with the increasing complexity and interrelatedness of different technologies and markets. We examine the technological and market motives for collaboration, and identify the organisational processes necessary to exploit it as an opportunity for knowledge acquisition and learning.

Organisations collaborate for many reasons, including efficiency and flexibility, but here we are concerned with gaining access to technological and market knowledge. Such relationships may take many forms, ranging from simple licensing agreements, loose coalitions or so-called strategic alliances, to more formal joint ventures. Therefore the technological and market competencies of a specific firm may be a less reliable indicator of innovative potential than its position in a network.

The concept of innovation networks has become popular in recent years, as it appears to offer many of the benefits of internal development, but with few of the drawbacks of collaboration. Networks have been claimed by some to be a new hybrid form of organisation that has the potential to replace both firms (hierarchies) and markets, in essence the 'virtual corporation', whereas others believe them to be simply a transitory form of organisation, positioned somewhere between internal hierarchies and external market mechanisms. Whatever the case, there is little agreement on what constitutes a network, and the term and alternatives such as 'web' and 'cluster' have been criticised for being too vague and all-inclusive.

Different authors adopt different meanings, levels of analysis and attribute networks with different characteristics. For example, academics on the Continent have focused on social, geographical and institutional aspects of networks, and the opportunities and constraints these present for innovation. In contrast, Anglo-Saxon studies have tended to take a systems perspective, and have attempted to identify how best to design, manage and exploit networks for innovation. Figure 3.4 presents a framework for the analysis of different network perspectives in innovation studies.

A network can be thought of as consisting of a number of positions or nodes, occupied by individuals, firms, business units, universities, governments, customers or other actors, and links or interactions between these nodes. A network perspective is concerned with how these economic actors are influenced by the social context in which they are embedded and how actions can be influenced by the position of actors. A network is more than an aggregation of bilateral relationships or dyads, and therefore the configuration, nature and content of a network impose additional constraints and present additional opportunities.

Innovation networks can exist at any level: global, national, regional, sector, organisational, or individual. For example, a National System of Innovation, which we discussed earlier, is an

	FOCUS ON GENERAL INNOVATIVENESS	FOCUS ON DISCRETE INNOVATIONS
SOCIAL NETWORK FOCUS	Regional and business groups; communities of scientists and engineers	Diffusion and commercialisation of innovations
ACTOR NETWORK FOCUS	Portfolios of strategic alliances	Networks mobilised for a specific innovation

FIGURE 3.4   Types of innovation network.

Source: Jones, O., Conway, S. and Steward, F. (2001) *Social Interaction and Organizational Change: Aston perspectives on innovation networks.* Imperial College Press, London.

example of an innovation network at a high level of aggregation – the country. Whatever the level of analysis, the most interesting attribute of an innovation network is the degree and type of interaction between actors, which results in a dynamic but inherently unstable set of relationships. Innovation networks are an organisational response to the complexity or uncertainty of technology and markets, and as such innovations are not the result of any linear process. This makes it very difficult, if not impossible, to predict the path or nature of innovation resulting from network interactions. The generation, application and regulation of an innovation within a network are unlike the trial-and-error process within a single firm or venture, or variation and selection within a market. Instead, actors in an innovation network attempt to reduce the uncertainty associated with complexity through a process of recursive learning and testing.

INNOVATION IN ACTION

An Environmental Innovation Network for IKEA

The catalogue of IKEA has one of the world's highest circulations, with a print run of more than 100 million per year, needing 50,000 tonnes of high-quality paper each year. However, in the 1990s there were growing environmental concerns about the discharge of chlorinated compounds from the processes used to create the relatively high-quality paper used in such promotional materials, as well as the more general issue of paper recycling. In response to these concerns, in 1992

(continued)

IKEA introduced two new goals for the production of its catalogue: be printed on paper that was totally chlorine-free (TCF), and to include a high proportion of recycled paper.

However, these goals demanded significant innovation. No such paper product existed at the time, and the dominant industry suppliers believed the combination of no chlorine and high levels of recycled pulp to be impossible. To achieve the necessary paper brightness for catalogue printing, a minimum of 50% chlorine-dioxide-bleached pulp had been used. Chlorine had been used for 50 years as the bleaching agent for high-quality paper. Moreover, the high-quality paper used for such catalogues consisted of a very thin paper base, which is coated with clay, which makes the insertion of recycled fibre very difficult. The manager of R&D at Svenska Cellulosa Aktiebolaget (SCA), one of Europe's largest producers of high-quality paper, argued that 'the high-quality demands and the large volume of filling substances is the main reason that it is neither realistic nor necessary to use recycled fibre'. SCA reinforced this view with the decision to build a new SEK 2.4 billion plant to produce conventional high-quality coated paper. At that time SCA was not a supplier to IKEA.

In Sweden, the paper manufacturer Aspa worked with the chemical firm Eka Nobel to develop an environmentally acceptable bleaching process with less damaging discharges, but this was still based on chlorine dioxide and failed to achieve the necessary brightness for use in high-quality paper, and was marketed as 'semi-bleached'. Following customer demand for a true TCF product, including a request from Greenpeace for TCF paper for production of its newsletter, Aspa was forced to develop a stable product with secure supplies. At this stage the pulp and fibre company Sodra Cell became involved, and identified the need to reach full brightness to create a broader market for TCF paper. Sodra worked with the German company Kvaerner to develop an alternative but equally effective bleaching process, and Kvaerner established a research project on ozone bleaching with Lentzing and STORA Billerud. The ozone bleaching process was adapted from an established process for water purification with the help of AGA Gas. However, the use of ozone in place of chlorine for bleaching required the quality of the pulpwood to be improved, so the harvesting system had to be changed to ensure that wood was better sorted and available within weeks of harvesting. To improve the brightness and strength of the paper, the impurities in the pulp from de-inked recycled paper had to be reduced, which required a new washing process. The changes in the chemistry of the pulp subsequently reduced the strength of the paper, which required changes in the paper production process. The printing processes had to be adapted to the characteristics of the new paper. Initially Sodra Cell supplied the new product to SCA through its relationship with Aspa, but also to the Italian paper producer Burgo, which provided the paper for the IKEA catalogue.

Thus the organisation evolved beyond a simple industrial supply relationship, to an innovation network including customers, printers, paper manufacturers, pulp and fibre producers, forestry companies, research institutes, environmental and lobby groups, across many different countries. At the same time, the intended innovation shifted from a high-quality TCF clay-coated paper, to a TCF uncoated fresh pulp and 10% de-inked recycled pulp product.

Source: H. Hakansson and A. Waluszewski (2003) *Managing Technological Development: IKEA, the Environment and Technology.* Routledge, London.

A network can influence the actions of its members in two ways. Firstly, through the flow and sharing of information within the network; secondly, through differences in the position of actors in the network, which causes power and control imbalances. Therefore the position an organisation occupies in a network is a matter of great strategic importance, and reflects its power and influence in that network. Sources of power include technology, expertise, trust, economic strength and legitimacy. Networks can be tight or loose, depending on the quantity (number), quality (intensity) and type (closeness to core activities) of the interactions or links. Such links are more than individual transactions, and require significant investment in resources over time. Types of interaction include:

Product interactions – products and groups of products and services interact, are adapted and evolve.

Process interactions – the interdependencies between product and process, and between different processes and production facilities are another interaction within a network, together with their use and utilisation.

Social interaction within the organisation – for example, business units are more than a combination of product and process facilities: they consist also of social interactions, with knowledge of, and an ability to work with, other business units within the organisation.

Social interaction between organisations – business relationships both restrict and provide opportunities for innovation, particularly for systemic innovations.

Historically, networks have evolved from long-standing business relationships. Any firm will have a group of partners that it does regular business with – universities, suppliers, distributors, customers and competitors. Over time mutual knowledge and social bonds develop through repeated dealings, increasing trust and reducing transaction costs. Therefore a firm is more likely to buy or sell technology from members of its network. Firms may be able to access the resources of a wide range of other organisations through direct and indirect relationships, involving different channels of communication and degrees of formalisation. Typically, this begins with a stronger relationship between a firm and a small number of primary suppliers, which share knowledge at the concept development stage. The role of the technology gatekeeper, or heavyweight project manager, is critical in this respect. In many cases organisational linkages can be traced to strong personal relationships between key individuals in each organisation. These linkages may subsequently evolve into a full network of secondary and tertiary suppliers, each contributing to the development of a subsystem or component technology, but links with these organisations are weaker and filtered by the primary suppliers. However, links amongst the primary, secondary and tertiary supplier groups may be stronger to facilitate the exchange of information.

This process is path-dependent in the sense that past relationships between actors increase the likelihood of future relationships, which can lead to inertia and constrain innovation. Indeed much of the early research on networks concentrated on the constraints networks impose on members, for example preventing the introduction of 'superior' technologies or products by controlling supply and distribution networks. Organisational networks have two characteristics that affect the innovation process: activity cycles and instability. The existence of activity cycles and transaction chains creates constraints within a network.

Different activities are systematically related to each other and through repetition are combined to form transaction chains. This repetition of transactions is the basis of efficiency, but systemic interdependencies create constraints to change.

For example, the Swiss watch industry was based on long-established networks of small firms with expertise in precision mechanical movements, but as a result was slow to respond to the threat of electronic watches from Japan. Similarly, in Japan the formal business groups dominate many traditional sectors, originally the family based *zaibatsu*, and more recently the more loosely connected *keiretsu* such as Mitsui, Mitsubishi, Sumitomo, Fuji, Sanwa and Dal Ichi Kangyo (DKB). Benefits of membership of a *keiretsu* include access to low-cost, long-term capital, and access to the expertise of firms in related industries. In practice, membership of *keiretsu* is associated with below-average profitability and growth, and independent firms like Honda and Sony are often cited as being more innovative than established members of *keiretsu*.

Networks are most appropriate where the benefits of sharing of joint infrastructure and standards and other network externalities outweigh the costs of network governance and maintenance. Where there are high transaction costs involved in purchasing technology, a network approach may be more appropriate than a market model, and where uncertainty exists a network may be superior to full integration or acquisition.

Go online to find a discussion of the importance of managing sustainability throughout the value chain in the case study *Green Supply Chain Management in the Automobile Industry*, written by Breno Nunes and David Bennett.

www.iande.info

However, no network can ever be optimal in any generic sense, as there is no single reference point. Therefore any network is inherently instable, but these imperfections mean that networks can evolve over time, for example, the evolution of innovation networks in a range of traditional industries in Italy. There are two distinct dynamics of formation and growth. The first type of network emerges and develops as a result of environmental interdependence, and through common interests – an *emergent* network. However, the other type of network requires some triggering entity to form and develop – an *engineered* network. In an engineered network a nodal firm actively recruits other members to form a network, without the rationale of environmental interdependence or similar interests. Different types of network may present different opportunities for learning. In a closed network, a company seeks to develop proprietary standards through scale economies and other actions, and thereby lock customers and other related companies into its network.

In such cases established companies are able to reinforce their positional advantage by adopting new technologies which have implications for compatibility, whereas new entrants or existing firms at the periphery of the network will find it extremely difficult to gain a positional advantage through innovation. Obvious examples include Microsoft in operating systems and Intel in microprocessors for PCs. In the case of open networks, complex products, services and businesses have to interface with others and it is in everyone's interest to share information and to ensure compatibility. Open networks or systems often involve multiple hierarchical levels or subsystems, each controlled by a different technical community.

Therefore innovations in one technical sub-field may influence some relationships within the network, but not the whole network. Therefore innovation by established firms at the periphery of the network or by new entrants is more common. Examples include many large socio-technical systems, such as telephony and power generation and distribution.

STRATEGIC AND SOCIAL IMPACT

In 2010 The Sussex Manifesto was launched to celebrate 40 years of policy research and practice at Sussex University linking science, technology and development. The United Nations commissioned a study which became known as the *Sussex Manifesto*, published in 1970. Today the STEPS Centre (Social, Technological and Environmental Pathways to Sustainability) is an interdisciplinary global research and policy hub uniting development studies with science and technology studies, which aims to shape future policy and practice towards a more sustainable and equitable future. STEPS is a joint venture of SPRU (Science and Technology Policy Research Unit) and the IDS (Institute of Development Studies), with global partners in Latin America, Asia and Africa.

Meeting the interlinked global challenges of poverty reduction, social justice and environmental sustainability is the great moral and political imperative of our age. STEPS argue that science, technology and innovation of many kinds have essential roles to play in this. But along with many others, the STEPS Centre believes that this imperative can only be fulfilled if there is a radical shift in how we think about and perform innovation. By innovation, they mean new ways of doing things. This includes not only science and technology, but – crucially – the related array of new ideas, institutions, practices, behaviours and social relations that shape scientific and technological patterns, purposes, applications and outcomes. Central to this is a move away from progress defined simply by the scale or rate of change – about who is 'ahead' or 'behind' in some presumed one-track race. Instead, attention must focus on the many alternative *directions* (emphasis added) for scientific, technological and associated institutional change. This is not about being 'pro' or 'anti' science or technology, but about addressing real questions of choice: 'which science?', 'what technology?' and, especially, 'whose innovation?' and 'what kinds of change?' In other words, we need to foster more diverse and far more fairly distributed forms of – and directions for – innovation, towards greater social justice.

This emphasis on *direction, distribution* and *diversity* is at the centre of a new *3D Agenda* for innovation. *Direction* matters because it shapes the distribution of benefits, costs and risks from innovation. Because marginal people and places so often lose out, the appraisal of alternative innovation pathways needs to focus specifically on the *distribution* of benefits and address questions of social difference, equity and justice. Growth in demand among relatively low-income groups near the 'bottom of the pyramid' worldwide presents a massive – and still under-recognised – opportunity for innovation processes linked to small businesses to foster more equally distributed economic growth. Deliberately pursuing a *diversity* of innovation pathways is the only way to prevent concentration and lock-in that close down and crowd out the paths favoured by more less dominant groups. Similarly, promotion of diversity is consistent with the needs of varied economic, ecological and cultural contexts.

Sources: www.steps-centre.org and http://anewmanifesto.org/

Chapter Summary

In formulating and executing their development and innovation strategies, business firms cannot ignore the national systems of innovation and international value chains in which they are embedded. Through their strong influences on demand and competitive conditions, the provision of human resources, and forms of corporate governance, national systems of innovation both open opportunities and impose constraints on what firms can do.

However, although firms' strategies are *influenced* by their own national systems of innovation, and their position in international value chains, they are not *determined* by them. Learning (i.e. assimilating knowledge) from competitors and external sources of innovation is essential for developing capabilities, but does require costly investments in R&D, training and skills development in order to develop the necessary absorptive capacity. This depends in part on what management itself does, by way of investing in complementary assets in production, marketing, service and support, and its position in local and international systems of innovation. It also depends on a variety of factors that make it more or less difficult to appropriate the benefits from innovation, such as intellectual property and international trading regimes, and over which management can sometimes have very little influence.

Innovation is too often portrayed as antagonistic to sustainability. However, in this chapter we have argued innovation has a central role to play in helping to create sustainable futures through conventional means such as new processes, products and services, and also through promoting change in organisation, business and behaviour. By better understanding the dynamics of innovation, including development, adoption and diffusion, the rate and direction of innovation can be influenced, and more sustainable trajectories explored. The process of innovation is much more complex than technology responding to market signals.

Discussion Questions

1. In what ways can innovation contribute to or potentially constrain sustainability?

2. What are the differences between 'open' and 'closed' types of innovation?

3. What characteristics do 'lead users' have, and why are they important?

4. What factors influence the location of innovation, and how might these constrain the globalisation of innovation?

5. What are the main components of a National Innovation System, and how do these interact?

6. How can firms learn from overseas sources of innovation?

7. How can firms limit the scope for competitors imitating their innovations, and therefore better appropriate the benefits of their innovations?

8. Beyond formal R&D investment, what types of capabilities and competencies do firms need in order to innovate?

9. Compare the development of capabilities in China and India. What are the key lessons for developing economies?

Team Exercise

Using Figure 3.3, identify a sustainable innovation for each of the four quadrants.

Assignment

Choose a country, industrialised or developing, and identify the key aspects of the National Innovation System. Compare these with any observed sectoral patterns of performance. What do you conclude about the respective role of government policy, national institutions and firm capabilities and behaviour?

Key Terms Defined

Bandwagons   may occur where an innovation is adopted because of pressure caused by the sheer number of those who have already adopted an innovation, rather than by individual assessments of the benefits of an innovation.

Corporate governance   the systems for exercising and changing corporate ownership and control.

Expeditionary marketing   with complex products and services potential users may not be aware of, or may be unable to articulate, their needs. In such cases it is not sufficient simply to understand or even to satisfy existing customers, but rather it is necessary to lead existing customers and identify potential new customers. Conventional market research techniques are of little use, and there will be a greater burden on developers to work with potential users.

Externalities   factors which influence the adoption and diffusion of an innovation, such as supporting infrastructure, complementary products and services, finance and new training and skills, or are created by the adoption of an innovation, for example, pollution. Therefore externalities can be positive or negative.

Lead users   demand new requirements ahead of the general market of other users, but are also positioned in the market to significantly benefit from the meeting of those requirements. Lead users are critical to the development and adoption of novel niches and systems innovations.

Position   the current endowment of technology and intellectual property of a firm, as well as its relations with customers and suppliers.

Spillovers   a term used by economists to describe the flow of know-how and other benefits from firm-specific investments, e.g. by MNCs, to the broader economy e.g. between firms and between sectors. This is often presented as being automatic, but demands a significant effort by domestic firms.

Value chain – or value network   the system of relationships to create and capture value, e.g. between suppliers and customers. These can constrain profoundly their ability to capture the benefits of their innovation and entrepreneurship.

Further Reading and Resources

There are a number of texts which describe and compare different systems of national innovation policy. In the edited text *National Systems of Innovation: Toward a Theory of Innovation and Interactive Learning* (2010), Lundvall provides an excellent up-to-date overview of the key theories and research (Anthem Press), and for a more specific focus see *Small Country Innovation Systems: Globalization, Change and Policy in Asia and Europe* (2008), edited by Charles Edquist and Leif Hommen (Edward Elgar). A more classic contribution is *National Innovation Systems* (Oxford University Press, 1993), edited by Richard Nelson, but all these have an emphasis on public policy rather than corporate strategy. Michael Porter's *The Competitive Advantage of Nations* (Macmillan, London, 1990) provides a useful framework in which to examine the direct impact on corporate behaviour of innovation systems. At the other extreme, David Landes' *Wealth and Poverty of Nations* (Little Brown, 1998) takes a broad (and stimulating) historical and cultural perspective. In *Globalisation, Poverty and Inequality* (Polity Press, 2005), Raphie Kaplinsky argues that macro-economic conditions can overwhelm the efforts of firms and countries to benefit from globalisation, and that global excess capacity in production and the terms of international trade mean that emerging economies may not benefit from further globalisation.

Comprehensive and balanced reviews of the arguments and evidence for product leadership versus follower positions is provided by G.J. Tellis and P.N. Golder, *Will and Vision: How latecomers grow to dominate markets* (McGraw-Hill, 2002) and *Fast Second: How Smart Companies Bypass Radical Innovation to Enter and Dominate New Markets* (Jossey-Bass/Wiley, 2004) by Constantinos C. Markides. More relevant to firms from emerging economies, and our favourite text on the subject, is Naushad Forbes and David Wield's *From Followers to Leaders: Managing technology and innovation* (Routledge, 2002), which includes numerous case examples. *Local Enterprises in the Local Economy: Issues of Governance and Upgrading* (Edward Elgar, 2004), edited by Hubert Schmitz of the Institute of

Development Studies, provides a summary of recent research on the influence of global standards and value chains on the development of firms from emerging economies. For recent reviews of the core competence and dynamic capability perspectives see David Teece's *Essays in Technology Management and Policy: Selected Papers* (World Scientific Press, 2004) and Connie Helfat's *Dynamic Capabilities: Understanding Strategic Change in Organizations* (Blackwell, 2006).

For a general introduction to the key issues in sustainable development, our favourite text is *The Principles of Sustainability* by Simon Dresner (Earthscan, London, 2002). Unlike most of the literature on the subject, this treatment is well-balanced and even includes some humour. Jennifer Elliott's *An Introduction to Sustainable Development* (Routledge, London, second edition 2005) is a more conventional academic approach, and focuses on the implications for developing nations. However, neither text is strong on the links between sustainability and innovation. The Special Issue of the *International Journal of Innovation Management* (2002) 6(3) on 'Innovation for Sustainability' is a useful place to begin, and is edited by two leading scholars in the field, Frans Berkhout and Ken Green.

The Natural Advantage of Nations: Business Opportunities, Innovations and Governance in the 21st Century by Amory B. Lovins (Earthscan Publications, 2005) is a collection of papers by leading authors, including Michael Porter, and makes the business case for sustainable development, including technological, structural and social change. The book has a useful companion website. *Sustainable Business Development: Inventing the Future Through Strategy, Innovation, and Leadership* by David L. Rainey (Cambridge University Press, 2006) provides a practical analysis of what sustainable business development (SBD) is and how companies do it, and includes many case studies from the US, Europe, Pacific Rim and South America. *Sustainable Innovation: The Organisational, Human and Knowledge Dimension* by Rene J. Jorna (Greenleaf Publishing, 2006) is a more theoretical and philosophical book, and looks at the human, social and management challenges and responses. The book argues that it is impossible to achieve the appropriate balance between the needs of people, planet and profit, and advocates a process of 'making sustainable', instead of trying to achieve 'sustainability'.

References

1. Cantwell, J. and J. Molero (2003) *Multinational Enterprises, Innovative Systems and Systems of Innovation*. Edward Elgar, Cheltenham; Granstrand, O., Hêakanson, L. and Sjèolander, S. (1992) *Technology Management and International Business: Internationalization of R&D and technology*. Wiley, Chichester, especially the chapter by Patel, P. and Pavitt, K., 'Large Firms in the Production of the World's Technology: An Important Case of Non-Globalization'.

2. Kim, L. and R.R. Nelson (2000) *Technology, Learning and Innovation: Experiences of Newly Industrializing Economies*. Cambridge University Press; Viotti, E.B. (2002) 'National Learning Systems: A new approach on technological change in late industrializing economies

and evidence from the cases of Brazil and South Korea', *Technological Forecasting and Social Change*, 69, 653–680; Bell, M. and K. Pavitt (1993) 'Technological accumulation and industrial growth: Contrasts between developed and developing countries', *Industrial and Corporate Change*, 2 (2), 157–210.

3. Schimtz, H. (2004) *Local Enterprises in the Global Economy*. Edward Elgar, Cheltenham; Sahay, A. and Riley, D. (2003) 'The role of resource access, market conditions, and the nature of innovation in the pursuit of standards in the new product development process', *Journal of Product Innovation Management*, 20, 338–355.

4. Tidd, J. and Bessant, J. (2009) *Managing Innovation: Integrating technological, market and organizational change*. Wiley, Chichester. Fourth edition.

5. Nelson, R. (1993) *National Innovation Systems*. Oxford University Press, Oxford; Edquist, C. (1997) *Systems of Innovation: Technologies, Institutions and Organisations* (Pinter, London); Lundvall, B.A. (1992) *National Systems of Innovation* (Pinter, London).

6. Porter, M. (1990) *The Competitive Advantage of Nations*. Macmillan, London.

7. Forbes, N. and D. Wield (2002) *From Followers to Leaders: Managing technology and innovation*. Routledge, London.

8. Prahalad, C. and Hamel, G. (1990) The core competence of the corporation. *Harvard Business Review*, May/June, 79–91.

9. Teece, D. (2004) *Essays in Technology Management and Policy: Selected Papers*. World Scientific Press, London; Helfat, C.E. (2006) *Dynamic Capabilities: Understanding Strategic Change in Organizations*. Blackwell.

10. Geels, F.W. (2002) 'Technological transitions as evolutionary reconfiguration processes: A multi-level perspective and a case study', *Research Policy*, 31 (8–9), 1257–1274.

11. Porter, M.E. and C. van der Linde (1995) 'Green and competitive: Ending the stalemate', *Harvard Business Review*, 73(5), 120-134.

12. Smith, A. (2004) 'Alternative technology niches and sustainable development', *Innovation: Management, Policy and Practice*, 6(2), 220–235; Smith, A., A. Stirling, and F. Berkhout (2005) 'The governance of sustainable socio-technical transitions', *Research Policy*, 34(10), 1491-1510.

13. Christensen, C.M. (2000) *The Innovator's Dilemma*. HarperCollins, New York.

14. Kemp, R., J. Schot and R. Hoogma (1998) 'Regime shifts to sustainability through processes of niche formation', *Technology Analysis and Strategic Management*, 10(2), 175-195.

15. Leonard-Barton, D. and D.K. Sinha (1993) 'Developer–user interaction and user satisfaction in internal technology transfer', *Academy of Management Journal,* **36** (5), 1125–1139; More, P.L.A. (1986) 'Developer/adopter relationships in new industrial product situations', *Journal of Business Research*, **14**, 501–517.

16. von Hippel, E. (2005) *Democratizing Innovation*. MIT Press, Cambridge.

17. Morrison, P.D., Roberts, J.H. and Midgley, D.F. (2004) 'The nature of lead users and measurement of leading edge status', *Research Policy*, **33**, 351–362; von Hippel, E. (1986) 'Lead users: A source of novel product concepts', *Management Science*, 32(7), 791–805; von Hippel, E. (1988) *The Sources of Innovation* (Oxford University Press, Oxford).

18. Chesborough, H. (2003) *Open Innovation: The new imperative for creating and profiting from technology*. Boston, Mass.: Harvard Business School Press; Trott, P. and Hartmann, D. (2009), 'Why Open Innovation is old wine in new bottles', *International Journal of Innovation Management*,13(4), 715–736.

CASE STUDY 3

Exploring Innovation in Action: Building BRICs — Innovation Capabilities in China

Since economic reform began in 1978, the Chinese economy has grown by about 9–10% each year, compared to 2–3% for the industrialised countries. As a result its GDP overtook Italy in 2004, France and the UK in 2005 and was expected to overtake Germany in 2008. China has a population of around 1.3 billion, and an economy valued at $2.3 trillion in 2006 (for comparison, the UK was $2.1 trillion, the USA $11.7 trillion, and Japan $4.9 trillion). China now has the world's second largest economy after the USA on a purchasing power (PPP) basis.

The Chinese government has followed a twin-track policy of exporting relatively low-technology products, while using various measures to protect its domestic economy, and providing subsidies to support selected state-owned firms, to build technological capability. This activist technology policy will be tightly constrained in future, after the completion of entry to the World Trade Organization in 2005, and implementation of TRIPS (Trade Related Intellectual Property System) in 2006. These will require stricter laws on intellectual property laws and their enforcement, and limit subsidies and interference with trade.

After two decades of providing the world economy with inexpensive labour, China is now starting to become a platform for innovation, research and development. The actual formal R&D expenditure is still comparatively small, about 1.3% of GDP (compared to an average of 2.3% of GDP in the advanced economies of the OECD, although Japan exceeds 3%), but the Chinese government aims to make China an 'innovation nation' by 2010, and a scientific power by 2050, and in 2006 increased government funding in R&D by 25% to $425 million. It plans to increase R&D expenditure to 2.5% of GDP by 2020, in line with expenditure in developed economies. China's science and technology output is already increasing, and was ranked fifth globally in terms of science papers produced between 2002 and 2005, which is impressive given the language disadvantage.

China's policy has followed the East Asian model in which success has depended on technological and commercial investment by and collaboration with foreign firms. Typically companies in the East Asian tiger economies such as South Korea and Taiwan developed technological capabilities on a foundation of manufacturing competence based on low-tech production, and developed higher levels of capability such as design and new product development, for example, through OEM (Own Equipment Manufacture) production for international firms. However, the flow of technology and development of capabilities are not automatic. Economists refer to 'spillovers' of know-how from foreign investment and collaboration, but this demands a significant effort by domestic firms.

Most significantly, China has encouraged foreign multinationals to invest in China, and these are now also beginning to conduct some R&D in China. Motorola opened the first foreign R&D lab in 1992, and estimates indicate there were more than 700 R&D centres in China in 2005, although care needs to be taken in the definitions used. The transfer of technology to China, especially in the manufacturing sector, is considered to be a major contributor to its recent economic growth. Around 80% of China's inward foreign direct investment (FDI) is 'technology' (hardware and software), and FDI inflows have continued to grow, to US$72bn in 2005. (For comparison, this is around ten times that attracted by India, whereas some advanced economies continue to attract significant FDI: for example, $165 billion was invested in the UK in 2005.) However, we must distinguish between technology transferred by foreign companies into their wholly or majority-owned subsidiaries in China, versus the technology acquired by indigenous enterprises. It is only through the successful acquisition of technological capability by indigenous enterprises, many of which still remain state-owned, that China can become a really innovative and competitive economic power.

The import of foreign technology can have a positive impact on innovation, and for large enterprises, the more foreign technology is imported, the more conducive to its own patenting. However, for the small and medium-sized enterprises this is not the case. This probably implies that larger enterprises possess certain absorptive capacity to take advantage of foreign technology which in turn leads to an enhancement of innovation capacity, whereas the small and medium-sized enterprises are more likely to rely on foreign technology due to the lack of appropriate absorptive capacity and the possibly huge gap between imported and its own technology. Buying bundles of technology has been encouraged. These included *embodied* and *codified* technology: hardware and licenses. If innovation expenditure is broken down by class of innovative activity, the costs of acquisition for *embodied* technology, such as machines and production equipment, account for about 58% of the total innovation expenditures, compared with 17% internal R&D, 5%

external R&D, 3% marketing of new product, 2% training cost and 15% engineering and manufacturing start-up.

It is clear that the large foreign MNCs are the most active in patenting in China. Foreign patenting began around 1995, and since 2000 patent applications have increased annually by around 50%. MNCs' patenting activities are highly correlated with total revenue, or the overall Chinese market size. This strongly supports the standpoint that foreign patents in China are largely driven by demand factors. China's specialisation in patenting does not correspond to its export specialisation. Automobiles, household durables, software, communication equipments, computer peripherals, semiconductors, telecommunication services are the primary areas. The semiconductor industry in 2005, for example, was granted as many as fourfold inventions of the previous year. Patents by foreign MNCs account for almost 90% of all patents in China, the most active being firms from Japan, the USA and South Korea. Thirty MNCs have been granted more than 1000 patents, and eight of these each have more than 5000: Samsung, Matsushita, Sony, LG, Mitsubishi, Hitachi, Toshiba, and Siemens. Almost half of these patents are for the application of an existing technology, a fifth for inventions, and the rest for industrial designs. Among the 18,000 patents for inventions with no prior-overseas rights, only 924 originate from Chinese subsidiaries of these MNCs, accounting for only 0.75% of the total. The average lag between patenting in the home country and in China is more than three years, which is an indicator of the technology lag between China and MNCs.

One reason for this pattern is the very low level of industry-funded R&D, as opposed to public-funded, but there has also been a failure of corporate governance in the large state-owned enterprises selected for support. When the economic reform programme began in 1978 it inherited the advantages and disadvantages of Maoist autarchy. China had enterprises producing across a very wide range of products, having spent heavily from the late 1950s to give itself a high degree of technological independence. The main disadvantage was that its technologies were out of date. The government promoted FDI through joint ventures, 51% owned by a 'national team' of about 120 large domestic state-owned enterprises. Pressures on and incentives for management in state-owned firms have encouraged them to rely on external sources of technology, rather than to develop their own internal capabilities. At the same time private Chinese firms have been constrained by a shortage of finance. However, in 2000 the government reviewed its policy and began to restructure the state-owned firms and to support the most successful private firms. There is a clear link between such restructuring and the development of capabilities.

Examples of companies which have gone through significant changes in governance or financial structure include Xiali, which was transformed into a joint venture with Toyota, TPCO, where debt funding was changed into equity and shareholding, which allowed higher investment in production capacity and technology development, and Tianjin Metal Forming, restructured to remove debt and in a stronger position to invest and be a more attractive candidate for a foreign investment. Private firms like Lenovo, TCL, (Ningbo) Bird and Huawei have since prospered and with belated government help, are successful overseas: Huawei, in 2004 gained 40% of its over $5bn revenues outside China; Haier has overseas revenues of over $1bn from its home appliances; Lenovo bought IBM's PC division in 2005; TCL made itself the largest TV maker in the world by buying Thomson of France's TV division in 2004; Wanxiang, a motor components manufacturer started by a farmer's son as a bicycle repair shop, had by 2004 $2bn annual sales.

However, there are significant differences of innovation and entrepreneurial activity in different areas of China. The eastern coastal region is higher than the other regions, especially in Shanghai, Beijing, Tianjin, whose entrepreneurial activity level is higher and continues to grow. Beijing and the Tianjin Region, Yangtze River Delta Region (Shanghai, Jiangsu, Zhejiang), Zhu Jiang Delta Region (Guangdong) are the most active regions. Shanghai ranks first in most surveys, followed by Beijing, but the disparity of the two areas has been expanding. For example, the local city government in Shanghai provides funds of $12 million each year to fund 'little giants', small high-technology firms which it hoped would contribute annual sales of $12 billion by 2010. In the middle region and the northeast region, entrepreneurial activity level is lower than the eastern coastal region, but is increasing. The western and north-west region is the lowest and least improving area for entrepreneurial activity level, and shows little change. Econometric models indicate that the main determinants for entrepreneurial activity are explained by regional market demand, industrial structure, availability of financing, entrepreneurial culture and human capital. Technology innovation and rate of consumption growth have no significant effects on the entrepreneurship in China.

Studies comparing successful and unsuccessful new ventures in China confirm the significance of entrepreneurial quality in explaining the success of new ventures, especially business and management skills, industrial experience and strength of social networks, the ubiquitous *guanxi*. However, there remain significant regulatory and institutional challenges with complex ownership structures, poor corporate governance and ambiguous intellectual property rights issues, especially with public research, former state enterprises and university spin-offs and academic-run enterprises.

Although some 200 million Chinese still live on $1 a day, China is also the largest market in the world for luxury goods. China is estimated to have 300,000 dollar millionaires, 400 entrepreneurs valued at $60 million each, and seven billionaires. Such disparities in income can create huge social and political tensions, and may result in a reaction against further growth unless governance and distribution are improved further.

Questions

1. In China, how has state policy promoted and constrained innovation?
2. What roles have MNCs had in the development of local capabilities?
3. In future, how might innovation and entrepreneurship contribute to development in China?

Sources: Qing Wang, Simon Collinson and Xiaobo Wu (eds.) *International Journal of Innovation Management* (2010) Special Issue on Innovation in China, 14(1); *East meets West: 15th International Conference on Management of Technology*, Beijing, May 2006.

ADVICE FOR ENTREPRENEURS

The competence or resource-based view is concerned essentially with identifying and building on strengths, preferably those which, for whatever reason, are unique to the firm. Every firm is unique by virtue of its history, value chain configuration, organisation culture etc. The challenge is to make the firm's uniqueness the source of its sustainable competitive advantage.

At one level the identification of competence appears to pose few difficulties. There are many cases which refer, for example, to the core competence of Honda in engines or Sony in miniaturisation and which explore why and how these firms have developed and maintain these competencies. But for core competence to be a tool of strategic analysis what is also required is a means for firms to analyse rigorously their own and their competitors' competencies. Yet, despite all the effort and attention, core competencies remain elusive, 'Few managers we have talked to could claim to have utilised core competence to achieve success in the marketplace, and even fewer to have built a core competence from scratch. Indeed, most were uncertain as to exactly what qualifies a core competence . . . it is like a mirage: something that from a distance appears to offer hope . . . but turns to sand when approached.'

Our own experience in working with the concept of core competence supports this view. Competencies disappear all too easily under close examination. A careful scrutiny of competence claims reveals, all too often, that they are neither firm-specific nor sustainable, that they convey functionality neither to the customer, nor generic qualities to the firm. A proven methodology to help to identify and assess the elusive competencies consists of three parts:

1. Identify the key attributes of the most successful products and services offered by the organization.
2. Map these attributes to the resources or competencies of the organisation, including tangible and intangible resources.
3. Assess the potential for sustaining, protecting and exploiting these resources, including knowledge management.

(continued)

1. Identifying key attributes

A pragmatic view on the nature of competitive advantage was advanced by Coyne (1986) whose argument starts with the observation that any company which is making repeat sales in a competitive market must enjoy an advantage in the eyes of the customers who are making the repeat purchases. He went on to argue that for a *sustainable* competitive advantage to exist three conditions must apply:

- Customers must perceive a consistent difference in important attributes between the producer's product/service and the attributes offered by competitors.
- This difference is the direct consequence of a capability gap between the producer and its competitors.
- Both the difference in important attributes and the capability gap can be expected to endure over time.

Types of resource capability:

- **Regulatory**: the possession of legal entities, e.g. patents and trademarks.
- **Positional**: the results of previous endeavour, e.g. reputation, trust, value chain configuration.
- **Business systems**: the ability to do things well, e.g. consistent conformance to specification.
- **Organisational** characteristics, e.g. the ability to manage change.

It is now possible to ask the question 'What is the nature of the package of product/delivery system attributes which customers value?' and to go on to ask the question 'What is responsible for producing the valued attributes'. The product/delivery system attributes will include factors such as: price, quality, specification, image, etc.

The Valued Attributes

Typical product/delivery system attributes which define competitive advantage.

Image What is the image of the product range? Is it important?

Price Is a low selling price a key buying criterion?

User friendliness Is it important for the product to be user friendly?

Availability Is product range availability crucial?

Rapid response to enquiry Is it important to produce designs, quotations etc. very quickly?

Quick response to customer demand Will sales be lost to the competition if they respond more quickly than you?

Width of product range Is it important to offer a wide range of products, and/or services to customers?

New product to market time How important is the product development time?

(continued)

Quality – the product's fitness for purpose Does the product, or service, deliver exactly the benefits which the customers want?

Quality – the consistent achievement of defined specification Is constant conformance to spec. vital?

Safety Is *safety in use* a major concern?

Regulatory requirements Does meeting regulatory requirements earlier/better than the competition give a competitive advantage?

Degree of innovation Is it important for the product or service to represent 'state of the art'?

Ability to vary product specification Is it important to complete product or service modifications easily and quickly?

Ability to vary product volume Is it important to be able to increase, or decrease, production volume easily?

Customer service Is the quality of the overall service which customers receive a key to winning business?

Pre- and after-sales service Is the supply of advice, spares, etc. a key aspect of winning business?

It may be necessary to identify different rankings for different categories of customers, e.g. new as opposed to long-standing customers, retailers as opposed to end users etc. In carrying out this analysis of attributes it is appropriate to seek consensus between the relevant executives with respect to questions such as:

- Can executives agree an importance weighting for each attribute?
- Can executives agree a benchmark score for each attribute compared with the competition?
- Can executives agree the *sustainability* of the advantage represented by each attribute?

The degree of congruence, or dissonance, in executives' perceptions of these issues can in itself be illuminating. In addition to identifying the current strengths in the marketplace it is also appropriate at this stage to identify known deficiencies in the product offering.

2. Mapping attributes to resources and competencies
The important characteristics of strategic competencies are:

- they are responsible for delivering a significant benefit to customers;
- they are idiosyncratic to the firm;
- they take time to acquire;
- they are sustainable because they are difficult and time consuming to imitate;
- they comprise *configurations* of resources;
- they have a strong tacit content and are socially complex – they are the product of experiential learning.

(*continued*)

The resources which produce product/delivery system attributes can now be placed in a framework of capabilities:

Regulatory capability – resources which are legal entities.

- tangible, on balance sheet, assets;
- intangible, off balance sheet, assets: e.g. patents
  licences
  trademarks
  contracts
  protectable data, etc.

Positional capability – resources which are not legal entities and which are the result of previous endeavour, i.e. with a high path dependency:

- reputation of company;
- reputation of product;
- corporate networks;
- personal networks;
- unprotectable data;
- distribution network;
- supply chain network;
- formal and informal operating systems;
- processes.

Functional capability

Comprises resources which are either individual skills and know-how or team skills and know-how, within the company, at suppliers, or at distributors etc.

- employee know-how and skills in:
  - operations
  - finance
  - marketing
  - R&D etc.
- supplier know-how;
- distributor know-how;
- professional advisers' expertise, etc.

Cultural Capability

Comprises resources which are the characteristics of the organisation:

- perception of quality standards;
- tradition of customer service;

(*continued*)

- ability to manage change;
- ability to innovate;
- team working ability;
- ability to develop staff, suppliers and distributors;
- automatic response mechanisms.

Whilst it is possible for a valued product/delivery system attribute to be the result of a tangible asset such as a building or a specialist manufacturing capability, research and experience suggest intangible resources, such as product reputation, employee know-how, etc., are the factors most often responsible for producing the attributes which are valued by customers.

The resources which occur frequently in the body of the matrix are those which, either by themselves, or in combination with others, constitute the organisation's strategic competencies.

3. Sustaining, protecting and exploiting competencies

Having identified the key resources it is appropriate to examine development scenarios in terms of protection, sustenance, enhancement and leverage.

Issues with respect to the development of intangible resources.

With respect to **protection**

- Do all concerned recognise the value of this intangible resource to the company?
- Can the resource be protected in law?

With respect to **sustainability**

- How long did it take to acquire this resource? Is it unique because of all that has happened in creating it?
- How durable is the resource? Will it decline with time?
- How easily may the resource be lost?
- How easily and quickly can others identify and imitate the resource?
- Can others easily 'buy' the resource?
- Can others easily 'grow' the resource?
- How appropriable is the resource? Can it 'walk away'?
- Is the resource vulnerable to substitution?

With respect to **enhancement**

- Is the 'stock' of this resource increasing?
- How can we ensure that the 'stock' of this resource *continues* to increase?

(*continued*)

*With respect to **exploitation***

- Are we making the best use of this resource?
- How else could it be used?
- Is the scope for **synergy** identified and exploited?
- Are we aware of the key linkages which exist between the resources?

Source: Adapted from J.Tidd (ed.) *From Knowledge Management to Strategic Competence.* Imperial College Press, London, 2006, in particular the chapter by Richard Hall. *See also:* Coyne, K.P. (1986) Sustainable competitive advantage – what it is and what it isn't, *Business Horizons,* January/February, Indiana University.

Team Exercise: Identifying Capabilities

Using the framework in *Advice for Entrepreneurs*, identify the capabilities and intangible resources of a chosen company. The exercise consists of three parts:

1. Identify the key attributes of the most successful products and services offered by the organisation.
2. Map these attributes to the resources or competencies of the organisation, including tangible and intangible resources.
3. Assess the potential for sustaining, protecting and exploiting these resources, including knowledge management.

Example of the Matrix of Attributes and Resources:

Key product/ delivery attributes	The resources which produce, or do not produce, the key attributes:			
	Regulatory capability	Positional capability	Functional capability	Cultural capability
Strengths				
1. e.g. availability		Value chain configuration	Forecasting skills	
2. e.g. quality				High perception of quality
3. e.g. specification	Patent 'abc'		Technology 'xyz'	

(continued)

Etc.				
Weaknesses				
1.				
2.				
Summary of the key resources				

Summary of Web Resources

Cases

- SPIRIT
- Aravind Eye Care
- Freeplay
- Green Building
- Green Supply Chain

Media

- Bottom of the Pyramid

PART II

RECOGNISING THE OPPORTUNITY

Part II Recognising the Opportunity

Innovative ideas can come from a wide range of sources and situations: from inspiration, transfer from another context, from listening to customer needs, from frontier research or by combining existing ideas into something new. And they could come through building alternative models of the future and exploring options opened up within these alternative worlds. But, if we are to succeed, we need to build rich and varied ways of picking up on all of the potential trigger signals that offer us interesting variation opportunities. What marks out successful individual entrepreneurs is often this ability to spot the key opportunity from a forest of possibilities.

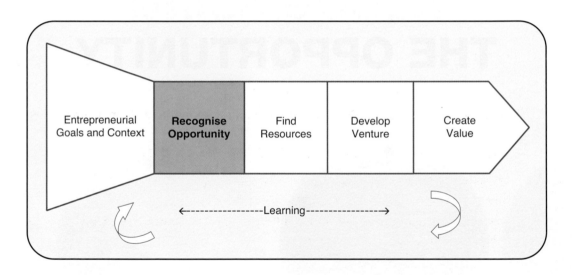

Chapter 4

Individual and Organisational Characteristics

Go online to find additional . . .

Cases

Tools

Media

www.iande.info

> 'Innovation is the specific tool of entrepreneurs, the means by which they exploit change as an opportunity for a different business or service. It is capable of being presented as a discipline, capable of being learned, capable of being practiced'
>
> —Peter Drucker

Innovation and entrepreneurship is not just about having a bright idea. Conventional approaches to entrepreneurship too often assume that the business idea and concept have already been identified, and that the main job to do is to develop a business plan and to raise resources to implement this. However, in our experience, identifying, assessing and refining an idea and developing this into a business concept is a big part of the problem. Many of the problems entrepreneurs and innovations experience can be traced to weaknesses in the early part of the process.

This has major implications for how we manage creativity and translate ideas into innovations. Whilst the initial idea may require a significant creative leap, much of the rest of the process will involve hundreds of small problem-finding and solving exercises – each of which needs creative input. And though the former may need the skills or inspiration of a particular individual the latter requires the input of many different people over a sustained period of time. Developing the light bulb or the Post-it note or any successful innovation is actually the story of the combined creative endeavour of many individuals.

Broadly speaking, the practice and study of innovation and entrepreneurship can be approached from three different perspectives:

1. Personal or individual, which emphasises the role of creativity and entrepreneurship.
2. Collective or social, which stresses the contribution of teams and groups.
3. Contextual, which focuses on the structures, climate, processes and tools.

One critical issue arising from these different perspectives is the relative effort needed between the individual, social and organisational contributions to innovation and entrepreneurship, and the interaction between these three levels.

Linking Creativity, Entrepreneurship and Innovation

We will use the following definition of creativity:

> Creativity is the making and communicating of meaningful new connections to help us think of many possibilities; to help us think and experience in varied ways and using different points of view; to help us think of new and unusual possibilities; and to guide us in generating and selecting alternatives. These new connections and possibilities must result in something of value for the individual, group, organization, or society.

Note that being creative at work is not the same as having a creative job. Jobs typically thought to be creative include design, development and advertising, but creativity in most organisations is essentially down to an individual choice between the routine and novel. It is based on the belief that one has the ability to produce productive creative outcomes. It includes the confidence to adopt non-conformist perspectives, to take risks and act without dependence on social approval, and can encourage broader information search and sustain effort. Also, the creativity of all workers responds positively to support for creativity from managers and co-workers.

Research has provided many insights into many aspects of creativity, the most relevant being an understanding and nurturing of the creative process. This focus includes consideration of mental operations, heuristics, and problem-solving strategies (among other items). Those who study creativity often refer to three overlapping themes:

1. *Personality,* which has led to the identification of many personality characteristics, cognitive abilities, and behavioural or biographical events associated with individual creativity.
2. *Process* of creative thinking, with various stages and strategies.
3. *Environmental* factors that facilitate or inhibit creative performance, such as climate and culture.

Together, these factors interact to either encourage, or to constrain, innovation and entrepreneurship (Figure 4.1).

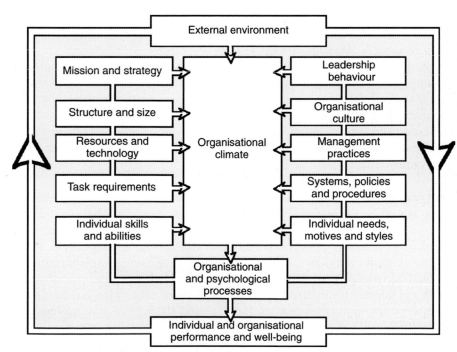

FIGURE 4.1 Factors which contribute to a creative organisation.
Source: Isaksen, S. and Tidd, J. (2006) *Meeting the Innovation Challenge.* Wiley.

Personality: Promoting Individual Creativity

Studies of innovation and entrepreneurship have tended to focus on the role of key individuals, in particular inherent or given traits of inventors or entrepreneurs. Archetypical inventors include Thomas Edison and Alexander Graham Bell, or more recently James Dyson or Steve Jobs. Each of these examples of inventors was also an innovator, translating the original technical inventions into new products, but each was also an entrepreneur, in the sense that they created and developed successful businesses based on the inventions and innovations.

Typical characteristics of an entrepreneur include:[1]

1. Passionately seek to identify new opportunities and ways to profit from change and disruption.
2. Pursue opportunities with discipline and focus on a limited number of projects, rather than opportunistically chasing every option.
3. Focus on action and execution, rather than endless analysis.
4. Involve and energise networks of relationships, exploiting the expertise and resources of others, while helping others to achieve their own goals.

These characteristics are consistent with what research tells us about the cognitive abilities necessary for creativity and innovation:

- Information acquisition and dissemination, including the capture of information from a wide range of sources, requiring attention and perception.
- Intelligence, the ability and capability to interpret, process and manipulate information.
- Sense making, giving meaning to information.
- Unlearning, the process of reducing or eliminating pre-existing routines or behaviours, including discarding information.
- Implementation and improvisation, autonomous behaviour, experimentation, reflection and action. Using information to solve problems, for example, during new product development or process improvement.

Personal orientation includes what is traditionally thought of as characteristics of the creative personas as well as the creative abilities associated with creativity. These include personality traits traditionally associated with creativity such as openness to experience, tolerance of ambiguity, resistance to premature closure, curiosity and risk-taking, among others. They also include such creative-thinking abilities as fluency, flexibility, originality and elaboration. Expertise, competence and knowledge base also contribute to creative efforts. Traditionally, people have been assessed and selected for different tasks on the basis of such characteristics, for example, using psychometric questionnaires or tests. For example, the Kirton Adapter-Innovator (KAI) scale assesses different dimensions of creativity, including originality, attention to detail and reliance on rules.

The Kirton Adapter-Innovator (KAI) scale is a psychometric approach for assessing the creativity of individuals. By a series of questions it seeks to identify an individual's attitudes towards originality, attention to detail and following rules. It seeks to differentiate 'adaptive' from 'innovative' styles:

- *Adaptors* characteristically produce a sufficiency of ideas based closely on existing agreed definitions of a problem and its likely solutions, but stretching the solutions. These ideas help to improve and 'do better'.
- *Innovators* are more likely to reconstruct the problem, challenge the assumptions and to emerge with a much less expected solution which very probably is also at first less acceptable. Innovators are less concerned with doing things better than with doing things differently.

It is important to recognise that creativity is an attribute that we all possess, but the preferred *style* of expressing it varies widely. Recognising the need for different kinds of individual creative styles is an important aspect of developing successful innovations and new ventures. It is clear from a wealth of psychological research that every human being comes with the capability to find and solve complex problems, and where such creative behaviour can be harnessed amongst a group of people with differing skills and perspectives extraordinary things can be achieved. Some people are comfortable with ideas which challenge the whole way in which the universe works, whilst others prefer smaller increments of change – ideas about how to improve the jobs they do or their working environment in small incremental steps.

A focus on creative style reveals more on preferred mode or manner of applying creativity. This distinction between the style of problem solving and level or capacity is important, and studies confirm that creative cognitive style and capacity are different. Once we understand our own style preferences, we can approach the task of challenging the way we think and respond more constructively, rather than viewing the task merely as attaining proficiency with an externally imposed, fixed set of tools or techniques. If we can better assess our own strengths and needs more effectively it becomes easier to understand and accept the principle that there is more than one 'right way'.

There is no doubt that certain individuals are more creative than others, but as with physical development and training, it is possible for almost anyone to improve their creativity. It can be encouraged by paying attention to the climate for creativity, the environment in which people work, the projects and challenges they face and the systems and techniques used to support them at work.

Creative productivity does not come about (or fail to come about) only as a result of what is present (or absent) within the individual; it is influenced by time, other people, places, settings, domain-specific knowledge and strategies that people can use individually or in groups. Therefore, no one is, in an absolute sense, always more or less creative. We must ask, creative at what, when, how, where, why, and with whom. We shouldn't 'look for' creativity as something fixed and static; it waxes and wanes dependent on a combination of multiple factors. Thus, the goal of profiling is ***not*** to ask, 'How creative is this person?', but 'How is the person creative?'. It is to help identify, for a particular task or goal, in a certain setting and under particular circumstances, the person's creative strengths or talents, the best ways to put them to use, and plans to enable us to incorporate those talents into a meaningful and effective instructional or training experience.

Go online to find the creativity assessment questionnaire, which will help you to identify your own creativity.

www.iande.info

Changing mind-set and refocusing organisational energies requires the articulation of a new vision, and there are many cases where this kind of leadership is credited with starting or turning round organisations. Examples include Jack Welch of GE, Steve Jobs (Pixar/Apple), Andy Groves (Intel) and Richard Branson (Virgin). Whilst we must be careful of vacuous expressions of 'mission' and 'vision', it is also clear that in cases like these there has been a clear sense of, and commitment to, shared organisational purpose arising from such leadership. Creativity is not just something that happens to people; it is actively and deliberately employed, monitored and managed. Creativity can be enhanced and nurtured. Research has demonstrated that specific process tools and strategies can be used to increase creative-thinking skills.

For example, research on successful entrepreneurs has identified some of the factors that affect the likelihood of establishing a venture, and these include a combination of those which are largely inherent or given, and those which can be more easily learnt or influenced:

- family and ethnic background;
- psychological profile;
- formal education and early work experience.

ENTREPRENEURSHIP IN ACTION

Personal Creativity and Entrepreneurship

A study of 800 senior managers revealed that there were significant differences between those in the top quartile (25%) and the rest of the sample. The more successful managers had achieved their goals within eight years, and most were in senior management positions by their early 30s. The key differences associated with the more successful managers were personality and cognitive, in particular the breadth and creativity of their thinking, and their social skills. However, the study does not conclude that creative thinking and social skills are inherent personality traits, but rather dispositions, which can be developed and improved significantly.

Such abilities are critical in many contexts, including large organisations and small start-up companies. For example, Eon, the world's largest energy services company has created a graduate training programme to help to assess and develop their new recruits. Following psychometric assessment, graduate recruits follow specific programmes aimed to improve their personal and social skills, including placements in different parts of the business. Alex Oakley, head of

(*continued*)

human resources at Eon believes 'in this way we get a balance between skills and personal attributes that helps people do the job. We don't just concentrate on skills.' Similarly, Jamie Malcolm, an entrepreneur who co-founded the garden centre Shoots in Sussex, argues that 'anything new and innovative, like a start-up business, needs to take risks – you just can't succeed without it. I'll always be prepared to take risk in order to innovate. The innovation required to grow the business is what drives me. Risk can be dangerous if you're taking it because of your personal desire to do so. You don't have to lower your appetite for risk as the business grows – you just have to analyse it more as there's more at stake.'

Source: Kaisen Consultants, 2006, www.kaisen.co.uk

Background

A number of other studies confirm that both family background and religion affect an individual's propensity to establish a new venture. A significant majority of technical entrepreneurs have a self-employed or professional parent. Studies indicate that between 50 and 80% have at least one self-employed parent. For example, one seminal study found that four times as many technical entrepreneurs have a parent who is a professional, compared with other groups of scientists and engineers.[2] The most common explanation for this observed bias is that the parent acts as a role model and may provide support for self-employment.

The effect of religious and ethnic background is more controversial, but it is clear that certain groups are over-represented in the population of entrepreneurs. For example, in the USA and Europe, Jews are more likely to establish new ventures, and the Chinese are more likely to in Asia. Whether this observed bias is the result of specific cultural or religious norms, or the result of minority status, is the subject of much controversy but little research. Research suggests that dominant cultural values are more important than minority status, but even this work indicates that the effect of family background is more significant than religion. In any case, and perhaps more importantly, there appears to be no significant relationship between family and religious background and the subsequent probability of success of a new venture.

Psychological Profile

Much of the research on the psychology of entrepreneurs is based on the experience of small firms in the USA, so the generalisability of the findings must be questioned. However, in the specific case of technical entrepreneurs there appears to be some consensus regarding the necessary personal characteristics. The two critical requirements appear to be an internal locus of control and a high need for achievement. The former characteristic is common in scientists and engineers, but the need for high levels of achievement is less common. Entrepreneurs are typically motivated by a high need for achievement (so-called 'n-Ach'), rather than a general desire to succeed. This behaviour is associated with moderate risk-taking, but not gambling or irrational risk-taking. A person with a high n-Ach:

- likes situations where it is possible to take personal responsibility for finding solutions to problems;
- has a tendency to set challenging but realistic personal goals and to take calculated risks;
- needs concrete feedback on personal performance.

However, a US study of almost 130 technical entrepreneurs and almost 300 scientists and engineers found that not all entrepreneurs have high n-Ach, only some do.[3] Technical entrepreneurs had only moderate n-Ach, but low need for affiliation (n-Aff). This suggests that the need for independence, rather than success, is the most significant motivator for technical entrepreneurs. Technical entrepreneurs also tend to have an internal locus of control. In other words, technical entrepreneurs believe that they have personal control over outcomes, whereas someone with an external locus of control believes that outcomes are the result of chance, powerful institutions or others. More sophisticated psychometric techniques such as the Myers–Briggs type indicators (MBTI) confirm the differences between technical entrepreneurs and other scientists and engineers. Attempts to measure more general entrepreneurial traits have been less successful. For example, the General Enterprise Tendency test assesses five types of trait – need for achievement, drive and ambition, risk-taking, autonomy and creativity and potential for innovation. This instrument has proven effective at identifying potential owner-mangers, but fails to distinguish these from successful entrepreneurs.

Studies of the traits of successful entrepreneurs identify very similar profiles in a wide range of contexts, which typically feature innovativeness, risk-taking and an ambition to achieve, compete and grow.[4] However, these are not the same characteristics as those who simply seek self-employment or manage small businesses, where the primary needs appear to be autonomy and independence.[5] These differences are critical, because too often entrepreneurs, the self-employed and SMEs are grouped together as a single group, whereas research confirms that these have very different characteristics, motives and outcomes. For example, the Global Entrepreneurship Monitor (GEM) tracks entrepreneurship at the national level, and in addition to cultural, demographic and educational factors, includes indicators of infrastructure and national context. However, the focus of the GEM is on start-up activity, rather than subsequent success or growth, so it also fails to differentiate small businesses from successful entrepreneurial activity. For example, despite their evident structural economic problems, the GEM ranked Greece and Ireland top of the EU for 'total entrepreneurial activity'.

Education and Experience

In general, the self-employed and managers of SMEs tend to be under-educated compared to the relevant population. One explanation for this is that either by choice or lack of ability or opportunity, those who do not pursue higher levels of education have fewer career options than those who do. This is often referred to as necessity-drive entrepreneurship, in contrast to opportunity-driven. Opportunity-driven entrepreneurs, in contrast to the self-employed and managers of SMEs, tend to be more educated than the relevant population, and technical entrepreneurs even more so: in general, those with a higher, college or university-level education are twice as likely to be successful entrepreneurs, and 85% of technical entrepreneurs have a degree.[6]

The levels of education of technical entrepreneurs do not differentiate them from other scientists and engineers, but education and training are major factors that distinguish the founders of technical ventures from other types of entrepreneur. The median level of education of technical entrepreneurs is a master's degree, and with the important exception of biotechnology-based new ventures, a doctorate was superfluous. Significantly, potential technical entrepreneurs tend to have higher levels of productivity than their technical work colleagues, measured in terms of papers published or patents granted. This suggests that potential entrepreneurs may be more driven than their corporate counterparts.

In addition to a master's-level education, on average, a technical entrepreneur will have around 13 years of work experience before establishing a new venture. In the case of Route 128, the entrepreneurs' work experience is typically with a single incubator organisation, whereas technical entrepreneurs in Silicon Valley tend to have gained their experience from a larger number of firms before establishing their own venture. This suggests that there is no ideal pattern of previous work experience. However, experience of development work appears to be more important than work in basic research. As a result of the formal education and experience required, a typical technical entrepreneur will be aged between 30 and 40 years when establishing his or her first venture. This is relatively late in life compared to other types of venture, and is due to a combination of ability and opportunity. On the one hand, it typically takes between 10 and 15 years for a potential entrepreneur to attain the necessary technical and business experience. On the other hand, many people begin to have greater financial and family responsibilities at this time, which reduces the appetite for risk. Thus there appears to be a window of opportunity to start a new venture some time in the mid-thirties. Moreover, different fields of technology have different entry and growth potential. Therefore the choice of a potential entrepreneur will be constrained by the dynamics of the technology and markets. The capital requirements, product lead times and potential for growth are likely to vary significantly between sectors.

Numerous surveys indicate that around three-quarters of technical entrepreneurs claim to have been frustrated in their previous job. This frustration appears to result from the interaction of the psychological predisposition of the potential entrepreneur and poor selection, training and development by the parent organisation. Specific events may also trigger the desire or need to establish a new venture, such as a major reorganisation or downsizing of the parent organisation (Figure 4.2).

Go online to hear Ken Robison discuss the characteristics of creativity.

www.iande.info

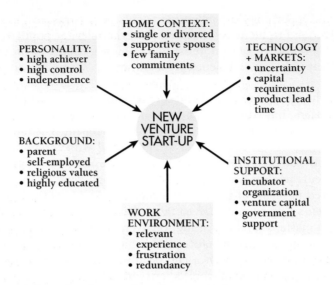

FIGURE 4.2   Factors influencing the creation of a new venture.

Source: From Tidd, J. and Bessant, J. (2009) *Managing Innovation: Integrating technological, market and organizational change.* John Wiley & Sons Ltd.

Processes: Strategies and Stages of Creativity

Stimulating creativity and innovation consists of much more than a set of tools and techniques to help generate ideas. The process focuses on the methodology and strategies needed, a pathway towards some solution or outcome. Effective practitioners have long since passed the view of the process as a fixed sequence of prescribed steps and activities, but to be effective, it is necessary to make deliberate decisions about the components, stages, and techniques that will be appropriate and valuable, given the purpose and intended outcomes of the process.

A number of models of the creative process can be helpful to those who need to engage in innovation and entrepreneurship. One proven and practical process for challenging the way we perceive things includes three main stages:[7]

1. Understanding the opportunity;
2. Generating ideas;
3. Planning for action.

1. Understanding the Opportunity

Understanding the opportunity or problem includes a systematic effort to define, construct, or formulate a problem. This is not necessarily the first step, nor is it necessarily undertaken by all people. Rather than prescribing an essential problem-finding process, this involves active construction by the individual or group through analysing the task at hand (including outcomes, people, context, and methodological options) to determine whether and when deliberate problem-structuring efforts are needed. This stage includes the three components:

* *Opportunity Construction* is a broad statement of a goal or direction that can be constructed as broad, brief, and beneficial. The opportunity generally describes the basic area of need or challenge on which the problem-solver's efforts will be focused, remaining broad enough to allow many perspectives to emerge as one (or a group) looks more closely at the situation.
* *Exploring Data* includes the generating and answering of questions to bring out key data (information, impressions, observations, feelings, etc.) to help the problem-solver(s) focus more clearly on the most challenging aspects and concerns of the situation.
* *Framing Problems* includes the seeking of a specified or targeted question (problem statement) on which to focus subsequent effort. Effectively worded problem statements invite an open or wide-ranging search for many, varied and novel options. They are stated concisely and are free from specific limiting criteria. This component has been widely applied to assist in strategic decision making and problem solving. Management teams have considered many, varied and unique opportunities and focused on those that offer the best future organisational results. These teams have explored a variety of data to better understand their market, competition and internal strengths and weaknesses.

For example, in quality management a number of proven tools and techniques exist to support a better understanding of problems or opportunities. These include tools such as Pareto analysis and cause and effect analysis.

Pareto analysis is used to prioritise areas for improvement by identifying the factors that will have the greatest impact on quality. A Pareto diagram simply ranks problems or causes of problems according to their frequency or significance. In some, but not all, cases, the frequency of a problem is a good guide to its significance; but in some cases, frequency and significance are not the same. Pareto analysis is useful as it helps to identify and focus attention on the critical few rather than the trivial but commonplace. A common interpretation of the Pareto principle is the 80/20 rule: in many cases 80% of errors or failures can be traced to 20% of the causes. For example, in Figure 4.3 the most common problem is delays to repairs which accounts for 75% of complaints to a car dealership. This analysis would suggest that quality improvement should begin with an identification of the root causes of such delays.

Having identified the most pressing quality problems using the Pareto analysis, we can now begin to search for their causes. Cause and effect diagrams are a useful way of searching for the root cause of a particular problem (Figure 4.4). They are also known as fish bone (because of the way the diagram looks) or Ishikawa diagrams (after the Japanese person who promoted the technique). There a number of simple steps in cause and effect analysis:

1. Clearly state a specific problem, that is, the 'effect'.
2. Next identify the main classes of potential causes. Commonly used classification schemes are 'methods, machinery, materials, manpower and money', or alternatively 'processes, people, materials and resources'.
3. Under each of these headings, identify potential causes by means of data collection and group discussion.

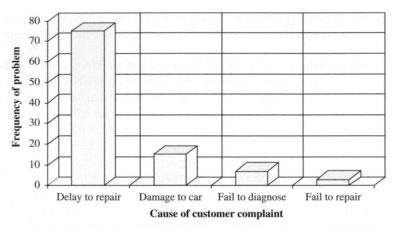

FIGURE 4.3 Example of a Pareto analysis for quality problems at a car dealership.

4. Change and refine the potential causes as necessary.
5. Finally, produce a shortlist of the most likely candidates for further analysis.

Another popular and proven method to assist problem definition is the mind map or spider diagram. This is simply a graphical way of identifying and exploring relationships between different factors. Mind or cognitive maps are a specific application of spider diagrams used to make explicit the relationships and assumptions within a given context. In both cases you begin with a central theme or key word which is written in the centre of a large sheet of paper, a white board, or screen. Next, generate related concepts or themes and write these around the central theme. Finally, draw lines to represent potential relationships between the different concepts. Used by an individual, this is a very effective way of clarifying thoughts. Used by a group, it helps to identify shared assumptions and to highlight differences in perceptions.

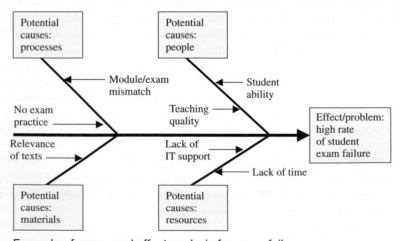

FIGURE 4.4 Example of cause and effect analysis for exam failure.

Cognitive mapping techniques aim to provide a tool for revealing peoples' subjective beliefs in a meaningful way so that they can be examined not only by the individual for whom the map is constructed, but also by other individuals and groups. Individual decision-makers might be encouraged to reflect on their own, perhaps rather narrow, understanding of a particular problem. The resultant cognitive map will not represent an entire belief system (this would be impossible), but hopes to portray those beliefs that are held to be most significant by the stakeholders concerned. In this way, valuable knowledge can be entered into the decision-making process that may otherwise remain hidden.

Another potential use of cognitive mapping techniques is to allow decision-makers to look at maps that have been constructed for other stakeholders so that they can begin to understand and appreciate alternative perspectives on the problem. This insight, however crude, into the way that others are thinking about the problem can encourage negotiation and help to reduce conflict. An advantage of cognitive mapping techniques (over, say, simply asking someone what they think) is that they allow knowledge to be externalised in some sort of graphical form that is then open for critical reflection. In this way subjective knowledge can be to some extent 'objectified' and therefore discussed in a less threatening way than direct questioning. In this way, if used as the decision-making process unfolds, cognitive mapping techniques may help the process to be managed.

2. *Generating Ideas*

Generating ideas includes the generating of options in answer to an open-ended or invitational statement of the problem. This stage contains both a generating and focusing phase. During the generating phase of this stage, the person or group produces many options (fluent thinking), a variety of possible options (flexible thinking), novel or unusual options (original thinking), or a number of detailed or refined options (elaborative thinking). The focusing phase of Generating Ideas provides an opportunity for examining, reviewing, clustering, and selecting promising options. Although this stage includes a focusing phase, its primary emphasis is generative.

Generating Ideas has also been widely applied to assist those who engage in strategic decision-making and problem solving. Brainstorming is the widely known tool to assist groups in generating ideas, but it can be applied whenever a group needs to consider many, varied and unusual alternatives.

A very wide range of specific tools and techniques has been developed to assist idea generation. Most are now available as software or as proprietary consultancy training packages. However, our experience suggests that simple, low-technology exercises are just as effective in practice. There is no mystery to applying these tools or techniques, and individuals and groups will improve with experience and practice.

There is no shortage of management consultants, gurus and training packages which claim to promote creativity. However, many of these consist of little more than team building or brainstorming. In addition, many advocate superficial and unproven methods, for example, drama workshops, humour workshops, or just being zany.

Whilst there may be some value in these, they should not be considered training in creativity and problem-solving. De Bono introduced the term **lateral thinking** to describe alternatives to logical thought, and has a long and distinguished career promoting applied creative thinking. In his 1996 book *Serious Creativity* he argues that creativity training in a business environment is not about artistic creativity/right-brain or simply being crazy/a rebel. Unlike most gurus of creativity, de Bono argues that most of us are not inherently creative, but rather that our brains are proficient at identifying, developing and subsequently following patterns or regularities. In most cases such mental models and patterned behaviour are efficient, but for problem-solving and creativity they can be dysfunctional. There is a great deal of research to support this view, and our experience confirms this. It follows that it is not sufficient to free the mind from constraints. Instead, we must force or provoke alternative ways of thinking. Specific methods of encouraging alternative ideas or solutions include the following:

- **Remove or suspend an assumption or goal** – what could we do differently if we temporarily ignore a key objective or assumption?
- **Reverse objectives or methods** – what would we do to achieve the exact opposite, and then reverse this?
- **Exaggerate the problem or goal** – what might we do if the goal or problem was much larger or smaller?
- **Distort the relationships or cause and effect** – what would the implications be?
- **Generate random inputs** – what new ideas does the introduction of a random word help create?
- **Use a metaphor or character** – what would a chosen famous character do in these circumstances?

In general, the more approaches used to generate ideas, the better. Planning and promotion of such schemes are critical to their success, and management support, feedback and rewards are associated with the successful idea generation (Table 4.1).

3. *Planning for Action*

Planning for action is appropriate when a person or group recognise a number of interesting or promising options that may not necessarily be useful, valuable or valid without extended effort and productive thinking. The need may be to make or develop effective choices, or prepare for successful implementation and acceptance by different stakeholders. This stage includes two components: Developing Solutions and Building Acceptance.

In Developing Solutions, promising options are analysed, refined or developed. If there are many options the emphasis may be compressing or condensing them so that they are more manageable. If there are only a few promising options, the challenge may be to strengthen each as much as possible. There may be a need to rank or prioritise a number of possible options. Specific criteria may be generated and selected upon which to evaluate and develop promising options or select from a larger pool of available alternatives. Although there may be some generating in this stage, the emphasis is primarily on focusing. Once the new concepts and ideas have been developed, the next logical focus of attention is to prepare them for the marketplace and acceptance from key stakeholders.

Building Acceptance involves searching several potential sources of assistance and resistance for possible solutions. The aim is to help prepare an option or alternative for

TABLE 4.1 Assessing the effectiveness of schemes to promote idea generation

Scheme Features:	Perceived Success of Scheme	Rate of Generation of new ideas
Planning of Scheme	17.6	8.5
Promotion of Scheme	31.2	21.5
Management support	28.6	3.2
Feedback to Staff	34.3	5.2
Rewards – recognition	23.8	3.8
Rewards – monetary	4.1	2.3 (+)
Rewards – non-monetary	31.3	9.3

N = 182, numbers are F values of the mean success scores, all are statistically significant at 5% level, except +

Source: Derived from Leach, D.J., Stride, C.B. and Wood, S.J. (2006) 'The effectiveness of idea capture schemes', *International Journal of Innovation Management*, 10(3), pp.325–350.

improved acceptance and value. This stage helps the problem-solver identify ways to make the best possible use of assisters and avoid or overcome possible sources of resistance. From considering these factors, a plan of action is developed and evaluated for implementation.

Although techniques to support more creative strategic decision-making and problem-solving can be taught and learned, they are best suited for the solution of real-life problems. This requires interest, influence and imagination. To be interesting, a problem must be 'real', and be owned by someone. A problem becomes 'real' only when it involves an emotional or affective commitment as well as an intellectual or cognitive one, it must have a personal frame of reference. The owners of the problem must also have some degree of influence, authority, and decision-making responsibility for implementing the solutions. It also means that the problem owner is motivated and willing to submit the challenge to systematic problem-solving efforts and is interested in following through on the results. Finally, the search and solutions must engage the imagination, and there must be a deliberate and explicit search for something new. The purpose of a 'real' problem is to contribute something new or bring about some sort of innovation. A good example of this process is the development of a business plan for a new venture.

Developing a Business Plan

The primary reason for developing a formal business plan for a new venture is to attract external funding. However, it serves an important secondary function. A business plan can provide a formal agreement between founders regarding the basis and future development of the venture. A business plan can help reduce self-delusion on the part of the founders, and avoid subsequent arguments concerning responsibilities and rewards. It can help to translate abstract or ambiguous goals into more explicit operational needs, and support subsequent decision-making and identify trade-offs. Of the factors *controllable* by entrepreneurs, business planning has the most significant positive effect on new venture performance. However, there are of course many *uncontrollable* factors, such as market opportunity, which have an even more significant influence on performance. Pasteur's advice still applies, '. . . chance favours only the prepared mind'. In such cases contingencies need to be identified and their potential impact on the venture assessed.

No standard business plan exists, but in many cases venture capitalists will provide a pro forma for the business plan. Typically a business plan should be relatively concise, say no more than 10 sides, begin with an executive summary, and include sections on the product, markets, technology, development, production, marketing, human resources, financial estimates with contingency plans, and the timetable and funding requirements. Most business plans submitted to venture capitalists are strong on the technical considerations, often placing too much emphasis on the technology relative to other issues. As Roberts notes, 'entrepreneurs propose that they can do *it* better than anyone else, but may forget to demonstrate that anyone wants *it*'.[8] He identifies a number of common problems with business plans submitted to venture capitalists: marketing plan, management team, technology plan and financial plan.

There were found to be serious inadequacies in all four of these areas, but the worst were in marketing and finance. Less than half of the plans examined provided a detailed marketing strategy, and just half included any sales plan. Three-quarters of the plans failed to identify or analyse any potential competitors. As a result most business plans contain only basic financial forecasts, and just 10% conducted any sensitivity analysis on the forecasts. The lack of attention to marketing and competitor analysis is particularly problematic as research indicates that both factors are associated with subsequent success.

Whilst there is general agreement about the main components of a good business plan, there are some significant differences in the relative weights attributed to each component. General venture capital firms typically only accept 5% of the technology ventures they are offered, and the specialist technology venture funds are even more selective, accepting around 3%. The main reasons for rejecting technology proposals compared to more general funding proposals are the lack of intellectual property, the skills of the management team, and size of the potential market. The criteria are similar to those discussed earlier, grouped into five categories:

1. The entrepreneur's personality.
2. The entrepreneur's experience.
3. Characteristics of the product.
4. Characteristics of the market.
5. Financial factors.

Overall, the surveys confirm the importance of a bundle of personal, market and financial factors, which were consistently ranked as being most significant: a proven ability to lead others and sustain effort; familiarity with the market; and the potential for a high return within 10 years. The personality and experience of the entrepreneurs were consistently ranked as being more important than either product or market characteristics, or even financial considerations. However, there were a number of significant differences between the preferences of venture capitalists from different regions. Those from the USA placed greater emphasis on a high financial return and liquidity than their counterparts in Europe or Asia, but less emphasis on the existence of a prototype or proven market acceptance. Perhaps surprisingly, all venture capitalists are averse to technological and market risks. Being described as a 'high-technology' venture was rated very low in importance by the US venture capitalists, and the European and Asian venture capitalists rated this characteristic as having a negative influence on funding. Similarly, having the potential to create an entirely new market was considered a drawback. We discuss these and other ingredients of a good business plan in detail in Chapter 7.

At each of the different stages of developing a new venture there are different significant challenges to overcome in order to make a successful transition to the next stage, what the researchers call 'critical junctures':

Opportunity recognition – at the interface of the research and opportunity framing phases. This requires the ability to connect a specific technology or know-how to a commercial application, and is based on a rather rare combination of skill, experience, aptitude, insight, and circumstances. A key issue here is the ability to synthesise scientific knowledge and market insights, which increases with the entrepreneur's social capital – linkages, partnerships and other network interactions.

Entrepreneurial commitment – acts and sustained persistence that bind the venture champion to the emerging business venture. This often demands difficult personal decisions to be made, for example, whether or not to remain an academic, as well as evidence of direct financial investments to the venture.

Venture credibility – is critical for the entrepreneur to gain the resources necessary to acquire the finance and other resources for the business to function. Credibility is a function of the venture team, key customers and other social capital and relationships. This requires close relationships with sponsors, financial and other, to build and maintain awareness and credibility. Lack of business experience, and failure to recognise their own limitations are a key problem here. One solution is to hire the services of a 'surrogate entrepreneur'. As one experienced entrepreneur notes 'the not so smart or really insecure academics want their hands over everything. These prima donnas make a complete mess of things, get nowhere with their companies and end up disappointed professionally and financially.'

ENTREPRENEURSHIP IN ACTION

Opportunity and Planning at Innocent

Innocent develops and sells fruit smoothies, healthy, premium pulped-fruit drinks, with no additives. The company was created in 1999 by three friends from university, Adam Balon, Richard Reed and Jon Wright. The company was founded with the help of £200,000 of venture capital,

(continued)

but Balon, Reed and Wright still own 70% of the company. In 2006 Innocent had sales of around £70 million, representing a market share of 60%, and the company was valued at £175 million. It has since recruited more experienced managers from larger firms, and now employs 100 staff in West London. It also has bases in France and Denmark, and planned to open offices in Germany and Austria in 2007. All production and packaging is outsourced, and the company focuses on development and marketing.

The company has cultivated a funky liberal image, in contrast to the large multinational firms that dominate the drinks market. They give 10% of company profits to charities, such as the Rainforest Alliance, and have developed a healthy dialogue with their customers through a weekly e-mail newsletter. In 2005 Reed won the title 'Most Admired Businessman' from the UK National Union of Students (NUS). However, beneath the hippy image there is a well-educated and experienced management team. After university Reed, now aged 33, gained experience in the advertising industry, and Balon and Wright both worked for large management consultants, respectively McKinsey and Bain. The likely exit or harvest for the business will be a trade sale, similar to other so-called 'ethical brands' such as Ben and Jerry's which was bought by Unilever, and Green and Blacks acquired by Cadbury. In preparation, in April 2009 the owners sold 18% of the company to Coca-Cola for £30 million.

Environment: Creating a Climate for Innovation

A climate for creativity and innovation is that which promotes the generation, consideration, and use of new products, services, and ways of working. This kind of climate supports the development, assimilation and utilisation of new and different approaches, practices and concepts. It is associated with a wide range of innovative outputs: new ideas, improved processes, new products or new ventures.

Many researchers have looked at the conditions under which creativity thrives or is suppressed. Kanter provides a list of environmental factors that contribute to stifling innovation; these include:[9]

- dominance of restrictive vertical relationships;
- poor lateral communications;
- limited tools and resources;
- top-down dictates;
- formal, restricted vehicles for change;
- reinforcing a culture of inferiority (i.e. innovation always has to come from outside to be any good);
- unfocused innovative activity;
- unsupported accounting practices.

The effect of these is to create and reinforce the behavioural norms which inhibit creativity and lead to a culture lacking in innovation. It follows from this that developing an innovative climate is not a simple matter since it consists of a complex web of behaviours and artefacts. And changing this culture is not likely to happen quickly or as a result of single initiatives (such as restructuring or mass training in a new technique).

Culture is a complex concept, but it basically equates to the pattern of shared values, beliefs and agreed norms which shape behaviour – in other words, it is 'the way we do things round here' in any organisation. Many writers have offered a variety of definition of culture. Thankfully, there are consistent themes among this diversity. Culture consists of deep and enduring patterns of how individuals and groups make decisions and demonstrate priorities about value differences. In general, culture is something that is shared by all or most of the members of some social group, and shapes behaviour and structures perceptions of the world.

As such culture can be described as collective programming of the mind or, as Geert Hofstede has called it, 'software of the mind'.[10] This collective software of the mind distinguishes the members of one social group from another. Many writers see culture as something that is stable, deep, and reinforced by a history of decisions, use of power, and learned strategies for answering fundamental questions. Schein suggests that culture can be understood as a hierarchy of interlinked levels.[11]

Values, Beliefs and Deeply Held Assumptions

Values are general beliefs that function to define what is right or wrong, or specify general preferences. They influence behaviour because they are broad tendencies to prefer certain states of affairs over others. They are similar to deeply held assumptions.

In an organisational context values can sometimes be specific and explicit. When we first started consulting with DuPont's Innovation Initiative in the early 1990s we were impressed with the many successes with new product development. There were, however, some challenges in implementing some of the strategies included within the innovation initiative. We also ran into a number of rules when we visited numerous factories and locations. We could not run on DuPont property, for example. When we looked deeper into the culture, it became very clear to us that DuPont held a strong value for safety. Later, we were able to visit the site of the founding of the E. I. Du Pont de Nemours gunpowder manufacturer in Wilmington, Delaware. It was a pretty location on the Brandywine River, which served as the power source in the early 1800s. We noticed that in the buildings in which the gunpowder was produced, three walls were made of very thick stone, but the side facing the river was made of thin wood. Not a single nail was used in the construction of these buildings for fear that a small piece of metal could fall and make a spark.

The family home was not very far from the buildings that made the gunpowder. So, from the very founding of the company, there was always a great concern for safe operations and limiting the risk of harm to people. This is how many deeply held values are embedded in organisations.

Rituals and Heroes

Rituals and customs are activities that seem non-essential to the actual functioning of the group, but they are considered socially necessary. These behaviours are reinforced over time – forming traditions that are filled with implicit meaning. In an organisational context this could include the way greetings and initial social exchanges occur during meetings. Heroes are people who can be either dead or living, real or imaginary, who possess highly valued characteristics. As such, they serve as role models for preferred or desired ways of behaving.

Symbols and Artefacts

Symbols are words, gestures, pictures, or other objects that carry and convey meaning to a particular group that share a common culture. In an organisational context they can include flags, status symbols, manner of dress, etc.

Rituals, heroes and symbols are visible to the observer, although their meaning is invisible and may require interpretation.

However, organisational culture is a different concept from national or social culture. Most people have exercised a choice to join a place of work whereas people are born into particular societies. People who work in organisations usually have limits on how much time they spend there (or at work) and have other discretionary time available. People are generally free to leave an organisation and may do so more easily than leaving a society. Organisational cultures should describe the shared mental programming of those within the same organisation, particularly if they share the same nationality. Research has shown that organisational cultures can and do differ in six important areas:

> *Process versus results orientation* – focus on the means or the way things are done, such as quality management or process improvement, versus a bias for action and results, such as 'management by objectives'.
>
> *Employee versus job* – the classic tension between concern for people versus concern for the task, for example, the so-called 'European Social Model' versus the 'Anglo-Saxon' liberal market approach.
>
> *Parochial versus professional* – identity derived from the internal organisation versus identity with a specific type of job.
>
> *Open versus closed systems* – broad definition of organisational boundaries with a high degree of interaction with the environment versus a narrow organisational focus, for example, the 'not invented here' syndrome.
>
> *Loose versus tight control* – a high degree of autonomy regarding ends and means versus a more prescriptive and directive approach.
>
> *Normative versus pragmatic* – a focus on following the bureaucratic rules and procedures versus meeting the needs of the task or customer.

Can Culture be Changed?

Culture is maintained over time through the attraction, selection and attrition of staff, and this provides clues to how culture may be changed over the longer term. This means that applicants are attracted to a certain type of organisation; and the organisation is more likely to select those that fit the organisation; and those that do not fit are more likely to leave, therefore reinforcing the existing culture. Since culture is such a deep, stable, complex set of shared assumptions that are built over relatively long periods of time, it is not an easy task to change it. Further, many definitions of culture specifically exclude behaviour.

When we see what leaders have done to actually influence culture change, they have actually focused their efforts more on the working climate. For example, Schein identified the primary mechanisms the leaders use to embed a culture. These include things like what leaders pay attention to, measure and control, as well as a number of other observed behaviours like the criteria leaders use to allocate scarce resources and rewards.

Given this model it is clear that management cannot directly change culture – but it can intervene at the level of artefacts – by changing structures or processes – and by providing models and reinforcing preferred styles of behaviour. Such 'culture change' actions are now widely tried in the context of change programmes towards total quality management and other models of organisation which require more participative culture.

Climate versus Culture

Climate is defined as the recurring patterns of behaviour, attitudes and feelings that characterise life in the organisation. At the individual level of analysis the concept is called psychological climate. At this level, the concept of climate refers to the intrapersonal perception of the patterns of behaviour, attitudes and feelings as experienced by the individual. When aggregated, the concept is called work unit or organisational climate. These are the objectively shared perceptions that characterise life within a defined work unit or in the larger organisation. Climate is distinct from culture in that it is more observable at a surface level within the organisation and more amenable to change and improvement efforts. Culture refers to the deeper and more enduring values, norms and beliefs within the organisation.

The two terms, culture and climate, have been used interchangeably by many writers, researchers, and practitioners. We have found that the following distinctions may help those who are concerned with effecting change and transformation in organisations:

Different levels of analysis.   Culture is a rather broad and inclusive concept. Climate can be seen as falling under the more general concept of culture. If your aim is to understand culture, then you need to look at the entire organization as a unit of analysis. If your focus is on climate, then you can use individuals and their shared perceptions of groups, divisions, or other levels of analysis. Climate is recursive or scalable.

Different disciplines involved.   Culture is within the domain of anthropology and climate falls within the domain of social psychology. The fact that the concepts come from different disciplines means that different methods and tools are used to study them.

Normative versus descriptive.   Cultural dimensions have remained relatively descriptive, meaning that one set of values or hidden assumptions was neither better nor worse than another. This is because there is no universally held notion or definition of the best society. Climate is often more normative in that we are more often looking for environments that are not just different, but better for certain things. For example, we can examine different kinds of climates and compare the results against other measures or outcomes like innovation, motivation, growth, etc.

More easily observable and influenced.   Climate is distinct from culture in that it is more observable at a surface level within the organisation and more amenable to change and improvement efforts.

What is needed is a commonsense set of levers for change that leaders can exert direct and deliberate influence over.

Climate and culture are different: traditionally studies of organisational culture are more qualitative, whereas research on organisational climate are more quantitative, but a multidimensional approach helps to integrate the benefits of each perspective.

Research indicates that organisations exhibit larger differences in practices than values, for example, the levels of uncertainty avoidance.

3M is the classic textbook (literally) example of a creativity organisation. Go online to find the case study to identify how climate contributes to this reputation.

www.iande.info

Table 4.2 summarises some research of how climate influences innovation. Many dimensions of climate have been shown to influence innovation and entrepreneurship, but here we discuss six of the most critical factors.

TABLE 4.2   Climate factors influencing innovation

Climate factor	Most Innovative (score)	Least Innovative (score)	Difference
Trust and Openness	253	88	165
Challenge and Involvement	260	100	160
Support and space for ideas	218	70	148
Conflict and Debate	231	83	148
Risk-taking	210	65	145
Freedom	202	110	92

Source: Derived for Scott Isaksen and Joe Tidd (2006) *Meeting the Innovation Challenge* (Wiley).

1. Trust and Openness

The trust and openness dimension refers to the emotional safety in relationships. These relationships are considered safe when people are seen as both competent and sharing a common set of values. When there is a strong level of trust, everyone in the organisation dares to put forward ideas and opinions. Initiatives can be taken without fear of reprisals and ridicule in case of failure. The communication is open and straightforward. Where trust is missing, count on high expenses for mistakes that may result. People also are afraid of being exploited and robbed of their good ideas.

Trust can make decision-making more efficient as it allows positive assumptions and expectations to be made about competence, motives and intentions, and thereby economises on cognitive resources and information-processing. Trust can also influence the effectiveness of an organisation through structuring and mobilising.

Trust helps to structure and shape the patterns of interaction and co-ordination within and between organisations. Trust can also motivate employees to contribute, commit and co-operate, by facilitating knowledge- and resource-sharing and joint problem-solving. When trust and openness are too low you may see people hoarding resources (i.e. information, software, materials, etc.). There may also be a lack of feedback on new ideas for fear of having concepts stolen. Management may not distribute the resources fairly among individuals or departments. One cause for this condition can be that management does not trust the capabilities and/or integrity of employees. It may help to establish norms and values that management can follow regarding the disbursement of resources, and a means to assure that resources are wisely used.

However, trust can bind and blind. If trust and openness are too high, relationships may be so strong that time and resources at work are often spent on personal issues. It may also lead to a lack of questioning each other that, in turn, may lead to mistakes or less productive outcomes. Cliques may form where there are isolated 'pockets' of high trust. One cause of this condition may be that people have gone through a traumatic organisational experience together and survived (i.e. down-sizing, a significant product launch, etc.). In this case it may help to develop forums for interdepartmental and intergroup exchange of information and ideas.

Trust is partly the result of individuals' own personality and experience, but can also be influenced by the organisational climate. For example, we know that the nature of rewards can affect some components of trust. Individual competitive rewards tend to reduce information-sharing and raise suspicions of others' motives, whereas group or co-operative rewards are more likely to promote information-sharing and reduce suspicions of motives. Similarly, the frequency of communication within an organisation influences trust, and in general the higher the frequency of communication, the higher the levels of trust. In a climate of low communication, the level of trust is much more dependent on the general attitudes of individuals towards their peers.

Trust is also associated with employees having some degree of role autonomy. Role autonomy is the amount of discretion that employees have in interpreting and executing their jobs. Defining roles too narrowly constrains the decision-making latitude. Role autonomy can also be influenced by the degree to which organisational socialisation encourages employees to internalise collective goals and values, for example, a so-called 'clan' culture focuses on developing shared values, beliefs and goals among members of an organisation so that appropriate behaviours are reinforced and rewarded, rather than specifying task-related behaviours or outcomes. This approach is most appropriate when tasks are difficult to anticipate or codify, and it is difficult to assess performance. Individual characteristics will also influence role autonomy, including the level of experience, competence and power accumulated over time working for the organisation.

Trust may exist at the personal and organisational levels, and researchers have attempted to distinguish different levels, qualities and sources of trust. For example, the following bases of organisational trust have been identified:

- **Contractual** – honouring the accepted or legal rules of exchange, but can also indicate the absence of other forms of trust.
- **Goodwill** – mutual expectations of commitment beyond contractual requirements.
- **Institutional** – trust based on formal structures.
- **Network** – because of personal, family or ethnic/religious ties.
- **Competence** – trust based on reputation for skills and know-how.
- **Commitment** – mutual self-interest, committed to the same goals.

These types of trust are not necessarily mutually exclusive, although over-reliance on contractual and institutional forms may indicate the absence of the other bases of trust. In the case of innovation, problems may occur where trust is based primarily on the network, rather than competence or commitment.

2. *Challenge and Involvement*

Challenge and involvement is the degree to which people are involved in daily operations, long-term goals, and visions. High levels of challenge and involvement means that people are intrinsically motivated and committed to making contributions to the success of the organisation. The climate has a dynamic, electric, and inspiring quality. People find joy and meaningfulness in their work, and therefore they invest much more energy. In the opposite situation, people are not engaged and feelings of alienation and indifference are present. The common sentiment and attitude is apathy and lack of interest in work and interaction is both dull and listless.

If challenge and involvement are too low, you may see that people are apathetic about their work, are not generally interested in professional development, or are frustrated about the future of the organisation. One of the probable causes for this might be that people are not emotionally charged about the vision, mission, purpose, and goals of the organisation. One of the ways to improve the situation might be to get people involved in interpreting the vision, mission, purpose, and goals of the organisation for themselves, and their work teams.

On the other hand, if the challenge and involvement are too high you may observe that people are showing signs of 'burn out', they are unable to meet project goals and objectives, or they spend 'too many' long hours at work. One of the reasons for this is that the work goals are too much of a stretch. A way to improve the situation is to examine and clarify strategic priorities.

Building and maintaining a challenging climate involves systematic development of organisational structures, communication policies and procedures, reward and recognition systems, training policy, accounting and measurement systems and deployment of strategy. Leaders who focus on work challenge and expertise, rather than formal authority, result in climates that are more likely to be assessed by members as being innovative and high performance. Studies suggest that output controls such as specific goals, recognition and rewards have a positive association with innovation. A balance must be maintained between creating a climate in which subordinates feel supported and empowered, with the need to provide goals and influence the direction and agenda. Leaders who provide feedback that is high on developmental potential, for example, provide useful information for subordinates to improve, learn and develop, result in higher levels of creativity.

Intellectual stimulation is one of the most underdeveloped components of leadership, and includes behaviours that increase others' awareness of and interest in problems, and develops their propensity and ability to tackle problems in new ways. Intellectual stimulation by leaders can have a profound effect on organisational performance under conditions of perceived uncertainty, and is also associated with commitment to an organisation.

However, innovation is too often seen as the province of specialists in R&D, marketing, design or IT, but the underlying creative skills and problem-solving abilities are possessed by everyone. If mechanisms can be found to focus such abilities on a regular basis across the entire organisation, the resulting innovative potential is enormous. Although each individual may only be able to develop limited, incremental innovations, the sum of these efforts can have far-reaching impacts.

Since much of such employee involvement in innovation focuses on incremental change it is tempting to see its effects as marginal. Studies show, however, that when taken over an extended period it is a significant factor in the strategic development of the organisation. For example, a study of firms in the UK that have acquired the 'Investors in People' award (an externally assessed review of employee involvement practices) showed a correlation between this and higher business performance. On average, these businesses increased their sales and profits per employee by three-quarters. Another study involved over 1000 organisations in a total of seven countries, and found that those that had formal employee involvement programmes, for example, featuring support and training in idea generation and problem-finding and solving, reported performance gains of 15–20%. But there is also an important secondary effect of high involvement: the more people are involved in change, the more receptive they become to it. Since the turbulent nature of most organisational environments is such that increasing levels of change are becoming the norm, greater formal involvement of employees may provide a powerful aid to effective management of change.

INNOVATION IN ACTION

Increasing Challenge and Involvement in an Electrical Engineering Division

The organisation was a division of a large, global electrical power and product supply company headquartered in France. The division was located in the South East of the USA and had 92 employees. Its focus was to help clients automate their processes, particularly within the automotive,

(continued)

pharmaceutical, microelectronics and food and beverage industries. For example, this division would make the robots that put cars together in the automotive industry or provide public filtration systems.

When this division was merged with the parent company, it was losing about $8 million a year. A new general manager was brought in to turn the division around and make it profitable quickly.

An assessment of the organisation's climate identified that they were strongest on the debate dimension but were very close to the stagnated norms when it came to challenge and involvement, playfulness and humour, and conflict. The quantitative and qualitative assessment results were consistent with their own impressions that the division could be characterised as conflict driven, uncommitted to producing results, and people were generally despondent. The leadership decided, after some debate, that they should target challenge and involvement, which was consistent with their strategic emphasis on a global initiative on employee commitment. It was clear to them that they also needed to soften the climate and drive a warmer, more embracing, communicative and exuberant climate.

The management team re-established training and development and encouraged employees to engage in both personal and business-related skills development. They also provided mandatory safety training for all employees. They committed to increase communication by holding monthly all-employee meetings, sharing quarterly reviews on performance, and using cross-functional strategy review sessions. They implemented mandatory 'skip level' meetings to allow more direct interaction between senior managers and all levels of employees. The general manager held 15-minute meetings will all employees at least once a year. All employee suggestions and recommendations were invited and feedback and recognition was required to be immediate. A new monthly recognition and rewards programme was launched across the division for both managers and employees that was based on peer nomination. The management team formed employee review teams to challenge and craft the statements in the hopes of encouraging more ownership and involvement in the overall strategic direction of the business.

In 18 months the division showed a $7 million turnaround, and in 2003 won a worldwide innovation award. The general manager was promoted to a national position.

Source: Scott Isaksen and Joe Tidd, *Meeting the Innovation Challenge: Leadership for Transformation and Growth* (John Wiley & Sons Ltd, 2006).

3. Support and Space for Ideas

Idea time is the amount of time people can (and do) use for elaborating new ideas. In the high idea-time situation, the possibilities exist to discuss and test impulses and fresh suggestions that are not planned or included in the task assignment and people tend to use these possibilities. When idea time is low, every minute is booked and specified. The time pressure makes thinking outside the instructions and planned routines impossible. Research confirms that individuals under time pressure are significantly less likely to be creative.

If there is insufficient time and space for generating new ideas you may observe that people are only concerned with their current projects and tasks. They may exhibit an unhealthy level of stress. People see professional development and training as hindrances to their ability to complete daily tasks and projects. You may also see that management avoids new ideas because they will take time away from the completion of day-to-day projects and schedules. One of the possible reasons for this could be that project schedules are so intense that they do not allow time to refine the process to take advantage of new ideas. Individuals are generally not physically or mentally capable of performing at 100%. A corrective action could be to develop project schedules that allow time for modification and development.

Conversely, if there is too much time and space for new ideas you may observe that people are showing signs of boredom that decisions are made through a slow, almost bureaucratic, process because there are too many ideas to evaluate, or the management of new ideas becomes such a task that short-term tasks and projects are not adequately completed. Individuals, teams and managers may lack the skills to handle large numbers of ideas and then converge on the most practical idea(s) for implementation. You may be able to provide training in creativity and facilitation, especially those tools and skills of convergence or focusing.

This suggests that there is an optimum amount of time and space to promote creativity and innovation. The concept of *organisational slack* was developed to identify the difference between resources currently needed and the total resources available to an organisation. When there is little environmental uncertainty or need for change, and the focus is simply on productivity; too much organisational slack represents a static inefficiency. However, when innovation and change are needed, slack can act as a dynamic shock absorber, and allows scope for experimentation. This process tends to be self-reinforcing due to positive feedback between the environment and organisation.

When successful, an organisation generates more slack, which provides greater resources (people, time, money) for longer term, significant innovation; however, when an organisation is less successful, or suffers a fall in performance, it tends to search for immediate and specific problems and their solution, which tends to reduce the slack necessary for longer term innovation and growth.

The research confirms that an appropriate level of organisational slack is associated with superior performance over the longer term. For high-performance organisations the relationship between organisational slack and performance is an inverted 'U' shape, or curvilinear: too little slack (for example, being too lean or too focused) does not allow sufficient time or resource for innovation, but too much provides little incentive or direction to innovation. However, for low-performance organisations any slack is simply absorbed and therefore simply represents an inefficiency rather than an opportunity for innovation and growth. Managers too often view time as a constraint or measure of outcomes, rather than as a variable to influence which can both trigger and facilitate innovation and change. By providing some, but limited, time and resources, individuals and groups can minimise the rigidity that comes from work overload, and the laxness that stems from too much slack.

Idea time helps to generate new ideas, but support is needed to assess and develop these ideas. In a supportive climate, ideas and suggestions are received in an attentive and kind way by bosses and workmates. People listen to each other and encourage initiatives. Possibilities for trying out new ideas are created. The atmosphere is constructive and positive.

When idea support is low, the reflexive 'no' prevails. Every suggestion is immediately refuted by a counter-argument. Fault-finding and obstacle-raising are the usual styles of responding to ideas. Where there is little idea support, people shoot each others' ideas down, keep ideas to themselves, and idea-suggestion systems are not well utilised. It could be that, based on past experience, people don't think anything will be done. You may need to carefully plan a re-launch of your suggestion system with a series of case studies of what has been acted upon and why.

A supportive climate is vital for gaining information, material resources, organisational slack and political support. This can reduce the energy wasted by individuals through non-legitimate acquisition and support strategies, such as bootlegging (within the organisation), or moonlighting (outside the organisation). Without appropriate support for new ideas, potential innovators grow frustrated: 'if they speak out too loudly, resentment builds towards them; if they play by the rules and remain silent, resentment builds inside them'. It is not sufficient simply to have a policy or process of support, it is necessary for managers to provide the time and resources to generate and test new ideas.

However, some situations may have too much idea support. In these cases you may observe that people are only deferring judgement. Nothing is getting done and there are too many options because appropriate judgement is not being applied. Too many people may be working in different directions. One of the reasons for this condition may be that people are avoiding conflict and staying 'too open'. You may need to help people apply affirmative judgement so that a more balanced approach to evaluation prevails.

In many cases innovation happens in spite of the senior management within an organisation, and success emerges as a result of guerrilla tactics rather than a frontal assault on the problem. Much has been made of the dramatic turnaround in IBM's fortunes under the leadership of Lou Gerstner who took the ailing giant firm from a crisis position to one of leadership in the IT services field and an acknowledged pioneer of e-business. But closer analysis reveals that the entry into e-business was the result of a bottom-up team initiative led by a programmer called Dave Grossman. It was his frustration with the lack of response from his line managers that eventually led to the establishment of a broad coalition of people within the company who were able to bring the idea into practice and establish IBM as a major e-business leader. The message for senior management is as much about leading through creating space and support within the organisation as it is about direct involvement.

4. Conflict and Debate

Conflict in an organisation refers to the presence of personal, interpersonal or emotional tensions. Although conflict is a negative dimension, all organisations have some level of personal tension.

Conflicts can occur over tasks, process or relationships. Task conflicts focus on disagreements about the goals and content of work, the 'what?' needs to be done and 'why?'. Process conflicts are around 'how?' to achieve a task; means and methods. Relationship or affective conflicts are more emotional, and characterised by hostility and anger. In general, some task and process conflict is constructive, helping to avoid groupthink and to considering more diverse opinions and alternative strategies. However, task and process conflict only have a positive effect on performance in a climate of openness and collaborative communication, otherwise it can degenerate into relationship conflict or avoidance. Relationship conflict is generally energy-sapping and destructive, as emotional disagreements create anxiety and hostility.

If the level of conflict is too high, groups and individuals dislike or hate each other and the climate can be characterised by 'warfare.' Plots and traps are common in the life of the organisation. There is gossip and back-biting going on. You may observe gossiping at water coolers (including character assassination), information hoarding, open aggression, or people lying or exaggerating about their real needs. In these cases, you may need to take the initiative to engender co-operation among key individuals or departments.

If conflict is too low you may see that individuals lack any outward signs of motivation or are not interested in their tasks. Meetings are more about 'tell' and not consensus. Deadlines may not be met. It could be that too many ineffective people are entrenched in an overly hierarchical structure. It may be necessary to restructure and identify leaders who possess the kinds of skills that are desired by the organisation.

So the goal is not necessarily to minimise conflict and maximise consensus, but to maintain a level of constructive conflict consistent with the need for diversity and a range of different preferences and styles of creative problem-solving. Group members with similar creative preferences and problem-solving styles are likely to be more harmonious but much less effective than those with mixed preferences and styles. So if the level of conflict is constructive, people behave in a more mature manner. They have psychological insight and exercise more control over their impulses and emotions.

Debate focuses on issues and ideas (as opposed to conflict which focuses on people and their relationships). Debate involves the productive use and respect for diversity of perspectives and points of view. Debate involves encounters, exchanges, or clashes among viewpoints, ideas, and differing experiences and knowledge. Many voices are heard and people are keen on putting forward their ideas. Where debates are missing, people follow authoritarian patterns without questioning. When the score on the debate dimension is too low you may see constant moaning and complaining about the way things are, rather than how the individual can improve the situation. Rather than open debate, you may see more infrequent and quiet one-on-one conversation in hallways. In these conditions, there will be a lack of willingness by individuals to engage others in conversation regarding new ideas, thoughts or concepts. One of the reasons for this situation is that people may have had bad experiences when they have interacted in the past. It may help to clarify the rationale of debate in the organisation and begin to model the behaviour.

However, if there is too much debate you are likely to see more talk than implementation. Individuals will speak with little or no regard for the impact of their statements. The focus on conversation and debate becomes more on individualistic goals than on co-operative and consensus-based action. One reason for this may be too much diversity or people holding very different value systems. In these situations it may be helpful to hold structured or facilitated discussions and affirm commonly held values.

The mandate for legitimating challenge to the dominant vision may come from the top – such as Jack Welch's challenge to 'destroy your business' memo. Perhaps building on their earlier experiences Intel now has a process called 'constructive confrontation', which essentially encourages a degree of dissent. The company has learned to value the critical insights which come from those closest to the action rather than assume senior managers have the 'right' answers every time.

This has important implications for managers trying to cope more effectively with complexity and change:

- given uncertainty, explore the implications of a *range* of possible future trends;
- ensure broad participation and informal channels of communication;
- encourage the use of multiple sources of information, debate and scepticism;
- expect to change strategies in the light of new (and often unexpected) evidence.

INNOVATION IN ACTION

Developing a Creative Climate in a Medical Technology Company

A Finnish-based global healthcare organisation had 55,000 employees and $50 billion in revenue. Its mission was to develop, manufacture and market products for anaesthesia and critical care.

The senior management team of one division conducted an assessment, and found that they had been doing well on quality and operational excellence initiatives in manufacturing and had improved their sales and marketing results, but were still concerned that there were many other areas on which they could improve, in particular creativity and innovation.

We held a workshop with the senior team to present the results and engage them to determine what they needed to do to improve their business. We met with the CEO prior to the workshop to highlight the overall results and share the department comparisons. She was not surprised by the results but was very interested to see that some of the departments had different results.

During the workshop, the team targeted challenge and involvement, freedom, idea time, and idea support as critical dimensions to improve to enable them to meet their strategic objectives. The organisation was facing increasing competition in their markets and significant advances in technology. Although major progress had been made in the manufacturing area, they needed to improve their product development and marketing efforts by broadening involvement internally and cross-functionally and externally by obtaining deep consumer insight. The main strategy they settled upon was to 'jump start' their innovation in new product development for life support.

Key personnel in new product development and marketing were provided training in creative problem-solving, and follow-up projects were launched to apply the learning to existing and new projects.

One project was a major investment in re-engineering their main product line. Clinicians were challenged with the current design of the equipment. The initial decision was to redesign the placement of critical control valves used during surgery. The project leader decided to use

(*continued*)

a number of the tools to go out and clarify the problem with the end users, involving project team members from research and development as well as marketing. The result was a redefinition of the challenge and the decision to save the millions of dollars involved in the re-engineering effort and instead develop a new tactile tool to help the clinicians' problem of having their hands full. Since the professionals in the research and development lab were also directly involved in obtaining and interpreting the consumer insight data, they understood the needs of the end users and displayed an unusually high degree of energy and commitment to the project.

We also observed a much greater amount of cross-functional and informal working across departments. Some human resource personnel were replaced and new forms of reward and recognition were developed. Not only was there more consumer insight research going on, but there were more and closer partnerships created with clinicians and end users of the products. During this period of time the CEO tracked revenue growth and profitability of the division and reported double-digit growth.

Source: Scott Isaksen and Joe Tidd, *Meeting the Innovation Challenge: Leadership for Transformation and Growth* (John Wiley & Sons Ltd, 2006).

5. *Risk-taking*

Tolerance of uncertainty and ambiguity constitutes risk-taking. In a high risk-taking climate, bold new initiatives can be taken even when the outcomes are unknown. People feel that they can 'take a gamble' on some of their ideas. People will often 'go out on a limb' and be first to put an idea forward.

In a risk-avoiding climate there is a cautious, hesitant mentality. People try to be on the 'safe side'. They decide 'to sleep on the matter'. They set up committees and they cover themselves in many ways before making a decision. If risk-taking is too low, employees offer few new ideas or few ideas that are well outside of what is considered safe or ordinary. In risk-avoiding organisations people complain about boring, low-energy jobs and are frustrated by a long, tedious process used to get ideas to action.

These conditions can be caused by the organisation not valuing new ideas, or having an evaluation system that is bureaucratic, or people being punished for 'drawing outside the lines'. It can be remedied by developing a company plan that would speed 'ideas to action'.

Conversely, if there is too much risk-taking, you will see that people are confused. There are too many ideas floating around, but few are sanctioned. People are frustrated because nothing is getting done. There are many loners doing their own thing in the organisation and no evidence of teamwork. These conditions can be caused by individuals not feeling they need a consensus or buy-in from others on their team in their department or organisation. A remedy might include some team building and improving the reward system to encourage co-operation rather than individualism or competition.

Go online to find a number of proven approaches to building more effective teams.

www.iande.info

A recent study of organisational innovation and performance confirms the need for this delicate balance between risk and stability.[12] Risk-taking is associated with a higher relative novelty of innovation (how different it was to what the organisation had done before), and absolute novelty (how different it was to what *any* organisation had done before), and that both types of novelty are correlated with financial and customer benefits. However, the same study concludes that 'incremental , safe, widespread innovations may be better for internal considerations, but novel, disruptive innovations may be better for market considerations . . . absolute novelty benefits customers and quality of life; relative innovation benefits employee relations (but) risk is detrimental to employee relations.'

This is consistent with the real options approach to investing in risky projects, because investments are sequential and managers have some influence on the timing, resourcing and continuation or abandonment of projects at different stages. By investing relatively small amounts in a wide range of projects, a greater range of opportunities can be explored. Once uncertainty has been reduced, only the most promising projects should be allowed to continue. The goal is not to calculate or optimise, but rather to help to identify risks and payoffs, key uncertainties, decision points and future opportunities that might be created. Combined with other methods, such as decision trees, a real options approach can be particularly effective where high volatility demands flexibility, placing a premium on the certainty of information and timing of decisions.

Research on new product and service development has identified a broad range of strategies for dealing with risk. Both individual characteristics and organisational climate influence perceptions of risk and propensities to avoid, accept or seek risks. Formal techniques such as Failure Mode and Effects Analysis (FMEA), Potential Problem Analysis (PPA) and Fault Tree Analysis (FTA) have a role, but the broader signals and support from the organisational climate are more important than the specific tools or methods used.

6. *Freedom*

Freedom is described as the independence in behaviour exerted by the people in the organisation. In a climate with much freedom, people are given autonomy to define much of their own work. They are able to exercise discretion in their day-to-day activities. They take the initiative to acquire and share information, make plans and decisions about their work. In a climate with little freedom, people work within strict guidelines and roles. They carry out their work in prescribed ways with little room to redefine their tasks.

If there is not enough freedom people demonstrate very little initiative for suggesting new and better ways of doing things. They may spend a great deal of time and energy obtaining permission and gaining support (internally and externally) or perform all their work 'by the book' and focus too much on the exact requirements of what they are told to do.

One of the many reasons could be that the leadership practices are very authoritarian or overly bureaucratic. It might be helpful to initiate a leadership improvement initiative including training, 360° feedback with coaching, skills of managing up, etc.

If there is too much freedom you may observe people going off in their own independent directions. They have an unbalanced concern weighted toward themselves rather than the work group or organisation. People may do things that demonstrate little or no concern for important policies/procedures, performing tasks differently and independently redefining how they are done each time. In this case people may not know the procedures, they could be too difficult to follow or the need to conform may be too low. You may start to reward improvement of manuals, process improvements, and ways to communicate and share best practices to help correct the situation.

Go online to find the case study of Cerulean for an example of how a creative climate can be developed in a smaller enterprise.

www.iande.info

Developing Personal Capabilities

Complete the questionnaire in the box, being as honest as possible. Then calculate your score using the guide in the answer. How innovative are you?

HOW CREATIVE ARE YOU?

(Please tick yes or no)   Yes   No

1. Are you constantly on the look-out for new ideas? ☐ ☐
2. Do you get bored with doing things in the same old ways? ☐ ☐
3. Do you get satisfaction from making improvements? ☐ ☐
4. Are you afraid of making mistakes? ☐ ☐
5. Do you worry about appearing foolish? ☐ ☐
6. Do you enjoy playing around with ideas? ☐ ☐
7. Do you resent criticism of your ideas? ☐ ☐
8. Do you welcome ideas from other people? ☐ ☐
9. Do you like solving problems in unorthodox ways? ☐ ☐
10. Do you give up early when you run into difficulties? ☐ ☐

(continued)

	Yes	No
11. Are you discouraged from acting because of lack of resources?	☐	☐
12. Should we have more respect for traditional methods?	☐	☐
13. Do you prefer a quiet *life* to a challenge?	☐	☐
14. Do you feel that it's not your job to be critical of established practice?	☐	☐
15. Do you fear new situations with unpredictable consequences?	☐	☐
16. Do you mistrust your own or other people's intuition?	☐	☐
17. Do you find it hard to accept disorder and confusion?	☐	☐
18. Do you dislike complexity?	☐	☐
19. Are you afraid of being looked upon as being pushy?	☐	☐
20. Are you reluctant to express your opinions?	☐	☐
21. Are you afraid of having your ideas ridiculed?	☐	☐
22. Are you easily discouraged by hostile criticism?	☐	☐
23. Do you have a difficulty in thinking broadly?	☐	☐
24. Are you quick to point out why an idea won't work?	☐	☐
25. Do you set yourself specific innovation objectives?	☐	☐
26. Do you keep abreast of new ideas in your field?	☐	☐

ADVICE FOR ENTREPRENEURS

Developing a business plan will not always be enough to ensure effective and successful implementation. Research has identified several factors to help increase the power of your implementation plan. For example, Everett Rogers identified five factors to increase the effectiveness of your planning and implementation. He suggested that if your plan shows the relative advantage of your solutions over previous approaches and their compatibility or consistency with existing values, experiences or needs, the likelihood of them being implemented increase. Also, as you make the plan easy to understand and use (less complex), observable, and give people a chance to try parts of it, the greater the change of successful implementation.[13]

We have used these five categories to develop a checklist to help you examine the effectiveness of your plan and to identify places where it might be strong or in need improvement or modification.

Relative Advantage. Being better than the previous solution: How well does my plan show how much better off people will be when they adopt the plan?

- Why is this plan better than what has been done before?
- What advantages or benefits might there be to accepting the plan?
- Who will gain from the implementation of the plan?

(continued)

- How will I (or others) be rewarded by adopting the plan?
- How might I emphasise the plan's benefits to all?

Compatibility. Consistent with values, experiences, and needs: How well does my plan demonstrate that it is compatible with current values, past experiences, and needs?

- Is the plan consistent with current practice?
- Does the plan meet the needs of a particular group?
- Does it offer better ways to reach our common goals?
- Who will naturally support and agree with the plan?
- Can it be favourably named, packaged, or presented?

Complexity. Being difficult to understand and use: How well does my plan provide for easy communication, comprehension, and use?

- Is the plan easy for others to understand?
- Can it be explained clearly to many different people?
- Will the plan be easily communicated?
- How might the plan be made more simple or easy to understand?
- Is the plan easy to use or follow?

Trialability. May be experimented with on a limited basis: How well does my plan allow for trialability?

- Can the plan be tried out or tested?
- Can uncertainty be reduced?
- Can we begin with a few parts of the plan?
- How might others be encouraged to try out the plan?
- Can the plan be modified by you or others?

Observability. Results are visible to others: How well does my plan provide results that are easily observed and visible to others?

- Is the plan easy for others to find or obtain?
- Can the plan be made more visible to others?
- How might I make the plan easier for others to see?
- Will others be able to see the effects of the plan?
- Are there good reasons for not making the entire plan visible?

Other questions. The following are some general questions that will help your planning and implementation efforts.

- What other resources will I need; how might I get them?
- What obstacles exist; how might we prevent or overcome them?
- What new challenges might be created; and dealt with?
- How might I encourage commitment to the plan?
- What feedback about the plan is needed?

Source: Isaksen, S. and J. Tidd (2006) *Meeting the Innovation Challenge: Leadership for Transformation and Growth*. John Wiley & Sons Ltd, Chichester.

STRATEGIC AND SOCIAL IMPACT

Managers are facing broadening demands on their time and attention to a dynamic and uncertain environment. No organisation is insulated from the requirements of being able to broaden their responsiveness to change. Organisations in both the private and public sectors face an increasingly ambiguous environment. Under these conditions, managers must learn how to become more flexible and agile in order to respond successfully.

Organisations have typically viewed creativity and entrepreneurial ability as belonging to a gifted few (usually placed within the design, research and development or marketing functions). As a result, the development and implementation of innovation has been limited. There is increasing recognition of the need to move beyond this narrow view of who has creative talent to how a broader range of talents might be applied. Organisations need to find ways to recognise and apply the full spectrum of creative talent represented in the entire employee population.

Innovation and change are at the forefront of the agenda for many who work within organisations, whether in the private or public sectors, or manufacturing or services, small or large. In his work on disruptive innovation, Christensen and Raynor identify the many challenges organisations now face, and why so many fail to respond to these.[14] Today everyone seems to be involved in planning or implementing some sort of change program or innovation initiative. At the same time organisations must competently manage existing operations and businesses, what Michael Tushman calls the 'ambidextrous organization'.[15]

However, organising innovation and change is not easy, and many fail. Research confirms what many of us already suspected. For example, a study of change efforts of Fortune 100 companies between 1980 and 1995 and found that virtually all had implemented at least one change programme with an average investment of one billion dollars per organisation, but only 30% produced an improvement in bottom line results that exceeded the company's cost of capital, and 50% failed to market performance.[16] Similarly, most major programmes of Business Process Reengineering (BPR) have failed to deliver the promised improvements in productivity or quality, for example two-thirds of 600 BPR cases studied experienced marginal or zero benefit, and many have simply been used as an excuse for rationalisation and down-sizing, e.g. typically 20% reduction in staff is experienced.[17] Most recently, many large private and public organisations have invested in some form of Enterprise Resource Planning (ERP) as a catalyst for change, but 'such systems force change on an organisation structure, working practices, policies and procedures that can hinder innovation'.[18]

In this chapter we have discussed the need for a more systemic approach, rather than simply trying to pull a single lever. Our research and experience confirm that those who initiate change need to have a good understanding of the nature of organisations, as well as the dynamics of innovation and change. This means that we must have a workable model for how organisations function that includes the key levers or factors for innovation and change.

Chapter Summary

The organisation of innovation and entrepreneurship is much more than a set of tools and techniques. Too often it is reduced to a simple methodology, such as developing a plan for a new business or development of a new product or service. However, in this chapter we have argued that the successful practice of innovation and entrepreneurship demands the interaction and integration of three different perspectives:

● Personal or individual, which focuses on creative style, and the ability to identify, assess and develop new ideas and concepts.
● Collective or social, which stresses the contribution of teams, groups and processes necessary to translate ideas and concepts into new products, services or businesses.
● Contextual, which focuses on the climate and resources needed to support the creation and growth of innovation and entrepreneurship.

Discussion Questions

1. What are the key similarities, differences and relationships between entrepreneurship and innovation?

2. Why is the creative style of an individual more important than any assessment of absolute creativity?

3. What are the relevant influences of an individual's characteristics and their environment on entrepreneurship?

4. List the key components of a process for identifying, developing and assessing new ideas, and suggest a tool or technique to support each stage.

5. What is the difference between culture and climate, and why is this distinction critical for innovation and entrepreneurship?

6. What factors contribute to the development of a creative climate – and what factors might block it?

Team Exercise: Brainstorming and Spider Diagrams

Construct a spider diagram to help to identify the key issues related to the implementation of a new IT system.

You will probably be familiar with brainstorming. However, it is often not conducted very well.

Brainstorming is the rapid generation and pooling of all and any ideas that a group of people can come up. It can be used to solve problems or to generate new ideas. Every idea is recorded no matter how obvious, irrational or bizarre. The critical thing to do when brainstorming, which is often not done well, is to *temporarily suspend any discussion or judgement*. This happens later. The keys to successful brainstorming are:

1. Keep a relaxed atmosphere. Meetings should be disciplined but informal. If possible, choose an informal venue.
2. Get the right size of team. The technique seems to work best with groups of 5 to 7 people.
3. Choose a neutral (ideally external) chairperson. The chair checks that everyone understands what is going on and why. Avoid senior managers, as this might restrict the flow of ideas.
4. Define the problem or objectives clearly.
5. Generate as many ideas as possible.
6. Do not allow any evaluation and discussion.
7. Give everyone equal opportunity to contribute.
8. Write down **every** idea — clearly and where everyone can see them.
9. When all the ideas are listed, review them for clarification, making sure everyone understands each item. At this point you can eliminate duplications and remove ideas the group feels are no longer appropriate.
10. Allow ideas to incubate. Brainstorm in sessions with perhaps a few days in between. This gives time for the team to let the ideas turn over in their mind, which often results in new ideas at a later session.

The evaluation of the ideas happens later, usually with a smaller group and using clear criteria for selection, review or rejection.

A spider diagram is simply a graphical way of identifying and exploring relationships between different factors. Mind or cognitive maps are a specific application of spider diagrams used to make explicit the relationships and assumptions within a given context. In both cases you begin with a central theme or key word which is written in the centre of a large sheet of paper, a white board, or screen. Next generate related concepts or themes and write these around the central theme. Finally, draw lines to represent potential relationships between the different concepts. Used by an individual, this is a very effective way of clarifying thoughts. Used by a group, it helps to identify shared assumptions and to highlight differences in perceptions. The process is less linear and logical than the cause and effect diagram discussed earlier in this chapter, and therefore is more suited to less well understood problems or for idea generation.

Here is a list of potential issues to get you started:

• Role of consultants.
• Maintenance and support.
• Financing and timing.
• Training and new skills.
• Software and data compatibility.

Assignment

1. Propose some new services for mobile telephony. Use each of the following six methods to help to provoke alternatives:
   - *Remove or suspend an assumption or goal* – what could we do differently if we temporarily ignore a key objective or assumption?
   - *Reverse objectives or methods* – what would we do to achieve the exact opposite, and then reverse this?
   - *Exaggerate the problem or goal* – what might we do if the goal or problem was much larger or smaller?
   - *Distort the relationships or cause and effect* – what would the implications be?
   - *Generate random inputs* – what new ideas does the introduction of a random word help create?
   - *Use a metaphor or character* – what would a chosen famous character do in these circumstances?

Key Terms Defined

Cause and effect diagram   a useful structured way of searching for the root cause of a particular problem, also known as fish bone (because of the way the diagram looks) or Ishikawa diagrams (after the Japanese person who promoted the technique).

Climate   recurring patterns of behaviour, attitudes and feelings that characterise life in the organisation. These are the objectively shared perceptions that characterise life within a defined work unit or in the larger organisation. Climate is distinct from culture in that it is more observable at a surface level within the organisation and more amenable to change and improvement efforts.

Cognitive mapping   techniques which aim to provide a tool for revealing peoples' subjective beliefs in a meaningful way so that they can be examined not only by the individual for whom the map is constructed, but also by other individuals and groups. Another potential use of cognitive mapping techniques is to allow decision-makers to look at maps that have been constructed for other stakeholders

Culture   the deeper and more enduring values, norms and beliefs within the organisation.

Creativity   the making and communicating of meaningful new connections to help us think of many possibilities; to help us think and experience in varied ways and using different points of view; to help us think of new and unusual possibilities; and to guide us in generating and selecting alternatives.

Lateral thinking   methods and tool to support alternatives to logic thought, to promote applied creative thinking.

Kirton Adapter-Innovator (KAI) scale   a psychometric approach for assessing the creativity of individuals. By a series of questions it seeks to identify an individual's attitudes towards originality, attention to detail and following rules. It seeks to differentiate 'adaptive' from 'innovative' styles.

Pareto analysis   used to prioritise areas for improvement by identifying the factors that will have the greatest impact on quality. A Pareto diagram simply ranks problems or causes of problems according to their frequency or significance.

Further Reading and Resources

The research and practice of organising innovation and entrepreneurship is rather fragmented, and tends to reflect the different disciplines relevant to the subject, ranging from psychology, which focuses on the individual issues such as cognition, sociology, which is more concerned with group processes and power, and economics, which only adequately deals with structures and exchanges or transaction between individuals and organisations. If you do not have a background in psychology, sociology or a dedicated course on organisational behaviour, we recommend you consult a good text on Organisational Behaviour. There are many suitable texts, but we would recommend David Buchanan and Andrzej Huczynski (2009) *Organizational Behaviour* (Sixth edition, FT-Prentice Hall), which provides an excellent synthesis of the main issues, with a good balance of managerial and more critical social science approaches.

A more detailed treatment of the issues covered in this chapter can be found in our recent text *Meeting the Innovation Challenge: Leadership for Transformation and Growth* (Wiley, 2006), written with Scott Isaksen. Ralph Katz *The Human Side of Managing Technological Innovation* (Oxford University Press, 2003) is an excellent collection of readings. Van de Ven, A.H., Polley, D., Angle, H.L. and Poole, M.S. *Research on the Management of Innovation* (Oxford University Press, 2000) provides a comprehensive review of a seminal study in the field, and includes a discussion of individual, group and organisational issues. For the more specific issue of entrepreneurial characteristics, a good start is E. Chell (2008) *The Entrepreneurial Personality* (Routledge, 2nd edn).

References

1. Kaplan, J.M. (2009) *Patterns of Entrepreneurship*. John Wiley & Sons Inc., New Jersey, 3rd edition.

2. Roberts, E.B. (1991) *Entrepreneurs in High Technology: Lessons from MIT and beyond*. Oxford University Press.

3. Ibid.

4. Mueller, S.L. and Thomas, A.S. (2001) Culture and entrepreneurial potential: A nine country study of locus of control and innovativeness, *Journal of Business Venturing*,

16(1), 51–75; Robichaud, Y., McGraw, E. and Roger, A. (2001) Towards development of a measuring instrument for entrepreneurial motivation, *Journal of Developmental Entrepreneurship*, 5(2), 189–202; Shane, S. and Venkataraman, S. (2000) The promise of entrepreneurship as a field of research, *Academy of Management Review*, 25, 217–226; Georgelli, Y.P., Joyce, B. and Woods, A. (2000) Entrepreneurial action, innovation and business performance, *Journal of Small Business and Enterprise Development*, 7(1), 7–17; Gartner, W.B. (1988) Who is an entrepreneur is the wrong question, *Entrepreneurship Theory and Practice*, 13(1), 47–64.

5. Sarason, Y., Dean, T. and Dillard, F. (2006) Entrepreneurship as the nexus of individual and opportunity, *Journal of Business Venturing*, 21, 286–305; Feldman, D.C. and Bolino, M.C. (2000) Career patterns of the self-employed, *Journal of Small Business Management*, 38(3), 53–68.

6. Harding, R. (2007) GEM: Global Entrepreneurship Monitor, London Business School; Storey, D. and Tether, B. (1998) New technology-based firms in the European Union, *Research Policy* 26, 933–946.

7. Isaksen, S. and J. Tidd (2006) *Meeting the Innovation Challenge: Leadership for Transformation and Growth*. John Wiley & Sons Ltd, Chichester.

8. Roberts, E.B. (1991) op cit.

9. Kanter, R.M. (2003) *Rosabeth Moss Kanter on the Frontiers of Management*. Harvard Business School Press; (1992) *The Change Masters: Corporate Entrepreneurs at Work*. International Thomson Business Press.

10. Hofstede, G. (2003) *Culture's consequences: Comparing values, behaviors, institutions, and organizations across nations*. Thousand Oaks, CA: Sage; Hofstede, G. (1994) *Cultures and organizations – Software of the mind: Intercultural cooperation and its importance for survival*. New York: McGraw-Hill.

11. Schein, E. H. (2004) *Organizational Culture and Leadership*. John Wiley & Sons Ltd.

12. Berglund, H. (2007) Risk conception and risk management in corporate innovation, *International Journal of Innovation Management*, 11(4), 497–514; Totterdell, P., D., Leach, K. Birdi, C. Clegg and T. Wall (2002) An investigation of the contents and consequences of major organizational innovation, *International Journal of Innovation Management*, 6(4), 343–368.

13. Rogers, E. M. (2003) *Diffusion of Innovations* (4th edn). New York: Simon & Schuster International.

14. Christensen, C. and M. Raynor (2003) *The Innovator's Solution: Creating and sustaining successful growth*. Boston: Harvard Business School Press.

15. Tushman, M.L. (2002) *Winning Through Innovation*. Harvard Business School Press.

16. Nohria, N. (1996). From the M-form to the N-form: Taking stock of changes in the large industrial corporation. *Harvard Business School Working Paper 96-054*.

17. CSC Index (1994) *The State of Re-Engineering*. CSC Index, London.

18. Trott, P. and Hoecht, A. (2004) 'Enterprise Resource Planning (ERP) and its impact on the innovative capability of the firm', *International Journal of Innovation Management*, 8(4), 380–398.

INNOVATION IN ACTION

Exploring Innovation in Action: Electronic Gaming

The global market for videogames has grown within a decade to US$40 billion and, in the UK, the handheld games market alone is worth £250 million a year. Although it can cost several million dollars to develop and distribute a new computer or console game, the industry still reflects its origins with individual users/developers and small groups of developers, but they now work with global manufacturers such as Sony, Nintendo and Microsoft, and major corporate publishers like Electronic Arts and Universal. The industry consists of a diverse 'eco-system', which has evolved as the industry has grown rapidly:

- *Super developers* – who develop games across different platforms and have their own intellectual property and brands.
- *Original IP developers* – who develop and seek to own their own intellectual property, but self-publish, or publish through other companies.
- *Specialist niche developers* – who specialise in a particular platform or genre.
- *Work-for-hire* – who compete for games development contracts from the publishers, and have no ownership of intellectual property.
- *Service providers* – who provide a range of services to developers and publishers throughout the development process.

This emerging sector integrates the combined creativity of individual and groups of developers and users with the more formal innovation processes of the hardware and publishing firms. The challenge is to translate creative ideas into commercially successful products on a consistent basis, which demands a systemic approach to entrepreneurship and innovation. As one analyst notes:

'Developers are highly regarded by the wider community for their creativity, originality and technical achievement . . . developers have the potential to leverage these technical and creative abilities, but only through the development of a range of complimentary business, management and personal competencies.'

Few of these firms have the critical strategic, commercial and financial capabilities needed to grow and prosper. The Super Developers may have up to five development teams and projects at any

(continued)

time, but the Original IP and Specialist Niche developers may have only one team. For example, most rely on advances from publishers to fund development, rather than debt or equity funding.

Although the design of any innovative game can often be traced to the creativity of just one or two people, its development into a commercially successful product involves the continuous improvement of the content that can only be achieved through collaboration with and continuous prototyping by a much bigger group of developers. The initial idea for any new game usually comes from one or two designers who outline the central concept and map out the game structure. If this is promising, it is developed by a larger team over a few months to create a more formal proposal that will normally include a prototype of section with art and code. This is pitched to potential publisher for funding, and if accepted will be developed by a large team over one or two years. Around two-fifths of these pitches are funded, and each proposal, whether or not successful, can cost a developer $200,000. If funded, the development budget is between $350,000 and $6 million, the average being around $2 million. The main cost is labour, around 70% of total costs, but the dedicated gamer/developers work long hours for modest income, with teams of 20–30 developers working on a typical development project.

The process of developing an electronic game is characterised by multiple design iterations and frequent milestones and testing. It is a strong combination of technology, creative games design and artistic content, and therefore demands complex concurrent multifunctional team development and the interaction and integration of design, content and technology. A typical profile for staff in a development team of 20 might be half working on artistic content, a third on programming and the rest on design. These interactions and interdependencies between design, content and technology require a highly iterative and evolutionary approach to games development, and can cause many problems in game function and development scheduling. Teams need to be co-ordinated on an almost daily basis; the integration of these components is critical. These relatively large, multidisciplinary teams require significant leadership, to maintain the vision and direction and to overcome the many decision deadlocks. This is a similar role to the producer in film or music development, what Baba refers to as a 'benevolent dictator keen on sustaining both the product's integrity and the egalitarian relationship among the project members'.

The game play experience and interactivity are crucial to success, and can only be tested and tuned by experience. The technical and creative nature of developers has restricted their ability to grow and evolve the game business. The predominately male, 20- to 30-year-old developers are increasingly isolated from broader market needs. For example, the traditional gamer/developer hero, such as Shigeru Miyamoto, the creator of classic Nintendo games such as *Donkey Kong* and *Super Mario Brothers*, may be less relevant exemplars than more sophisticated marketing approaches. Nintendo has recently targeted those who do not currently play computer games, and has explicitly developed games beyond the typical 18–35 male demographic market. The value of this central market has continued to grow with the development of new consoles and games, but the number of core users has stabilised at around a third of the population. Therefore any further growth will demand expanding beyond the core gamer community. For example, games for the DS handheld console have been developed specifically for female users, such as *Nintendogs*, and the brain-testing and developing game *Brain Training* for older users. *Nintendogs* sold

(continued)

4 million units in 2005, and *Brain Training*, aimed at the over 45-year-olds, was launched in the UK in 2006, following a successful launch in Japan in May 2005.

The increasing cost of development and need for global sales has resulted in a significant consolidation of the sector. For example, the development of a game for the Playstation 3 platform is estimated to cost around US$12 million. As a result major console manufacturers and independent publishers currently dominate the industry, and these largely dictate what games will reach the market, and drive the cost, quality and development times. However, the industry continues to evolve, which presents further opportunities for entrepreneurship and innovation:

- Potentially disruptive innovations, such as web-based and mobile interactive gaming, which may challenge the big publisher business model.
- New software automation modules, middleware, which may change relationships and create new specialist niche suppliers.
- The availability of low-cost but experienced software development talent from India and Eastern Europe, leading to new models of development and new markets and competitors in the games industry.

Questions

1. In the computer games industry, what are the respective roles of individual developers, small firms and large international companies?
2. What are the potential conflicts between the need for creativity and more formal development processes in the industry?
3. Given trends in the structure and funding of the industry, what future opportunities are there for innovation and entrepreneurship?

Sources: Andrew Grantham and Raphael Kaplinsky (2005) 'Getting the measure of the electronic games industry: Developer and the management of innovation', *International Journal of Innovation Management*, 9(2), 183–214; F. Ted Chang (2005) 'Videogames as interactive experiential products and their manner of development', *International Journal of Innovation Management*, 9(1), 103–131; Yasonori Baba and F. Ted Tschang (2001) 'Product development in Japanese TV game software', *International Journal of Innovation Management*, 5(4), 487–515.

CASE STUDY 4

Bob Noyce, the Pod-father

Robert (Bob) Noyce was one of the pioneers of microelectronics, whose contribution can be traced all the way forward to current entrepreneurs such as Steve Jobs of Apple fame. He has been referred to as the Thomas Edison and the Henry Ford of Silicon Valley: Edison for his invention and technological innovations, including the co-invention of the integrated circuit; and Ford for his process and corporate innovations, including the creation of Fairchild Semiconductor and Intel.

A first degree in Physics and Maths, followed by a PhD in Physics from MIT, upon graduation in 1953 he gained three years' experience as a research engineer, and then at age 29 he joined the then newly established but prestigious Shockley Semiconductor Laboratory in California. William Shockley had won the Nobel Prize for his co-development of the transistor. However, Noyce was very unhappy with the management style at Shockley, and left in 1957 with the so-called 'Traitorous Eight' to form Fairchild Semiconductor, a new division of Fairchild Camera and Instruments.

Sherman Fairchild agreed to fund the 'Traitorous Eight's' new venture on the basis of Noyce's reputation and vision. Noyce convinced Fairchild that the key was the manufacturing process, and that silicon-based components could become low-cost and widely used in a range of electronic devices. At Fairchild, Noyce created a climate in which talent thrived: it was much less structured, more relaxed, team-based and less hierarchical than at Shockley. Arguably this was the archetype for the future culture of Silicon Valley.

In 1958 the new venture developed the key planar technology which made higher-performance transistors easier and cheaper to manufacture. In July 1959 he filed for the patent for the Integrated Circuit, essentially multiple transistors on a single wafer of silicon, which was the next significant technological breakthrough. Between 1954 and 1967 he accumulated 16 patents. The first sales were to IBM, and sales of Fairchild's semiconductor division doubled each year until the mid-1960s by which time the company had grown from 12 to 12,000 employees, and was earning $130 million a year. By 1966, the sales of Fairchild were second to Texas Instrument's, followed in third place by Motorola. Noyce was rewarded with the position of corporate vice-president, and the *de facto* head of the semiconductor division.

These devices were analogue, but Fairchild was less successful with its digital devices. Some of its early digital circuits were used in the Apollo Space Guidance computer, but generally these were not suited to other military applications and were not a commercial success. Texas Instruments and a number of new start-up companies offered superior designs, and in 1967 Fairchild suffered its first loss, of US$7.6 million. When the CEO resigned, the board did not promote Noyce. As a consequence, in 1968 Noyce left Fairchild to form a new venture with Gordon Moore (also one of the original 'Traitorous Eight' from Shockley, and originator of 'Moore's Law'). Five of the original founders of Fairchild Semiconductor funded the creation of Intel (INTgrated ELectronics). Intel's third employee was Andy Grove, a chemical engineer and credited as its key business and strategic leader.

For the first few years, Intel's business was based on the low-cost manufacture of Random Access Memory (RAM) devices. Noyce oversaw the development of the next major milestone in the industry, the microprocessor, invented by Ted Hoff in 1971. The processor was developed to replace a number of components for an electronic calculator developed for a Japanese client. However, the microprocessor did not become central to Intel's business until much later. Increasing competition from Japan reduced the profitability of memory devices, and Intel changed strategy to pursue the development microprocessor which would be critical to the growth of the nascent PC industry. In July 1979 Intel launched its 8088 processor, a new variant of its 8086, accompanied by a major marketing and sales campaign 'Operation Crush', to promote widespread adoption and application. An early win was as a supplier to IBM. In August 1981 IBM launched its PC based upon the Intel processor. In 1982, Intel introduced the 80286 processor, and subsequently the 80386 in 1985, first used by Compaq in its PC-clones and later by IBM. The 386 was also a milestone as it was the first processor to be single-sourced from Intel. Before this, customers would source critical components from several competing manufacturers to ensure deliveries and reduce risk, but for the 386 Intel refused to license its design and instead manufactured the chips at three separate sites. This strategy established Intel at the heart of the PC industry.

Noyce's charisma and powers of persuasion made him an inspiring leader, but he was a less effective manager. He was criticised by Grove and others for his indecisiveness and dislike of confrontation, a trait that kept him from making difficult decisions and taking tough actions. He resigned as President in 1975, transferring the role to Moore. However, Noyce maintained a mentoring role at Intel and more broadly, and provided advice and seed capital to promising entrepreneurs.

One of these aspiring entrepreneurs was Steve Jobs, who Noyce met during the first year of Apple Computer, in 1977. Jobs deliberately sought out Noyce as a mentor. 'Steve would regularly appear at our house on his motorcycle . . . he and Bob were disappearing into the basement, talking about projects.' Noyce answered Jobs's phone calls – which invariably began with, 'I've been thinking about what you said' or 'I have an idea' – even when they came at midnight. This relationship continued for over a decade.

Clearly then, Bob Noyce has contributed to almost all aspects of innovation in Silicon Valley – technological, process, product, corporate and cultural. As

Noyce advised budding entrepreneurs: 'Optimism is an essential ingredient for innovation . . . go off and do something wonderful'.

Case Questions

1. What were the key characteristics which contributed to the success of Bob Noyce?
2. What other individuals contributed, and in what ways?
3. Identify the types of innovation and their impact on the development of the new ventures and industry.

Sources: BBC Productions (2009) *The Podfather;* Leslie Berlin (2007) Focus on Robert Noyce, *Core*, Spring-Summer (www.computerhistory.org/core/backissues/pdf/core_2007.pdf); Leslie Berlin (2005) *The Man Behind the Microchip: Robert Noyce and the Invention of Silicon Valley*. Oxford University Press; T.R. Reid (2001) *The Chip: How to Americans Invented the Microchip and Launched a Revolution*. Random House.

Summary of Web Resources

Cases

- 3M
- Cerulean

Media

- Ken Robison

Tools

- Creativity assessment questionnaire
- Team building

Chapter 5

Sources of Innovation

LEARNING OBJECTIVES

By the end of this chapter you will develop an understanding of:

- Where innovations come from – the wide range of different sources which can trigger the process.

- The different ways in which sources of innovation can open up opportunities for change.

- A framework for looking at sources in terms of 'push' and 'pull' forces.

- The different importance of different sources over time.

- Where and when you might search for opportunities to innovate.

Go online to find additional . . .

Cases

Tools

Media

www.iande.info

Introduction

One definition of an entrepreneur is someone who sees an opportunity – and does something about it. Whether it's an individual looking to find a new product or service to make his or her fortune, a social entrepreneur trying to change the world or a large established organisation looking for new market space, the challenge is one of finding opportunities for innovation. And whilst there is always the possibility of a stroke of luck, the reality is that this first step in the innovation process will require extensive search. To help guide this process it is useful to look at where innovations come from – and that is the aim of this chapter.

Where Do Innovations Come From?

Where do innovations come from? For many people that question will evoke images like that of Archimedes, jumping up from his bath and running down the street, so enthused by his new idea that he forgot to get dressed. Or Newton, dozing under the apple tree until a falling apple helped kick his brain into thinking about the science of gravity. Or James Watt, also asleep, until woken by the noise of a boiling kettle. Such 'Eureka' moments are certainly a part of innovation folklore – and they underline the importance of flashes of insight which make new connections. They form the basis of the cartoon model of innovation which usually involves thinking bubbles and flashing light bulbs. And from time to time they do happen – for example, Percy Shaw's observation of the reflection in a cat's eye at night led to the development of one of the most widely used road safety innovations in the world. Or George de Mestral, on a walk in the Swiss Alps noticing the way plant burrs became attached to his dog's fur and developing from that inspiration the highly successful 'Velcro' fastener.

But of course there is much more to it than that. Innovation is a process of taking ideas forward, revising and refining them, weaving the different strands of 'knowledge spaghetti' together towards a useful product, process or service. Triggering that process is not just about occasional flashes of inspiration – innovation comes from many other directions, and if we are to manage it effectively we need to remind ourselves of this diversity. Figure 5.1 indicates some of the wide range of stimuli which can begin the innovation journey. In the following sections we will explore some of these in more detail.

Knowledge Push . . .

One obvious source of innovation is the possibilities which emerge as a result of scientific research. Although there have always been solo researchers we should remember that from a very early stage this process of exploring and codifying at the frontiers of knowledge became a systematic activity – and one which involved a wide network of people sharing their ideas. In the twentieth century the rise of the modern large corporation brought with it the emergence of the research laboratory as a key instrument of progress. Bell Labs, ICI, Bayer, BASF, Philips, Ford, Western Electric, DuPont – all were founded in the early 1900s as powerhouses

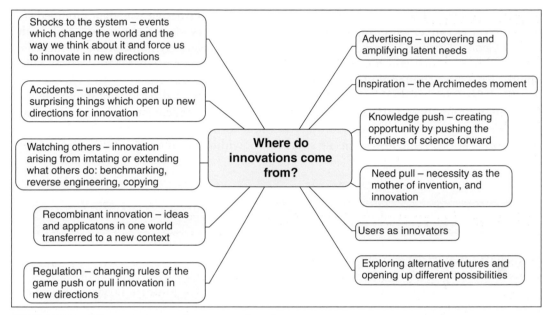

FIGURE 5.1   Where do innovations come from?

of ideas. Their output wasn't simply around product innovation – many of the key technologies underpinning *process* innovations, especially around the growing field of automation and information/communications technology also came from such organised R&D effort.

Organised R&D became a systematic commitment of specialist staff, equipment, facilities and resources targeted at key technological problems or challenges. Much of this effort is about incremental innovation, moving forward slowly and systematically along the knowledge frontier. But every so often there is a major breakthrough, one which sets the direction for the next wave of incremental innovation activity.

For example, the rise of the huge global pharmaceutical industry was essentially about big R&D expenditure, much of it spent on development and elaboration punctuated by the occasional breakthrough into 'blockbuster' drug territory. The semiconductor and the computer and other industries which depend on it have become linked to a long-term trajectory which followed from the early 'breakthrough' years of the industry. Moore's Law (named after one of the founders of Intel), essentially sets up a trajectory which shapes and guides innovation based on the idea that the size will shrink and the power will increase by a factor of 2 every two years. This affects memory, processor speed, display drivers and various other components which in turn drives the rate of innovation in computers, digital cameras, mobile phones and thousands of other applications.

The same pattern can be seen in products. For example, the original design for a camera is something which goes back to the early nineteenth century and – as a visit to any science museum will show – involved all sorts of ingenious solutions. The dominant design gradually emerged with an architecture which we would recognise – shutter and lens arrangement, focusing principles, back plate for film or plates, etc. But this design was then modified still further – for example, with different lenses, motorised drives, flash technology – and, in the case of George Eastman's work, to creating a simple and relatively 'idiot-proof' model camera (the Box Brownie) which opened up photography to a mass market. More recent development has seen a similar fluid phase around digital imaging devices.

This idea of occasional breakthroughs followed by extended periods of exploring and elaboration along those paths helps us deal with the key management question of how and where to direct our search activity for innovation. It forms the basis of much R&D strategy in big corporations – and also opens up space for individual inventors to spot niches and new directions.

INNOVATION IN ACTION

Bags of Ideas – the Case of James Dyson

In October 2000 the air inside Court 58 of the Royal Courts of Justice in London rang with terms like 'bagless dust collection', 'cyclone technology', 'triple vortex' and 'dual cyclone' as one of the most bitter of patent battles in recent years was brought to a conclusion. On one side was Hoover, a multinational firm with the eponymous vacuum suction sweeper at the heart of a consumer appliance empire. On the other was a lone inventor – James Dyson – who had pioneered a new approach to the humble task of house cleaning and then seen his efforts threatened by an apparent imitation by Hoover. Eventually the court ruled in Dyson's favour.

This represented the culmination of a long and difficult journey which Dyson travelled in bringing his ideas to a wary marketplace. It began in 1979 when Dyson was using, ironically, a Hoover Junior vacuum cleaner to dust the house. He was struck by the inefficiency of a system which effectively reduced its capability to suck the more it was used since the bag became clogged with dust. He tried various improvements such as a finer mesh filter bag but the results were not promising. The breakthrough came with the idea of using industrial cyclone technology applied in a new way – to the problem of domestic cleaners.

Dyson was already an inventor with some track record and one of his products was a wheelbarrow which used a ball instead of a front wheel. In order to spray the black dust paint in a powder coating plant they had installed a cyclone – a well-established engineering solution to the problem of dust extraction. Essentially a mini-tornado is created within a shell and the air in the vortex moves so fast that particles of dust are forced to the edge where they can be collected whilst clean air moves to the centre. Dyson began to ask why the principle could not be applied in vacuum cleaners – and soon found out why. His early experiments – with the Hoover – were not entirely successful but eventually he applied for a patent in 1980 for a vacuum cleaning appliance using cyclone technology.

It took another four years and 5127 prototypes and even then he could not patent the application of a single cyclone since that would only represent an improvement on an existing and

(continued)

proven technology. He had to develop a dual cyclone system which used the first to separate out large items of domestic refuse – cigarette ends, dog hairs, cornflakes, etc. – and the second to pick up the finer dust particles. But having proved the technology he found a distinct cold shoulder on the part of the existing vacuum cleaner industry represented by firms like Hoover, Philips and Electrolux. In typical examples of the 'not invented here' effect they remained committed to the idea of vacuum cleaners using bags and were unhappy with bagless technology. (This is not entirely surprising since suppliers such as Electrolux make a significant income on selling the replacement bags for their vacuum cleaners.)

Eventually Dyson began the hard work of raising the funds to start his own business – and it gradually paid off. Launched in 1993 – 14 years after the initial idea – Dyson now runs a design-driven business worth around £530m and has a number of product variants in its vacuum cleaner range; other products under development aim to re-examine domestic appliances like washing machines and dishwashers to try to bring similar new ideas into play. The basic dual cyclone cleaner was one of the products identified by the UK Design Council as one of its 'millennium products'.

Perhaps the greatest accolade though is the fact that the vacuum cleaner giants like Hoover eventually saw the potential and began developing their own versions. Although Hoover lost the case they are planning to appeal, arguing that their version used a different technology developed for the oil and gas industry by the UK research consultancy BHR. Whoever wins, Dyson has once again shown the role of the individual champion in innovation – and that success depends on more than just a good idea. Edison's famous comment that it is '1% inspiration and 99% perspiration' seems an apt motto here!

Go online to find a case study of an entrepreneur-driven success story. SPIRIT is a Russian company started in 2000 which continues to use its R&D strengths to provide a range of voice collaboration solutions for major players like Oracle and Macromedia.
Other cases on website – Corning, 3M, Philips – show the continuing importance of R&D/knowledge push.

www.iande.info

Need Pull . . .

Knowledge creation provides a push, creating an 'opportunity field' which sets up possibilities for innovation. But simply having a bright idea is no guarantee of adoption. The American writer Ralph Waldo Emerson is supposed to have said 'build a better mousetrap and the world will beat a path to your door' – but the reality is that there are plenty of bankrupt mousetrap salesmen around! Knowledge push creates a field of possibilities – but not every idea finds successful application and one of the key lessons is that innovation requires some form of demand if it is to take root. Bright ideas are not, in themselves, enough – they may not meet a real or perceived need and people may not feel motivated to change.

A second key source of innovation is need pull – the complementary pull to the knowledge push. In its simplest form it is captured in the saying that *'necessity is the Mother of invention'* – innovation is often the response to a real or perceived need for change. So we need to develop a clear understanding of needs and finding ways to meet those needs. For example, Henry Ford was able to turn the luxury plaything that was the early automobile into something which became 'a car for Everyman', whilst Procter & Gamble began a business by meeting a need for domestic lighting (via candles) and moved across into an ever-widening range of household needs from soap to nappies to cleaners, toothpaste and beyond. Low-cost airlines have found innovative solutions to the problem of making flying available to a much wider market, whilst micro-finance institutions have developed radical new approaches to help bring banking and credit within the reach of the poor.

INNOVATION IN ACTION

Two hundred years ago Churchill Potteries began life in the UK making a range of crockery and tableware. That it is still able to do so today, despite a turbulent and highly competitive global market, says much for the approach which they have taken to ensure a steady stream of innovation. Chief Executive Andrew Roper highlights the way in which listening to users and understanding their needs has changed the business. 'We have taken on a lot of service disciplines, so you could think of us as less of a pure manufacturer and more as a service company with a manufacturing arm.' Staff spend a significant proportion of their time talking to chefs, hoteliers and others. '. . . sales, marketing and technical people spend far more of their time than I could ever have imagined checking out what happens to the product in use and asking the customer, professional or otherwise, what they really want next.'

'Ingredients for success on a plate', Peter Marsh, *Financial Times*, 26/3/08, p.16

Just as the knowledge push model involves a mixture of occasional breakthrough followed by extensive elaboration, so the same is true of need. Occasionally it involves a new to the world idea but mostly it is extensions, variations and adaptations around those core ideas. Figure 5.2 indicates a typical breakdown – and we could construct a similar picture for process innovations.

Understanding buyer/adopter behaviour has become a key theme in marketing studies since it provides us with frameworks and tools for identifying and understanding user needs. Advertising and branding plays a key role in this process, essentially using psychology to tune into – or even stimulate and create – basic human needs. And much recent research has focused on detailed ethnographic studies of what people actually do and how they actually use products and services – using the same approaches which anthropologists use to study strange new tribes – to uncover hidden and latent needs.

Need pull innovation is particularly important at mature stages in industry or product life cycles when there is more than one offering to choose from – competing depends on

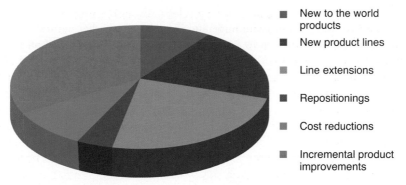

■ New to the world products

■ New product lines

■ Line extensions

■ Repositionings

■ Cost reductions

■ Incremental product improvements

FIGURE 5.2 Types of new product.

 Go online to find the cases of RED and Open Door projects and the Tesco Fresh 'n' easy example, which give illustrations of taking the use of ethnographic tools to get closer to user needs.

www.iande.info

differentiating on the basis of needs and attributes, and/or segmenting the offering to suit different adopter types. There are differences between business-to-business markets (where emphasis is on needs amongst a shared group, e.g. along a supply chain) and consumer markets where the underlying need may be much more basic – food, shelter, mobility – and appeal to a much greater number of people.

Sometimes the increase in the urgency of a need or the extent of demand can have a forcing effect on innovation – the example of wartime and other crises supports this view. For example, the demand for iron and iron products increased hugely in the Industrial Revolution and exposed the limitations of the old methods of smelting with charcoal – it created the pull which led to developments like the Bessemer converter. In similar fashion the emerging energy crisis with oil prices reaching unprecedented levels has created a significant pull for innovation around alternative energy sources – and an investment boom for such work.

A powerful example of the impact crisis can have on driving innovation can be seen in the context of major humanitarian crises – for example, after devastating earthquakes or hurricanes. The need to improvise solutions around logistics, shelter, healthcare, water and sanitation and energy force a rapid pace of innovation.

INNOVATION IN ACTION

ALNAP is a learning network of humanitarian agencies including organisations like the Red Cross, UNICEF, Médecins Sans Frontières and Christian Aid. It aims to share and build on

(continued)

experience gained through coping with humanitarian crises – whether natural or man-made – and has spent time reflecting on how many of the innovations developed as a response to urgent needs can be spread to others. Examples include high-energy biscuits which can be quickly distributed or building materials which can be deployed and assembled quickly into makeshift shelters. Their website gives a wide range of examples of such crisis-driven innovations.

www.alnap.org/resources/innovations.aspx

It's also important to recognise that innovation is not always about commercial markets or consumer needs. There is also a strong tradition of social need providing the pull for new products, processes and services – as we saw in Chapter 2 in talking about social entrepreneurship. Whether it is social needs like provision of healthcare or clean water in developing countries or more effective education or social services in established industrial economies, the need for change is clear and provides an engine for increasing innovation.

Making Processes Better

Of course, needs aren't just about external markets for products and services – we can see the same phenomenon of need pull working inside the business, as a driver of *process* innovation. 'Squeaking wheels' and other sources of frustration provide rich signals for change – and this kind of innovation is often something which can engage a high proportion of the workforce which experiences these needs first hand. (The successful model of 'kaizen' which underpins the success of firms like Toyota is fundamentally about sustained, high involvement incremental process innovation along these lines.) It provided the basic philosophy behind the 'total quality management' movement in the 1980s, the 'business process re-engineering' ideas of the 1990s and the current widespread application of concepts based on the idea of 'lean thinking' – essentially taking waste out of existing processes.

Go online to find some case examples of innovation in public sector services. More detailed examples and a wider discussion of 'high involvement innovation' can also be found. The video of Veeder Root, for instance, features a case example, and Emma Taylor, training manager at Denso, the giant Japanese manufacturer, talks in a video interview about her experiences in enabling high involvement/kaizen innovation.

www.iande.info

INNOVATION IN ACTION

'Pretty in Pink'

Walking through the plant belonging to Ace Trucks (a major producer of forklift trucks) in Japan the first thing which strikes you is the colour scheme. In fact you would need to be blind not to notice it – amongst the usual rather dull greys and greens of machine tools and other equipment there are flashes of pink. Not just a quiet pastel tone but a full-blooded, shocking pink which would do credit to even the most image-conscious flamingo. Closer inspection shows these flashes and splashes of pink are not random but associated with particular sections and parts of machines – and the eye-catching effect comes in part from the sheer number of pink-painted bits, distributed right across the factory floor and all over the different machines.

What is going on here is not a bizarre attempt to redecorate the factory or a failed piece of interior design. The effect of catching the eye is quite deliberate – the colour is there to draw attention to the machines and other equipment which have been modified. Every pink splash is the result of a kaizen project to improve some aspect of the equipment, much of it in support of the drive towards 'total productive maintenance' (TPM) in which every item of plant is available and ready for use 100% of the time. This is a goal like 'zero defects' in total quality – certainly ambitious, possibly an impossibility in the statistical sense, but one which focuses the minds of everyone involved and leads to extensive and impressive problem-finding and solving. TPM programmes have accounted for year on year cost savings of 10–15% in many Japanese firms and these savings are being ground out of a system which is already renowned for its lean characteristics.

Painting the improvements pink plays an important role in drawing attention to the underlying activity in this factory, in which systematic problem-finding and solving is part of 'the way we do things around here'. The visual cues remind everyone of the continuing search for new ideas and improvements, and often provide stimulus for other ideas or for places where the displayed pink idea can be transferred to. Closer inspection around the plant shows other forms of display – less visually striking but powerful nonetheless – charts and graphs of all shapes and sizes which focus attention on trends and problems as well as celebrating successful improvements. There are photographs and graphics which pose problems or offer suggested improvements in methods or working practices, and flipcharts and whiteboards covered with symbols and shapes of fish bones and other tools being used to drive the improvement process forward.

This kind of process improvement is of particular relevance in the public sector where the issue is not about creating wealth but providing value for money in service delivery. Many applications of 'lean' and similar concepts can be found which apply this principle – for example in reducing waiting times or improving patient safety in hospitals, in speeding up delivery of services like car taxation and passport issuing and even in improving the collection of taxes!

INNOVATION IN ACTION

Mindlab is a Danish organisation set up to promote and enable public sector innovation in Denmark. 'Owned' by the Ministries of Taxation, Employment and Economic Affairs, it has pioneered a series of initiatives engaging civil servants and members of the public in a wide range of social innovation which have raised productivity, improved service quality and cut costs across the public sector. Case studies of their activities can be found at their website: www.mind-lab.dk/en

Whose Needs? – Working at the Edge

One very interesting source of innovation lies at the edges of existing markets. Disruptive innovation is often associated with entrepreneurs working at the fringes of a mainstream market and finding groups whose needs are not being met. It poses a problem for existing players because the needs of such fringe groups are not seen as relevant to their 'mainstream' activities – and so they tend to ignore them or to dismiss them as not being important. But working with these users and their different needs creates different innovation options – and sometimes what has relevance for the fringe begins to be of interest to the mainstream. US professor Clayton Christensen in his many studies of such 'disruptive innovation' shows this has been the pattern across industries as diverse as computer disk drives, earth moving equipment, steel making and low-cost air travel.

For much of the time there is stability around markets where innovation of the 'do better' variety takes place and is well-managed. Close relationships with existing customers are fostered and the system is configured to deliver a steady stream of what the market wants – and often a great deal more! (What he terms 'technology overshoot' is often a characteristic of this, where markets are offered more and more features which they may not ever use or place much value on but which come as part of the package).

But somewhere else there is another group of potential users who have very different needs – usually for something much simpler and cheaper – which will help them get something done. For example the emergent home computer industry began amongst a small group of hobbyists who wanted simple computing capabilities at a much lower price than was available from the mini-computer suppliers. In turn the builders of those early PCs wanted disk drives which were much simpler technologically but – importantly – much cheaper and so were not really interested in what the existing disk drive industry had to offer. It was too high tech, massively over-engineered for their needs and, most important, much too expensive.

Although they approached the existing drive makers none of them was interested in making such a device – not surprisingly since they were doing very comfortably supplying expensive high-performance equipment to an established mini-computer industry. Why should they worry about a fringe group of hobbyists as a market? Steve Jobs described in an interview their attempts to engage interest, '. . . So we went to Atari and said, "Hey, we've got this amazing thing, even built with some of your parts, and what do you think about funding us? Or we'll give it to you. We just want to do it. Pay our salary, we'll come work for you." And they said,

"No." So then we went to Hewlett-Packard, and they said, "Hey, we don't need you. You haven't got through college yet."

Consequently the early PC makers had to look elsewhere – and found entrepreneurs willing to take the risks and experiment with trying to come up with a product which did meet their needs. It didn't happen overnight and there were plenty of failures on the way – and certainly the early drives were very poor performers in comparison with what was on offer in the mainstream industry. But gradually the PC market grew, moving from hobbyists to widespread home use and from there – helped by the emergence and standardisation of the IBM PC – to the office and business environment. And as it grew and matured so it learned and the performance of the machines became much more impressive and reliable – but coming from a much lower cost base than mini-computers. The same thing happened to the disk drives within them – the small entrepreneurial firms who began in the game grew and learned and became large suppliers of reliable products which did the job – but at a massively lower price.

Eventually the fringe market which the original disk drive makers had ignored because it didn't seem relevant or important enough to worry about grew to dominate – and by the time they realised this it was too late for many of them. The best they could hope for would be to be late entrant imitators, coming from behind and hoping to catch up.

This pattern is essentially one of *disruption* – the rules of the game changed dramatically in the marketplace with some new winners and losers. It can be seen in many industries – think about the low-cost airlines, for example. Here the original low-cost players didn't go head to head with the national flag carriers who offered the best routes, high levels of service and prime airport slots – all for a high price. Instead they sought new markets at the fringe – users who would accept a much lower level of service (no food, no seat allocation, no lounges, no frills at all) but for a basic safe flight would pay a much lower price. As these new users began to use the service and talk about it, so the industry grew and came to the attention of existing private and business travellers who were interested in lower cost flights at least for short-haul because it met their needs for a 'good enough' solution to their travel problem. Eventually the challenge hit the major airlines who found it difficult to respond because of their inherently much higher cost structure – even those like BA and KLM which set up low-cost subsidiaries found they were unable to manage with the very different business model low-cost flying involved.

Low-end market disruption of this kind is a potent threat – think what a producer in China might do to an industry like pump manufacturing if they began to offer a simple, low-cost, 'good enough' household pump for $10 instead of the high-tech high performance variants available from today's industry at prices 10 to 50 times as high? Or how will manufacturers of medical devices like asthma inhalers need to respond once they have come off-patent – a challenge already being posed in markets such as generic pharmaceuticals?

INNOVATION IN ACTION

India represents an interesting laboratory for the development of radically different products and services configured for a large but not particularly wealthy population. Examples include the

(continued)

Tata Nano car, which is now on sale for around $3000, and a mobile phone which retails at $20. In 2010 the country's Human Resources Development minister unveiled a $35 computer, targeted first at the school market (which is huge, around 110 million children in the first instance) and to be followed by higher education students. The minister commented that: 'The solutions for tomorrow will emerge from India. We have reached a stage that today, the motherboard, its chip, the processing, connectivity, all of them cumulatively cost around $35 [£23], including memory, display, everything.'

By way of comparison this tablet-style computer will compete with Apple's iPad currently retailing in the USA for $450. It will be a simple but robust device, running on open source Linux operating system, using Open Office software and can be powered by solar panel or batteries as well as mains electricity. It will have no hard drive but additional functionality can be provided via a USB port.

But it is also important to recognise that similar challenges to existing market structures can happen through 'high-end' disruption – as James Utterback, a key innovation researcher at MIT, points out. Where a group of users require something at a higher level than the current performance this can create new products or services which then migrate to mainstream expectations – for example, in the domestic broadband or mobile telephone markets.

Disruptive innovation examples of this kind focus attention on the need to look for needs which are not being met, or poorly met or sometimes where there is an overshoot. Each of these can provide a trigger for innovation – and often involve disruption because existing players don't see the different patterns of needs. This thinking is behind, for example, the concept of 'Blue Ocean' strategy, which argues for firms to define and explore uncontested market space by spotting latent needs which are not well-served.

INNOVATION IN ACTION

Gaining Competitive Edge through Meeting Unserved Needs

An example of the 'blue ocean' approach is the Nintendo Wii which has carved a major foothold in the lucrative computer games market – a business which is in fact bigger than Hollywood in terms of overall market value. The Wii console is not a particularly sophisticated piece of technology – compared to the rivals (Sony PS3 or the Microsoft Xbox) it has less computing power, storage or other features and the games graphics are much lower resolution than major sellers like 'Grand Theft Auto'. But the key to the phenomenal success of the Wii has been its appeal to an under-served market. Where computer games were traditionally targeted at boys the Wii extends – by means of a simple interface wand – their interest to all members of the family.

(continued)

Add-ons to the platform like the Wii board for keep fit and other applications and the market reach extends – for example to include the elderly or patients suffering the after-effects of stroke.

Nintendo has performed a similar act of opening up the marketplace with its DS handheld device – again by targeting unmet needs across a different segment of the population. Many DS users are middle-aged or retired and the best-selling games are for brain training and puzzles.

Over-served markets might include those for office software or computer operating systems where the continuing trend towards adding more and more features and functionality has possibly outstripped users' needs for or ability to use them all. Linux and open office applications such as 'Star Office' represent simpler, 'good enough' solutions to the basic needs of users – and are potential disruptive innovations for a player like Microsoft

Central to this idea is the role of entrepreneurs – by definition established players find it difficult to look at and work with the fringe since it is not their core business or main focus of attention. But entrepreneurs are looking for new opportunities to create value and working at the fringe may provide them with such inspiration. So the pattern of disruptive innovation is essentially one where entrepreneurs play a role in changing and reshaping business and social markets through often radical innovation. Smart organisations look to defend themselves against disruption to their world by setting up small entrepreneurial units with the licence to explore and behave exactly as free agents, challenging conventional approaches and looking at the edges of what the business does.

Go online to find the Philips and Cerulean cases for examples of disruptive innovation challenges and responses.

An audit tool is also available: 'How well do we manage discontinuous innovation'?

www.iande.info

Emerging Markets and the 'Bottom of the Pyramid'

One way in which this idea of looking at the edge of existing social and business markets comes sharply into focus is in considering the major growth in the world economy coming from what are termed 'emerging markets' – especially in the BRICs group of economies (Brazil, Russia, India and China). These contain large, young and increasingly affluent populations who are fuelling the demand for products and services and whose needs will increasingly shape the innovation agenda. But their needs may be fundamentally different to those of the markets we have traditionally focused upon – in other words, they may represent a 'fringe' group around whom radical innovations are created.

For example, India's giant Tata Corporation has been developing the '1 lakh car' – essentially a car for the Indian market which would retail for around $3000. Despite considerable cynicism from the industry the Nano has been launched at close to this price and represents the first response to a classic extreme environment challenge. Producing something at this target cost which also meets emission controls and provides a level of features to satisfy the growing Indian middle class is already a significant innovation achievement given that the closest competitor cars retail for nearly twice that price. Creating the wider system for service and support, for insurance, for financing purchase, for driver training and so on imply a very different approach to bringing driving within the reach of a large population. As low-cost airline and other disruptive innovators found, the learning effects across large volumes of rapidly growing markets mean that many innovative solutions are developed and create a business model which has significant challenges for established incumbents. Arguably this is not simply a local innovation but an experiment towards the kind of industry-changing system which Henry Ford pioneered a century ago.

Taking this idea further opens up the fascinating discussion first surfaced by the writer C.K. Prahalad who coined the phrase 'the fortune at the bottom of the pyramid'. He argued that nearly 80% of the world's population live on incomes below the poverty line – around $2 per day – and therefore do not represent 'markets' in the traditional sense. But seeing them as a vast reservoir of unserved needs opens up a significant challenge and opportunity for innovation. In the context of our discussion they are currently at the fringe of existing search – but there is a huge untapped source of opportunity there.

Solutions to meeting these needs will have to be highly innovative, but the prize is equally high – access to a high-volume, low-margin marketplace. For example Unilever realised the potential of selling their shampoos and other cosmetic products not in 250 ml bottles (which were beyond the price range of most 'bottom of the pyramid' (BoP) customers) but in single sachets. The resulting market growth has been phenomenal – and examples like this are fuelling major activity amongst large corporations looking to adapt their products and services to serve the BoP market.

As G. Gilbert Cloyd, Chief Technology Officer, Procter & Gamble commented in a *Business Week* interview, '. . . We've put more emphasis on serving an even broader base of consumers. We have the goal of serving the majority of the world's consumers someday. Today, we probably serve about 2 billion-plus consumers around the globe, but there are 6 billion consumers out there. That has led us to put increased emphasis on low-end markets and in mid- and low-level pricing tiers in developed geographies. That has caused us to put a lot more attention on the cost aspects of our products. . .'

For example in the Philippines there is little in the way of a formal banking system for the majority of people – and this has led to users creating very different applications for their mobile phones where pay as you go credits become a unit of currency to be transferred between people and used as currency for various goods and services. In Kenya it is used to increase security – if a traveller wishes to move between cities he or she will not take money but instead forward it via mobile phone in the form of credits which can then be collected from the phone recipient at the other end. This is only one of hundreds of new applications being developed in extreme conditions and by under-served users – and represents a powerful laboratory for new concepts which companies like Nokia and Vodafone are working closely to explore. The potential exists to use this kind of extreme environment as a laboratory to test and develop concepts for wider application – for example, Citicorp has been experimenting with a design of ATM based on biometrics for use with the illiterate population in rural India.

The pilot involves some 50,000 people but as a spokesman for the company explained, 'we see this as having the potential for global application'.

Go online to find an example of 'bottom of the pyramid' social innovation using mobile phones together with a podcast interview with Suzana Moreira, the founder.

www.iande.info

Significantly the needs of this BoP market cover the entire range of human wants and needs, from cosmetics and consumer goods through to basic healthcare and education. Prahalad's original book contains a wide range of case examples where this is beginning to happen and which indicate the huge potential of this group – but also the radical nature of the innovation challenge. Subsequently there has been significant expansion of innovative activity in these emerging market areas – driven in part by a realisation that the major growth in global markets will come from regions with a high BoP profile.

Go online to find the Aravind eye clinics case.
There is a case study of some examples written by Girish Prabhu, a director of Srishti Labs in Bangalore, specialists in developing 'bottom of pyramid' solutions.

www.iande.info

Importantly many companies are actively using 'bottom of pyramid' markets as places to search for weak signals of potentially interesting new developments. For example, Nokia has been sending scouts to study how people in rural Africa and India are using mobile phones and the potential for new services which this might offer, whilst the pharmaceutical firm Novo-Nordisk has been learning about low-cost provision of diabetes care in Tanzania as an input to a better understanding of how such models might be developed for different regions. We'll return to this theme when we look at the idea of 'extreme users' as sources of innovation.

Towards Mass Customisation

Another important source of innovation – and a key trend – is the rise of a desire for *customisation*. We can see this in the case of the motor car as one simple example. Arguably Henry Ford's plant, based on principles of mass production, represented the most efficient response to the market environment of its time. But that environment changed rapidly during the 1920s, so that what had begun as a winning formula for manufacturing began gradually to represent a major obstacle to change. Production of the Model T began in 1909 and for 15 years or so it was the market leader.

Despite falling margins the company managed to exploit its blueprint for factory technology and organisation to ensure continuing profits. But growing competition (particularly from General Motors with its strategy of product differentiation) was shifting away from trying to offer the customer low-cost personal transportation and towards other design features – such as the closed body – and Ford was increasingly forced to add features to the Model T. Eventually it was clear that a new model was needed and production of the Model T stopped in 1927.

Go online to find the Model T case.

www.iande.info

The trouble is that markets are not made up of people wanting the same thing – and there is an underlying challenge to meet their demands for variety and increasing customisation. This represents a powerful driver for innovation – as we move from conditions where products are in short supply to one of mass production so the demand for differentiation increases. There has always been a market for personalised custom made goods and, similarly, custom configured services – for example, personal shoppers, personal travel agents, personal physicians, etc. But until recently there was an acceptance that this customisation carried a high price tag and that mass markets could only be served with relatively standard product and service offerings.

ADVICE FOR FUTURE ENTREPRENEURS

One of the common mistakes we make in thinking about innovation is that we assume users are passive. But whilst not everyone may be able to design and build their own motor car, people do have wishes and aspirations which they'd like to see built into products. And they often have good ideas about particular features which they'd find useful or valuable – and which they would be prepared to pay for if they could see them implemented somewhere. So increasingly smart firms are realising the potential of working with users, capturing their ideas and co-creating products and services. This isn't going to happen just by advertising slogans – firms need to develop ways of finding who are the 'lead users' whose ideas and wishes would be worth capturing because they reflect the wider needs of a particular market. And they need new ways of working alongside them – for example via design studios, using the web to get ideas and discuss new concepts, etc. In the future an increasingly important skill set will be around:

- lead user identification;
- lead user design methods;
- co-design and co-creation tools;
- deployment of technologies like rapid prototyping, computer-aided design and manufacture.

However, a combination of enabling technologies and rising expectations has begun to shift this balance and resolve the trade-off between price and customisation. 'Mass customisation' (MC) is a widely used term which captures some elements of this. MC is the ability to offer highly configured bundles of non-price factors configured to suit different market segments (with the ideal target of total customisation: i.e. a market size of 1) – but to do this without incurring cost penalties and the setting up of a trade-off of agility vs. prices.

Of course there are different levels of customising – from simply putting a label 'specially made for . . . . . (insert your name here)' on a standard product right through to sitting down with a designer and co-creating something truly unique. Table 5.1 gives some examples of this range of options.

TABLE 5.1 Options in customisation (after Mintzberg and Lampel[1])

Type of customisation	Characteristics	Examples
Distribution customisation	Customers may customise product/service packaging, delivery schedule and delivery location but the actual product/service is standardised	Sending a book to a friend from Amazon.com. They will receive an individually wrapped gift with a personalised message from you – but it's actually all been done online and in their distribution warehouses. iTunes appears to offer personalisation of a music experience but in fact it does so right at the end of the production and distribution chain
Assembly customisation	Customers are offered a number of predefined options. Products/services are made to order using standardised components	Buying a computer from Dell or another online retailer. Customers choose and configure to suit their exact requirements from a rich menu of options – but Dell only start to assemble this (from standard modules and components) when your order is finalised. Banks offering tailor-made insurance and financial products are actually configuring these from a relatively standard set of options

(continued)

TABLE 5.1	(*Continued*)	
Type of customisation	**Characteristics**	**Examples**
Fabrication customisation	Customers are offered a number of predefined designs. Products/services are manufactured to order	Buying a luxury car like a BMW, where the customers are involved in choosing ('designing') the configuration which best meets their needs and wishes – for engine size, trim levels, colour, fixtures and extras, etc. Only when they are satisfied with the virtual model they have chosen does the manufacturing process begin – and they can even visit the factory to watch their car being built
		Services allow a much higher level of such customisation since there is less of an asset base needed to set up for 'manufacturing' the service – examples here would include made to measure tailoring, personal planning for holidays, pensions, etc.
Design customisation	Customer input stretches to the start of the production process. Products do not exist until initiated by a customer order	Co-creation, where end users may not even be sure what it is they want but where – sitting down with a designer – they co-create the concept and elaborate it. It's a little like having some clothes made but rather than choosing from a pattern book they actually have a designer with them and create the concept together. Only when it exists as a firm design idea does it then get made. Co-creation of services can be found in fields like entertainment (where user-led models like YouTube are posing significant challenges to mainstream providers) and in healthcare where experiments towards radical alternatives for healthcare delivery are being explored – see, for example, the Design Council RED project which is discussed on the website

This trend has important implications for services, in part because of the difficulty of sustaining an entry barrier for long. Service innovations are often much easier to imitate and the competitive advantages which they offer can quickly be competed away because there are fewer barriers to entry or options for protecting intellectual property. The pattern of airline innovation on the transatlantic route provides a good example of this – there is a fast pace of innovation but as soon as one airline introduces something like a flat bed, others will quickly emulate it. Arguably the drive to personalisation of the service experience will be strong because it is only through such customised experiences that a degree of customer 'lock on' takes place.

Certainly the experience of internet banking and insurance suggests that, despite attempts to customise the experience via sophisticated web technologies, there is little customer loyalty and a high rate of churn. However the lower capital cost of creating and delivering services and their relative simplicity makes co-creation more of an option. Where manufacturing may require sophisticated tools like computer-aided design and rapid prototyping, services lend themselves to shared experimentation at relatively lower cost. There is growing interest in such models involving active users in design of services – for example, in the open source movement around software or in the digital entertainment and communication fields where community and social networking sites like Facebook, Flickr and YouTube have had a major impact.

Go online to find an extended discussion of agility and mass customisation. You will also find a link to Frank Piller's own website where he discusses this concept and gives a rich set of case examples.

www.iande.info

Once again we should be clear that this is not simply a trend in the commercial marketplace; social innovation is increasingly about trying to match particular needs of different groups in society with solutions that work for them. Customising solutions for the delivery of public services to different groups is becoming a major agenda item, particularly as governments and service providers recognise that 'one size fits all' is not a model which applies well.

Go online to find website links to the Threadless and the Lego cases.

www.iande.info

Understanding what it is that customers value and need is critical in pursuing a customisation strategy – and it leads, inevitably, to the next source of innovation in which the users themselves become the source of ideas.

Users as Innovators

It is easy to fall into the trap of thinking about need pull innovation as involving a process in which user needs are identified and then something is created to meet those needs. This assumes that users are passive recipients – but this is often not the case. In many cases users are ahead of the game – their ideas plus their frustrations with existing solutions lead them to experiment and create something new. And sometimes these prototypes eventually become mainstream innovations.

Eric von Hippel[2] of Massachusetts Institute of Technology has made a lifelong study of this phenomenon and gives the example of the pickup truck – a long-time staple of the world automobile industry. This major category did not begin life on the drawing boards of Detroit, but rather on the farms and homesteads of a wide range of users who wanted more than a family saloon. They adapted their cars by removing seats, welding new pieces on and cutting off the roof – in the process prototyping and developing the early model of the pickup. Only later did Detroit pick up on the idea and then begin the incremental innovation process to refine and mass produce the vehicle. A host of other examples support the view that user-led innovation matters – for example, petroleum refining, medical devices, semiconductor equipment, scientific instruments, a wide range of sports goods and the Polaroid camera. Importantly, active and interested users – 'lead users' – are often well ahead of the market in terms of innovation needs.

 Go online to find the website link to 3M videos on user-led innovation.

www.iande.info

One of the fields where this has played a major role is in medical devices where active users amongst medical professionals have provided a rich source of innovations for decades. Central to their role in the innovation process is that they are very early on the adoption curve for new ideas – they are concerned with getting solutions to particular needs and prepared to experiment and tolerate failure in their search for a better solution. One strategy – which we will explore later – around managing innovation is thus to identify and engage with such 'lead users' to co-create innovative solutions.

Tim Craft, a practising anaesthetist, developed a range of connectors and other equipment as a response to frustrations and concerns about the safety aspects of the equipment he was using in operating theatres. He describes the birth of the company and the underlying philosophy in the podcast interview on the website.

Go online to find the podcast interview with Tim Craft, founder of Anaesthetic Medical Systems and a classic 'user-innovator'.

www.iande.info

INNOVATION IN ACTION

User Involvement in Innovation

One of the key lessons about successful innovation is the need to get close to the customer. At the limit the user can become a key part of the innovation process, feeding in ideas and improvements to help define and shape the innovation. The Danish medical devices company, Coloplast, was founded in 1954 on these principles when nurse Elise Sorensen developed the first self-adhering ostomy bag as a way of helping her sister, a stomach cancer patient. She took her idea to various plastics manufacturers, but none showed interest at first. Eventually one, Aage Louis-Hansen, discussed the concept with his wife, also a nurse. She saw the potential of such a device and persuaded her husband to give the product a chance. Hansen's company, Dansk Plastic Emballage, produced the world's first disposable ostomy bag in 1955. Sales exceeded expectations and in 1957, after having taken out a patent for the bag in several countries, the Coloplast company was established. Today the company has factories in five countries around the world, and subsidiaries in 20, with specialist divisions dealing with incontinence care, wound care, skin care, mastectomy care, consumer products (specialist clothing etc.) as well as the original ostomy care division.

Keeping close to users in a field like this is crucial and Coloplast has developed novel ways of building in such insights by making use of panels of users, specialist nurses and other health-care professionals located in different countries. This has the advantage of getting an informed perspective from those involved in post-operative care and treatment and who can articulate needs which might for the individual patient be difficult or embarrassing to express. By setting up panels in different countries the varying cultural attitudes and concerns could also be built into product design and development.

An example is the Coloplast Ostomy Forum (COF) Board approach. The core objective within COF Boards is to try to create a sense of partnership with key players, either as key customers or key influencers. Selection is based on an assessment of their technical experience and competence but also on the degree to which they will act as opinion leaders and gatekeepers – for example, by influencing colleagues, authorities, hospitals and patients. They are also a key link in the clinical trials process. Over the years Coloplast has become quite skilled in identifying relevant people who would be good COF Board members – for example, by tracking people who author clinical articles or who have a wide range of experience

(*continued*)

across different operation types. Their specific role is particularly to help with two elements in innovation:

- identify, discuss and prioritise user needs;
- evaluate product development projects from idea generation right through to international marketing.

Importantly COF Boards are seen as integrated with the company's product development system and they provide valuable market and technical information into the stage gate decision process. This input is mainly associated with early stages around concept formulation (where the input is helpful in testing and refining perceptions about real user needs and fit with new concepts). There is also significant involvement around project development where involvement is concerned with evaluating and responding to prototypes, suggesting detailed design improvements, design for usability, etc.

Go online to find an extended case study of Coloplast.

www.iande.info

Sometimes user-led innovation involves a community which creates and uses innovative solutions on a continuing basis – a state which has been called 'perpetual beta', referring to the old idea of testing new software modules across a community to get feedback and development ideas. Good examples of this include communities around Linux software, Apache servers, Mozilla (with Firefox, Thunderbird and other open source tools), Propellerhead and other music software communities and the emergent group around Apple's i-platform devices like the iPhone.

Increasing interest is being shown in 'crowdsourcing' approaches to co-creating innovations – essentially new ways of creating and working with such communities. The principle extends beyond software and virtual applications – for example, Lego makes extensive use of communities of developers in its Lego Factory and other online activities linked to its manufactured products. Adidas has taken the model and developed its *'mi Adidas'* concept where users are encouraged to co-create their own shoes using a combination of website (where designs can be explored and uploaded) and in-store mini-factories where user created and customised ideas can then be produced.

Such engagement may provide a powerful new resource for the 'front end' of innovation. One example is Goldcorp – a struggling mining company which threw open its geological data and asked for ideas about where it should prospect. Tapping into the combined insights of 1200 people from 50 countries helped them find 110 new sites, 80% of which produced gold. The business has grown from $100m in 1999 to over $9bn today. Companies like Swarowski have recruited an army of new designers using 'crowdsourcing' approaches – and in the process have massively increased their design capacity. Organisations like the BBC, Lego and Ordnance Survey are increasingly engaging communities of software developers, sharing source code and inviting them to 'use our stuff to build your stuff'.

INNOVATION IN ACTION

Open Collective Innovation

An increasingly important element in the innovation equation is *co*-creation – using the ideas, experience and insights of many people across a community to generate innovation. For example, Encyclopaedia Britannica was founded in and currently has around 65,000 articles. Until 1999 it was available only in print version but, in response to a growing number of CD and online based competitors (such as Microsoft's Encarta) it now has an online version. Encarta was launched in 1993 and offered many new additions to the Britannica model, through multimedia illustrations carried on a CD/DVD; like Britannica it was available in a limited number of different languages.

By contrast Wikipedia is a newcomer, launched in 2004 and available free on the Internet. It has become the dominant player in terms of online searches for information and is currently the sixth most visited site in the world. Its business model is fundamentally different – it is available free and is constructed through the shared contributions and updates offered by members of the public.

A criticism of Wikipedia is that this model means that inaccuracies are likely to appear but, although the risk remains, there are self-correcting systems in play, which mean that if it is wrong it will be updated and corrected quickly. A study by the journal *Nature* in 2005 (15 December) found it to be as accurate as *Encyclopaedia Britannica* yet the latter employs around 4000 expert reviewers and a rewrite (including corrections) takes around 5 years to complete.

Encarta closed at the end of 2009 but *Encyclopaedia Britannica* continues to compete in this knowledge market. After 300 years of an expert-driven model it moved, in January 2009, to extend its model and invite users to edit content using a variant on the Wikipedia approach. Shortly after that (February 2010) it discovered an error in its coverage of a key event in Irish history which had gone uncorrected in all its previous editions and only emerged when users pointed it out!

In similar fashion Facebook chose to engage its users in helping to translate the site into multiple languages rather than commission an expert translation service. Its motive was to try and compete with MySpace, which in 2007 was the market leader, available in five languages. The Facebook 'crowdsource' project began in December 2007 and invited users to help translate around 30,000 key phrases from the site: 8000 volunteer developers registered within 2 months and within 3 weeks the site was available in Spanish, with pilot versions in French and German also online. Within a year Facebook was available in over 100 languages and dialects – and like Wikipedia it continues to benefit from continuous updating and correction via its user community.

We will return to this theme in more detail in Chapter 8 where we look at the increasingly important role of external networks in innovation.

Extreme Users

An important variant which picks up on both the lead user and the fringe needs concepts lies in the idea of extreme environments as a source of innovation. The argument here is that the users in the toughest environments may have needs which by definition are at the edge – so any innovative solution which meets those needs has possible applications back in the mainstream. An example would be antilock braking systems (ABS) which are now a commonplace feature of cars but which began life as a special add-on for premium high-performance cars. The origins of this innovation came from a more extreme case, though – the need to stop aircraft safely under difficult conditions where traditional braking might lead to skidding or other loss of control. ABS was developed for this extreme environment and then migrated across to the (comparatively) easier world of automobiles.

Looking for extreme environments or users can be a powerful source of stretch in terms of innovation – meeting challenges which can then provide new opportunity space. The message is clear from the title of a famous paper by Rothwell and Gardiner,[3] 'tough customers mean good designs'. For example, stealth technology arose out of a very specific and extreme need for creating an invisible aeroplane – essentially something which did not have a radar signature. It provided a powerful pull for some radical innovation which challenged fundamental assumptions about aircraft design, materials, power sources etc. and opened up a wide frontier for changes in aerospace and related fields. The 'bottom of the pyramid' concept mentioned earlier also offers some powerful extreme environments in which very different patterns of innovation are emerging. And the crisis innovations emerging from sites of disasters via humanitarian agencies offer another powerful set of examples.

Watching Others

Innovation is essentially a competitive search for new or different solutions – whether in the sense of commercial enterprises competing with each other for market share or in the wider sense of creating social value, where the competition is for doing more with limited resources, or between law and order vs. crime, or education and illiteracy. In such a contest one important strategy involves learning from others – imitation is not only the sincerest form of flattery but also a viable and successful strategy for sourcing innovation. For example, reverse engineering of products and processes and development of imitations – even around impregnable patents – is a well-known route to find ideas. Much of the rapid progress of Asian economies in the post-war years was based on a strategy of 'copy and develop', taking Western ideas and improving on them.

For example much of the early growth in Korean manufacturing industries in fields like machine tools came from adopting a strategy of 'copy and develop' – essentially learning (often as a result of taking licences or becoming service agents) by working with established products and understanding how they might be adapted or developed for the local market. Subsequently this learning could be used to develop new generations of products or services.

A wide range of tools for competitor product and process profiling has been developed which provide structured ways of learning from what others do or offer.

Go online to find tools for competitiveness profiling.

www.iande.info

One powerful variation on this theme is the concept of benchmarking. In this process enterprises make structured comparisons with others to try to identify new ways of carrying out particular processes or to explore new product or service concepts. The learning triggered by benchmarking may arise from comparing between similar organisations (same firm, same sector, etc.), or it may come from looking outside the sector but at similar products or processes.

For example, Southwest Airlines became the most successful carrier in the USA by dramatically reducing the turnaround times at airports – an innovation which it learned from studying pit stop techniques in the Formula 1 Grand Prix events. Similarly the Karolinska Hospital in Stockholm made significant improvements to its cost and time performance through studying inventory management techniques in advanced factories.

Go online to find the Karolinska Hospital case.

www.iande.info

Benchmarking of this kind is increasingly being used to drive change across the public sector, both via 'league tables' linked to performance metrics which aim to encourage fast transfer of good practice between schools or hospitals and also via secondment, visits and other mechanisms designed to facilitate learning from other sectors managing similar process issues such as logistics and distribution. One of the most successful applications of benchmarking has been in the development of the concept of 'lean' thinking, now widely applied to a many public and private sector organisations. The origins were in a detailed benchmarking study of car manufacturing plants during the 1980s which identified significant performance differences and triggered a search for the underlying process innovations which were driving the differences.

Go online to find benchmarking tools.

www.iande.info

Recombinant Innovation

Another easy assumption to make about innovation is that it always has to involve something new to world. The reality is that there is plenty of scope for cross-over – ideas and applications which are commonplace in one world may be perceived as new and exciting in another. This is an important principle in sourcing innovation where transferring or combining old ideas in new contexts – a process called' recombinant innovation' by US researcher Andrew Hargadon – can be a powerful resource. The Reebok pump running shoe, for example, was a significant product innovation in the highly competitive world of sports equipment – yet although this represented a breakthrough in that field it drew on core ideas which were widely used in a different world. Design Works, the agency which came up with the design, brought together a team which included people with prior experience in fields like paramedic equipment (from which they took the idea of an inflatable splint providing support and minimising shock to bones) and operating theatre equipment (from which they took the micro-bladder valve at the heart of the pump mechanisms).

Many businesses – as Hargadon points out – are able to offer rich innovation possibilities primarily because they have deliberately recruited teams with diverse industrial and professional backgrounds and thus bring very different perspectives to the problem in hand. His studies of the design company IDEO show the potential for such recombinant innovation work.

Nor is this a new idea. Thomas Edison's famous 'Invention Factory' in New Jersey was founded in 1876 with the grand promise of *'a minor* invention *every ten days and a big thing every six month or so'*. They were able to deliver on that promise not because of the lone genius of Edison himself but rather from taking on board the recombinant lesson – Edison hired scientists and engineers from all the emerging new industries of early twentieth-century USA. In doing so he brought experience in technologies and applications like mass production and precision machining (gun industry), telegraphy and telecommunications, food processing and canning, automobile manufacture, etc. Some of the early innovations which built the reputation of the business – for example the teleprinter for the New York Stock Exchange – were really simple cross-over applications of well-known innovations in other sectors.

Regulation

Photographs of the industrial towns around the Midlands of the UK taken in the early part of the twentieth century would not be much use in tracing landmarks or spotting key geographical features. The images in fact would reveal very little at all, not because of a limitation in the photographic equipment or processing but because the subject matter itself – the urban landscape – was rendered largely invisible by the thick smog which regularly enveloped the area. Yet 60 years later the same images would show up crystal clear, not because the factories had closed (although there are fewer of them) but because of the continuing effects of the Clean Air Act and other legislation. They provide a clear reminder of another important source of innovation – the stimulus given by changes in the rules and regulations which define the various 'games' for business and society. The Clean Air Act didn't specify how but only what had to change – achieving the reduction in pollutants emitted to the atmosphere involved extensive innovation in materials, processes and even in product design made by the factories.

Regulation in this way acts as a double-edged sword – it both restricts certain things (and closes off avenues along which innovation had been taking place) and opens up new ones along which change is mandated to happen. One of the powerful drivers for moving into environmentally sustainable 'clean' technologies is the increasingly tough legislation in areas like carbon emissions and pollution.

And it works the other way – deregulation, the slackening off of controls, may open up new innovation space. The liberalisation and then privatisation of telecommunications in many countries led to rapid growth in competition and high rates of innovation, for example.

Given the pervasiveness of legal frameworks in our lives we shouldn't be surprised to see this source of innovation. From the moment we get up and turn the radio on (regulation of broadcasting shaping the range and availability of the programmes we listen to) to eating our breakfast (food and drink is highly regulated in terms of what can and can't be included in ingredients, and how foods are tested before being allowed for sale, etc.) to climbing into our cars and buckling on our safety belt whilst switching on our hands-free phone devices (both the result of safety legislation), the role of regulation in shaping innovation can be seen.

Regulation can also trigger counter-innovation – solutions designed to get round existing rules or at least bend them to advantage. The rapid growth in speed cameras as a means of enforcing safety legislation on roads throughout Europe has led to the healthy growth of an industry providing products or services for detecting and avoiding cameras. And, at the limit, changes in the regulatory environment can create radical new space and opportunity. Although Enron ended its days as a corporation in disgrace due to financial impropriety it is worth asking how a small gas pipeline services company rose to become such a powerful beast in the first place. The answer was its rapid and entrepreneurial take up of the opportunities opened up by deregulation of markets for utilities like gas and electricity.

Futures and Forecasting

Another source of stimuli for innovation comes through imagining and exploring alternative trajectories to the dominant version in everyday use. Various tools and techniques for forecasting and imagining alternative futures are used to help strategy-making – but can also be used to stimulate imagination around new possibilities in innovation. For example, Shell has a long history of exploring future options and driving innovations, most recently through its Game changer programme. Sometimes various 'transitional objects' are used, like concept models and prototypes in the context of product development, to explore reactions and provide a focus for various different kinds of input which might shape and co-create future products and services.

Go online to find a podcast interview with Helen King of the Irish Food Board, who describes how they make use of futures to help alert the industry to new challenges. The Philips case study shows how a large company makes use of futures tools. Some examples of futures tools can also be found on the website.

www.iande.info

There is more about futures tools and their use in Chapter 7.

Accidents

Accidents and unexpected events happen – and in the course of a carefully planned R&D project they could be seen as annoying disruptions. But on occasion accidents can also trigger innovation, opening up surprisingly new lines of attack. The famous example of Fleming's discovery of penicillin is but one of many stories in which mistakes and accidents turned out to trigger important innovation directions. For example, the famous story of 3M's 'Post-it' notes began when a polymer chemist mixed an experimental batch of what should have been a good adhesive but which turned out to have rather weak properties – sticky but not very sticky. This failure in terms of the original project provided the impetus for what has become a billion dollar product platform for the company.

In another example from the late 1908s, scientists working for Pfizer began testing what was then known as compound UK-92,480 for the treatment of angina. Although promising in the lab and in animal tests, the compound showed little benefit in clinical trials in humans. Despite these initial negative results the team pursued what was an interesting side-effect which eventually led to UK-92,480 becoming the blockbuster drug Viagra.

The secret is not so much recognising that such stimuli are available but rather in creating the conditions under which they can be noticed and acted upon. As Pasteur is reputed to have said, 'chance favours the prepared mind'. Using mistakes as a source of ideas only happens if the conditions exist to help it emerge. A study by Chesbrough[4] of Xerox highlighted the fact that they developed many technologies in its laboratories in Palo Alto which did not easily fit their image of themselves as 'the document company'. These included Ethernet (later successfully commercialised by 3Com and others) and PostScript language (taken forward by Adobe Systems). In fact 11 of 35 rejected projects from Xerox's labs were later commercialised with the resulting businesses having a market capitalisation of twice that of Xerox itself.

In similar fashion shocks to the system which fundamentally change the rules provide not only a threat to the existing status quo but a powerful stimulus to find and develop something new. The tragedy of the 9/11 bombing of the Twin Towers served to change fundamentally public sense of security – but it has also provided a huge stimulus to innovate in areas like security, alternative transportation, fire safety and evacuation, etc.

INNOVATION IN ACTION

Cleaning Up by Accident

Audley Williamson is not a household name of the Thomas Edison variety but he was a successful innovator whose UK business sold for £135m in 2004. The core product which he invented was called 'Swarfega' and offered a widely used and dermatologically safe cleaner for skin. It is a greenish gel which has achieved widespread use in households as a simple and robust aid with

(continued)

the advertising slogan 'clean hands in a flash!' But the original product was not designed for this market at all – it was developed in 1941 as a mild detergent to wash silk stockings. Unfortunately the invention of Nylon and its rapid application in stockings meant that the market quickly disappeared and he was forced to find an alternative. Watching workers in a factory trying to clean their hands with an abrasive mixture of petrol, paraffin and sand which left their hands cracked and sore led him to rethink the use of his gel as a safer alternative.

(*The Independent*, 28/2/2006, p.7)

A Framework for Looking at Innovation Sources

Push or Pull Innovation?

If we take a broad overview we can see that all of these sources can be looked at as either a 'push' or a 'pull' stimulus for innovation. And this raises the question: which is more important? This has been the subject of many innovation studies over the years, using a variety of different methods to try and establish which is more important (and therefore where organisations might best place their resources). The reality is that innovation is never a simple matter of push or pull but rather their interaction: as Chris Freeman said, 'Necessity may be the mother of invention but procreation needs a partner!' Innovations tend to resolve intovectors – combinations of the two core principles. And these direct our attention in two complementary directions – creating possibilities (or at least keeping track of what others are doing along the R&D frontier) and identifying and working with needs.

Importantly the role of needs in innovation is often to translate or select from the range of knowledge push possibilities the variant which becomes the dominant strain. Out of all the possible bicycle ideas we eventually got to the dominant design – which is with us today. The iPod wasn't the first MP3 player but it somehow clicked as the one which resonated best with user needs.

In fact most of the sources of innovation we mentioned above involve both push and pull components – for example, 'applied R&D' involves directing the push search in areas of particular need. Regulation both pushes in key directions and pulls innovations through in response to changed conditions. User-led innovation may be triggered by user needs but it often involves them creating new solutions to old problems – essentially pushing the frontier of possibility in new directions.

There is a risk in focusing on either of the 'pure' forms of push or pull sources. If we put all our eggs in one basket we risk being excellent at invention but without turning our ideas into successful innovations – a fate shared by too many would-be entrepreneurs. But equally too close an ear to the market may limit us in our search – as Henry Ford is reputed to have said, 'If I had asked the market they would have said they wanted faster horses!' The limits of even the best market research lie in the fact that they represent sophisticated ways of asking people's reactions to something which is already there – rather than allowing for something completely outside their experience so far.

Incremental or Radical?

Another key dimension is around incremental or radical innovation. We've seen that there is a pattern of what could be termed 'punctuated equilibrium' with innovation – most of the time innovation is about exploiting and elaborating, creating variations on a theme within an established technical, market or regulatory trajectory. But occasionally there is a breakthrough which creates a new trajectory – and the cycle repeats itself. This suggests that much of our attention in searching for innovation triggers will be around incremental improvement innovation – the different versions of a piece of software, the Mk 2, 3, 4 of a product or the continuing improvement of a business process to make it closer to lean. But we will need to have some element of our portfolio focused on the longer range, higher risk which might lead to the breakthrough and set up a new trajectory.

Timing

A third issue is around timing – at different stages in the product or industry life cycle the emphasis may be more or less on push or pull. For example, mature industries will tend to focus on pull, responding to different market needs and differentiating by incremental innovation in key directions of user need. By contrast a new industry – for example, the emergent industries based on genetics or nano materials technology – is often about solutions looking for a problem. So we would expect a different balance of resources committed to push or pull within these different stages.

This kind of thinking is reflected in models of the 'innovation life cycle' which see innovation as moving through different stages. It begins with an early 'fluid' stage, characterised by extensive experimentation and with emphasis on product – creating a radical new offering. As the dominant design emerges attention shifts towards more incremental variation around the core trajectory – and as the industry matures so emphasis shifts to process innovation aimed at improving parameters like cost and quality. Once again this helps allocate scarce search resources in particular ways.

INNOVATION IN ACTION

The Innovation Life Cycle

Sometimes it is helpful to understand a little about timing in innovation strategy – at what stage in the innovation life cycle are we and what implications does that have for the kind of projects we might undertake? Back in the 1970s two US researchers (William Abernathy and James Utterback) developed a model which has three different phases with important lessons for how we think about managing innovation. In the early stage – the 'fluid' phase – there is a lot of uncertainty and emphasis is placed on product innovation. Typically entrepreneurs have lots of ideas (most of which fail)

(continued)

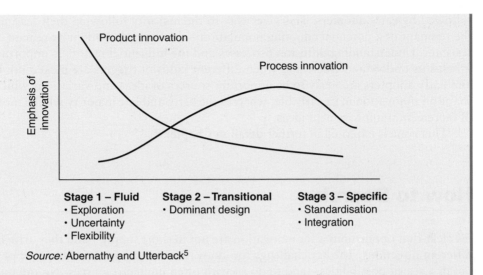

Stage 1 – Fluid
- Exploration
- Uncertainty
- Flexibility

Stage 2 – Transitional
- Dominant design

Stage 3 – Specific
- Standardisation
- Integration

Source: Abernathy and Utterback[5]

about the ways to use new market and technological opportunities. (Think about the rise of the Internet and the continuing proliferation of entrepreneurial ideas as an example of a fluid phase.)

But after a while there is a stabilisation around a particular configuration – the 'dominant design' (which may not always be the best in technical terms but which is the one which matches the markets' needs and aspirations) and then emphasis shifts away from more product variety to process innovation. How can we make this in volume, to a low price, consistent quality, etc? (Think of Henry Ford – he was a latecomer to the business of car design but his Model T became the dominant design and succeeded principally because of the extensive process innovations around mass production.)

Finally there is a third, 'mature' phase in which innovation is incremental in both product and process, there is extensive competition – and the scene is set for another breakthrough and return to the fluid stage.

What this model means is that we might particularly look for radical product innovation ideas in the fluid phase but in the mature stage we would be better placed concentrating on incremental improvement innovations.

 Go online to find an example that illustrates a pattern of innovation life cycles associated with the bicycles industry.

www.iande.info

Adoption and Diffusion

A fourth and related issue is around diffusion – the adoption and elaboration of innovation over time. Innovation adoption takes place gradually over time, following some version of an S-curve. At the early stages innovative users with high tolerance for failure will explore to be followed by early adopters. This gives way to the majority following their lead until finally the remnant of a potential adopting population – the laggards – adopt or remain stubbornly resistant. Understanding diffusion processes and the influential factors is important because it helps us understand where and when different kinds of triggers are picked up. Lead users and early adopters are likely to be important sources of ideas and variations which can help shape an innovation in its early life, whereas the early and late majority will be more a source of incremental improvement ideas.

This issue is explored in further detail in Chapter 7.

How to Search

It's clear that opportunities for innovation are not in short supply – and they arise from many different directions. The key challenge for innovation management is how to spot the potential in a sea of possibilities – and to do so with often limited resources. No organisation can hope to cover all the bases so there needs to be some underlying strategy to how the search process is undertaken. Whether it is our entrepreneur seeking to find some innovation space to start a new venture which will change the world, or an intrapreneur inside a giant corporation seeking to renew and regenerate itself, there is a need to explore in a systematic rather than a random way. That's the subject of the next chapter.

STRATEGIC AND SOCIAL IMPACT

Faced with the challenge of a widely differing workforce, many of whom lacked manufacturing skills and in a lot of cases spoke poor English as a second language, Henry Ford and his engineers used 'scientific management' principles to develop an alternative approach to making cars. From a highly variable activity with low productivity and variable quality the 'mass production' system changed car manufacturing dramatically.

There is little doubt that this was a 'better' way of making cars – at least in terms of the overall production figures (although the question of whether the conditions under which manufacturing took place is perhaps more open to question), but the trap it set was to help embed the powerful beliefs that this was something which only specialists could be involved in designing and refining. Henry Ford is reputed to have once complained 'How come when I want a pair of hands I get a human being as well?'

The justification for this separation of hand and brain was that a well-designed system should not be interfered with through the introduction of unnecessary variation. A consequence – easy to see with hindsight but less so in the context of what were significant improvements in productivity and quality – was that many early mass production factories came to resemble giant

(continued)

machines staffed by an army of human robots. The images in Charlie Chaplin's famous film 'Modern Times' provide a picture of this kind of work which is not heavily exaggerated!

The trouble is that many of the underlying beliefs about how far employees can be trusted to make improvements remain in the twenty-first century. The paradox which this raises is simple to express but hard to understand. Organisations need creativity and active learning in order to survive in a hostile environment. In today's turbulent times with challenges coming from all directions – uncertainty in competing in a global market, uncertainty in political and social stability, technological frontiers being pushed back at a dizzying pace – the one certainty is that we need all the creativity and learning capacity that we can get.

The idea that people can contribute to innovation through suggesting and implementing their ideas isn't new. Attempts to utilise this approach in a formal way can be traced back to the eighteenth century, when the 8th shogun Yoshimune Tokugawa introduced the suggestion box in Japan. In 1871 Denny's shipyard in Dumbarton, Scotland, employed a programme of incentives to encourage suggestions about productivity-improving techniques; they sought to draw out *'any change by which work is rendered either superior in quality or more economical in cost'*.

These days many organisations try to implement some form of employee involvement and the gains from doing so are becoming increasingly apparent. For example, the national UK Workplace Employee Relations Survey found a link between the use of more human resource management (HR) practices and a range of positive outcomes, including greater employee involvement, satisfaction and commitment, productivity and better financial performance.

DEVELOPING PERSONAL CAPABILITIES

Implementing high involvement innovation will need skills in dealing with questions like these:

Question	Response required
What's in it for people?	Putting in place some form of recognition/reward system which acknowledges their contribution
How to do it?	Training and skills development around problem-finding and solving and related innovation capabilities
	Setting up suitable vehicles – problem-solving teams, quality circles or whatever – to carry through innovation activities

(continued)

Question	Response required
Who is going to help support them?	Identification and training of suitable facilitators Commitment of senior management to support and champion the cause
How will this fit in?	Ensuring that organisational structures and systems support rather than block innovation behaviour Making space and time available to carry out innovation activities
How will the flow of ideas be managed?	Putting in place some form of idea management system
How to maintain momentum?	Ensuring this is more than another 'fashion statement' by the organisation Planning for long-term strategic development of innovation capability
Where and how to get started?	Identifying suitable pilot areas/teams/projects

Chapter Summary

1   Innovations don't just appear perfectly formed – and the process is not simply a spark of imagination giving rise to changing the world. Instead, innovations come from a number of sources and these interact over time.

2   Sources of innovation can be resolved into two broad classes – knowledge push and need pull – although they almost always act in tandem. Innovation arises from the interplay between them.

3   There are many variations on this theme – for example, 'need pull' can include social needs, market needs, latent needs ('squeaking wheels'), crisis needs, etc.

4   Whilst the basic forces pushing and pulling have been a feature of the innovation landscape for a long time it involves a moving frontier in which new sources of push and pull come into play. Examples include the emerging demand pull from the 'bottom of the pyramid' and the opportunities opened up by an acceleration in knowledge production in R&D systems around the world.

5   Regulation is also an important element in shaping and directing innovative activity – by restricting what can and can't be done for legal reasons, new trajectories for change are established, which entrepreneurs can take advantage of.

6   Entrepreneurs need some form of framework to make sense of the multiple sources of innovation open to them. Dimension of this could include:
   - push or pull?
   - incremental or radical?
   - timing across the innovation life cycle?
   - how do adoption and diffusion shape innovation trajectories?

Key Terms Defined

Benchmarking   approach to learning from others by systematic comparison of products, services or processes – can provide rich source of innovative ideas.

Bottom of the pyramid   term coined to describe the 5 billion people in the global population on low incomes. Innovations to meet their needs are likely to be significantly different to those for 'mainstream' industrialised country markets.

Disruptive innovation   innovation triggered by developments at the edge of existing markets and/or technologies which migrates to the centre stage and disrupts the current game.

Extreme users   fringe markets with very different and often difficult conditions which force radically different innovation directions.

High involvement innovation   pattern in which the majority of the workforce engage in contributing ideas for innovation.

Innovation life cycle   model proposed by Abernathy and Utterback to describe the different patterns of innovation over time in particular technology/market contexts.

Kaizen   Japanese term for continuous improvement, systematic pattern of sustained incremental innovation.

Knowledge push   innovation triggered by advances in science and technology which enables new possibilities.

Mass customisation   providing innovative solutions tailored to individual preferences but delivered at low cost and to high volume of users.

Need pull   innovation triggered by social or market need.

Open collective innovation   pattern of co-creation amongst wide range of users enabled by Web 2.0 and other communication technologies.

Recombinant innovation   transferring an idea from one context where it is well understood and applied into a new setting.

Regulation   source of innovation triggered by changes in legislation forcing new directions – for example, in safety or pollution control.

User-led innovation   pattern in which users create ideas – and often prototypes – for innovations rather than acting as consumers of other people's ideas.

Discussion Questions

1. Where do innovations come from? Generate a list of as many categories of trigger as you can think of – with examples for each one.

2. Push and pull – which is more important? This question has worried managers and policy-makers for decades – and having an idea of the answer would help focus support for the innovation process more effectively. Using examples, try to show how each is important under certain conditions but that it is their interplay which really shapes innovation.

3. Taking each of the '4Ps' of innovation which we introduced in Chapter 1, try to identify examples of 'product', 'process', 'position' and 'paradigm' innovation – and in each case list the sources which gave rise to those innovations.

4. Julia Wilson is keen to use her skills in creating social enterprises. Where might she look for sources of inspiration on which to focus her entrepreneurial enthusiasm?

Team Exercises

1. Choose some examples of product, service or social innovation – for example, a smart phone, an electric car, online booking of hospital appointments or enabling literacy programmes in Africa via mobile phones. Now try to work backwards – draw out the 'family tree' of triggers which brought that innovation into being. What were the enabling 'pushes' – for example, where did the technology come from, and what were the 'need pulls'?

2. Innovations don't just appear – sometimes they involve a lot of competing ideas before a 'dominant design' emerges. Henry Ford wasn't the first car maker but his was the design which 'clicked' with the market. Apple's iPod wasn't the first MP3 player – but it became the dominant architecture which others then copied. South West Airlines weren't the first low-cost carrier but they established the model which other successful players like Ryanair, EasyJet, Air Berlin and Air Europa have followed. Taking an example of an established innovation category like these, try to reconstruct the case history. Where did the original idea come from and what forces – pushes and pulls – shaped its emergence into a dominant design?

Further Reading and Resources

In this chapter we've looked at the many ways in which the innovation process can be triggered. The long-running debate about which sources – demand pull or knowledge push – are most important is well covered in Freeman and Soete's book *The Economics of Industrial Innovation* (Cambridge: MIT Press, 3rd edn, 1997). Particular discussion of fringe markets and unmet or poorly met needs as a source of innovation is covered by Christensen and colleagues and by Ulnwick (Christensen, C., S. Anthony and E. Roth, *Seeing What's Next* (Boston: Harvard Business School Press, 2007); Utterback, J., High End Disruption, *International Journal of Innovation Management*, 2007: Ulnwick, A., *What Customers Want: Using outcome-driven innovation to create breakthrough products and services,* (New York: McGraw-Hill, 2005.) whilst the 'bottom of the pyramid' and extreme user potential is explored in Prahalad's work (Prahalad, C.K., *The fortune at the bottom of the pyramid* (New Jersey: Wharton School Publishing, 2006). The website Next Billion (www.**nextbillion**.net) provides a wide range of resources and information about 'bottom of the pyramid' and extreme user activity including video and case studies. 'Blue ocean' strategy is described in Kim, W. and R. Mauborgne, *Blue Ocean Strategy: How to create uncontested market space and make the competition irrelevant* (Boston, Mass.: Harvard Business School Press, 2005) and on their accompanying website. User-led innovation has been researched extensively by Eric von Hippel and his books and website (http://web.mit.edu/evhippel/www/) provide an excellent starting point for further exploration of this approach. Frank Piller, Professor at Aachen University in Germany, has a rich website around the theme of mass customisation with extensive case examples and other resources (http://www.mass-customization.de/); the original work on the topic is covered in Joseph Pine's book (Pine, B.J., *Mass Customisation: The new frontier in business competition,* Cambridge, Mass.: Harvard University Press, 1993). High involvement innovation is covered in Bessant, J., *High Involvement Innovation* (Chichester: John Wiley and Sons Ltd, 2003) and lean thinking ideas and tools in Dan Jones and Jim Womack, *Lean solutions* (New York: Free Press, 2005. Andrew Hargadon has done extensive work on 'recombinant innovation' (*How Breakthroughs Happen,* Boston: Harvard Business School Press, 2003) and Mohammed Zairi provides a good overview of benchmarking (*Effective Benchmarking: Learning from the best,* London: Chapman and Hall, 1996). Searching at the frontier is one of the questions being addressed by the Discontinuous Innovation Laboratory, a network of around 30 academic institutions and 150 companies – see www.innovation-lab.org for more details. Downloadable reports on their work are available at www.aim-research.org

References

1. Mintzberg, H. and Lampel, J. (1996) Customising customisation, *Sloan Management Review,* **38**(1), 21–30.

2. Von Hippel, E. (2005) *The Democratization of Innovation.* Cambridge, Mass.: MIT Press.

3. Rothwell, R. and P. Gardiner (1983) Tough customers: good design, *Design Studies,* 4(3), 161–169.

4. Chesbrough, H. (2003) Managing your false negatives, *Harvard Management Updates,* 8(8).

5. Abernathy, W. and Utterback, J. (1978) Patterns of industrial innovation, *Technology Review,* 80, 40–47.

CASE STUDY 5

Exploring Innovation in Action: The Dimming of the Light Bulb

In the beginning. . . .

God said let there be light. And for a long time this came from a rather primitive but surprisingly effective method – the oil lamp. From the early days of putting simple wicks into congealed animal fats, through candles to more sophisticated oil lamps, people have been using this form of illumination. Archaeologists tell us this goes back at least 40,000 years so there has been plenty of scope for innovation to improve the basic idea! Certainly by the time of the Romans, domestic illumination – albeit with candles – was a well-developed feature of civilised society.

Not a lot changed until the late eighteenth century when the expansion of the mining industry led to experiments with uses for coal gas – one of which was as an alternative source of illumination. One of the pioneers of research in the coal industry – Humphrey Davy – invented the carbon arc lamp and ushered in a new era of safety within the mines, but also opened the door to alternative forms of domestic illumination and the era of gas lighting began.

But it was not until the middle of the following century that researchers began to explore the possibilities of using a new power source and some new physical effects. Experiments by Joseph Swann in England and Moses Farmer in the USA (amongst others) led to the development of a device in which a tiny metal filament enclosed within a glass envelope was heated to incandescence by an electric current. This was the first electric light bulb – and it still bears more than a passing resemblance to the product found hanging from millions of ceilings all around the world.

By 1879 it became clear that there was significant commercial potential in such lighting – not just for domestic use. Two events occurred during that year which were to have far-reaching effects on the emergence of a new industry. The first was that the city of Cleveland – although using a different lamp technology (carbon arc) – introduced the first public street lighting. And the second was that patents were registered for the incandescent filament light bulb by Joseph Swann in England and one Thomas Edison in the USA.

Needless to say the firms involved in gas supply and distribution and the gas lighting industry were not taking the threat from electric light lying down and they responded with a series of improvement innovations which helped retain gas lighting's popularity for much of the late nineteenth century. Much of what happened over the next 30 years is a good example of what is sometimes called the 'sailing ship effect'. That is, just as in the shipping world the invention of steam power did not instantly lead to the disappearance of sailing ships but instead triggered a whole series of improvement in that industry, so the gas lighting industry consolidated its position through incremental product and process innovations.

But electric lighting was also improving and the period between 1886 and 1920 saw many important breakthroughs and a host of smaller incremental performance improvements. In a famous and detailed study (carried out by an appropriately named researcher called Bright) there is evidence to show that little improvements in the design of the bulb and in the process for manufacturing it led to a fall in price of over 80% between 1880 and 1896 (A. Bright, *The Electric Lamp Industry Technological change and economic development from 1800 to 1947*, Macmillan, New York). Examples of such innovations include the use of gas instead of vacuum in the bulb (1913 Langmuir) and the use of tungsten filaments.

Innovation theory teaches us that after an invention there is a period in which all sorts of designs and ideas are thrown around before finally a 'dominant design' settles out and the industry begins to mature. So it was with the light bulb; by the 1920s the basic configuration of the product – a tungsten filament inside a glass gas-filled bulb – was established and the industry began to consolidate. It is at this point that the major players with whom we associate the industry – Philips, General Electric (GE), Westinghouse – become established.

Technological Alternatives

Although the industry then entered a period of stability in the marketplace there was still considerable activity in the technology arena. Back in the nineteenth century Henri Becquerel invented the fluorescent lamp and in 1911 Georges Claude invented the neon lamp – both inventions which would have far-reaching effects in terms of the industry and its segmentation into different markets.

The neon lamp started a train of work based on forming different glass tubes into shapes for signs and in filling them with a variety of gases with similar properties to neon but which gave different colours.

The fluorescent tube was first made commercially by Sylvania in the USA in 1938 following extensive development work by both GE and Westinghouse. The technology had a number of important features including low power consumption and long life – factors which led to their widespread use in office and business environments although less so in the home. By the 1990s this product had matured alongside the traditional filament bulb and a range of compact and shaped fittings were available from the major lighting firms.

Meanwhile, in Another Part of the World . . .

Whilst neon and fluorescent tubes were variations on the same basic theme of lights, a different development began in a totally new sector in the 1960s. In 1962 work on the emerging solid state electronics area led to the discovery of a light emitting diode – LED – a device which would, when a current passed through it, glow in red or green colour. These lights were bright and used little power; they were also part of the emerging trend towards miniaturisation. They quickly became standard features in electronic devices and today the average household will have hundreds of LEDs in orange, green or red to indicate whether devices such as TV sets, mobile phones or electric toothbrushes are on and functioning.

Development and refinement of LEDs took place in a different industry for a different market and in particular one line of work was followed in a small Japanese chemical company supplying LEDs to the major manufacturers like Sony. Nichia Chemical began a programme of work on a type of LED which would emit blue light – something much more difficult to achieve and requiring complex chemistry and careful process control. Eventually they were successful and in 1993 produced a blue LED based on gallium arsenide technology. The firm then committed a major investment to development of both product and process technology, amassing around 300 patents along the way. Their research culminated in the development in 1995 of a white light LED – using the principle that white light is made up of red, green and blue light mixed together.

So what? The significance of Shuji Nakamura's invention may not be instantly apparent – and for a long time the only products which could be bought utilising it were small high power torches. But think about the significance of this discovery. White LEDs offer the following advantages:

- 85% less power consumption;
- 16 times brighter than normal electric lights;
- tiny size;
- long life – tests suggest the life of an LED could be 100,000 hours (about 11 years);
- can be packaged into different shapes, sizes and arrangements;
- will follow the same economies of scale in manufacturing that led to the continuing fall in the price of electronic components, so and become very cheap very quickly.

If people are offered a low-cost, high-power, flexible source of white light they are likely to adopt it – and for this reason the lighting industry is feeling some sense of threat. The likelihood is that the industry as we know it will be changed dramatically by the emergence of this new light source – and whilst the names may remain the same they will have to pay a high price for licensing the technology. They may try to get around the patents – but with 300 already in place and the experience of the complex chemistry and processing which go into making LEDs, Nichia have a long head start. When Dr Nakamura left Nichia Chemical for a chair at University of California, Santa Barbara, sales of blue LEDs and lasers were bringing the firm more than $200m a year and the technology is estimated to have earned Nichia nearly $2bn.

Things are already starting to happen. Many major cities are now using traffic lights which use the basic technology to make much brighter green and red lights since they have a much longer life than conventional bulbs. One US company, Traffic Technology Inc., has even offered to give away the lights in return for a share of the energy savings the local authority makes! Consumer products like torches are finding their way into shops and online catalogues whilst the automobile industry is looking at the use of LED white light for interior lighting in cars. Major manufacturers such as GE are entering the market and targeting mass markets such as street lighting and domestic applications, a market estimated to be worth $12bn in the USA alone.

Go online to find the case study of Philips Atmosphere Provider, which gives a deep insight into the innovation thinking around this revolution in lighting.

www.iande.info

Reflection Questions/Assignments Linked to the Case

(1) Looking at the case study, try to identify the different sources of innovation and the changing pattern of threats (to existing players) and opportunities (for new entrant entrepreneurs). What are the implications of the latest developments for different players in terms of the likely threat to them and the ways in which they could respond?

Use the following framework to capture your answers.

	Architectural innovation	*Component innovation*
Likely threat/opportunity for player 1 – and why		
Likely threat/opportunity for player 2 – and why		
Etc.		

(2) Competence-destroying and competence-enhancing innovation

Try to review the case in terms of the following questions.

- To what extent are the changes involved competence-enhancing (i.e. building on what a player in the industry already knows so they can strengthen their position) or competence-destroying (i.e. something completely new which requires learning some new tricks) innovations?
- And for whom? (Think about the different players in the lighting industry – who are the likely winners and losers?)
- What strategies might a firm use to exploit the opportunities? (Again think about the different players in the industry and how they might defend their positions or open up new opportunities.)

Use the following framework to capture your answers.

	An established record company	A newcomer wanting to offer entertainment on the Web	A music publishing company (responsible for copyrights on sheet music, etc.)	Other examples. . . .
Is the change competence enhancing? Why?				
Is it competence destroying? Why?				
What might you do about this to secure and improve your position?				

(3) Can you map the different kinds of innovation in the case study? Which were incremental and which radical/discontinuous? Why? Give examples to support your answer.

(4) Is the 'revolution' in the lighting industry a result of the development of new technologies? Or is it happening because of changes on the demand side – shifts in what people want and are prepared to pay for? Or is it a mixture of both? What lessons might that offer to someone wanting to enter the industry as a new player? And what might an established player do to preserve their position? Illustrate your answer with examples.

Summary of Web Resources

- SPIRIT
- Corning
- 3M
- Philips
- RED
- Open Door
- Tesco
- Public sector/high innovation
- Cerulean
- Aravind

Cases
- Model T Ford
- Threadless
- Lego
- Coloplast
- Karolinska Hospital
- Bicycles industry
- Philips Atmosphere

Media

- Veeder Root video
- Emma Taylor interview
- Suzana Moreira interview
- Frank Piller on mass customisation
- 3M video/user-led innovation
- Tim Craft podcast
- Helen King interview

Tools

- Discontinuous innovation audit tool
- Competitiveness profiling
- Benchmarking
- Futures tools

Chapter 6

Searching for Opportunities

Go online to find additional . . .

Cases

Tools

Media

www.iande.info

In Chapter 5 we saw that innovation can be triggered by a wide range of stimuli – knowledge push, need pull, regulation, users insights, learning from other sectors and many more besides. With this forest of possibilities the problem becomes one of too much opportunity rather than a lack of it – and the challenge is in organising the search process. Simply taking a random walk in the field of opportunities may result in a lucky chance encounter – but to sustain a steady stream of innovation requires a more organised approach. Even the largest organisation can't afford to search in haphazard fashion and for the solo start-up entrepreneur managing the scarce resources means that he or she must take care in developing an effective search approach. So how could we manage the search stage of the innovation process to help find opportunities?

The Innovation Treasure Hunt

As we saw in Chapter 1 innovation can take a variety of forms – 'product', 'process', 'position' and 'paradigm' – and comes in incremental or radical flavours. So it would help to have a map of innovation search space – the ground we want to cover – before we start out on our journey. We'll build it with two axes to create a simple view of the search space – then look at how we can cover it.

Incremental/Radical Innovation – Do Better/Do Different

Innovation can happen along a spectrum of incremental to radical – from 'do what we do but better' to 'do different'. Table 6.1 gives some examples to remind us of this distinction.

For all but the smallest start-up we will be looking to balance a portfolio of ideas – most of them 'do better' incremental improvements on what has gone before but with a few which are more radical and may even be 'new to the world'. The big advantage of innovation of this kind is that there is a degree of familiarity, the risk is lower, we are moving forward along a path which has already been trodden. The benefits from doing so may be small in themselves but their effect is cumulative. And the ways in which we can search for such opportunities – tools and directions – are essentially well established and systematic.

By contrast taking a leap forward could bring big gains – but also carries higher risk. Since we are moving into unknown territory there will be a need to experiment – and a good chance that much of that experimentation will fail. We won't be clear about the directions in which we want to go and so there is a real risk of going up blind alleys or getting trapped in one-way streets. Essentially the kind of searching we do – and the tools we use – will be different.

Established Frame/New Frame

We like to think that we have powerful brains which can handle the huge range of information coming into it through our various senses – sight, sound, smell, touch, etc. The reality is different – there is simply too much information 'out there' and so our brains don't actually process everything – instead they have well-developed rules which help us decide what to pay attention to. This idea of selective attention is important because it means that under 'normal'

TABLE 6.1 From incremental to radical

Innovation type	Incremental – do what we do but better	Radical – do something different
'Product' – what we offer the world	Windows Vista replacing XP – essentially improving on an existing software idea	New to the world software – for example, the first speech recognition program
	VW EOS replacing the Golf – essentially improving on established car design	Toyota Prius – bringing a new concept: hybrid engines
	Improved performance of incandescent light bulbs	LED-based lighting, using completely different and more energy efficient principles
Process – how we create and deliver that offering	Improved fixed-line telephone services	Skype and other VOIP systems
	Extended range of stock broking services	Online share trading eBay
	Improved auction house operations	Toyota Production System and other 'lean' approaches
	Improved factory operations efficiency through upgraded equipment	Mobile banking in Kenya, Philippines – using phones as an alternative to banking systems
	Improved range of banking services delivered at branch banks	
Position – where we target that offering and the story we tell about it	Haagen Dazs changing the target market for ice cream from children to consenting adults	Addressing under-served markets – for example, the Tata Nano which targets the huge but relatively poor Indian market using the low-cost airline model – target cost is 1 lakh (around $3000)
	Low-cost airlines	
	University of Phoenix and others, building large education businesses via online approaches to reach different markets	'Bottom of the pyramid' approaches using a similar principle – Aravind Eye Care, Cemex construction products
	Dell and others segmenting and customising computer configuration for individual users	One laptop per child project – the $100 universal computer
	Banking services targeted at key segments – students, retired people, etc.	Micro-finance – Grameen Bank opening up credit for the very poor

(continued)

TABLE 6.1 (*Continued*)		
Innovation type	**Incremental – do what we do but better**	**Radical – do something different**
Paradigm – how we frame what we do	Bausch and Lomb – moved from 'eye wear' to 'eye care' as their business model, effectively letting go of the old business of spectacles, sunglasses (Raybans) and contact lenses all of which were becoming commodity businesses. Instead they moved into newer high-tech fields like laser surgery equipment, specialist optical devices and research in artificial eyesight IBM moving from being a machine maker to a service and solution company – selling off its computer making and building up its consultancy and service side. VT moving from being a shipbuilder with roots in Victorian times to a service and facilities management business	Grameen Bank and other micro-finance models – rethinking the assumptions about credit and the poor iTunes platform – a complete system of personalised entertainment Rolls Royce – from high quality aero engines to becoming a service company offering 'power by the hour' Cirque de Soleil – redefining the circus experience

circumstances we see (and hear, touch, etc.) what we expect to see based on an internal model of how we expect the world to behave. For most of the time that works really well for us, but occasionally we can be deceived or simply have a blind spot – we just don't 'see' what is out there, or rather we don't pay attention to it.

Just as human beings need to develop mental models to simplify the 'blooming, buzzing confusion' which the rich stimuli in their environment offer them, so individual entrepreneurs and established organisations make use of simplifying frames. They 'look' at the environment and take note of elements which they consider relevant – threats to watch out for, opportunities to take advantage of, competitors and collaborators, etc. Constructing such frames helps give the organisation some stability but it also defines the space within which it will search for innovation possibility.

In practice these models often converge around a core theme – although organisations might differ, they often share common models of how their world behaves. So most firms in a particular sector will adopt similar ways of framing – assuming certain 'rules of the game', following certain trajectories in common. And this will shape where and how they tend to search for opportunities.

These frames are accepted 'architectures' – the ways in which players see the configuration within which they innovate. The dominant architecture emerges over time but once established becomes the 'box' within which further innovation takes place.

It's difficult to think and work outside this box because it is reinforced by the structures, processes and tools which the organisation uses in its day to day work. The problem is also that such ways of working are linked to a complex web of other players in the organisation's 'value network' – its key competitors, customers and suppliers – who reinforce further the dominant way of seeing the world.

Powerful though they are, such frames are only models of how individuals and organisations think the world works. It is possible to see things differently, take into account new elements, pay attention to different things and come up with alternative solutions. This is, of course, exactly what entrepreneurs do when they try to find opportunities – they look at the world differently and see opportunity in a different way of framing things. And sometimes their new way of looking at things becomes a widely accepted one – and their innovation changes the game.

This poses one of the big challenges in innovation – within an existing frame where everyone plays by the shared and accepted rules it is usually the established players who do well because they have the resources and experience and they have built up strong networks all playing the same game. But precisely because of this they find it very difficult to unravel this and reframe the world with a new model. We talk about them needing to 'think outside the box' – but that box has very strong and well-reinforced walls.

Rather like the drunk who has lost his keys on the way home and is desperately searching for them under the nearest lamp-post 'because there is more light there', firms have a natural tendency to search in spaces which they already know and understand. But we know that the weak early warning signals of the emergence of totally new possibilities – radically different technologies, new markets with radically different needs, changing public opinion or political context – won't happen under our particular lamp-post. Instead they are out there in the darkness – so we have to find new ways of searching in space we aren't familiar with. To make it even worse we have no real idea what we are looking for – it will only become clear as it emerges and the best we can hope for is to spot it early in its emergence and develop our response alongside it.

How can this be done? By luck, sometimes – except that simply being in the right place at the right time doesn't always help. History suggests that even when the new possibility is presented to the firm on a plate its internal capacity to see and act on the possibilities is often lacking. For example, the famous 'not invented here' effect has been observed on many occasions where an otherwise well-established and successful innovative firm rejects a new opportunity which turns out to be of major significance.

The problem of framing is a big one – it takes insight and courage to see a mistake or failure as an opportunity – although when this does happen it can have spectacular results. Viagra, for example, began life as a failure in terms of its original indication as a vasoconstrictor whilst 3M's Post-it notes are based on an adhesive with decidedly non-sticky properties! What emerges from stories like these is that firms need more than luck – they need to be prepared and equipped. As Pasteur put it, chance favours the prepared mind.

INNOVATION IN ACTION

Technological Excellence May Not Be Enough . . . .

In the 1970s, Xerox was the dominant player in photocopiers, having built the industry from its early days when it was founded on the radical technology pioneered by Chester Carlsen and the Battelle Institute. But despite their prowess in the core technologies and continuing investment in maintaining an edge it found itself seriously threatened by a new generation of small copiers developed by new entrant Japanese players. Despite the fact that Xerox had enormous experience in the industry and a deep understanding of the core technology it took them almost eight years of mishaps and false starts to introduce a competitive product. In that time Xerox lost around half its market share and suffered severe financial problems.

In similar fashion, in the 1950s, the electronics giant RCA developed a prototype portable transistor-based radio using technologies which it had come to understand well. However it saw little reason to promote such an apparently inferior technology and continued to develop and build its high-end range of devices. By contrast Sony used it to gain access to the consumer market and to build a whole generation of portable consumer devices – and in the process acquired considerable technological experience which enabled them to enter and compete successfully in higher value more complex markets.

A Map of Innovation Search Space

Putting these two together gives us a framework map of search space, see Figure 6.1.

The vertical axis refers to the familiar 'incremental/radical' dimension in innovation whilst the second relates to the way we frame things.

Having drawn the map we can begin to look at strategies which individuals and organisations might use to search across it. And that raises an important theme – do we exploit or explore?

Exploit and Explore

One way we can innovate is by moving forward from what we already know. Individuals and organisations can deploy knowledge resources and other assets to secure returns and a 'safe' way of doing so is to harvest a steady flow of benefits derived from 'doing what we do better'. This has been termed 'exploitation' by innovation researchers, and it essentially involves using what we already know as the foundation for further incremental innovation. It builds strongly on what is already well-established – but in the process leads to a high degree of what is called 'path dependency'. Essentially what we did in the past will play a strong role in shaping what we do next.

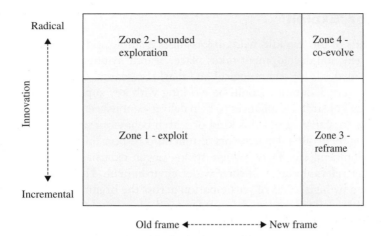

FIGURE 6.1   A map of innovation search space.

The trouble is that in an uncertain environment the potential to secure and defend a competitive position depends on 'doing something different', i.e. radical product or process innovation rather than imitations and variants of what others are also offering. This kind of search had been termed 'exploration' and is the kind which involves big leaps into new knowledge territory – risky but they enable the organisation to do new and very different things.

Whether we are talking about private sector competition or public service reform we need to recognise that 'exploit' may not always be a sufficient strategy. In the UK, for example, the National Health Service in 2010 was tasked with finding £20bn of savings within four years – and whilst efficiency improvements will certainly contribute a proportion of this through incremental 'do better' innovation, the reality is that some radically different things will be needed. So the challenge is one of exploit *and* explore, with the need to learn some new search approaches and tools to help do that.

Once again we find ourselves looking at entrepreneurship as something which is carried through by individuals and small groups looking for new opportunities to start value creating ventures by exploring space which others haven't yet found. But we also find the same need within established organisations needing to find radical new opportunities and wanting to draw on the reframing and searching skills associated with entrepreneurs on the inside.

Innovation Search Strategies

Of course in reality the lines between these 'zones' are not clear cut, but the idea behind the map is that we are likely to experience very different challenges in each area. Finding opportunities is going to need different strategies – and in the following section we'll look at the challenges in a little more detail.

Strategies for 'Exploit'

Zone 1 corresponds to the 'exploit' field and assumes a stable and shared frame within which adaptive and incremental development takes place. Search 'routines' here are associated with *refining* tools and methods for technological and market research, deepening relationships with established key players. Examples would be working with key suppliers, getting closer to customers and building key strategic alliances to help deliver established innovations more efficiently.

The structures for carrying out this kind of search behaviour are clearly defined with relevant actors carrying them out – departments or functions responsible for market research, product (service) development, etc. They involve strong ties in external networks with customers, suppliers and other relevant actors in their wider environment. The work of core groups like R&D is augmented by high levels of participation across the organisation – because the search questions are clearly defined and widely understood high involvement of non-specialists is possible. So procurement and purchasing can provide a valuable channel as can sales and marketing – since these involve contact with external players. Process innovation can be enabled by inviting suggestions for incremental improvement across the organisation – a high involvement kaizen model.

Go online to find the Kumba and NPI cases, which are examples of companies that make use of incremental process innovation.
Emma Taylor, training manager at Denso, the giant Japanese manufacturer, talks in a video interview about her experiences in enabling high involvement/kaizen innovation. See also the Veeder Root video.

www.iande.info

This kind of searching favours established organisations because they have the resources to organise and manage a systematic search across the territory. Start-up entrepreneurs simply don't have the capacity to cover all the ground – so their opportunities in Zone 1 tend to come through spotting a niche, and gap which no one else has seen.

Go online to find the Coloplast case, which gives some good insights into how a company searches this space. There are some links to relevant tools for market research, quality function, and deployment.

www.iande.info

Innovation Search Strategies for Explore

Zone 2 involves search into new territory, pushing the frontiers of what is known and deploying different search techniques for doing so. But this still takes place within an established framework – a shared mental model which we could term 'business model as usual'. R&D investments here are on big bets with high strategic potential, patenting and intellectual property (IP) strategies aimed at marking out and defending territory, riding key technological trajectories (such as Moore's Law in semiconductors). Market research similarly aims to get close to customers but to push the frontiers via empathic design, latent needs analysis, etc. Although the activity is risky and exploratory it is still governed strongly by the frame for the sector – common patterns which shape the behaviour of all the players in terms of their innovation strategies.

The structures involved in such exploration are, of necessity, highly specialised. Formal R&D and within that sophisticated specialisation is the pattern on the science/technology frontier, often involving separate facilities. Here too there is mobilisation of a network of external but similarly specialised researchers – in university, public and commercial laboratories – and the formation of specific strategic alliances and joint ventures around a particular area of deep technology exploration. The highly specialised nature of the work makes it difficult for others in the organisation to participate – and indeed this gap between worlds can often lead to tensions between the 'operating' and the 'exploring' units and the boardroom battles between these two camps for resources are often tense. In similar fashion, market research is highly specialised and may include external professional agencies in its network with the task of providing sophisticated business intelligence around a focused frontier.

From the standpoint of the entrepreneur this zone is interesting since there may be significant opportunities. Individuals and start-up businesses with highly specialised knowledge assets – for example, hi-tech spin-outs from universities – may feature strongly on the radar screens of large established organisations looking to explore. This pattern of 'symbiosis' – mutual dependency and advantage for new and established players – is a common pattern in fields like pharmaceuticals, electronics, software and biotechnology. (A good example is the Chiroscience case presented in Chapter 12.)

Go online to find cases on Corning, 3M, P&G and Tesco, which all give insights into how this search process takes place.

www.iande.info

Breaking Out of the Frame

Zone 3 is essentially associated with *reframing*. It involves searching a space where alternative architectures are generated, exploring different permutations and combinations of elements in the environment. Importantly this often happens by working with elements in the environment not embraced by established business models – for example, working with fringe markets, looking at the 'bottom of the pyramid' or collaborating with 'extreme users'. (We discussed these novel sources of innovation in Chapter 5.)

For example, the low-cost airline industry was not a development of new product or process – it still involves airports, aircraft, etc. Instead the innovation was in position and paradigm, reframing the business model by identifying new elements in the markets – students, pensioners, etc. – who did not yet fly but might if the costs could be brought down. Rethinking the business model required extensive product and process innovation to realise it – for example, in online booking, fast turnaround times at airports, multi-skilling of staff, etc. – but the end result was a reframing and creation of new innovation space.

This zone often favours entrepreneurs on the outside of established organisations because they can see and frame the world differently, see ways of putting the pieces together differently. Importantly this may not involve pushing the technological frontiers with radical innovation in the core offering or process – it is often about change in the ways the architecture works.

Sometimes an organisation needs to change its perspective in radical fashion – to reframe what it does in order to survive and compete under very different conditions. (This corresponds to radical 'paradigm' innovation of the kind which we saw in Chapter 1.) Fuji Film is a Japanese company which has been a key player in the world of photography and imaging (printers, scanners, cameras, etc.). But in recent years it has been extending its sphere of activity through some radical reframing – using the fact that it has a deep knowledge base underpinning its established business based on particles coated on surfaces. As Stefan Kohn explains in the case on the website they have begun to play a major role in the world of skin care – and in the process of reframing have opened up considerable new innovation space.

Go online to find more on the Fuji Film case.

www.iande.info

Exploring Complexity – Working at the Edge of Chaos

Zone 4 represents the 'edge of chaos' complex environment where innovation emerges as a product of a process of co-evolution. In this space many different elements are involved and each affects the other so that it becomes impossible to predict the outcome. Think about the emerging future for healthcare – it's unlikely that the current models (whether publicly or privately funded) will survive long into the future because of the pressures of greater demand, ageing population, spending cuts etc. But any new model is going to be hard to predict because so many factors are involved – technology, markets, global distribution, public/ private sector split, increasing lobbying by different interest groups, etc. Instead we should see it as a complex system in which there is extensive interaction and where what happens in one part of the system will affect the others.

Under conditions like these it is easy to assume that there is nothing we can do – and more importantly for our entrepreneurs, nowhere in which they could find opportunities except by accident or by waiting until the new game has fully emerged. But we do know something about these situations – there is a body of knowledge around 'complexity theory' which specialises in them. And there are some simple principles which can help us work in innovation space of this kind. In particular there is a pattern of what is called 'co-evolution' in which different interacting elements begin to converge on a particular solution. (An example in nature is the way ice crystals can form into the particular and organised pattern of a snowflake.)

As this pattern begins to emerge so it can be amplified through feedback, making the signal about the pattern clearer than all the other competing background signals. And gradually the system acquires momentum to move in a particular direction – and a dominant pattern emerges. We see this a lot in what is sometimes called the 'fluid phase' in the innovation life cycle, when new combinations of technologies and markets swirl around and entrepreneurs try out many different ideas. Eventually out of the turbulent and unpredictable set of possibilities a dominant design emerges which sets the pattern for future innovation – think about the motor car or the bicycle as simple examples.

So for entrepreneurs to work in this complex space there are some simple rules.

- Be in the game early – the signals about the emergence of the dominant design will be weak at first and hard to spot from the outside.
- Be in there actively and prepared to experiment – there is no 'right' answer but a lot of playing with possibilities.
- Be prepared for failure – essentially working in zone 4 is about probe and learn, mostly about what won't work.
- Be aware of others in the system picking up weak signals and amplifying what seems to work.

Once again the need to be flexible about how the world is framed – in this case it is particularly important since there is no clearly established pattern – is a key resource. This favours an entrepreneurial mindset, prepared to look at things differently and make use of new opportunities which emerge. Think about the way in which the Internet has opened up space for radically different ways of carrying out many established activities but is now moving to enable completely new ones. Whilst many of them fail – the 'dotcom bubble' is a healthy reminder of this – there is considerable space for exploration and emergence of new opportunities.

Table 6.2 gives some examples of such 'discontinuous' shifts which open up opportunities for entrepreneurial mindsets.

TABLE 6.2 Sources of discontinuity

Triggers/ sources of discontinuity	Explanation	Problems posed	Examples (of good and bad experiences)
New market emerges	Most markets evolve through a process of growth, segmentation, etc. But at certain times completely new markets emerge which can not be analysed or predicted in advance or explored through using conventional market research/ analytical techniques	Established players don't see it because they are focused on their existing markets May discount it as being too small or not representing their preferred target market – fringe/cranks dismissal Originators of new product may not see potential in new markets and may ignore them, e.g. text messaging	Disk drives, excavators, mini-mills Mobile phone/ SMS where market which actually emerged was not the one expected or predicted by originators
New technology emerges	Step change takes place in product or process technology – may result from convergence and maturing of several streams (e.g. industrial automation, mobile phones) or as a result of a single breakthrough (e.g. LED as new white light source)	Don't see it because beyond the periphery of technology search environment. Not an extension of current areas but completely new field or approach Tipping point may not be a single breakthrough but convergence and maturing of established technological streams, whose combined effect is underestimated	Ice harvesting to cold storage Valves to solid state electronics Photos to digital images Voice over internet protocol telephony Filament light bulbs to LED sources

TABLE 6.2   (*Continued*)

Triggers/ sources of discontinuity	Explanation	Problems posed	Examples (of good and bad experiences)
		Not invented here effect – new technology represents a different basis for delivering value: e.g. telephone vs. telegraphy	
New political rules emerge	Political conditions which shape the economic and social rules may shift dramatically: for example, the collapse of communism meant an alternative model – capitalist competition, as opposed to central planning – and many ex-state firms couldn't adapt their ways of thinking	Old mindset about how business is done, rules of the game, etc. are challenged and established firms fail to understand or learn new rules	Centrally planned to market economy e.g. former Soviet Union Apartheid to post-apartheid South Africa Free trade/globalisation results in dismantling protective tariff and other barriers and new competition basis emerges
Running out of road	Firms in mature industries may need to escape the constraints of diminishing space for product and process innovation and the increasing competition of industry structures by either exit or by radical reorientation of their business	Current system is built around a particular trajectory and embedded in a steady-state set of innovation routines which militate against widespread search or risk-taking experiments	Encyclopaedia Britannica finally running out of road as it is displaced by first CD-based, then online and now open source encyclopaedias like Wikipedia Sometimes the firms manage to break out and establish a new trajectory – e.g. Nokia from timber products to mobile phones or Preussag from metals and commodities to tourism

(*continued*)

TABLE 6.2   (*Continued*)

Triggers/ sources of discontinuity	Explanation	Problems posed	Examples (of good and bad experiences)
Sea change in market sentiment or behaviour	Public opinion or behaviour shifts slowly and then tips over into a new model – for example, the music industry is in the midst of a (technology-enabled) revolution in delivery systems from buying records, tapes and CDs to direct download of tracks in MP3 and related formats. Long-standing issues of concern to a minority accumulate momentum (sometimes through the action of pressure groups) and suddenly the system switches/tips over – for example, social attitudes to smoking or health concerns about obesity levels and fast-foods	Don't pick up on it or persist in alternative explanations – cognitive dissonance – until it may be too late Rules of the game suddenly shift and then new pattern gathers rapid momentum wrong-footing existing players working with old assumptions	Apple, Napster, Dell, Microsoft vs. traditional music industry McDonald's, Burger King and obesity concerns Tobacco companies and smoking bans Oil/energy and others and global warming Opportunity for new energy sources like wind power where Danish firms have come to dominate
Deregulation/shifts in regulatory regime	Political and market pressures lead to shifts in the regulatory framework and enable the emergence of a new set of rules – e.g. liberalisation, privatisation or deregulation	New rules of the game but old mind-sets persist and existing players unable to move fast enough or see new opportunities opened up	Old monopoly positions in fields like telecommunications and energy were dismantled and new players/combinations of enterprises emerged. In particular, energy and bandwidth become

TABLE 6.2   (*Continued*)

Triggers/ sources of discontinuity	Explanation	Problems posed	Examples (of good and bad experiences)
			increasingly viewed as commodities. Innovations include skills in trading and distribution – a factor behind the considerable success of Enron in the late 1990s as it emerged from a small gas pipeline business to becoming a major energy trader
Business model innovation	Established business models are challenged by a reframing, usually by a new entrant who redefines/reframes the problem and the consequent rules of the game	New entrants see opportunity to deliver product/service via new business model and rewrite rules – existing players have at best to be fast followers	Amazon.com in retailing Charles Schwab in share trading Southwest and other low-cost airlines Direct Line insurance
Unthinkable events	Unimagined and therefore not prepared for events which – sometimes literally – change the world and set up new rules of the game.	New rules may disempower existing players or render competencies unnecessary	9/11
Shifts in 'techno-economic paradigm' – systemic changes which impact whole sectors or even whole societies	Change takes place at system level, involving technology and market shifts. This involves the convergence of a	Hard to see where new paradigm begins until rules become established. Existing players tend to reinforce their	Industrial Revolution Mass production

(continued)

TABLE 6.2 *(Continued)*			
Triggers/ sources of discontinuity	Explanation	Problems posed	Examples (of good and bad experiences)
	number of trends which result in a 'paradigm shift' where the old order is replaced	commitment to old model, reinforced by 'sailing ship' effects	

ADVICE TO FUTURE ENTREPRENEURS

The pattern can be seen in many studies and its implications for innovation management are important. In particular it helps us understand why established organisations often find it hard to deal with discontinuous change. Organisations build capabilities around a particular trajectory and those who may be strong in the later (specific) phase of an established trajectory often find it hard to move into the new one. (The example of the firms which successfully exploited the transistor in the early 1950s is a good case in point – many were new ventures, sometimes started by enthusiasts in their garage, yet they rose to challenge major players in the electronics industry like Raytheon.)

So one important management skill is to develop the ability to look with more than one pair of eyes at the industry in which you operate. What's going on at the edges? How could someone else reframe this line of business and create a new fluid state? If such a state starts to emerge can we develop an approach more like that of a new entrant firm?

Navigating the Search Space

Table 6.3 below summarises the challenges of navigating this search space.

Part of the problem in trying to deal with the search space is that we may need two different kinds of innovation organisation – one aimed at 'exploit' activities where there is a high degree of stability in the frame and one where we need more flexibility because of the high uncertainty as we move to the right-hand side of our search space. Table 6.4 summarises this distinction and highlights the need for different tools and techniques.

TABLE 6.3 Challenges in navigating innovation search space

Zone	Search challenges
1 'Business as usual' – innovation but under 'steady-state conditions, little disturbance around core business model	Exploit – extend in incremental fashion boundaries of technology and market. Refine and improve. Build close links/strong ties with key players. Favours established organisations with resources – start-up entrepreneurs are looking to spot niches within the mainstream
2 'Business model as usual' – bounded exploration within this frame	Exploration – pushing frontiers of technology and market via advanced techniques. Build close links with key strategic knowledge sources, inside and especially outside the organisation. Entrepreneurs with key knowledge assets – for example, spin-off ventures from a university research lab – can benefit from this search process and link their ideas with the resources which a major organisation can bring
3 Alternative frame – taking in new/different elements in environment. Variety matching, alternative architectures	Reframing – explore alternative options, introduce new elements. Experimentation and open-ended search. Breadth and periphery important. Entrepreneurs have a significant advantage here since they can bring fresh thinking and perspectives to an established game. Mainstream organisations often seek to explore here through setting up internal entrepreneurial groups – corporate venturing, 'intrapreneurs', etc.
4 Radical – new to the world – possibilities. New architecture around as yet unknown and established elements	Emergence – need to co-evolve with stakeholders • Be in there • Be in there early • Be in there actively Entrepreneurs have advantages here since this resembles the 'fluid' state in innovation life cycle and requires flexibility in thinking, tolerance for failure, willingness to take risks, etc. Big problem is the high rate of failure here which established organisations have some capacity to absorb but which is an issue for start-up entrepreneurs

---

TABLE 6.4 Two different types of innovation organisation for steady-state and discontinuous innovation

Type 1 Innovation organisation	Type 2
Operates within mental framework based on clear and accepted set of rules of the game	*No clear rules – these emerge over time* *High tolerance for ambiguity*

(continued)

TABLE 6.4 (Continued)	
Type 1 Innovation organisation	**Type 2**
Strategies path dependent	*Path independent, emergent, probe and learn*
Clear selection environment	*Fuzzy, emergent selection environment*
Selection and resource allocation linked to clear trajectories and criteria for fit	*Risk taking, multiple parallel bets, tolerance of (fast) failure*
Operating routines refined and stable	*Operating patterns emergent and 'fuzzy'*
Strong ties and knowledge flows along clear channels	*Weak ties and peripheral vision important*

Implementing Search Strategies

Faced with the challenge of covering all of the search space how do organisations and individuals go about it? A good place to start understanding broad strategies is to look at what organisations actually do in searching for innovation triggers. There are many large-scale innovation surveys which ask around this theme – for example, the European Community Innovation Survey regularly looks at the innovative behaviour of firms across 27 EU states.

Information of this kind gives us a broad picture – in this case showing that ideas for innovation come from many different sources – suppliers, universities, etc. It reinforces the view that successful innovation is about spreading the net as widely as possible, mobilising multiple channels. Although surveys of this kind tell us a lot they also miss important elements – for example:

- incremental innovation and how it is triggered lies beneath their radar screen, and there is a bias towards product innovation;
- they don't capture much of the organisational change;
- they don't capture 'position' or business model innovation so well, again especially at the incremental end;
- they tend to focus on the 'obvious' search agents like R&D or market research departments – but leave out others who may be involved, e.g. purchasing – and within the business the idea of suggestion schemes and high involvement innovation;
- they deal with established organisations so such surveys tell us very little about where and how new start-ups seek out their opportunities;
- they mainly tell us about the 'exploit' area and give less detail about the 'explore' side of things.

We can also look at individual cases and see in detail how they carry out search. Cases like Tesco and Cerulean give us clues about the actual approaches organisations take, and the combinations of tools which they employ.

 Go online to find the cases on Tesco and Cerulean.

www.iande.info

What these different studies highlight is the need to cast the net widely – and one of the core themes in innovation and entrepreneurship has been the importance of building rich and diverse networks and linkages to help this process.

Casting the Net Widely – Opening Up the Game

Building rich and extensive linkages with potential sources of innovation has always been important – for example, studies in the UK in the 1950s identified one key differentiator between successful and less successful innovating firms as the degree to which they were 'cosmopolitan' as opposed to 'parochial' in their approach towards sources of innovation. Entrepreneurs starting up new ventures know the importance of building networks – the essence of what they do in spotting opportunities is to make connections which others might have missed.

There are, of course, arguments for keeping a relatively closed approach – for example, there is a value in doing your own R&D and market research because the information collected is then available to be exploited in ways which the business can control. It can choose to push certain lines, hold back on others, keep things essentially within a closed system. But as we've seen the reality is that innovation is triggered in all sorts of ways and a sensible strategy is to cast the new as widely as possible.

This is especially true when we move into our 'explore' spaces on the map. We are going to need different knowledge sets and perspectives – and this requires learning new search strategies. Innovation has always been a multi-player game, one which involves weaving together many different strands of what could be termed 'knowledge spaghetti' to create something new. What's different about today's context is the sheer volume and distribution of that knowledge – for example, it's estimated that nearly $750bn of new knowledge is being created every year in public and private sector R&D around the world. Keeping track of growth on this scale – especially when this R&D is increasingly globalised and coming from an ever-wider range of players – becomes a major headache even for major technology-based firms.

US professor Henry Chesbrough coined the term *'open innovation'* to describe the challenge facing even large organisations in keeping track of and accessing external knowledge rather than relying on internally generated ideas. Put simply open innovation involves the recognition that 'not all the smart guys work for us'.

Of course it is not simply new R&D knowledge about science and technology which is exploding – there are similar seismic shifts on the market demand side, and on the interests of users in greater customisation and even participation in the innovation game. Table 6.5 indicates some of the big shifts in the context for innovation.

TABLE 6.5   Changing context for innovation (Source: Bessant and Venables[1])

Context change	Indicative examples
Acceleration of knowledge production	OECD estimates that close to $750bn is spent each year (public and private sector) in creating new knowledge – thus extending the frontier along which 'breakthrough' technological developments may happen
Global distribution of knowledge production	Knowledge production is increasingly involving new players, especially in emerging market fields like the BRIC (Brazil, Russia, India, China) nations – hence the need to search for innovation opportunities across a much wider space. One consequence of this is that 'knowledge workers' are now much more widely distributed and concentrated in new locations – for example, Microsoft's third largest R&D Centre employing thousands of scientists and engineers is now in Shanghai
Market fragmentation	Globalisation has massively increased the range of markets and segments so that these are now widely dispersed and locally varied, putting pressure on innovation search activity to cover much more territory, often far from 'traditional' experiences – such as the 'bottom of the pyramid' conditions in many emerging markets
Market virtualisation	Increasing use of Internet as marketing channel means different approaches need to be developed. At the same time emergence of large-scale social networks in cyber-space pose challenges in market research approaches – for example, Facebook currently has over 500 million subscribers. Further challenges arise in the emergence of parallel world communities as a research opportunity – for example, Second Life now has over 6 million 'residents'
Rise of active users	Although users have long been recognised as a source of innovation there has been an acceleration in the ways in which this is now taking place – for example, the growth of Linux has been a user-led open community development. In sectors like media the line between consumers and creators is increasingly blurred – for example, You Tube has around 100 million videos viewed each day but also has over 70,000 new videos uploaded every day from its user base
Development of technological and social infrastructure	Increasing linkages enabled by information and communications technologies around the Internet and broadband have enabled and reinforced alternative social networking possibilities. At the same time the increasing availability of simulation and prototyping tools has reduced the separation between users and producers

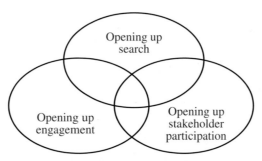

FIGURE 6.2   Convergence around 'open innovation'.

What this means is a significant acceleration in the opening up of the innovation search game in a number of converging areas – as indicated by Figure 6.2.

- *Opening up of search*

    This corresponds to Chesbrough's 'open innovation' model and strategies here require new ways of accessing a wide and diverse set of ideas and connecting these to sites within the organisation which can make effective use of them. In turn this raises questions of networking and knowledge management, issues identified as far back as the 1970s but coming to the fore in an era of social networking and enabling technologies. Much of the new challenge is about combining and creating communities of practice around key themes which transcend traditional organisational boundaries.

- *Opening up engagement*

    Extensive research on 'high involvement innovation' – engaging employees in organised innovative activities across an organization – suggests this offers a powerful source of ideas Until recently this emphasised incremental improvements – kaizen – but recent work, enabled by corporate intranets and the trend to social networking have shifted the focus to more radical innovation, tapping into internal entrepreneurship through innovation competitions etc. There has also been extensive interest in social entrepreneurship and tapping into change ideas within large public sector organisations.

- *Opening up stakeholder participation*

    User-led innovation highlights the active role played by users as active initiators of change. The emergence of powerful communication technologies which enable active co-operation of user communities in co-creation and diffusion of innovations has accelerated the trend. At the limit this involves communities creating innovation amongst and for themselves and the resulting innovations only then being appropriated by the traditional corporate agents in public and private sector – a significant reversal of the traditional innovation model.

Traditional models of innovation implied a separation between design and adoption but there is growing use of increasingly sophisticated techniques to collect intelligence about user concerns and wishes – what is often called 'user-centred design'. Further work has demonstrated the potential contribution of users as active co-creators of innovation, a trend reflected in much of the work on 'mass customisation'.

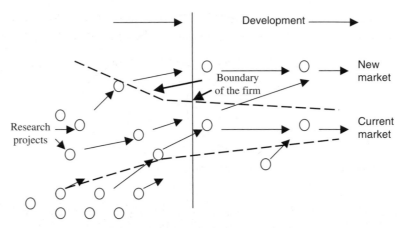

FIGURE 6.3 The open innovation model (based on Chesbrough[2]).

Moving to this new model is not without its difficulties. On the one hand it makes sense to recognise that, in a knowledge-rich world, *'not all the smart guys work for us'*. Even large R&D spenders like Procter & Gamble (annual R&D budget around $3bn and about 7000 scientists and engineers working globally in R&D) are fundamentally rethinking their models – in their case switching from 'Research and Develop' to *'Connect and Develop'* as the dominant slogan, with the strategic aim of moving from closed innovation to sourcing 50% of their innovations from outside the business. But on the other we should recognise the tensions that appear around intellectual property (how do we protect and hold on to knowledge when it is now much more mobile – and how do we access other people's knowledge?), around appropriability (how do we ensure a return on our investment in creating knowledge?) and around the mechanisms to make sure we can find and use relevant knowledge (when we are now effectively sourcing it from across the globe and in all sorts of unlikely locations?). In this context innovation management emphasis shifts from knowledge creation to knowledge trading and managing knowledge flows.

The 'open innovation' model essentially involves opening up the enterprise to flows of knowledge into and out from the organisation – as indicated in Figure 6.3.

Go online to find podcast interviews with David Simoes-Brown and Richard Philpott, both of whom are entrepreneurs who have set up businesses based on exploiting the 'open innovation' opportunity.

www.iande.info

It offers significant opportunities for entrepreneurs since it implies new ways of connecting – small enterprises with key knowledge assets may become attractive to large players who need that knowledge, whilst small enterprises can now access a wide range of knowledge resources, providing they are well-networked. Inevitably this raises big questions, though, around how those connections can be made, who and what broker mechanisms come into play – and how intellectual property rights can be managed in such a knowledge-trading world.

We will return to this theme in more detail in Chapter 8 where we look at the key role being played by networks as a source of ideas and resources.

INNOVATION IN ACTION

Connect and develop at Procter & Gamble

One of the early users of the 'open innovation' model was Procter & Gamble whose Chief Executive set the ambitious target for the business of sourcing 50% of its innovations from outside – a big shift for a company which had traditionally done everything itself. In Chapter 8 there is a case study of 'Connect and Develop' – their name for their open innovation programme – and on the website Roy Sandbach, a senior manager within the business explains in a podcast some of the challenges which this posed for them.

 Go online to find the podcast interview with P&G's Roy Sandbach.

www.iande.info

In the next section we will look at some of the major tools and techniques which individuals and organisations can use to help carry through their search strategies in trying to find innovation opportunities.

Tools, Structures and Mechanisms to Enable Search

Managing innovation is something which individuals and organisations learn to do through a mixture of trial and error, imitation and borrowing of good practices, improvisation, etc. Over time they accumulate experience about what works best for them – and this becomes a highly specific approach, almost like a personality. The idea of 'routines' – repeated, learned and embedded patterns of behaviour – is one we introduced in Chapter 1 and it very much applies here in the area of search tools. Individuals and organisations develop and refine the tools they use to trawl the innovation space, building on tried and tested techniques but also experimenting and adding new ones to deal with new challenges in their search space.

For example, much experience has been gained in how R&D units can be structured to enable a balance between applied research (supporting the 'exploit' type of search) and more wide-ranging, 'blue sky' activities (which facilitate the 'explore' side of the equation). These approaches have been refined further along 'open innovation' lines where the R&D work of others is brought into play, and by ways of dealing with the increasingly global production of knowledge – for example, the pharmaceutical giant GSK deliberately pursues a policy of R&D competition across several major facilities distributed around the world.

In similar fashion, market research has evolved to produce a rich portfolio of tools for building a deep understanding of user needs – and which continues to develop new and further refined techniques (for example, empathic design, lead user methods and increasing use of ethnography).

Choice of techniques and structures depends on a variety of strategic factors like those explored above – balancing their costs and risks against the quality and quantity of knowledge they bring in. Throughout the book we have stressed the idea that managing innovation is a *dynamic* capability – something which needs to be updated and extended on a continuing basis to deal with the 'moving frontier' problem. As markets, technologies, competitors, regulations and all sorts of other elements in a complex environment shift so we need to learn new tricks and sometimes let go of older ones which are no longer appropriate.

In this section we'll look at some examples of tools and mechanisms for innovation search which are emerging in response to a context which sees very high levels of knowledge production, global distribution of such production and of the marketplaces providing the demand signals, increasing virtualisation of those markets, growing involvement of users in shaping and 'co-creating' innovation, etc.

Searching Inside – and Opening it Up

One area which has seen growing activity addresses a fundamental knowledge management issue which is well expressed in the statement – 'If only xxx (insert the name of any large organization) knew what it knows'! In other words, how can organisations tap into the rich knowledge (and potential innovation triggers) within its existing structures and amongst its workforce? We saw in Chapter 5 that knowledge of this kind can be a valuable resource in incremental process innovation, for example, where the engagement of employees in local level problem-solving has brought significant productivity gains across all sectors.

Go online to find several cases that illustrate this, including Cerulean. Also, see the video of Veeder Root.

www.iande.info

Of course, using ideas from outside is powerful – but only if the right connections are made back into the organisation. For example, in assessing technological opportunities it's also important that the user perspective is communicated to all the different functions and disciplines within the organisation. Amongst recipes for achieving this are to rotate staff so that they spend some time out working with and listening to customers, and the introduction of the concept that 'everybody is someone's customer'.

An increasing number of tools and structured frameworks are now available for trying to identify, clarify, articulate and communicate 'the voice of the customer' throughout the organisation. Based on the principles of quality function deployment (QFD) these tools usually take as their starting point the customer needs as expressed in the customer's own words or images and gradually and systematically decompose them into tasks for the various elements within the organisation.

Go online to find a description of QFD (along with many other tools) and an interactive tool to explore how it works.

www.iande.info

We're also making much more use of our understanding of social networks and how ideas flow within and across organisations. Of particular significance in this context is the role played by various forms of 'gatekeeper' in the organisation. This concept – which goes back to the pioneering work of Thomas Allen in his studies within the aerospace industry of the 1970s – relates to a model of communication in which ideas flow via key individuals to those who can make use of them in developing innovation.

Gatekeepers are often well-positioned in the informal communication networks and have the facility to act as translators and brokers of key information. Studies of the operation of such communication networks stress the informal flows of knowledge and have led to a variety of architectural changes in research laboratories and other knowledge environments. These are essentially variants around the 'village pump' idea where environments are configured to allow plenty of space for informal encounter (such as by the coffee machine or in a relaxation area) where key exchange of information can take place. Significantly the rise of distributed working and the use of virtual teams have spawned an extension to these ideas making use of advanced communications to enable such networking across geographical and organisational boundaries.

This has led to renewed efforts to deal with what is an old problem – for example, Procter & Gamble's successes with 'connect and develop' owe much to their mobilising rich linkages between people who know things *within* their giant global operations and increasingly outside it. They use 'communities of practice' – Internet-enabled 'clubs' where people with different knowledge sets can converge around core themes, and the deploy a small army of innovation 'scouts' who are licensed to act as prospectors, brokers and gatekeepers for knowledge to flow across the organisation's boundaries. Intranet technology links around 10,000 people in an internal 'ideas market' – and some of their significant successes have come from making better internal connections. (There is an extended discussion of 'communities of practice' in Chapter 11.)

3M – another firm with a strong innovation pedigree dating back over a century – similarly put much of their success down to making and managing connections. Larry Wendling, Vice President for Corporate Research talks of 3M's 'secret weapon' – the rich formal and informal networking which links the thousands of R&D and market-facing people across the organisation. Their long-history of breakthrough innovations – from masking tape, through Scotchgard, Scotch tape, magnetic recording tape to Post-Its and their myriad derivatives – arise primarily out of people making connections.

Go online to find the 3M case.

www.iande.info

It's important to recognise that much of the knowledge lies in the experience and ideas of 'ordinary' employees rather than solely with specialists in formal innovation departments like R&D or market research. Increasingly organisations are trying to tap into such knowledge as a source of innovation via various forms of what can be termed 'high involvement innovation' systems such as suggestion schemes, problem-solving groups and innovation 'jams'. Innovation contests – which we discuss in more detail in Chapter 8 – offer a powerful twenty-first century mechanism to tap into the enthusiasm and creativity of employees.

This becomes important in trying to search for the unexpected – essentially moving into 'explore' mode. One rich source of internal innovation lies in the entrepreneurial ideas of employees – projects which are not formally sanctioned by the business but which build on the energy, enthusiasm and inspiration of people passionate enough to want to try out new ideas. Encouraging internal entrepreneurship – 'intrapreneurship' as it has been termed – is increasingly popular and organisations like 3M and Google make attempts to manage it in a semi-formal fashion, allocating a certain amount of time/space to employees to explore their own ideas.

Managing this is a delicate balancing act – on the one hand there is a need to give both permission and resources to enable employee-led ideas to flourish, but on the other there is the risk of these resources being dissipated with nothing to show for them. In many cases there is an attempt to create a culture of what can be termed 'bootlegging' in which there is tacit support for projects which go against the grain. An example in BMW – where these are called 'U-boat projects' – was the Series 3 Estate version, which the mainstream company thought was not wanted and would conflict with the image of BMW as a high-quality, high-performance and somewhat 'sporty' car. A small group of staff worked on a U-Boat project, even using parts cannibalised from an old VW Rabbit to make a prototype – and the model has gone on to be a great success and opened up new market space.

Searching Outside – Open Search

As we have seen, the principle of spreading the net widely is well-established in innovation studies as a success factor – and places emphasis on building strong relationships with

INNOVATION IN ACTION

How We Search for Innovation

We look in the usual places for our industry. We look at our customers. We look at our suppliers. We go to trade bodies. We go to trade fairs. We present technical papers. We have an input coming from our customers. What we also try to do is develop inputs from other areas. We've done that in a number of ways. Where we're recruiting, we try to bring in people who can bring a different perspective. We don't necessarily want people who've worked in the type of instruments we have in the same industry. . . . certainly in the past we've brought in people who bring a completely different perspective, almost like introducing greensand into the oyster. We deliberately look outside. We will look in other areas. We will look in areas that are perhaps different technology. We will look in areas that are adjacent to what we do, where we haven't normally looked. And we also do encourage the employees themselves to come forward with ideas.

Some of our product ideas have come from an individual who was sitting as a peripheral part of a little project team that was looking at different project ideas, different products for the future of the business. He had an idea. He created something in his garage. He brought it into me and says, what about this? And we looked at it. We had a quick discussion about it, talked to the management team and initiated a development that we did for one of our suppliers. That came right from outside the area we normally operate in. It came through one of our employees, a long-service employee, so not someone who was recent to the business. But it was triggered by him thinking in a different way. An idea came that he has married up to a potential market need because of the job he worked in when he was working in the service and repair area. He said, right, there's an opportunity for this product. He created a prototype out of a piece of drainpipe and some pieces he had taken from the repair area and made a functional model and said, what about this? And from that, we actually created a product that has spawned a product range of small manual instruments, which traditionally the business hasn't been involved with for probably 20 years. So, that's an idea that came from within the business. It came from an existing employee, but it's not something that we would have thought of as part of our normal pipeline.

We didn't immediately see, oh, there's a demand for this, let's do that. This came from him having some local knowledge and talking to customers at lower levels and saying, there's actually a demand for this small product. It's small, it's relatively niche, it's not going to set the world alight, but it enhances our product range and it puts us into an area where we've never been before. So, we're very receptive to those ideas coming forward. We create an environment where we encourage people to question and challenge. We've actually got an appraisal system where we look at people's competencies rather than performance, and one of the competencies we want is, is that person going to question and challenge? Are they willing to say, how can we do this better, how can we do this more effectively? So, continuous improvement is something we look for. But we also want people to hold up hands and say, hang on a minute, why are you doing it that way? What about this? I've seen this because of something I've done, one of my hobbies or in some of

(continued)

the social activities, and we encourage people to bring those ideas in and work with us to develop that into a product idea. We've actually set up a mechanism where we run a project team where we take people from all areas of the business . . . this is no longer just a product development area. We then put them in a room with all the resources they need for three or four days and say, what we want out of this is a number of product ideas that are different to what we do. Where can we go in the future? Where can you take this little business? Working within the limits of what we're capable of they will come up with product ideas, and the last one that we ran, we had seven or eight product ideas came out . . .

(Patrick McLaughlin, Managing Director, Cerulean)

 Go online to find a full video transcript of the interview with Cerulean's Patrick McLaughlin.

www.iande.info

key stakeholders. For example, in a recent IBM survey of 750 CEOs around the world, 76% ranked business partner and customer collaboration as top sources for new ideas whilst internal R&D ranked only eighth. The study also indicated that 'outperformers' – in terms of revenue growth – used external sources 30% more than underperformers. It's not hard to see why – the managers interviewed listed the clear benefits from collaboration with partners as things like reduced costs, higher quality and customer satisfaction, access to skills and products, increased revenue, and access to new markets and customers. As one CEO put it, 'We have at our disposal today a lot more capability and innovation in the marketplace of competitive dynamic suppliers than if we were to try to create on our own', while another stated simply 'If you think you have all of the answers internally, you are wrong'.

This emphasises the need both for better use of existing mainstream innovation agents – for example, sales or purchasing as channels to monitor and bring back potential sources of innovation – and for establishing new roles and structures. In the former case there is already strong evidence of the importance of customers and suppliers as sources of innovation and the key role which relevant staff have in managing these knowledge sources. In the field of process innovation for example, where the 'lean' agenda of improving on cost, quality and delivery is a key theme, there is strong evidence that diffusion can be accelerated through supply chain learning initiatives like the UK Industry Forum in the auto components, aerospace, textiles and other sectors.

The importance of building and managing external networks is even more significant in a start-up where the challenge – as we'll see in Chapter 8 – is about trying to mobilise scarce resources. Engaging others to help you search for opportunities is an important strategy.

As we move from the 'exploit' to the 'explore' side of our innovation space so the need for different and sometimes unexpected perspectives becomes greater. At the same time the 'open innovation' opportunity (recognising that the smart guys don't all work for us and so trying to mobilise outside sources of knowledge) also points us to where further experimentation is needed to make new connections. Table 6.6 identifies some of these experimental approaches which we'll look at in a little more detail.

TABLE 6.6 Developing new ways of searching
(for more details on these, see J. Bessant and B. von Stamm[3]; www. aimresearch.org)

Search Strategy	Mode of operation
Sending out scouts	Dispatch idea hunters to track down new innovation triggers.
Exploring multiple futures	Use futures techniques to explore alternative possible futures; and develop innovation options from that.
Using the Web	Harness the power of the Web, through online communities, and virtual worlds, for example, to detect new trends.
Working with active users	Team up with product and service users to see the ways in which they change and develop existing offerings.
Deep diving	Study what people actually do, rather than what they say they do.
Probe and learn	Use prototyping as a mechanism to explore emergent phenomena and act as boundary object to bring key stakeholders into the innovation process.
Mobilise the mainstream	Bring mainstream actors into the product and service development process.
Corporate venturing	Create and deploy venture units.
Corporate entrepreneurship and intrapreneuring	Stimulate and nurture the entrepreneurial talent inside the organisation.
Use brokers and bridges	Cast the ideas net far and wide and connect with other industries.
Deliberate diversity	Create diverse teams and a diverse workforce.
Idea generators	Use creativity tools.

Sending Out Scouts

This is a widely used strategy which involves sending out people (full- or part-time) whose role is to search actively for new ideas to trigger the innovation process. (In Germany they are called *ideenjager* – idea hunters – a term which captures the concept well.) They could be searching for technological triggers, emerging markets or trends, competitor behaviour, etc., but what they have in common is a remit to seek things out, often in unexpected places. Search is not restricted to the organisation's particular industry; on the contrary, the fringes of an industry or even currently entirely unrelated fields can be of interest.

INNOVATION IN ACTION

Scouting for Ideas

The mobile phone company O2 has a trend-scouting group of about 10 people who interpret externally identified trends into their specific business context whilst BT has a scouting unit in Silicon Valley which assesses some 3000 technology opportunities a year in California. The four-man operation was established in 1999 to make venture investments in promising telecom start-ups, but after the dotcom bubble burst it shifted its mission towards identifying partners and technologies that BT was interested in. The small team looks at more than 1000 companies per year and then, based on their deep knowledge of the issues facing the R&D operations back in England, they target the small number of cases where there is a direct match between BT's needs and the Silicon Valley company's technology. While the number of successful partnerships that result from this activity is small – typically four or five per year – the unit serves an invaluable role in keeping BT abreast of the latest developments in its technology domain.

Exploring Multiple Futures

Futures studies of various kinds can provide a powerful source of ideas about possible innovation triggers, especially those which do not necessarily follow the current trajectory. Shell's 'Gamechanger' programme is a typical example which makes extensive use of alternative futures as a way of identifying domains of interest for future business which may lie outside the 'mainstream' of their current activities. Increasingly these rich 'science fiction' views of how the world might develop (and the threats and opportunities which it might pose in terms of discontinuous innovations) are being constructed by using a wide and deliberately diverse set of inputs rather than using the relatively narrow frame of reference which company staff might bring. One consequence has been the growth of specialist service companies which offer help in building and exploring models of alternative futures.

INNOVATION IN ACTION

Novo Nordisk, a major Danish pharmaceuticals business makes use of a company-wide scenario-based programme to explore radical futures around their core business. Its 'Diabetes 2020' process involved exploring radical alternative scenarios for chronic disease treatment and the roles which a player like Novo-Nordisk could play. As part of the follow-up from this initiative, in 2003 the company helped set up the Oxford Health Alliance, a non-profit collaborative entity which brought together key stakeholders – medical scientists, doctors, patients and government officials – with views and perspectives which were sometimes quite widely separated. To make it

(continued)

happen, Novo Nordisk made clear that its goal was nothing less than the prevention or cure of diabetes – a goal which if it were achieved would potentially kill off the company's main line of business. As Lars Rebien Sørensen, the CEO of Novo Nordisk, explained:

> 'In moving from intervention to prevention – that's challenging the business model where the pharmaceuticals industry is deriving its revenues! . . . We believe that we can focus on some major global health issue – mainly diabetes – and at the same time create business opportunities for our company.'

Another related approach is to build 'concept' models and prototypes to explore reactions and provide a focus for various different kinds of input which might shape/co-create future products and services. Concept cars are commonly used in the automotive industry not as production models but as stepping stones to help understand and shape what will be products in the future. Similarly Airbus and other aerospace firms have concept aircraft whilst Toyota is working on concept projects around housing, transportation and energy systems.

More recently companies have started to see value in developing such scenarios jointly with other organisations and discover exciting opportunities for cross-industry collaboration (which often means the creation of an entirely new market).

Using the Web

At one level the Internet offers a vast library – and the mechanisms to make new connections to and amongst the information it contains. This is, naturally, a widely used approach but it is interesting to look a little more deeply at how particular forms are developing and shaping this powerful tool.

In its simplest form the Web is a passive information resource to be searched – an additional space into which the firm might send its scouts. Increasingly there are professional organisations which offer focused search capabilities to help with this hunting – for example, in trying to pick up on emerging 'cool' trends among particular market segments. High-velocity environments like mobile telecoms, gaming and entertainment depend on picking up early warning signals and often make extensive use of these search approaches across the Web.

Developments in communications technology also make it possible to provide links across extranets and intranets to speed up the process of bringing signals into where they are needed. Firms like Zara and Benetton have sophisticated IT systems giving them early warning of emergent fashion trends which can be used to drive a high-speed flexible response on a global basis.

 Go online to find the Zara case study.

www.iande.info

This rich information source aspect can quickly be amplified in its potential if it is seen as a two-way or multi-way information marketplace. One of the first companies to take advantage of this was Ely Lilly who set up *Innocentive.com* as a matchmaking tool, connecting those with scientific problems with those being able to offer solutions. As Innocentive CEO Darrel Carroll says, 'Lilly hires a large number of extremely talented scientists from around the world, but like every company in its position, it can never hire all the scientists it needs. No company can.'

There are now multiple sites offering a brokering service, linking needs and means and essentially creating a global marketplace for ideas – in the process providing a rich source of early warning signals.

A further extension of this is to use websites in a more open-ended fashion, as laboratories in which experiments can be conducted or prototypes tested. For example, a site which is growing in popularity is www.secondlife.com – essentially a role playing game with over a million users. In this alternative world people can create different characters for themselves and interact in an alternative world – in the process creating a powerful laboratory for testing out ideas. Since by definition Second Life is the result of people projecting their aspirations and interests in a different space it offers significant scope for early warning about or even creating new trends.

The potential of 'advergaming' is being explored, for example, by US clothing retailer American Apparel which opened a virtual store in Second Life in 2006. In similar fashion social networking sites such as Facebook and MySpace have become powerful channels for finding and developing music and other entertainment ideas, challenging 'traditional' marketing approaches.

Beyond these uses come those which bring users into the equation as 'co-creators' – a theme we discussed earlier. For example, BMW makes use of the Web to enable a 'Virtual Innovation Agency' – a forum where suppliers from outside the normal range of BMW players can offer ideas which BMW may be able to use. These can be both product related and also process-related – for example a recent suggestion was for carbon recycling out of factory waste. Although this carries the risk that many 'cranks' will offer ideas these may also provide stepping stones to new domains of interest.

In many ways we are still at the beginning of using the interactive Internet – Web 2.0 – as an enabler of innovation search. We will look at the use of such networks in more detail in Chapter 8.

Working with Active Users

As we saw earlier, an increasingly significant strategy involves seeing users not as passive consumers of innovations created elsewhere but rather as active players in the process. Their ideas and insights can provide the starting point for very new directions and create new markets, products and services. The challenge now is to find ways of identifying and working with such lead users.

One of the clues is that active users are often at the fringes of the mainstream – in diffusion theory they are not even early adopters but rather active innovators. They are tolerant of failure, prepared to accept that things go wrong but through mistakes they can get to something better – hence the growing interest in participating in 'perpetual beta' testing and development of software and other online products. More often than not active users love to get involved because they feel strongly about the product or service in question; they really want to help and improve things. Lego found that the prime motivator amongst its communities of user-developers was the recognition which came with having their products actually made and distributed.

Go online to find the Lego case study.

www.iande.info

INNOVATION IN ACTION

The German firm Webasto makes a wide range of roofing systems for cars including the sophisticated cabriolet features on luxury cars like the Porsche, Volvo, Saab and Ferrari. They went through a systematic approach to understand what lead users are and how to identify them. Building on existing literature they identified four aspects that really drive people's propensity to innovate (cognitive complexity, team expertise, general knowledge, willingness to help). Based on those aspects they developed a questionnaire that they sent out, depending on the project in question, to up to 5000 people from their database. About 20% returned the questionnaires. There were several selection steps (e.g. age bracket, innovation potential) before they arrived at a lead user group of between 10 and 30. The lead users committed to come for an entire weekend, and without pay.

We will look at more examples of mobilising user networks in Chapter 8.

'Deep Diving'

Modern market research has become adept at hearing the 'voice of the customer' via interviews, focus groups, panels, etc. But sometimes what people say and what they actually do is different. In recent years there has been an upsurge in the use of anthropological style techniques to get closer to what people need/want in the context in which they operate. 'Deep dive' is one of many terms used to describe the approach – 'empathic design' and 'ethnographic methods' are others. (There is more discussion of this approach and a short case about IDEO in Chapter 11.)

Much of the research toolkit here originates from the field of anthropology where the researcher aims to gain insights primarily through observation and immersing him- or herself in the day to day life of the object of study – rather than through questioning only.

INNOVATION IN ACTION

For example, the German software company Hyve has developed sophisticated tools for carrying out market research using 'ethnography' – studying what groups of people do and how they interact with products and services. Their particular toolkit uses 'netnography' and studies online communities which, by definition, have multiple members exchanging experiences, ideas, concerns, tips, recommendations, etc. They have worked with a number of clients to develop new insights and identify opportunities for innovation – for example, looking at new tanning products on behalf of the cosmetics company Nivea.

This kind of approach is widely used by designers but in recent years has become a powerful innovation tool. For example, to ensure their new terminal at Heathrow would address user needs well into the future **BAA** commissioned some research into what the profile of users in 2020 might look like, and what their needs might be. Of course the ageing population came up as an issue; focusing on the behaviour of old people at the airport they noticed old people tend to go to the toilet rather frequently. So, the conclusion was to plan for more toilets at Terminal 5. However, when someone really followed people around they noted that many people going to the restrooms did not actually go to the toilet – but went there because it was quiet, and they could actually hear the announcements!

 Such ideas have considerable potential in public service applications – both for improving and also radically transforming them through involving users and meeting their needs more accurately. For example, healthcare work in the UK has focused on 'experience-based design' as a way of bringing patient insights into the design of services and on the website there is a podcast with Lynne Maher where she gives some examples.

www.iande.info

Probe and Learn

One of the problems about a radically different future is that it is hard to imagine it and hard to predict how things will play out. Sometimes a powerful approach is to try something out – probe – and learn from the results, even if they represent a 'failure'. In this way emergent trends, potential designs, etc. can be explored and refined in a continuous learning process.

There are two complementary dimensions here – the concept of 'prototyping' as a means of learning and refining an idea, and the concept of pilot-scale testing before moving across to a mainstream market. In both cases the underlying theme is essentially one of 'learning as you go', trying things out, making mistakes but using the experience to get closer to what is needed and will work. As Geoff Penney, Chief Information Officer of the US-based investment house Charles Schwab, once said, 'To avoid running too much risk we run pilots, and everyone knows it is 'just' a pilot and is not afraid of making suggestions for improvement – or killing it.'

Not surprisingly prototyping is particularly relevant in product-based firms. For example, **Bang & Olufsen** have revitalised their prototyping department and made it the innovation hub of the company. The prototyping department is engaged in new ideas as early as possible and the experiences are that this strongly supports the process. And, after a period with disappointing results in applying electronics in toys **LEGO** made a change in their development approach towards more intensive use of prototypes. Prototypes were created within days – often within hours – after the ideas matured. The result was a much more precise dialogue both within the organisation and with the main customers. Eventually, this led to more simple technology – and more success in terms of sales.

But the principles also apply in services – for example, the UK National Health Service and the **Design Council** have been prototyping new options for dealing with chronic diseases like diabetes, heart conditions and Alzheimer's disease. The aim is to learn by doing and also by engaging with the multiple stakeholders who will be part of whatever new system co-evolves.

 Go online to find the RED and Open Door case studies.

www.iande.info

This is one area where what have been called 'innovation technologies ' – simulation, rapid prototyping, interactive design, virtual worlds, etc. – can play an important role since they allow many different players to experiment with alternative models of what future innovations might look like. And they allow this to happen at an early enough stage in the innovation process so that there is a better chance of getting the most appropriate design before expensive resources are committed.

Corporate Venturing

For large organisations a major difficulty in search strategies is to find ways of 'getting out of the box' – as we saw earlier they are very good at searching within the mental frame in which they have traditionally operated. So they need to deploy new approaches to try to get outside this way of looking – and one powerful tool is to try to re-create entrepreneurship within the organisation. One widely used approach involves setting up of special units with the remit – and more importantly the budget – to explore new diversification options. Loosely termed 'corporate venture' (CV) units they actually cover a spectrum ranging from simple venture capital funds (for internal and externally generated ideas) through to active search and implementation teams, acquisition and spin-out specialists, etc. For example, **Nokia** has a very interesting corporate venturing approach for finding innovation. They have moved beyond 'not invented here' and are embracing 'let's find the best ideas whereever they are'. Nokia Venturing Organisation is focused on corporate venturing activities that include identifying and developing new businesses, or as they put it 'the renewal of Nokia'. Nokia Venture Partners invests exclusively in mobile and Internet protocol (I/P) related start-up businesses. They have a very interesting third group called Innovent that directly supports and nurtures nascent innovators with the hope of growing future opportunities for Nokia.

INNOVATION IN ACTION

The software company SAP has set up a venture unit called **SAP Inspire** to fund start-ups with interesting technologies. The mission of the group is to 'be a world-class corporate venturing group that will contribute, through business and technical innovation, to SAP's long-term growth and leadership'. It does so by:

- seeking entrepreneurial talent within SAP and providing an environment where ideas are evaluated on an open and objective basis;
- actively soliciting and cultivating ideas from the SAP community as well as effectively managing the innovation process from idea generation to commercialisation;
- looking for growth opportunities that are beyond the existing portfolio but within SAP's overall vision and strategy.

The purpose of corporate venturing is to provide some ring-fenced funds to invest in new directions for the business. Such models vary from being tightly controlled (by the parent organisation) to being fully autonomous.

Use Brokers and Bridges

As we saw in Chapter 5, innovation can often take a 'recombinant' form – and the famous saying of writer William Gibson is relevant here – 'the future is already here, it's just unevenly distributed'. Much recent research work on networks and broking suggests that a powerful search strategy involves making or facilitating connections – 'bridging small worlds'. Increasingly organisations are looking outside their 'normal' knowledge zones as they begin to pursue 'open innovation' strategies. But sending out scouts or mobilising the Internet can result simply in a vast increase in the amount of information coming at the firm – without necessarily making new or helpful connections. There is a clear message that networking – whether internally across different knowledge groups, or externally – is one of the big management challenges in the twenty-first century. Increasingly organisations are making use of social networking tools and techniques to map their networks and spot where and how bridges might be built – and this is a source of a growing professional service sector activity. Firms like **IDEO** and Whatif? specialise in being experts in nothing except the innovation process itself – their key skill lies in making and facilitating connections.

Brokering of this kind is particularly relevant in social entrepreneurship. Often the problem here is that an individual or group has a good idea and can make something happen at a local level. Examples might be self-help groups, or community activists, where solutions which meet the needs of a small group can be generated and developed. The problem is often one of scaling – of spreading these to the point where they might have a widespread impact and create significant social value. Brokering is a model increasingly used to help connect such social entrepreneurs with sources of further resources – money, knowledge, staff, etc. and also with those who commission services on the part of a wider social community. An example might be healthcare in the UK where an increasing amount of specialist provision is being delivered by entrepreneurial providers who are commissioned to deliver services on behalf of the wider National Health Service.

A number of new brokers today use the Internet to facilitate innovation. We have already mentioned Innocentive in the 'Using the Web' strategy above. Other web-based brokers are companies like YET2.com, who provide bridging capabilities that link (external) inventors with ideas or concepts to corporate development units. Chapter 8 looks at the whole idea of networks and links across them as a key approach in innovation search and development.

Searching the Innovation Space

If we return to the map of innovation space which we set out earlier in the chapter we can see that the search challenge requires different approaches – structures, tools and techniques – as we move across the different zones. Table 6.7 presents these in outline.

TABLE 6.7   Searching the innovation space

Zone	Search challenges	Tools and methods	Enabling structures
1 'Business as usual' – innovation but under steady-state conditions, little disturbance around core business model	Exploit – extend in incremental fashion boundaries of technology and market Refine and improve Close links/strong ties with key players	'Good practice' new product/service development Close to customer Technology platforms and systematic exploitation tools	Formal and main-stream structures High involvement across organisation Established roles and functions (including production, purchasing, etc.)
2 'Business model as usual' – bounded exploration within this frame	Exploration – pushing frontiers of technology and market via advanced techniques. Close links with key strategic knowledge sources	Advanced tools in R&D, market research. Increasing 'open innovation' approaches to amplify strategic knowledge search resources	Formal investment in specialised search functions – R&D, market research, etc.

(*continued*)

TABLE 6.7 (Continued)			
Zone	**Search challenges**	**Tools and methods**	**Enabling structures**
3 Alternative frame – taking in new/different elements in environment Variety matching, alternative architectures	Reframe – explore alternative options, introduce new elements Experimentation and open-ended search Breadth and periphery important	Alternative futures, weak signal detection User-led innovation Extreme and fringe users Prototyping – probe and learn Creativity techniques Bootlegging, etc.	Peripheral/ad hoc Challenging – 'licensed fools' CV units Internal entrepreneurs, scouts Futures groups, brokers, boundary spanning and consulting agencies
4 Radical – new to the world – possibilities. New architecture around as yet unknown and established elements	Emergence – need to co-evolve with stakeholders • Be in there • Be in there early • Be in there actively	Complexity theory – feedback and amplification, probe and learn, prototyping and use of boundary objects	Far from mainstream 'Licensed dreamers' Outside agents and facilitators

Absorptive Capacity – Developing the Capability to Search and Use Knowledge

One more broad strategic point concerns the question of where, when and how organisations make use of external knowledge to grow. It's easy to make the assumption that because there is a rich environment full of potential sources of innovation that every organisation will find and make use of these. The reality is, of course, that they differ widely in their ability to make use of such trigger signals – and the measure of this ability to find and use new knowledge has been termed 'absorptive capacity'.

The concept is essentially concerned with 'the ability of a firm to recognize the value of new, external information, assimilate it, and apply it to commercial ends ' and it is important because it shifts our attention to how well individuals and organisations are equipped to search out, select and implement knowledge.

Absorptive capacity is clearly not evenly distributed across a population. For various reasons firms may find difficulties in growing through acquiring and using new knowledge. Some may simply be unaware of the need to change never mind having the capability to manage such change. Such firms – a classic problem of small business growth, for example – differ from those which recognise in some strategic way the need to change, to acquire and use new knowledge but lack the capability to target their search or to assimilate and make effective use of new knowledge once identified. Others may be clear what they need but lack capability in finding and acquiring it. And others may have well-developed routines for dealing with all of these issues and represent resources on which less experienced firms might draw – as is the case with some major supply chains focused around a core central player.

The key message from research on absorptive capacity is that acquiring and using new knowledge involves multiple and different activities around search, acquisition, assimilation and implementation. It's essentially about learning to learn – building capabilities for search, acquire, assimilate, etc. which allow organisations to repeat the trick. Developing AC involves two complementary kinds of learning. Type 1 – adaptive learning – is about reinforcing and establishing relevant routines for dealing with a particular level of environmental complexity, and type 2 – generative learning – for taking on new levels of complexity.

We return to this discussion in Chapter 11 where we look in more detail at the question of knowledge management.

Chapter Summary

1 Faced with a rich environment full of potential sources of innovation, individuals and organisations need a strategic approach to searching for opportunities.

2 We can imagine a search space for innovation within which we look for opportunities. There are two dimensions – 'incremental/do better vs radical/do different innovation, and 'existing frame/new frame'.

3 Looking for opportunities can take us into the realms of 'exploit' – innovations built on moving forward from what we already know in mainly incremental fashion. Or it can involve 'explore' innovation, making risky but sometimes valuable leaps into new fields and opening up innovation space.

4 Exploit innovation favours established organisations and start-up entrepreneurs mostly find opportunities within niches in an established framework.

5 Bounded exploration involves radical search but within an established frame. This requires extensive resources – for example in R&D – but although this again favours established organisations there is also scope for knowledge-rich entrepreneurs – for example in high-tech start-up businesses.

6 Reframing innovation requires a different mindset, a new way of seeing opportunities – and often favours start-up entrepreneurs. Established organisations find this area difficult to search in because it requires them to let go of the ways they have traditionally worked – in response many set up internal entrepreneurial groups to bring the fresh thinking they need.

7 Exploring at the edge of chaos requires skills in trying to 'manage' processes of co-evolution. Again this favours start-up entrepreneurs with the flexibility, risk-taking and tolerance for failure to create new combinations and the agility to pick up on emerging new trends and ride them.

8 Search strategies require a combination of exploit and explore approaches but these often need different organisational arrangements.

9 There are many tools and techniques available to support search in exploit and explore directions; increasingly the game is being opened up and networks (and networking approaches and technologies) are becoming increasingly important.

10 Absorptive capacity – the ability to absorb new knowledge – is a key factor in the development of innovation management capability. It is essentially about learning to learn.

Key Terms Defined

Absorptive capacity   the ability of an organisation to take on and use new knowledge from outside.

Bootlegging   innovation projects which take place without the formal backing of the host organisation.

Brokering   ways of connecting different players in a network, for example linking start-up entrepreneurs with sources of resources.

Communities of practice   groups of individuals with common interests who co-operate to share knowledge within and across organisations.

Complexity/co-evolution   situation where multiple elements interact with each other making it impossible to predict their future development, instead it emerges as a result of interaction – co-evolution.

Corporate entrepreneurship   attempt on the part of established organisations to re-create entrepreneurial characteristics like agility, new perspectives and risk-taking by licensing a specific group to operate in different fashion.

Deep diving   deep immersion in the context within which innovations might be used.

Discontinuous innovation   innovation which occasionally takes place and changes the rules of the game – for example, through radical new technology, emergence of new markets, unexpected physical crisis, etc.

Ethnography   approaches to understanding user needs through observation, using approaches similar to those employed by anthropologists.

Exploit   innovation based on doing what we do but better, moving forward along established trajectories.

Explore   innovation involving jumps and leaps into new fields and opening up new space for innovation.

Fluid phase innovation   in innovation life cycle the early period when all sorts of technological and market possibilities co-exist, before a dominant design emerges.

Framing/reframing   the ways in which organisations and individuals make sense of a complex environment by simplifying it, using mental lenses to decide on what they pay attention to and what solutions they look at.

Gatekeepers   people within an organisation or network who help facilitate connections to others

High involvement innovation   innovation which involves a high proportion of the workforce or other population in contributing their ideas for change.

Intrapreneurship   internal entrepreneurship, as corporate entrepreneurship.

Lead users   early and active users within a population who can contribute ideas which shape the final version of an innovation.

Open innovation   model of innovation which allows for much more emphasis on knowledge flows rather than on knowledge production.

Scouts   individuals or groups who search out new technologies and/or markets.

STRATEGIC AND SOCIAL IMPLICATIONS

Innovation futures are likely to be very different from the current context – the trouble is that we don't know how! Trajectories in technologies and markets may play out in ways we can anticipate and plan for – that's the model which has driven the semiconductor industry, following 'Moore's Law' (which 'predicts' that the price of chips will halve as their power doubles on a regular basis) for example. But often there is interaction between different elements so we need to look for more complex and emergent patterns.

Two major research projects have been trying to develop alternative pictures of how innovation will work in the future in terms of challenges, solutions – and how we might approach managing it. How will we search, what opportunities (and threats) might emerge and what changes might we need to make to take advantage of them?

In the first, Anna Trifilova and Bettina von Stamm have pulled together a book and website drawing on the insights of nearly 400 innovation researchers from around 60 countries to paint a picture of the different ways in which 'the future of innovation' can be seen. (www.thefutureofinnovation.org)

The second is a European Union funded programme – INFU (Innovation Futures for Europe) with multiple partners aiming at developing scenarios for the future of innovation. They present a variety of different scenarios and invite further elaboration and addition through an interactive website – www.innovation-futures.org

Try visiting both websites and exploring the range of alternative futures being presented. How might you elaborate further on these search directions? What threats – and more importantly, opportunities – might be found in them?

DEVELOPING PERSONAL CAPABILITIES

Innovation is about finding opportunities so it is a good idea to try to develop some systematic search skills – 'rules of thumb' – which help begin the process of spotting niches and gaps where new possibilities might exist. For example:

- Sometimes innovation opportunities can be found by asking 'what business are we in?' This sounds an obvious question, but sometimes innovation can take the form of repositioning – offering the same basic product or service but addressed in a new way to different markets. For example, Amazon.com began as an online retailer but is trying to broaden its business by positioning itself also as a software developer and supplier. Google began as a search engine but has moved into advertising and now into mass communication.
- Another approach is to use market research tools to understand the shape, size, dynamics of the market. For example, the cellular phone business has moved from a specialist, high-price

(*continued*)

business tool into the general marketplace as a result of both technological and cultural change. Similarly low cholesterol and other healthy foods are increasingly becoming relevant to a large segment of the population as a result of changing social attitudes and education.

- A wide range of techniques is available for trying to understand the likely future dynamics of new markets, running from simple extrapolation of current trends through to complex techniques for handling discontinuous change, such as Delphi panels and scenario writing. Such forecasting needs to move beyond sales-related information to include other features which will influence the potential market – for example, demographic, technological, political and environmental issues. For example, the present concern for environmentally friendly 'green' products is likely to increase and will be shaped by a variety of these factors. From this information come valuable clues about the type of performance which the market expects from a particular manufacturer or service provider – and hence the targets for process innovation.

- One difficulty in exploring a market space arises when the market does not exist or where it suddenly takes a turn in a new direction. Developing antennae to pick up on the early warnings of trends is important, particularly in consumer-related innovation. For example, much of the development of the mobile phone industry has been on the back of the different uses to which schoolchildren put their phones and delivering innovations which support this. Examples include text messaging, image/video exchange and downloadable personal ring tones where the clues to the emergence of these innovation trajectories were picked up by monitoring what such children were doing or aspiring to.

Further Reading and Resources

The concept of 'exploit' vs 'explore' was first discussed by James March and has formed the basis for many studies since then – see March, J., *Exploration and exploitation in organizational learning*. Organization Science, **2**(1), p. 71–87 and Benner, M.J. and M.L. Tushman, *Exploitation, exploration, and process management: The productivity dilemma revisited*, Academy of Management, *The Academy of Management Review*, **28**(2), pp. 238.

Tushman and Anderson explored the challenges for organisations in the midst of major technological upheavals – see Tushman, M. and P. Anderson, Technological discontinuities and organizational environments, *Administrative Science Quarterly*, **31**(3), pp. 439–465.

The difficulties of reframing are well explored by Day and Shoemaker who argue the need for 'peripheral vision' amongst entrepreneurs, see Day, G. and P. Schoemaker, *Peripheral Vision: Detecting the weak signals that will make or break your company* (Boston: Harvard Business School Press, 2006). This theme is also picked up in Foster, R. and S. Kaplan, *Creative Destruction* (Cambridge: Harvard University Press, 2002).

Christensen, C., S. Anthony and E. Roth, *Seeing What's Next* (Boston: Harvard Business School Press, 2007).

Searching at the frontier is one of the questions being addressed by the Discontinuous Innovation Laboratory, a network of around 30 academic institutions and 150 companies – see www.innovation-lab.org for more details. Reports on their work are available for download at www.aim-research.org

Looking at the edge of familiar markets and how to find unexploited space are discussed in Ulnwick, A., *What Customers Want: Using outcome-driven innovation to create breakthrough products and services* (New York: McGraw-Hill, 2005) and Kim, W. and R. Mauborgne, *Blue Ocean Strategy: How to create uncontested market space and make the competition irrelevant* (Boston, Mass.: Harvard Business School Press, 2005).

Open innovation was originated by Henry Chesbrough but has been elaborated in a number of other studies. Case examples include the Procter & Gamble story and Alan Lafley's book provides a readable account from the perspective of the CEO: Lafley, A. and R. Charan, *The Game Changer* (New York: Profile, 2008).

The concept of absorptive capacity was originated by Cohen and Levinthal and developed by Zahra and George: Zahra, S.A. and G. George, Absorptive capacity: A review, reconceptualization and extension, *Academy of Management Review*, 27, pp. 185–194.

References

1. Bessant, J. and T. Venables (2008) *Creating Wealth from Knowledge: Meeting the innovation challenge*. Cheltenham: Edward Elgar.
2. Chesbrough, H. (2003) *Open Innovation: The new imperative for creating and profiting from technology*. Boston, Mass.: Harvard Business School Press.
3. Bessant, J. and B. von Stamm (2007) *Twelve Search Strategies Which Might Save Your Organization*. London: AIM Executive Briefing.

Discussion Questions

1. Where and how might you organise search for innovation opportunities for the following businesses?
   a. A fast food restaurant chain
   b. An electronic test equipment maker
   c. A hospital
   d. An insurance company
   e. A new entrant biotechnology firm.

2. Using the list of innovation sources in Chapter 5, how would you organise search to pick up trigger signals from these?

3. If innovation is increasingly a matter of knowledge management, what sorts of challenges does this approach pose for managing the process?

4. How might you search for innovation opportunities in the public sector? Using examples indicate how and where it can be an important strategic issue.

5. You are a newly appointed director for a small charity which supports homeless people. How could innovation improve the ways in which your charity operates in terms of finding new opportunities for raising support?

6. What are the challenges which managers might face in trying to organise to find a long-term steady stream of incremental innovation ideas?

Team Exercises

1. You have been appointed as a team to search for radical/disruptive ideas for your company. How would you organise the search process – where would you look, how would you bring the messages back to the mainstream?

2. Looking at the innovation search space in Figure 6.1, how would you organise to explore each of the four areas?

3. You've been asked as a team to come up with 'learning partners' – organizations outside of your sector – from whom you could learn and pick up different ideas. Who might you look at and what kinds of ideas might you get from this.

4. Pick a sector and then discuss how you might reframe the way it operates. How could you find new opportunities and how might you change the rules of the game?

CASE STUDY 6

Exploring Innovation in Action

Sewing up the competition – innovation in the textile and clothing industry

Manufacturing doesn't get much older than the textile and clothing industry. Since the earliest days when we lived in caves there's been a steady demand for something to wrap around us to keep warm and to protect the more sensitive bits of our anatomy from the worst of the elements. What began with animal hides and furs gradually moved into a more sophisticated activity with fabrics woven from flax or wool – and with people increasingly specialising in the business.

In its early days this was very much a cottage industry – quite literally people would spin wool gathered from sheep and weave simple cloths on home-made looms. But the skill base – and the technology – began to develop and many of the family names we still have today – Weaver, Dyer, Tailor, for example – remind us of the importance of this sector. And where there were sufficient cottages and groups of people with such skill we began to see concentrations of manufacturing – for example, the Flemish weavers or the lace makers in the English Midlands. As their reputation – and the quality of their goods – grew so the basis of trading internationally in textile and clothing was established.

The small-scale nature of the industry changed dramatically during the Industrial Revolution. Massive growth in population meant that markets were becoming much bigger whilst at the same time significant developments in technology (and the science underpinning the technology) meant that making textiles and clothing became an increasingly industrialised process. Much of the early Industrial Revolution was around the cotton and wool industries in England and many of the great innovations and machinery – such as the Spinning Jenny – were essentially innovations to support a growing international industry. And the growth of the industry fuelled scientific research and led to developments like the invention of synthetic dyes (which allowed a much broader range of colour) and the development of bleaching agents.

There's a pattern in this in which certain manufacturing innovation trajectories play a key role. For example, the growing mechanisation of operations, their linking together into *systems* of production and the increasing attempts to take human intervention out through automation. Of course this was easier to do in some cases than others – for example, one of the earliest forms of programmable control, long before the invention of the computer, was the Jacquard punched card system which could control the weaving of different threads across a loom. But actually making material into various items of clothing is more difficult, simply because material doesn't have a fixed and controllable shape – so this remained increasingly a labour-intensive process.

By the twentieth century the industries had become huge and well-established, with growing international trade in raw materials such as cotton and in finished goods. The role of design became increasingly important as basic demand was satisfied and certain regions – for example, France and Italy – began to assume strong reputations for design. Branding became increasingly important in a world where mass communications began to make the telling of stories and the linking of images and other elements into advertising which fuelled demand for clothing as much more than a basic necessity purchase.

Mass production methods and the scientific management approaches underpinning them diffused rapidly – and in the case of clothing assembly which remained a labour-intensive process – led to the quest for lower wage cost locations. So began the migration of clothing manufacture around the world, visiting and settling in ever cheaper locations across the Far East, through much of Africa and Latin America to its present home in China.

Today this is a global industry embracing design activities, cutting and processing operations, assembly, distribution and sales – all fuelled by a huge demand for differentiation and personalisation. This is an industry in which price is only one element – non-price factors such as variety, speed, brand and quality matter. And it's an industry dominated by the need for high-frequency product innovation – fashion collections no longer run along the old seasonal track with winter and summer collections. In some cases the range is changed every month and innovation in information and communications technology means that this cycle is getting shorter still.

All of this has shaped an industry which is highly networked across global 'value chains' and co-ordinated by a few major players. Much of the 'front' end of the industry is about major brands and retail chains whilst the 'backroom' operations are often small-scale subcontractors often in low wage cost areas of the world. Like so many industries it has become somewhat footloose and wandered from its origins – leaving behind only a small reminder of its original dominance. Compared with countries like India and China, today's European clothing industry is a small player on the global stage.

There are some exceptions to this – and they underline the power of innovation and entrepreneurship. Just because the dominant trends lead in one direction does not mean that there isn't scope for someone to spot and deploy ways of bucking this trend. One such player was a young clerk working in a small clothing retailing business in northern Spain. Frustrated with his career prospects Amancio Ortega Gaona decided to strike out on his own and in 1963 invested his savings – the princely sum of $25 – into a small manufacturing operation making pyjamas and lingerie. In classic fashion he peddled (and pedalled – his earliest transport was a bicycle!) his wares around the region and built the business over the next ten years and then decided to move into retailing as well, opening his first shop in the north-western town of La Coruna in 1975.

Things have moved on somewhat since then. Industria de Diseno Textil – Inditex – the holding company which he established – is now worth around $8 billion and has just opened its 2000th store in Hong Kong. Active in nearly 70 countries this textile and clothing business has eight key brand groups, each targeted at particular segments or product types – for example, 'Pull and Bear' for children, 'Massimo Dutti' for older men and women or 'Oysho' in lingerie. Best known of these is 'Zara' – a global brand with strong design and fashion identity running through both the clothes and the stores in which they are sold.

Its clothes combine stylish designs with a strong link to current high-fashion themes with moderate prices. As Lotte Freddie, fashion editor of the Danish daily newspaper *Berlingske Tidende*, commented 'If you want a classic, Italianate look in tune with current styles and at a reasonable price go to Zara'.

Zara's successful growth is not simply a matter of low cost or of standardisation but rather of *innovation*. The company has become a leader by exploiting some of the key non-price trends in the industry – for example, variety and product innovation. For example over 10,000 different clothing models are created and sold every year – this is most certainly not a case of 'one size fits all' or of long-lasting product types! Ortega has taken the entire system for creating clothes and built a business – and originally did so in an area which did not previously have any textile tradition.

At an early stage in the development of the manufacturing business he moved back into textile finishing operations to make sure that the colours and quality of the material he used to make the clothes were up to scratch. Not only did this give better quality control but it also opened up the road to offering exciting and different fabric designs and textures. There are now 18 textile designing and finishing operations in the group as well as the clothing manufacturing.

A major part of the company's success comes from a strong commitment to design – they employ over 200 designers and make extensive play of this commitment. It's a theme which doesn't stop with the clothes themselves but also extends to the presentation of the stores, their window displays, their catalogues, Internet advertising and so on. Part of the headquarters building in Arteixo La Coruna, Spain, contains 25 full-size shop windows with display platforms and lighting which allow the team to see what real store windows would look like – not only under normal conditions but also on rainy days, at night and so on.

Another key aspect of Zara's success is the flexibility which comes from having a very different model for manufacturing. Around 2500 employees work directly in manufacturing operations – but behind them is a much larger workforce spread across villages and small communities in Spain and northern Portugal. Once the new design has been approved the fabric is cut and then distributed to this network of small workshops – and these represent an outsource capability delivering a high degree of flexibility. Pre-cut pieces and easy to follow instructions are given to workers in what is still largely an informal economy – and their output then flows back into the massive Zara distribution centre like tributaries to a fast-flowing river. (This is not a small operation – the centre has around 200 kilometres of moving rails on which the products flow. Highly automated and with extensive in-line quality checking the process transfers the incoming pieces into production lots which are then allocated to a fleet of trucks for fast shipment, mostly by air from the nearby airport at Santiago de Compostella.)

Needless to say this places significant demands on a highly flexible and innovative co-ordination system which Zara have developed in-house. In this way they make use of a model which dates back hundreds of years (the idea of industrial districts and clusters) but use twenty-first century technologies to make it work to give them huge flexibility in both the volume and variety of the things they make. Where competitors such as H&M and Gap have to start planning and producing their new lines three to five months before goods finally make it to the stores, Zara manages the whole process in less than three weeks!

Their flexibility is also based on rapid response and extensive use of information and communication technologies. At the end of the day as the customers leave their 950 stores around the world the sales staff use wireless handsets to communicate inventory levels to the store manager who then transmits this intelligence back to Spain as a feed into the design order and distribution system. This gives an up-to-the-minute idea of what is selling – and what isn't – so the stores can be highly responsive to customer preferences – which colours 'work', which themes are popular, which designs aren't hitting the spot. But it's not just following the market – Zara can also push the game by making sure that no model is kept on sale for more than four weeks – no matter how well it is selling. This has a strong impact on their brand – they are seen as very original and design-led – but it puts even more pressure on their ability to be agile in design and manufacture.

Questions Linked to Case Study

1. Zara is a late but successful entrant to the global textile market. How did it search for – and create – opportunities to give it a niche? Is the Zara model sustainable? What would you do to preserve their edge over the next 5–10 years, given that many other players are now looking to follow their example? If you don't think it can survive, give your reasons for why you think the model is unsustainable and will fail.

2. You have been hired as a consultant to a small clothing manufacturer who wants to emulate the success of Zara and Benetton. She wants advice on an innovation strategy which takes the key lessons from these successful firms. What would you offer?

3. Zara Home has just opened using the same basic business model and deploying the same innovative approach as the rest of the business but in the home goods field. Do you think it might succeed and why?

5. How might Zara search at the edge of its current business to avoid being surprised or disrupted by a new entrant entrepreneur reframing the business?

Summary of Web Resources

Cases

- Kumba
- Corning
- NPI
- Lego
- RED
- Open Door
- Coloplast
- 3M
- Tesco
- P&G
- Cerulean
- Zara
- Lego

Media

- Emma Taylor, video interview
- Veeder Root, video interview
- Podcasts for David Simoes-Brown and Richard Philpott
- Roy Sandbach, podcast interview
- Patrick McLaughlin, video interview
- Lynne Maher, podcast interview

Tools

- QFD
- Market research
- 12 search strategies

PART III

FINDING THE RESOURCES

Part III Finding the Resources

Making it happen is critical and will need time, money, different knowledge sets etc. But before we even begin to assemble the resources, we need a plan. What will we need and when? And before that we need to be clear about which opportunity we will develop and why. Out of all the things we could do, what are we going to do—and why? Selecting the best of these sounds simple enough, except that we don't know which of them is best until we try. Innovation is fraught with uncertainty and guesswork, and the only way to find out whether or not something is a good bet is to start developing it. So the process of strategic choice—which of the many possibilities should we back, given that we only have limited resources—is a big challenge.

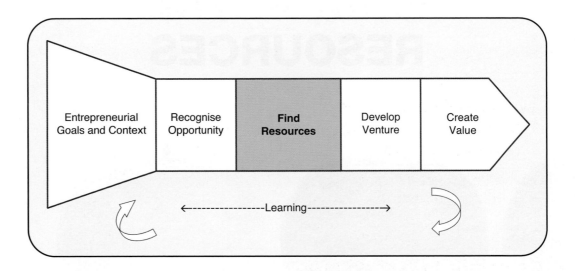

Chapter 7

Building the Case

LEARNING OBJECTIVES

By the end of this chapter you will be able to:

- Develop and use a business plan to attract resources.
- Choose and apply the most appropriate forecasting methods.
- Develop innovations to improve the likelihood of adoption and diffusion.
- Identify and manage risk and uncertainty.

Go online to find additional . . .

Cases

Tools

Media

www.iande.info

tive for developing a formal business plan is to secure support or funding for a ture. However, research is not unanimous on the role and effectiveness of busi- me studies indicate a positive relationship between the development of a formal and the ability to attract external funding,[1] whereas others find no significant relationship.[2] Whatever the reality, the development of a convincing plan has become a rite of passage for a new venture. In practice business planning serves a much broader function than funding, and can help to translate abstract or ambiguous goals into more explicit operational needs, and support subsequent decision making and identify trade-offs. A business plan can help to make more explicit the risks and opportunities, expose any unfounded optimism and self-delusion, and avoid subsequent arguments concerning responsibilities and rewards.

Developing the Business Plan

No standard business plan exists, but in many cases venture capitalists will provide a pro forma for their business plan. Typically a business plan should be relatively concise, say no more than 10–20 pages, begin with an executive summary, and include sections on the product, markets, technology, development, production, marketing, human resources, financial estimates with contingency plans, and the timetable and funding requirements. A typical formal business plan will include the following sections:[3]

1. Details of the product or service.
2. Assessment of the market opportunity.
3. Identification of target customers.
4. Barriers to entry and competitor analysis.
5. Experience, expertise and commitment of the management team.
6. Strategy for pricing, distribution and sales.
7. Identification and planning for key risks.
8. Cash-flow calculation, including break-even points and sensitivity.
9. Financial and other resource requirements of the business.

Most business plans submitted to venture capitalists are strong on the technical considerations, often placing too much emphasis on the technology relative to other issues. As Roberts notes, 'entrepreneurs propose that they can do *it* better than anyone else, but may forget to demonstrate that anyone wants *it*'.[4] He identifies a number of common problems with business plans submitted to venture capitalists: marketing plan, management team, technology plan and financial plan. The management team will be assessed against their commitment, experience and expertise, normally in that order. Unfortunately, many potential entrepreneurs place too much emphasis on their expertise, but have insufficient experience in the team, and fail to demonstrate the passion and commitment to the venture (Table 7.1).

There are common serious inadequacies in all four of these areas, but the worst are in marketing and finance. Less than half of the plans examined provide a detailed marketing strategy,

TABLE 7.1 Criteria used by venture capitalists to assess proposals

Criteria	European (n = 195)	American (n = 100)	Asian (n = 53)
Entrepreneur able to evaluate and react to risk	3.6	3.3	3.5
Entrepreneur capable of sustained effort	3.6	3.6	3.7
Entrepreneur familiar with the market	3.5	3.6	3.6
Entrepreneur demonstrated leadership ability*	3.2	3.4	3.0
Entrepreneur has relevant track record*	3.0	3.2	2.9
Product prototype exists and functions*	3.0	2.4	2.9
Product demonstrated market acceptance*	2.9	2.5	2.8
Product proprietary or can be protected*	2.7	3.1	2.6
Product is 'high technology'*	1.5	2.3	1.4
Target market has high growth rate*	3.0	3.3	3.2
Venture will stimulate an existing market	2.4	2.4	2.5
Little threat of competition within 3 years	2.2	2.4	2.4
Venture will create a new market*	1.8	1.8	2.2
Financial return >10 times within 10 years*	2.9	3.4	2.9
Investment is easily made liquid* (e.g. made public or acquired)	2.7	3.2	2.7
Financial return >10 times within 5 years*	2.1	2.3	2.1

1 = irrelevant, 2 = desirable, 3 = important, 4 = essential. * Denotes significant at the 0.05 level.

Source: Adapted from Knight, R. (1992) Criteria used by venture capitalists. In T. Khalil and B. Bayraktar, eds, *Management of Technology III: The Key to Global Competitiveness* (pp. 574–583), Industrial Engineering & Management Press, Georgia.

and just half include any sales plan. Three-quarters of the plans fail to identify or analyse any potential competitors. As a result most business plans contain only basic financial forecasts, and just 10% conduct any sensitivity analysis on the forecasts. The lack of attention to marketing and competitor analysis is particularly problematic as research indicates that both factors are associated with subsequent success.

Go online to find the Clearvue case study.

www.iande.info

The Clearvue case study illustrates many of the practical difficulties in developing a robust business plan, even in more mature markets and technologies.

For example, in the early stages many new ventures rely too much on a few major customers for sales, and are therefore very vulnerable commercially. As an extreme example, around half of technology ventures rely on a single customer for more than half of their first-year sales. An overdependence on a small number of customers has three major drawbacks:

1. Vulnerability to changes in the strategy and health of the dominant customer.
2. A loss of negotiating power, which may reduce profit margins.
3. Little incentive to develop marketing and sales functions, which may limit future growth.

Therefore it is essential to develop a better understanding of the market, and technological inputs to a business plan. The financial estimates flow from these critical inputs relatively easily, although risk and uncertainty still need to be assessed. This chapter focuses only on the most important, but often poorly executed, aspects of business planning for innovations. We first discuss approaches to forecasting markets and technologies, and then identify how a better understanding of the adoption and diffusion of innovations can help us to develop more successful business plans. Finally, we look at how to assess the risks and resources required to finalise a plan.

ENTREPRENEURSHIP IN ACTION

What Is the 'Fuzzy Front End', Why Is It Important, and How Can It be Managed?

Technically, new product development (NPD) projects often fail at the end of a development process. The foundations for failure, however, often seem to be established at the very beginning of the NPD process, often referred to as the 'fuzzy front end'. Broadly speaking, the fuzzy front

(continued)

end is defined as the period between when an opportunity for a new product is first considered, and when the product idea is judged ready to enter 'formal' development. Hence, the fuzzy front end starts with a firm having an idea for a new product, and ends with the firm deciding to launch a formal development project or, alternatively, decides not to launch such a project.

In comparison with the subsequent development phase, knowledge on the fuzzy front end is severely limited. Hence, relatively little is known about the key activities that constitute the fuzzy front end, how these activities can be managed, which actors participate, as well as the time needed to complete this phase. Many firms also seem to have great difficulties managing the fuzzy front end in practice. In a sense this is not surprising: the fuzzy front end is a crossroads of complex information processing, tacit knowledge, conflicting organisational pressures, and considerable uncertainty and equivocality. In addition, this phase is also often ill-defined and characterised by ad hoc decision making in many firms. It is therefore important to identify success factors which allow firms to increase their proficiency in managing the fuzzy front end. This is the purpose of this research note.

In order to increase knowledge on how the fuzzy front end can be better managed, we conducted a large-scale survey of the empirical literature on the fuzzy front end. In total, 39 research articles constitute the base of our review. Analysis of these articles identified 17 success factors for managing the fuzzy front end. The factors are not presented in order of importance, as the present state of knowledge makes such an ordering judgemental at best.

1. *The presence of idea visionaries or product champions.* Such persons can overcome stability and inertia and thus secure the progress of an emerging product concept.
2. *An adequate degree of formalisation.* Formalisation promotes stability and reduces uncertainty. The fuzzy front end process should be explicit, widely known among members of the organisation, characterised by clear decision-making responsibilities, and contain specific performance measures.
3. *Idea refinement and adequate screening of ideas.* Firms need mechanisms to separate good ideas from the less good ones, but also to screen ideas by means of both business and feasibility analysis.
4. *Early customer involvement.* Customers can help to construct clear project objectives, reduce uncertainty and equivocality, and also facilitate the evaluation of a product concept.
5. *Internal cooperation among functions and departments.* A new product concept must be able to 'survive' criticism from different functional perspectives, but cooperation among functions and departments also creates legitimacy for a new concept and facilitates the subsequent development phase.
6. *Information processing other than cross-functional integration and early customer involvement.* Firms need to pay attention to product ideas of competitors, as well as legally mandated issues in their emerging product concepts.
7. *Senior management involvement.* A pre-development team needs support from senior management to succeed, but senior management can also align individual activities which cut across functional boundaries.

(continued)

8. *Preliminary technology assessment.* Technology assessment means asking early whether the product can be developed, what technical solutions will be required, and at what cost. Firms need also to judge whether the product concept, once turned into a product, can be manufactured.

9. *Alignment between NPD and strategy.* New concepts must capitalise on the core competence of their firms, and synergy among projects is important.

10. *An early and well-defined product definition.* Product concepts are representations of the goals for the development process. A product definition includes a product concept, but in addition provides information about target markets, customer needs, competitors, technology, resources, etc. A well-defined product definition facilitates the subsequent development phase.

11. *Beneficial external co-operation with stakeholders other than customers.* Many firms benefit from a 'value-chain perspective' during the fuzzy front end, e.g. through collaboration with suppliers. This factor is in line with the emerging literature on 'open innovation'.

12. *Learning from experience capabilities of the pre-project team.* Pre-project team members need to identify critical areas and forecast their influence on project performance, i.e. through learning from experience.

13. *Project priorities.* The pre-project team needs to be able to make trade-offs among the competing virtues of scope (product functionality), scheduling (timing) and resources (cost). In addition, the team also needs to use a priority criteria list, i.e. a rank ordering of key product features, should it be forced to disregard certain attributes due to e.g. cost concerns.

14. *Project management and the presence of a project manager.* A project manager can lobby for support and resources, and coordinate technical as well as design issues.

15. *A creative organisational culture.* Such a culture allows a firm to utilise the creativity and talents of employees, as well as maintaining a steady stream of ideas feeding into the fuzzy front end.

16. *A cross-functional executive review committee.* A cross-functional team for development is not enough – cross-functional competence is also needed when evaluating product definitions.

17. *Product portfolio planning.* The firm needs to assure sufficient resources to develop the planned projects, as well as 'balancing' its portfolio of new product ideas.

Although successful management of the fuzzy front end requires firms to excel in individual factors and activities, this is a necessary rather than sufficient condition. Firms must also be able to integrate or align different activities and factors, as reciprocal interdependencies exist among different success factors. This is often referred to as 'a holistic perspective', 'interdependencies among factors', or simply as 'fit'. To date, however, nobody seems to know exactly which factors should be integrated, and how this should be achieved. In addition, specific guidelines on how to measure performance in the fuzzy front end are also lacking. Hence, only fragments of a 'theory' for managing the fuzzy front end can be said to be in place.

To make things even more complicated, the fuzzy front end process seems to vary not only among firms, but also among projects within the same firm where activities, their sequencing,

(continued)

degree of overlap and relative time duration differ from project to project. Therefore, capabilities for managing the fuzzy front end are both highly valuable yet difficult to obtain. Developing firms therefore need first to obtain proficiency in individual success factors. Second, they need to integrate and arrange these factors into a coherent whole aligned to the circumstances of the firm. And finally, they need to master several trade-off situations which we refer to as 'balancing acts'.

As a first balancing act, firms need to ask if screening of ideas should be made gentle or harsh. On the one hand, firms need to get rid of bad ideas quickly, to save the costs associated with their further development. On the other hand, harsh screening may also kill good ideas too early. Ideas for new products often refine and gain momentum through informal discussion, a fact which forces firms to balance too gentle and too harsh screening. Another balancing act concerns formalisation. The basic proposition is that formalisation is good because it facilitates transparency, order and predictability. However, in striving to enforce effectiveness, formalisation also risks inhibiting innovation and flexibility. Even if evidence is still scarce the relationship between formality and performance seems to obey an inverted U-shaped curve, where both too little and too much formality has a negative effect on performance. From this it follows that firms need to carefully consider the level of formalisation they impose on the fuzzy front end.

A third balancing act concerns the trade-off between uncertainty and equivocality reduction. Market and technological uncertainty can often be reduced through environmental scanning and increased information processing in the development team, but more information often increases the level of equivocality. An equivocal situation is one where multiple meanings exist, and such a situation implies that a firm needs to construct, cohere or enact a reasonable interpretation to be able to move on, rather than to engage in information seeking and analysis. Therefore, firms need to balance their need to reduce uncertainty with the need to reduce equivocality, as trying to reduce one often implies increasing the other. Furthermore, firms need to balance the need for allowing for flexibility in the product definition with the need to push it to closure. A key objective in the fuzzy front end is a clear, robust and unambiguous product definition as such a definition facilitates the subsequent development phase. However, product features often need to be changed during development as market needs change or problems with underlying technologies are experienced. Finally, a final balancing act concerns the trade-off between the competing virtues of innovation and resource efficiency. In essence, this concerns balancing competing value orientations, where innovation and creativity in the front end are enabled by organisational slack and an emphasis on people management, while resource efficiency is enabled by discipline and an emphasis on process management.

In addition, the fuzzy front end process needs to be adapted to the type of product under development. For physical products, different logics apply to assembled and non-assembled products. Emerging research shows that a third logic applies to the development of new service concepts. To conclude, managing the fuzzy front end is indeed no easy task, but can have an enormous positive impact on performance for those firms that succeed.

Source: Frishammar, J. and H. Florén (2008). Where new product development begins: success factors, contingencies and balancing acts in the fuzzy front end. Paper presented at the IAMOT conference in Dubai, 5–8 April. Reproduced by permission of Johan Frishammar (Luleå University of Technology, Sweden) and Henrik Florén (Halmstad University, Sweden).

Forecasting Innovation

Forecasting the future has a pretty bad track record, but nevertheless has a central role in business planning for innovation. In most cases the outputs, that is the predictions made, are less valuable than the process of forecasting itself. If conducted in the right spirit, forecasting should provide a framework for gathering and sharing data, debating interpretations and making assumptions, challenges and risks more explicit.

The most appropriate choice of forecasting method will depend on:

- What we are trying to forecast.
- Rate of technological and market change.
- Availability and accuracy of information.
- The company's planning horizon.
- The resources available for forecasting.

In practice there will be a trade-off between the cost and robustness of a forecast. The more common methods of forecasting such as trend extrapolation and time series are of limited use for new products, because of the lack of past data. However, regression analysis can be used to identify the main factors driving demand for a given product, and therefore provide some estimate of future demand, given data on the underlying drivers.

For example, a regression might express the likely demand for the next generation of digital mobile phones in terms of rate of economic growth, price relative to competing systems, rate of new business formation, and so on. Data are collected for each of the chosen variables and coefficients for each derived from the curve that best describes the past data. Thus the reliability of the forecast depends a great deal on selecting the right variables in the first place. The advantage of regression is that, unlike simple extrapolation or time-series analysis, the forecast is based on cause and effect relations. Econometric models are simply bundles of regression equations, including their interrelationship. However, regression analysis is of little use where future values of an explanatory value are unknown, or where the relationship between the explanatory and forecast variables may change.

Leading indicators and analogues can improve the reliability of forecasts, and are useful guideposts to future trends in some sectors. In both cases there is a historical relationship between two trends. For example, new business start-ups might be a leading indicator of the demand for fax machines in six months' time. Similarly, business users of mobile telephones may be an analogue for subsequent patterns of domestic use.

Such 'normative' techniques are useful for estimating the future demand for existing products, or perhaps alternative technologies or novel niches, but are of limited utility in the case of more radical systems innovation. Exploratory forecasting, in contrast, attempts to explore the range of future possibilities. The most common methods are:

- customer or market surveys
- internal analysis, e.g. brainstorming
- Delphi or expert opinion
- scenario development.

ENTREPRENEURSHIP IN ACTION

Limits of Forecasting

In 1986, Schnaars and Berenson published an assessment of the accuracy of forecasts of future growth markets since the 1960s, with the benefit of over 20 years of hindsight. The list of failures is as long as the list of successes. Below are some of the failures.

The 1960s were a time of great economic prosperity and technological advancement in the United States . . . One of the most extensive and widely publicised studies of future growth markets was TRW Inc. 'Probe of the Future'. The results . . . appeared in many business publications in the late 1960s . . . Not all . . . were released. Of the ones that were released, nearly all were wrong! Nuclear-powered underwater recreation centers, a 500 kilowatt nuclear power plant on the moon, 3D color TV, robot soldiers, automatic vehicle control on the interstate system, and plastic germproof houses were amongst some of the growth markets identified by this study.

In 1966, industry experts predicted, 'The shipping industry appears ready to enter the jet age.' By 1968, large cargo ships powered by gas turbine engines were expected to penetrate the commercial market. The benefits of this innovation were greater reliability, quicker engine starts and shorter docking times.

Even dentistry foresaw technological wonders . . . in 1968, the Director of the National Institute of Dental Research, a division of the US Public Health Service, predicted that 'in the next decade, both tooth decay and the most prevalent form of gum disease will come to a virtual end'. According to experts at this agency, by the late 1970s false teeth and dentures would be 'anachronisms' replaced by plastic teeth implant technology. A vaccine against tooth decay would also be widely available and there would be little need for dental drilling.'

Source: Schnaars, S. and C. Berenson (1986) Growth market forecasting revisited: a look back at a look forward. *California Management Review*, 28, 71–88.

Customer or Market Surveys

Most companies conduct customer surveys of some sort. In consumer markets this can be problematic simply because customers are unable to articulate their future needs. For example, Apple's iPod was not the result of extensive market research or customer demand, but largely because of the vision and commitment of Steve Jobs. In industrial markets, customers tend to be better equipped to communicate their future requirements, and consequently, business-to-business innovations often originate from customers. Companies can also consult their direct sales force, but these may not always be the best guide to future customer requirements. Information is often filtered in terms of existing products and services, and biased in terms of current sales performance rather than long-term development potential.

There is no 'one best way' to identify novel niches, but rather a range of alternatives. For example, where new products or services are very novel or complex, potential users may not be aware of, or able to articulate, their needs. In such cases traditional methods of market research are of little use, and there will be a greater burden on developers of radical new products and services to 'educate' potential users.

Our own research confirms that different managerial processes, structures and tools are appropriate for routine and novel development projects. We discuss this in detail in Chapter 9, when we examine new product and service development. For example, in terms of frequency of use, the most common methods used for high novelty projects are segmentation, prototyping, market experimentation and industry experts; whereas for the less novel projects the most common methods are partnering customers, trend extrapolation and segmentation. The use of market experimentation and industry experts might be expected where market requirements or technologies are uncertain, but the common use of segmentation for such projects is harder to justify. However, in terms of usefulness, there are statistically significant differences in the ratings for segmentation, prototyping, industry experts, market surveys and latent needs analysis. Segmentation is more effective for routine development projects; and prototyping, industry experts, focus groups and latent needs analysis are all more effective for novel development projects.[5]

Internal Analysis, e.g. Brainstorming

Structured idea generation, or brainstorming, aims to solve specific problems or to identify new products or services. Typically, a small group of experts is gathered together and allowed to interact. A chairman records all suggestions without comment or criticism. The aim is to identify, but not evaluate, as many opportunities or solutions as possible. Finally, members of the group vote on the different suggestions. The best results are obtained when representatives from different functions are present, but this can be difficult to manage. Brainstorming does not produce a forecast as such, but can provide useful input to other types of forecasting.

We discussed a range of approaches to creative problem solving and idea generation in Chapter 3. Most of these are relevant here, and include ways of:[6]

- *Understanding the problem* – the active construction by the individual or group through analysing the task at hand (including outcomes, people, context and methodological options) to determine whether and when deliberate problem-structuring efforts are needed. This stage includes constructing opportunities, exploring data and framing problems.
- *Generating ideas* – to create options in answer to an open-ended problem. This includes generating and focusing phases. During the generating phase of this stage, the person or group produces many options (fluent thinking), a variety of possible options (flexible thinking), novel or unusual options (original thinking) or a number of detailed or refined options (elaborative thinking). The focusing phase provides an opportunity for examining, reviewing, clustering and selecting promising options.
- *Planning for action* – is appropriate when a person or group recognise a number of interesting or promising options that may not necessarily be useful, valuable or valid. The aim is to make or develop effective choices, and to prepare for successful implementation and social acceptance.

External Assessment, e.g. Delphi

The opinion of outside experts, or Delphi method, is useful where there is a great deal of uncertainty or for long time horizons.[7] Delphi is used where a consensus of expert opinion is required on the timing, probability and identification of future technological goals or consumer needs and the factors likely to affect their achievement. It is best used in making long-term forecasts and revealing how new technologies and other factors could trigger discontinuities in technological trajectories. The choice of experts and the identification of their level and area of expertise are important; the structuring of the questions is even more important. The relevant experts may include suppliers, dealers, customers, consultants and academics. Experts in non-technological fields can be included to ensure that trends in economic, social and environmental fields are not overlooked.

The Delphi method begins with a postal survey of expert opinion on what the future key issues will be, and the likelihood of the developments. The response is then analysed, and the same sample of experts resurveyed with a new, more focused questionnaire. This procedure is repeated until some convergence of opinion is observed, or conversely if no consensus is reached. The exercise usually consists of an iterative process of questionnaire and feedback among the respondents; this process finally yields a Delphi forecast of the range of experts' opinions on the probabilities of certain events occurring by a quoted time. The method seeks to nullify the disadvantage of face-to-face meetings at which there could be deference to authority or reputation, a reluctance to admit error, a desire to conform or differences in persuasive ability. All of these could lead to an inaccurate consensus of opinion. The quality of the forecast is highly dependent on the expertise and calibre of the experts; how the experts are selected and how many should be consulted are important questions to be answered. If international experts are used, the exercise can take a considerable length of time, or the number of iterations may have to be curtailed. Although seeking a consensus may be important, adequate attention should be paid to views that differ radically 'from the norm' as there may be important underlying reasons to justify such maverick views. With sufficient design, understanding and resources, most of the shortcomings of the Delphi technique can be overcome and it is a popular technique, particularly for national foresight programmes.

In Europe, governments and transnational agencies use Delphi studies to help formulate policy, usually under the guise of 'Foresight' exercises. In Japan, large companies and the government routinely survey expert opinion in order to reach some consensus in those areas with the greatest potential for long-term development. Used in this way, the Delphi method can to a large extent become a self-fulfilling prophecy.

Scenario Development

Scenarios are internally consistent descriptions of alternative possible futures, based upon different assumptions and interpretations of the driving forces of change.[8] Inputs include quantitative data and analysis, and qualitative assumptions and assessments, such as societal, technological, economical, environmental and political drivers. Scenario development is not strictly speaking prediction, as it assumes that the future is uncertain and that the path of current developments can range from the conventional to the revolutionary. It is particularly good at incorporating potential critical events which might result in divergent paths or branches being pursued.

Scenario development can be normative or explorative. The normative perspective defines a preferred vision of the future and outlines different pathways from the goal to the present. For example, this is commonly used in energy futures and sustainable futures scenarios. The explorative approach defines the drivers of change, and creates scenarios from these without explicit goals or agendas.

For scenarios to be effective they need to inclusive, plausible and compelling (as opposed to being exclusive, implausible or obvious), as well as being challenging to the assumptions of the stakeholders. They should make the assumptions and inputs used explicit, and form the basis of a process of discussion, debate, policy, strategy and ultimately action. The output is typically two or three contrasting scenarios, but the process of development and discussion of scenarios is much more valuable.

Scenario development may involve many different forecasting techniques, including computer-based simulation. Typically, it begins with the identification of the critical indicators, which might include use of brainstorming and Delphi techniques. Next, the reasons for the behaviour of these indicators is examined, perhaps using regression techniques. The future events which are likely to affect these indicators are identified. These are used to construct the best, worst and most-likely future scenarios. Finally, the company assesses the impact of each scenario on its business. The goal is to plan for the outcome with the greatest impact, or better still, retain sufficient flexibility to respond to several different scenarios. Scenario development is a key part of the long-term planning process in those sectors characterised by high capital investment, long lead times and significant environmental uncertainty, such as energy, aerospace and telecommunications.

Factors Influencing Adoption of Innovations

Numerous variables have been identified as affecting the diffusion and adoption of innovations, but these can be grouped into three clusters: characteristics of the innovation itself; characteristics of individual or organisational adopters; and the characteristics of the environment.[9] Characteristics of an innovation found to influence adoption include relative advantage, compatibility, complexity, observability and trialability. Individual characteristics include age, education, social status and attitude to risk. Environmental and institutional characteristics include economic factors such as the market environment and sociological factors like communications networks. However, whilst there is a general agreement regarding the relevant variables, there is very little consensus on the relative importance of the different variables, and in some cases disagreements over the direction of relationships.

Characteristics of an Innovation

A number of characteristics of an innovation have been found to affect diffusion and adoption:[10]

- relative advantage
- compatibility

- complexity
- trialability
- observability.

Relative Advantage

Relative advantage is the degree to which an innovation is perceived as better than the product it supersedes, or competing products. Relative advantage is typically measured in narrow economic terms, for example cost or financial payback, but non-economic factors such as convenience, satisfaction and social prestige may be equally important. In theory, the greater the perceived advantage, the faster the rate of adoption.

It is useful to distinguish between the primary and secondary attributes of an innovation. Primary attributes, such as size and cost, are invariant and inherent to a specific innovation irrespective of the adopter. Secondary attributes, such as relative advantage and compatibility, may vary from adopter to adopter, being contingent upon the perceptions and context of adopters. In many cases, a so-called 'attribute gap' will exist. An attribute gap is the discrepancy between a potential user's perception of an attribute or characteristic of an item of knowledge and how the potential user would prefer to perceive that attribute. The greater the sum of all attribute gaps, the less likely a user is to adopt the knowledge. This suggests that preliminary testing of an innovation is desirable in order to determine whether significant attribute gaps exist. Not all attribute gaps require changes to the innovation itself – a distinction needs to be made between knowledge content and knowledge format. The idea of pre-testing information for the purposes of enhancing its value and acceptance is not widely practised.

Compatibility

Compatibility is the degree to which an innovation is perceived to be consistent with the existing values, experience and needs of potential adopters. There are two distinct aspects of compatibility: existing skills and practices; and values and norms. The extent to which the innovation fits the existing skills, equipment, procedures and performance criteria of the potential adopter is important, and relatively easy to assess.

However, compatibility with existing practices may be less important than the fit with existing values and norms. Significant misalignments between an innovation and an adopting organisation will require changes in the innovation or organisation, or both. In the most successful cases of implementation, mutual adaptation of the innovation and organisation occurs. However, few studies distinguish between compatibility with value and norms, and compatibility with existing practices. The extent to which the innovation fits the existing skills, equipment, procedures and performance criteria of the potential adopter is critical. Few innovations initially fit the user environment into which they are introduced. Significant misalignments between the innovation and the adopting organisation will require changes in the innovation or organisation, or in the most successful cases of implementation, mutual adaptation of both. Initial compatibility with existing practices may be less important, as it may provide limited opportunity for mutual adaptation to occur.

Complexity

Complexity is the degree to which an innovation is perceived as being difficult to understand or use. In general, innovations which are simpler for potential users to understand will be adopted more rapidly than those which require the adopter to develop new skills and knowledge.

However, complexity can also influence the direction of diffusion. Evolutionary models of diffusion focus on the effect of 'network externalities'. That is the interaction of consumption, pecuniary and technical factors which shape the diffusion process. For example, within a region the cost of adoption and use, as distinct from the cost of purchase, may be influenced by: the availability of information about the technology from other users, of trained skilled users, technical assistance and maintenance, and of complementary innovations, both technical and organisational.

Trialability

Trialability is the degree to which an innovation can be experimented with on a limited basis. An innovation that is trialable represents less uncertainty to potential adopters, and allows learning by doing. Innovations which can be trialled will generally be adopted more quickly than those which cannot. The exception is where the undesirable consequences of an innovation appear to outweigh the desirable characteristics. In general, adopters wish to benefit from the functional effects of an innovation, but avoid any dysfunctional effects. However, where it is difficult or impossible to separate the desirable from the undesirable consequences trialability may reduce the rate of adoption.

Developers of an innovation may have two different motives for involving potential users in the development process. First, to acquire knowledge from the users needed in the development process, to ensure usability and to add value. Second, to attain user 'buy-in', that is user acceptance of the innovation and commitment to its use. The second motive is independent of the first, because increasing user acceptance does not necessarily improve the quality of the innovation. Rather, involvement may increase users' tolerance of any inadequacies. In the case of point-to-point transfer, typically both motives are present.

However, in the case of diffusion it is not possible to involve all potential users, and therefore the primary motive is to improve usability rather than attain user buy-in. But even the representation of user needs must be indirect, using surrogates such as specially selected user groups. These groups can be problematic for a number of reasons. First, because they may possess atypically high levels of technical knowledge, they are therefore not always representative. Second, where the group must represent diverse user needs, such as both experienced and novice users, the group may not work well together. Finally, when user representatives work closely with developers over a long period of time they may cease to represent users, and instead absorb the developer's viewpoint. Thus, there is no simple relationship between user involvement and user satisfaction. Typically, very low levels of user involvement are associated with user dissatisfaction, but extensive user involvement does not necessarily result in user satisfaction.

Observability

Observability is the degree to which the results of an innovation are visible to others. The easier it is for others to see the benefits of an innovation, the more likely it will be adopted.

The simple epidemic model of diffusion assumes that innovations spread as potential adopters come into contact with existing users of an innovation.

Peers who have already adopted an innovation will have what communication researchers call 'safety credibility', because potential adopters seeking their advice will believe they know what it is really like to implement and utilise the innovation. Therefore early adopters are well positioned to disseminate 'vicarious learning' to their colleagues. Vicarious learning is simply learning from the experience of others, rather than direct personal experimental learning. However, the process of vicarious learning is neither inevitable nor efficient because, by definition, it is a decentralised activity. Centralised systems of dissemination tend to be designed and rewarded on the basis of being the source of technical information, rather than for facilitating learning among potential adopters.

Over time, learning and selection processes foster both the evolution of the technologies to be adopted and the characteristics of actual and potential adopters. Thus an innovation may evolve over time through improvements made by early users, thereby reducing the relative cost to later adopters. In addition, where an innovation requires the development of complementary features, for example a specific infrastructure, late adopters will benefit. This suggests that instead of a single diffusion curve, a series of diffusion curves will exist for the different environments. However, there is a potential drawback to this model. The short-term preferences of early adopters will have a disproportionate impact on the subsequent development of the innovation, and may result in the establishment of inferior technologies and abandonment of superior alternatives. In such cases interventionalist policies may be necessary to postpone the lock-in phenomenon.

From a policy perspective, high visibility is often critical. However, high visibility, at least initially, may be counter-productive. If users' expectations about an innovation are unrealistically high and adoption is immediate, subsequent disappointment is likely. Therefore in some circumstances it may make sense to delay dissemination or to slow the rate of adoption. However, in general, researchers and disseminators are reluctant to withhold knowledge.

The choice between the different models of diffusion and factors that will most influence adoption will depend on the characteristics of the innovation and nature of potential adopters. The simple *epidemic model* appears to provide a good fit to the diffusion of new processes, techniques and procedures, whereas the *Bass model* appears to best fit the diffusion of consumer products. However, the mathematical structure of the epidemic and Bass models tends to overstate the importance of differences in adopter characteristics, and tends to underestimate the effect of macroeconomic and supply-side factors. In general, both these models of diffusion work best where the total potential market is known, that is for derivatives of existing products and services, rather than totally new innovations.

In the case of systemic or network innovations, a wider range of factors has to be managed to promote adoption and diffusion. In such cases a wider set of actors and institutions on the supply and demand side are relevant, in what has been called an adoption network. On the supply side, other organisations may provide the infrastructure, support and complementary products and services which can promote or prevent adoption and diffusion. For example, in 2008 the two-year battle between the new high-definition DVD formats was decided not by price or any technical superiority, but rather because the Blu-ray consortium managed to recruit more film studios to its format than the competing HD-DVD format. As soon as the uncertainty over the future format was resolved, there was a step change increase in the rate of adoption.

On the demand side, the uncertainty of potential adopters, and communication with and between them needs to be managed. Whilst early adopters may emphasise technical performance and novelty above other factors, the mainstream mass market is more likely to be concerned with factors such as price, quality, convenience and support. This transition from the niche market and needs of early adopters, through to the requirements of more mass markets has been referred to as crossing the chasm by Moore.[11] Moore studied the successes and many more failures of Silicon Valley and other high-technology products, and argued that the critical success factors for early adopters and mass markets were fundamentally different, and most innovations failed to make this transition. Therefore the successful launch and diffusion of a systemic or network innovation demands attention to traditional marketing issues such as the timing and positioning of the product or service, but also significant effort to demand-side factors such as communication and interactions between potential adopters.

INNOVATION IN ACTION

Why Innovations Fail to be Adopted

This research examined the factors which influence the adoption and diffusion of innovations drawing upon case studies of successful and less successful consumer electronics products, such as the Sony PlayStation and MiniDisc, Apple iPod and Newton, TomTom GO, TiVo and RIM BlackBerry.

The study finds that a critical factor influencing successful diffusion is the careful management of acceptance by the early adopters, which in turn influences the adoption by the main market. Strategic issues such as positioning, timing and management of the adoption network are identified as being important. The adoption network is defined as a configuration of users, peers, competitors, and complementary products and services and infrastructure. However, the positioning, timing and adoption networks are different for the early and main market adopters, and failure to recognize these differences is a common cause of the failure of innovations to diffuse widely. Also, innovation contingencies such as the degree of radicalness and discontinuity affect how these factors interact and how these need to be managed to promote acceptance. The relevant assessment of the radicalness and discontinuity of an innovation is not based on the technological aspects, but rather the effects on user behaviour and consumption.

To promote use by early adopters, the research recommends that four enabling factors need to be managed: legitimate the innovation through reference customers and visible performance advantage; trigger word of mouth within specialist communities of practice; stimulate imitation to increase the user base and peer pressure; and collaborate with opinion leaders. Significantly, the study argues that the subsequent successful diffusion of an innovation into the mainstream

(*continued*)

market has very little to do with the merits of the product itself, and much more to do with the positive acceptance of early adopters and repositioning and targeting for the main market by influencing the relevant adoption network.

Source: Frattini, F. (2010) The commercialisation of innovation in high-tech markets, in Tidd, J. (ed.) *Gaining Momentum: managing the diffusion of innovations*. Imperial College Press, London.

Assessing Risk, Recognising Uncertainty

Dealing with risk and uncertainty is central to the assessment of most innovative projects. Risk is usually considered to be possible to estimate, either qualitatively – high, medium, low – or ideally by probability estimates. Uncertainty is by definition unknowable, but nonetheless the fields and degree of uncertainty should be identified to help to select the most appropriate methods of assessment and plan for contingencies. Traditional approaches to assessing risk focus on the probability of foreseeable risks, rather than true uncertainty, or complete ignorance – what Donald Rumsfeld memorably called the 'unknown unknowns' (12 February 2002, US Department of Defense news briefing).

Research on new product development and R&D project management has identified a broad range of strategies for dealing with risk. Both individual characteristics and organisational climate influence perceptions of risk and propensities to avoid, accept or seek risks. Formal techniques such as failure mode and effects analysis (FMEA), potential problem analysis (PPA) and fault tree analysis (FTA) have a role, but the broader signals and support from the organisational climate is more important than the specific tools or methods used. For example, too many organisations emphasise project management in order to contain internal risks in the organisation, but as a result fail to identify or exploit opportunities to take acceptable risks and to innovate.

There are many approaches to risk assessment, but the most common issues to be managed include:

- Probabilistic estimates of technical and commercial success.
- Psychological (cognitive) and sociological perceptions of risk.

A number of approaches exist to help entrepreneurs to assess risk in a balanced way.

Go online to find tools for assessing risk, both at the project and portfolio levels.

www.iande.info

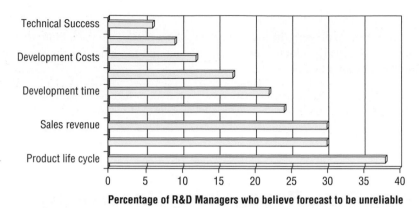

FIGURE 7.1   Managers' perceptions of sources of uncertainty.

Risk as Probability

Research indicates that 30–45% of all projects fail to be completed, and over half of projects overrun their budgets or schedules by up 200%. Figure 7.1 presents the results of a survey of R&D managers. Whilst most appear to be relatively confident when predicting technical issues such as the development time and costs, a much smaller proportion are confident when forecasting commercial aspects of the projects.

We examined how commonly different approaches to project assessment were used in practice. We surveyed 50 projects in 25 companies, and assessed how often different criteria were used, and how useful they were thought to be. Table 7.2 summarises some of the results. Clearly probabilistic estimates of technical and commercial success are near universal, and considered to be of critical importance in all types of project assessment. These are usually combined with some form of financial assessment, and fit with the company strategy and capabilities.

Given the complexities involved, the outcomes of investments in innovation are uncertain, so that the forecasts (of costs, prices, sales volume, etc.) that underlie project and programme evaluations can be unreliable. According to Joseph Bower, management finds it easier, when appraising investment proposals, to make more accurate forecasts of reductions in production cost than of expansion in sales, whilst their ability to forecast the financial consequences of new product introductions is very limited indeed.[12] This last conclusion is confirmed by the study by Edwin Mansfield and his colleagues of project selection in large US firms.[13] By comparing project forecasts with outcomes, Mansfield showed that managers find it difficult to pick technological and commercial winners:

- Probability of *technical* success of projects $(P_t) = 0.80$
- Subsequent probability of *commercial* success $(P_c) = 0.20$
- Combined probability for all stages: $0.8 \times 0.2 = 0.16$

TABLE 7.2   Use and usefulness of criteria project screening and selection

	High novelty		Low novelty	
	Usage (%)	Usefulness	Usage (%)	Usefulness
Probability of technical success	100	4.37	100	4.32
Probability of commercial success	100	4.68	95	4.50
Market share*	100	3.63	84	4.00
Core competencies*	95	3.61	79	3.00
Degree of internal commitment	89	3.82	79	3.67
Market size	89	3.76	84	3.94
Competition	89	3.76	84	3.81
NPV/IRR	79	3.47	68	3.92
Payback period/break-even*	79	3.20	58	4.27

Usefulness score: 5 = critical; 0 = irrelevant. * denotes difference in usefulness rating is statistically significant at 5% level.

Source: Adapted from Tidd, J. and K. Bodley (2002) Effect of novelty on new product development processes and tools. *R&D Management*, 32 (2), 127–38.

He also found that managers and technical managers cannot predict accurately the *development costs*, *time periods*, *markets* and *profits* of R&D projects. On average, costs were greatly *underestimated*, and time periods *overestimated* by 140–280% in incremental product improvements, and by 350–600% in major new products. Other studies have found that:

- About half business R&D expenditures are on *failed* R&D projects. The higher rate of success in *expenditures* than in *projects* reflects the weeding out of unsuccessful projects at their early stages and before large-scale commercial commitments are made to them.
- R&D scientists and engineers are often deliberately overoptimistic in their estimates, in order to give the illusion of a high rate of return to accountants and managers.

Trying to get involved in the right projects is worth an effort, both to avoid wasting time and resources in meaningless activities, and to improve the chances of success. Project appraisal and evaluation aims to:

1. Profile and gain an overall understanding of potential projects.
2. Prioritise a given set of projects, and where necessary reject projects.
3. Monitor projects, e.g. by following up the criteria chosen when the project was selected.

4. Where necessary, terminate a project.
5. Evaluate the results of completed projects.
6. Review successful and unsuccessful projects to gain insights and improve future project management, i.e. learning.

Project evaluation usually assumes that there is a choice of projects to pursue, but where there is no choice project evaluation is still important to help to assess the opportunity costs and what might be expected from pursuing a project. Different situations and contexts demand different approaches to project evaluation. We argued earlier that complexity and uncertainty are two of the most important dimensions for assessing projects. Different types of project will demand specific techniques, or at least different criteria for assessment. A large number of techniques have been developed over the years, and are still being developed and used today. Most of these can be described by means of some common elements which form the core of any project evaluation technique:

- *Inputs* into the assessment include likely costs and benefits in financial terms, probability of technical and market success, market attractiveness, and the strategic importance to the organisation.
- *Weighting*: as certain data may be given more relevance than other (e.g. of market inputs compared with technical factors), in order to reflect the company's strategy or the company's particular views. The data is then processed to arrive at the outcomes.
- *Balancing* a range of projects, as the relative value of a project with respect to other projects is an important factor in situations of competition for limited resources. Portfolio management techniques are specifically devoted to deal with this factor.

Economic and cost–benefit approaches are usually based on a combination of expected utility or Bayesian assumptions. Expected utility theory can take into account probabilistic estimates and subjective preferences, and therefore deals well with risk aversion, but in practice utility curves are almost impossible to construct and individual preferences are different and highly subjective. Bayesian probability is excellent at incorporating the effects of new information, as we discussed earlier under the diffusion of innovations, but is very sensitive to the choice of relevant inputs and the weights attached to these.

As a result no technique should be allowed to determine outcomes, as these decisions are a management responsibility. Many techniques used today are totally or partially software based, which have some additional benefits in automating the process. In any case, the most important issue, for any method, is the managers' interpretation.

There is no single 'best' technique. The extent to which different techniques for project evaluation can be used will depend upon the nature of the project, the information availability, the company's culture and several other factors. This is clear from the variety of techniques that are theoretically available and the extent to which they have been used in practice. In any case, no matter which technique is selected by a company, it should be implemented, and probably adapted, according to the particular needs of that organisation. Most of the techniques in practical use incorporate a mixture of financial assessment and human judgement.

Perceptions of Risk

Probability estimates are only the starting point of risk assessment. Such relatively objective criteria are usually significantly moderated by psychological (cognitive) perceptions and bias, or overwhelmed altogether by sociological factors, such as peer pressure and cultural context. Studies suggest that different people (and animals) have different perceptions and tolerances for risk taking. For example, a study comparing the behaviours of chimpanzees and bonobos apes found that the chimps were more prepared to gamble and take risks.[14] At first sight this appears to support the personality explanation for risk taking, but actually the two types of ape share more than 99% of their DNA. A more likely explanation is the very different environments in which they have evolved: in the chimp environment food is scarce and uncertain, but in the bonobo habitats food is plentiful. We are not suggesting that entrepreneurs are chimp-like, or accountants are ape-like, but rather that experience and context have a profound influence on the assessment of, and appetite for, risk.

At the individual, cognitive level, risk assessment is characterised by overconfidence, loss aversion and bias. Overconfidence in our ability to make accurate assessments is a common failing, and results in unrealistic assumptions and uncritical assessment. Loss aversion is well documented in psychology, and essentially means that we tend to prefer to avoid loss rather than to risk gain. Finally, cognitive bias is widespread and has profound implications for the identification and assessment of risk. Cognitive bias results in us seeking and overemphasising evidence which supports our beliefs and reinforces our bias, but at the same time leads us to avoid and undervalue any information which contradicts our view. Therefore we need to be aware of and challenge our own biases, and encourage others to debate and critique our data, methods and decisions.

Studies of research and development confirm that measures of cognitive ability are associated with project performance. In particular, differences in reflection, reasoning, interpretation and sense-making influence the quality of problem formulation, evaluation and solution, and therefore ultimately the performance of research and development. A common weakness is the oversimplification of problems characterised by complexity or uncertainty, and the simplification of problem-framing and evaluation of alternatives. This includes adopting a single prior hypothesis, selective use of information that supports this, and devaluing alternatives, and illusion of control and predictability. Similarly, marketing managers are likely to share similar cognitive maps, and make the same assumptions concerning the relative importance of different factors contributing to new product success, such as the degree of customer orientation versus competitor orientation, and the implications of relationship between these factors, such as the degree of interfunctional co-ordination. So the evidence indicates the importance of cognitive processes at the senior management, functional, group and individual levels of an organisation. More generally, problems of limited cognition include:[15]

- *Reasoning by analogy*, which oversimplifies complex problems.
- *Adopting a single, prior hypothesis bias*, even where information and trails suggest this is wrong.
- *Limited problem set*, the repeated use of a narrow problem-solving strategy.

- *Single outcome calculation*, which focuses on a simple single goal and a course of action to achieve it, whilst denying value trade-offs.
- *Illusion of control and predictability*, based on an overconfidence in the chosen strategy, a partial understanding of the problem and limited appreciation of the uncertainty of the environment.
- *Devaluation of alternatives*, emphasising negative aspects of alternatives.

At the group or social level, other factors also influence our perception and response to risk. How managers assess and manage risk is also a social and political process. It is influenced by prior experience of risk, perceptions of capability, status and authority, and the confidence and ability to communicate with relevant people at the appropriate times. In the context of managing innovation, risk is less about personal propensity for risk taking or rational assessments of probability, and more about the interaction of experience, authority and context. In practice, managers deal with risk in different ways in different situations. General strategies include delaying or delegating decisions, or sharing risk and responsibilities. Generally, when mangers are performing well, and achieving their targets, they have less incentive to take risks. Conversely, when under pressure to perform, managers will often accept higher risks, unless these threaten survival.

The inherent uncertainty in some projects limits the ability of managers to predict the outcomes and benefits of projects. In such cases changes to project plans and goals are commonplace, being driven by external factors, such as technological breakthroughs or changes in markets, as well as internal factors, such as changes in organisational goals. Together the impact of changes to project plans and goals can overwhelm the benefits of formal project planning and management (Table 7.3).

TABLE 7.3   Management of conventional and risky projects.

Conventional project management	Management of risky projects
Modest uncertainty	Major technical and market uncertainties
Emphasis on detailed planning	Emphasis on opportunistic risk taking
Negotiation and compromise	Autonomous behaviour
Corporate interests and rules	Individualistic and ad hoc
Homogeneous culture and experience	Heterogeneous backgrounds

Anticipating the Resources

Given their mathematical skills, one might have expected R&D managers to be enthusiastic users of quantitative methods for allocating resources to innovative activities. The evidence suggests otherwise: practising R&D managers have been sceptical for a long time. An exhaustive report by practising European managers on R&D project evaluation classifies and assesses more than 100 methods of evaluation and presents 21 case studies on their use.[16] However, it concludes that no method can guarantee success, that no single approach to pre-evaluation meets all circumstances, and that – whichever method is used – the most important outcome of a properly structured evaluation is improved communication. These conclusions reflect three of the characteristics of investments in innovative activities:

1. They are uncertain, so that success cannot be assured.
2. They involve different stages that have different outputs that require different methods of evaluation.
3. Many of the variables in an evaluation cannot be reduced to a reliable set of figures to be plugged into a formula, but depend on expert judgements: hence the importance of communication, especially between the corporate functions concerned with R&D and related innovative activities, on the one hand, and with the allocation of financial resources, on the other.

Financial Assessment of Projects

As we showed earlier, financial methods are still the most commonly used method of assessing innovative projects, but usually in combination with other, often more qualitative approaches. The financial methods range from simple calculation of payback period or return on investment, to more complex assessments of net present value (NPV) through discounted cash flow (DCF).

Project appraisal by means of DCF is based on the concept that money today is worth more than money in the future. This is not because of the effect of inflation, but reflects the difference in potential investment earnings, that is the opportunity cost of the capital invested.

The NPV of a project is calculated using:

$$NPV = \Sigma_0^T P_t / (1 + i)^t - C$$

where:

P_t = Forecast cash flow in time period t
T = Project life
i = Expected rate of return on securities equivalent in risk to project being evaluated
C = Cost of project at time $t = 0$

In practice, rather than use this formula, it is easy to create standard NPV templates in a spreadsheet package such as Excel.

How to Evaluate Learning?

However, the potential benefits of innovative activities are twofold. First, *extra profits* derived from increased sales and/or higher prices for superior products, and from lower costs and/or increased sales from superior production processes. Conventional project appraisal methods can be used to compare the value of these benefits against their cost. Second, *accumulated firm-specific knowledge* ('learning', 'intangible assets') that may be useful for the development of *future* innovations (e.g. new uses for solar batteries, carbon fibre, robots, word processing). This type of benefit is relatively more important in R&D projects that are more long term, fundamental and speculative. Conventional techniques cannot be used to assess this second type of benefit, because it is an 'option' – in other words, it creates the *opportunity* for the firm to invest in a potentially profitable investment, but the realisation of the benefits still depends on a decision to commit further resources. Conventional project appraisal techniques cannot evaluate options.

This approach can be developed further and the analysis interaction and feedback can be easily managed using simple information technology. Ways to make the evaluation more sophisticated include:

- To include some quantitative factors among the whole list of factors.
- To assign different weights to different factors.
- To develop a systematic way of arriving at an overall opinion on the project, such as a score or index.

A simple checklist could be one made up of a range of factors which have been formed to affect the success of a project and which need to be considered at the outset. In the evaluation procedure a project is evaluated against each of these factors using a linear scale, usually 1 to 5 or 1 to 10. The factors can be weighted to indicate their relative importance to the organisation.

The value in this technique lies in its simplicity, but by the appropriate choice of factors it is possible to ensure that the questions address, and are answered by, all functional areas. When used effectively this guarantees a useful discussion, an identification and clarification of areas of disagreement and a stronger commitment, by all involved, to the ultimate outcome. Table 7.4 shows an example of a checklist, developed by the Industrial Research Institute, which can be adapted to almost any type of project.

TABLE 7.4   List of potential factors for project evaluation.

	Score (1–5)	Weight (%)	S × W
Corporate objectives Fits into the overall objectives and strategy Corporate image			
Marketing and distribution Size of potential market Capability to market product Market trend and growth Customer acceptance Relationship with existing markets Market share Market risk during development period			

(continued)

TABLE 7.4 (*Continued*)			
	Score (1–5)	Weight (%)	S × W
Pricing trend, proprietary problem, etc. Complete product line Quality improvement Timing of introduction of new product Expected product sales life			
Manufacturing Cost savings Capability of manufacturing product Facility and equipment requirements Availability of raw material Manufacturing safety			
Research and development Likelihood of technical success Cost Development time Capability of available skills Availability of R&D resources Availability of R&D facilities Patent status Compatibility with other projects			
Regulatory and legal factors Potential product liability Regulatory clearance			
Financial Profitability Capital investment required Annual (or unit) cost Rate of return on investment Unit price Payout period Utilisation of assets, cost reduction and cash-flow			

As with all techniques, there is a danger that project appraisal becomes a routine that a project has to suffer rather than an aid to designing and selecting appropriate projects. If this happens people may fail to apply the techniques with the rigour and honesty required, and can waste time and energy trying to 'cheat' the system. Care needs to be taken to communicate the reasons behind the methods and criteria used, and where necessary these should be adapted to different types of project and to changes in the environment.[17]

Limitations of Conventional Project and Product Assessment

Clayton Christensen and colleagues argue that three commonly used means of assessment discourage expenditure on innovation. Firstly, conventional means of assessing projects, such as discounted cash flow (DCF) and the treatment of fixed costs, favour the incremental exploitation of existing assets rather than the more risky development of new capabilities. Secondly, methods such as the stage-gate process demand data on estimated markets, revenues and costs, which are much more difficult to generate for more radical innovations. Finally, senior managers and publically quoted firms are typically assessed by improvements in the earning per share (EPS), which encourages short-term investments and returns – most institutional investors hold shares for only 10 months in the USA, and the tenure of CEOs is shrinking.

Whilst they appreciate the benefits of such financial methods of assessment, they argue that such techniques should be adjusted to redress the balance for risk taking and expenditure on innovation. For example, when using DCF, comparative assessments should be made with the option of doing nothing, or not investing in an innovative project, rather than assuming a decision not to invest will result in no loss of competitiveness. Similarly, for the stage-gate process, they propose focusing less on the (unreliable) quantitative forecasts, and much more on challenging and testing the assumptions made in business planning. Finally, they believe that the use of short-term measurers such as EPS is no longer appropriate because it provides perverse incentives. The original rationale for this type of approach was the principal–agent problem – to try to align the interests of the principals (owners/shareholders) and their agents (managers). However, the growth of collective institutional ownership of most public firms has created an agent–agent problem, and the interests of the agents need to be more aligned to promote innovation.

Source: Christensen, C.M, S.P. Kaufmann and W.C. Shih (2008) Innovation killers: how financial tools destroy your capacity to do new things. *Harvard Business Review*, January, 98–105.

How Practising Managers Cope

These two sets of difficulties – in evaluating the potential contributions of technological investments to firm-specific intangible assets, and in dealing with uncertainty – are reflected in how successful managers allocate resources to technological activities. In particular, they:

- Encourage *incrementalism* – step-by-step modification of objectives and resources, in the light of new evidence.
- Use *simple rules* models for allocating resources, so that the implications of changes can be easily understood.
- Make explicit from the outset criteria for *stopping* the project or programme.

- Use *sensitivity analysis* to explore if the outcome of the project is 'robust' (unchanging) to a range of different assumptions (e.g. 'What if the project costs twice as much, and takes twice as long, as the present estimates?').
- Seek the reduction of *key uncertainties* (technical and – if possible – market) before any irreversible commitment to full-scale – and costly – commercialisation.
- Recognise that *different types* of innovation should be evaluated by *different criteria*.

Go online to see how the development and growth of Glasses Direct shows how web-based businesses can reduce risk and uncertainty by starting modestly with minimal resources, but grow by adopting a scalable business model.

www.iande.info

Chapter Summary

The process of innovation is much more complex than technology responding to market signals. Effective business planning under conditions of uncertainty demands a thorough understanding and management of the dynamics of innovation, including conception, development, adoption and diffusion.

    The adoption and diffusion of an innovation depend on the characteristics of the innovation, the nature of potential adopters and the process of communication. The relative advantage, compatibility, complexity, trialability and observability of an innovation all affect the rate of diffusion. The skills, psychology, social context and infrastructure of adopters also affect adoption. Epidemic models assume that innovations spread by communication between adopters, but bandwagons do not require this. Instead, early adopters influence the development of an innovation, but subsequent adopters may be more influenced by competitive and peer pressures. Forecasting the development and adoption of innovations is difficult, but participative methods such as Delphi and scenario planning are highly relevant to innovation and sustainability. In such cases the process of forecasting, including consultation and debate, is probably more important than the precise outcomes of the exercise.

Discussion Questions

1. Which components of a business plan are most important to attract resources?

2. How can forecasting be used to identify and reduce risk and uncertainty?

3. What factors influence the adoption of innovations, and which of these can be managed?

4. What is meant by the 'fuzzy front end' and how can it be better managed?

5. What is the difference between risk and uncertainty?

6. What are the relative advantages and disadvantages of using quantitative and qualitative methods for assessing projects?

Key Terms Defined

Bandwagons   occur during the diffusion of an innovation when an innovation is adopted because of the cumulative volume of previous adoptions, through peer pressure and expectations, rather than by any individual rational assessment of costs and benefits.

Bass model   this model of diffusion assumes that potential adopters are influenced by two processes: by individual independent decisions and by interpersonal communications and channels.

Delphi   is a forecasting method which surveys expert opinion on the timing, probability and identification of future technological goals or consumer needs and the factors likely to affect their achievement.

Diffusion   is the process by which a focal innovation is adopted by a focal social system or market segment, and includes the rate and direction of change.

Fuzzy Front End   in new product and service development is the very early phase in which an idea is developed into a concept, and is usually poorly managed.

Risk   is usually considered to be possible to estimate, either qualitatively – high, medium, low – or ideally by probability estimates. However, in practice different stakeholders' perceptions of risk and hazard influence decisions more than simple probabilistic assessments.

Scenarios   are internally consistent descriptions of alternative possible futures, based upon different assumptions and interpretations of the driving forces of change. Scenario development can be normative or explorative.

Uncertainty   is by definition unknowable, but nonetheless the sources, fields and degree of uncertainty can be identified to help to select the most appropriate methods of assessment and plan for contingencies.

Further Reading and Resources

More generally, the problems of forecasting the future development, adoption and diffusion of innovations are dealt with by many authors in the innovation field. Everett Roger's classic text *The Diffusion of Innovations*, first published in 1962, remains the best overview of this subject, the most recent and updated edition being published in 2003 (Simon and Schuster). More up-to-date accounts can be found in *Determinants of Innovative Behaviour*, edited by Cees van Beers, Alfred Kleinknecht, Roland Ortt and Robert Verburg (Palgrave, 2008), and our own *Gaining Momentum: Managing the Diffusion of Innovations*, edited by Joe Tidd (Imperial College Press, 2010).

In *Democratizing Innovation* (MIT Press, 2005, and free online) Eric von Hippel builds on his earlier concept of 'lead users' in innovation, and argues that innovation is becoming more democratic, with users increasingly being capable of developing their own new products and services. He believes that such user innovation has a positive impact on social welfare as innovating users – both individuals and firms – often freely share their innovations with others, creating user-innovation communities and a rich intellectual commons. Examples provided range from surgical equipment to surfboards to software security. A broader review of user innovation is provided by the special issue of the *International Journal of Innovation Management*, **12** (3), 2008, edited by Steve Flowers.

Clayton Christensen's (with S.D. Anthony and E.A. Roth) *Seeing What's Next: Using the Theories of Innovation to Predict Industry Change* (Harvard Business School Press, 2005) is a useful up-to-date review of methods for forecasting radical and potentially disruptive innovations.

A special issue of the journal *Long Range Planning*, **37** (2), 2004, is devoted to forecasting, and provides a good overview of current thinking. *Scenario Planning* by Gill Ringland (John Wiley & Sons, Ltd, 2nd edition, 2006) and *Scenario Planning: The Link Between Future and Strategy* by Mats Lindgren (Palgrave Macmillan, 2002) are both detailed and practical guides to conducting scenario planning, which is probably one of the most relevant methods for understanding innovation planning. For a comprehensive overview of international research and practice refer to *The Handbook of Technology Foresight*, edited by Luke Georghiou (Edward Elgar, 2008).

References

1. Delmar, F. and S. Shane (2003) Does business planning facilitate the development of new ventures? *Strategic Management Journal*, 24(12), 1165–1185.

2. Kirsch, D.B., B. Goldfarb and A. Gera (2009) Form or substance? The role of business plans in venture capital decision making, *Strategic Management Journal*, 30(5), 487–515.

3. Kaplan, J.M. and A.C. Warren (2009) *Patterns of Entrepreneurship*, John Wiley & Sons, Inc., New York.

4. Roberts, E.B. (1991) *Entrepreneurs in High Technology: Lessons from MIT and Beyond*, Oxford University Press, Oxford.

5. Tidd, J. and K. Bodley (2002) Effect of novelty on new product development processes and tools, *R&D Management*, **32** (2), 127–138.

6. Isaksen, S. and J. Tidd (2006) *Meeting the Innovation Challenge: Leadership for Transformation and Growth*, John Wiley & Sons, Ltd, Chichester.

7. Landeta, J. (2006) Current validity of the Delphi method in social sciences, *Technological Forecasting and Social Change*, **73** (5), 467–482; Fuller, T. and L. Warren (2006) Entrepreneurship as foresight: a complex social network perspective on organisational foresight, *Futures*, **38** (8), 956–971; Gupta, U.G. and R.E. Clarke (1996) Theory and applications of the Delphi technique: a bibliography (1975–1994), *Technological Forecasting and Social Change*, **53** (2), 185–212.

8. Ringland, G. (2006) *Scenario Planning*, second edition, John Wiley & Sons, Ltd, Chichester; Chermack, T.J. (2005) Studying scenario planning: theory, research suggestions, and hypotheses, *Technological Forecasting and Social Change*, **72** (1), 59–73; Burt, G. and K. van der Heijden (2003) First steps: towards purposeful activities in scenario thinking and future studies, *Futures*, **35** (10), 1011–1026.

9. Tidd, J. (2010) The commercialisation of innovation in high-tech markets, in Tidd, J. (ed.) *Gaining Momentum: managing the diffusion of innovations*, Imperial College Press, London; Rogers, E.M. (2003) *Diffusion of Innovations*, Free Press, New York.

10. Rogers, E.M. (2003) *Diffusion of Innovations*, Free Press, New York.

11. Moore, G. (1991) *Crossing the Chasm: Marketing and Selling Technology Products to Mainstream Customers*, HarperBusiness, New York; (1998) *Inside the Tornado: Marketing Strategies from Silicon Valley's Cutting Edge*, John Wiley & Sons, Ltd, Chichester.

12. Bower, J. (1986) *Managing the Resource Allocation Process*, Harvard Business School, Boston, MA.

13. Mansfield, E., J. Raporport, J. Schnee, S. Wagner and M. Hamburger (1972) *Research and Innovation in the Modern Corporation*, Macmillan, London.

14. Heilbronner, S.R. (2008) A fruit in the hand or two in the bush? Divergent risk preferences in chimpanzees and bonobos, *Biology Letters*, **4** (3) 246–249.

15. Walsh, J.P. (1995) Managerial and organizational cognition: notes from a field trip. *Organization Science*, **6** (1), 1–41; Genus, A. and A.M. Coles (2006) Firm strategies for risk management in innovation, *International Journal of Innovation Management*, **10** (2), 113–126; Berglund, H. (2007) Risk conception and risk management in corporate innovation, *International Journal of Innovation Management*, **11** (4), 497–514.

16. EIRMA (1995) *Evaluation of R&D Projects*, European Industrial Research Management Association, Paris.

17. Laslo, Z. and A.I. Goldberg (2008) Resource allocation under uncertainty in a multi-project matrix environment: is organizational conflict inevitable? *International Journal of Project Management*, 26(4).

CASE STUDY 7

Pre-Launch Decisions which Influence Innovation Success

It has been extensively documented in management literature that an incredibly large share of firms' investments in technological innovation do not generate substantial financial returns. Three main reasons underlying this phenomenon can be identified. First, technological innovation creates knowledge and technological assets that often remain largely unexploited. Various studies show that between 70 and 90% of corporate technology assets often never get used in core products or lines of business. Second, the likelihood that an innovation project reaches completion and that the new product is introduced into the market is strikingly low. It has been estimated that the probability of new product commercialisation is about 40% in many industries, with some cases (e.g., pharmaceutics) where the mortality of innovation projects is much higher. Finally, a large share of the innovations that ultimately reach the market do not experience a satisfactory diffusion and their sales are discontinued. Empirical studies have shown indeed that on average 40–50% of fully commercialised new products turn out to be commercial failures.

An important managerial question is however left unanswered: which are the levers a manager can act upon to achieve adoption network acceptance and early adopters' acceptance for a high-tech innovation, having a given functional content and a set of technical specifications, which is introduced within the scope of a given competitive and product strategy (Table 7.5)?

TABLE 7.5 Commercialisation factors influencing the adoption of innovations

Variable	Description
Timing	– When will the innovation first be launched into the market? – Will the firm announce the innovation to the press long before its market launch? – Will the firm partner with external organisations long before the official market launch?
Targeting and positioning	– Which market segments will the innovation will be addressed to? – Which will be the position of the innovation in the eyes of potential adopters in each of the targeted market segments? – Will the firm target different segments as long as the commercialisation process progresses?
Inter-firm relationships	– Which external organisations will the firm partner with during the commercialisation of the innovation? – Which forms of relationships will be most appropriate (e.g., licensing agreements, strategic, long-term partnerships) to organise such relationships?
Product	– Which bundle of additional adds-on, services and functionalities surrounding the 'core' innovation will be included in the basic configuration of the new product?
Distribution	– Which type of distribution strategy (e.g., push or pull) will be needed to streamline the market penetration of the innovation? – Which types of distribution channels will be chosen to deliver the innovation to market (e.g., retail or specialised distributors)? – Which critical functions (e.g., customer education) will they be required to perform?
Advertising and promotion	– Which message will be communicated during the pre-announcement and post-launch advertising campaign? – Which types of communication channels will be employed for these advertising and promotion initiatives (e.g., mass or specialised channels)?
Pricing	– Which pricing strategy (e.g., skimming or penetration) will be used for the market introduction of the new product? – Which pricing strategy will be adopted for complementary goods and additional services?

The commercialisation processes of 11 technological innovations, launched in high-technology markets in the past 30 years, were investigated using this approach (Table 7.6).

TABLE 7.6   Successful and unsuccessful innovation examined

	Radical innovations	**Systemic innovations**
Unsuccessful innovations	Apple Newton IBM PC-Junior Sony Betamax	3DO Interactive Multiplayer Sony MiniDisc Apple Newton Sony Betamax
Successful innovations	Tom Tom GO Sony Walkman RIM BlackBerry	Palm Pilot Nintendo NES Apple iPod

Comparing the commercialisation of the successful and unsuccessful systemic innovations in the sample, a number of decisions were taken along the dimensions.

Inter-Firm Relationships

Our analysis indicates that obtaining the support from the critical members of innovation's adoption network requires chiefly a careful administration of the inter-firm relationships that are established before and along the commercialisation process.

The decision to prevent other companies (e.g., competitors and suppliers of complementary hardware and software) from manufacturing products based on the innovation's underlying technology is likely to be a first detrimental decision for the large-scale adoption of a high-technology innovation. This is due to the strong network externalities that high-tech markets, because of their tight interconnectedness, are currently experiencing. Accordingly, letting the actors of the adoption network manufacture products based on the innovation's technology (e.g., through advantageous out-licensing agreements) increases the availability of complementary products and the chances that a potential adopter chooses to purchase the innovation. This in turn exponentially enhances the value of the innovation in the eyes of both subsequent adopters and the other members of the adoption network, in a self-reinforcing double-loop cycle. The effects of this commercialisation decision are very clear when comparing the cases of the Palm Pilot (whose OS operating system was released for free to all manufacturers of adds-on and software applications) with that of Sony Betamax (with the Japanese firm that accepted to licence the underlying technology to Zenith only more than one year after launch, when the incoming success of the VHS by JVC was already undisputable).

It also emerges as a critical approach to win the support of the critical members of the adoption network to enter into long-term, strategic partnerships with them. This allows firms to share the risks and the costs they incur when supporting a systemic innovation (e.g., developing and manufacturing ad hoc, specialised, complementary devices or pieces of software). This is what Palm did, in 1996, when commercialising its Pilot: it decided to sign a €20 million agreement with Circuit City to ensure adequate shelf space and customer education services for its new product. Similarly Apple, to streamline the acceptance of the iPod and the associated iTunes Music Store service, was able to convince a number of record labels (e.g., Sony Music Entertainment, BMG, EMI, Universal and Warner) to endorse the new service provision model ensuring a 65% compensation for each song sold through iTunes. In a similar vein, Nintendo invested heavily in order to obtain the full support for its NES from the most important game developers (e.g., Taito, Bandai, Capcom). This required the Japanese firm to grant above the average money compensation for each game sold. Sometimes the innovating firm instead refuses to establish any partnerships with the members of the adoption network, or simply sets up arm's-length, commercial relationships with them, with the aim of maximising its potential profits from the innovation. This is evident in the case of 3DO, which failed to establish any forms of relationship with the developers of software titles and the manufacturers of consoles for its new Interactive Multiplayer. A similar phenomenon is clear in the commercialisation of the Betamax, where Sony refused to partner with video rental channels and film producers (with the exception of Paramount Home Video, with which a Joint Venture was established).

A critical member of the adoption network for content-based innovations is the community of small and highly creative software and application developers. In order to secure their support, it is especially critical to develop an easy to use software authoring kit that is made available for free or at a very low price. This is what Palm did when it released for free the application development kit for its Pilot. 3DO, on the other hand, decided to sell the authoring system for the Interactive Multiplayer for several thousand dollars.

Timing

Besides the form of the inter-firms relationships with the critical members of the adoption network, it seems that the timing with which they are established is important in determining the degree of support they ensure to the innovation. The analysis indicates that sometimes firms deliberately postpone the establishment of strategic partnerships with the adoption network on the assumption that, once the innovation has taken off in the market, its critical players will support it of their own accord. However, it often happens that, after an initial, unexpected growth of the new product's sales, the innovation never diffuses in the largest part of the target market. This is what happened in the commercialisation of the MiniDisc: Sony refused to partner with consumer electronics outlets (which played a critical role in ensuring a wide availability of recorded music albums) in the belief that the new format would diffuse into the mass market and, as a result, force outlets to provide the required shelf space. This phenomenon is due to the fact that the bulk of a high-tech consumer innovation's target market is made of people who resist new products and experience a high level of uncertainty when evaluating the opportunity to buy them. Although early adopters might be willing to purchase the new product whilst it is not backed up by the critical members of the adoption network (because they are mainly attracted by the technical content and degree of sophistication of the innovation and are able to more objectively assess its advantages), this represents an important signal to later adopters of the value of the innovation, which helps reduce their resistance and customer uncertainty.

Therefore, although a high-tech innovation may experience an unexpected sales growth immediately after launch without support from the critical players of the adoption network, it is of paramount importance to rapidly secure this support, through the establishment of long-term, strategic partnership, if large-scale adoption is to be achieved. All firms whose innovations had experienced a relevant and rapid diffusion in the bulk of their target market started very early indeed to work with the adoption network's critical players. This is clear in the cases of the Pilot by Palm, the NES by Nintendo and the iPod by Apple.

It often happens that firms rush to market their high-tech innovations in an attempt to establish them as technological standards and to quickly recover their R&D investments. This sometimes leads to the launch of an incomplete product, with some functionalities not working perfectly, as a result of the acceleration of development and testing activities. This seems to have a very negative effect on the attitude developed by early adopters. Companies sometimes prefer shortening time to market at the expense of product completeness on the assumption that the potential technical problems will not affect the purchasing decision and the satisfaction of the average member of the target market. In doing so they overlook that the innovation is adopted immediately after launch by those customer segments that are most sensitive to the new product's technical content and sophistication, and whose opinion about the new product is key in affecting subsequent purchases. This erroneous conduct is clear in the commercialisation of the IBM PC-Junior and the Apple Newton, while there is no sign of new product acceleration for the successful radical innovations in the sample (e.g., Tom Tom GO, Sony Walkman and RIM BlackBerry).

It should be noted that the negative impact of the launch of an incomplete product is exacerbated by an overblown pre-announcement campaign, which raises the expectations of early adopters and leaves them disappointed when a deficient version reaches the market: their attitudes to the innovation as a whole are thereby negatively affected. This happened with the Apple's Newton, which was announced

18 months before the actual launch and was known as one of the most-hyped and postponed products for years. Similarly, the PC-Junior was pre-announced about 12 months before the launch, which fuelled the curiosity, rumours and enthusiasm that accompanied the new product. Analysts started referring to the PC-Junior by the nickname 'Peanut'. Interestingly, IBM itself contributed to nurturing these expectations by drawing a thick curtain of secrecy over the new product after having pre-announced it.

Targeting and Positioning

Especially for content-based innovations, it seems that a firm more easily succeeds in orchestrating the behaviour of the adoption network's players and in securing their support if the positioning of the new product is unambiguous. The experience of 3DO in the commercialisation of the Interactive Multiplayer is paradigmatic in this respect. The new, revolutionary console always lacked a library of software titles that were able to fully exploit its graphic capabilities. This was partly due to its un-clear positioning: the Multiplayer was sold as a gaming platform with advanced interactive, learning and educational capabilities, enabled by its CD-Rom support, that caused confusion in the developers community about the exact applications that were required for its commercial success. On the other hand, the NES by Nintendo was unambiguously positioned as a gaming system, and the Palm Pilot as a substitute for personal paper-based organisers.

The incapability to understand that an incomplete new product is likely to elicit a very negative reaction in the first market segments that adopt it is also due to a lack of pro-active targeting of these early adopters. The firms in the sample that failed to raise a positive post-purchase attitude of early adopters had not targeted the innova-tion at any specific market segments after launch. This is clear in the cases of Apple's Newton and IBM's PC-Junior that were aimed at a broadly defined market made of mass consumers and families with children. It was only after the first months of sales that managers realised the new products were being purchased by people with a very different profile than the average target customer (namely, executives and companies looking for sales force automation applications, and managers used to working with a traditional PC at the office who wanted to bring some work at home). On the other hand, when commercialising the Walkman, Sony realized that it was going to be initially purchased by young men fond of sport and outdoor living, and that the 'near CD quality' of sound reproduction associated with advanced portability of the device was key in affecting their post-purchase attitude. Similarly, RIM targeted its BlackBerry immediately after launch to top executives (e.g., Chief Information Officers, Chief Financial Officers) or sales agents who had a compelling reason to receive e-mail messages in real time while travelling for work, and ensured that this functionality was working perfectly from a technical point of view.

Product

The aforementioned lack of targeting of the innovation's early adopters is detrimental also because it often prevents firms from devising a configuration of the whole product at launch that meets early adopters' expectations, which are usually very different from the intended average target customer's. For instance, the IBM PC-Junior was not compatible with many of the applications available for the traditional PC, and the Apple Newton lacked connectivity with PC and Macintosh at launch. It is noteworthy and seemingly nonsensical that both IBM and Apple had sponsored these capabilities of the new products during the pre-announcement campaign, which exacerbates the negative effect of an inappropriate product configuration at launch over early adopters' satisfaction. This might be the result of the attempt to anticipate the launch of the innovation without a clear targeting of the early customers.

On the other hand, the successful innovations in the sample do not seem to have missed any critical functionalities to satisfy early adopters' expectations. How could this be achieved? The analysis suggests that an effective commercialisation strategy could need to include a limited number of simple functionalities in the configuration of the new product at launch, designed to satisfy the compelling reason to purchase of early adopters. The product configuration is enriched with additional functionalities as long as the innovation diffuses in the less innovative segments of the target market. An essential prerequisite for successfully adopting this approach, which increases the likelihood that the new product is complete at launch despite a firm's attempt to rush it to market, is a careful targeting of the innovation's early customers. This approach was for instance adopted by RIM in the commercialisation of the BlackBerry. In order to improve the chances of satisfying the new product's early customers, RIM decided to design and launch a simplified version of the BlackBerry, called Desktop Redirector, that could work using as a mail server any PCs or laptops and only featured the revolutionary 'push' approach to mail delivery. Agenda, address book, and synchronisation with PC were added as long as the BlackBerry diffused in the market. On the other hand, Apple tried to include as many complex functionalities as possible in the first version of the Newton (e.g., infrared communication, advanced handwriting recognition, contact manager, organiser, synchronisation with both PC and Macintosh, traditional and wireless phone connectivity), some of which were absent or did not function perfectly at launch, resulting in a very negative attitude from early adopters.

Advertising and Promotion

The role of the pre-announcement campaign in influencing the post-purchase attitude of early adopters has already been discussed in this section of the chapter. In particular, it has emerged that an early pre-announcement of the new product generates great expectations in the innovation's early adopters. If the new product at launch fails to fulfil these expectations, because it is incomplete as a result of a rush to market, or because it lacks some functionalities that are critical for early adopters, the latter turn out to be highly dissatisfied with the innovation, and their opinion about it freezes any further diffusion of the new product. Therefore, if a firm chooses to pre-announce early a high-tech innovation, it must be sure to arrive on the market with a complete product having the few, critical functionalities that are necessary to satisfy the compelling reason to buy of early adopters. This is consistent with literature on New Product Pre-announcements (NPPAs), which indicates that pre-announcing and then missing introduction dates for new products is not detrimental per se in terms of customer acceptance. It becomes problematic only in the case when the new product, once it reaches the market, fails to fulfil the expectations of early adopters nurtured by the pre-announcement campaign. This is exactly what happened with the commercialisation of the Apple Newton and the IBM PC-Junior.

Case Questions

1. What are the respective roles of early adopters and network development in the market acceptance of innovations?
2. What are the critical differences in the timing and positioning of successful versus unsuccessful innovations?
3. Product and Promotion are standard parts of the 'Marketing Mix'. How do these contribute to market acceptance of an innovation?

Source: Federico Frattini (2010) Achieving adoption network and early adopters acceptance for technological innovations, in Tidd, J. (ed.) *Gaining Momentum: managing the diffusion of innovations.* Imperial College Press, London.

Summary of Web Resources

Cases

• Clearvue

Media

• Glasses Direct

Tools

• Risk Assessment

Chapter 8

Exploiting Networks

Go online to find additional . . .

Cases

Tools

Media

www.iande.info

No Man is an Island . . .

Eating out in the days of living in caves was not quite the simple matter it has become today. For a start there was the minor difficulty of finding and gathering the roots and berries – or, being more adventurous, hunting and (hopefully) catching your mammoth for the stew pot. And cold meat isn't necessarily an appetising or digestible dish so cooking it helps – but for that you need fire and for that you need wood, not to mention cooking pots and utensils. If any single individual tried to accomplish all of these tasks alone they would quickly die of exhaustion, never mind starvation! We could elaborate but the point is clear – like almost all human activity, it is dependent on others. But it's not simply about spreading the workload – for most of our contemporary activities the key is shared creativity – solving problems together, and exploiting the fact that different people have different skills and experiences which they can bring to the party.

INNOVATION IN ACTION

Take any group of people and ask them to think of different uses for an everyday item – a cup, a brick, a ball, etc. Working alone they will usually develop an extensive list – but then ask them to share the ideas they have generated. The resulting list will not only be much longer but will also contain much greater diversity of possible classes of solution to the problem. For example, uses for a cup might include using it as a container (vase, pencil holder, drinking vessel, etc.), a mould (for sandcastles, cakes, etc.), a musical instrument, a measure, a template around which one can draw, a device for eavesdropping (when pressed against a wall) and even , when thrown, a weapon!

The psychologist J.P. Guilford classed these two traits as 'fluency' – the ability to produce ideas – and 'flexibility' – the ability to come up with different types of idea.[1] The above experiment will quickly show that working as a group people are usually much more fluent and flexible than any single individual. When working together people spark each other off, jump on and develop each other's ideas, encourage and support each other through positive emotional mechanisms like laughter and agreement – and in a variety of ways stimulate a high level of shared creativity.

(This is the basis of 'brainstorming' and a wide range of creativity enhancement techniques which have been developed over many years).

It's easy to think of innovation as a solo act – the lone genius, slaving away in his or her garret or lying, Archimedes-like, in the bath before that moment of inspiration when they run through the streets proclaiming their 'Eureka!' moment. But although that's a common image it lies a long way from the reality. In reality taking any good idea forward relies on all sorts of inputs from different people and perspectives.

For example, the technological breakthrough which makes a better mousetrap is only going to mean something if people can be made aware of it and persuaded that this is something they cannot live without – and this requires all kinds of inputs from the marketing skill set. Making it happen is going to need skills in manufacturing, in procurement of the bits and pieces to make it, in controlling the quality of the final product. None of this will happen without some funding so other skills in getting access to finance – and the understanding of how to spend the money wisely – become important. And co-ordinating the diverse inputs needed to turn the mousetrap into a successful reality rather than a gleam in the eye will require project management skills, balancing resources against the clock and facilitating a team of people to find and solve the thousand and one little problems which crop up as you make the journey.

Innovation is not a solo act but a multi-player game. Whether it is the entrepreneur who spots an opportunity or an established organisation trying to renew its offerings or sharpen up its processes, making innovation happen depends on working with many different players. This raises questions about team working, bringing the different people together in productive and creative ways inside an organisation – a theme we discussed in Chapter 2. But increasingly it's also about links *between* organisations, developing and making use of increasingly wide *networks*. Smart firms have always recognised the importance of linkages and connections – getting close to customers to understand their needs, working with suppliers to deliver innovative solutions, linking up with collaborators, research centres, even competitors to build and operate innovation systems. But in an era of global operations and high-speed technological infrastructures populated by people with highly mobile skills, building and managing networks and connections becomes *the* key requirement for innovation. It's not about knowledge creation so much as knowledge *flows*. Even major research and development players like Siemens or GlaxoSmithKline are realising that they can't cover all the knowledge bases they need and instead are looking to build extensive links and relationships with players around the globe.

Networking is important right across the innovation process – from finding opportunities, through pulling together the resources to develop the venture, to making it happen and diffusing the idea – and capturing value at the end of the process.

This chapter explores some of the emerging themes around the question of innovation as a network-based multi-player game. And of course, in the twenty-first century this game is being played out on a vast global stage but with an underlying networking technology – the Internet – which collapses distances, places geographically far-flung locations right alongside each other in time and enables increasingly exciting collaboration possibilities. However, just because we have the technology to make and live in a global village doesn't necessarily mean we'll be able to do so – much of the challenge, as we'll see, lies in organising and managing networks so that they perform. Rather than simply being the coming together of different people and organisations, successful networks have what are called *emergent properties* – the whole is greater than the sum of the parts.

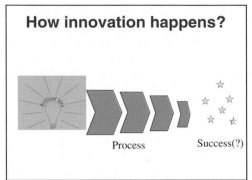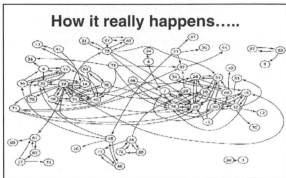

FIGURE 8.1   Spaghetti model of innovation

The Spaghetti Model of Innovation

As we showed in Chapter 1, innovation is a core process with a defined structure and a number of influences. That's helpful in terms of simplifying the picture into some clear stages and recognising the key levers we might have to work with if we are going to manage the process successfully. But like any simplification, the model isn't quite as complex as the reality. Figure 8.1 provides an illustration of this complexity.

Whilst our model works as an aerial view of what goes on and has to be managed, the close-up picture can look a lot more like the picture on the right. The ways knowledge actually flows around an innovation project are complex and interactive, woven together in a kind of social spaghetti where different people talk to each other in different ways, more or less frequently, and about different things.

This complex interaction is all about *knowledge* and the ways it flows and is combined and deployed to make innovation happen. Whether it's our entrepreneur building a network to help him get his mousetrap to market or a company like Apple bringing out the latest generation iPhone the process will involve building and running knowledge networks. And as the innovation becomes more complex so the networks have to involve more different players, many of whom may lie outside the firm. By the time we get to big complex projects – like building a new aeroplane or hospital facility – the number of players and the management challenges the networks pose get pretty large. There is also the complication that increasingly the networks we have to learn to deal with are becoming more virtual, a rich and global set of human resources distributed and connected by the enabling technologies of the Internet, broadband and mobile communications and shared computer networks.

Networking as the Latest Generation Innovation Model

It could be agued that innovation and entrepreneurship is evolving – from a world of centuries ago which saw the sole inventor/entrepreneur as the key player, through one in the last century in which major corporations came to dominate the landscape to today's picture which is

TABLE 8.1	Rothwell's five generations of innovation models
Generation	**Key features**
First/second	Simple linear models – need pull, technology push
Third	Coupling model, recognising interaction between different elements and feedback loops between them
Fourth	Parallel model, integration within the company, upstream with key suppliers and downstream with demanding and active customers, emphasis on linkages and alliances
Fifth	Systems integration and extensive networking, flexible and customised response, continuous innovation

becoming massively networked, globally distributed and connected via communication and information processing technologies which enable a very different approach.

Networking of this kind is something which Roy Rothwell, for many years a key researcher at Sussex University's Science Policy Research Unit, foresaw in his pioneering work on models of innovation which predicted a gradual move away from thinking about (and organising) a linear science/technology push or demand pull process to one which saw increasing interactivity.[2] At first, this exists across the company with cross-functional teams and other boundary-spanning activities. Increasingly, it then moves outside it with links to external actors. Rothwell's vision of the 'fifth generation' innovation is essentially the one in which we now need to operate, with rich and diverse network linkages accelerated and enabled by an intensive set of information and communication technologies (Table 8.1).

Types of Innovation Networks

If networking is becoming the dominant mode for innovation and entrepreneurship then it would be useful to begin with a clear understanding of our terms. A network can be defined as 'a complex, interconnected group or system', and networking involves using that arrangement to accomplish particular tasks. As we've suggested innovation has always been a multi-player game and we can see a growing number of ways in which such networking takes place. At its simplest networking happens in an informal way when people get together and share ideas as a by-product of their social and work interactions. But we'll concentrate our attention on more formal networks which are deliberately set up to help make innovation happen, whether it is creating a new product or service or learning to apply some new process thinking more effectively within organisations.

Innovation networks are more than just ways of assembling and deploying knowledge in a complex world. They can also have what are termed 'emergent properties' – that is, the potential for the whole to be greater than the sum of its parts. Being in an effective innovation network can deliver a wide range of benefits beyond the collective knowledge efficiency mentioned above. These include getting access to different and complementary knowledge sets, reducing risks by sharing them, accessing new markets and technologies and otherwise pooling complementary skills and assets. Without such networks it would be nearly impossible for the lone inventor to bring his or her idea successfully to market. And it's one of the main reasons why established businesses are increasingly turning to co-operation and alliances – to extend their access to these key innovation resources.

Participating in innovation networks can help companies bump into new ideas and creative combinations – even for mature businesses. It is well known in studies of creativity, that the process involves making associations. And sometimes, the unexpected conjunction of different perspectives can lead to surprising results. The same seems to be true at the organisational level; studies of networks indicate that getting together in such a fashion can help open up new and productive territory.

INNOVATION IN ACTION

Networking for Innovation

Cosworth is a well-known producer of high-performance engines for motor racing and performance car applications. They were seeking a source of aluminium castings which were cheap enough for volume use but of high enough precision and quality for their product; having searched throughout the world they were unable to find anyone suitable. Either they took the low-price route and used some form of die-casting which often lacked the precision and accuracy, or they went along the investment casting route which added significantly to the cost. Eventually they decided to go right back to basics and design their own manufacturing process; they set up a small pilot facility and employed a team of metallurgists and engineers with the brief to come up with an alternative approach that could meet their needs. After three years' work and a very wide and systematic exploration of the problem the team came up with a process which combined conventional casting approaches with new materials (especially a high grade of sand) and other improvements. The breakthrough was, however, the use of an electromagnetic pump which forced molten metal into a shell in such a way as to eliminate the air which normally led to problems of porosity in the final product. This innovation came from well outside the foundry industry, from the nuclear power field where it had been used to circulate the liquid sodium coolant used in the fast breeder reactor programme! The results were impressive; not only did Cosworth meet their own needs, they were also able to offer the service to other users of castings and to license the process to major manufacturers such as Ford and Daimler-Benz.

Consider another example from the motor sport industry: leading race car makers are continually seeking innovation in support of enhanced performance and may take ideas, materials,

(continued)

technology or products from very different sectors. Indeed some have people (called 'technological antennae') whose sole responsibility is to search for new technologies that might be used. For instance, recent developments in the use of titanium components in Formula 1 engines have been significantly advanced by lessons learned about the moulding process from a company producing golf clubs.[3]

Another way in which networking can help innovation is in providing support for shared learning. A lot of process innovation is about configuring and adapting what has been developed elsewhere and applying it to your processes – for example, in the many efforts which organisations have been making to adopt world-class manufacturing (and increasingly, service) practice. While it is possible to go it alone in this process, an increasing number of companies are seeing the value in using networks to give them some extra traction on the learning process.

INNOVATION IN ACTION

Networking for Learning

Learning together has its advantages. For example, in the UK, the Society of Motor Manufacturers and Traders has run the successful Industry Forum for many years, helping a wide range of businesses adopt and implement process innovations around world-class manufacturing. This model has been rolled out (with support from the government) to sectors as diverse as ceramics, aerospace, textiles and tourism. Many regional development agencies now try to use networks and clusters as a key aid to stimulating economic growth through innovation. The same principles can help to diffuse innovative practices along supply chains; companies such as IBM and BAE Systems have made extensive efforts to make 'supply chain learning' the next key thrust in their supplier development programmes.

Go online to find more case examples of 'learning networks'.

www.iande.info

Innovation is about taking risks and deploying what are often scarce resources on projects which may not succeed. So, another way in which networking can help is by helping to spread the risk and, in the process, extending the range of things which might be tried. This is particularly useful in the context of smaller businesses where resources are scarce and it is one of the key features behind the success of many industrial clusters.

INNOVATION IN ACTION

The case of the Italian furniture industry is one in which a consistently strong export perform-ance has been achieved by companies with an average size of less than 20 employees. Keeping their position at the frontier in terms of performance is the result of sustained innovation in design and quality enabled by a network-based approach. This isn't an isolated case – one of the most respected research institutes in the world for textiles is CITER, based in Emilia Romagna. Unlike so many world-class institutions, this was not created in top-down fashion but evolved from the shared innovation concerns of a small group of textile producers who built on the network model to share risks and resources. Their initial problems with dyeing and with computer-aided design helped them to gain a foothold in terms of innovation in their processes. In the years since its founding in 1980, it has helped its 500 (mostly small business) members develop a strong inno-vation capability.

Long-lasting innovation networks can create the capability to ride out major waves of change in the technological and economic environment. We think of places like Silicon Valley, Cambridge in the UK or the island of Singapore as powerhouses of innovation but they are just the latest in a long-running list of geographical regions which have grown and sustained themselves through a continuous stream of innovation.

INNOVATION IN ACTION

Networking for Collective Efficiency

Michael Best's fascinating account of the ways in which the Massachusetts economy managed to reinvent itself several times is one which places innovation networking at its heart.[4] In the 1950s the state suffered heavily from the loss of its traditional industries of textiles and shoes but by the early 1980s the 'Massachusetts miracle' led to the establishment of a new high-tech industrial dis-trict. It was a resurgence enabled in no small measure by an underpinning network of specialist skills, high-tech research and training centres (the Boston area has the highest concentration of col-leges, universities, research labs and hospitals in the world) and by the rapid establishment of en-trepreneurial firms keen to exploit the emerging 'knowledge economy'. But in turn this miracle turned to dust in the years between 1986 and 1992 when around one third of the manufacturing jobs in the region disappeared as the minicomputer and defence-related industries collapsed. Despite gloomy predictions about its future the region built again on its rich network of skills, tech-nology sources and a diverse local supply base which allowed rapid new product development to emerge again as a powerhouse in high technology such as special purpose machinery, optoelec-tronics, medical laser technology, digital printing equipment and biotech.

Table 8.2 gives an idea of the different ways in which networks can be configured to help with the innovation process. In the following section we'll look a little more closely at some of these, how they operate and the benefits they can offer.

Let's explore some of these in detail.

TABLE 8.2   Types of innovation networks

Network type	Examples
Entrepreneur-based	Bringing different complementary resources together to help take an opportunity forward. Often a combination of formal and informal, depends a lot on the entrepreneur's energy and enthusiasm in getting people interested to join – and stay in – the network.
Internal project teams	Formal – and informal – networks of knowledge and key skills which can be brought together to help enable some opportunity to be taken forward. Essentially like entrepreneur networks but on the inside of established organisations. May run into difficulties because of having to cross internal organisational boundaries.
Communities of practice	These are networks which can involve players inside and across different organisations – what binds them together is a shared concern with a particular aspect or area of knowledge.
Spatial clusters	Networks which form because of the players being close to each other – for example, in the same geographical region. Silicon Valley is a good example of a cluster which thrives on proximity – knowledge flows amongst and across the members of the network but is hugely helped by the geographical closeness and the ability of key players to meet and talk.
Sectoral networks	Networks which bring different players together because they share a common sector – and often have the purpose of shared innovation to preserve competitiveness. Often organised by sector or business associations on behalf of their members. Shared concern to adopt and develop innovative good practice across a sector or product market grouping – for example, the SMMT Industry Forum or Logic (Leading Oil and Gas Industry Competitiveness), a gas and oil industry forum.
New product or process development consortium	Sharing knowledge and perspectives to create and market a new product or process concept – for example, the Symbian consortium (Sony, Ericsson, Motorola and others) worked towards developing a new operating system for mobile phones and PDAs.

(continued)

TABLE 8.2 (*Continued*)	
Network type	**Examples**
Sectoral forum	Working together across a sector to improve competitiveness through product, process and service innovation.
New technology development consortium	Sharing and learning around newly emerging technologies – for example, the pioneering semiconductor research programmes in the US and Japan.
Emerging standards	Exploring and establishing standards around innovative technologies – for example, the Motion Picture Experts Group (MPEG) working on audio and video compression standards.
Supply chain learning	Developing and sharing innovative good practice and possibly shared product development across a value chain – for example, the SCRIA initiative in UK aerospace.

Networks at the Start-Up

The idea of the lone inventor pioneering his or her way through to market success is something of a myth – not least because of the huge efforts and different resources needed to make innovation happen. Whilst individual ideas, energy and passion are key requirements, most successful entrepreneurs recognise the need to network extensively and to collect the resources they need via complex webs of relationships. They are essentially highly skilled at networking, both in building and in maintaining those networks to help build a sustainable business model.

INNOVATION IN ACTION

Many Minds Make Light Work . . .

Say the name 'Thomas Edison, and people instinctively imagine a great inventor, the lone genius who gave us so many twentieth-century products and services – the gramophone, the light bulb, electric power, etc. But he was actually a very smart networker. His 'invention factory' in Menlo Park, New Jersey, employed a team of engineers in a single room filled with workbenches, shelves of chemicals, books and other resources. The key to their undoubted success was to bring together a group of young, entrepreneurial, enthusiastic men from very diverse backgrounds, and allow the emerging community to tackle a wide range of problems. Ideas flowed across the group and were combined and recombined into an astonishing array of inventions.

If we look at some cases of entrepreneur-driven start-ups it quickly becomes possible to see their evolution as one of growing networks. Take the wind-up radio story featured in Chapter 2 – a great idea and an interesting invention required an extensive network of finance, logistics, distribution, marketing and manufacturing to enable it to come to scale and sustainability. Or Mike Lynch's Autonomy – another brilliant technological idea, which provided the basis for what is now a key global player in the information management world, but it began with a process of network building, linking up with key players able to provide the complementary skills and resources to get the innovation established. (This case is discussed in detail in Chapter 12.)

These days one of the most powerful companies in the electronics world is ARM whose chips are in almost all mobile phones and a host of other devices. Now a global player, ARM began as a spin-off from Cambridge University in the 1980s. But its evolution was not a one-man show but the building and development of a complex network with links across countries, sectors and technologies.

Networks on the Inside . . .

'If only x knew what x knows . . . ' You can fill the x in with the name of almost any large contemporary organisation (Siemens, Philips, GSK, Citibank), they all wrestle with the paradox that they have hundreds or thousands of people spread across their organisations with all sorts of knowledge. The trouble is that – apart from some formal project activities which bring them together – many of these knowledge elements remain unconnected, like a giant jigsaw puzzle in which only a small number of the pieces have so far been fitted together. This kind of thinking was behind the fashion for 'knowledge management' in the late 1990s and one response, popular then, was to make extensive use of information technology to try to improve the connectivity. Trouble is that, whilst the computers and database systems were excellent at storage and transmission, they didn't necessarily help make the connections that turned data and information into useful – and used – knowledge. Increasingly firms are recognising that, whilst advanced information and communications technology can support and enhance, the real need is for improved knowledge networks inside the organisation.

It's back to the spaghetti model of innovation – how to ensure that people get to talk to others and share and build on each other's ideas. This might not be too hard in a three or four person business but it gets much harder across a typical sprawling multinational corporation. Although this is a long-standing problem there has been quite a lot of movement in recent years towards understanding how to build more effective innovation networks within such businesses.

Chapter 6 (search) gave some examples of using such internal networks to find opportunities and others can be found on the website.

Go online to find case studies on 3M, P&G and Kumba, along with the Roy Sandbach podcast.

www.iande.info

Networks on the Outside

Creating and combining different knowledge sets has always been the name of the game both inside and outside the firm. But there has been a dramatic acceleration in recent years led by major firms like Procter & Gamble, GSK, 3M, Siemens and GE towards what has been termed 'open innovation'. The idea – first put forward by US professor Henry Chesbrough – is that even large-scale R&D in a closed system like an individual firm isn't going to be enough in the twenty-first century environment.[5] Knowledge production is taking place at an exponential rate and the OECD countries spend getting on for $750bn per year on R&D in the public and private sector – a figure which is probably an underestimate since it ignores the considerable amount of 'research' which is not captured in official statistics. How can any single organisation keep up with – or even keep tabs on – such a sea of knowledge? And this is happening in widely distributed fashion – R&D is no longer the province of the advanced industrial nations like USA, Germany or Japan but is increasing most rapidly in the newly growing economies like India and China. In this kind of context it's going to be impossible to pick up on every development and even smart firms are going to miss a trick or two.

And of course innovation isn't just about the R&D side – it's also about market knowledge around customer needs and wishes. Globalisation has meant that markets are increasingly fragmented so understanding the demand side for innovation becomes massively more complex. Not to mention the fact that the rapid rise of the Internet as a virtual marketplace changes the rules radically – new markets emerge with high speed out of nowhere as information flows in and across complex networks. When bands can rise to prominence and top the album charts with products originally available only in digital download form and when they can build reputations not via conventional PR and publicity but by the sheer pace and scale of viral marketing via the Web, then the game becomes much more open and unpredictable. When YouTube can capture videos of all manner of events – news, entertainment, comedy, tragedy – and distribute it via the Internet, which allows rapid diffusion around the world, it changes the relationship between producers, consumers and intermediate agencies involved in broadcasting. What will this mean for players in the media, information and entertainment industries in the near future? How does even an established player like the BBC in the UK try and deal with the challenge of new digital media – who creates it, with what content, for which audience reached by what route?

INNOVATION IN ACTION

BBC Backstage is an example of one of the projects which is trying to do with new media development what the open source community did with Linux and other software development. The model is deceptively simple – developers are invited to make free use of various elements of the BBC's site (such as live news feeds, weather, TV listings, etc.) to integrate and shape innovative applications. The strap line is 'use our stuff to build your stuff' – and since the site was launched in May 2005 it has already attracted the interest of hundreds of software developers and led to some high-potential product ideas. Ben Metcalf, one of the programme's founders, summed up the approach. 'Top line, we are looking to be seen as promoting innovation and creativity on the Internet, and if we can be seen to be doing that, we will be very pleased. In terms of projects coming out of it, if we can see a few examples that offered real value to our end users to build something new, we would be happy with that as well. And if someone is doing something really innovative, we would like to invite them into the BBC and see if some of that value can be incorporate into the BBC's core propositions.'

Go online to find a podcast interview with David Overton that gives an illustration of how the UK's Ordnance Survey organisation is using a similar approach to the BBC's.

www.iande.info

The logic of open innovation is that organisations need to open up their innovation processes, searching widely outside their boundaries and working towards managing a rich set of network connections and relationships right across the board. Their challenge becomes one of improving the knowledge *flows* in and out of the organisation, trading in knowledge as much as goods and services. Great in theory – but what it implies is that firms need to raise their game around finding and forming relevant connections and networks, and in building high-performance relationships with which to enable innovation.

Similarly this open environment offers rich opportunities for start-up entrepreneurs. You no longer need to have all the knowledge resources in one place but rather the challenge is knowing where they are and how to get at them. But once again this means learning a whole new set of skills around making and managing connections.

In some ways the traditional boundaries are becoming blurred – for example, between established organisations and start-ups, or between public and private sector. Instead it is a pattern of new relationships across which knowledge spaghetti is combined in new ways. But underlying this is the need to learn new ways of working – or rather new ways of 'networking'. Social entrepreneurship has always depended on networking to help make change happen, but it is now able to take advantage of rich social and technological tools to help make those connections. Organisations like the Young Foundation or the Innovation Exchange in the UK specialise in helping to make connections and broker networks.

 Go online to find a podcast interview with Simon Tucker of the Young Foundation.

www.iande.info

For example, Procter & Gamble's successes with 'connect and develop' (which we looked at briefly in Chapter 6) owe much to their mobilising rich linkages between people who know things within their giant global operations and increasingly outside it. They use communities of practice – Internet-enabled 'clubs' where people with different knowledge sets can converge around core themes, and they deploy a small army of innovation 'scouts' who are licensed to act as prospectors, brokers and gatekeepers for knowledge to flow across the organisation's boundaries. Intranet technology links around 10,000 people in an internal 'ideas market' whilst sites like InnoCentive.com extend the principle outside the firm and enable a world of new collaborative possibilities.

 Go online to find a podcast interview with Roy Sandbach giving more details of the P&G experience.

www.iande.info

3M – another firm with a strong innovation pedigree dating back over a century – similarly put much of their success down to making and managing connections. Larry Wendling, Vice President for Corporate Research, talks of 3M's 'secret weapon' – the rich formal and informal networking which links the thousands of R&D and market-facing people across the organisation. Their long-history of breakthrough innovations – from masking tape, through Scotchgard, Scotch tape, magnetic recording tape, to Post-its and their myriad derivatives – arise primarily out of people making connections.

The process of opening up the game is not without its problems – first of all in finding new ways to enable connections. There has been a huge rise in the role played by social and technological networking as mechanisms which enable closer linkages – and with it have sprung up new roles and groupings within organisations (gatekeepers, information managers, knowledge hubs, etc.) and new service businesses on the outside specialising in brokering and connecting. But improving knowledge flows also opens a can of worms as far as managing intellectual property is concerned – in a world of open source who owns what and how might you protect your hard-won knowledge assets?

For the lone entrepreneur this raises a tantalising mixture of threat and opportunity. On the one hand he or she can make effective connections to resources and can mobilise them and act on a global basis. We've seen examples of this in the field of Internet businesses which operate often with very small groups of people and amplify their efforts and presence through networking to a global community sometimes running into billions of people. Developments around networking mean that the old problem for small businesses – their isolation – is removed. But on the other hand the sheer scale and number of potential connections requires learning new skills in finding, forming and getting networks to perform.

 Go online to find podcast interviews with David Simoes-Brown and Richard Philpott that give examples of entrepreneurs who are trying to take advantage of this open innovation opportunity.

www.iande.info

INNOVATION IN ACTION

Netflix and Open Collective Innovation

Netflix is a major player in the growing film rental business in the USA; the business works by online and mail-order distribution of DVDs and other media. Its business model depends on having a good understanding of what people want and – like Amazon – trying to tailor advertising and offers to their preferences. It was already a successful business but in 2006 decided to try to improve the algorithm it used to develop these recommendations by opening up the challenge to the wider community. It offered a $1m reward – the Netflix Prize – to anyone who could improve the performance of its algorithm by 10% or better.

In running the competition it had to open up its current customer database of around 100 million people to anyone registering for the competition. The work involved was complex – the data file which contestants had to work with was around 10 gigabytes and the statistical techniques needed to work with it were sophisticated. Within 3 months over 18,000 contestants from 125 countries had registered – effectively creating a temporary R&D laboratory on a huge and globally distributed scale.

In addition to the $1m prize Netflix offered 'progress prizes' where they would pay $50,000 for a non-exclusive licence to use any interesting new algorithms. Importantly they published these so that others in the competition would have access to them and employ them to make their own efforts even better.

After one year it became clear that 'not all the smart guys work for us' – Netflix found over 7000 people had a better algorithm than the one they had originally been using. Within three years 51,000 contestants had joined the competition from 186 countries, and they had created 44,000 valid entries. A winner was announced which demonstrated a better than 10% improvement; significantly, the strategy employed was not one of lone expertise but rather continuous co-creation, in which groups of developers learned from each other and improved on a continuing basis.

Using Networks to Help Learning

We saw in Chapter 6 that a problem in innovation arises because although individuals and organisations operate in a world full of external knowledge which they could access they are, in practice, limited by their 'absorptive capacity' – their ability to make sense of it, acquire it and put it to effective use. They need to learn to learn, building a capability for innovating, which can take advantage of the open innovation environment. Once again networking can help enable even very small organisations and individuals to obtain traction on this problem.

In principle firms have a number of opportunities available to them to enable learning – through experiment (e.g. R&D), through transfer of ideas from outside, through working with different players (suppliers, partners, customers), through reflecting and reviewing previous projects, and even through failure. Studies of organisational learning suggest that it can be supported by structures, procedures, etc. to facilitate the operation of the learning cycle – for example, through challenging reflection, facilitated sharing of experiences or planned experimentation.

Experience and research suggests that shared learning can help deal with some of the barriers to learning which individual firms might face. For example,

- in shared learning there is the potential for challenge and structured critical reflection from different perspectives;
- different perspectives can bring in new concepts (or old concepts which are new to the learner);
- shared experimentation can reduce perceived and actual costs or risks in trying new things;
- shared experiences can provide support and open new lines of inquiry or exploration;
- shared learning helps explicate the systems principles, seeing the patterns – separating 'the wood from the trees';
- shared learning provides an environment for surfacing assumptions and exploring mental models outside of the normal experience of individual organisations – helps prevent 'not invented here' and other effects;
- shared learning can reduce costs (for example, in drawing on consultancy services and learning about external markets) which can be particularly useful for small/medium-sized enterprises (SMEs) and for developing country firms.

A key element in shared learning is the active participation of others in the process of challenge and support. Its potential as an aid to firms trying to cope with a challenging and continuing learning agenda has led to a number of attempts to establish formal arrangements for interorganisational learning. For example, the experience of regional clusters of small firms, which have managed to share knowledge about product and process technology and to extend the capabilities of the sector as a whole, is recognised as central to their abilities to achieve export competitiveness. In work on supply chain development there is a growing recognition that the next step after moving from confrontational to co-operative relationships within supply chains is to engage in a process of shared development and learning.

Learning is often involved as a 'by-product' of network activities – for example, emerging through exchange of views or through shared attempts at problem-solving. But it is also possible to see learning as the primary purpose around which a network is built; this concept of a 'learning network' can be expressed as *a network formally set up for the primary purpose of increasing knowledge'*. Such networks share a number of characteristics:

- they are formally established and defined;
- they have a primary learning target – some specific learning/knowledge which the network is going to enable;
- they have a structure for operation, with boundaries defining participation;
- they involve processes which can be mapped on to the learning cycle;
- they use measurement of learning outcomes which feeds back to operation of the network and which eventually decides whether or not to continue with the formal arrangement.

Examples include 'best practice' clubs (whose members have formed together to try to understand and share experiences about new production concepts), 'co-laboratories' (shared pre-competitive R&D projects), supplier associations and sectoral research organisations (where the aim is to upgrade knowledge across a system of firms). Learning may also involve 'horizontal' collaboration (between like firms) or 'vertical' co-operation (as in supply chain learning programmes), or a combination of the two.

Go online to find a tool/resource that describes in detail how to set up and run learning networks. Several case examples are also available.

www.iande.info

INNOVATION IN ACTION

'The trouble with small firms isn't that they're small, it's that they're isolated!' A powerful point – we know that small firms have lots of advantages in terms of focus, energy and fast decision-making. But they often lack resources to achieve their full potential. This is where a concept which the economists call 'collective efficiency' comes in – the idea that you don't have to have all the resources under your own roof, only to know where and how to get hold of them. Working with others can get you a lot further. As highlighted earlier, the world-beating Italian furniture industry shows how a network of small companies can compete in the high end of the market not through individual excellence but through sharing design expertise and facilities, and with collective materials purchasing and marketing. The same is true around the world. For example, 12% of the world's surgical instruments are made in one town in Pakistan. This isn't a case of low-cost manufacturing; it is a high-precision, design-intensive business and the small firms involved prosper by working together in a co-operative cluster.

Using Networks for Exploration

As we've seen, for much of the time the challenge in innovation is one of 'doing what we do, but better' – continuously improving products and services and enhancing our processes. The scope here is enormous – both in terms of incremental modifications and additions of features and enhancements and in delivering on cost savings and quality improvements. Taken on their own these may not be as eye-catching as the launch of a radically new product but the historical evidence is that continuous incremental innovation of this kind has enormous economic impact. It's the glacier model rather than the violently fast-running stream – but in the long run the impact on the economic geography is significant.

We've learned a lot about how to manage this kind of 'steady state' innovation and the kinds of thing which make for 'good practice'. The trouble is that from time to time there are *discontinuous* shifts in the environment – events which pull the carpet out from under our feet and rewrite the rules of the game. For example, some bright spark invents a radical new technology which changes the underlying knowledge base on which the firm operates. Or a completely new market emerges at the fringes and becomes mainstream – in the process disrupting the cosy arrangements amongst established players who are suddenly wrong-footed. Or business models change – as we have seen with low-cost airlines, the music industry or across the Internet. Or government changes the rules of the game through the regulatory environment. Discontinuities arise from many sources and we know they will happen – we just don't know when or where!

But we also know we can't simply ignore the possibility – the evidence is clear that when discontinuous events occur existing players do badly and it is the new kids on the block who succeed. Under these conditions the natural reaction is often to redouble our efforts along tried and tested pathways – to work twice as hard to get close to customers and build their requirements into our products and services. We do even better at our existing technologies, wringing extra performance out of them and we persevere with established business models refining them with even more bells and whistles. Unfortunately the evidence is that enhancing our ways of managing 'steady-state' innovation may not help but even actively hinder our abilities to deal with new challenges. As Clayton Christensen showed in his work on disruptive innovation, when new markets emerge they do so at the fringe of existing ones and are often easy to ignore and dismiss as not being relevant.[6] So working on getting even closer to existing customers actually takes you further away from what becomes the site of the real action.

One big problem with such change is that it challenges our established networks. The people we work with, talk to, buy from, sell to, are all – by definition – within the same frame and may see the world in the same way. Discontinuous change requires a new frame – and making it happen requires building new kinds of networks.

Under these conditions organisations need a different approach to managing innovation – much more exploratory, agile, flexible in thinking and deciding, being able to turn on organisational sixpence. In short they need to be like a new entrant firm, an entrepreneurial opportunity seeker but backed with more extensive resources and experience.

How do firms deal with this kind of innovation – how do they work at the edge of chaos where new threats and opportunities are only dimly visible? And how do they search for innovation triggers or pick up on weak signals about emerging – but possibly radically different – futures? One way is to mobilise 'open innovation' approaches – to cast the net wide and concentrate on finding and forming new networks – with different suppliers, customers, users.

Chapter 6 looked at some of the powerful ways this can happen. The box below gives some more examples, as does the website.

Go online to find cases on open collective innovation.

www.iande.info

INNOVATION IN ACTION

A Framework for Open Collective Innovation

The potential of information and communication technology (ICT) and the Internet in particular have led to an explosion of new kinds of innovation network. Interactive web applications (Web 2.0) mean that many previously isolated individuals and groups can be brought into the innovation equation, especially at the early stages of idea generation and elaboration, at low cost. In the process there is scope for considerable 'collective efficiency' around innovation and entrepreneurship.

In work with colleagues at the University of Erlangen-Nuremburg in Germany and at the Centre for Leading Innovation and Change at Leipzig Business School, Kathrin Moeslein has developed a framework for viewing such developments.[7]

Tools for enabling OCI can be grouped into five clusters:

- Innovation contests – not a new idea (Napoleon's offer of a prize led to the development of margarine as a substitute for butter whilst in the UK the development of the maritime chronometer was as a result of an open contest won by Thomas Harrison). The basic principle is to offer a prize and then invite ideas via a Web 2.0 portal on which others can vote, make comments, etc. A twenty-first century example is the $20m prize Lunar X competition to develop a robot which can explore the surface of the moon; it must travel at least 500m and send pictures back to earth. Many public and private sector organisations are using versions of innovation contests to increase the front-end flow of ideas, ranging from jewellery design (Swarovski), car design (Smart) and even public service design (Bavarian State government).
- Innovation markets – these essentially work by bringing 'seekers' and 'solvers' together via an eBay-style marketplace enabled by Web 2.0. The pioneer of this approach and still widely used is InnoCentive.com (which brings together 165,000 innovators in 175 countries) but many others now exist. Research suggests that such markets are particularly valuable in dealing with persistent problems which internal innovation teams have been unable to solve.

(continued)

- Innovation communities – unite interested and often experienced and skilled innovators sharing common interests. User groups and online communities are examples and such groups are often a rich source of co-operative innovation in which ideas from one member are built on by others. Linux is a good example of this process, as is the growing developer community around Apple's i-phone platform.
- Innovation toolkits – enable users to engage with developing their ideas – for example through configuration and self-build toolkits. Lego Factory offers a good example of this approach where users are encouraged to create their own designs which software on the Web helps them work with.
- Innovation technologies – offer tools to realise design and production by user creators, for example, through online computer-aided design and rapid prototyping technologies.

Making Networks Happen – Networks by Design

Whatever the purpose in setting it up, actually operating within an innovation network is not easy – it needs a new set of management skills and it depends on the starting point. For example, there is a big difference between the demands for an innovation network working at the frontier where issues of intellectual property management and risk are critical, and one where there is an established innovation agenda. But the challenges are about building trust and sharing key information – as might be the case in using supply chains to enhance product and process innovation. We can map some of these different types of innovation network on to a simple diagram (Figure 8.2) which positions them in terms of:

- how radical the innovation target is with respect to current innovative activity;
- the similarity of the participating companies.

By making this distinction, we can see that different types of networks have different issues to resolve. For example, in zone 1 we have individuals and organisations with a broadly

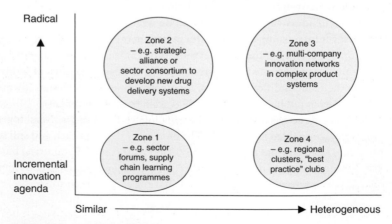

FIGURE 8.2   Types of innovation network.

similar orientation working on tactical innovation issues. Typically, this might be a cluster or sector forum concerned with adopting and configuring 'good practice' manufacturing or a group of innovation managers in the health sector trying to improve productivity. Issues here would involve enabling them to share experiences, disclose information, develop trust and transparency and build a system-level sense of shared purpose around innovation.

Zone 2 activities might involve players from a sector working to explore and create new product or process concepts – for example, the emerging biotechnology/pharmaceutical networking around frontier developments and the need to look for interesting connections and synthesis between these adjacent sectors. Here, the concern is exploratory and challenges existing boundaries but will rely on a degree of information sharing and shared risk-taking, often in the form of formal joint ventures and strategic alliances.

In Zone 3, the players are highly differentiated and bring different key pieces of knowledge to the party. Their risks in disclosing can be high so ensuring careful IP management and establishing ground rules will be crucial. At the same time, this kind of innovation is likely to involve considerable risk and so putting in place risk- and benefit-sharing arrangements will also be critical.

Zone 4 involves the kind of shared learning across organisations which we saw earlier – essentially building on regional or sect oral links to focus a shared learning effort. In a review of such 'high value innovation networks' in the UK, researchers from the Advanced Institute of Management Research (AIM)[8] found the following characteristics were important success factors:

- Highly diverse: network partners from a wide range of disciplines and backgrounds who encourage exchanges about ideas across systems.
- Third-party gatekeepers: science partners such as universities but also consultants and trade associations, who provide access to expertise and act as neutral knowledge brokers across the network.
- Financial leverage: access to investors via business angels, venture capitalists and corporate venturing, which spreads the risk of innovation and provides market intelligence.
- Proactively managed: participants regard the network as a valuable asset and actively manage it to reap the innovation benefits.

ADVICE FOR FUTURE ENTREPRENEURS

We have enough difficulties trying to manage within the boundaries of a typical business. So, the challenge of innovation networks takes us well beyond this. The challenges include:

- how to manage something we don't own or control;
- how to see system-level effects not narrow self-interests;
- how to build trust and shared risk-taking without tying the process up in contractual red tape;
- how to avoid 'free riders' and information 'spillovers'.

It's a new game and one in which a new set of management skills becomes important.

Learning to Manage Innovation Networks

Innovation networks can be broken down into three stages of a life cycle – set up, operate and sustain. In this section we'll consider some of the key management questions associated with each stage.

(a) Set-up stage

Issues here are around providing the momentum for bringing the network together and clearly defining its purpose. It may be crisis triggered – for example, perception of the urgent need to catch up via adoption of innovation. Equally, it may be driven by a shared perception of opportunity – the potential to enter new markets or exploit new technologies. Key roles here will often be played by third parties – network brokers, gatekeepers, policy agents and facilitators.

(b) Operate stage

The key issues here are about trying to establish some core operating processes about which there is support and agreement. These need to deal with:

- Network boundary management – how the membership of the network is defined and maintained.
- Decision-making – how (where, when, who) decisions get taken at the network level.
- Conflict resolution – how conflicts are resolved effectively.
- Information processing – how information flows among members and is managed.
- Knowledge management – how knowledge is created, captured, shared and used across the network.
- Motivation – how members are motivated to join/remain within the network.
- Risk/benefit sharing – how the risks and rewards are allocated across members of the network.
- Co-ordination – how the operations of the network are integrated and co-ordinated.

(c) Sustain stage

Networks need not last for ever – sometimes they are set up to achieve a highly specific purpose (e.g. development of a new product concept) and once this has been done the network can be disbanded. In other instances there is a case for sustaining the networking activities for as long as members see benefits. This may require periodic review and 're-targeting' to keep the motivation high. For example, CRINE, a successful development programme for the offshore oil and gas industry, was launched in 1992 by key players in the industry such as BP, Shell and major contractors (and with support from the government), with the target of cost reduction. Using a network model, it delivered extensive innovation in product/services and processes over a ten-year period. Having met its original cost-reduction targets, the programme moved to a second phase with a focus aimed more at capturing a bigger export share of the global industry through innovation.

DEVELOPING PERSONAL CAPABILITIES

Innovation isn't a solo act – it's a multi-player game. But that means we need to develop skills around networking – and in particular to think about three key tasks:

Finding – who should we recruit and why: for example, sources of complementary expertise, finance, access to key markets, opinion leaders, etc.

Forming – how will we establish a working relationship with them? What's in it for them? Do we need to tie this up with some form of contract or is the network more open-ended, as in a learning network, where people share on a voluntary basis? How do we build trust and manage the core processes of decision-making, conflict resolution, risk- and benefit-sharing, etc.?

Performing – how can we retain and develop the relationship over the long-term? How do we sustain things after the initial project? Is there a point where we need to end the relationship and move on?

Using this simple checklist – finding, forming, performing – allows us to build a map of the networks we need to build, or as a checklist to ensure we have a rich enough and robust network already in place.

STRATEGIC AND SOCIAL IMPACT

Innovation is a multi-player game. And the theory of systems and networks talks about 'emergent properties' – essentially where the whole is greater than the sum of the parts. In innovation networks there are plenty of ways such emergent properties might help – for example:

- bringing together different knowledge sets to solve a particular complex problem;
- maximising problem-solving capabilities by getting more (and different) minds on the job;
- sharing the risks around exploring and exploiting new ideas;
- transmitting learning across a group of players – for example, improving quality or delivery performance across a whole supply chain.

Given the scale of many of today's innovation challenges it is unlikely that any single enterprise – and certainly no single individual – will be able to deal with them. But networking offers the chance to leverage other kinds of resources – knowledge, skills, finance, distribution, etc. – to help make things happen. It's particularly an opportunity for small firms – competing in a turbulent global marketplace can be very tough, not to mention lonely. As one commentator put it – 'the problem for small firms isn't so much that they're small as that they're isolated'. Networking offers the chance to build 'collective efficiency' – a model which has been used with great success in small firm clusters around the world.

And in the field of social entrepreneurship, where the challenge isn't so much about making money as creating social value – changing the world – the potential of networking is equally powerful. As we saw in Chapter 2, mobilising the kinds of resources to make a difference, often against the odds, depends critically on the skills and abilities to engage others in the network.

Chapter Summary

1 Innovation is not a solo act but a multi-player game. Whether it is the entrepreneur who spots an opportunity or an established organisation trying to renew its offerings or sharpen up its processes, making innovation happen depends on working with many different players. This raises questions about *between* organisations, developing and making use of increasingly wide *networks*.

2 The ways knowledge actually flows around an innovation project are complex and interactive, woven together in a kind of social spaghetti where different people talk to each other in different ways, more or less frequently, and about different things. As the innovation becomes more complex so the networks have to involve more different players, many of whom may lie outside the firm.

3 Increasingly the networks we have to learn to deal with are becoming more virtual, a rich and global set of human resources distributed and connected by the enabling technologies of the Internet, broadband and mobile communications and shared computer networks.

4 Innovation networks are more than just ways of assembling and deploying knowledge in a complex world. They can also have what are termed 'emergent properties' – that is, the potential for the whole to be greater than the sum of its parts. These include getting access to different and complementary knowledge sets, reducing risks by sharing them, accessing new markets and technologies and otherwise pooling complementary skills and assets.

5 Operating within an innovation network is not easy – it needs a new set of management skills and it depends on the starting point. The challenges include:
  * how to manage something we don't own or control;
  * how to see system-level effects not narrow self-interests;
  * how to build trust and shared risk-taking without tying the process up in contractual red tape;
  * how to avoid 'free riders' and information 'spillovers'.

Key Terms Defined

Clusters networks which form because of the players being close to each other – for example, in the same geographical region. Silicon Valley is a good example of a cluster which thrives on proximity – knowledge flows amongst and across the members of the network but is hugely helped by the geographical closeness and the ability of key players to meet and talk.

Collective efficiency where a group of (often small) players work together to share resources, risks, etc.

Communities of practice networks which can involve players inside and across different organisations – what binds them together is a shared concern with a particular aspect or area of knowledge.

Emergent properties   principle in systems that the whole is greater than the sum of the parts.

Learning network   'a network formally set up for the primary purpose of increasing knowledge'.

Network   'a complex, interconnected group or system', and networking involves using that arrangement to accomplish particular tasks.

Open innovation   approach which seeks to mobilise innovation sources inside and outside the enterprise.

Supply chain learning   developing and sharing innovative good practice and possibly shared product development across a value chain.

Further Reading and Resources

The work of Andrew Hargadon has highlighted the importance of networks and brokers going back to the days of Edison and Ford (Hargadon, A. (2003) *How Breakthroughs Happen*, Boston, Harvard Business School Press). One of the strong examples of this approach today is IDEO the design consultancy which Kelley and colleagues have described in detail (Kelley, T., J. Littman, et al. (2001) *The Art of Innovation: Lessons in Creativity from Ideo, America's Leading Design Firm,* New York, Currency). Conway and Steward ((1998) Mapping innovation networks,' *International Journal of Innovation Management* (2), 165–196) look at the concept of innovation networks and this theme is also picked up by Swan, Newell et al. ((1999) Knowledge management and innovation: networks and networking,' *Journal of Knowledge Management* 3(4): 262). Learning networks are discussed in Bessant and Tsekouras ((2001) 'Developing learning networks,' *A.I. and Society* 15(2), 82–98) and their use in sectors, supply chains and regional clusters in Morris, Bessant et al. ((2006) 'Using learning networks to enable industrial development: Case studies from South Africa,' *International Journal of Operations and Production Management* 26(5), 557–568). High value innovation networks in several reports form AIM – the Advanced Institute for Management Research (www.aimresearch.org).

References

1. Guilford, J.P. (1967) *The Nature of Human Intelligence.* McGraw-Hill, New York.
2. Rothwell, R. (1992). 'Successful industrial innovation: Critical success factors for the 1990s.' *R&D Management* 22(3): 221–239.
3. Delbridge, R. (2004). How motorsport companies collaborate and share knowledge. London, AIM and Government Motorsport Unit.
4. Best, M. (2001). *The New Competitive Advantage.* Oxford, Oxford University Press.
5. Chesbrough, H. (2003). *Open Innovation: The new imperative for creating and profiting form technology.* Boston, Mass., Harvard Business School Press.

6. Christensen, C. (1997). *The Innovator's Dilemma*. Cambridge, Mass., Harvard Business School Press.
7. Moeslein, K. and J. Bessant (2011). 'Open collective innovation', AIM Executive Briefing, Advanced Institute of Management Research, London.
8. AIM (2004). i- works: How high value innovation networks can boost UK productivity. London, ESRC/EPSRC Advanced Institute of Management Research.
9. Huston, L. and N. Sakkab (2006). 'Connect and Develop: Inside Procter & Gamble's New Model for Innovation.' *Harvard Business Review* (March).

Discussion Questions

1. Michael Dell didn't invent the computer – but he built one of the most successful businesses selling them. Discuss how he makes use of a networking approach to build and sustain a competitive edge in his business.

2. Why might Joe Bloggs, famous inventor, need help in getting his great idea into widespread use? And how might a networking approach help him?

3. Is innovation a solo act – the product of the lone genius? Show how successful entrepreneurs make use of networks to help take their ideas forward.

4. List three advantages of co-operating across networks in innovation as opposed to a 'go it alone' approach.

5. Jane Wilson has come up with a great new idea for a medical sensor to help in monitoring babies while they sleep. How could she improve her chances of success with her new product idea by using a networking approach to taking it forward?

Team Exercises

1. 'Many hands make light work' – or 'Too many cooks spoil the broth'? Using examples show why networking may be a positive or negative element in enabling successful innovation. Split the group to present both sides of this argument and run the discussion as a debate.
2. Try to construct a map of the innovation network which leads to creating and delivering a new product like a new mobile phone or MP3 player.

Assignment Questions

1. 'The problem for small firms isn't that they're small – it's that they're isolated.' How might networking help deal with the challenges of being an innovative small firm and what advantages might this approach offer?

2. XYZ Electronics want to launch a supplier development programme to get their 180 suppliers to participate more fully in the innovation process – contributing new ideas for products and services and helping improve processes around quality, delivery and cost reduction. What issues should they think about in designing and implementing such a programme?

3. 'Open innovation' is becoming a fashionable approach to innovation, building on the advantages of networking. But what problems might the implementation of such an approach throw up?

CASE STUDY 8

Exploring Innovation in Action: 'Connect and Develop' at Procter & Gamble

Next time you go into a supermarket, think about innovation. Not only are you likely to encounter a massive range of products – food, drink, homecare, personal care, luxury goods, etc. – but you're likely to find them constantly changing. Watch any category and see how much the offer changes – the range, the packaging, the branding and advertising/ promotional storyline and, of course, the products themselves. Most of this change is incremental – you'll have to look closely to pick up on the minor shifts in the shape of the coffee jar or the improved seal on a toothpaste cap. But from time to time there are radical shifts – a new generation of an established product but embodying new technology or sometimes the emergence of a whole new product category.

Now think about the challenge this poses for the manufacturers of those products – a game played out every week in thousands of supermarkets where they compete with other manufacturers for the attention (and hopefully the purchases) of an army of shoppers. Innovation is very much the name of the game and it's a relentless quest for novelty. It's a powerful force driving a company like Procter & Gamble (P&G) forward – as their Chief Technology Officer, G. Gilbert Cloyd comments, 'we're facing an ever-faster pace of innovation in consumer-product markets. We think the pace of innovation has roughly doubled in the past 10 years. So when we make an innovation and bring it into the marketplace, it has a much shorter market life than what it had previously. We need to be moving to upgrade our brands even more frequently . . . the competition is very fierce. Fifteen years ago, when we had a lot of generic brands or private labels, they were often not true brands; they were products. Now the brands that we face from retailers, from regional competitors, are very well-developed brands.'

P&G have been players in the household and consumer goods market for nearly 200 years. They started life making candles at a time when these were still a common source of domestic lighting. But they moved on from those to other, related products – soaps and cleaning products. Today their range is a little wider – P&G have around 300 brands, including Crest oral care, Pampers nappies and baby products, Tide and Ariel washing powders, Tampax sanitary products, Flash and Vanish cleaners – the list goes on a long way!

To keep a range as wide as this refreshed and to develop new and improved products to feature on the supermarket stages around the world needs a powerful innovation engine. P&G have built a world-wide R&D operation which involves some 7500 scientists and a spend of around $3bn per year: maybe not as much as the high-technology pharmaceutical industry but still very impressive for its sector. Nor is it simply throwing money at the problem – P&G have some very effective systems and structures to ensure efficient project selection and progression.

The engine has worked well for them. They have an impressive record on new product launches and many of their new categories have gone on to reach the magic number of becoming billion dollar brands – products whose annual sales can be as high as $150–200m.

The Birth of 'Connect and Develop'

But in the late 1990s there were concerns about this approach to innovation. Whilst it worked there were worries – not least the rapidly rising costs of carrying out R&D. In a world where technology is changing so fast and across so many frontiers it becomes increasingly hard to keep up. It's important in a diverse product company to try to cover all the bases – but which bases? – and how do you afford to cover all of them when getting on them carries a significant price tag? And what about the ones that get away – the new product ideas which are offered to the firm, or even developed in its own labs but which don't appear to have enough market promise and so are not backed? For P&G there were many instances of innovations which they might have made but which they passed on – only to find someone else doing so and succeeding. As CEO Alan Lafley explained in a recent article, 'Our R&D productivity had levelled off, and our innovation success rate – the percentage of new products that met financial objectives – had stagnated at about 35 percent. Squeezed by nimble competitors, flattening sales, lacklustre new launches, and a quarterly earnings miss, we lost more than half our market cap when our stock slid from $118 to $52 a share. Talk about a wake-up call.'[9]

Thinking along these lines led them to take a radically different approach to innovation. Instead of their traditional 'research and develop' model they moved to what they have called 'connect and develop' – an innovation process based on the principles of 'open innovation'. This idea originated in the work of Henry Chesbrough and basically challenges the dominant mode in which firms operate a 'closed' system, carrying out R&D but keeping it in-house so that they can exploit the benefits and control the use of ideas. This works but creates the kind of rising costs and insulation from new ideas which P&G were experiencing.

They recognised that much important innovation was being carried out in small entrepreneurial firms, or by individuals, or in university labs – essentially there was a great deal going on outside the company. They also saw other major players like IBM, Cisco, Eli Lilly and Microsoft beginning to go down the route of opening up their innovation systems.

That rang bells with their own experience as well. They recognised that in the past some of their best innovations had come from connecting ideas across internal businesses. So the idea of 'Connect and develop' was born – not with the intention of 'outsourcing R&D' but rather to increase their leverage in innovation by working better across internal and external networks.

Did it work? Lafley's original stretch goal was to get 50% of innovations coming from outside the company; by 2006 more than 35% of new products had elements which originated from outside, compared with 15% in 2000. Over 100 new products in the past 2 years came from outside the firm and 45% of innovations in the new product pipeline have key elements which were discovered or developed externally. They estimate that R&D productivity has increased by nearly 60% and their innovation success rate has more than doubled. One consequence is that they have increased innovation whilst *reducing* their R&D spend, from 4.8% of turnover in 2000 to 3.4%. And five years after the stock suffered a serious setback, the share price doubled and they now have a portfolio of 22 billion dollar brands.

How Does it Work?

Pretty successful on anyone's scale – but how have they made it happen? How does the new innovation engine operate? The key lies in harnessing the power of innovation networks. As Cloyd explained, 'It has changed how we define the organization, . . . We have 9000 people on our R&D staff and up to 1.5 million researchers working through our external networks. The line between the two is hard to draw . . . We're . . . putting a lot more attention on what we call 360-degree innovation.'

Amongst their successes in internal networking was the Crest Whitestrips product – essentially linking oral care experts with researchers working on film technology and others in the bleach and household cleaning groups. Another is Olay Daily Facials which linked the surface active agents expertise in skin care with people from the tissue and towel areas and from the fabric property enhancing skills developed in 'Bounce', a fabric softening product.

Making it happen as part of daily life rather than as a special initiative is a big challenge. They use multiple methods including extensive networking via an intranet site called 'Ask me' which links 10,000 technical people across the globe. It acts as a signposting and Web-market for ideas and problems across the company. They also operate 21 'communities of practice' built around key areas of expertise such as polymer chemists, biological scientists, people involved with fragrances. And they operate a global-technology council, which is made up of representatives of all of their business units.

External links are built through an increasingly diverse set of mechanisms. One powerful approach is a group of 80 'technology entrepreneurs' whose task is to roam the globe and find and make interesting connections. They visit conferences and exhibitions, talk with suppliers, visit universities, scour the Internet – essentially a no-holds-barred approach to searching for new possible connections.

They also make extensive use of the Internet. One is their involvement as founding members of a site called InnoCentive (www.innocentive.com), originally set up by the pharmaceutical giant Eli Lilly in 2001. This is essentially a Web-based marketplace where problem-owners can link up with problem-solvers – and it currently has around 90,000 solvers available around the world. The business model is simple – companies post their problems on the site and if any of the solvers can help, they pay for the idea. Payments can range from $10,000 to $100,000 – and the model appears to work. From the outset, InnoCentive threw open the doors to other firms eager to access the network's trove of ad hoc experts. Companies like Boeing, DuPont, and Procter & Gamble now post their most ornery scientific problems on InnoCentive's website; anyone on InnoCentive's network can take a shot at cracking them. Importantly the solvers are a very wide mix, from corporate and university lab staff through to lone inventors, retired scientists and engineers and professional design houses. Jill Panetta, InnoCentive's chief scientific officer, says more than 30% of the problems posted on the site have been cracked, 'which is 30% more than would have been solved using a traditional, in-house approach.'

Other mechanisms include a website called Yourencore which allows companies to find and hire retired scientists for one-off assignments. NineSigma is an online marketplace for innovations, matching seeker companies with solvers in a marketplace similar to InnoCentive. As Chief Technology Officer Gil Cloyd comments, 'NineSigma can link us to solutions that are more cost efficient, give us early access to potentially disruptive technologies, and facilitate valuable collaborations much faster than we imagined.' And yet2com looks for new technologies and markets across a broad frontier, involving around 40% of the world's major R&D players in their network.

What is significant about the P&G use of these mechanisms is that it is part of a deliberate networking strategy to open up their innovation system. As Larry Huston comments, 'People mistake this for outsourcing, which it most definitely is not . . . Outsourcing is when I hire someone to perform a service and they do it and that's the end of the relationship. That's not much different from the way employment has worked throughout the ages. We're talking about bringing people in from outside and involving them in this broadly creative, collaborative process. That's a whole new paradigm.'

Questions on Case Study

1 'Open innovation' is becoming a fashionable approach to innovation, building on the advantages of networking. But what problems might the implementation of such an approach throw up?
2 ABC Electronics has heard about 'open innovation' and sees this as a possible solution to its flagging innovation efforts. How might they think about implementing such a programme – and what issues would they watch out for?
3 What might the downside be for taking an open innovation approach like that of P&G?

Summary of Web Resources

Cases

- Open Collective Innovation
- Learning networks
- 3M
- P&G
- Kumba

Media

- Roy Sandbach podcast
- David Overton podcast
- Simon Tucker podcast
- David Simoes-Brown and Richard Philpott podcast

Tools

- Setting up and running a learning network

PART IV

DEVELOPING THE VENTURE

Part IV Developing the Venture

How do we go about taking a concept from a gleam in the eye into a fully fledged process, product, service or business? It's not just a matter of project management – balancing resources against time and budget – but doing so against a backdrop of uncertainty. We need to understand the factors that influence the success and failure of innovations and new ventures. Even if we can steer a project through the rocks to make it real, there's no guarantee that people will use it or that it will diffuse widely. This often demands alliance to promote acceptance and widespread adoption.

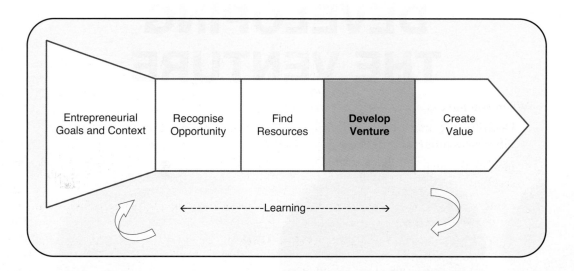

Chapter 9

Developing New Products and Services

Go online to find additional . . .

Cases

Tools

Media

www.iande.info

In this chapter we examine the process of new product and service development. We review a very large body of management research on the subject, and identify a number of generic factors that influence success (and failure). Based on this evidence we identify a 'good practice' process for developing new products and services which includes a number of distinct stages separated by decision points or gates at which selection criteria are applied. However, the generic factors and process needs to be adapted for different contexts, and the specific context will influence the most appropriate factors, process and organisation for new product and service development. Therefore we begin with a discussion of the main differences between products and services. Finally, we review a range of tools and methods to support the development process, and identify how the novelty of the product or service affects the utility of these tools.

Service versus Product Development

Employment trends in all the so-called advanced countries indicate a move away from manufacturing, construction, mining and agriculture, towards a range of services, including retail, finance, transportation, communication, entertainment, professional and public services. This trend is in part because manufacturing has become so efficient and highly automated, and therefore generates proportionately less employment; and partly because many services are characterised by high levels of customer contact and are reproduced locally, and are therefore often labour intensive.

In the most advanced service economies such as the USA and UK, services create up to three-quarters of the wealth and 85% of employment, and yet we know relatively little about managing innovation in this sector. The critical role of services, in the broadest sense, has long been recognised, but service innovation is still not well understood.

Innovation in services in much more than the application of information technology (IT). In fact, the disappointing returns to IT investments in services has resulted in a widespread debate about its causes and potential solutions – the so-called 'productivity paradox' in services. Frequently service innovations, which make significant differences to the ways customers use and perceive the service delivered, will demand major investments in process innovation and technology by service providers, but also demand investment in skills and methods of working to change the business model, as well as major marketing changes. Estimates vary, but returns on investment on IT alone are around 15%, with a typical lag of two to three years, when productivity often falls, but when combined with changes in organisation and management these returns increase to around 25%.[1]

In the service sector the impact of innovation on growth is generally positive and consistent, with the possible exception of financial services. The pattern across retail and wholesale distribution, transport and communication services, and the broad range of business services is particularly strong (Figure 9.1).

Most research and management prescriptions have been based on the experience of manufacturing and high-technology sectors. Most simply assume that such practices are equally applicable to managing innovation in services, but some researchers argue that services are

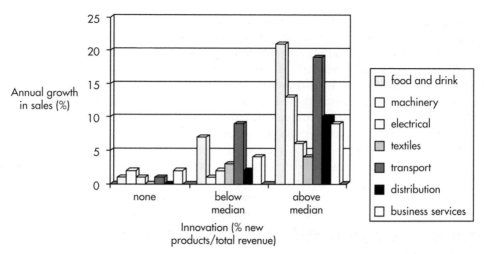

FIGURE 9.1   Innovation and growth in the service sector.
Source: EU Community Innovation Survey, 2000. Based on a survey of 2000 UK service businesses.

fundamentally different. There is a clear need to distinguish what aspects, if any, of what we know about managing innovation in manufacturing are applicable to services, what must be adapted, and what is distinct and different.

We will argue that generic good practices do exist, which apply to both the development of manufactured and service offerings, but that these must be adapted to different contexts, specifically the scale and complexity, degree of customisation of the offerings, and the uncertainty of the technological and market environments. It is critical to match the configuration of management and organisation of development to the specific technology and market environment.

The service sector includes a very wide range and a great diversity of different activities and businesses, ranging from individual consultants and shopkeepers, to huge multinational finance firms and critical non-profit public and third sector organisations such as government, health and education. Therefore great care needs to be taken when making any generalisation about the service sectors. We will introduce some ways of understanding and analysing the sector later, but it is possible to identify some fundamental differences between manufacturing and service operations:

- **Tangibility** – goods tend to be tangible, whereas services are mostly intangible, even though you can usually see or feel the results. Therefore **perceptions** of performance are more often important than more objective measures.
- **Perceptions** of performance and quality are more important in services, in particular the difference between expectations and perceived performance. A customer is likely to regard a service as being good if it exceeds their expectations. Perceptions of service quality are affected by
  - tangible aspects – appearance of facilities, equipment and staff;
  - responsiveness – prompt service and willingness to help;

- competence – the ability to perform the service dependably;
- assurance – knowledge and courtesy of staff and ability to convey trust and confidence;
- empathy – provision of caring, individual attention.
- **Simultaneity**. The lag between production and consumption of goods and services is different. Most goods are produced well in advance of consumption, to allow for distribution, storage and sales. In contrast, many services are produced and almost immediately consumed. This creates problems of quality management and capacity planning. It is harder to identify or correct errors in services, and more difficult to match supply and demand.
- **Storage**. Services cannot usually be stored, for example a seat on an airline, although some, such as utilities, have some potential for storage. The inability to hold stocks of services can create problems matching supply and demand – capacity management. These can be dealt with in a number of ways. Pricing can be used to help smooth fluctuations in demand, for example by providing discounts at off-peak times. Where possible, additional capacity can be provided at peak times by employing part-time workers or outsourcing. In the worst cases, customers can simply be forced to wait for the services, by queuing.
- **Customer contact**. Most customers have low or no contact with the operations which produce goods. Many services demand high levels of contact between the operations and ultimate customer, although the level and timing of such contact varies. For example, medical treatment may require constant or frequent contact, but financial services only sporadic contact.
- **Location**. Because of the contact with customers and near simultaneous production and consumption of services, the location of service operations is often more important than for operations which produce goods. For example, restaurants, retail operations and entertainment services all favour proximity to customers. Conversely, manufactured goods are often produced and consumed in very different locations. For these reasons the markets for manufactured goods also tend to be more competitive and global, whereas many personal and business services are local and less competitive. For example, only around 10% of services in the advanced economies are traded internationally.

These service characteristics should be taken into account when designing and managing the organisation and processes for new service development, as some of the findings from research on new product development will have to be adapted or may not apply at all. Also, because of the diversity of service operations, we need to tailor the organisation and management to different types of service context.

Services differ from manufactured goods in many ways, but the two characteristics that most influence innovation management are their intangibility and the interaction between production and consumption. The intangibility of most services makes differentiation more difficult as it is harder to identify and control attributes. The near simultaneous production and consumption of many service offerings blurs the distinction between process (how) and product (what) innovation, and demands the integration of back-end (support services) and front-end (customer-facing) operations.

For example, in our study of 108 service firms in the UK and USA, we found that a strategy of rapid, reiterative redevelopment ('RRR') was associated with higher levels of new service development success and higher service quality. This approach to new service development combines many of the benefits of the polar extremes of radical and incremental innovation, but with lower costs and risks. This strategy is less disruptive to internal functional relationships than infrequent but more radical service innovations, and encourages knowledge reuse through the accumulation of numerous incremental innovations. For example, the American Express Travel Service Group implemented a strategy of RRR. A vice-president of product development was created, cross-functional teams were established, a formal development process adopted, and computer tools, including prototyping and simulation, were deployed. In the previous decade, the group had introduced only two new service products. Since the strategy was implemented the group has developed and launched more than 80 new service offerings, and has become the market leader.[2]

In practice, most operations produce some combination of goods and services, as we discussed in the previous chapter. It is possible to position any operation on a spectrum from 'pure' products or goods, through to 'pure' services. For example, a restaurant or retail operation both have real goods on offer, but in most cases the service provided is at least equally important. Conversely, most manufacturers now offer some after-sales service and support to customers.

However, the distinction between goods and services remains important because the differences in their characteristics demand a different approach to management and organisation. It is perhaps better to think of any business or operation as offering a bundle of benefits, some of which will be tangible, some not, and from this decide the appropriate mix of products and services to be produced.

The service sector includes a wide range of very different operations, including low-skilled personal services such as cleaners, higher skilled personal services such as tradesmen, business services such as lawyers and bankers, and mass consumer services such as transportation, telecommunications and public administration. The service–process matrix provides a useful way of identifying the key management challenges of an operation. The matrix classifies operations in terms of two dimensions (Figure 9.2). The first dimension is the labour intensity of the operations, that is the ratio of labour costs to equipment costs. The second dimension is the degree of customisation or interaction with customers. Combining these dimensions produces four distinct types of service operation, which demand different approaches to OM.

This framework is useful for two purposes. Firstly, to help characterise different types of service operation, even within the same business. Secondly, and more importantly, to help to identify the scope for improvement or change. For example, if the levels of customisation and labour intensity are both high, what is the scope to reduce the level of customisation or labour intensity to help reduce costs? In the UK, the national health service (NHS) asked a similar question. It was able to identify a range of services which did not necessarily require direct contact with the customer, such as standard health advice, and automated these using a website – NHS Direct. This helped to free resources for those operations that did require customer contact and are difficult to automate.

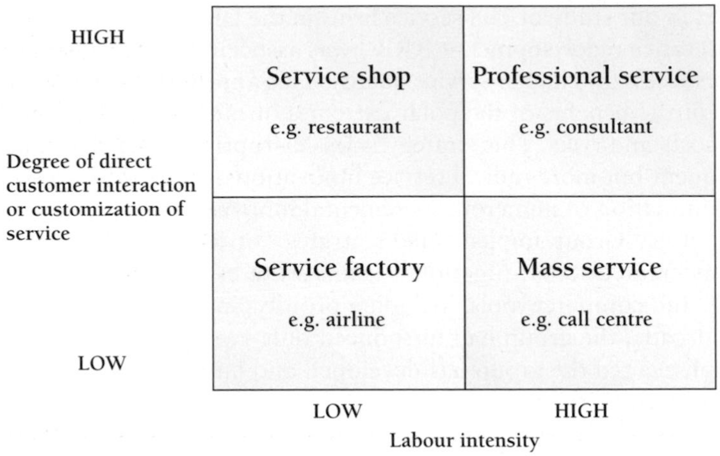

FIGURE 9.2 Characterising service operations based on labour intensity and degree of customer interaction or customisation.
Source: Derived from Schmenner (1986) 'How can service businesses survive and prosper?', *Sloan Management Review,* 27(3), 21–32.

INNOVATION IN ACTION

Innovation in Services

The legal profession is not the most obvious place to find service innovation, but in 2006 the *Financial Times* invited submissions from lawyers and law firms in the UK and attracted 300 entries. The submissions were rated on the basis of rationale, originality, and impact, and 33 were rated as 'outstanding'. The conclusion was that increased international competition, changes in regulation, and the expectations of customers, were driving innovation in legal services. This has increased the commoditisation of legal services.

Some law firms have responded to this by developing more standardised offerings and introducing more formal processes and by investing in IT, while others have attempted to move away from these markets, and have begun to offer bundles of services, and more bespoke and customised services, similar to consultancy. Law firms can be innovative in the legal expertise and advice they offer (equivalent to product innovation), the way they deliver these services (service innovation), or they way they run their businesses (process innovation).

For example, Mishcon de Reya developed a new offering, the Tulip service, which combines the two distinct areas of legal expertise in financial fraud and intellectual property law, to assess whether and how best to pursue claims. Norton Rose has developed the Takaful insurance service product aimed at the 20% of the population that is Muslim to comply with Sharia Law.

(continued)

Wragge developed a free service to offer unbiased strategic IT advice to the legal departments of client firms, which helps to add value to clients and deepen relationships. Withy King established a network of retail-style law centres, called 'Complete', to offer routine legal advice using non-lawyers. Pannone and Partners franchised its 'Connet2Law' service which clusters local smaller firms around a larger main firm to provide a full range of services, and has recruited more than 500 law firms.

However, the report warns that these examples are not typical, and that most lawyers and law firms do not have a culture of innovation, and few have any formal processes or investments for innovation.

Source: Financial Times *Special Report: Innovative Lawyers*, 29 June 2006.

Go online to find the Bank of Scotland case study, which provides a good example of the challenges in developing new services.

www.iande.info

Products and Service Development Strategies: Success Factors

The main contribution new product and service development makes is to increase differentiation in the market. Differentiation measures the degree to which competitors differ from one another in a specific market. In general, higher differentiation is associated with higher market share and high return on investment at the product level.

These ideas were developed around the creation and development of new physical products – but with the rise in the service economy attention has moved to their application in service innovation. Sectors like financial services or retailing are increasingly concerned with offering variations on their existing range and also totally new service concepts – and with this has come a realisation that managing these innovations requires a systematic process.

There have been numerous studies that have investigated the factors affecting the success of new products. Most have adopted a 'matched-pair' methodology in which similar new products are examined, but one is much less successful than the other. This allows us to discriminate between good and poor practice, and helps to control for other background factors.

These studies have differed in emphasis and sometimes contradicted each other, but despite differences in samples and methodologies it is possible to identify some consensus of what the best criteria for success are:

- *Product advantage* – product superiority in the eyes of the customer, real differential advantage, high performance-to-cost ratio, delivering unique benefits to users – appears to be the primary factor separating winners and losers. Customer perception is the key.

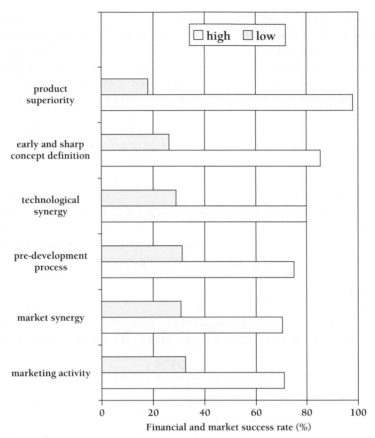

FIGURE 9.3 Factors influencing new product success.
Source: Derived from Cooper[3]

- *Market knowledge* – the homework is vital: better pre-development preparation, including initial screening, preliminary market assessment, preliminary technical appraisal, detailed market studies and business/financial analysis. Customer and user needs assessment and understanding is critical. Competitive analysis is also an important part of the market analysis.
- *Clear product definition* – this includes: defining target markets, clear concept definition and benefits to be delivered, clear positioning strategy, a list of product requirements, features and attributes or use of a priority criteria list agreed before development begins.
- *Risk assessment* – market-based, technological, manufacturing and design sources of risk to the development project must be assessed, and plans made to address them. Risk assessments must be built into the business and feasibility studies so they are appropriately addressed with respect to the market and the firms' capabilities.
- *Project organisation* – the use of cross-functional, multidisciplinary teams carrying responsibility for the project from beginning to end.

- *Project resources* – sufficient financial and material resources and human skills must be available; the firm must possess the management and technological skills to design and develop the new product.
- *Proficiency of execution* – quality of technological and production activities, and all pre-commercialisation business analyses and test marketing; detailed market studies underpin new product success.
- *Top management support* – from concept through to launch. Management must be able to create an atmosphere of trust, co-ordination and control; key individuals or champions often play a critical role during the innovation process.

These factors have all been found to contribute to new product success, and should therefore form the basis of any formal process for new product development. Note from this list, and the factors illustrated in Figures 9.3 and 9.4, that successful new product and service development requires the management of a blend of product or service characteristics, such as product focus, superiority and advantage, and organisational issues, such as project resources, execution and leadership. Managing only one of these key contributions is unlikely to result in consistent success.

The organisational issues appear to dominate even more in the case of more radical product or service offerings. This is probably because it is much more difficult in such cases to specify, in advance, the product or service characteristics in any detail, and instead managers have to rely more on getting the organisation right and influencing the direction of development.

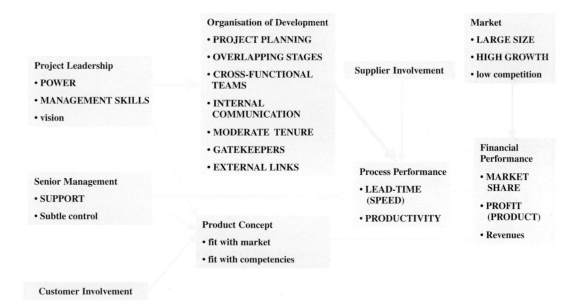

FIGURE 9.4   Key factors influencing the success of new products.
Source: Derived from Brown, S.L. and Eisenhardt, K.M. (1995) Product development: Past research, present findings and future directions, *Academy of Management Review*, 20, 343–378.

When we have asked managers to describe how radical products and services are developed, the answers include the mysterious and intuitive, and many highlight the importance of luck, accident and serendipity. Of course, there are examples of radical technologies or products that have begun life by chance, like the discovery of penicillin, but, as ever, Pasteur's advice applies: 'chance favours the prepared mind'.

INNOVATION IN ACTION

Intangible Product Advantage

Engineers (and consumer associations) tend to focus too much on the measurable and tangible features of products and services, but as we saw in the case of services, intangibles can be important differentiators.

Branding and price can be a proxy for product or service quality, but more often it is much more profound than this. Customers associate brands with certain attributes which can create additional value by providing benefits such as 'comfort' or 'coolness'. For example, there are hundreds of competent MP3 players on the market, but in the USA at least, Apple's iPod still has 70% of the market partly because of its perceived 'coolness'.

Since 2001 the advertising consultancy CoolBrands, a spin-off from brand consultants SuperBrands, has created global rankings of brand 'coolness'. In the past this has been based on the views of a select band of 'style leaders', but in 2006 for the first time it also took into account an online pole of 1725 consumers. However, the results are still weighted 70:30 in favour of nominated style leaders, so the results need to be interpreted with caution. The top ten ranks for 2006 were:

1. Aston Martin
2. Alexander McQueen
3. iPod
4. Agent Provocateur
5. Bang & Oulfsen
6. Google
7. Green & Black's
8. Tate Modern
9. Jimmy Choo
10. Vivienne Westwood

Other members of CoolBrands include Asahi and Cobra beers, Boxfresh sportswear, Gaggia and DeLonghi coffee machines, PJ and Innocent's fruit drinks and Smile and First Direct banking. Make your own judgements about the precise rankings, but there is little doubt that each brand does create additional value by being 'cooler' in their respective markets.

Source: Sunday Times, Cool Brands, September 24, 2006; www.superbrands.uk.com.

Go online to listen to the case study of the creation and development of Innocent Smoothies, which demonstrates the importance of intangible factors, even in the success of tangible products.

www.iande.info

Gary Lynn and Richard Reilly have tried to identify in a systematic way the most common factors that contribute to successful product development, focusing on what they call 'blockbuster' products – more radical and successful than most new products. Over ten years they studied more than 700 teams and nearly 50 detailed cases of some of the most successful products ever developed, and compared and contrasted these organisations with less successful counterparts. They identify five key practices that contribute to the successful development of 'blockbuster' products:[4]

- commitment of senior management;
- clear and stable vision;
- improvisation;
- information exchange;
- collaboration under pressure.

All five practices operate as a system, and blockbuster development teams must adopt all five practices. Size of the organisation did not seem to matter; neither did the type of product.

Commitment of Senior Management

Those teams that developed blockbusters had full support and co-operation from senior management. These senior managers functioned as sponsors for the project and took on an active and intimate role. Senior managers would often have a more 'hit and run' kind of involvement with those teams that did not produce blockbusters.

Clear and Stable Vision

It is important for the development team to have a clear and stable vision to guide them, with specific and enduring parameters, something called 'project pillars,' to follow. These pillars are the key requirements, or 'must haves' for the new product. Mission awareness is a strong predictor of the success of R&D projects, the degree to which depending on the stage of the project. For example, in the planning and conceptual stage, mission awareness explains around two-thirds of the subsequent project success. Leadership clarity is also associated with clear team objectives, high levels of participation, commitment to excellence, and support for innovation. Leadership clarity, partly mediated by good team processes, is a good predictor of team innovation.

Improvisation

A clear and stable vision is necessary, but nobody is so brilliant that they can see the end product from the beginning. They may have a vision of what the end product may look like or what the experience of using it will be (or must be) like. It's more like having a dialogue with the product – in trying to get the end results you may ditch what you've done and try something else. You may just have to accept that you may come up with something you never thought you would produce and you might be better off for it. Teams that produce blockbuster products complete the traditional stages of product development, but they take a different approach to the process. Although this may appear to be undisciplined, the teams nearly always have to meet a hard and fast deadline, and are more likely to monitor their progress and costs than the less successful teams.

Information Exchange

Effective communication and information exchange is another key practice. Many blockbuster outcomes require the use of cross-functional teams. Exchanging information openly and clearly on a cross-functional team can be challenging to say the least. Not only do specific functions have their own specialised language, they also often have conflicting interests. Team members call on each other through a variety of informal and personal ways like casual conversation, phone calls, and meetings. In addition more formal knowledge exchange happens through a system for recording, storing, retrieving and reviewing information (see Chapter 6 for more on knowledge management). Both types of information exchange can be enabled for virtual team working, but all teams need some face-to-face time.

Collaboration Under Pressure

Blockbuster development teams are generally cross-functional, but must also often deal with outsiders to bring in a new perspective or expertise. Collaboration in the face of conflicting functions and other sources of internal and external pressure requires a number of facilitating factors. Teams that produced blockbuster products complete the traditional stages of product development, but take a different approach to the process. Rather than going through the gates step-by-step, waiting for a final decision to be made about going forward, they focus on getting an early prototype out quickly to learn how customers might respond. Once they learned how customers responded, they then continued to take new prototypes out for more continuous feedback. The teams need to be able to balance the insights they gained from the customers with the desired outcome. This constant balance allowed them to adjust and fine-tune their understanding of both the market need and the product concept. This fast, iterative process was critical to their success.

To identify common characteristics of service innovators, we have examined over 100 service businesses from the PIMS (Profit Impact of Market Strategy) database, and separated out those which have the highest sustained new service content in their revenue (Table 9.1).

Not surprisingly, high innovators spend more on R&D, to change both what they deliver to customers, and how they deliver it. In addition, they have often experienced technology change, and invested in fixed assets to do so. They usually take less than a year to bring new

TABLE 9.1   Characteristics of 'High Innovators'

Business Descriptor	No/Low Innovators	High Innovators
Innovation Outcomes		
– % sales from services introduced <3 years ago	<1%	17%
– % new services vs. competitors	>0	5%
Customer Base		
– Focus on key customers	Average	High
– Relative customers base	Similar to competitors	More focused than competitors
Value Chain		
– Focus on key suppliers	Average	High/strategic
– Value added/sales %	72%	60%
– Operating cost added/sales	36%	25%
– Vertical integration vs. competitors	Same or more	Same or less
Innovation input		
– 'What' R&D	0.1% sales	0.7% sales
– 'How' R&D	0.1% sales	0.5% sales
– Fixed Assets/sales	growing at 10% pa	growing at > 20% pa
– Overheads/sales %	8%	11%
Innovation context		
– Recent technology change	20%	40%
– Time to market	> 1 year	< 1 year
Competition		
– Competitor entry	10%	40%
– Imports/Exports vs. market	2%	12%
Quality of offer		
– Relative quality vs. competitors	Declining	Improving
– Value for money	Just below competitors	Better than competitors
Output		
– Real sales	9%	15%

Source: From Clayton (2003) in Tidd, J. and Hull, F.M. (eds) *Service Innovation: Organizational Responses to Technological Opportunities and Market Imperatives.* Imperial College Press, London.

service concepts to market. Competition is also an important factor. The highest innovating firms are more than likely to have experienced entry into their markets by a significant new competitor. They are also much more likely to compete in open markets where international trade – both imports and exports – play an important role.

The data also indicate that focus is an important discriminating factor between high and low service innovators. First, those businesses with the highest level of new service content tend to avoid overcomplicating their customer base. They are usually firms for which fewer key customer segments account for a higher proportion of their total revenue. This suggests that customer complexity can be a barrier to effective innovation in service businesses. This 'focus' service strategy is well demonstrated by the rise of 'no frills' air services in the USA and Europe since the mid-1990s, such as South West, Ryanair and EasyJet. Second, it seems that focus in the procurement and service delivery process is also an aid to stronger innovation performance. High innovators tend to focus their purchases on fewer, larger suppliers, and are less vertically integrated – and therefore focused on fewer internal processes within the overall value chain.

However, persuading customers to buy new services at a premium can be difficult. Most of our 'innovation winners' operate with a policy of parity pricing, with a policy of using their service advantage to go for growth, rather than to exploit it for maximum immediate profits. They grow real sales significantly faster; they grow share of their target markets faster than their direct competitors, and faster than non-innovators generally; and in addition they increase their returns on capital employed and assets.

INNOVATION IN ACTION

Charcol On-Line

As financial services move online, again the most successful are those with a very clear view of which customer segments to aim for. In the words of the MD of Charcol On-line (one of the UK's largest Internet mortgage companies), 'Segmentation is key to any business seeking to transform itself, and its market, through e-commerce. Understanding how groups of consumer behave, and what they are most likely to value, is a critically important factor for the business in gaining competitive advantage in constructing offers to customers.'

Charcol's strategy in creating a successful online business has been to move incrementally from its original base in traditional mortgage broking, maintaining its focus on higher net worth individuals while developing methods for communicating with them in different ways. The firm has created relatively simple online advice systems, easy to use and designed to build trust in the brand, and then to offer a limited range of options, with selected, high-quality product suppliers.

Understanding customer needs, in terms of the preference for personal advice vs. the ability or inclination to use 'self service', is one important dimension for Charcol in filtering its customers to online purchasing or towards direct contact with a sales adviser. Another is the requirement for a simple transactional product vs. more complex overall solutions, which depends on the clients' circumstances. In the 'self service / transactional product' corner of this matrix the possibilities of delivering reliable service are high, and the strategy behind Charcol's innovation approach is to offer this group the best value proposition in the market. Growing the business depends on new propositions to extend the envelope, rather than attacking directly the traditional customers with very different needs.

Source: From Clayton (2003) in Tidd, J. and Hull, F.M. (eds) *Service Innovation: Organizational Responses to Technological Opportunities and Market Imperatives.* Imperial College Press, London.

Organisation for Development and Delivery of New Products and Services

We discussed the broader organisational factors to support innovation in Chapter 2, but here we explore the more specific needs of new product and service development. Successful product and service development requires much more than the application of a set of tools and techniques, and in addition requires an appropriate organisation to support innovation and an explicit process to manage development. In this section we examine the critical role of organisation, and the various options available in the case of new product and service development. The purpose of this section is not, however, to provide a more general overview of the theory and practice organisational behaviour and development, and we assume that you are familiar with the basics of this field.

One of the key challenges facing the organisation of new product and process development is that most organisations have not evolved or been designed to do this, but are structured for a different purpose, usually to serve some operational need. In most organisations new product or service development is a rather unusual and infrequent requirement, so in most organisations the first decision is what sort of team to put together to do this.

Essentially the choice is between functional teams, cross-functional project teams or some form of matrix between the two. For example, the team might be within a single function or department such as research, marketing or design. Alternatively, a special cross-functional team might be established, including representatives from many (but not all) functional groups. In a matrix organisation a dedicated team is not formed; rather, members remain in their functional or departmental groups, but are designated to a project group. Studies of new product development suggest four main types of team structure:

(i) *Functional structure* – a traditional hierarchical structure where communication between functional areas is largely handled by function managers and according to standard and codified procedures.

(ii) *Lightweight product manager structure* – again a traditional hierarchical structure but where a project manager provides an overarching co-ordinating structure to the inter-functional work.

(iii) *Heavyweight product manager structure* – essentially a matrix structure led by a product (project) manager with extensive influence over the functional personnel involved but also in strategic directions of the contributing areas critical to the project. By its nature this structure carries considerable organisational authority.

(iv) *Project execution teams* – a full-time project team where functional staff leave their areas to work on the project, under project leader direction.

Project management structure is strongly correlated with product success, and, of the available options, the functional structures are the weakest. Associated with these different structures are different roles for team members and particularly for project managers. For example, the 'heavyweight project manager' has to play several different roles, which include extensive interpreting and communication between functions and players. Similarly, team members have multiple responsibilities. This implies the need for considerable efforts at team building and development – for example, to equip the team with the skills to explore problems, to resolve the inevitable conflicts that will emerge during the project, and to manage relationships inside and outside the project.

More generally, different combinations organisational structure, processes and tools create a number of possible coherent configurations with different properties and performance advantages.

INNOVATION IN ACTION

Types of Service Organisation and Innovation

Client Project-orientation

Project leaders organise the involvement of everyone early on to reduce hand-overs, the essence of concurrent product development. Structured processes, such as QFD (Quality Function Deployment), are used to identify and influence customer requirements. Processes are mapped and continuously improved. The system is integrated by the voice of the customer and early involvement of the customer in need fulfilment. This configuration is strong on organisation, but weaker on tools/technology, such as technological sophistication in either knowledge or IT. However, the art and craft of project management, which is somewhat analogous to batch production in goods industries, provides a strong yet flexible type of enabling control over the development and delivery of customer-focused services. It can achieve high levels of service delivery, and on time to market and cost reduction. These effects on performance are consistent with the inherent flexibility of project-based systems, and is effective in dynamic environments.

Many consultancies and technology-based firms fit this profile. For example, Arup is an international engineering consultancy firm that provides planning, designing, engineering and project management services. The business demands the simultaneous achievement of innovative solutions and significant time compression imposed by client and regulatory requirements. The organisation has established a wide range of knowledge management initiatives to encourage sharing of know-how and experience across projects. These initiatives range from organisational processes and mechanisms, such as cross-functional communications meetings and skills networks, to technology-based approaches such as a project database and expert intranet. To date, the former have been more successful than the latter. This may be due to the difficulty of codifying tacit knowledge, which is difficult to store and retrieve electronically, and the unique environmental context of each project limiting the scope for the reuse of standardised knowledge and experience.

Mechanistic Customisation

This is organised by the involvement of external customers in product development and delivery process decisions. Standardisation is a key factor in controlling the relationship, and electronic

(continued)

links are used to exchange data with customers and suppliers. Setting standards for projects and products is a key method of process control, and customers help set these standards in conformance with their requirements. The electronic interchange with customers provides the capability for routinely adapting them to market demand. In addition, this type also has a significant positive effect on product innovation and quality, and the locus in both cases is external – the customer.

For example, in British Gas Trading (BGT) standardised documentation and processes are used as an instrument of management control, and yet many different types of contract exist. Within BGT, there are formal procedures for assessing the financial performance of projects, and all projects over a certain threshold require the business owner to prepare a completion report within three months of completion. A project is complete when all physical work is completed, all costs relating to the work have been incurred, and all benefits have been delivered.

Hybrid Knowledge-sharing

In this type of organisation people are cross-trained and co-rewarded and organized in groups, which reinforces their team identity. Electronic tools are distributed to all and enable team members to map processes, share best practices, and communicate lessons learned online. Group systems are typically rather self-contained which may be one reason companies in this factor are more likely to value knowledge, reuse it, and share it for achieving a balanced portfolio of performance advantages. It is strong in organisation, tools, and system integration, but lacks formal processes. Its use of tools compensates for a lack of processes, and these focus on knowledge management, e.g., distributed databases, templates for process mapping, etc. To the extent it represents a hybrid system, it can achieve different types of performance advantage simultaneously, but is not optimal for anything, and has only a weak association with product innovation and quality, time to market, and service delivery. The Hybrid Knowledge-sharing configuration enables a relatively self-contained group of people to become experts in developing and delivering products as quasi professionals. This type of organisation thereby provides some of the advantages of codified knowledge with far less hierarchical control by bureaucratic forms, consistent with the view that most service innovations demand greater knowledge-sharing than in conventional product development.

For example, Cable & Wireless Global Markets (CWGM), a division of the UK telecom operator Cable & Wireless, is a systems integrator and service provider which designs, integrates and operates telecommunications networks for multinational clients. CWGM was established to deal with the increasing number of non-standard and highly complex outsourcing projects. The common processes and standards developed by the parent company were found to be inappropriate for this type of business. In contrast to the formal business processes and matrix structure used for simpler management network services, CWGM has adopted a more flexible teaming approach, which includes a 'war room' to help build relationships and promote communication between team members and customers. In this way teams can more easily work closely with customers to develop innovative service packages of standardised products and customised applications to achieve the required service level agreements for outsourcing.

(continued)

Integrated Innovative

The Integrated Innovative organisation is characterised by co-located, cross-functional teams in a flattened hierarchy. Communications are open regardless of rank, both face-to-face and via e-mail. Its technical base utilises expert systems and management information systems. Responsibility for work is shared and partnering is practised throughout the value chain. The organic design has many advantages for creativity and innovation. They have dense communications facilitated by cross-functional teams and physical collocation. Cross-functional teaming, whereby different specialists are assigned to work on the same project simultaneously, has been advocated and widely adopted in many companies as a strategy to improve their product development process. Collaboration among diverse functions typically provides better solutions to complex design problems. Physical co-location involves aggregating project team members in common space to enhance rich communications among group members. Accordingly, it ranks significantly higher than other configurations in innovation, but lowest in all other performance measures.

For example, in BBC Worldwide (BBCW) speed/timeliness is essential to the processes given its strategic nature. Processes are strongly time-driven – indeed, diagrammatically they are captured in a timeline. A series of discrete steps is defined, beginning with the initial receipt of programme treatment, to the final sign-off by a senior management committee. The process documentation at BBCW has in-built financial measures as well as benchmarks against the success of previous programmes. The quality of a bid is dependent on individuals and departments providing the required information on a timely basis, together with robust ROI analyses and sales projections. However, processes are able to evolve reactively to emergent business needs. For example, if a new means of exploiting programmes arises (video on demand, broadband video) these additional media can be included in the necessary documentation. In the case of an emergency item that requires urgent approval, informal contacts are exploited to minimise timescales, which is indicative of flexibility and the use of networking.

None of these different service organisations is optimal in every context, and instead different organisational configurations perform best in different cases or contingencies. The integrated innovative is the most innovative; the mechanistic customisation is the most cost efficient; hybrid knowledge-sharing is best for overall performance; and the client project-orientated is best at service delivery.

Sources: Tidd, J. and Hull, F.M. (2006) 'Managing Service Innovation: The need for selectivity rather than 'best-practice', *New Technology, Work and Employment,* 21(2), 139–161; Tidd, J. and Hull, F.M. (2003) *Service Innovation: Organizational Responses to Technological Opportunities and Market Imperatives.* Imperial College Press, London.

All four configurations have one or more significant effects on performance. Each appears to have evolved or acquired sufficient good practices to be viable at least in niche markets. The client project-orientation reduces time to market and improves service delivery by focusing on customer requirements and project management; the mechanised customisation reduces costs by setting standards and through the involvement of suppliers and customers; the hybrid knowledge-sharing provides a combination of innovation and efficiency by promoting team work and knowledge-sharing; and the integrated innovative raises innovation and quality by means of cross functional groups supported by groupware and other tools and technology, but this increased co-ordination raises the time and cost of service development.

Examination of the actual measures suggests that each of the four organisational configurations provide several common elements, including:

- organisational mode of bringing people together;
- control mechanisms, either impersonal (standards, documentation, common software) or interpersonal (collocated teams);
- shared knowledge and/or technical information base;
- external linkages, e.g., customers and/or partners/suppliers.

In terms of performance, innovation and quality appear to be improved by cross-functional teams and sharing information, raised by involvement with customers and suppliers, and by encouraging collaboration in teams. Service delivery is improved by customer focus and project management, and by knowledge sharing and collaboration in teams. Time to market is reduced by knowledge sharing and collaboration, and customer focus and project organisation, but cross-functional teams can prolong the process. Costs are reduced by setting standards for projects and products, and by involvement of customers and suppliers, but can be increased by using cross-functional teams. Although individual practices can make a significant contribution to performance (Figure 9.5), it is clear that it is the coherent combination of practices and their interaction that creates superior performance in specific contexts.

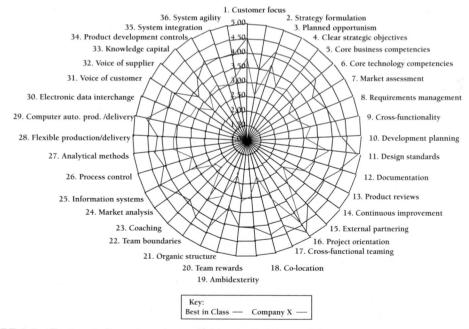

FIGURE 9.5 Factors influencing successful innovation in services.
Source: Tidd, J. and Bessant, J. (2009) *Managing Innovation: Integrating technological, market and organizational change.* John Wiley & Sons Ltd.

Processes for New Product and Service Development

The process of new product or service development – moving from idea through to successful products, services or processes – is a gradual process of reducing uncertainty through a series of problem-solving stages, moving through the phases of scanning and selecting and into implementation – linking market and technology-related streams along the way.

At the outset anything is possible, but increasing commitments of resources during the life of the project makes it increasingly difficult to change direction. Managing new product or service development is a fine balancing act, between the costs of continuing with projects which may not eventually succeed (and which represent opportunity costs in terms of other possibilities) and the danger of closing down too soon and eliminating potentially fruitful options. With shorter life cycles and demand for greater product variety pressure is also placed upon the development process to work with a wider portfolio of new product opportunities and to manage the risks associated with progressing these through development to launch.

These decisions can be made on an *ad hoc* basis but experience and research suggests some form of structured development system, with clear decision points and agreed rules on which to base go/no go decisions, is a more effective approach. Attention needs to be given to reconfiguring internal mechanisms for integrating and optimising the process such as concurrent engineering, cross-functional working, advanced tools, early involvement, etc. To deal with this attention has focused on systematic screening, monitoring and progression frameworks such as Cooper's 'stage-gate' approach (Figure 9.6).

 The stage-gate process is used widely, but in various forms. Go online to find further details.

www.iande.info

As Cooper suggests, successful product development needs to operate some form of structured, staging process. As projects move through the development process, there are a number of discrete stages, each with different decision criteria or 'gates' which they must pass. Many variations on this basic idea exist (e.g. 'fuzzy gates'), but the important point is to ensure that there is a structure in place which reviews both technical and marketing data at each stage. A common variation is the 'development funnel', which takes into account the reduction in uncertainty as the process progresses, and the influence of real resource constraints (Figure 9.7).[5]

The development of new products and services is inherently a complex and iterative process, and this makes it difficult to model for practical purposes. There are numerous models in the literature, incorporating various stages ranging from three to thirteen. Such models are essentially linear and unidirectional, beginning with concept development and ending with commercialisation.

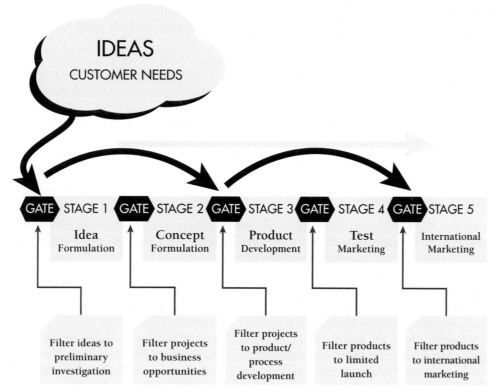

FIGURE 9.6 Stage-gate process for new product development.
Source: Tidd, J. and Bessant, J. (2009) *Managing Innovation: Integrating technological, market and organizational change.* John Wiley & Sons Ltd.

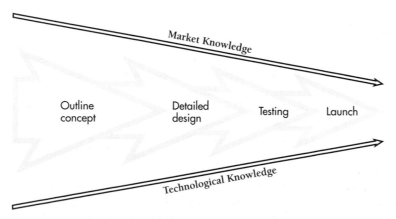

FIGURE 9.7 Development funnel model of new product development.
Source: Tidd, J. and Bessant, J. (2009) *Managing Innovation: Integrating technological, market and organizational change.* John Wiley & Sons Ltd.

For ease of discussion and analysis, we will adopt a simplified four-stage model which I believe is sufficient to discriminate between the various factors which must be managed at different stages:

1. *Concept generation* – identifying the opportunities for new products and services.
2. *Project assessment and selection* – screening and choosing projects which satisfy certain criteria.
3. *Product development* – translating the selected concepts into a physical product (we'll discuss services later).
4. *Product commercialisation* – testing, launching and marketing the new product.

Concept Generation

Much of the marketing and product development literatures concentrate on monitoring market trends and customer needs to identify new product concepts. However, there is a well-established debate in the literature about the relative merits of 'market pull' versus 'technology push' strategies for new product development. A review of the relevant research suggests that the best strategy to adopt is dependent on the relative novelty of the new product. For incremental adaptations or product line extensions, 'market pull' is likely to be the preferred route, as customers are familiar with the product type and will be able to express preferences easily. However, there are many 'needs' that the customer may be unaware of, or unable to articulate, and in these cases the balance shifts to a 'technology push' strategy. Nevertheless, in most cases customers do not buy a technology, they buy products for the benefits that they can receive from them; the 'technology push' must provide a solution for their needs. Thus some customer or market analysis is also important for more novel technological projects. A number of tools are available to help systematically identify new product concepts, and these are described below.

Project Selection

This stage includes the screening and selection of product concepts prior to subsequent progress through to the development phase. Two costs of failing to select the 'best' project set are: the actual cost of resources spent on poor projects; and the opportunity costs of marginal projects which may have succeeded with additional resources.

There are two levels of filtering. The first is the aggregate product plan, in which the new product development portfolio is determined. The aggregate product plan attempts to integrate the various potential projects to ensure the collective set of development projects will meet the goals and objectives of the firm, and help to build the capabilities needed. The first step is to ensure resources are applied to the appropriate types and mix of projects. The second step is to develop a capacity plan to balance resource and demand. The final step is to analyse the effect of the proposed projects on capabilities, to ensure this is built up to meet future demands.

The second lower level filters are concerned with specific product concepts. The two most common processes at this level are the development funnel and the stage-gate system.

The development funnel is a means to identify, screen, review and converge development projects as they move from idea to commercialisation. It provides a framework in which to review alternatives based on a series of explicit criteria for decision-making. Similarly, the stage-gate system provides a formal framework for filtering projects based on explicit criteria. The main difference is that where the development funnel assumes resource constraints, the stage-gate system does not.

Product Development

This stage includes all the activities necessary to take the chosen concept and deliver a product for commercialisation. It is at the working level, where the product is actually developed and produced, that the individual R&D staff, designers, engineers and marketing staff must work together to solve specific issues and to make decisions on the details. Whenever a problem appears, a gap between the current design and the requirement, the development team must take action to close it. The way in which this is achieved determines the speed and effectiveness of the problem-solving process. In many cases this problem solving routine involves iterative design – test – build cycles, which make use of a number of tools.

Product Commercialisation and Review

In many cases the process of new product development blurs into the process of commercialisation. For example, customer co-development, test marketing and use of alpha, beta and gamma test sites yield data on customer requirements and any problems is use, but also help to obtain customer buy-in and prime the market. It was not the purpose of this study to examine the relative efficacy of different marketing strategies, but rather to identify those factors which influence directly the process of new product development. We were primarily interested in what criteria firms use to evaluate the success of new products, and how these criteria might differ between low- and high-novelty projects. In the former case we expected more formal and narrow financial or market measures, but in the latter case we hoped to find a broader range of criteria to reflect the potential for organisational learning and future new product options.

Tools and Technology to Support Service Innovation

Despite their intangibility, many services are knowledge-based and/or are heavily dependent upon IT (Information Technology). Improvements in computers and software for storing and sharing information have increased capabilities for conceiving of new kinds of services as well as for managing development and delivery processes. Tools that were once hard to change and difficult to distribute are now soft, flexible, and easily shared via electronic networks. IT can act as an enabler of continually updated processes and instant exchanges among cross-functional team members, regardless of distance.

Concept Generation

Most studies have highlighted the importance of understanding users' needs. Designing a product to satisfy a perceived need has been shown to be an important discriminator of commercial success. Common approaches include:

- *Surveys and focus groups* – where a similar product exists surveys of customers' preferences can be a reliable guide to development. Focus groups allow developers to explore the likely response to more novel products where a clear target segment exists.
- *Latent needs analysis* – are designed to uncover the unarticulated requirements of customers by means of their responses to symbols, concepts and forms.
- *Lead users* – are representative of the needs of the market, but some time ahead of the majority, and so represent future needs. Lead users are one of the most important sources of market knowledge for product improvements.
- *Customer-developers* – in some cases new products are partly or completely developed by customers. In such cases the issue is how to identify and acquire such products.
- *Competitive analysis* – of competing products, by reverse engineering or benchmarking features of competing products.
- *Industry experts or consultants* – who have a wide range of experience of different users' needs. The danger is that they may have become too immersed in the user's world to have the breadth of vision required to assess and evaluate the potential of the innovation. The use of 'proxy experts' can help overcome the problem. They suggest selecting a specific group of respondents who have knowledge of the product category or usage context.
- *Extrapolating trends* – in technology, markets and society to guess the short- to medium-term future needs.
- *Building scenarios* – alternative visions of the future based on varying assumptions to create robust product strategies. Most relevant to long-term projects and product portfolio development.
- *Market experimentation* – testing market response with real products, but able to adapt or withdraw rapidly. Only practical where development costs are low, lead times short and customers tolerant of product underperformance or failure. Sometimes referred to as 'expeditionary marketing', or more modestly 'test marketing'.

Go online to find the case study of Coloplast, which illustrates the importance of capturing users' needs in new product development.

www.iande.info

Go online to watch the video of Eric von Hippel discussing the role of lead users in new product development.

www.iande.info

Project Selection

Different combinations of criteria are used to screen and assess projects prior to development. The most common are based on discounted cash flows, such as Net Present Value/Internal Rate of Return, followed by cost – benefit analysis, and simple calculations of the payback period. In addition to these financial criteria, most organisation also use a range of additional measures:

- *Ranking* – a means of ordering a list of candidate projects in relative value or worthiness of support, broken down into several factors, so both objective and judgemental data can be assessed. These techniques are likely to be of most use in the early stages of the process, since they are fairly 'rough-cut' methods.
- *Profiles* – projects are given scores on each of several characteristics, and are rejected if they fail to meet some predetermined threshold. The projects which dominate on all or most of the factor scores are selected. These methods can be used at all stages of the development process.
- *Simulated outcomes* – alternative outcomes to which probabilities can be attached, or alternate paths depending on chance outcomes and when the projects have different payoffs for different outcomes. The range of possible outcomes and the likelihood of a specific outcome are found. It is used especially in the analysis of sets of projects which are interdependent (the aggregate project plan).
- *Strategic clusters* – projects not selected solely for maximisation of some financial measure, but for the support they give to the strategic position. Groups are clustered according to their support for specific objectives, and then these groups are rated according to strategic importance and funded accordingly (again, this is important at the aggregate project plan level).
- *Interactive* – an iterative process between the R&D Director and project managers, where project proposals are improved at each stage to more closely align with the objectives. The aim of this is to develop projects that more nearly fit the strategic and tactical objectives of the firm. These methods are used mainly at the aggregate project plan level, or at the early stages of specific projects.

Product Development

There are a number of tools, or methodologies, which have been developed to help solve the problems, and most require the integration of different functions and disciplines. The most significant tools and methods used are:

- *Design for Manufacture (DFM)* – 'the full range of policies, techniques, practices and attitudes that cause a product to be designed for the optimum manufacturing cost, the optimum achievement of manufactured quality, and the optimum achievement of life-cycle support (serviceability, reliability and maintainability)'. It includes Design for Assembly (DFA), Design for Producibility (DFP) and other Design Rule approaches. Studies from the car industry indicate that up to 80% of the final production costs are determined at the design stage.

- *Rapid Prototyping* – is the core element of the design – build – test cycle, and can increase the rate and amount of learning that occurs in each cycle. The first design is unlikely to be complete, and so designers go through several iterations learning more about the problem and alternative solutions each time. The number of iterations will depend on the time and cost constraints of the project. One study found that frequent prototyping proved useful for intra-team communication, obtaining customer feedback and manufacturing process development. Having an actual prototype as a visual model enables more reliable assessment of preferences and suggestions.
- *Computer-Aided Techniques (CAD/CAM)* – potential benefits include reduction in development lead times, economies in design, ability to design products too complex to do manually and the combination of CAD with production automation, computer-aided manufacture (CAM), to achieve the benefits of integration. However, these benefits are not always realised due to organisational shortcomings.
- *Quality Function Deployment (QFD)* – is a set of planning and communications routines, which are used to identify critical customer attributes and create a specific link between these and design parameters (Figure 9.8); it focuses and co-ordinates the skills within the organisation to design, manufacture and then market products that customers want. The aim is to answer three primary questions: What are the critical attributes for customers? What design parameters drive these attributes? What should the design parameter targets be for the new design?

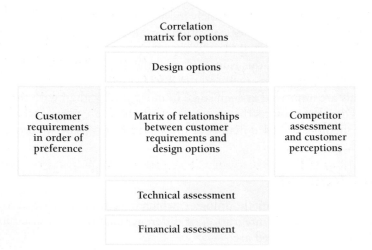

FIGURE 9.8 Quality Function Deployment (QFD) matrix for new product development.
Source: Tidd, J. and Bessant, J. (2009) *Managing Innovation: Integrating technological, market and organizational change.* John Wiley & Sons Ltd.

Quality function deployment is a useful technique for translating customer requirements into development needs, and encourages communication between engineering, production and marketing. Unlike most other tools of quality management, QFD is used to identify opportunities for product improvement or differentiation, rather than to solve problems. Customer-required characteristics are translated or 'deployed' by means of a matrix into language which engineers can understand. The construction of a relationship matrix – also known as 'the house of quality' – requires a significant amount of technical and market research. Great emphasis must be placed on gathering market and user data in order to identify potential design trade-offs, and to achieve the most appropriate balance between cost, quality and performance. The construction of a QFD matrix involves the following steps:

1. Identify customer requirements, primary and secondary, and any major dislikes.
2. Rank requirements according to importance.
3. Translate requirements into measurable characteristics.
4. Establish the relationship between the customer requirements and technical product characteristics, and estimate the strength of the relationship.
5. Choose appropriate units of measurement and determine target values based on customer requirements and competitor benchmarks.

Symbols are used to show the relationship between customer requirements and technical specifications, and weights attached to illustrate the strength of the relationship. Horizontal rows with no relationship symbol indicate that the existing design is incomplete. Conversely, vertical columns with no relationship symbol indicate that an existing design feature is redundant as it is not valued by the customer. In addition, comparisons with competing products, or benchmarks, can be included. This is important because relative quality is more relevant than absolute quality: customer expectations are likely to be shaped by what else is available, rather than some ideal.

QFD was originally developed in Japan, and is claimed to have helped Toyota to reduce its development time and costs by 40%. More recently many leading American firms have adopted QFD, including AT&T, Digital and Ford, but results have been mixed: only around a quarter of projects have resulted in any quantifiable benefit. In contrast, there has been relatively little application of QFD by European firms. This is not the result of ignorance, but rather recognition of the practical problems of implementing QFD.

 Go online to find an interactive Flash version of QFD to help assess new product concepts.

www.iande.info

In addition to these discrete techniques, the efficiency and effectiveness of new product development will also be influenced by the internal organisation and relationships with other organisations. Both internal and external integrity determine the dynamic capability of the organisation, in exploiting the existing technology and marketing capabilities in response to the changing market and technological environment. There is substantial agreement in the literature on the need for effective integration of all the stakeholders in the new product development process, and this the rationale for multifunctional project teams. The other aspect of organisation is concerned with the relationships with suppliers, customers and other external sources of innovation. For example, working closely with key suppliers may reduce the cost, time and effectiveness of product development, and exploiting other external sources of technology and market know-how allows a firm to focus on its own competencies.

Development projects range from simple improvements to existing products, through to radical 'new to the world' products. What matters to practising managers is how close a project is to their existing skills and past experience, which is a relative, not an absolute, matter. Clearly, what is novel for one firm may be routine for another, which is reflected in the common distinction between 'new to the firm', 'new to the market' and 'new to the world'. For example, the development of a new electronic control unit might be considered routine by a large electronics firm, but perceived as highly novel by a small manufacturer of machine tools or large manufacturer of automobiles. This approach is consistent with the test of 'inventive step' for a new patent application, which is relative to the industry, being based on what is obvious to a 'skilled practitioner' in the same industry. Therefore we might expect managers to use different tools and approaches depending on the novelty of the products *relative* to the firm.

The use and usefulness of various techniques are shown in Table 9.2. In terms of frequency of use, the most common methods used for high-novelty projects are segmentation, market experimentation and industry experts, whereas for the less complex projects the most common methods are partnering customers, trend extrapolation and segmentation. The use of market experimentation and industry experts might be expected where market requirements or technologies are uncertain, but reasons for the use of segmentation for such projects are less obvious. Segmentation is also commonly used for the low-novelty projects, but in this case technologies and market demand are more clearly defined, and therefore extrapolation of trends and customer requirements more reliable. In terms of the usefulness, there are statistically significant differences in the ratings for segmentation, focus groups, customer partnerships and user-developers. Segmentation is more useful for low-novelty projects, essentially product extensions where a reliable basis of segmenting markets is available, but for the novel projects deeper market analysis and closer relationships with lead customers are more important.[6]

In practice, most organisations use only three or four different techniques to support development, the most common being prototyping and market experimentation. Both of these techniques also received high ratings for usefulness, prototyping being even more critical for novel projects. In contrast, the relatively low use and usefulness rating of Quality Function Deployment (QFD) is surprising. The low take-up may be due the fact that QFD demands close integration between functional groups, in particular design, development and marketing, which is still not commonplace. The low rating for usefulness may reflect the difficulty in measuring some of the benefits of QFD, especially in the short term. QFD requires the compilation of a lot of marketing and technical data, and more importantly the close co-operation of the development and marketing functions. Indeed, the process of constructing the relationship matrix provides a structured way of getting people from development and marketing to

TABLE 9.2   Use and usefulness of techniques for product and service development

	High Novelty		Low Novelty	
	Usage (%)	Usefulness	Usage (%)	Usefulness
Segmentation*	89	3.42	42	4.50
Market Experimentation	63	4.00	53	3.70
Industry Experts	63	3.83	37	3.71
Surveys/Focus groups*	52	4.50	37	4.00
User-practice Observation	47	3.67	42	3.50
Partnering Customers*	37	4.43	58	3.67
Lead Users*	32	4.33	37	3.57
Probability of technical success	100	4.37	100	4.32
Probability of commercial success	100	4.68	95	4.50
Market share*	100	3.63	84	4.00
Core competencies*	95	3.61	79	3.00
Degree of internal commitment	89	3.82	79	3.67
Market size	89	3.76	84	3.94
Competition	89	3.76	84	3.81
Gap Analysis	79	2.73	84	2.81
Strategic Clusters*	42	3.63	32	2.67
Prototyping*	79	4.33	63	4.08
QFD	47	3.33	37	3.43
Cross-functional Teams*	63	4.47	37	3.74
Project Manager (Heavyweight)*	52	3.84	32	3.05

Usefulness Scale: 1–5, 5=critical, based on manager assessments of 50 development projects in 25 firms.
* denotes difference in usefulness rating is statistically significant at 5% level

Source: Adapted from Tidd, J. and Bodley, K. (2002) 'The effect of project novelty on the new product development process', *R&D Management,* 32(2), 127–138.

communicate, and therefore is as valuable as any more quantifiable outputs. However, where relations between the technical and marketing groups are a problem, which is too often the case, the use of QFD may be premature.

Table 9.2 confirms that cross-functional teams are essential to new product and service development. However, there are significant differences in the management and usefulness of such teams. Heavyweight project managers and cross-functional teams appear to be a more effective combination for high-novelty projects, whereas lower weight co-ordination mechanisms may be sufficient for more routine projects. The involvement of external organisations in different stages of the product development process is common. Customers are twice as likely to be involved in the development and commercialisation of novel products and services, compared to low-novelty projects, and the involvement of lead users is significantly more effective in the development of novel products and services.

DEVELOPING PERSONAL CAPABILITIES

Problem-solving style is an important part of new product and service development. Information from different functions and disciplines – especially the constant challenge of 'doing more with less', and the always present need to anticipate, create, innovate, and manage change from both internal and external sources.

Problem-solving style can be defined as '*consistent individual differences in the ways people prefer to plan and carry out the generating and focusing of ideas, in order to gain clarity, or prepare for action when solving problems or managing change.*'

An important dimension of problem-solving style is personal **orientation to change**, which focuses on a person's preferences for managing change and solving problems creatively. How someone perceives opportunities and challenges surrounding change is based on three main issues:

1. How much structure do you need in order to understand and deal effectively with the change?
2. How much will you need to have the guidance and direction from sources of authority.
3. What kind of novelty or originality do you prefer to pay attention to?

The two contrasting styles are the *Explorer* and the *Developer*. An 'explorer' is someone who prefers to venture into uncharted directions and follows possibilities wherever they might lead.

Explorers enjoy initiating many tasks. They thrive on novel, ambiguous situations and challenges. They seek to create many original options that, if developed and refined, might provide the foundation for valuable contributions. Explorers see unusual possibilities, patterns, and relationships. These highly novel alternatives may not be very workable or easy to implement. Explorers often 'plunge right in', feeding on risk and uncertainty, and improvising as situations unfold. They often find externally imposed plans, procedures, and structures confining. Explorers prefer that sources of authority maintain their distance and limit their influence on their thinking and doing.

A 'developer' is someone who prefers to bring tasks to fulfilment, or who organises, synthesises, refines, and enhances basic ingredients, shaping them into a more complete and useful result. Developers are concerned with practical applications and the reality of the task. They think creatively by emphasising workable possibilities and successful implementation. They are usually careful and well organised, seek to minimise risk and uncertainty, and are comfortable with plans, details, and structures. They are able to move tasks or projects forward efficiently and deliberately, and they appreciate close guidance from sources of authority.

Neither style is superior, but the two different perspectives result in different ways of seeing and solving problems. It is important to be aware of your own preferences and style so that you can compensate for this by forcing yourself to consider other perspectives and if necessary involve others with different styles.

Adapted from Isaksen, S. and Tidd, J. (2006) *Meeting the Innovation Challenge: Leadership for Transformation and Growth*. John Wiley & Sons Ltd, Chichester.

ADVICE FOR ENTREPRENEURS

Effective teamwork is critical for new product and service development. An effective team is one that has a mutual and shared accountability for its goal – the outcomes of the project will affect the evaluation of the individuals and the team as a whole.

When you work in a team, or are responsible for building or guiding a team, you will face a number of challenges and opportunities. To be effective, a team must be able to maintain collaboration, communication, and positive interactions over a sustained period of time. One of the most significant issues is helping team members understand and deal effectively with differences, rather than viewing others with differing preferences as 'odd', 'wrong', or 'ineffective'. Team members need to understand that 'differences are not deficits'. Group members can also sustain their team's working relationship when they are able to celebrate each other's strengths and use their differences to complement each other. In general, there is a need to provide for participation to increase acceptance, and to exploit a diverse range of experiences and perspectives. In general, an effective development team needs:

Competent team members, respectful of each other.
Adequate, but not excessive, resources.
A clear, common and elevating goal.
Unified commitment and shared standards.
A collaborative climate and participation in decision-making.
Principled leadership.
External support and recognition.

Adapted from Isaksen, S. and Tidd, J. (2006) *Meeting the Innovation Challenge: Leadership for Transformation and Growth*. John Wiley & Sons Ltd, Chichester.

STRATEGIC AND SOCIAL IMPACT

The traditional model for many public services – in the UK and elsewhere – has been the vertically integrated 'command and control' model, in which organisations undertake most of the steps involved in delivering not just the service to final consumers, but also many of the intermediate and support services required. In addition, most public services are – in principle – available to all. The concept of customer selection is in many cases either inappropriate or difficult to enforce. Given the evidence we have shown about private sector success rules for innovation, we should not be surprised if these structural characteristics of public sector organisations have made the delivery of innovation difficult, and slow.

(continued)

In the process of privatising UK public sector services, in energy, telecommunications and transport, and in attracting private capital into health, education and administrative support, some of these issues have been addressed. For example, in energy the electricity and gas industries have been 'vertically disintegrated', with primary energy assets separated from transmission, distribution and end user supply. In transport, track ownership was split from maintenance, train ownership and train operation. The record of achievement across these examples has been – to say the least – mixed.

Comparing the successes with the failures, it seems at least arguable that the best-performing services are those which have used their new structures to innovate and improve customer value. This is true of some of the energy and telecommunications supply businesses, which have chosen to focus on specific customer groups through targeted marketing, and deliver a set of modular services which can be tailored through 'mass customisation' and sourced from a limited range of suppliers.

The most spectacular failure – rail – was saddled with a new business structure which was itself much too complex, because of the number of relationships created by cutting the service into so many small entities. Some of the train operating companies have succeeded in creating new and improved services by targeted investments and new operating practices. However, for the most part they have been handicapped by the strategy of the main infrastructure owner – Railtrack – to concentrate on cost reduction rather than value creating innovation. Railtrack also miscalculated the importance of intangible assets – information, knowledge and skills – which were essential to improve the quality of its offer to immediate customers. The case of rail illustrates the necessity, in designing new business models for the public sector, to ensure that participants at every step in the value chain have clear incentives to innovate, and to develop the means to do so.

In health, the effects of recent changes in organisation and governance are only now beginning to become apparent. The budget of the UK National Health Service is around £76 billion, larger than the GDP of 155 member states of the United Nations. It is a large, complex organisation involving many stakeholders with diverse, and sometimes conflicting, goals. The initial simplistic approach of creating internal markets was replaced with a rather optimistic faith in the potential benefits of automation using IT. The current, more integrated strategy of organisational change, service innovation and selected investment in technology may be more complex to plan and manage, but is more likely to yield improvements in performance.

From Clayton (2003) in Tidd, J. and Hull, F.M. (eds) *Service Innovation: Organizational Responses to Technological Opportunities and Market Imperatives*. Imperial College Press, London.

Chapter Summary

There is a vast amount of management research on the subject of new product and service development, and we are now pretty certain what works and what does not. There are no guarantees that following the suggestions in this chapter will produce a blockbuster product, service or business, but if these elements are not managed well, your chances of success will be much lower. This is not supposed to discourage experimentation and calculated risk-taking, but rather to provide a foundation for evidence-based practice.

Research suggests that a range of factors affect the success of a potential new product or service, including product advantage, clear target market and attention to pre-development activities. Services and products are different in a number of ways, some of which will demand the adaptation of the standard models and prescriptions for new product development. A formal process for new product and service development should consist of distinct stages, such as concept development, business case, product development, pilot and commercialisation, separated by distinct decision points or gates, which have clear criteria such as product fit, product advantages and so on. Different stages of the process demand different criteria and different tools and methods. Useful tools and methods at the concept stage include segmentation, experimentation, focus groups and customer-partnering; and at the development stage useful tools include prototyping, design for production and QFD.

If you want to develop blockbuster products and services, you will need to attend to all elements of the system. Only paying attention to one element of the system will decrease significantly the likelihood of success. You must be clear about the desired outcome, at least in terms of what needs to be done to meet consumers' needs and kind of innovation you desire as a result. You will need to establish and manage a deliberate process that promotes cross-functional teamwork and integrate the practices outlined above. The right people must be on the team and they need to be supported by appropriate leadership and sponsorship. The working environment must support the people and the process. The climate within the team is critical, but a broader organisational climate conducive to innovation is optimal.

Discussion Questions

1. What are the key differences between managing operations in services and manufacturing? Think of a business, and identify the relative contributions to value-added of the service and physical product components.

2. To what extent do you think that manufacturing and services are converging? Try to think of an example of a manufacturing operation that increasingly features a service. Conversely, identify a service operation that is becoming more product-based.

3. In what ways do you think the development of new products differs from the development of new services?

4. Identify the relative importance of product/service attributes and organisational factors in successful development.

5. In practice, how many stages and gates do you think a process for new product development should have?

6. What is the different between the 'stage-gate' and 'development funnel' models of the new product development process?

7. What effect does the novelty of the new product or service have on the development process?

Team Exercise

Apply QFD to a real example of a new product or service. In a group, take the following steps:

1. Identify the target customer requirements, by market research or in class by 'brain-storming'. Try to include both tangible and intangible elements.
2. Rank or weight these requirements, based on your best knowledge of the target market segment.
3. Where possible, translate the requirements into measurable characteristics.
4. Identify different technical or design options to deliver these characteristics.
5. Compare or benchmark against real-life competing products.

See website for more information.
www.iande.info

Assignment

Prepare a 20 minute presentation which critically assesses the reasons for the success or failure of a new product, service or technology. 'New' in this context means something which was launched within the past five years or so, so that sufficient data and material exists to assess its success. For these reasons please avoid very recent innovations, or generic non-proprietary technologies such as 'the Internet'. The product or service should be sufficiently well-documented or known to you so that you can differentiate between controllable and uncontrollable factors:

Controllable	Uncontrollable
Technology or market strategy	Market potential
Product advantage	Market attractiveness
Pre-development activities	Competitor behaviour
Proficiency of development process	Capital requirements
Proficiency of marketing	Regulation or legislation

This should not simply be an assessment of the marketing and commercialisation of the product or service, but should include an analysis of as many as possible of the factors listed.

Key Terms Defined

Development funnel   an alternative to the stage-gate model, which takes into account the reduction in uncertainty as the process progresses, and the influence of real resource constraints.

Quality Function Deployment (QFD)   is a set of planning and communications routines, which are used to identify critical customer attributes and create a specific link between these and design parameters. It aims to answer three primary questions: What are the critical attributes for customers? What design parameters drive these attributes? What should the design parameter targets be for the new design?

Problem-solving style   individual differences in the ways people frame, perceive and attempt to solve problems: a 'developer' is someone who prefers to bring tasks to fulfilment, or who organises, synthesises, refines, and enhances basic ingredients, shaping them into a more complete and useful result; an 'explorer' is someone who prefers to venture into uncharted directions and follow possibilities wherever they might lead.

Stage-gate process   a structured process for new product or service development, which features a number of discrete stages, each with different decision criteria or 'gates' which they must pass.

Further Reading and Resources

The classic texts on new product development are those by Robert Cooper, for example, *Winning at New Products: Accelerating the Process from Idea to Launch* (Perseus Books, 2001), or Cooper, R.G. (2000) 'Doing it right: winning with new products', *Ivey Business Journal*, 64(6) (July/August), pp. 1–7 [available online: http://www.iveybusinessjournal.com/article.asp? intArticle_ID=235], or anything by Kim Clark and Steven Wheelwright, such as Wheelwright,

Steven C. and Clark, Kim B. (1997) 'Creating Project Plans to Focus Product Development', *Harvard Business Review*, September–October, or their book *Revolutionizing Product Development* (1992, Free Press). Paul Trott provides a good review of research in his text *Innovation Management and New Product Development* (2008, FT Prentice Hall, fourth edition), but for a more up to date review of the research, see Panne, van der, G., Beers, C. van and Kleinknecht, A. (2003) 'Success and failure of innovation: A literature review', *International Journal of Innovation Management*, 7(3), 309–338.

For more focused studies of new service development, see Berry, L. L., Shankar, V., Parish, J.T., Cadwallader, S. and Dotzel, T. (2006) 'Creating New Markets Through Service Innovation', *MIT Sloan Management Review*, 47(2), Winter. More comprehensive overviews of service innovation are provided by Ian Miles in the Special Issue on Innovation in Services, *International Journal of Innovation Management*, December, 2000, or in the books Tidd, J. and Hull, F.M. (2003) *Service Innovation: Organizational Responses to Technological Opportunities and Market Imperatives,* Imperial College Press, London; and Richard Normann's (2000) *Service Management – Strategy and leadership in service business*, Wiley, Chichester, third edition. Recent comprehensive handbooks on service development, both of which we have contributed to, are: F. Djellal and C. Gallouj (eds) *The Handbook of Innovation and Services* (Edward Elgar, 2010), and Gavriel Salvendy and Waldemar Karwowski (eds) *Introduction to Service Engineering* (Wiley, 2010).

References

1. Crespi, G., Criscuolo, C., and Haskel, J. (2006) Information Technology, Organisational Change and Productivity Growth: Evidence from UK Firms, *The Future of Science, Technology and Innovation Policy: Linking Research and Practice*, SPRU 40th Anniversary Conference, Brighton, UK, September 2006.

2. Tidd, J. and Hull, F.M. (2006) 'Managing Service Innovation: The need for selectivity rather than 'best-practice', *New Technology, Work and Employment*, 21(2), 139–161; Tidd, J. and Hull, F.M. (2003) *Service Innovation: Organizational Responses to Technological Opportunities and Market Imperatives.* Imperial College Press, London.

3. Cooper, R.G. (2000) 'Doing it right: winning with new products', *Ivey Business Journal*, 64(6) (July/August), pp. 1–7 [available online: http://www.iveybusinessjournal.com/article.asp?intArticle_ID=235]

4. Lynn, G.S. and Reilly, R.R. (2002). *Blockbusters: The five keys to developing great new products*. New York: HarperBusiness.

5. Wheelwright, Steven C. and Clark, Kim B. (1997) 'Creating Project Plans to Focus Product Development', *Harvard Business Review*, September–October.

6. Tidd, J. and Bodley, K. (2002) 'The effect of project novelty on the new product development process', *R&D Management*, 32(2), 127–138.

CASE STUDY 9
New Concept Development at Philips

Philips

Philips has a proud history of innovation and has been responsible for launching several 'new to the world' product categories, like X-ray tubes in its early days, the Compact Cassette in the 1960s followed by the Compact Disc in the 1980s, and more recently Ambilight TV. These successes are linked to Philips' deep understanding of innovation, enabled notably by significant R&D investments and strong traditions in design.

Since 2003, Philips has been engaged in a market-driven change programme to rejuvenate its brand and approach to new product innovation with expertise on end-user insights. Six years later, the end-user insights approach has significantly influenced the way Philips innovates, in line with the new brand promise of 'sense and simplicity'. Yet in 2000, new product innovation was still predominantly shaped by R&D, particularly in its lighting business. In that same year, Philips incurred a net loss of EUR 3206 million. Management was focused on dissolving the Components business, returning the Semiconductor business to profitability, simplifying the organisation and making cost savings.

Philips' role in the global lighting industry had always been dominant. Philips Lighting was Philips' 'cash cow'; it operated in a mature, low-growth oligopoly market in which finding new approaches to realise bottom-line growth was the main challenge. End-user driven innovation was a new approach to innovation, perhaps truly a 'radical' one given the division's history. How was this new approach piloted?

Exploratory Stages

Following Albert Einstein's notion that 'insanity is doing the same things over and over again and expecting different results', senior management realised that something had to change. Consequently, in early 2001 the Chief Technology Officer of the Lamps business initiated a set of complementary activities of an exploratory nature in order to catalyse learning opportunities and help shape a platform for a future vision. These activities were:

☐ A vision team in the Central Lighting Development Lab. This involved four employees with an equal male and female representation, two of the people were new to the development lab, the other two were well established and anchored informal leaders. The team's role was to bring outside inspiration into the development organisation via lectures, workshops, visits and books. These activities resulted in the start of two 'out of the box' innovation projects in 2002, one of which led to the invention of Ambilight TV.

☐ An exploratory automotive project for car headlights. This involved piloting a combination of the Dialog Decision Process (DDP)1 and a Philips Design innovation process based on socio-cultural insights.

☐ A Philips Lighting 'New Business Creation' (NBC) group. This involved a team of four senior managers and one lateral thinker, whose role was to challenge mainstream business assumptions by asking simple questions. Established as a new organisational unit in a six month period, the NBC group was set up to provide the environment for 'out of the box' business development. Once the unit was created, the main open question was how to fill the NBC idea pipeline?

Think the Lighting Future Project

Building on the experiences of these three exploratory projects and using other Philips knowledge on radical innovation, the 'Think the Lighting Future' project (TTLF) was defined at the end of 2001. It was established in response to the CEO's ambition to identify a 10% top-line growth opportunity (approximately EUR 500 million) which could be achieved in a five to seven year time-frame. Senior management was instrumental in initiating the TTLF project. The project had three tangible deliverables for the end of 2002:

☐ Clarify alternative scope definitions for Philips Lighting that could deliver 10% top-line growth in the longer term.

☐ Define two to three New Business Creation projects.

☐ Define a process for knowledge sharing and updating the NBC long-list.

In addition there were several 'intangible' aspirations for the project – for example, it was envisaged that it would:

☐ Provide a 'growing in opportunity' for the senior management team, thus creating commitment for additional scope.

☐ Prepare for implementation (avoid 'not invented here syndrome') for critical mass of colleagues.

☐ Radiate, let involved colleagues experience that the whole exercise is about doing different things . . . and doing them differently . . .

☐ Create the confidence to deal with a stretching vision.

'Think the Lighting Future' was a 'presidential project' with core team participation from each Lighting business group, Philips Design and Philips Research:

which was – next to its scope of 10 years ahead – an innovation in itself. In addition, special attention was put on forming a diverse team to enable different views to be captured. Importantly this project provided opportunities for learning and improvement of the corporate innovation process – for example, the original three-step design process (information sharing, ideation, idea development and concept definition) was expanded by a fourth step (translation to action).

Emphasis was also placed on creating broad ownership from the beginning both in management via the DDP approach and in the executing functions via multi-functional workshops. Subsequently the dialogue decision process was further expanded to a 'trialog' process involving the decision team, the core team (i.e. the decision preparation team) and the implementation team.

Vital to orchestrating communication was the set-up of Think the Lighting Future as an extended Dialogue (trialog) Decision Process around three key innovation dimensions:

☐ People – understanding and serving both end-users' explicit current as well as their implicit emerging needs.
☐ Technology – understanding and using current and emerging technology options to enable user relevant functionality.
☐ Business – understanding current and emerging market characteristics and dynamics; applying appropriate and future-proof business models.

Thirty-two colleagues were invited to two workshops. They came from different innovation backgrounds (marketing, business development, R&D) and from different Lighting businesses, Design and Research teams. Maximal possible global presence was established. Since TTLF was a highly visible presidential project, workshop participation was seen as an honour. The workshops served several tangible and intangible purposes, including:

☐ Enriching the core-team work by existing corporate knowledge.
☐ Generation of business ideas seeds.
☐ Preparing for later implementation.
☐ Building a 'performing' team around a shared vision.

All workshop flows and all tools used during the workshops were especially designed such that the holistic outcomes became highly probable by equally and simultaneously focusing on the different dimensions: people and their needs, technology enabling new solution spaces and business including generic competition and existing next to emerging business models facilitating value creation.

By the end of 2002, TTLF was concluded and was regarded as a successful exploration and visioning project. It led to the selection of a 'theme' for new business: Atmosphere Provider, which was about 'empowering people to become their own light designers'. It also led to three new business creation projects and delivered a list of ideas for New Business Creation. However, no additional turnover had yet been generated. The real work was about to start . . .

Atmosphere Provider Programme

In July 2003 senior management launched the 'Atmosphere Provider' programme. The programme lasted two and half years and was given some explicit and several implicit deliverables:

- □ Bring 'Atmosphere Provider' as a theme to life.
  - ○ Create a 'need-scape' for the new innovation area.
  - ○ Envisage the boundaries/solution space of the innovation and growth opportunities.
- □ Initiate the creation of a related patent portfolio.
- □ Prove the business potential by piloting the three new business creation projects.
- □ Exploration towards new business proposition definition including initial product concepts.
  - ○ Prototyping and market testing.
  - ○ Business case development and transfer to mainstream business.

And implicitly –

- □ Prepare for transfer and scaling up.
- □ Initiate the building of an Atmosphere Provider network (with shared vision, creativity, cross-functional and discipline perspectives, embracing the required new way of working, etc.).
- □ Pioneer the end-user driven innovation approach.

The programme's architecture was designed to ensure cross-fertilisation between the development of the broader business theme and the three new business creation projects; emerging insights from creating the new business were captured via foundation documents; general observations derived from the theme development were fed back into NBC projects.

The core of the programme comprised a team of four people: the overall programme manager who had led the TTLF project and three project managers, of whom one had been a TTLF core team member whilst the other two were new to Philips Lighting. Over time, a small support team became involved: a lighting designer, an experienced market researcher, a marketing specialist and several colleagues from Philips Design. The team was small and flexible; additional skills and capacity were brought in on an as-needed basis, which in turn required good communication skills from the project managers and the commitment from senior management to ensure the needed resources were made available to the team when required.

Initiation:
☐ 10 July 2003 in the Philips Lighting Senior Management meeting.

Deliverables:
☐ Bring the Atmosphere Provider theme to life.
☐ Show proof points via business potential in the three selected projects.
☐ Investment: EUR 2.85 million from August 2003 to December 2005.

Context of assignment:
☐ Cross-functional with impact on Philips Lighting level beyond a single Business Group, positioned under Global Marketing, unclear ownership on executive level, no standard processes or tools => learn as you go.

Characteristics of assignment:
☐ Innovation for additional profitable growth (out of the box), market-led, pioneering, emphasis on results in the form of content, high risk and high reward, phase 1 of change management.

Core team:
☐ Dorothea Seebode, Gerard Harkin, Benedicte van Houtert, Paul Brulez, followed up by Stefan Verbrugh (from April 2004).

Extended team:
☐ Markus Reisinger, Liesbeth Ploeg (from Dec.04), Ronald Dalderup (from Jan.05).

Mindset:
☐ Focus on results, commitment, dialogue.

By the end of 2005:
☐ In total over 1800 people had been involved globally, across and beyond Philips Lighting.
☐ Three foundation documents were published with over 1000 copies distributed.
☐ Patents: > 50 IDs submitted, > 25 patents filed, > 10 patents in pipeline.

Case Questions

1. Identify the key stages in the development process, starting at the initial brief to the final selection of the three business cases.
2. What role did senior management and leadership play in the development of the new concepts?
3. How did cross-functional teams contribute to the translation of concepts into business cases?

Source: Extract from Dorothea Seebode, Gerard Harkin and John Bessant (2009) *Radical Innovation at Philips Lighting.*

 Go online to find the full version of the Philips Lighting case study.

www.iande.info

Summary of Web Resources

Cases

- Bank of Scotland
- Coloplast
- Philips Lighting

Media

- Innocent Smoothies
- Von Hippel on lead users

Tools

- Stage-gate process
- Quality function deployment

Chapter 10

Creating New Ventures

Go online to find additional . . .

Cases

Tools

Media

www.iande.info

Types of New Venture

In the UK, between 400,000 and 500,000 new businesses are created each year. At the same time, each year around 300,000 firms fail, suggesting a net annual rate of new business creation of some 100,000 to 200,000 firms. However, most of these new businesses are not very creative or innovative, and entrepreneurship is much more than the creation of a new business.

Contrary to popular belief, the majority of small firms are not particularly innovative. The goal of most entrepreneurs is to achieve independence of employment, rather than the creation of innovative businesses. However, here we focus on the creation and development of *innovative* new ventures, those which aim to offer new products or services, or are based on novel processes or ways of creating value. These are not necessarily, or even frequently, based on inventions, new technology or scientific breakthroughs. Instead, the entrepreneur has chosen or been forced to create a new business in order to exploit the innovation.

People create new ventures for many different reasons, and it is critical to understand the different motives and mechanisms of entrepreneurship:

Lifestyle entrepreneurs – those who seek independence, and wish to earn a living based around their personal circumstances and values, for example, individual professional consulting practices, or home-based craft businesses. Statistically speaking, these are the most common type of new venture, and are an important source of self-employment in almost all economies. Contrary to popular belief, the majority of such small firms are not particularly creative or innovative, and instead are simply exploiting an asset (e.g. a shop), or expertise (e.g. IT consulting).

Growth entrepreneurs – those who aim to become wealthy and powerful through the creation and aggressive growth of new businesses (plural, as they are often serial entrepreneurs who create a string of new ventures). They are more likely to measure their success in terms of wealth, influence and reputation. Although we tend to think of people like Bill Gates or Steve Jobs, more typical examples are in relatively conservative, capital-intensive and well-understood sectors such as retail, property and commodities. Successful growth entrepreneurs tend to create very large corporations through acquisitions, which may dominate national markets, and the founders may become very wealthy and influential.

Innovative entrepreneurs – individuals who are driven by the desire to create or change something, whether in the private, public or third sectors. Independence, reputation and wealth are not the primary goals in such cases, although are often achieved anyway. Rather, the main motivation is to actually change or create something new. Innovative entrepreneurs include technological entrepreneurs and social entrepreneurs, but such ventures are rarely based on inventions, new technology or scientific breakthroughs. Instead, the entrepreneur has chosen or been forced to create a new venture in order to create or change something. These are the focus of this chapter.

Social Entrepreneurs

We discussed social innovation and entrepreneurship in Chapter 2, but much of this takes place in large, established public, private or third-sector organisations. Here we focus on new venture creation. There are numerous definitions of social entrepreneurship, but most include two critical elements:

1. The aim is to create social change and value, rather than commercial innovation and financial value. Conventional commercial entrepreneurship often results in new products and services and growth in the economy and employment, but social benefits are not the explicit goal.
2. It involves business, public and third-sector organisations to achieve this aim. Conventional commercial entrepreneurship tends to focus on the individual entrepreneur and new venture, which occupy the business sector, although organisations in the public or third sectors may be stakeholders or customers.

Examples of applications of social entrepreneurship include:

- poverty relief;
- community development;
- health and welfare;
- environment and sustainability;
- arts and culture;
- education and employment.

However, social entrepreneurship is not simply entrepreneurship in a different context. Traditional public and third-sector organisations have often failed to deliver improvement or change because of the constraints of organisation, culture, funding or regulation. For example, in many public and third-sector organisations the needs of the funders or employees may become more important to satisfy then the needs of their target community.

Therefore social entrepreneurs share most of the characteristic of entrepreneurs, but are different is some important respects:

- *Motives and aims* – less concerned with independence and wealth, and more on social means and ends.
- *Time-frame* – less emphasis on short-term growth and longer term harvesting of the venture, and more concern on long-term change and enduring heritage.
- *Resources* – less reliance on the firm and management team to execute the venture, and greater reliance on a network of stakeholders and resources to develop and deliver change.

Key characteristic which appear to distinguish social entrepreneurs from their commercial counterparts include a high level of empathy and need for social justice. The concept of empathy is complex, but includes the ability to recognise and emotionally share the feelings and needs of others, and is associated with a desire to help. However, whilst empathy and a need for social justice may be necessary attributes of a social entrepreneur, they are not sufficient. These may make a social venture desirable, but not necessarily feasible.[1] The feasibility will be influenced by the more conventional personal characteristics of an entrepreneur, such as background and personality, but also some contextual factors more common in public and third sector. Potential barriers to social entrepreneurship:

- Access to and support of local networks of social and community-based organisations, e.g. relationships and trust in informal networks.
- Access to and support of government and political infrastructure, e.g. nationality or ethnic restrictions.

ENTREPRENEURSHIP IN ACTION

Marc Koska and Star Syringe

Marc Koska founded Star Syringe in 1996 to design and develop disposable, single-use or so-called 'auto-disable syringes' (ADS) to help prevent the transmission of diseases like HIV/AIDS. For example, over 23 million infections of HIV and Hepatitis are given to otherwise healthy patients through syringe reuse every year.

Marc had no formal training in engineering, but had relevant design experience from previous jobs in modelling and plastics design. He designed the ADS according to the following basic principles:

Cheap: The same price as a standard disposable plastic syringe
Easy: Manufactured on existing machinery, to cut setup costs
Simple: Used as closely as possible in the same way as a standard disposable plastic syringe
Scalable: Licensed to local manufacturers, leveraging resources in a sustainable way.

The ADS is not manufactured in-house, but by Star licensees based all over the world. The company now licenses the technology to international aid agencies and is recognised by the UNICEF and the World Health Organisation (WHO). Star alliance is the network which connects the numerous manufacturing licensees to the global marketplace. The alliance includes 19 international manufacturing partners, and serves markets in over 20 countries. The combined capacity of the alliance licensees is close to 1 billion annual units.

His dedication and persistent drive over the last 20 years have earned him respect from leaders in state health services as well as industry: in February 2005 for example the Federal Minister for Health in Pakistan presented Marc with an award for Outstanding Contribution to Public Health for his work on safer syringes, and in 2006 the company won the UK Queen's Award for Enterprise and International Trade.

Sources: www.starsyringe.com, web.mac.com/marckoska/

 Go online to listen to Carmel McConnell discuss how business skills can be applied to social businesses.

www.iande.info

Technological Entrepreneurs

The creation of a technology venture is the interaction of individual skills and disposition and the technological and market characteristics. The US studies emphasise the role of personal characteristics, such as family background, goal orientation, personality and motivation, whereas the European studies stress the role of the environment, including institutional support and resources.[2]

The decision to start a technology venture typically begins with a desire to gain independence and to escape the bureaucracy of a large organisation, whether it is in the public or private sector. Thus the background, psychological profile and work and technical experience of a technical entrepreneur all contribute to the decision to create a new venture.

Education and training are major factors that distinguish the founders of technology ventures from other entrepreneurs. The median level of education of technical entrepreneurs in the US study was a master's degree, and with the important exception of biotechnology-based ventures, a doctorate was superfluous. Significantly, the levels of education of technical entrepreneurs do not differentiate them from other scientists and engineers. However, potential technical entrepreneurs tend to have higher levels of productivity than their technical work colleagues, measured in terms of papers published or patents granted. This suggests that potential entrepreneurs may be more driven than their corporate counterparts.

In addition to a master's-level education, on average, a technical entrepreneur will have around 13 years of work experience before establishing a new venture. In the case of Route 128, the entrepreneurs' work experience is typically with a single incubator organisation, whereas technical entrepreneurs in Silicon Valley tend to have gained their experience from a larger number of firms before establishing their own business. This suggests that there is no ideal pattern of previous work experience. However, experience of development work appears to be more important than work in basic research. As a result of the formal education and experience required, a typical technical entrepreneur will be aged between 30 and 40 years when establishing his or her first technology venture. This is relatively late in life compared to other types of venture, and is due to a combination of ability and opportunity. On the one hand, it typically takes between 10 and 15 years for a potential entrepreneur to attain the necessary technical and business experience. On the other hand, many people begin to have greater financial and family responsibilities at this time. Thus there appears to be a window of opportunity to start a technology venture, some time in the mid-thirties. Moreover, different fields of technology have different entry and growth potential. Therefore the choice of a potential entrepreneur will be constrained by the dynamics of the technology and markets. The capital requirements, product lead times and potential for growth are likely to vary significantly between sectors.

Unlike general entrepreneurs, technology entrepreneurs appear to have only moderate n-Ach, but a low need for affiliation (n-Aff). This suggests that the need for independence, rather than success, is the most significant motivator for technical entrepreneurs. Technology entrepreneurs also tend to have an internal locus of control. In other words, they believe that they have personal control over outcomes, whereas someone with an external locus of control believes that outcomes are the result of chance, powerful institutions or others. More sophisticated psychometric techniques such as the Myers–Briggs type indicators (MBTI) confirm the differences between technology entrepreneurs and other scientists and engineers.

Numerous surveys indicate that most technology entrepreneurs claim to have been frustrated in their previous job. This frustration appears to result from the interaction of the psychological predisposition of the potential entrepreneur and poor selection, training and development by the parent organisation. Specific events may also trigger the desire or need to establish a technology venture, such as a major reorganisation or downsizing of the parent organisation.

ENTREPRENEURSHIP IN ACTION

Mike Lynch and Autonomy

Mike Lynch founded the software company Autonomy in 1994, a spin-off from his first start-up Neurodynamics. Lynch, a grammar school graduate, studied information science at Cambridge where he carried out PhD research on probability theory. He rejected a conventional research career as he had found his summer job at GEC Marconi a 'boring, tedious place'. In 1991, aged 25, he approached the banks to raise money for his first venture, Neurodynamics, but 'met a nice chap who laughed a lot and admitted that he was only used to lending money to people to open newsagents'. He subsequently raised the initial £2000 from a friend of a friend. Neurodynamics developed pattern recognition software which it sold to specialist niche users such as the UK police force for matching fingerprints and identifying disparities in witness statements, and banks to identify signatures on cheques.

Autonomy was spun off in 1994 to exploit applications of the technology in Internet, intranet and media sectors, and received the financial backing of venture capitalists Apax, Durlacher and Enic. Autonomy was floated on the Easdaq in July 1998, on the Nasdaq in 1999, and in February 2000 was worth US$5bn, making Lynch the first British software billionaire. Autonomy creates software which manages unstructured information, which accounts for 80% of all data. The software applies Bayesian probabilistic techniques to identify patterns of data or text, and compared to crude keyword searches can better take into account context and relationships. The software is patented in the US, but not in Europe as patent law does not allow patent protection of software. The business generates revenues through selling software for cataloguing and searching information direct to clients such as the BBC, Barclays, BT, Eli Lilly, General Motors, Merril Lynch, News Corporation, Nationwide, Proctor & Gamble and Reuters. In addition, it has more than 50 licensing agreements with leading software companies to use its technology, including Oracle, Sun and Sybase. A typical licence will include a lump sum of US$100,000 plus a royalty on sales of 10–30%. By means of such license deals Autonomy aims to become an integral part of a range of software and the standard for intelligent recognition and searching. In the financial year ending March 2000 the company reported its first profit of US$440,000 on a turnover of $11.7 million. The company employs 120 staff, split between Cambridge in the UK and Silicon Valley, and spends 17% of its revenues on R&D. In 2004 sales were around $60 million, with an average licence costing $360,000, and high gross margins of 95%. New customers included AOL, BT, CitiBank, Deutsche Bank, Ford, the 2004 Greek Olympics, and the defence agencies in the USA, Spain, Sweden and Singapore. Repeat customers accounted for 30% of sales.

Internet entrepreneurs and web businesses are the most common type of technology-based venture today. Go online to see the case studies ihavemoved.com and threadless.com for two very different examples.

www.iande.info

Context for Entrepreneurship

Most of what we know about innovative new ventures is based on the experience of start-up firms in the USA, in particular the growth of biotechnology, semiconductor and software firms. Many of these originated from a parent or 'incubator' organisation, typically either an academic institution or large well-established firm. Examples of university incubators include Stanford which spawned much of Silicon Valley, the Massachusetts Institute of Technology (MIT) which spawned Route 128 in Boston, and Imperial and Cambridge in the UK. MIT in particular has become the archetype academic incubator, and in addition to the creation of Route 128, its alumni have established some 200 new ventures in northern California, and account for more than a fifth of employment in Silicon Valley. The so-called MIT model has been adopted worldwide, so far with limited success. For example, in 1999 Cambridge University in the UK formed a UK government-sponsored joint venture with MIT to help develop spin-offs in the UK. However, to put such initiatives into perspective, Hermann Hauser, a venture capitalist, notes 'Stanford alumni have produced companies worth a trillion dollars. MIT half a trillion dollars. If Cambridge is getting to $20bn we will be lucky.' One reason is the differences in scale. Mike Lynch, founder of the software company Autonomy, observes 'Silicon Valley is 60 miles long and in the last few months there will have been 70 to 80 money raisings in the $50 million to $200 million range. In Cambridge we might think of one, perhaps.'

ENTREPRENEURSHIP IN ACTION

Boston's Route 128

The cluster of universities in Boston and Cambridge in the USA, which includes the Massachusetts Institute of Technology (MIT), Harvard, Boston University and 70 other colleges and universities, has a long tradition of spawning spin-off firms.

The success of the region can be traced back to the defence-related investments in computing and software which helped to create incubator firms such as Compaq, Digital, Data General, Lucent, Lotus, Raytheon and Wang in the 1970s, and more recently the creation of many life sciences-based ventures in biotechnology and medical devices.

For several decades now, the venture capital industry has consistently funded the creation or growth of around 200 to 300 new firms each year with annual funding of around US$2 billion

(continued)

(this more than quadrupled during the Internet Boom/Bubble of 1998/2000). To date MIT alone has helped to create 4000 new firms worldwide with total revenues of US$232 billion, with more than a thousand of these firms still based in Massachusetts

Source: Wonglimpiyarat, J. (2006) 'The Boston Route 128 Model of High-Tech Industry Development', *International Journal of Innovation Management*, 10(1), 47–64.

Examples of large incubator firms include the Xerox PARC and Bell Laboratories in the USA, which spawned Fairchild Semiconductor, which in turn led to numerous spin-offs including Intel, Advanced Memory Systems, Teledyne and Advanced Micro-Devices. Similarly, Engineering Research Associates (ERA) led to more than 40 new firms, including Cray, Control Data Systems, Sperry and Univac. In many cases, incubator firms provide the technical entrepreneurs, and the associated academic institutions provide the additional qualified manpower.

ENTREPRENEURSHIP IN ACTION

Spin-off Companies from Xerox's PARC Labs

Xerox established its Palo Alto Research Center (PARC) in California in 1970. PARC was responsible for a large number of technological innovations in the semiconductor lasers, laser printing, Ethernet networking technology and web indexing and searching technologies, but it is generally acknowledged that many of it most significant innovations were the result of individuals who left the company and firms which spun-off from PARC, rather than developed via Xerox itself. For example, many of the user-interface developments at Apple originated at Xerox, as did the basis of Microsoft's Word package. By 1998 Xerox PARC had spun-out 24 firms, including ten which went public such as 3Com, Adobe, Documentum, and SynOptics. By 2001 the value of the spin-off companies was more than twice that of Xerox itself.

A debate continues to the reasons for this, most attributing the failure to retain the technologies in-house to corporate ignorance and internal politics. However, most of the technologies did not simply 'leak out', but instead were granted permission by Xerox, which often provided non exclusive licenses and an equity stake in the spin-off firms. This suggests that Xerox's research and business managers saw little potential for exploiting these technologies in its own businesses. One of the reasons for the failure to commercialise these technologies in-house was that Xerox had been highly successful with its integrated product-focused strategy, which made it more difficult to recognise and exploit potential new *businesses*.

Source: Chesbrough, H. (2003) *Open Innovation: The new imperative for creating and profiting from technology* (Harvard Business School Press, Boston, Massachusetts).

Spin-off firms tend to cluster around their respective incubator organisations, forming regional networks of expertise. The firms tend to remain close to their parents for a number of technical and personal reasons. Most spin-offs retain contacts with their parent organisations to gain financial and technical support, and are often reluctant to disrupt their social and family lives whilst establishing a new venture. Perhaps surprisingly, the mortality rate of spin-offs is lower than that of most types of new firm, around 20–30% in 10 years compared to more than 80% for other types of new business. One explanation for their higher survival rate is that the barriers to entry are higher than for many other businesses, in terms of expertise and capital. Therefore those new ventures that are able to overcome such barriers are more likely to survive. The concentration of start-ups in a region can create positive feedback, through demonstration effects and by increasing the demand for, and experience of, supporting institutions, such as venture capitalists, legal services and contract research and production, thereby improving the environment and probability of success of subsequent start-ups. Failures are an inherent part of such a system, and provided a steady stream of new venture proposals exists and venture capitalists maintain diverse investment portfolios and are ruthless with failed ventures, the system continues to learn from both good and bad investments.

However, given the unique circumstances of the US environment in the 1970s and 1980s, we should question the generalisability of the lessons of Silicon Valley and Route 128. Specifically, the role of the defence industry investment, liberal tax regimes and sources of venture capital were unique. In addition, it is important to distinguish the evolutionary growth of such regional clusters of innovative new ventures from more recent attempts to establish science parks based around universities. For example, success of science parks in Europe and Asia in the 1990s, and other attempts to emulate the early US experiences, has been limited, and studies comparing firms located on and off university science parks conclude that there were no statistically significant differences between their technological inputs, such as expenditure on R&D, and outputs, such as new products and patents. Often such science parks provide little more than cheap, short-term leases and a prestigious address.

In addition to individual entrepreneurs, a successful entrepreneurial system needs the broad participation of a diversity of entrepreneurial actors and institutions, including small and larger firms, universities, and sources of funding and support.

Broad participation refers to the need for an inclusive system of development, production and consumption of innovations. Early innovations can be traced to individual inventors or more often a combination of an inventor and entrepreneur, and their efforts were often only affordable by the wealthy elite. This system is often referred to as the Schumpeter Model 1 of innovation, after the economic historian Joseph Schumpeter. However, as Schumpeter and others noted, innovation became more and more the province of larger organisations, characterised by greater economies of research, development, production and sales. This is often referred to as the Schumpeter Model 2 of innovation. It is characterised by mass production and consumption, but more fundamentally by workers and consumers who believe that growth and innovation are both inevitable and desirable. In this system the sources of innovation are more distributed, for example, it is difficult to trace individual inventors, and educated users play a more significant part in the development and evolution of innovations.

The diversity of the entrepreneurial species refers to the co-existence of both Schumpeterian models of innovation. Individual inventors and entrepreneurs, small and large firms co-exist and make different contributions. For example, in the computer games industry, large firms are necessary to test, distribute and support games, but the design, development and improvement of games is the result of inputs of numerous developers and users.

Roles of Small and Large Firms

The relationship between the size of firm and degree of innovation is unclear. In theory, large and small firms have different advantages and disadvantages:[3]

- Larger firms are more able to exploit economies of scale and scope in innovation, including research, development, production and sales. For example, large firms dominate where large expenditures on R&D are necessary, such as in aerospace or pharmaceuticals, where there are significant production economies of scale, as in automobile or consumer electronics, or where high-volume global sales are necessary, as in fast-moving consumer goods (FMCGs). However, larger firms suffer from high levels of bureaucracy and may neglect higher risk or lower volume opportunities.
- Small firms are less bureaucratic, and are able to flourish in smaller market niches which may be unattractive to larger firms. Motivation is typically much higher in such organisations. However, they lack internal resources and must therefore rely more on external sources of innovation and partnerships to develop and exploit innovations.

In practice, this means that neither large nor small firms are inherently more or less innovative. Instead, they tend to exhibit different patterns of innovation due to these different relative advantages.

In terms of innovation, the performance of SMEs is easily exaggerated. Early studies based on innovation counts consistently indicated that when adjusted for size, smaller firms created more new products than their larger counterparts. However, methodological shortcomings appear to undermine this clear message. When the divisions and subsidiaries of larger organisations are removed from such samples, and the innovations weighted according to their technological merit and commercial value, the relationship between firm size and innovation is reversed: larger firms create proportionally more significant innovations than SMEs.

Research over the past decade or so suggests that the innovative activities of SMEs exhibit broadly similar characteristics across sectors. They:

- are more likely to involve product innovation than process innovation;
- are focused on products for niche markets, rather than mass markets;
- will be more common amongst producers of final products, rather than producers of components;
- will frequently involve some form of external linkage;
- tend to be associated with growth in output and employment, but not necessarily profit.

Unlike large firms, small firms tend to be specialised rather than diversified in their technological competencies and product range. However, as with large firms, it is impossible to make robust generalisations about their technological trajectories and innovation strategies.

TABLE 10.1   Types of innovative new ventures

	Superstars: small firms into big since 1950	New technology-based firms (NTBFs)	Specialized	Supplier-dominated
Examples	Polaroid, DEC, TI, Xerox, Intel, Microsoft, Compaq, Sony, Casio, Benetton	Start-ups in electronics, biotechnology and software	Producer of goods (machines, components, instruments, software)	Traditional products (e.g. textiles, wood products, food products) and many services
Sources of competitive advantage	Successful exploitation of major invention or technological trajectory	1. Product or process development in fast-moving and specialised area 2. Privatising academic research	Combining technologies to meet users' needs	Integration and adaptation of innovations by suppliers
Main tasks of innovation strategy	Preparing replacements for the original invention (or inventor)	1. 'Superstar' or 'specialised supplier'? 2. Knowledge or money?	Links to advanced users and pervasive technologies	Exploiting new IT-based opportunities in design, distribution and co-ordination

Kurt Hoffman and his colleagues have recently pointed out that relatively little research has been undertaken on innovation in small firms: what research has been done tends to concentrate on the small group of spectacular high-tech successes (or failures) rather than the much more numerous run-of-the-mill small firms coping (say) with the introduction of IT into their distribution systems.[4]

Table 10.1 tries to categorise these differences. Until recently, attention has been focused on the left-hand side of the table – the spectacular and visible successes amongst small innovating firms: in particular, the 'superstars' that became big, and those of the technology-based firms that often want to become big. As we have seen earlier in this chapter, recent more systematic surveys of innovative activities and of small firms show two other classes of small firm with less spectacular innovation strategies, but of far greater importance to the overall economy: specialised suppliers of production inputs, and firms whose sources of innovation are mainly their suppliers.

Superstars are large firms that have emerged from small beginnings, through high rates of growth based on the exploitation of a major invention (e.g. instant photography, reprography), or a rich technological trajectory (e.g. semiconductors, software), enabling small firms to exploit first-mover advantages like patent protection (see Chapter 6). Successful innovators often either accumulated their technological knowledge in large firms before leaving to start their own, or they offered their invention to large firms but were refused (examples: Polaroid, Xerox). Few superstars have emerged either in the chemical industry over the past 50 years, or – contrary to expectations – out of biotechnology firms over the past 15 years, probably because the barriers to entry (in R&D, production, or marketing) remain high.

The examples in Table 10.1 show that many superstars are from the USA, although we can find European and Japanese examples. Experience suggests that one of the main challenges facing the management of superstars is their transition from the original innovator and the original innovation to new management and a new line of products. Beyond the period of spectacular growth, the characteristics behind the original success can become sources of 'core rigidities'. Successful innovators are often strong characters who do not necessarily encourage diversity in ideas and approaches within the firm. Successful innovations are often well protected by patents and other first-comer advantages, which can blunt the drive for improvement and change. These difficulties have beset companies like DEC, Polaroid and Xerox. An interesting exercise is to speculate about the future of today's superstars: what will happen to Microsoft after Bill Gates, or Apple after Steve Jobs?

New technology-based firms (NTBFs) are small firms that have emerged recently from large firms and large laboratories in such fields as electronics, software and biotechnology. They are usually specialised in the supply of a key component, subsystem, service or technique to larger firms, who may often be their former employers. Contrary to a widespread belief, most of the NTBFs in electronics and software have emerged from corporate or government laboratories involved in development and testing activities. It is only with the advent of biotechnology (and, more recently software), that university laboratories have become regular sources of NTBFs, thereby strengthening the strong direct links that have always existed between university-based research and the pharmaceutical industry. However, some observers criticise this trend, and fear the 'privatisation' of university research in biotechnology will in the long term reduce the rate of scientific progress and innovation and their contribution to economic and social welfare.

The management of NTBFs faces two sets of strategic problems:

1. The first relates to long-term prospects for growth. Very few technology-based small firms can become superstars, since they provide mainly specialised 'niche' products with no obvious or spectacular synergies with other markets. How far the firm will grow, or how long it will survive, will often depend on its ability to negotiate the transition from the first to the second (improved) generation of products, and to develop the supporting managerial competencies.
2. How far the NTBF will grow depends on the second strategic choice: whether the management is aiming to maximise long-term value of the business, or merely seeking an increase in income and independence. Thus, owners of small firms often sell their firms after a few years and live off their investments. And university researchers set up consultancy firms,

either to increase their personal income (the BMW effect), or to find supplementary income for their university-based research and teaching activities in times of increasing financial stringency.

Specialised supplier firms design, develop and build specialised inputs into production, in the form of machinery, instruments and (increasingly) software, and interact closely with their (often large) technically progressive customers. They perform relatively little formal R&D, but are nonetheless a major source of the active development of significant innovations, with major contributions being made by design and production staff.

Finally, most small firms fall into the *supplier-dominated* category, with their suppliers of production inputs as their main sources of new technology. These firms depend heavily on their suppliers for their innovations, and therefore are often unable to appropriate firm-specific technology as a source of competitive advantage. Technology will become more important in future, with the growing range of potential IT applications offered by suppliers, especially in service activities like distribution and co-ordination. An increasing range of small firms will therefore need to obtain the technological competencies to be able to specify, purchase, install and maintain software systems that help increase their competitiveness. Whether these competencies will become distinctive, *core* competencies is less clear, given that they can be adopted by all small firms. Distinctive advantage will emerge only where the software competencies are difficult to imitate, namely in developing and operating complex systems. Amongst small firms, such competencies are less likely to emerge in those *using* software than amongst those *supplying* software services.

Role of University Incubators

The creation and sharing of intellectual property is a core role of a university, but managing it for commercial gain is a different challenge. Most universities with significant commercial research contracts understand how to license, and the roles of all parties – the academics, the university and the commercial organisation – are relatively clear. In particular, the academic will normally continue with the research whilst possibly having a consultancy arrangement with the commercial company. However, forming an independent company is a different matter. Here both the university and the scientist must agree that spin-out is the most viable option for technology commercialisation and must negotiate a spin-out deal. This may include questions of, for example, equity split, royalties, academic and university investment in the new venture, academic secondment, identification and transfer of intellectual property and use of university resources in the start-up phase. In short, it is complicated. As Chris Evans, founder of Chiroscience and Merlin Ventures notes: 'Academics and universities . . . have no management, no muscle, no vision, no business plan and that is 90% of the task of exploiting science and taking it to the marketplace. There is a tendency for universities to think, "we invented the thing so we are already 50% there". The fact is they are 50% to nowhere' (*Times Higher*, 27 March 1998). A characteristically provocative statement, but it does highlight the gulf between research and successful commercialisation.

Many universities have accepted and followed the fashion for the commercial exploitation of technology, but typically put too much emphasis on the importance of the technology and ownership of the intellectual property, and 'fail to recognise the importance and sophistication of the business knowledge and expertise of management and other parties who contribute to the non-technical aspects of technology shaping and development . . . the linear model gives no insight into the interplay of technology push and market pull'.

Since the mid-1980s the role of universities in the commercialisation of technology has increased significantly. For example, the number of patents granted to US universities doubled between 1984 and 1989, and doubled again between 1989 and 1997. In 1979 the number of patents granted to US universities was only 264, compared to 2436 in 1997. There are a number of explanations for this significant increase in patent activity. Changes in government funding and intellectual property law played a role, but detailed analysis indicates that the most significant reason was technological opportunity.

Changes in funding and law in the 1980s clearly encouraged many more universities to establish licensing and technology transfer departments, but the impact of these has been relatively small. For example, there is strong evidence that the scientific and commercial quality of patents has fallen since the mid-1980s as a result of these policy changes, and that the distribution of activity has a very long tail. Measured in terms of the number of patents held or exploited, or by income from patent and software licences, commercialisation of technology is highly concentrated in a small number of elite universities which were highly active prior to changes to funding policy and law: the top 20 US universities account for 70% of the patent activity. Moreover, at each of these elite universities a very small number of key patents account for most of the licensing income: the five most successful patents typically account for 70–90% of total income.[5] This suggests that a (rare) combination of research excellence and critical mass is required to succeed in the commercialisation of technology. Nonetheless, technological opportunity has reduced some of the barriers to commercialisation. Specifically, the growing importance of developments in the biosciences and software present new opportunities for universities to benefit from the commercialisation of technology.

University spin-outs are an alternative to exploitation of technology through licensing, and involve the creation of an entirely new venture based upon intellectual property developed within the university. Estimates vary, but between 3–12% of all technologies commercialised by universities are via new ventures. As with licensing, the propensity for success of these ventures varies significantly. For example, MIT and Stanford University each create around 25 new start-ups each year, whereas Columbia and Duke Universities and rarely generate any start-up companies. Studies in the USA suggest that the financial returns to universities are much higher from spin-out companies than from the more common licensing approach. One study estimated that the average income from a university license was $63,832, whereas the average return from a university spin-out was more than ten times this – $692,121. When the extreme cases were excluded from the sample, the return from spin-outs was still $139,722, more than twice that for a licence.[6] Apart from these financial arguments, there are other reasons why forming a spin-out company may be preferable to licensing technology to an established company:

- No existing company is ready or able to take on the project on a licensing basis.
- The invention consists of a portfolio of products or is an 'enabling technology' capable of application in a number of fields.

- The inventors have a strong preference for forming a company and are prepared to invest their time, effort and money in a start-up.

As such they involve the 'academic entrepreneur' more fully in the detail of creating and managing a market entry strategy than is the case for other forms of commercialisation. They also require major career decisions for the participants. Consequently, they highlight most clearly the dilemmas faced as the scientist tries to manage the interface between academia and industry. The extent to which an individual is motivated to attempt the launch of a venture depends upon three related factors – antecedent influences, the incubator organisation and environmental factors:

- *Antecedent influences*, often called the 'characteristics' of the entrepreneur, including genetic factors, family influences, educational choices, and previous career experiences, all contribute to the entrepreneur's decision to start a venture.
- *Individual incubator experiences* immediately prior to start-up include the nature of the physical location, the type of skills and knowledge acquired, contact with possible fellow founders, the type of new venture or small business experience gained.
- *Environmental factors* include economic conditions, availability of venture capital, entrepreneurial role models, availability of support services.

 Go online to listen to David Hall who identifies some of the common characteristics of entrepreneurs.

www.iande.info

There are relatively few data on the characteristics of the academic entrepreneur, partly due to the low numbers involved, but also because the traditional context within which they have operated, particularly as they apply to IPR and equity sharing, has meant that many have been unwilling to be researched. It is also probable that this is compounded by inadequate university data capture systems. Nevertheless, it is clear that in the USA, scientists and engineers working in universities have long become disposed towards the commercialisation of research. Studies in the USA reveal an increasing legitimisation of university–industry research interactions. However, academic entrepreneurs are still not the norm, even in the USA. A study of 237 scientists working in three large national laboratories in the USA found clear differences between the levels of education in inventors in national laboratories and those in a study of technical entrepreneurs from MIT. The study found significant differences between entrepreneurs and non-entrepreneurs in terms of situational variables such as the level of involvement in business activities outside the laboratory or the receipt of royalties from past inventions.[7] Studies of academic scientists and engineers in the UK identify similar relationships between attitudes to industry, number of industry links and commercial activity.[8] This begs the question: what is the direction of causation? Do entrepreneurial researchers seek more links outside the organisation, or do more links encourage entrepreneurial behaviour?

Entrepreneurs, academic or otherwise, require a supportive environment. Surveys indicate that two-thirds of university scientists and engineers now support the need to commercialise their research, and half the need for start-up assistance. There are two levels of analysis of the university environment, the formal institutional rules, policies and structures, and the 'local norms' within the individual department. There are a number of institutional variables which might influence academic entrepreneurship:

1. Formal policy and support for entrepreneurial activity from management.
2. Perceived seriousness of constraints to entrepreneurship, e.g. IPR issues.
3. Incidence of successful commercialisation, which demonstrates feasibility and provides role models.

Formal policies to encourage and support entrepreneurship can have both intended and unintended consequences. For example, a university policy of taking an equity stake in new start-ups in return for paying initial patenting and licensing expenses seems to result in a higher number of start-ups, whereas granting generous royalties to academic entrepreneurs appears to encourage licensing activity, but tends to suppress significantly the number of start-up companies.[9] In addition, some very common university policies appear to have little or no positive effect on the number or subsequent success of start-ups, including university incubators and local venture capital funding. Moreover, badly targeted and poorly monitored financial support may encourage 'entrepreneurial academics', rather than academic entrepreneurs – scientists in the public sector who are not really committed to creating start-ups, but rather are seeking alternative support for their own research agendas. This can result in start-ups with little or no growth prospects, remaining in incubators for many years. Simply encouraging commercially oriented or industry-funded research also appears to have no effect on the number of start-ups, whereas a university's intellectual eminence has a very strong positive effect.[10] There are two explanations for this effect: more prestigious universities typically attract better researchers and higher funding; and other commercial investors use the prestige or reputation of the institution as a signal or indicator of quality.

Formal policies may send a signal to staff, but the effect on individual behaviour depends very much on whether these policies are reinforced by behavioural expectations. Individual characteristics and local norms appear to be equally effective predictors of entrepreneurial activity, but only provide weak predictions of the forms of entrepreneurship. Where successful, this can create a virtuous circle, the demonstration effect of a successful spin-out encouraging others to try. This leads to clusters of spin-outs in space and time, resulting in entrepreneurial departments or universities, rather than isolated entrepreneurial academics. Local norms or culture at the departmental level will influence the effectiveness of formal policies by providing a strong mediating effect between the institutional context and individual perceptions. Local norms evolve through self-selection during recruitment, resulting in staff with similar personal values and behaviour, and reinforced by peer pressure or behavioural socialisation resulting in a convergence of personal values and behaviour. However, there is a real potential conflict between the pursuit of knowledge and its commercial exploitation, and a real danger of lowering research standards exists.

Therefore it is essential to have explicit guidelines for the conduct of business in a university environment:

1. Specific guidelines on the use of university facilities, staff and students and intellectual property rights.
2. Specific guidelines for, and periodic reviews of, the dual employment of scientist-entrepreneurs, including permanent part-time positions.
3. Mechanisms to resolve issues of financial ownership and the allocation of research contracts between the university and the venture.

ENTREPRENEURSHIP IN ACTION

License or Spin-out? The Lambert Review of Business – University Collaboration in the UK

In the UK, the Lambert Review of Business – University Collaboration reported in December 2003. It reviewed the commercialisation of intellectual property by universities in the UK, and also made international comparisons of policy and performance. The UK has a similar pattern of concentration of activity as the USA: in 2002, 80% of UK universities made no patent applications, whereas 5% filed 20 or more patents; similarly, 60% of universities issued no new licences, but 5% issued more than 30. However, in the UK there has been a bias towards spin-outs rather then licensing, which the Lambert Report criticises. It argues that spin-outs are often too complex and unsustainable, and of low quality – a third in the UK are fully funded by the parent university and attract no external private funding. In 2002, universities in the UK created over 150 new spin-out firms, compared to almost 500 by universities in the USA; the respective figures for new licences that year were 648 and 4058. As a proportion of R&D expenditure, this suggests that British universities place greater emphasis on spin-outs than their North American counterparts, and less on licensing. Lambert argues that universities in the UK may place too high a price on their intellectual property, and that contracts often lack clarity of ownership. Both of these problems discourage businesses from licensing intellectual property from universities, and may encourage universities to commercialise their technologies through wholly owned spin-outs.

Process and Stages for Creating a New Venture

Typical stages of creating a new venture include: ✗

1. Assessing the opportunity for a new venture – generating, evaluating and refining the business concept.
2. Developing the business plan and deciding the structure of the venture.

3. Acquiring the resources and funding necessary for implementation – including expert support and potential partnerships.
4. Growing and harvesting the venture – how to create and extract value from the business.

A new venture will face different challenges at different stages in order to make a successful transition to the next stage, what the researchers call 'critical junctures':

- *Opportunity recognition* – at the interface of the research and opportunity framing phases. This requires the ability to connect a specific technology or know-how to a commercial application, and is based on a rather rare combination of skill, experience, aptitude, insight, and circumstances. A key issue here is the ability to synthesise scientific knowledge and market insights, which increases with the entrepreneur's social capital – linkages, partnerships and other network interactions.
- *Entrepreneurial commitment* – acts and sustained persistence that bind the venture champion to the emerging business venture. This often demands difficult personal decisions to be made, for example, whether or not to remain an academic, as well as evidence of direct financial investments to the venture.
- *Venture credibility* – is critical for the entrepreneur to gain the resources necessary to acquire the finance and other resources for the business to function. Credibility is a function of the venture team, key customers and other social capital and relationships. This requires close relationships with sponsors, financial and other, to build and maintain awareness and credibility. Lack of business experience and failure to recognise their own limitations are a key problem here. One solution is to hire the services of a 'surrogate entrepreneur'. As one experienced entrepreneur notes: 'The not-so-smart or really insecure academics want their hands over everything. These prima donnas make a complete mess of things, get nowhere with their companies and end up disappointed professionally and financially'.

Assessing the Opportunity

One of the failures of many discussions of entrepreneurship is that they assume that the opportunity has already been identified, and all that remains is to develop and resource this. However, in practice a budding entrepreneur may have only a vague idea of the basis of a new venture. Common sources of ideas for new ventures include:

- Extensions or adaptations of existing products or services.
- Application of existing products or services in different or newly created market segments, or at different price points: for example, low-cost airlines such as Ryanair and EasyJet, or Dyson's household cleaner, which adapted centrifugal technology from industrial applications.
- Adding value to an existing product or service: for example, web search engines for specialist fields like travel and insurance, such as TravelJungle.co.uk or Confused.com.
- Developing a completely new product or service.

The more fundamental drivers of opportunities for new ventures are:

- Economic factors – for example, changes in disposable income.
- Technological developments – which may reduce (or increase) barriers to entry.
- Demographic trends – for example, the ageing population, more leisure time.
- Regulatory changes – for example, environmental requirements, health and safety.

All of these potential sources can be more readily identified and assessed by using the systematic approaches to scanning and searching that we advocated in Chapters 5 and 6. One useful source of ideas is to examine how potential users live and work, and identify un-met needs or better ways of providing existing products and services. We introduced Quality Function Deployment in Chapter 9, but it is also useful here to help to assess opportunities and compare these with existing competing offerings.

INNOVATION IN ACTION

Learning from Users at IDEO

IDEO is one of the most successful design consultancies in the world. Based in Palo Alto, California, and London, UK, it helps large consumer and industrial companies worldwide to design and develop innovative new products and services. Behind its rather typical Californian wackiness lies a tried and tested process for successful design and development:

1. Understand the market, client and technology.
2. Observe users and potential users in real-life situations.
3. Visualise new concepts and the customers who might use them, using prototyping, models and simulations.
4. Evaluate and refine the prototypes in a series of quick interations.
5. Implement the new concept for commercialisation.

The first critical step is achieved through close *observation* of potential users in context. As Tom Kelly of IDEO argues: 'We're not big fans of focus groups. We don't much care for traditional market research either. We go to the source. Not the 'experts' inside a (client) company, but the actual people who use the product or something similar to what we're hoping to create . . . we believe you have to go beyond putting yourself in your customers' shoes. Indeed we believe it's not even enough to *ask* people what they think about a product or idea . . . customers may lack the vocabulary or the palate to explain what's wrong, and especially what's *missing*.'

The next step is to develop prototypes to help evaluate and refine the ideas captured from users: 'an iterative approach to problems is one of the foundations of our culture of prototyping . . . you can prototype just about anything – a new product or service, or a special promotion. What counts is moving the ball forward, achieving some part of your goal.'

Source: T. Kelly (2002) *The Art of Innovation: Lessons in Creativity from IDEO* (HarperCollinsBusiness)

INNOVATION IN ACTION

Using Quality Function Deployment to Assess Opportunities

Quality function deployment (QFD) is a useful technique for translating customer requirements into development needs, and encourages communication between engineering, production and marketing. Unlike most other tools of quality management, QFD is used to identify opportunities for product improvement or differentiation, rather than to solve problems. Customer-required characteristics are translated or 'deployed' by means of a matrix into language which engineers can understand. The construction of a relationship matrix – also known as 'the house of quality' – requires a significant amount of technical and market research. Great emphasis must be placed on gathering market and user data in order to identify potential design trade-offs, and to achieve the most appropriate balance between cost, quality and performance. The construction of a QFD matrix involves the following steps:

1. Identify customer requirements, primary and secondary, and any major dislikes.
2. Rank requirements according to importance.
3. Translate requirements into measurable characteristics.
4. Establish the relationship between the customer requirements and technical product characteristics, and estimate the strength of the relationship.
5. Choose appropriate units of measurement and determine target values based on customer requirements and competitor benchmarks.

Symbols are used to show the relationship between customer requirements and technical specifications, and weights attached to illustrate the strength of the relationship. Horizontal rows with no relationship symbol indicate that the existing design is incomplete. Conversely, vertical columns with no relationship symbol indicate that an existing design feature is redundant as it is not valued by the customer. In addition, comparisons with competing products, or benchmarks, can be included. This is important because relative quality is more relevant than absolute quality: customer expectations are likely to be shaped by what else is available, rather than some ideal.

In some cases potential users may have latent needs or requirements which they cannot articulate. In such cases three types of user needs can be identified: 'must be's', 'one-dimensionals' and attractive features or 'delighters'. Must be's are those features which must exist before a potential customer will consider a product or service. For example, in the case of an executive car it must be relatively large and expensive. One-dimensionals are the more quantifiable features which allow direct comparison between competing products. For example, in the case of an executive car, the acceleration and braking performance. Finally, the delighters which are the most subtle means of differentiation. The inclusion of such features delights the target customers, even if they do not explicitly demand them. For example, delighters in the case of an executive car include ultrasonic parking aids, rain-sensitive windscreen wipers and photochromatic mirrors. Such features are rarely demanded by customers or identified by regular market research. However, indirect questioning can be used to help identify latent requirements.

Developing the Business Plan

We discussed this in detail in Chapter 7, so here we only review the main considerations when developing a plan. The primary reason for developing a formal business plan for a new venture is to attract external funding. However, it serves an important secondary function. A business plan can provide a formal agreement between founders regarding the basis and future development of the venture. A business plan can help reduce self-delusion on the part of the founders, and avoid subsequent arguments concerning responsibilities and rewards. It can help to translate abstract or ambiguous goals into more explicit operational needs, and support subsequent decision-making and identify trade-offs. Of the factors *controllable* by entrepreneurs, business planning has the most significant positive effect on new venture performance. However, there are of course many *uncontrollable* factors, such as market opportunity, which have an even more significant influence on performance. Pasteur's advice still applies, '. . . chance favours only the prepared mind'.

A typical formal business plan will include the following sections:

1. Details of the product or service.
2. Assessment of the market opportunity.
3. Identification of target customers.
4. Barriers to entry and competitor analysis.
5. Experience, expertise and commitment of the management team.
6. Strategy for pricing, distribution and sales.
7. Identification and planning for key risks.
8. Cash-flow calculation, including break-even points and sensitivity.
9. Financial and other resource requirements of the business.

No standard business plan exists, but in many cases venture capitalists will provide a pro forma for the business plan. Typically a business plan should be relatively concise, say no more than 10 to 20 pages, begin with an executive summary, and include sections on the product, markets, technology, development, production, marketing, human resources, financial estimates with contingency plans, and the timetable and funding requirements. Most business plans submitted to venture capitalists are strong on the technical considerations, often placing too much emphasis on the technology relative to other issues. As Ed Roberts notes, 'entrepreneurs propose that they can do *it* better than anyone else, but may forget to demonstrate that anyone wants *it*'. He identifies a number of common problems with business plans submitted to venture capitalists: marketing plan, management team, technology plan and financial plan. The management team will be assessed against their commitment, experience, and expertise, normally in that order. Unfortunately, many potential entrepreneurs place too much emphasis on their expertise, but have insufficient experience in the team, and fail to demonstrate the passion and commitment to the venture.

There are common serious inadequacies in all four of these areas, but the worst are in marketing and finance. Less than half of the plans examined provide a detailed marketing strategy, and just half include any sales plan. Three-quarters of the plans fail to identify or analyse any potential competitors. As a result most business plans contain only basic financial forecasts, and just 10% conduct any sensitivity analysis on the forecasts. The lack of attention to marketing and competitor analysis is particularly problematic as research indicates that both factors are associated with subsequent success.

For example, in the early stages many new ventures rely too much on a few major customers for sales, and are therefore very vulnerable commercially. As an extreme example, around half of technology ventures rely on a single customer for more than half of their first-year sales. This over-dependence on a small number of customers has three major drawbacks:

1. Vulnerability to changes in the strategy and health of the dominant customer.
2. A loss of negotiating power, which may reduce profit margins.
3. Little incentive to develop marketing and sales functions, which may limit future growth.

Risk assessment is a critical element of good business planning. The goal is not to eliminate risk, but rather to identify the type and source of risks, and plan how best to deal with these. Go online to find tools to support this.

www.iande.info

Acquiring the Resources and Funding

The potential sources of initial funding for creating a new venture include (Figure 10.1):

- self-funding;
- family and friends;
- business angels;
- bank loans;
- government schemes.

The initial funding to establish a new venture is rarely a major problem. Almost all are funded from personal savings or loans from family or friends. At this stage few professional sources of capital will be interested, with the possible exception of government support schemes. However, a new venture is likely to require financial restructuring every three years, if it is to develop and grow. Studies identify stages of development, each having different financial requirements:

1. Initial financing for launch.
2. Second-round financing for initial development and growth.

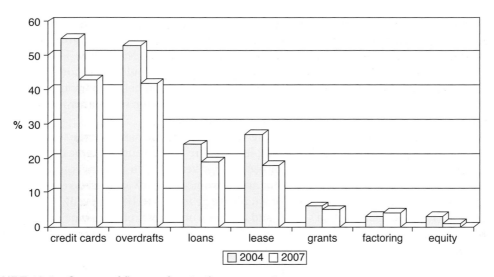

FIGURE 10.1   Source of finance for starting new ventures.

Source: Centre for Business Research (2008) 'Financing UK small and medium-sized enterprises', CBR, Cambridge.

3. Third-round financing for consolidation and growth.
4. Maturity or exit.

In general, professional financial bodies are not interested in initial funding because of the high risk and low sums of money involved. It is simply not worth their time and effort to evaluate and monitor such ventures. However, as the sums involved are relatively small, typically of the order of tens of thousands of pounds, personal savings, re-mortgages and loans from friends and relatives are often sufficient. In contrast, third-round finance for consolidation is relatively easy to obtain, because by that time the venture has a proven track record on which to base the business plan, and the venture capitalist can see an exit route.

Given their strong desire for independence, most entrepreneurs seek to avoid external funding for their ventures. However, in practice this is not always possible, particularly in the later growth stages. The initial funding required to form a new venture includes the purchase of accommodation, equipment and other start-up costs, plus the day-to-day running costs such as salaries, heating, light and so on – usually referred to as the working capital. For these reasons, many ventures begin life as part-time businesses, and are funded by personal savings, loans from friends and relatives, and bank loans, in that order. Around half also receive some funding from government sources, but in contrast receive next to nothing from venture capitalists. Venture capital is typically only made available at later stages to fund growth on the basis of a proven development and sales record.

Technology ventures are different from other new ventures in that there is often no marketable product available before or shortly after formation. Therefore, initial funding of the venture cannot normally be based on cash flow derived from early sales. The precise cash flow profile will be determined by a number of factors, including development time and cost, and the volume and profit margin of sales. Different development and sales strategies exist, but to some extent these factors are determined by the nature of the technology and markets. For example, biotechnology ventures typically require more start-up capital than electronics or software-based ventures, and have longer product development lead times. Therefore, from the perspective of a potential entrepreneur, the ideal strategy would be to conduct as much development work as possible within the incubator organisation before starting the new venture. However, there are practical problems with this strategy, in particular ownership of the intellectual property on which the venture is to be based.

The extent of the need for external funding will depend on the nature of the technology and the market strategy of the venture. For example, software-based ventures typically require less start-up capital than either electronics or biotechnology ventures – it is more common for such firms to rely solely on personal funding – but an electronics or software-based venture will also demand high initial funding if a strategy of aggressive growth is to be achieved. Biotechnology firms tend to have the highest R&D costs, and consequently most require some external funding. In contrast, software firms typically require little R&D investment, and are less likely to seek external funds. Almost three-quarters of software start-ups were funded by profits after three years, whereas only a third of the biotechnology firms had achieved this.

Venture capitalists are keen to provide funding for a venture with a proven track record and strong business plan, but in return will often require some equity or management involvement. Moreover, most venture capitalists are looking for a means to make capital gains after about five years. However, almost by definition technical entrepreneurs seek independence and control, and there is evidence that some will sacrifice growth to maintain control of their ventures. For the same reason, few entrepreneurs are prepared to 'go public' to fund further growth. Thus many entrepreneurs will choose to sell the business and found another. In fact, the typical technical entrepreneur establishes an average of three new ventures. Therefore the biggest funding problem is likely to be for the second-round financing to fund development and growth. This can be a time-consuming and frustrating process to convince venture capitalists to provide finance. The formal proposal is critical at this stage. Professional investors will assess the attractiveness of the venture in terms of the strengths and personalities of the founders, the formal business plan and the commercial and technical merits of the product, probably in that order.

ENTREPRENEURSHIP IN ACTION

Reuters' Corporate Venture Funds

Reuters established its first fund for external ventures, Greenhouse 1, in 1995. It has since added a further two venture funds, which aim to invest in related businesses such as financial services, media, and network infrastructure. By 2001 it had invested US$432 million in 83 companies, and these investments contributed almost 10% to its profits. However, financial return was not the primary objective of the funds. For example, it invested $1 million in Yahoo! in 1995, and consequently Yahoo! acquired part of its content from Reuters. This increased the visibility of

(continued)

Reuters in the growing Internet markets, particularly in the USA where it was not well-known, and resulted in other portals following Yahoo!'s lead with content from Reuters. By 2001 Reuters' content was available on 900 web services, and had an estimated 40 million users per month.

Source: A. Loudon (2001) *Webs of Innovation: The networked economy demands new ways to innovate* (FT.com, Pearson Education, Harlow)

Venture Capital

An important issue is the influence of venture capitalists on the success of new ventures. They can play two distinct roles. The first is to identify or select those ventures that have the best potential for success, that is 'picking winners' or 'scouting'. The second role is to help develop the chosen ventures, by providing management expertise and access to resources other than financial, that is a 'coaching' role. Distinguishing between the effects of these two roles is critical for both the management of and policy for business. For managers, it will influence the choice of venture capital firm, and for policy, the balance between funding and other forms of support.

Information asymmetry between entrepreneurs and potential professional investors can make external funding difficult – entrepreneurs have information potential investors lack, are reluctant to fully disclose this and may engage in opportunistic behaviour. Analysis of a survey of 136 venture capitalists, each with an average of 17 years' investment experience, identified five factors that influence funding: direct or indirect social ties between entrepreneur and potential investor, the business plan, the technology, size of funding, and sector. The average size of the seed-stage funding was just under $1m (in 1998).[11] This demonstrates the critical importance of social ties, direct and indirect, to promote the flow of 'private' knowledge from entrepreneurs to potential investors, 'while VCs receive many cold deals (without introduction), they rarely invest in them . . . most funded proposals come by referral' (p. 377). However, these social ties become less significant when the knowledge becomes more 'public', for example, through the reputation of the entrepreneur or venture.

When selecting start-ups to invest in, the most significant criteria used by venture capitalists are a broad, experienced top management team, a large number of recent patents, and downstream industry alliances (but not upstream research alliances, which had a negative effect on selection). The strongest effect on the decision to fund was the first criterion, and the human capital in general. However, subsequent analysis of venture performance indicates that this factor has limited effect on performance, and that the few significant effects are split equally between improving and impeding the performance of a venture. The effects of technology and alliances on subsequent performance are much more significant and positive. In short, in the *selection* stage, venture capitalists place too much emphasis on human capital, specifically the top management team. In the development or coaching stages, venture capitalists do contribute to the success of the chosen ventures, and tend to introduce external professional management much earlier than if the venture is not funded by venture capital. Taken together, this suggests that the coaching role of venture capitalists is probably as important, if not more so, than the funding role, although policy interventions to promote the creation of venture often focus on the latter.

Whilst there is general agreement about the main components of a good business plan, there are some significant differences in the relative weights attributed to each component. General venture capital firms typically only accept 5% of the ventures they are offered, and the specialist technology venture funds are even more selective, accepting around 3%. The main reasons for rejecting proposals are the lack of intellectual property, the skills of the management team, and size of the potential market. The criteria are similar to those discussed earlier, grouped into five categories:

1. The entrepreneur's personality.
2. The entrepreneur's experience.
3. Characteristics of the product.
4. Characteristics of the market.
5. Financial factors.

ENTREPRENEURSHIP IN ACTION

Andrew Rickman and Bookham Technology.

Andrew Rickman founded Bookham Technology in 1988, aged 28. Rickman has a degree in mechanical engineering from Imperial College London, a PhD in integrated optics from Surrey University, an MBA and has worked as a venture capitalist. Unlike many technology entrepreneurs, he did not begin with the development of a novel technology and then seek a means to exploit it. Instead, he first identified a potential market need for optical switching technology for the then fledgling optical fibre networks, and then developed an appropriate technological solution. The market for optical components is growing fast as the use of Internet and other data-intensive traffic grows. Rickman aimed to develop an integrated optical circuit on a single chip to replace a number of discrete components such as lasers, lenses and mirrors. He chose to use silicon rather than more exotic materials to reduce development costs and exploit traditional chip production techniques. The main technological developments were made at Surrey University and the Rutherford Appleton Laboratory, where he had worked, and 27 patents were granted and a further 140 applied for. Once the technology had been proven, the company raised US$110m over several rounds of funding from venture capitalist 3i, and leading electronics firms Intel and Cisco. The most difficult task was scale-up and production: 'Taking the technology out of the lab and into production is unbelievably tough in this area. It is infinitely more difficult than dreaming up the technology.' Bookham Technology floated in London and on the Nasdaq in New York April 2000 with a market capitalization of more than £5bn, making Andrew Rickman, with 25% of the equity, a paper billionaire. Bookham is based in Oxford, and employs 400 staff. The company acquired the optical component businesses of Nortel and Marconi in 2002, and in 2003 the US optical companies Ignis Optics and New Focus, and the latter included chip production facilities in China. This puts Bookham in the top three in the global opto-electronics sector.

Overall, a bundle of personal, market and financial factors are consistently ranked as being most significant: a proven ability to lead others and sustain effort; familiarity with the market; and the potential for a high return within 10 years. The personality and experience of the entrepreneurs are consistently ranked as being more important than either product or market characteristics, or even financial considerations. However, there were a number of significant differences between the preferences of venture capitalists from different regions. Those from the USA place a greater emphasis on a high financial return and liquidity than their counterparts in Europe or Asia, but less emphasis on the existence of a prototype or proven market acceptance. Perhaps surprisingly, all venture capitalists are averse to technological and market risks. Being described as a 'high-technology' venture was rated very low in importance by the US venture capitalists, and the European and Asian venture capitalists rated this characteristic as having a negative influence on funding. Similarly, having the potential to create an entirely new market is considered a drawback because of the higher risk attached. In short, venture capitalists are not particularly adventurous.

Venture capital in the UK invests relatively little in technology-based ventures. Over the 1990–2005 period, investment in technology-based firms as a percentage of total venture capital remained stable at around 10% of the total by value. In absolute terms this still represents a significant sum, almost £7 billion in 2005, as the UK has a very large venture capital market. Of the total venture capital investment in UK of £6.8 billion in the year 2005 (Table 10.2), only 5% was for early stage funding (by value, or 38% by number of firms), 29% for expansion (by value, or 44% by number of firms), and the rest for management buy-outs or buy-ins (MBO/MBI). The average funds for a start-up or early stage venture was £800,000 (in 2005). The USA has the largest venture capital industry (Figure 10.2) with investments of around US$ 340 billion in 2004.

As venture capital firms have gained experience of this type of funding, and the opportunities for flotation have increased due to the new secondary financial markets in Europe such as the AIM, TechMARK and Neur Markt, their returns on investment have increased significantly.

TABLE 10.2   Structure of venture capital in the UK, by stage and sector

	All ventures	Software	e-commerce	Biotechnology	Telecoms
Early/start-up	£382m (5%) n = 491 (38%)	£52m n = 88	£21m n = 46	£34m n = 36	£12m n = 27
Expansion	£1,951m (29%) n = 573 (44%)	£82m n = 82	£24m n = 81	£23m n = 28	£24m n = 23
Management Buy-out/in	£4,480m (66%) n = 308 (24%)	£16m n = 14	£117m n = 31	£1m n = 3	£161m n = 9
Totals	£6,813m n = 1,307	£150m n = 180	£162m n = 157	£58m n = 67	£197m n = 58

Note: Totals do not always sum to 100% as firms may receive multiple funding.
Source: British Venture Capital Association (2006)

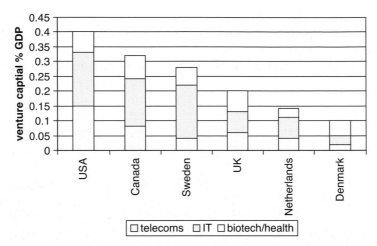

FIGURE 10.2   Breakdown of main venture funding capital by country and field.
Source: OECD (2007) Science, Technology and Industry Scoreboard. OECD, Paris.

ENTREPRENEURSHIP IN ACTION

Alternative Investment Market (AIM)

The Alternative Investment Market (AIM) was established in London, UK, in 1995 as an alternative to the London Stock Exchange. It is designed to be more simple and cheaper than the main market, and to have a less restrictive regulatory regime than the main exchange, and therefore more suited to smaller firms at an earlier stage of development. AIM began with just 10 UK-based companies in 1995, but by 2006 had 1500 firms listed, including 250 from overseas. The total market capitalisation was £72 billion in 2006. About half of all firms on the AIM have a market capitalisation of less than £15 million, and a quarter of firms less than £5 million.

Listing on AIM is easier and cheaper than on most other exchanges, and costs around 5% of the funds raised on flotation. Admission to AIM takes around four months, and involves a number of prescribed steps:

1. Development of the business plan.
2. Appointment of the advisers – Nomad (nominated adviser, a unique and critical feature of AIM, regulated by the London Stock Exchange), broker, accountant and lawyer.
3. Nomad prepares the timetable for admission.
4. Accountants prepare financial due diligence, including historical trading record.
5. Lawyers conduct the legal due diligence, including a review of all contracts, titles and any litigation.

(continued)

6. Accountants prepare the 18-month working capital requirements for the admission document.
7. Formal Admission Document is developed.
8. Marketing and completion, including institutional road-show and public relations.

There is no minimum capitalisation or trading record requirement, and no minimum proportion of shares which have to be held by the public. Institutional investors have been attracted to invest in AIM companies because of the many tax breaks available to investors, such as Venture Capital Trusts. However, a listing on AIM requires greater transparency than a private company, for example, in terms of accounting standards, corporate governance and communication with investors.

In 2005, 29 Chinese or China-focused firms were listed on the London AIM, but regulation, language and distance can make this more difficult and expensive than for local firms. The cost of listing is typically between £500,000 and £1 million, around twice that of a UK-based firm. AIM-style markets have been launched in Asia, including the SESDAQ in Singapore, Growth Enterprise Market in Hong Kong, and Mother Market in Japan.

Business Angels

Business angels are successful entrepreneurs who wish to re-invest in others new ventures, usually in return for some management role. The sums involved are usually relatively small (by venture capital standards), in the range £100,000–£250,000, but in addition they can bring experience and expertise to a new venture. They are usually able to introduce a venture to an established network of professional advisers and business contacts. In this way they can provide a critical knowledge bridge between the venture and potential customers and investors.

Government Funding

There are a number of reasons why governments become involved in promoting and providing resources for new ventures:[12]

- There is an 'equity gap' between the costs and risks involved in assessing and funding a new venture, and its potential return. The costs associated with the 'due diligence' of assessing a venture and its subsequent management are relatively high and fixed, therefore professional venture capitalists are unlikely to consider proposals below a certain threshold, typically around £0.5 to £1 million. Similarly, where the risk of a new venture exceeds the expected return, professional venture capital is unlikely to be available. Table 10.3 indicates that this is a common problem, particularly in the UK and the rest of Europe. This suggests that government schemes may provide support and funding for smaller or higher risk ventures.
- Professional venture capital tends to gravitate to fashionable fields, for example IT or biotechnology, and favour established centres of excellence, for example, Cambridge and Oxford in the UK, or Boston in the USA. Table 10.3 indicates that this is a common

TABLE 10.3   Comparative venture capital structures

Country	% funding for seed/start-up	% funding for technology ventures
Singapore	40	85
USA	31	80
EU	13	26
UK	8	13

problem, particularly in the USA and some emerging economies, where venture capital quickly follows technology trends and fads. This suggests there is a role for policy to broaden the availability of funding for ventures in a wider range of fields and regions.[13]

- Broader need to promote an entrepreneurial culture within a country or region, to provide management support and to establish equity funding (as opposed to debt) as a legitimate source of venture funding. This includes the non-financial support often provided by venture capitalists, including advice and mentoring.[14]

Harvesting the Venture: Growth and Exit Strategies

We will identify the factors that contribute to successful value creation and growth in the next chapter. However, a high proportion of new ventures fail to grow and prosper. Estimates vary by type of business and national context, but typically 40% of new businesses fail in their first year, and 60% within the first two. In other words, around 40% survive the first two years. Common reasons for failure include:

- poor financial control;
- lack of managerial ability or experience;
- no strategy for transition, growth or exit.

There are many ways that a new venture can grow and create additional value:

- organic growth through additional sales and diversification;
- acquisition of or merger with another company;
- sale of the business to another company, or private equity firm;
- an initial public offering (IPO) on a stock exchange.

For example, The UK *Sunday Times* Profit Track estimates that of the 500 fastest grow-ing private firms in the UK, over five years around 100 have merged with or been acquired

Name	Date founded	Business	Profit, 2005, £millions	Annual growth, %
Betfair	1999	Online bookmaker	23.2	146
Invotec	2001	Circuit boards	3.4	88
Azzurri	2000	Telecoms services	8.0	77
Unicom	1998	Telecoms services	3.3	86
Regard	1994	Care homes	4.0	76
Spearhead	2000	Farm produce	5.2	74
Baxter	2000	Contract caterer	4.1	66
Ingenious media	1998	Media adviser	35.7	56
Ineos	1998	Chemicals	191	56
Esri	1993	Software	5.2	79

TABLE 10.4. Some of the fastest growing private firms in the UK.

Source: Sunday Times Profit Track, April 2006.

by other companies or private equity firms, but only 10 or so have been floated (Table 10.4). This is consistent with recent research which shows that contrary to the high visibility of IPOs, this route is relatively rare: less than 2% of VC-funded new ventures in the UK exit via an IPO, compared to more than a quarter by trade sale.[15]

ENTREPRENEURSHIP IN ACTION

Chris Evans and Chiroscience

Chiroscience Plc is one of the nearly 20 biotechnology firms founded by the microbiologist/entrepreneur Chris Evans. Evans, PhD, and since OBE, formed his first new venture, Enzymatix Ltd, in 1987, aged 30. His business plan was rejected by venture capitalists, so he was forced to sell his house for £40 000 to raise the initial finance. Subsequent finance of £1m was provided by the commodities group Berisford International, but following financial problems in the property market, the company was divided into Celsis Plc, which makes contamination testing equipment, and Chiroscience, which exploits chiral technology, the basis of which is that most molecules have mirror images that have different properties, essentially a right-hand sense and a

(continued)

left-hand sense. Isolating the more effective mirror image in an existing drug formulation can improve its efficacy, or reduce unwanted side effects.

Chiroscience was formed in 1990, other directors being recruited from large established pharmaceutical firms such as Glaxo, SmithKline Beecham and Zeneca. The company was floated on the London Stock Exchange in 1994. This was only possible because in 1992 the Stock Exchange relaxed its requirements for market entry, and no longer required three consecutive years' profits before listing. The biotechnology company applies chiral technology to the purification of existing drugs and design of new drugs. Chiroscience has three potential applications of chiral technology: first, and most immediately, the improvement of existing drugs by isolating the most effective sense of molecules; second, the development of alternative processes for the production of existing drugs as they come off patent and, finally, the design of new drugs by means of single isomer technology.

Chiroscience was the first British biotechnology firm to be granted approval for sale of a new product, Dexketoprofen, in 1995. This is a non-steroidal anti-inflammatory drug, based on a right-handed version of the older drug ketoprofen. The drug is marketed by the Italian firm Menarini. Chiroscience has been involved in a number of collaborative development and marketing deals. In 1995 it formed an alliance with the Swedish pharmaceutical group Pharmacia, to develop and market its local anaesthetic, Levobupivacaine. It also forged a more general strategic alliance with Medeva, the pharmaceutical group which performs no primary research, but specialises in taking products to market.

Biotechnology stocks are more volatile than most other investments, and it is difficult to use conventional techniques to assess their current value or future potential. Expenditure on R&D in the initial years typically results in significant losses, and sales may be negligible for up to 10 years. Therefore there are no price–earnings ratios or future revenues to discount. For example, in its first two years after flotation Chiroscience reported cumulative losses of £3.7m, due largely to research spending of £12.4m. Nevertheless, Chiroscience has outperformed the financial markets, and most other biotechnology stock. The company was floated in 1994 at 150p, and quickly fell to below 100p. However, by December 1995 shares had reached 364p. As a result, Chris Evans's personal fortune was estimated to have reached £50m by 1995.

In January 1999 Chiroscience merged with Celltech to form Celltech Chiroscience, which subsequently acquired Medeva to become the Celltech Group. The new company has some 400 research staff, an R&D budget of £51m and adds much-needed sales and marketing competencies with a sales force of 550. Celltech Group is three times the size of Chiroscience, and reached a market capitalisation of £3bn in 2000. It is one of the few British biotechnology companies to gain regulatory approval for its products in the USA, and the first to achieve profitability. Sir Chris Evans (he was knighted in 2001) now runs the biotechnology venture capital firm Merlin Biosciences.

Successful, high-growth new ventures are associated with:

- Strong emphasis on design and innovation, but not necessarily technology or formal R&D.
- Extensive external links, including contract research organisations, suppliers, customers and universities.

Design and Innovation

Innovation, broadly defined, is found to be statistically three times more important to growth than other attributes or factors. Innovativeness, including a propensity to engage in new idea generation and experimentation is associated with performance, and so is pro-activeness, defined as the firm's approach to market opportunities through active market research and the introduction of new products and services. The amount of expenditure by a new venture on design and engineering generally has a positive effect on the share of exports in sales, but formal R&D appears to be only weakly associated with profitability, and is not correlated with growth. Moreover, expenditure on R&D and investment in technology do not appear to discriminate between the success and failure of ventures. Instead, other factors have been found to have a more significant effect on profitability and growth, in particular the contributions of technically qualified owner-managers and their scientific and engineering staff, and attention to product planning and marketing.

Where a new venture has a niche product strategy and relies too much on close relationships with a small number of customers, it may have little incentive or scope for further innovation, and therefore may pay relatively little attention to formal product development or marketing. Such ventures form dependent relationships and are likely to have limited potential for future growth, and may remain permanent infants or subsequently be acquired by competitors or customers.

External Links

Innovative new ventures are likely to have diverse and extensive linkages with a variety of external sources of innovation, and in general there is a positive association between the level of external scientific, technical and professional inputs and the performance of an SME. The sources of innovation and precise types of relationship vary by sector, but links with contract research organisations, suppliers, customers and universities are consistently rated as being highly significant, and constitute the 'social capital' of the firm. However, such relationships are not without cost, and the management and exploitation of these linkages can be difficult for an SME, and can overwhelm the limited technical and managerial resources of SMEs. As a result, in some cases the cost of collaboration may outweigh the benefits and in the specific case of collaboration between SMEs and universities there is an inherent mismatch between the short-term, near-market focus of most SMEs and the long-term, basic research interests of universities.[16]

Links with sponsors, including venture capital, play an important developmental role, as discussed earlier. The size and location of new ventures also has an effect on performance. Geographic closeness increases the likelihood of informal linkages and encourages the mobility of skilled labour across firms. However, the probability of a start-up benefiting from such local knowledge exchanges appears to decrease as the venture grows. This growing inability to exploit informal linkages is a function of organisational size, not the age of the venture, and suggests that as ventures grow and become more complex, they begin to suffer many of the barriers to innovation faced by larger firms.

In general, larger SMEs are associated with a greater spatial reach of innovation-related linkages, and with the introduction of more novel product or process innovations for international markets. In contrast, smaller SMEs are more embedded in local networks, and are more likely to be engaged in incremental innovations for the domestic market. It is always difficult to untangle cause and effect relationships from such associations, but it is plausible that as the more innovative start-ups begin to outgrow the resources of their local networks, they actively replace and extend their networks, which both creates the opportunity and demand for higher levels of innovation. Conversely, the less innovative start-ups fail to move beyond their local networks, and therefore are less likely to have either the opportunity or need for more radical innovation.

However, different contingencies will demand different innovation strategies. For example, for software start-ups five factors appear to influence success most strongly: level of R&D expenditure, how radical new products were, the intensity of product upgrades, use of external technology and management of intellectual property.[17] In contrast, in biotechnology start-ups three factors are associated with success: location within a significant concentration of similar firms, quality of scientific staff (measured by citations) and the commercial experience of the founder. In biotechnology ventures, the number of scientific staff in the top management team had a negative association, suggesting that the scientists are best kept in the laboratory. Other studies of biotechnology start-ups confirm this pattern, and suggest that maintaining close links with universities reduces the level of R&D expenditure needed, increases the number of patents produced, and moderately increases the number of new products under development. However, as with more general alliances, the *number* of university links has no effect on the success or performance of biotechnology start-ups, but the *quality* of such relationships does.[18]

ENTREPRENEURSHIP IN ACTION

Technology-based High-growth Ventures

Since 2001 the Oxford-based research company Fast Track has compiled a report for the newspaper the *Sunday Times* on the top 100 technology-based new ventures in the UK, sponsored by consultants PriceWaterhouseCoopers and Microsoft.

Following the collapse of the dot-com bubble, the annual survey provides an excellent barometer of the more robust and consistent technology-based new ventures, which, without reaching the headlines, continue to be created, grow and prosper.

Of the 100 firms studies, 48 have been funded by venture capital or private equity funds. As might be expected, many of the most successful new ventures are based on software or telecommunications technologies, so-called Information Communication Telecommunications (ICT) technologies, but the commercial applications are increasingly dynamic and diverse, including gaming, gambling, music, film, fashion and education. Although most of these firms are only five or six years old, annual sales average £5 million, with annual growth of 60%. Examples include:

> Gamesys, a gaming website operator created in 2001, now with 50 staff and sales of £9.4 million.
>
> The Search Works, an advertising consultant for search engines, founded in 1999, now employing more than 50 staff, with sales of $18.6 million.

(continued)

Redtray, an e-learning software developer, formed in 2002, which now has 30 staff and sales of £4.5 million.

Ocado, the delivery business for online orders to supermarket Waitrose, created in 2000, and now employing almost 1000, with 3 million deliveries each week, and turnover of $143 million.

Wiggle, an online retailer of sports goods, founded in 1998, now with 50 staff and sales of £9.2 million.

Betfair, an online bookmaker and betting website, established in 1999, now with turnover of £107 million and employing more than 400.

Source: Sunday Times Tech Track 100, September 24, 2006; www.fasttrack.co.uk;www.pwc.com

Developing Personal Capabilities

The following framework is useful for structuring the assessment and development of ideas for a new business.

Criterion	Initial Opportunity	Stronger Opportunity
Customers and market segments		
Needs		
Benefits		
Differentiation		
Competition		
Industry structure		
Barriers to entry		
Regulation/IPR		
Market size		
Market growth		
Potential market share		
Gross margins		
Profits		

(continued)

Criterion	Initial Opportunity	Stronger Opportunity
Return on capital		
Break-even time		
Capital requirements		
Cash flow needs		
Management team		
Contacts and networks		
Exit options		
Assumptions		
Critical risks		

Source: Derived from Kaplan, J.M., and A.C. Warren (2009) *Patterns of Entrepreneurship.* John Wiley & Sons Inc., New York.

ADVICE FOR ENTREPRENEURS

One of the early decisions an entrepreneur will have to make is the type of business structure to use. When deciding what type of company to form, you need to consider:

1. How much capital is needed to start the business?
2. How much control and ownership do you want?
3. How much risk are you willing to take on, in the case of failure?
4. How large could the business become, and how fast?
5. What are the registration, reporting and tax implications of different structures?
6. What are the proposed harvest strategies or exit routes?
7. Who might become the beneficiary of the business?

The basic options are:

Sole proprietorship – the advantages are the relatively light regulation and reporting, autonomy of decision-making and total control, direct personal incentive to succeed, and easy to exit. However, this exposes the owner to unlimited personal liability, provides only limited access to external capital and development, and relies on the skills and talent of only one person.

(continued)

Partnership – the advantages are: easy to establish; larger pool of expertise and capital; partners share all profits; flexibility to extend partnerships as the business develops. However, potential for personality and decision-making conflicts, buying out partners who wish to leave, joint unlimited liability of partners.

Company – easy and cheap to establish, better access to capital for growth, and exposes owners to only a limited liability. The disadvantages are the reporting requirements, rules of operations, different shareholder interests and restrictions on the sale and transfer of assets.

Source: Derived from Kaplan, J.M., and A.C. Warren (2009) *Patterns of Entrepreneurship*. John Wiley & Sons Inc., New York.

STRATEGIC AND SOCIAL IMPACT

UnLtd – The UK Foundation for Social Entrepreneurs

UnLtd aims to support social entrepreneurs by providing funding and support to help these individuals start up and run projects that deliver social benefit.

It was established in 2000 through a partnership between seven leading UK non-profit organisations, including the School for Social Entrepreneurs, Ashoka, Senscot, The Scarman Trust, The Community Action Network, Comic Relief, and Changemakers, and funded by an endownment of £100 million from the UK Millennium Commission Award Scheme. The Foundation invests the money awarded to generate an income of £5 million a year to provide grants to individuals with projects to improve their community. These individual grants were launched in 2002, and range from £2500 to £15,000.

In addition to funding, UnLtd provides advice, training and support, using its extensive network of resources and partner organisations throughout the UK. It has formed an Institute for Social Entrepreneurs to help to raise the effectiveness of the sector by building a deeper understanding of what works and what does not, translating that understanding into tools and performance measures, and promoting public and media awareness.

In future UnLtd plans to establish a Social Venture Fund to link social investors to more mature social entrepreneurs, whose projects have the potential to develop in scope and/or geography with significant financial backing. Current plans range from becoming a broker between different venture philanthropy funds to establishing its own VP fund.

Sources: www.unltd.org.uk, www.aworldconnected.org, www.howtochangetheworld.org, www.socialent.org

Chapter Summary

In this chapter we have explored the rationale, characteristics and management of innovative new ventures. Typically an innovative entrepreneur will establish a venture primarily to create something new or to change something, rather than a means to achieve independence or wealth, although both of these may follow as a consequence. A range of factors influences the creation of innovative new ventures, some contextual, such as institutional support, availability of capital and culture, others more personal, such as personality, background and relevant skills and experience. Therefore entrepreneurship is not just simply an individual act, driven by psychology, but also a profoundly social process. The process of creating an innovative new venture requires careful business planning, and also the systematic assessment and acceptance of opportunities and risks. Innovative entrepreneurs need to be able to identify and exploit a broader range of external resources and sources of knowledge than their more conventional counterparts, including diverse networks of those in the private, public and third sectors.

Discussion Questions

1. In what ways do social entrepreneurs and technology entrepreneurs differ from other types of entrepreneur?

2. What are the main funding options for a new venture, and what are the advantages and disadvantages of each?

3. What should be included in a business plan, and what do venture capitalists look for?

4. In each of the different stages in the development of a new venture, what are the different management requirements?

5. What factors affect the decision of what type of company to form?

6. What are the relative advantages and drawbacks of different sources of finance?

Team Exercise

Identify an idea for a new venture, and develop a business plan to attract external funding. This should include:

1. Details of the product or service.
2. Assessment of the market opportunity.

3. Identification of target customers.
4. Barriers to entry and competitor analysis.
5. Experience, expertise and commitment of the management team.
6. Strategy for pricing, distribution and sales.
7. Identification and planning for key risks.
8. Cash-flow calculation, including break-even points and sensitivity.
9. Financial and other resource requirements of the business.

Assignment

In your university, find out what the policies, incentives, resources and support are for commercialising technology, including patenting, licensing and the creation of new venture firms. Identify a recent new venture and interview the founders to find out why and how they created the business, and what their plans are for its development and growth.

Key Terms Defined

Alternative Investment Market (AIM)   was established as a simpler and cheaper alternative to the London Stock Exchange.

Business angels   successful entrepreneurs who wish to re-invest in new ventures, usually in return for some management role. They are usually able to introduce a venture to an established network of professional advisers and business contacts.

Incubator organisation   a private firm, university or public organisation which provides resources and support for the generation of spin-out firms.

New technology-based firms (NTBFs)   small firms that have emerged recently from large firms or public laboratories in such fields as electronics, software and biotechnology. They are usually specialised in the supply of a key component, subsystem, service or technique to larger firms, who may often be their former employers.

Social entrepreneur   those whose aim is to create social change and value, rather than commercial innovation and financial value. They engage business, public and third-sector organisations to achieve this aim.

Superstars   large firms that have grown rapidly from small beginnings, through high rates of growth based on the exploitation of a major invention.

Further Reading and Resources

There are many books and journal articles on the subject of entrepreneurship, but relatively little has been produced on the more specific subject of innovative new ventures. We believe one of the best general texts on entrepreneurship is Jack Kaplan's *Patterns of Entrepreneurship*, written with A.C. Warren (Wiley, New York, 2009, third edition), which adopts a very practical approach. Also recommended are Paul Burns (2008) *Entrepreneurship and Small Businesses* (second edition, Palgrave Macmillan), which unusually includes a discussion of creativity and innovation. Alex Nicholls (2006) *Social Entrepreneurship: New Paradigms of Sustainable Social Change* (Oxford University Press), and Mair, J., Robinson, J. and Hockets, K. (2006) *Social Entrepreneurship* (Palgrave Macmillan) are both edited texts, and rather academic, but both discuss the definitions, boundaries and some of the problems of research and practice in the emerging field of social entrepreneurship. John Elkington and Pamela Hartigan (2008) provide a lively account of social entrepreneurship which focuses on the contributions of individuals in *Power of Unreasonable People: How Social Entrepreneurs Create Markets That Change the World* (Harvard Business School Press), but for a more balanced and academic approach see Alex Nicholls (2008) *Social Entrepreneurship: New Models of Sustainable Social Change* (Oxford University Press).

For a more specialist treatment of technology-based entrepreneurship, Ed Roberts's *Entrepreneurs in High Technology: Lessons from MIT and beyond* (Oxford University Press, Oxford, 1991) is an excellent study of the MIT experience, albeit a little dated, but perhaps places too much emphasis on the characteristics of individual entrepreneurs rather than the unique context. The broader role of the Boston Route 128 is discussed in the paper 'The Boston Route 128 Model of High-Tech Industry Development' by J. Wonglimpiyarat (2006) *International Journal of Innovation Management*, 10(1), 47–64. For a more comprehensive study of technology-based new ventures in the USA, see Martin Kenny (ed.), *Understanding Silicon Valley: Anatomy of an entrepreneurial region* (Stanford University Press, 2000). For a review of recent research on the broader issue of innovative small firms, see 'Small firms, R&D, technology and innovation: a literature review' by Kurt Hoffman *et al.*, published in *Technovation*, **18** (1), 39–55, 1998. A special issue of the *Strategic Management Journal* (volume 22, July 2001) examined entrepreneurial strategies, and includes a number of papers on technology-based firms. The journal *Research Policy* has a number of relevant special issues: 38(6), 2009, on Academic Entrepreneurship; and 32(2), 2003, on entrepreneurship.

The literature in this field is dominated by the US experience, but other models exist. Ray Oakey's *High-technology New Firms* (Paul Chapman, London, 1995) is a study of technology-based new ventures in the UK, and places greater emphasis on how different technologies constrain the opportunities and success. Acs, Z.J. and Audretsch, D.B. (2005) *Entrepreneurship, Innovation and Technological Change* (Foundations and Trends in Entrepreneurship, Now Publishers, Hanover, MA) provide a short but excellent review of the theories and evidence linking the fields of entrepreneurship and innovation, and in Audretsch, D.B, M.C. Keilbach and E.E. Lehman (2006) *Entrepreneurship and Economic Growth*

(Oxford University Press) they examine the evidence in Germany. Vinig, T. and van der Voort, R. (2005) *The Emergence of Entrepreneurial Economics* (Elsevier, Amsterdam) is an edited book, with a strong historical perspective in part I, and recent country studies in part II, including less commonly studied countries such as Russia, New Zealand and France. *Country Studies in Entrepreneurship*, edited by Y. Cassis and I.P. Minoglou (2006, Palgrave Macmillan, Basingstoke), includes case studies of the USA, UK, France, Italy, Germany, and, most interesting of all, Singapore.

For studies of the influence of venture capital, Simon Barnes, with Rupert Pearce, gives a rare practitioner's account of the workings of venture capital in *Raising Venture Capital* (John Wiley & Sons Ltd, Chichester, 2006). Our colleagues assess the UK context in detail in Paul Nightingale, Gordon Murray, Marc Cowling, Charles Baden-Fuller, Josh Siepel, and Michael Hopkins (2009) *From funding gaps to thin markets: UK Government support for early-stage venture capital*, NESTA/BVCA, London www.nesta.org.uk/publications. For a more critical assessment of the role of venture capital and in particular the limitations of venture capitalists, see any of Scott Shane's various accounts, such as (2009) *The Illusions of Entrepreneurship* (Yale University Press).

References

1. Mair, J., Robinson, J. and Hockets, K. (2006) *Social Entrepreneurship*. Palgrave Macmillan, Basingstoke. An edited book which discusses the definitions, boundaries and some of the problems of research and practice in the emerging field of social entrepreneurship.

2. Wonglimpiyarat, J. (2006) 'The Boston Route 128 Model of High-Tech Industry Development', *International Journal of Innovation* Management, 10(1), 47–64; Kenny, M. (2000) *Understanding Silicon Valley: Anatomy of an entrepreneurial region*. Stanford University Press, California; Roberts, E. (1991) *Entrepreneurs in High Technology: Lessons from MIT and beyond*. Oxford University Press, Oxford.

3. Audretsch, D.B, M.C. Keilbach and E.E. Lehman (2006) *Entrepreneurship and Economic Growth*. Oxford University Press.

4. Hoffman, K., M. Parejo, J. Bessant and L. Perren (1998) 'Small firms, R&D, technology and innovation in the UK: a literature review', *Technovation*, **18**(1), 39–55.

5. Mowery, D.C., R.R. Nelson, B.N. Sampat and A.A. Ziedonis (2001) 'The growth of patenting and licensing by U.S. Universities: an assessment of the effects of the Bayh–Dole Act of 1980', *Research Policy*, **30**; Henderson, R., A.B. Jaffe and M. Trajtenberg (1998) 'Universities as a source of commercial technology: a detailed analysis of university patenting 1965–1988', *The Review of Economics and Statistics*, 80(1), 119–127.

6. Bray, M.J. and Lee, J.N. (2000) 'University revenues from technology transfer: Licensing fees versus equity positions', *Journal of Business Venturing*, 15, 385–392.

7. Kassicieh, S.K., R. Radosevich and J. Umbarger (1996) 'A comparative study of entrepreneurship incidence among inventors in national laboratories', *Entrepreneurship Theory and Practice*, Spring, 33–49.

8. Meyer, M. (2004) 'Academic entrepreneurs or entrepreneurial academics? Research-based ventures and public support mechanisms', *R&D Management*, 33 (2), 107–115; Butler, S. and S. Birley (1999) 'Scientists and their attitudes to industry links', *International Journal of Innovation Management*, 2(1), 79–106.

9. Lee, Y. S. (1996) 'Technology transfer and the research university: a search for the boundaries of university–industry collaboration', *Research Policy*, **25**, 843–863.

10. Di Gregorio, D. and Shane, S. (2003) 'Why do some universities generate more start-ups than others?', *Research Policy*, 32, 209–227.

11. Shane, S. and Cable, D. (2002) Network ties, reputation and the financing of new ventures, *Management Science*, 48(3), 364–381.

12. Harding, R. (2000) *Venturing Forward: the role of venture capital in enabling entrepreneurship*. Institute for Public Policy Research, London.

13. Lockett, A., Murray, G. and Wright, M. (2002) 'Do UK venture capitalists still have a bias against investment in new technology firms?', *Research Policy*, 31, 1009–1030.

14. Baum, J.A.C. and Silverman, B.S. (2004) 'Picking winners or building them? Alliance, intellectual and human capital as selection criteria in venture financing and performance of biotechnology startups', *Journal of Business Venturing*, 19, 411–436.

15. Siepel, J. (2010) *Capabilities, Policy and Institutions in the Emergence of Venture Capital in the UK and US*, unpublished DPhil thesis, SPRU, University of Sussex, UK.

16. Almeida, P., Dokko, G. and Rosenkopf, L. (2003) 'Startup size and the mechanisms of external learning: Increasing opportunity and decreasing ability?', *Research Policy*, 32, 301–315; Freel, M.S. (2003) 'Sectoral patterns of small firm innovation, networking and proximity', *Research Policy*, 32, 751–770; Lee, C., Lee, K. and Pennings, J.M. (2000) 'Internal capabilities, external networks, and performance: A study of technology-based ventures', *Strategic Management Journal*, 22, 615–640.

17. Gans, J.S. and Stern, S. (2003) 'The product and the market for "ideas": commercialization strategies for technology entrepreneurs', *Research Policy*, 32, 333–350; Zahra, S.A. and W.C. Bogner (2000) 'Technology strategy and software new ventures performance', *Journal of Business Venturing*, 15(2), 135–173.

18. Deeds, D.L., D. DeCarolis and J. Coombs (2000) 'Dynamic capabilities and new product development in high technology ventures: an empirical analysis of new biotechnology firms', *Journal of Business Venturing*, 15(3), 211–229; George, G., Zahra, S.A., and Robley Wood, D. (2002) 'The effects of business – university alliances on innovative output and financial performance: A study of publicly traded biotechnology companies', *Journal of Business Venturing*, 17, 577–609.

CASE STUDY 10

Exploring Innovation in Action – Evolving Knowledge Needs of a New Venture

Helax AB was founded in 1986 by three staff of Uppsala University in Sweden. The three founders had degrees in physics, mathematics and computer science, and had experience of using IT in medical applications, in particular radiotherapy. The founders successfully raised US$3 million of venture capital from private and government sources, enough for three years of working capital without any additional revenues.

The idea for the business originated in a public-funded research project called CART (Computer Aided Radio Therapy), which aimed to create an integrated information management system for the records of cancer patients. This was believed to be desirable because such patients usually undertook a wide range of different examinations, scans, diagnosis and treatments over an extended period. By combining and tracking these data, it was hoped that the overall effectiveness of the therapy would be improved. The CART project successfully demonstrated that the success of therapy could be improved through better management of the patient data, identified user requirements for such a system, and had developed a number of the software subsystems and components necessary to begin building a more integrated information management system. However, CART did not go as far as hoped, and never developed a functioning integrated system. Helax AB was created to take the work further, and to develop commercial applications.

So at start-up the three founders of the company inherited knowledge of the problem area, user requirements, and most importantly had formal knowledge relevant to potential solutions within the combined fields of computer science, mathematics and physics. Based on the results of the CART project, a process map of the clinical process was developed, independent of any systems design. This was circulated to 30 international cancer centres for feedback, and this quasi-Delphi survey also helped to create potential customer awareness and buy-in for the future. The feedback was positive, and provided the basis for further development of the system. In 1988 the technology was installed in two hospitals for clinical trials and evaluation. At the core of this design was the dose planning system, later to be renamed the TMS (Treatment Management System). This architecture allowed Helax AB to act as a systems integrator by adding further components from other providers and partners.

The potential solution had two very different components. The first was specific to radiotherapy and concerned the planning of dosage levels. Dose planning requires knowledge of the relationship between radiation levels and patterns and their effects on biological tissues and cells. This subject had been explored in a PhD project jointly funded by Helax AB and Uppsala University. The second area of knowledge was more generic, and concerned with information management. These two fields of knowledge evolved in different ways as the new venture developed. The first was based on the knowledge generated and accumulated from the CART research, plus access to an extended external network of scientific research and clinical expertise. The second was more internal, but required extension by further recruitment.

Development was grouped into three different areas: hardware and operating systems architecture; software for the user interfaces; and quite separately, the development of the algorithms for calculating the doses, which required access to more basic science. Within a year the whole CART project group of 13 from Uppsala University had joined Helax AB, and in addition engineers with product development and commercial experience were recruited to help in design and development, bringing the total number of employees to 20 by 1990. Almost all employees had degrees, mainly in the physical sciences or engineering, but the company decided not to recruit medical expertise. Instead, it relied on a network of contacts in the medical community. By this time the original venture capital funding had been exhausted, and arguments between the founders and venture capital owners over the future direction of the firm resulted in the founders buying out the venture capitalists interest in the firm.

By 1994 the company had installed its system in 11 of the 15 radiotherapy centres in Sweden, and had also achieved some sales in Germany and the UK. During this period the company developed some new knowledge and capabilities in production, and had an annual capacity to build 12 systems. However, in product development most of the knowledge-seeking effort was within the existing system design, and was aimed at fixing bugs and improving performance of the existing system by refining the dose algorithms. To extend its sales and international reach further, it established partnerships with Siemens, Philips and General Electric. This was rather too successful, and in the first six months of the Siemens partnership 60 new systems were ordered, equivalent to five years of production. Therefore Helax had to fundamentally change how it produced and installed the systems, and the increasing customer base demand created a need for maintenance, service and support for the installed systems. Initially the system developers had undertaken the new service and support function, but this placed strains on product development, and so the firm had to create a new service division and recruit new personnel with the relevant skills and experience.

The additional revenues from these sales allowed Helax to invest in research and development, and two product extensions were successfully launched between 1994 and 1998. Customers were demanding more standard interfaces compatible with Windows PCs, rather than the purpose-built and non-standard interface offered. These more fundamental attempts to upgrade and change the software failed, and Helax experienced significant problems recruiting and retaining the necessary staff experienced in more structured software development. The legacy of the unstructured development approach of the original founders and CART team resulted in under-investment in formal software engineering, and attempts to out-source this development had also failed.

The company continued to develop sales subsidiaries in Northern Europe, and extended its product market into other fields such as oncology with the development of the HOME (Helax Oncology Management Environment) system. However, efforts to enter the critical US market were not successful, and in return for access to North America Helax sold out to the Canadian firm MDS Nordion. Helax in Uppsala is now a division of MDS Nordion, and a centre of excellence for the development of the HOME concept. The identity and knowledge of the founding group remains, but autonomy and control do not: 'the 20 first employees have become, and still are, the core of the company. [But they have not] broadened their core function since they started, but have become mentors in the company's main process, i.e. the devel-opment of a system of radiography . . . but I don't think it is possible to break up and get the individuals to work together in a different perspective. (p. 422)

Therefore over its 15-year life as an independent new venture, the knowledge needs of Helax have changed significantly. The new venture was founded based on the formal knowledge outputs of the CART research project, and the explicit knowledge of the three founders in the fields of physics, computer science and mathematics, plus their experience in the domains of informatics and radiography. The core knowledge base of the new venture was, and largely remained, a detailed knowledge of the whole radiography process, combined with the specific knowledge of dose planning. Over time, the need for new internal knowledge of production systems and formal soft-ware development and engineering grew, and to a great extent these had to be satis-fied by the recruitment of new staff with knowledge and experience of these fields. In addition, a wide range of external sources of knowledge had to be utilised to help translate the technology into a successful commercial venture. These included the local networks within medical research and clinical practice, and international networks for cancer treatment. The need for specialist national and product market knowledge and access demanded partnerships with large multinationals, and culminated in the sale of the company and loss of control.

Questions

1. Identify the different types of knowledge needed throughout the growth of the new venture.
2. What was the balance of internal and external sources of knowledge at different stages of the venture's development?
3. How else might Helax have commercialised its knowledge?

Source: From R.J. Saemundsson (2004) 'Technical Knowledge-Seeking in a Young and Growing Technology-Based Firm', *International Journal of Innovation Management*, 8(4), 399–430.

Summary of Web Resources

Cases

- ihavemoved.com
- threadless.com

Media

- David Hall on entrepreneurs
- Carmel McConnell on social businesses

Tools

- Risk assessment

PART V

CREATING VALUE

Part V Creating Value

There is a significant difference between generating an innovation or new venture and creating and capturing the value from it. How do we ensure the social gains are there if we are trying to change the world? How do we make sure there is a stream of income from its widespread use? How do we recover our – and other people's – investment of time, energy and money? How do we protect ourselves from people copying our idea and capitalising on all our pioneering? And even if we fail, how do we capture the learning about how the innovation process works so that next time we try something we can increase our chances of success?

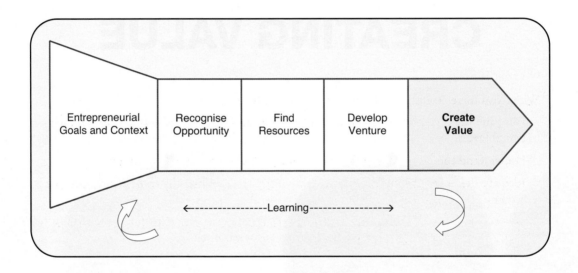

Chapter 11

Exploiting Knowledge and Intellectual Property

Go online to find additional . . .

Cases

Tools

Media

www.iande.info

In this chapter we discuss how individuals and organisations identify 'what they know' and how best to exploit it. We examine the related fields of knowledge management, organisational learning and intellectual property. Key issues include the nature of knowledge, for example explicit versus tacit knowledge; the locus of knowledge, for example individual versus organisational; and the distribution of knowledge across an organisation. More narrowly, knowledge management is concerned with identifying, translating, sharing and exploiting the knowledge within an organisation. One of the key issues is the relationship between individual and organisational learning, and how the former is translated into the latter, and ultimately into new processes, products and businesses. Finally, we review different types of formal intellectual property, and how these can be used in the development and commercialisation of innovations.

In essence managing knowledge involves five critical tasks:

1. Generating and acquiring new knowledge.
2. Identifying and codifying existing knowledge.
3. Storing and retrieving knowledge.
4. Sharing and distributing knowledge across the organisation.
5. Exploiting and embedding knowledge in processes, products and services.

Generating and Acquiring Knowledge

Organisations can acquire knowledge by experience, experimentation or acquisition. Of these, learning from experience appears to be the least effective. In practice, organisations do not easily translate experience into knowledge. Moreover, learning may be unintentional or it may not result in improved effectiveness. Organisations can incorrectly learn, and they can learn harmful things, such as learning faulty or irrelevant skills or self-destructive habits. This can lead an organisation to accumulate experience of an inferior technique, and may prevent it from gaining sufficient experience of a superior procedure to make it rewarding to use, sometimes called the 'competency trap'.

Experimentation is a more systematic approach to learning. It is a central feature of formal R&D activities, market research and some organisational alliances and networks, as we examined in Chapter 8. When undertaken with intent, a strategy of learning through incremental trial and error acknowledges the complexities of existing technologies and markets, as well as the uncertainties associated with technology and market change and in forecasting the future. The use of alliances for learning is less common and requires an intent to use them as an opportunity for learning, a receptivity to external know-how and partners of sufficient transparency. Whether the acquisition of know-how results in organisational learning depends on the rationale for the acquisition and the process of acquisition and transfer. For example, the cumulative effect of outsourcing various technologies on the basis of comparative transaction costs may limit future technological options and reduce competitiveness in the long term.

A more active approach to the acquisition of knowledge involves scanning the internal and external environments. As we discussed in Chapter 6, scanning consists of searching, filtering and evaluating potential opportunities from outside the organisation, including related and emerging technologies, new markets and services, which can be exploited by applying or combining with existing competencies. Opportunity recognition, which is a precursor to entrepreneurial behaviour, is often associated with a flash of genius, but in reality is probably more often the end result of a laborious process of environmental scanning. External scanning can be conducted at various levels. It can be an operational initiative with market- or technology-focused managers becoming more conscious of new developments within their own environments, or a top-driven initiative where venture managers or professional capital firms are used to monitor and invest in potential opportunities.

INNOVATION IN ACTION

Identifying Different Types of Knowledge

The concept of disembodied knowledge can become a very abstract idea, but it can be assessed in practice. Here are some types of knowledge identified in a study of the biotechnology and telecommunications industries:

- variety of knowledge;
- depth of knowledge;
- source of knowledge, internal and external;
- evaluation of knowledge and awareness of competencies;
- knowledge management practices, the capability to identify, share and acquire knowledge;
- use of IT systems to store, share and reuse knowledge;
- identification and assimilation of external knowledge;
- commercial knowledge of markets and customers;
- competitor knowledge, current and potential;
- knowledge of supplier networks and value chain;
- regulatory knowledge;
- financial and funding stakeholder knowledge;
- knowledge of intellectual property rights (IPR), own and others;
- knowledge practices, including documentation, intranets, work organisation and multi-disciplinary teams and projects.

The study concluded that each of these contributed to the intellectual assets and innovative performance of companies, but in different ways. In general, the less tangible and more tacit knowledge of individuals, groups and practices are necessary to exploit the more explicit and tangible types of knowledge, such as R&D and IPR, and these in turn can lead to better use and access to external sources of knowledge, due to a strengthening of position, reputation and trust.

Source: Derived form Marques, D.P., Simon, F.J.G. and Caranana, C.D. (2006) 'The effect of innovation on intellectual capital: An empirical evaluation in the Biotechnology and Telecommunications industries', *International Journal of Innovation Management*, 10(1), 89–112.

Identifying and Codifying Knowledge

It is useful to begin with a clearer idea of what we mean by 'knowledge'. It has become all things to all people, ranging from corporate IT systems to the skills and experience of individuals. There is no universally accepted typology, but the following hierarchy is helpful:

- **Data** are a set of discrete raw observations, numbers, words, records and so on. Typically, they are easy to structure, record, store and manipulate electronically.
- **Information** is data that have been organised, grouped or categorised into some pattern. The organisation may consist of categorisation, calculation or synthesis. This organisation of data endows information with relevance and purpose, and in most cases adds value to data.
- **Knowledge** is information that has been contextualised, given meaning and therefore made relevant and easier to operationalise. The transformation of information into knowledge involves making comparisons and contrasts, identifying relationships and inferring consequences. Therefore knowledge is deeper and richer than information, and includes framed expertise, experience, values and insights.

There are essentially two different types of knowledge, each with different characteristics:

- **explicit** knowledge, which can be codified, that is expressed in numerical, textual or graphical terms, and therefore is more easily communicated, for example, the design of a product;
- **tacit** or implicit knowledge, which is personal, experiential, context-specific and hard to formalise and communicate, for example, how to ride a bicycle.

Note that the distinction between explicit and tacit is not necessarily the result of the difficulty or complexity of the knowledge, but rather how easy it is to express that knowledge. Blackler develops a finer typology of knowledge, which identifies five types:[1]

- **Embrained** knowledge, which depends on conceptual skills and cognitive abilities, and emphasises the value of abstract knowledge.
- **Embodied** knowledge, which is action-oriented but likely to be only partly explicit, for example problem-solving ability and learning by doing, and is highly context-specific.
- **Encultured** knowledge, which is the process of achieving shared understanding and meaning. It is socially constructed and open to negotiation, and involves socialisation and acculturation.
- **Embedded** knowledge, which resides in systematic routines and processes. It includes resources and relationships between roles, procedures and technologies and is related to the notion of organisational capabilities or competencies.
- **Encoded** knowledge, which is represented by symbols and signs, and includes designs, blueprints, manuals and electronic media.

None of these types of knowledge is inherently superior, and the most relevant type will be contingent upon the organisational and environmental needs. It is also possible to add a sixth type of knowledge, **commodified** knowledge, which is embodied in the outputs of an organisation, for example products and services. This is a critical point, because much of the writing and practice of knowledge management treats the creation and sharing of knowledge as an end in itself. However, in most organisations, perhaps with the exceptions of (some) schools and universities, this is not the case. Knowledge is simply an input or means to achieve some organisational goal.

It is useful to distinguish between learning 'how' and learning 'why'. Learning 'how' involves improving or transferring existing skills, whereas learning 'why' aims to understand the underlying logic or causal factors with a view to applying the knowledge in new contexts.

Neither form of learning is inherently superior, and each will be important in different circumstances. For example, learning 'how' is more relevant where speed or quality is critical, but learning 'why' will be necessary to apply skills and know-how in new situations.

Much of the research on innovation management and organisational change has failed to address the issue of organisational learning. Instead, it has focused on learning by individuals within organisations: '. . . it is important to recognise that organisations do not learn, but rather the people in them do';[2] 'an organisation learns in only two ways: (i) by the learning of its members; or (ii) by ingesting new members . . . '.[3]

Clearly, individuals do learn within the context of organisations. This context affects their learning which, in turn, may affect the performance of the organisation. However, individuals and organisations are very different entities, and there is no reason why organisational learning should be conceptually or empirically the same as learning by individuals or individuals learning within organisations. Existing theory and research on organisational learning has been dominated by a weak metaphor of human learning and cognitive development, but such simplistic and inappropriate anthropomorphising of organisational characteristics has contributed to confused research and misleading conclusions.

Using the dimensions of individual versus collective knowledge, and routine versus novel tasks, it is possible to identify four organisational configurations (Figure 11.1). This framework is useful because rather than advocate a simplistic universal trend towards 'knowledge

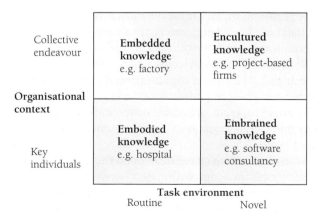

FIGURE 11.1   Task environment, organisational context and knowledge types.
Source: Derived from Blackler[1]

workers', it allows different types of knowledge to be mapped onto different organisational and task requirements.

For example, this framework suggests that, under conditions of environmental uncertainty, embrained and encultured knowledge are more relevant than embedded or embodied knowledge. The choice between the two approaches will depend on the organisational culture and context. We might expect a small, entrepeneurial firm to rely more on embrained knowledge, and a large established firm on encultured knowledge.

As we have seen, knowledge can be embodied in people, organisational culture, routines and tools, technologies, processes and systems. Organisations consist of a variety of individuals, groups and functions with different cultures, goals and frames of reference. Knowledge management consists of identifying and sharing knowledge across these disparate entities. There is a range of integrating mechanisms which can help to do this. Mobilising and managing knowledge should become a primary task and many of the recipes offered for achieving this depend upon mobilising a much higher level of participation in innovative problem-solving and on building such routines into the fabric of organisational life.

Nonaka and Takeuchi argue that the conversion of tacit to explicit knowledge is a critical mechanism underlying the link between individual and organisational knowledge. They argue that all new knowledge originates with an individual, but that through a process of dialogue, discussion, experience sharing and observation such knowledge is amplified at the group and organisational levels. This creates an expanding community of interaction, or **knowledge network**, which crosses intra- and interorganisational levels and boundaries. Such knowledge networks are a means to accumulate knowledge from outside the organisation, share it widely within the organisation, and store it for future use. This transformation of individual knowledge into organisational knowledge involves four cycles:[4]

- **Socialisation** – tacit to tacit knowledge, in which the knowledge of an individual or group is shared with others. Culture, socialisation and communities of practice are critical for this.
- **Externalisation** – tacit to explicit knowledge, through which the knowledge is made explicit and codified in some persistent form. This is the most novel aspect of Nonaka and Takeuchi's model. They argue that tacit knowledge can be transformed into explicit knowledge through a process of conceptualisation and crystallisation. Boundary objects are critical here.
- **Combination** – explicit to explicit knowledge, where different sources of explicit knowledge are pooled and exchanged. The role of organisational processes and technological systems are central to this.
- **Internalisation** – explicit to tacit, whereby other individuals or groups learn through practice. This is the traditional domain of organisational learning.

Max Boisot and Dorothy Griffiths have developed the similar concept of C-space (culture space) to analyse the flow of knowledge within and between organisations. It consists of two dimensions: codification, the extent to which information can be easily expressed, and diffusion, the extent to which information is shared by a given population. Using this framework he proposes a social learning cycle which involves four stages: scanning, problem-solving, diffusion and absorption (Figure 11.2).[5]

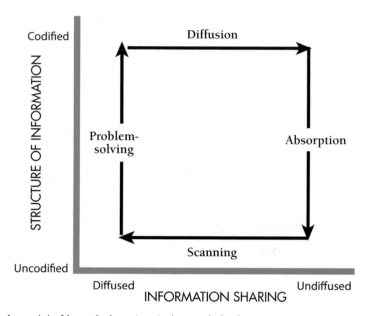

FIGURE 11.2   A model of knowledge structuring and sharing.

Source: Boisot, M. and Griffiths, D. (2006) in J. Tidd (ed.) *From Knowledge Management to Strategic Competencies.* Imperial College Press, second edition.

C-Space is a useful conceptual framework for this analysis. It focuses on the structuring and flow of knowledge within and between organisations. It consists of two dimensions: **codification** and **diffusion**. Codifying knowledge involves taking information that human agents carry in their heads and find hard to articulate, and structuring it in such a way that its complexity is reduced. This enables it to be incorporated into physical objects or described on paper. Once this has occurred, it will develop a life of its own and can diffuse quite rapidly and extensively. Knowledge moves around the C-Space in a cyclical fashion as shown in Figure 11.2.

INNOVATION IN ACTION

An Example of Codification and Diffusion Scales

Codified

Can be totally automated
Can be partially automated

(continued)

Can be systematically described
Can be described and put down on paper
Can be shown and described verbally
Can be shown
Inside someone's heard

Uncodified

Diffused

Known by all firms in all industries
Known by many firms in all industries
Known by many firms in many industries
Known by many firms in a few industries
Known by a handful of firms in a few industries
Known by only a handful of firms in one industry
Known only by one firm in one industry

Undiffused

This methodology can be used to map knowledge in an organisation or industry. This framework can help define what an organisation needs to do over time to maintain and renew resources and competencies. Effective management is about knowing where to locate knowledge resources and the organisational linkages that integrate them together to create competencies. The objectives of the framework are:

1. to enable an organisation to map its resources and the key linkages between them onto the C-Space;
2. to act as an elicitation device to facilitate a discussion about the meaning and action required – in terms of core competencies and knowledge resources.

Storing and Retrieving Knowledge

Storing knowledge is not a trivial problem, even now that the electronic storage and distribution of data is so cheap and easy. The biggest hurdle is the codification of tacit knowledge. The other common problem is to provide incentives to contribute, retrieve and reuse relevant knowledge. Many organisations have developed excellent knowledge intranet systems, but these are often under-utilised in practice.

> ## INNOVATION IN ACTION
>
> ## Knowledge Management at Arup
>
> Arup is an international engineering consultancy firm which provides planning, designing, engineering and project management services. The business demands the simultaneous achievement of innovative solutions and significant time compression imposed by client and regulatory requirements.
>
> Since 1999, the organisation has established a wide range of knowledge management initiatives to encourage sharing of know-how and experience across projects. These initiatives range from organisational processes and mechanisms, such as cross-functional communications meetings and skills networks, to technology-based approaches such as the Ovebase database and intranet.
>
> To date, the former have been more successful than the latter. For example, a survey of engineers in the firm indicated that in design and problem-solving, discussions with colleagues were rated as being twice as valuable as knowledge databases, and consequently engineers were four times as likely to rely on colleagues. Two primary reasons were cited for this. First, the difficulty of codifying tacit knowledge. Engineering consultancy involves a great deal of tacit knowledge and project experience which is difficult to store and retrieve electronically. Second, the complex engineering and unique environmental context of each project limits the reuse of standardised knowledge and experience.

In practice, there are two common but distinct approaches to knowledge management. The first is based on investments in IT, usually based on groupware and intranet technologies. This is the favoured approach of many management consultants. But introducing knowledge management into an organisation consists of much more than technology and training. It can require fundamental changes to organisational structure, processes and culture. The second approach is more people and process based, and attempts to encourage staff to identify, store, share and use information throughout the organisation. Research suggests that as in previous cases of process innovation, the benefits of the technology are not fully realised unless the organisational aspects are first dealt with.[6]

Therefore the storage, retrieval and reuse of knowledge demands much more than good IT systems. It also requires incentives to contribute to and use knowledge from such systems, whereas many organisations instead encourage and promote the generation and use of new knowledge.

Organisational memory is the process by which knowledge is stored for future use. Such information is stored either in the memories of members of an organisation or in its operating procedures and routines. The former suffers from all of the shortcomings of human memory, with the additional organisational problem of personnel loss or turnover. However, over time, these behavioural routines create and are reinforced by artefacts such as organisational structures, procedures and policies. In these terms, competencies become highly firm-specific combinations of behavioural routines and artefacts. This specificity questions the validity of the current fashion for benchmarking 'best practice' processes and structures: what works for one firm may not work for another. Conversely, the difficulty in anticipating future needs.

Richard Hall goes some way towards identifying the components of organisational memory. His main purpose is to articulate intangible resources and he distinguishes between intangible assets and intangible competencies. Assets include intellectual property rights and reputation. Competencies include the skills and know-how of employees, suppliers and distributors, as well as the collective attributes which constitute organisational culture. His empirical work, based on a survey and case studies, indicates that managers believe that the most significant of these intangible resources are the company's reputation and employees' know-how, both of which may be a function of organisational culture. These include:[7]

- Intangible, off balance sheet assets, such as patents, licences, trademarks, contracts and protectable data.
- Positional, which are the result of previous endeavour, that is, with a high path-dependency, such as processes and operating systems, and individual and corporate reputation and networks.
- Functional, which are either individual skills and know-how or team skills and know-how, within the company, at the suppliers or distributors.
- Cultural, including traditions of quality, customer service, human resources or innovation.

The key questions in each case are:

i. Are we making the best use of this resource?
ii. How else could it be used?
iii. Is the scope for synergy identified and exploited?
iv. Are we aware of the key linkages which exist between the resources?

Go online to find a framework for identifying innovative capabilities that helps to identify different types of knowledge and how these contribute to performance.

www.iande.info

Sharing and Distributing Knowledge

In practice, large organisations often do not know what they know. Many organisations now have databases and groupware to help store, retrieve and share data and information, but such systems are often confined to 'hard' data and information, rather than more tacit knowledge.

As a result functional groups or business units with potentially synergistic information may not be aware of where such information could be applied.

Knowledge sharing and distribution is the process by which information from different sources is shared and, therefore, leads to new knowledge or understanding. Greater organisational learning occurs when more of an organisation's components obtain new knowledge and recognise it as being of potential use. Tacit knowledge is not easily imitated by competitors because it is not fully encoded, but for the same reasons it may not be fully visible to all members of an organisation. As a result, organisational units with potentially synergistic information may not be aware of where such information could be applied. The speed and extent to which knowledge is shared between members of an organisation is likely to be a function of how codified the knowledge is.

There is a large number permutations of the processes required for converting and connecting knowledge from different parts of an organisation:[8]

- **Converting data and information to knowledge** – for example identifying patterns and associations in databases.
- **Converting text to knowledge** – through synthesis, comparison and analysis.
- **Converting individual to group knowledge** – sharing knowledge requires a supportive culture, appropriate incentives and technologies.
- **Connecting people to knowledge** – for example through seminars, workshops or software agents.
- **Connecting knowledge to people** – pushing relevant information and knowledge through intranets, agent systems.
- **Connecting people to people** – creating expert and interest directories and networks, mapping who knows what and who knows who.
- **Connecting knowledge to knowledge** – identifying and encouraging the interaction of different knowledge domains, for example through common projects.

This process of conversion and connection is underpinned by **communities of practice**. A community of practice is a group of people related by a shared task, process or the need to solve a problem, rather than by formal structural or functional relationships.[9] Through practice, a group within which knowledge is shared becomes a community of practice through a common understanding of what it does, of how to do it, and how it relates to other communities of practice.

Within communities of practice, people share tacit knowledge and learn through experimentation. Therefore the formation and maintenance of such communities represents an important link between individual and organisational learning. These communities naturally emerge around local work practice and so tend to reinforce functional or professional silos, but also can extend to wider, dispersed networks of similar practitioners.

The existence of communities of practice facilitates the sharing of knowledge within a community, due to both the sense of collective identity, and the existence of a significant common knowledge base. However, the sharing of knowledge between communities is much more problematic, due to the lack of both these elements. Thus the dynamics of knowledge sharing within and between communities of practice are likely to be very different, with the sharing of knowledge between communities typically much more complex, difficult and problematic.

Taking the issue of identity first, differences between different communities of practice will complicate the process of knowledge-sharing because of perceived or real differences of interest between communities, resulting in potential conflict. We discussed the benefits and drawbacks of conflict in Chapter 2. If conflict is too high, you may see information hoarding, open aggression, or people lying or exaggerating about their real needs. These conditions could be caused by power struggles of both a personal and professional nature. However, if conflict is too low, individuals and groups may lack motivation or interest in their tasks, and meetings are about one-way communication or reporting, rather than discussion and debate.

The other factor which can prevent the sharing of knowledge between communities of practice is the distinctiveness of different knowledge bases, and the lack of common knowledge, goals, assumptions, and interpretative frameworks. These differences significantly increase the difficulty not just of sharing knowledge between communities, but appreciating the knowledge of another community.

There are a few proven mechanisms to help knowledge transfer between different communities of practice:[10]

1. An organisational **translator**, who is an individual able to express the interests of one community in terms of another community's perspective. Therefore the translator must be sufficiently conversant with both knowledge domains and trusted by both communities. Examples of translators include the 'heavyweight product manager' in new product development, who bridges different technical groups and the technical and marketing groups.
2. A knowledge **broker**, who differs from a translator in that they participate in different communities rather than simply mediate between them. They represent overlaps between communities, and are typically people loosely linked to several communities through **weak ties** who are able to facilitate knowledge flows between them.[11] An example might be a quality manager responsible for the quality of a process that crosses several different functional groups.
3. A **boundary object or practice**, which is something of interest to two or more communities of practice. Different communities of practice will have a stake in it, but from different perspectives. A boundary object might be a shared document, for example a quality manual; an artefact, for example a prototype; a technology, for example a database; or a practice, for example a product design. A boundary object provides an opportunity for discussion, debate (and conflict) and therefore can encourage communication between different communities of practice.

For example, formally appointed 'knowledge brokers' can be used to systematically scavenge the organisation for old or unused ideas, to pass these around the organisation and imagine their application in different contexts. For example, Hewlett-Packard created a SpaM group to help identify and share good practice among its 150 business divisions. Before the new group was formed, divisions were unlikely to share information because they often competed for resources and were measured against each other. Similarly, Skandia, a Swedish insurance company active in overseas markets, attempts to identify, encourage and measure its intellectual capital, and has appointed a 'knowledge manager' who is responsible for this. The company has developed a set of indicators that it uses both to manage knowledge internally, and for external financial reporting.

More generally, cross-functional team-working can help to promote this inter-communal exchange. Functional diversity tends to extend the range of knowledge available and increase the number of options considered, but also can have a negative effect on group cohesiveness and the cost of projects and efficiency of decision-making. However, a major benefit of cross-functional team-working is the access it provides to the bodies of knowledge that are external to the team. In general a high frequency of knowledge sharing outside of a group is associated with improved technical and project performance, as gatekeeper individuals pick up and import vital signals and knowledge. In particular, cross-functional composition in teams is argued to permit access to disciplinary knowledge outside. Therefore cross-functional team-working is a critical way of promoting the exchange of knowledge and practice across disciplines and communities.

A wide range of strategies for introducing knowledge management is available, and no single approach will be appropriate in all circumstances. The most appropriate strategy will depend on the existing organisational culture, structure, processes and culture, the nature of knowledge, and the availability of resources and urgency of action.

It follows from this that developing a climate conducive to knowledge sharing is not a simple matter since it consists of a complex web of behaviours and artefacts. And changing this culture is not likely to happen quickly or as a result of single initiatives, such as restructuring or mass training in a new technique. Given this, it is clear that management cannot directly change culture but it can intervene at the level of artefacts – by changing structures or processes – and by providing models and reinforcing preferred styles of behaviour. Instead, building a culture supportive of knowledge management involves systematic development of organisational structures, communication policies and procedures, reward and recognition systems, training policy, accounting and measurement systems and deployment of strategy.

Go online to watch the video of how Xerox developed a knowledge management system.

www.iande.info

Table 11.1 provides a useful way of understanding the advantages and disadvantages of different ways of implementing knowledge management. It identifies five different strategies for introducing knowledge management to an organisation:[12]

- ripple;
- flow;
- embedding;

- bridge;
- transfer.

The **ripple** approach is the most basic, and consists of a knowledge centre or core of one specific discipline, technology or skill, which is developed incrementally over time. An example might be quality management, or the experience curve in mass production, or robust designs. The impact over time can be great, but the danger is that the knowledge will become detached from market needs and technological opportunities.

The **flow** approach involves projects being handed from one knowledge centre to another, often sequentially. This is similar to the traditional new product or service development process, and one of the biggest problems is managing the interfaces and integration between the knowledge centres, for example, the design, production and marketing functions.

The **embedding** approach brings different knowledge centres into a broader framework, without any major changes to the centres. An example would be the electronic data interchange

TABLE 11.1   Knowledge management strategies

Strategy	Characteristics	Requirements	Risks
Ripple	Bottom-up, continuous improvement, e.g. quality management	Process tools, sustained motivation	Isolation from technical excellence
Flow	Integration of functional knowledge within processes, e.g. product development	Improved interfaces, early involvement, overlapping phases	Conformity, co-ordination burden
Embedding	Coupling of systems, products and services, e.g. enterprise resource planning (ERP)	Common information systems and technology, motivation and rewards	Loss of autonomy, system complexity
Bridge	New knowledge by novel combination of existing competencies, e.g. architectural innovations	Common language and objectives	High control needs, technical feasibility, market failure
Transfer	Exploiting existing knowledge in a new context, e.g. related diversification	New market knowledge	Inappropriate technology, customer support and service

Source: Adapted from den Hertog, J.F. and Huizenga, E. (2000) *The Knowledge Enterprise*. Imperial College Press, London.

(EDI) between a supplier and retailer to reduce stocks and improve responsiveness. Potential problems include asymmetric cost and benefits between the centres, and fear of control or leakage of information.

The **bridge** approach merges two or more different knowledge centres to create a whole new knowledge domain. This may be a merger of disciplines, for example mechanical and electrical engineering to form mechatronics, which is sometimes referred to as **technology fusion**, or may involve the combination of two organisations in a joint venture or merger. This is a very risky strategy, as such bridges typically have significant technological, organisational and commercial uncertainties, but when successful can result in radically new knowledge and high rewards.

The **transfer** approach is more selective, and consists of taking a useful element of one knowledge domain and adapting it for use in another. The knowledge transferred might be technology, market knowledge or organisational know-how or processes. Process benchmarking is an example of a knowledge transfer strategy.

This framework is useful because it helps us to understand better the needs and limits of different approaches to knowledge management, beyond the usual, but often unsuccessful 'technology and training' approach.

Translating Knowledge into Innovation

Knowledge management has all the characteristics of a management fad or fashion. However, successful management practice is never fully reproducible. In a complex world, neither the most scrupulous practising manager nor the most rigorous management scholar can be sure of identifying – let alone evaluating – all the necessary ingredients in real examples of successful management practice. In addition, the conditions of any (inevitably imperfect) reproduction of successful management practice will differ from the original, whether in terms of firm, country, sector, physical conditions, state of technical knowledge, or organisational skills and cultural norms. Therefore in real life there are no easily applicable recipes for successful management practice. This is one of the reasons why there are continuous swings in management fashion.

INNOVATION IN ACTION

Management Fads and Fashion Statements versus Behavioural Change in Organisations

The problem with routines is that they have to be learned – and learning is difficult. It takes time and money to try new things, it disrupts and disturbs the day-to-day working of the firm, it can

(continued)

upset organisational arrangements and require efforts in acquiring and using new skills. Not surprisingly most firms are reluctant learners – and one strategy which they adopt is to try to short cut the process by borrowing ideas from other organisations.

Whilst there is enormous potential in learning from others, simply copying what seems to work for another organisation will not necessarily bring any benefits and may end up costing a great deal and distracting the organisation from finding its own ways of dealing with a particular problem. The temptation to copy gives rise to the phenomenon of particular approaches becoming fashionable – something which every organisation thinks it needs in order to deal with its particular problems.

Over the past 20 years we have seen many apparent panaceas for the problems of becoming competitive. Organisations are constantly seeking for new answers to old problems, and the scale of investment in the new fashions of management thinking have often been considerable. The *original* evidence for the value of these tools and techniques was strong, with case studies and other reports testifying to their proven value within the context of origin, but there is also extensive evidence to suggest that these changes do not always work, and in many cases lead to considerable dissatisfaction and disillusionment.

Examples include:

- advanced manufacturing technology (AMT – robots, flexible machines, integrated computer control, etc.), lean and agile production;
- quality circles, total quality management (TQM), ISO9000;
- business process re-engineering (BPR), Enterprise Resource Planning (ERP);
- benchmarking best practice;
- networking/clustering;
- knowledge management.

What is going on here demonstrates well the principles behind behavioural change in organisations. It is not that the original ideas were flawed or that the initial evidence was wrong, rather it was that other organisations assumed they could simply be copied, without the need to adapt them, to customise them, to modify and change them to suit their circumstances. In other words, there was no learning, and no progress towards making them become routines, part of the underlying culture within the firm.

However, innovation and entrepreneurship are about knowledge – creating new possibilities through combining different knowledge sets. These can be in the form of knowledge about what is technically possible or what particular configuration of this would meet an articulated or latent need. Such knowledge may already exist in our experience, based on something we have seen or done before. Or it could result from a process of search – research into technologies, markets, competitor actions, etc. And it could be in explicit form, codified in such a way that others can access it, discuss it, transfer it, etc. – or it can be in tacit form, known about but not actually put into words or formulae.

The process of weaving these different knowledge sets together into a successful new process, product or business is one which takes place under highly uncertain conditions. We often don't know about what the final configuration will look like, or precisely how we will get there. In such cases managing knowledge is about committing resources to reduce the uncertainty.

 We have developed two interactive Flash Innovation Audits to help to identify how different types of knowledge contribute to innovation. Go online to find them.

www.iande.info

A key contribution to our understanding here comes from the work of Henderson and Clark who looked closely at the kinds of knowledge involved in different kinds of innovation. They argue that innovation rarely involves dealing with a single technology or market but rather a bundle of knowledge which is brought together into a configuration. Successful innovation management requires that we can get hold of and use knowledge about *components* but also about how those can be put together – what they termed the *architecture* of an innovation (Figure 11.3).

Figure 11.3 highlights the issues for managing innovation. In zone 1 the rules of the game are clear – this is about steady-state improvement to products or processes and uses knowledge accumulated around core components.

In zone 2 there is significant change in one element but the overall architecture remains the same. Here there is a need to learn new knowledge but within an established and clear

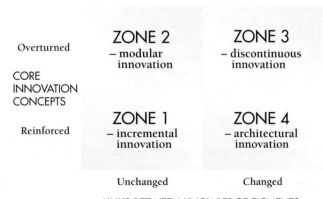

FIGURE 11.3   Architectural innovation and knowledge components.
Source: Tidd, J. and Bessant, J. (2009) *Managing Innovation: Integrating technological, market and organizational change.* John Wiley & Sons Ltd.

framework of sources and users – for example, moving to electronic ignition or direct injection in a car engine, the use of new materials in airframe components, the use of IT systems instead of paper processing in key financial or insurance transactions, etc. None of these involves major shifts or dislocations.

In zone 3 we have discontinuous innovation where neither the end state nor the ways in which it can be achieved are known about – essentially the whole set of rules of the game change and there is scope for new entrants.

In zone 4 we have the condition where new combinations – architectures – emerge, possibly around the needs of different groups of users (as in the disruptive innovation case). Here the challenge is in reconfiguring the knowledge sources and configurations. We may use existing knowledge and recombine it in different ways or we may use a combination of new and old. Examples might be low-cost airlines, direct-line insurance, others.

We can see this more clearly with an example. Change at the component level in building a flying machine might involve switching to newer metallurgy or composite materials for the wing construction or the use of fly-by-wire controls instead of control lines or hydraulics. But the underlying knowledge about how to link aerofoil shapes, control systems, propulsion systems, etc. at the *system* level is unchanged – and being successful at both requires a different and higher order set of competencies.

One of the difficulties with this is that innovation knowledge flows – and the structures which evolve to support them – tend to reflect the nature of the innovation. So if it is at component level then the relevant people with skills and knowledge around these components will talk to each other – and when change takes place they can integrate new knowledge. But when change takes place at the higher system level – 'architectural innovation' – then the existing channels and flows may not be appropriate or sufficient to support the innovation and the firm needs to develop new ones. This is another reason why existing incumbents often fare badly when major system level change takes place – because they have the twin difficulties of learning and configuring a new knowledge system and 'unlearning' an old and established one.

A variation on this theme comes in the field of 'technology fusion', where different technological streams converge, such that products which used to have a discrete identity begin to merge into new architectures. An example here is the home automation industry, where the fusion of technologies like computing, telecommunications, industrial control and elementary robotics is enabling a new generation of housing systems with integrated entertainment, environmental control (heating, air conditioning, lighting, etc.) and communication possibilities.

Similarly, in services a new addition to the range of financial services may represent a component product innovation, but its impacts are likely to be less far-reaching (and the attendant risks of its introduction lower) than a complete shift in the nature of the service package – for example, the shift to direct-line systems instead of offering financial services through intermediaries.

David Tranfield and his colleagues map the different phases of the innovation process to identify the knowledge routines in each of three innovation phases: Discovery, Realisation and Nurture (Figure 11.4 and Table 11.2):[13]

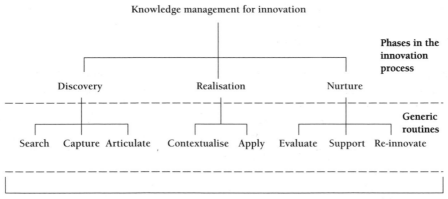

FIGURE 11.4   Hierarchical process model of knowledge management for innovation.
Source: From David Tranfield, Malcolm Young, David Partington, John Bessant and Jonathan Sapsed (2006) 'Knowledge Management Routines for Innovation Projects: Developing a Hierarchical Process Model', in J. Tidd (ed.) *From Knowledge Management to Strategic Competence.* Imperial College Press, second edition.

- *Discovery* – scanning and searching the internal and external environments, and to pick up and process signals about potential innovation. These could be needs of various kinds, opportunities arising from research activities, regulative pressures, or the behaviour of competitors.
- *Realisation* – how the organisation can successfully implement the innovation, growing it from an idea through various stages of development to final launch as a new product or service in the external marketplace or a new process or method within the organisation. Realisation requires selecting from this set of potential triggers for innovation those activities to which the organisation will commit resources.
- *Nurturing* the chosen option by providing resources, developing (either by creating through R&D or acquiring through technology transfer) the means for exploration. It involves not only codified knowledge formally embodied in technology, but also tacit knowledge in the surrounding social linkage which is needed to make the innovation work. The nurture phase involves maintaining and supporting the innovation through various improvements and also reflecting upon previous phases and reviewing experiences of success and failure in order to learn about how to manage the process better, and capture relevant knowledge from the experience. This learning creates the conditions for beginning the cycle again, or 're-innovation'.

Go online to find the case study of how the UK retailer Tesco entered the US market. It demonstrates how different types of knowledge transfer contributed to success in a different context.

www.iande.info

TABLE 11.2 Process model linking innovation phase to knowledge management activities

Phase in the innovation process	Generic routines	Description	Examples of detailed knowledge management activities
Discovery	Search	The passive and active means by which potential knowledge sources are scanned for items of interest	Active environmental scanning (technological, market, social, political, etc.) Active future scanning Experiment – R&D, etc.
	Capture	The means by which knowledge search outcomes are internalised within the organisation	Picking up relevant signals and communicating them within and across the organisation to relevant players
	Articulate	The means by which captured knowledge is given clear expression	Concept definition – what might we do? Strategic and operational planning cycles – from outline feasibility to detailed operational plan
Realisation	Contextualise	The means by which articulated knowledge is placed in particular organisational contexts	Resource planning and procurement – inside and outside the organisation Prototyping and other concept refining activities Early mobilisation across functions – design for manufacture, assembly, quality, etc.
	Apply	The means by which contextualised knowledge is applied to organisational challenges	Project team mobilisation Project planning cycles Project implementation and modification – 'cycles of mutual adaptation' in technological, market, organisational domains Launch preparation and execution
Nurture	Evaluate	The means by which the efficacy of knowledge applications is assessed	Post-project review Market/user feedback Learning by using/making/etc.

(continued)

Phase in the innovation process	Generic routines	Description	Examples of detailed knowledge management activities
	Support	The means by which knowledge applications are sustained over time	Feedback collection Incremental problem-solving and debugging
	Re-innovate	The means by which knowledge and experience are re-applied elsewhere within the organisation	Pick up relevant signals to repeat the cycle Mobilise momentum for new cycle

TABLE 11.2 (*Continued*)

Source: From David Tranfield, Malcolm Young, David Partington, John Bessant and Jonathan Sapsed (2006) 'Knowledge Management Routines for Innovation Projects: Developing a Hierarchical Process Model', in J. Tidd (ed.) *From Knowledge Management to Strategic Competence*. Imperial College Press, second edition.

Exploiting Intellectual Property

In some cases knowledge, in particular in its more explicit or codified forms, can be commercialised by licensing or selling the intellectual property rights (IPR), rather than the more difficult and uncertain route of developing new processes, products or businesses.

For example, in one year IBM reported license income of US$1bn, and in the USA the total royalty income of industry from licensing is around US$100bn. Much of this is from payments for licenses to use software, music or films. For example, in 2005 the global sales of legal music downloads exceeded US$1 billion (although illegal downloads are estimated to be worth three to four times this figure), still only around 5% of all music company revenue, with music downloaded to mobile phones accounting for almost a quarter of this. Patterns of use vary by country: for example, in Japan 99.8% of all music downloads are to mobile phones rather than to dedicated MP3 players. However, despite the growth of legal sites for downloading music and an aggressive programme of pursuing users of illegal file-sharing sites, the level of illegal downloads has not declined.

This clearly demonstrates two of the many the problems associated with intellectual property: these may provide some legal rights, but such rights are useless unless they can be effectively enforced; and once in the public domain, imitation or illegal use is very likely. For these reasons, secrecy is often a more effective alternative to seeking IPR.

However, IPR can be highly effective in some circumstances, and as we will argue later, can be used in less obvious ways to help to identify innovations and assess competitors. A range of IPR exist, but those most applicable to technology and innovation are patents, copyright and design rights and registration.

Patents

All developed countries have some form of patent legislation, the aim of which is to encourage innovation by allowing a limited monopoly, usually for 20 years, and more recently many developing and emerging economies have been encouraged to sign up to the TRIPS (Trade Related Intellectual Property System). Legal regimes differ in the detail, but in most countries the issue of a patent requires certain legal tests to be satisfied:

- *Novelty* – no part of 'prior art', including publications, written, oral or anticipation. In most countries the first to file the patent is granted the rights, but in the USA it is the first to invent. The American approach may have the moral advantage, but results in many legal challenges to patents, and requires detailed documentation during R&D.
- *Inventive step* – 'not obvious to a person skilled in the art'. This is a relative test, as the assumed level of skill is higher in some fields than others. For example, Genentech was granted a patent for the plasminogen activator t-PA which helps to reduce blood clots, but despite its novelty, a Court of Appeal revoked the patent on the grounds that it did not represent an inventive step because its development was deemed to be obvious to researchers in field.
- *Industrial application* – utility test requires the invention to be capable of being applied to a machine, product or process. In practice a patent must specify an application for the technology, and additional patents sought for any additional application. For example, Unilever developed Ceramides and patented their use in a wide range of applications. However, it did not apply for a patent for application of the technology to shampoos, which was subsequently granted to a competitor.
- *Patentable subject* – for example, discoveries and formulae cannot be patented, and in Europe neither can software (the subject of copyright) nor new organisms, although both these are patentable in the USA. For example, contrast of the mapping of the human genome in the USA and Europe: in the USA the research is being conducted by a commercial laboratory which is patenting the outcomes, and in Europe by a group of public laboratories which is publishing the outcomes on the Internet.
- *Clear and complete disclosure.* Note that a patent provides only certain legal property rights, and in the case of infringement the patent holder needs to take the appropriate legal action. In some cases secrecy may be a preferable strategy. Conversely, national patent databases represent a large and detailed reservoir of technological innovations which can be interrogated for ideas.

Apart from the more obvious use of patents as IPR, they can be used to search for potential innovations, and to help identify potential partners or to assess competitors.

 Go online to listen to Roy Sandbach discuss how Procter & Gamble exploit a wide range of external sources of knowledge and technology.

www.iande.info

For example, the TRIZ system developed by Genrich Altshuller identifies standard solutions to common technical problems distilled from an analysis of 1.5 million patents, and applies these in different contexts. Many leading companies use the system, including 3M, Rolls-Royce and Motorola.

Patents can also be used to identify and assess innovation, at the firm, sector or national level. However, great care needs to be taken when making such assessments, because patents are only a partial indicator of innovation.

The main advantages of patent data are that they reflect the corporate capacity to generate innovation, are available at a detailed level of technology over long periods of time, are comprehensive in the sense that they cover small as well as large firms, and are used by practitioners themselves. However, patenting tends to occur early in the development process, and therefore can be a poor measure of the output of development activities, and tells us nothing about the economic or commercial potential of the innovation.

Crude counts of the number of patents filed by a firm, sector or country reveal little, but the quality of patents can be assessed by a count of how often a given patent is cited in later patents. This provides a good indicator of its technical quality, albeit after the event, although not necessarily commercial potential. Highly cited patents are generally of much greater importance than patents which are never cited, or are cited only a few times. The reason for this is that a patent which contains an important new invention – or major advance – can set off a stream of follow-on inventions, all of which may cite the original, important invention upon which they are building.

Using such patent citations, the quality distribution of patents tends to be very skewed: there are large numbers of patents that are cited only a few times, and only a small number of patents cited more than 10 times. For example, half of patents are cited two or fewer times, 75% are cited five or fewer times, and only 1% of the patents are cited 24 or more times. Overall, after 10 or more years, the average cites/patent is around six.[14]

The most useful indicators of innovation based on patents are (Table 11.3):

i. *Number of patents*. Indicates the level of technology activity, but crude patent counts reflect little more than the propensity to patent of a firm, sector or country.

ii. *Cites per patent*. Indicates the impact of a company's patents.

iii. *Current impact index (CII)*. This is a fundamental indicator of patent portfolio quality, it is the number of times the company's previous five years of patents, in a technology area, were cited from the current year, divided by the average citations received.

iv. *Technology strength (TS)*. Indicates the strength of the patent portfolio, and is the number of patents multiplied by the current impact index, that is, patent portfolio size inflated or deflated by patent quality.

v. *Technology cycle time (TCT)*. Indicates the speed of invention, and is the median age, in years, of the patent references cited on the front page of the patent.

vi. *Science linkage (SL)*. Indicates how leading edge the technology is, and is the average number of science papers referenced on the front page of the patent.

vii. *Science strength (SS)*. Indicates how much the patent applies basic science, and is the number of patents multiplied by science linkage, that is, patent portfolio size inflated or deflated by the extent of science linkage.

TABLE 11.3 Patent indicators for different sectors			
	Current impact index (expected value 1.0)	Technology life cycle (years)	Science linkage (science references/ patents)
Oil and gas	0.84	11.9	0.8
Chemicals	0.79	9.0	2.7
Pharmaceuticals	0.79	8.1	7.3
Biotechnology	0.68	7.7	14.4
Medical equipment	2.38	8.3	1.1
Computers	1.88	5.8	1.0
Telecoms	1.65	5.7	0.8
Semiconductors	1.35	6.0	1.3
Aerospace	0.68	13.2	0.3

Source: Derived from Narin, F. (2006) in J. Tidd (ed.) *From Knowledge Management to Strategic Competence.* Imperial College Press, second edition.

Companies whose patents have above average current impact indices (CII) and science linkage indicators (SL) tend to have significantly higher market-to-book ratios and stock market returns. However, having a strong intellectual property portfolio does not, of course, guarantee a company's success. Many additional factors influence the ability of a company to move from quality patents to innovation and financial and market performance. The decade of troubles at IBM, for example, is certainly illustrative of this, since IBM has always had very high-quality and highly cited research in its laboratories. As Chris Evans, founder of Chiroscience and Merlin Ventures, notes: 'Academics and universities . . . have no management, no muscle, no vision, no business plan and that is 90% of the task of exploiting science and taking it to the marketplace. There is a tendency for universities to think, "we invented the thing so we are already 50% there". The fact is they are 50% to nowhere' (*Times Higher*, 27 March 1998).

At the firm level, rather than at the industry level, there is a lot of variability in the productivity of technological inputs, that is, how effectively these are translated into technological outputs. Research suggests at least three reasons for the differences in the ability of firms to translate inputs into outputs: scale, technological opportunity and organisation and management. However, few managers are interested in improved measures of technological inputs, and instead need ways to assess the *efficiency* and *effectiveness* of the innovation process: efficiency in the sense of how well companies translate technological and commercial inputs into new products, processes and businesses; effectiveness in the sense of how successful such innovations are in the market and their contribution to financial performance. Our own research, using various combinations of inputs, outputs and indicators of performance, suggests that some ratio of outputs (e.g. new product announcements) to input (e.g. patents or R&D) provides a good proxy for innovation efficiency, and is associated with a range of financial and market measures of performance, such as value-added and market-to-book value.

Therefore care needs to be taken when using patent data as an indicator of innovation. The main advantages of patents are:

i. Patents represent the output of the inventive process, specifically those inventions which are expected to have an economic benefit.
ii. Obtaining patent protection is time consuming and expensive. Hence applications are only likely to be made for those developments which are expected to provide benefits in excess of these costs.
iii. Patents can be broken down by technical fields, thus providing information on both the rate and direction of innovation.
iv. Patent statistics are available in large numbers and over very long time series.

The main disadvantages of patents as indicators of innovation are:

i. Not all inventions are patented. Firms may chose to protect their discoveries by other means, such as through secrecy. It has been estimated that firms apply for patents for 66% to 87% of patentable inventions.
ii. Not all innovations are technically patentable – for example, software development (outside the USA), and some organisms.
iii. The propensity to patent varies considerably across different sectors and firms. For example, there is a high propensity to patent in the pharmaceutical industry, but a low propensity in fast-moving consumer goods.
iv. Firms have a different propensity to patent in each national market, according to the attractiveness of markets.
v. A large proportion of patents are never exploited, or are applied for simply to block other developments. It has been estimated that between 40% and 60% of all patents issued are used.

There are major intersectoral differences in the relative importance of patenting in achieving its prime objective, namely, to act as a barrier to imitation. For example, patenting is relatively unimportant in automobiles, but critical in pharmaceuticals. Moreover, patents do not yet fully measure technological activities in software since copyright laws are often used as the main means of protection against imitation outside the USA.

There are also major differences among countries in the procedures and criteria for granting patents. For this reason, comparisons are most reliable when using international patenting or patenting in one country. The US patenting statistics are a particularly rich source of information, given the rigour and fairness of criteria and procedures for granting patents, the strong incentives for firms to get IPR in the world's largest market. More recently, data from the European Patent Office are also becoming more readily available.

Copyright

Copyright is concerned with the expression of ideas, and not the ideas themselves. Therefore the copyright exists only if the idea is made concrete, for example, in a book or recording. There is no requirement for registration, and the test of originality is low compared to patent law, requiring only that 'the author of the work must have used his own skill and effort to create the work'. Like patents, copyright provides limited legal rights for certain types of material for a specific term. For literary, dramatic, musical and artistic works copyright is normally for 70 years after the death of the author, 50 in the USA, and for recordings, film, broadcast and cable programmes 50 years from their creation. Typographical works have 25 years copyright. The type of materials covered by copyright include:

- 'original' literary, dramatic, musical and artistic works, including software and in some cases databases;
- recordings, films, broadcasts and cable programmes;
- typographical arrangement or layout of a published edition.

Design Rights

Design rights are similar to copyright protection, but mainly apply to three-dimensional articles, covering any aspect of the 'shape' or 'configuration', internal or external, whole or part, but specifically excludes integral and functional features, such as spare parts. Design rights exist for 15 years and 10 years if commercially exploited. Design registration is a cross between patent and copyright protection, is cheaper and easier than patent protection, but more limited in scope. It provides protection for up to 25 years, but covers only visual appearance – shape, configuration, pattern and ornament. It is used for designs that have aesthetic appeal, for example, consumer electronics and toys. For example the knobs on top of Lego bricks are functional, and would therefore not qualify for design registration, but were also considered to have 'eye appeal', and therefore granted design rights.

INNOVATION IN ACTION

Open Source Software

Proprietary software usually restricts imitation by retaining the source code and by enforcing intellectual property rights such as patents (mainly the USA) or copyright (elsewhere). However, Open Source Software has many characteristics of a public good, including non-excludability and non-rivalry, and developers and users of OSS have a joint interest in making OSS free and

(continued)

publicly available. The open software movement has grown since the 1980s when the programmer Richard Stallman founded the Free Software Foundation, and the General Public License (GPL) is now widely used to promote the use and adaptation of open source software. The GPL forms the legal basis of three-quarters of all OSS, including Linux.

Therefore firms active in the field of Open Source Software have to create value and appropriate private benefits in different ways. The ineffectiveness of traditional intellectual property rights in such cases means that firms are more likely to rely on alternative ways of appropriating the benefits of innovation, such as being first to the market or by using externalities to create value. More generic strategies include product and service approaches:

Products – adding a proprietary part to the open code and licensing this, or black-boxing by combining several pieces of OSS into a solution package.
Services – consultancy, training or support for OSS.

Linux is a good example of a successful OSS which firms have developed products and services around. It has been largely developed by a network of voluntary programmers, often referred to as the 'Linux community'. Linus Torvalds first suggested the development of a free operating system to compete with the DOS/Windows monopoly in 1991, and quickly attracted the support of a group of volunteer programmers: 'having those 100 part-time users was really great for all the feedback I got. They found bugs that I hadn't because I hadn't been using it the way they were . . . after a while they started sending me fixes or improvements . . . this wasn't planned, it just happened.' Thus Linux grew from 10,000 lines of code in 1991 to 1.5 million lines by 1998. Its development coincided with and fully exploited the growth of Internet and later web forms of collaborative working. The provision of the source code to all potential developers promotes continuous incremental innovation, and the close and sometimes indistinguishable developer and user groups promote concurrent development and debugging. The weaknesses are potential lack of support for users and new hardware, availability of compatible software and forking in development.

By 1998 there were estimated to be more than 7.5 million users and almost 300 user groups across 40 countries. Linux has achieved a 25% share of the market for server operating systems, although its share of the PC operating system market was much lower, and Apache, a Linux application Web server program, accounted for half the market. Although Linux is available free of charge, a number of businesses have been spawned by its development. These range from branding and distribution of Linux, development of complementary software and user support and consultancy services. For example, although Linux can be downloaded free of charge, RedHat Software provides an easier installation program and better documentation for around US$50, and in 1998 achieved annual revenues of more than US$10 m. Red Hat was floated in 1999. In China, the lack of legacy systems, low costs and government support have made Linux-based systems popular on servers and desktop applications. In 2004 Linux began to enter consumer markets, when Hewlett-Packard launched its first Linux-based notebook computer, which helped to reduce the units cost by US$60.

Source: L. Dahlander (2005) 'Appropriation and Appropriability in Open Source Software', *International Journal of Innovation Management*, 9(3), 259–286.

Licensing IPR

Once you have acquired some form of formal legal IPR, you can allow others to use it in some way in return for some payment (a licence), or sell the IPR outright (or assign it). Licensing IPR can have a number of benefits:

- reduce or eliminate production and distribution costs and risks;
- reach a larger market;
- exploit in other applications;
- establish standards;
- gain access to complementary technology;
- block competing developments;
- convert competitor into defender.

Considerations when drafting a licensing agreement include degree of exclusivity, territory and type of end use, period of licence and type and level of payments – royalty, lump sum or cross-licence. Pricing a licence is as much an art as a science, and depends on a number of factors such as the balance of power and negotiating skills. Common methods of pricing licences are:

- Going market rate – based on industry norms, e.g. 6% of sales in electronics and mechanical engineering.
- 25% rule – based on licensee's gross profit earned through use of the technology.
- Return on investment – based on licensor's costs.
- Profit-sharing – based on relative investment and risk. First, estimate total life-cycle profit. Next, calculate relative investment and weight according to share of risk. Finally, compare results to alternatives, e.g return to licensee, imitation, litigation.

There is no 'best' licensing strategy, as it depends on the strategy of the organisation and the nature of the technology and markets. For example, Celltech licensed its asthma treatment to Merck for a single payment of $50 m, based on sales projections. This isolated Celltech from the risk of clinical trials and commercialisation, and provided a much-needed cash injection. Toshiba, Sony and Matsushita license DVD technology for royalties of only 1.5% to encourage its adoption as the industry standard . Until the recent legal proceedings, Microsoft applied a 'per processor' royalty to its OEM (original equipment manufacturer) customers for Windows to discourage its customers from using competing operating systems.

 Go online to find the case study of Joint Solutions, which illustrates the complexities of managing licensing agreements.

www.iande.info

For example, since the mid-1980s the universities have increasingly used IPR in an effort to commercialise technology and increase income. Changes in funding and law have clearly encouraged many more universities to establish licensing and technology transfer departments, but whilst the level of patenting has increased significantly as a result, the income and impact has been relatively small. The number of patents granted to US universities doubled between 1984 and 1989, and doubled again between 1989 and 1997. In 1979 the number of patents granted to US universities was only 264, compared with 2436 in 1997.

There are a number of explanations for this significant increase in patent activity. Changes in government funding and intellectual property law played a role, but detailed analysis indicates that the most significant reason was technological opportunity. For example, there is strong evidence that the scientific and commercial quality of patents has fallen since the mid-1980s as a result of these policy changes, and that the distribution of activity has a very long tail.

Measured in terms of the number of patents held or exploited, or by income from patent and software licences, commercialisation of technology is highly concentrated in a small number of elite universities which were highly active prior to changes to funding policy and law: the top 20 US universities account for 70% of the patent activity. Moreover, at each of these elite universities a very small number of key patents account for most of the licensing income, the five most successful patents typically account for 70–90% of total income. The average income from a university licence is only around $60,000, whereas the average return from a university spin-out firm was more than ten times this.

This suggests that a (rare) combination of research excellence and critical mass is required to succeed in the commercialisation of technology. Nonetheless, technological opportunity has reduced some of the barriers to commercialisation. Specifically, the growing importance of developments in the biosciences and software present new opportunities for universities to benefit from the commercialisation of technology.

The successful exploitation of IPR also incurs costs and risks:

- cost of search, registration and renewal;
- need to register in various national markets;
- full and public disclosure of your idea;
- need to be able to enforce.

INNOVATION IN ACTION

ARM Holdings

ARM Holdings designs and licenses high-performance, low-energy-consumption 16- and 32-bit RISC (reduced instruction set computing) chips, which are used extensively in mobile devices such as cell phones, cameras, electronic organisers and smart cards. ARM was established in

(continued)

1990 as a joint venture between Acorn Computers in the UK and Apple Computer. Acorn did not pioneer the RISC architecture, but it was the first to market a commercial RISC processor in the mid-1980s. Perhaps ironically, the first application of ARM technology was in the relatively unsuccessful Apple Newton PDA (Personal Digital Assistant). One of the most recent successful applications has been in the Apple i-Pod and i-Pad. ARM designs but does not manufacture chips, and receives royalties of between 5 cents and US$2.50 for every chip produced under licence. Licensees include Apple, Ericsson, Fujitsu, H-P, NEC, Nintendo, Sega, Sharp, Sony, Toshiba and 3Com. In 1999, it announced joint ventures with leading chip manufacturers such as Intel and Texas Instruments to design and build chips for the next generation of hand-held devices. It is estimated that ARM-designed processors were used in more than 2 billion devices by 2006, representing around 80% of all mobile devices. In 1998, the company was floated in London and on the Nasdaq in New York, and it achieved a market capitalisation of £3bn in December 1999, with an annual revenue growth of 40%. The company has created 30 millionaires amongst its staff.

In July 2010, Microsoft signed a licensing deal with ARM, building on a relationship going back to 1997. This gave Microsoft greater access to the chip architecture and the instruction set to allow it to further develop mobiles and embedded devices with ARM-designed processors inside, such as the Zune media player, smartphones running Windows Mobile and the new Windows Phone 7. Other leading firms, such as Apple, Amazon, Google, Samsung and Sony Ericsson also incorporate ARM designs in their tablets, e-readers and netbooks. The company shipped its 10 billionth processor in 2008, and claims that there is an average of 2.6 ARM processors in every mobile phone sold today. It spends around 25% of its annual income of US $300 million on R&D. By mid-2010, ARM had 1775 full-time employees, 726 based in the UK, 485 in the US, 207 in Europe, 267 in India and 90 in the Asia Pacific region.

http://www.arm.com/

In most countries the basic registration fee for a patent is relatively modest, but in addition applying for a patent includes the cost of professional agents, such as patent agents, translation for foreign patents, official registration fees in all relevant countries and renewal fees. As a result the lifetime cost for a single non-pharmaceutical patent in the main European markets would be around £80,000, and the addition of the USA and Japan some £40,000 more. Patents in the other Asian markets are cheaper, at up to £5000 per country, but the cumulative cost becomes prohibitive, particularly for lone inventors or small firms. Pharmaceutical patents are much more expensive, up to five times more, due to the complexity and length of the documentation. In addition to these costs, firms must consider the competitive risk of public disclosure, and the potential cost of legal action should the patent be infringed (Figure 11.5). Costs vary by country, because of the size and attractiveness of different national markets, and also because of differences in government policy. For example, in many Asian countries the policy is to encourage patenting by domestic firms, so the process is cheaper. An exception is Japan, which historically has discouraged patenting to allow local firms to legally develop and exploit technologies from overseas (Figure 11.6).

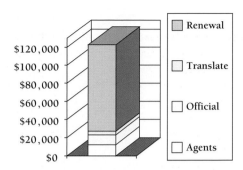

FIGURE 11.5 Typical lifetime cost of a single patent from the European Patent Office.

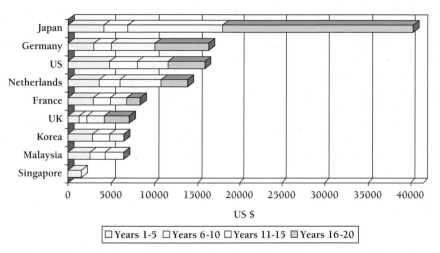

FIGURE 11.6 Lifetime patent costs in different national markets.

DEVELOPING PERSONAL CAPABILITIES

We have argued in this chapter that knowledge is created, shared and exploited by interaction with different groups or communities of practice, both within and external to an organisation. It is all too easy to mix with those with similar backgrounds, education or professions as our own, but this is unlikely to stimulate innovation and entrepreneurship. Here are a hundred different

(*continued*)

ways of interacting with other individuals and groups, to help stimulate knowledge creation and transfer:

1. One-on-one conversation.
2. A small group.
3. Multiple small groups.
4. Across functions.
5. Within functions.
6. Organisation wide.
7. Across organisations.
8. At workplaces.
9. Between workplace and home.
10. At homes.
11. Conferences.
12. Training courses.
13. Workshops.
14. Conventions.
15. Trade shows.
16. E-mail.
17. Letters through the mail.
18. Phone conversations one-on-one.
19. Video conferences.
20. Telephone conferences.
21. Web or Internet.
22. Bookmarks.
23. Signs.
24. Clothing.
25. Flipcharts.
26. Music.
27. Dance.
28. Games.
29. Role-playing.
30. Arena or stadium events.
31. Outdoors.
32. Indoors.
33. Smoke signals.
34. Sign language.
35. Braille.
36. Audio tapes.
37. Compact disc (CD).
38. Within cultures.
39. Across cultures.
40. On pens.
41. Paging systems.
42. Cell phones.
43. Answering machines.
44. Voice mail.
45. Articles.
46. Fax.
47. Intercom.
48. FedEx.
49. DHL.
50. UPS.
51. Networks (people).
52. Bulletin boards.
53. Mailboxes.
54. Notes.
55. AOL Instant message.
56. Groupware.
57. Body language.
58. Newsletters.
59. Brochures.
60. Place mats.
61. Advertisements.
62. Magazines.
63. Books.
64. Billboards.
65. TV.
66. Radio.
67. White boards.
68. Posters.
69. Flyers.
70. Parties.
71. PowerPoint presentations.
72. Paintings, art and sculpture.
73. Drawings and illustrations.
74. Graphic images and icons.
75. Cafes.
76. Over meals.

(continued)

77. On planes.	89. Focused on others.
78. On trains.	90. Talking.
79. On buses.	91. Listening.
80. In cars.	92. Whispering.
81. On boats.	93. Shouting.
82. Lounges, pubs and bars.	94. Seeing.
83. Sending messages with flowers.	95. Tasting.
84. Singing telegrams.	96. Smelling.
85. Telex.	97. With content.
86. LAN.	98. With silence.
87. Carrier pigeons.	99. With meaning.
88. Focused on self (introspection).	100. Story-telling.

Source: From Scott Isaksen and Joe Tidd (2006) *Meeting the Innovation Challenge: Leadership for Transformation and Growth.* John Wiley & Sons.

ADVICE FOR FUTURE ENTREPRENEURS

When you need to contact a potential financial backer, manufacturer or other partner, or need to share your ideas with someone about a new product, process or business, you should consider a confidentiality or non-disclosure agreement of some kind.

Such confidential ideas, or 'trade-secrets', cannot be patented, but can be equally important commercially. Also, outside the USA (which has a 'first to invent' system, rather than the more common 'first to file' patent system), if you tell anyone about your invention before a patent application has been filed then this will invalidate the application.

A non-disclosure agreement (NDA) is a legally binding document that records the terms under which you exchange secret information. This does not mean that a duty of confidence does not arise in the absence of a NDA, but a written agreement gives added legal weight. Also, having a signed NDA means you will be able to share more with a potential partner, and are therefore more likely to secure their support.

However, some professional advisers and organisations will be unable or unwilling to sign a NDA. This is often because they do not want to receive any confidential information which might prejudice or conflict with projects they may already be working on. In such cases it is best to describe and discuss a potential innovation in more general terms of its business benefits, rather than in more detailed technical features and functions.

(continued)

If you do decide to apply for a patent, the process in most countries is relatively simple, but can be time-consuming and will require the involvement (and payment!) of professional advisers, including the services of a registered patent agent. The basic process is as follows:

1. First prepare a **patent specification**, including drawings if these are useful in describing the invention. The specification should contain a full description of your invention, and it is important that this is as complete a description as possible, as you cannot make any changes to your specification once you have filed your application.
2. Complete a **formal application** form, with two copies of your patent specification, and with the appropriate fees, request a search. This must be done by a given date, usually within a year of your filing date, to avoid the application being terminated.
3. The Patent Office conducts a **preliminary examination** to make sure your application meets certain formal requirements and searches through published patents to assess whether or not the invention is new and inventive. This can take time, typically many months, and in some countries the backlog is years.
4. If you satisfy the formal requirements, you pay another fee and the Patent Office **publishes your patent application** around 18 months from your filing date (or sooner if you have requested a priority date).
5. Finally, you complete and file an **examination form**, together with the appropriate fee, within six months of publication of the application. The Patent Office then examines your application, and advises you of any necessary revisions. If your application meets all the requirements of the relevant Patents Acts, they will grant your patent, publish your application in its final form and send you a certificate. So from start to finish the process will take two or more years.

For further advice in the UK, see www.patent.gov.uk, or the relevant patent office in your country.

STRATEGIC AND SOCIAL IMPACT

The UK Treasury established the agency Partnerships UK (PUK) in 2000 to help commercialise public sector knowledge. It is a public–private venture, 49% owned by the UK government and 51% by private sector firms, including Abbey, British Land, Group 4 Securicor, Prudential, Serco and Sun Life. It has acted as an adviser in many public–private partnerships infrastructure projects in the health and education sectors, but has also made more targeted investments in higher-risk technologies from the biotechnology and defence sectors. For example, medical diagnostics technologies from the Defence Science and Technology labs have received funding of £1–2 million per project, and innovations from various universities have received similar levels of funding,

(continued)

such as £1.5 million for the *Smart Hologram* project towards the development of sensor holograms at Cambridge and £750,000 to the *CellTran* project developing skin regeneration technology at Sheffield.

In the UK, the Lambert Review of Business–University Collaboration reported in December 2003. It reviewed the commercialisation of intellectual property by universities in the UK, and also made international comparisons of policy and performance. The UK has a similar pattern of concentration of activity as the USA: in 2002, 80% of UK universities made no patent applications, whereas 5% filed 20 or more patents; similarly, 60% of universities issued no new licences, but 5% issued more than 30. However, in the UK there has been a bias towards spin-outs rather then licencing, which the Lambert Report criticises. It argues that spin-outs are often too complex and unsustainable, and of low quality – a third in the UK are fully funded by the parent university and attract no external private funding. In 2002, universities in the UK created over 150 new spin-out firms, compared to almost 500 by universities in the USA; the respective figures for new licences that year were 648 and 4058. As a proportion of R&D expenditure, this suggests that British universities place greater emphasis on spin-outs than their North American counterparts, and less on licencing. Lambert argues that universities in the UK may place too high a price on their intellectual property, and that contracts often lack clarity of ownership. Both of these problems discourage businesses from licensing intellectual property from universities, and may encourage universities to commercialise their technologies through wholly owned spin-outs.

Chapter Summary

The generation, acquisition, sharing and exploitation of knowledge are central to the successful practice of innovation and entrepreneurship. However, there is a wide range of different types of knowledge, and each plays a different role. Tacit knowledge is critical, but is difficult to capture, and draws upon individual expertise and experience. Therefore, where possible tacit knowledge needs to be made more explicit and codified to allow it to be more readily shared and applied to different contexts. One of the key challenges is to identify and exchange knowledge across different groups and organisations, and a number of mechanisms can help, mostly social in nature, but supported by technology. In limited cases, codified knowledge can form the basis of legal intellectual property rights (IPR), and these can form a basis for the commercialisation of knowledge. However, care needs to be taken when using IPR, as these can divert scarce management and financial resources, and can expose the organisation to imitation and illegal use of IPR.

Discussion Questions

1. Consider a university. What types of data, information and knowledge might be relevant to its management and performance?

2. For an organisation with which you are familiar, identify an example of each of these six types of knowledge.

    Embrained: _____

    Embodied: _____

    Enclutured: _____

    Embedded: _____

    Encoded: _____

    Commodified: _____

3. In what ways can tacit knowledge be made explicit and codified?

4. What mechanisms exist to help the sharing and transfer of knowledge within an organisation?

5. What are the similarities and differences between Nonaka and Takeuchi's and Boisot and Griffiths's models of knowledge generation and transfer?

6. What are the advantages and disadvantages of using formal IPR to commercialise an innovation?

Team Exercise

For each of the following cases suggest a possible boundary object or practice to encourage knowledge sharing:

(a) the design and production groups in a car company;
(b) the operations and marketing groups in a service organisation and different research groups in a technical centre.

Assignment

Using the framework in Figure 11.1, identify the most important types of knowledge in the following cases.

(a) a hospital;
(b) a factory;
(c) a construction company;
(d) a software consultancy.

Key Terms Defined

Boundary object or practice   something of interest to two or more communities of practice. Different communities of practice will have a stake in it, but from different perspectives. A boundary object might be a shared document, for example a quality manual; an artefact, for example a prototype; a technology, for example a database; or a practice, for example a product design.

Codified knowledge   knowledge that has been structured and simplified, which facilitates its transfer and use in different contexts.

Community of practice   a group of people related by a shared task, process or the need to solve a problem, rather than by formal structural or functional relationships.

Copyright   legal rights associated with the *expression* of ideas, and not the ideas themselves, only available if the idea is made explicit or codified, for example, in a book or recording, and can demonstrate some effort or skill used. There is no requirement for registration, and the test of originality is low compared to patent law.

Explicit knowledge   can be codified, that is expressed in numerical, textual or graphical terms, and therefore is more easily communicated, for example, the design of a product.

Intellectual Property Rights (IPR)   includes all formal legal means of identifying or registering rights, including patents, copyright, design rights and trademarks.

Knowledge translator   an individual able to express the interests of one community in terms of another community's perspective. Therefore the translator must be sufficiently conversant with both knowledge domains and trusted by both communities.

Knowledge broker   differs from a translator in that they participate in different communities rather than simply mediate between them. They represent overlaps between communities, and are typically people who are loosely linked to several communities and are able to facilitate knowledge flows between them. An example might be a quality manager responsible for the quality of a process that crosses several different functional groups.

Patent   a limited legal monopoly, usually for 20 years, provided an invention satisfies certain requirements, including novelty, inventive step and application.

Tacit or **implicit knowledge** – personal, experiential, context-specific and hard to articulate, formalise and communicate.

TRIZ   a system of problem-solving and opportunity-seeking developed by Genrich Altshuller identifies standard solutions to common technical problems distilled from an analysis of 1.5 million patents, and applies these in different contexts.

Further Reading and Resources

Knowledge management and intellectual property are both very large and complex subjects. For knowledge management, we would recommend the books by den Hertog and Huizenga's *The Knowledge Enterprise* (Imperial College Press, 2000) for applications and examples, and for theory Nonaka and Takeuchi's *The Knowledge Creating Company* (Oxford, 1995). We provide a good combination of theory, research and practice of knowledge management in *From Knowledge Management to Strategic Competence*, edited by Joe Tidd (Imperial College Press, 2006, second edition), which tries to establish the links between knowledge, innovation and performance. However, the best student texts on the subject are Donald Hislop's (2009) *Knowledge Management in Organizations: A Critical Introduction* (Oxford University Press) and *Knowledge at Work: Creative Collaborative in a Global Economy* by Bob Defillippi, Michael Arthur, and Valerie Lindsay (2006, Wiley-Blackwell).

   More critical accounts of the concept and practice of knowledge management can be found in the editorial by Jack Swan and Harry Scarbrough (2001) 'Knowledge management: concepts and controversies', *Journal of Management Studies*, 38(7), 913–921; Storey, J. and Barnett, E. (2000) 'Knowledge management initiatives: learning from failure', *Journal of Knowledge Management*, 4(2), 145–156; and Pritchard, C., R. Hull, M. Chumer and H. Willmott (2000) *Managing Knowledge: Critical Investigations of Work and Learning*, Macmillan, London. Harry Scarbrough also edits *The Evolution of Business Knowledge*

(Oxford University Press, 2008), which reports the findings of the UK national research programme on the relationships between business and knowledge (including one of our research projects).

For understanding the role and limitations of intellectual property, we like the theoretical approach adopted by David Teece, for example, in his book *The Transfer and Licensing of Know-how and Intellectual Property* (World Scientific, 2006), or for a more applied treatment of the topic, see *Licensing Best Practices: Strategic, Territorial and Technology Issues*, edited by Robert Goldscheider and Alan Gordon (Wiley, 2006), which includes practical case studies of licensing from many different countries and sectors. There are lots of texts for lawyers, but a good management student text is *Intellectual Property Management: A Guide for Scientists, Engineers, Financiers, and Managers* by Claas Junghans *et al.* (Wiley, 2006).

The Open Source movement is covered widely, but often in a partisan way, and a good balanced discussion which links this to innovation can be found in *Open Source: A Multidisciplinary Approach*, by Moreno Muffatto (Imperial College Press, London, 2006), and *Innovation without Patents*, edited by Uma Suthersansen, Graham Dutfield and Kit Boey Chow (Edward Elgar, 2007), which examines the policy aspects, especially for developing economies.

References

1. Blackler, F. (1995) Knowledge, knowledge work and organizations: an overview and interpretation, *Organization Studies*, 16(60), 1021–1046.

2. Bessant, J. (2003) *High Involvement Innovation*. Wiley, Chichester.

3. Simon, H.A. (1996) 'Bounded rationality and organizational learning', in M.D. Cohen and L.S. Sproull (eds) *Organizational Learning*, Sage, London, pp. 175–187.

4. Nonaka, I. and Takeuchi, H. (1995) *The Knowledge Creating Company*. Oxford University Press.

5. Boisot, M. and Griffiths, D. (2006) 'Are there any competencies out there? Identifying and using Technical Competencies', in J. Tidd (ed.) *From Knowledge Management to Strategic Competence*. Imperial College Press, London, second edition, pp. 249–307.

6. Crespi, G., Criscuolo, C., and Haskel, J. (2006) Information Technology, Organisational Change and Productivity Growth: Evidence from UK Firms, *The Future of Science, Technology and Innovation Policy: Linking Research and Practice*, SPRU 40th Anniversary Conference, Brighton, UK, September 2006.

7. Hall, R. (2006) 'What are Strategic Competencies?', in J. Tidd (ed.) *From Knowledge Management to Strategic Competence*. Imperial College Press, London, second edition, pp. 26–49.

8. O'Leary, D. (1998) Knowledge management systems: converting and connecting, *IEEE Intelligent Systems*, 13(3), 30–33; Becker, M. (2001) Managing dispersed knowledge: organizational problems, managerial strategies and their effectiveness, *Journal of Management Studies*, 38(7), 1037–1051.

9. Brown, J.S. and Duguid, P. (2001) Knowledge and organization: a social practice perspective, *Organization Science*, **12**(2), 198–213; Brown, J.S. and Duguid, P. (1991) Organizational learning and communities of practice: towards a unified view of working, learning and organization, *Organizational Science*, 2(1), 40–57; Hildreth, P., Kimble, C. and Wright, P. (2000) Communities of practice in the distributed international environment, *Journal of Knowledge Management*, 4(1), 27–38.

10. Star, S.L. and Griesemer, J.R. (1989) Institutional ecology, translations and boundary objects, *Social Studies of Science*, 19, 387–420; Carlile, P.R. (2002) A pragmatic view of knowledge and boundaries: boundary objects in new product development, *Organization Science*, **13**(4), 442–455.

11. Granovetter, M. (1976) The strength of weak ties, *American Journal of Sociology*, 1360–1380; Cummings, J.N. (2004) Work groups, structural diversity, and knowledge sharing in a global organization, *Management Science*, 50(3), 352–364.

12. den Hertog, J.F. and Huizenga, E. (2000) *The Knowledge Enterprise*. Imperial College Press, London.

13. Tranfield, David, Malcolm Young, David Partington, John Bessant and Jonathan Sapsed (2006) 'Knowledge Management Routines for Innovation Projects: Developing a Hierarchical Process Model', in J. Tidd (ed.) *From Knowledge Management to Strategic Competence*, Imperial College Press, London, second edition, pp. 126–149; Coombs, R. and Hull, R. (1998) 'Knowledge management practices and path-dependency in innovation', *Research Policy*, 237–253.

14. Narin, F. (2006) 'Assessing Technological Competencies', in J. Tidd (ed.) *From Knowledge Management to Strategic Competence*, Imperial College Press, London, second edition, pp. 179–219.

CASE STUDY 11

Apple's Apps

Apple launched its iPod in 2003. Much has been written on the attractions of the device itself, especially its user interface and ease of use. However, less well-documented was the novel business model which accompanied Apple's entry into media devices.

With the iPod, Apple created a closed service system which excluded non-Apple software, and gave Apple control over the choice and price of music purchased. Before this, personal music players used industry-standard software and allowed users to purchase music from a range of legal and illegal sources. Apple's strategy is very different to the traditional Web ethos of being 'open and free'.

In July 2007, Apple extended its empire with the introduction of the iPhone, which relied on applications written specifically for Apple by its chosen partners. After lobbying from software developers, Apple created the App Store to distribute apps developed by third-party developers. This allowed third-party developers, subject to certification and contract, to develop and submit applications to for Apple's approval.

The Software Development Kit for iPhone was announced in 2008, later to become the iPhone Developer progam, aimed at third-party developers to create applications using Wcode, which iPhone, iPod Touch and iPad all run on natively. This means that developers can potentially reach a large established market and do not have to adapt their apps for use on a wide range of different platforms, which is currently an issue with Google's competing Android operating system which is used on more than 60 different devices. Developers pay an annual fee to Apple to use the development kit and to maintain the right to submit apps, but they receive 70% of revenues from any of their apps which are approved by Apple for sale on the App Store, Apple keeping the remaining 30%.

This proved to be a clever strategy as it added an estimated 125,000 third-party developers to Apple's internal workforce of 34,000. Within two months, 100 million apps had been downloaded. By March 2010, 185,000 apps were available, and Apple had sold more than 85 million iPhones and iPod Touches, and users had downloaded 10 billion songs, 4 billion apps, 250 million TV shows and 33 million films. In 2009, Apple earned an estimated 500 million euros from its App Store alone. By 2013, Apple is forecast to achieve 9 billion downloads and earn almost 2 billion euros from these.

However, Apple has achieved this dominance by maintaining strict control over third-party developers through its contract, certification and approval processes. Apple's standard contract with app developers forbids the use of Adobe's Flash technology, or even the use of software which translates Flash-based apps into Apple-approved one. This means apps developed for Apple will not run on other platforms, and *vice versa*. Flash is used by 75% of video and games on the Internet. The argument is that Flash on portable devices can be buggy and battery-draining, but this also reflects a long and bitter battle between the two companies. Clearly, if Flash was implemented on the iPad and iPhone platform, users could consume video and games without going through iTunes. Apple also collects data on users buying habits, but prevents third-party developers from incorporating their own software to capture information on the use of their apps. Apple also retains the right of approval or rejection of any app submitted. For example, it has rejected apps which it deemed 'ridiculed a public figure'. The Electronic Frontier Foundation (EFF) has assessed Apple's standard developer program licence and found many of the conditions 'troubling', for example, a 'ban on public statements' which prohibits developers from speaking about the contents of the agreement itself.

Despite its huge sales success, the iPhone only represents 2% of global mobile phone sales, and 15% of smartphone sales (25% in the USA). In 2010, Apple launched the iPad to extend the market for its apps, exploiting the existing apps available, plus newer custom-made apps to exploit the larger 9.7 inch screen, such as enhanced gaming. New deals were being made with publishers of books, magazines, newspapers and video to distribute their media. This move threatens Amazon's Kindle e-reader, and the growing e-book and newspaper business. For the first time Apple also included new contract terms for advertising, which prevent other ad networks from capturing data on ad effectiveness and requires Apple to retains 40% of revenues. This extends Apple's control from mobile devices potentially to devices which can replace netbooks and laptops, and may challenge the guiding philosophy and direction of the Web.

Case Questions

1. How is Apple's business model different from competitors'?
2. As the App Store relies on third-party developers, is this an example of Open Innovation?
3. Why has it proven so difficult for other powerful innovative firms such as Amazon and Google to compete with and copy Apple's strategy?

Sources: Peter Burrows (2010) Apple's Expanding App Universe, *Business Week*, April 22; Daniel Lyons (2010) Fortress Apple, *Newsweek*, May 3.

Summary of Web Resources

Cases

- Joint Solutions
- Tesco

Tools

- Identifying Innovative Capabilities
- Innovation Audits

Media

- Roy Sandbach of Procter & Gamble
- Xerox

Chapter 12

Creating Value and Growing Ventures

LEARNING OBJECTIVES

When you have completed this chapter you will be able to:

- Identify the different ways in which innovation and entrepreneurship can create economic and social value.

- Select and build the most appropriate business model to exploit an innovation or new venture.

- Understand what factors promote the growth of new ventures.

Go online to find additional . . .

Cases

Tools

Media

www.iande.info

In this chapter we examine how organisations, private and public, can better create value through innovation and entrepreneurship. We begin by identifying the relationships between different types of innovation and various forms of financial and market performance. Next we review different business models used to exploit innovation and new ventures. Finally, we identify the factors which influence the growth of new ventures.

Creating Economic and Social Value

One of the central problems of managing innovation is how to create and capture value. For example, in Chapter 1 we discussed the recent transitions in the music industry, and changes in how music is produced, distributed, consumed and paid for (or not, in many cases). Video content is facing a similar challenge to the dominant business model, and the producers, distributors and users are experimenting with a range of new ways of generating an income to pay for the production and distribution of video content.

INNOVATION IN ACTION

Profiting from Digital Media

The business model for capturing the value from video is simple but conservative: own and enforce the copyright, global cinema release, followed by DVD rental and sale, and lastly TV and other broadcast. The DVD stage is critical, as it generates income of $23.4 billion in the USA, compared with $9.6 billion from cinema release. Note that when DVD was introduced in 1997, three of the major studios initially refused to publish on it, as they feared losing revenue from the existing proven VHS tape format.

However, annual DVD sales have begun to stabilise at around 9 billion units worldwide, and in some markets have begun to decline. Therefore the industry has begun to promote the successor to DVD, the high-definition DVD. After a stupid format war, Blu-ray became the new standard for high-definition disks early in 2008. Initial sales of the new format have been slow, not helped by uncertainty of the format war, with 9 million Blu-ray discs shipped in 2007, compared with 9 billion conventional DVDs – just 0.1% of the market. (In addition, some 40 million Blu-ray PS3 games were sold – since its launch in 2006, the Sony PlayStation 3 has sold some 11 million games consoles which also play Blu-ray discs.) Surveys in the USA and Europe suggest that 80% of consumers are happy with the picture and sound quality of DVD and standard definition broadcast. Therefore formats such as Blu-ray and high-definition satellite and cable broadcasts are aimed at the 20% 'early adopters' who value (i.e. are prepared to pay a premium for) higher definition pictures and sound, primarily for films and sports coverage.

(continued)

However, for the majority who favour cost and convenience over quality, the Internet is the current preferred medium, legal or otherwise. Illegal sites lead the way, such as ZML which offers 1700 movies for (illegal) download, whereas to date the legal services like MovieFlix and FilmOn tend to be restricted to independent or amateur content. Hollywood has been slow to adapt its business model, and still relies on cinema releases, followed by DVD rental and sales, and finally broadcast. Legal download and streaming offer the potential for lower cost (and prices), as this removes much of the cost of creating, distributing and selling physical media, as well as greater convenience for consumers in terms of choice and flexibility. However, DVD sales depend on the major chain stores for distribution: for example, in the USA Wal-Mart accounts for around 40% of sales, and this represents a powerful resistance to change. As a result, in 2008, legal online film distribution was only around $58 million in the USA, less than 5% of total film sales. Television broadcasters have been faster to adopt such services, such as the BBC i-Player in the UK, mainly because their current business model is based on subscription or advertising, without the film studios' legacy of reliance on physical media and retail distributors. In the USA, Apple iTunes and TV and the Microsoft Xbox have begun to dominate the emerging market for download video rental, but copyright issues have restricted the legal sale of video by download.

As a result of the growing importance of Internet sales of video material, in 2007 the Writers' Guild of America went on strike for better payment terms for electronic distribution and sales. The Hollywood studios' offer was for the payments for Internet sales to be based on the precedent set by DVD – 1.2% of gross receipts – whereas the writers wanted something closer to book or film publishing – 2.5% of gross. The final settlement, reached in February 2008, was a compromise, with a royalty on download rentals of 1.2% of gross, and 0.36–0.70% of gross on download sales, and up to 2% where video streaming is part-funded by advertising. A partial victory for the authors, but this compares with 20% of gross receipts claimed by some leading actors of blockbusters. Clearly there is work to be done on the final business model for the creation, sales and distribution of digital video. Greater clarity of the regime for managing intellectual property is a start, and faster broadband will soon make higher quality download practical for the mass markets, so all that remains is a little innovation in the business model.

Sources: The Economist, 23 February 2008, Volume 386, Issue 8568; *ALCS News*, Spring 2008.

According to the conventional wisdom of strategic management, firms must decide between two broad innovation strategies:

1. *Innovation 'leadership'* – where firms aim at being first to market, based on technological leadership. This requires a strong corporate commitment to creativity and risk taking, with close linkages both to major sources of relevant new knowledge, and to the needs and responses of customers.
2. *Innovation 'followership'* – where firms aim at being late to market, based on imitating (learning from) the experience of technological leaders. This requires a strong commitment to competitor analysis and intelligence, to reverse engineering (i.e. testing, evaluating and

taking to pieces competitors' products, in order to understand how they work, how they are made and why they appeal to customers), and to cost cutting and learning in manufacturing.

However, in practice the distinction between 'innovator' and 'follower' is much less clear. For example, market pioneers often continue to have high expenditures on R&D, but this is most likely to be aimed at minor, incremental innovations. A pattern emerges where pioneer firms do not maintain their historical strategy of innovation leadership, but instead focus on leveraging their competencies in minor incremental innovations. Conversely, late entrant firms appear to pursue one of two very different strategies. The first is based on competencies other than R&D and new product development: for example, superior distribution or greater promotion or support. The second, more interesting, strategy is to focus on major new product development projects in an effort to compete with the pioneer firm.

It is not necessarily a great advantage to be a technological leader in the early stages of the development of radically new products, when the product performance characteristics, and features valued by users, are not always clear, either to the producers or to the users themselves. Especially for consumer products, valued features emerge only gradually through a process of dynamic competition, which involves a considerable amount of trial, error and learning by both producers and users. New features valued by users in one product can easily be recognised by competitors and incorporated in subsequent products. This is why market leadership in the early stages of the development of personal computers was so volatile, and why pioneers are often displaced by new entrants. In such circumstances, product development must be closely coupled with the ability to monitor competitors' products and to learn from customers. In fact, pioneers in radical consumer innovations rarely succeed in establishing long-term market positions. Success goes to so-called 'early entrants' with the vision, patience and flexibility to establish a mass consumer market. For example, studies of the PIMS (Profit Impact of Market Strategy) database indicate that (surviving) product pioneers tend to have higher quality and a broader product line than followers, whereas followers tend to compete on price, despite having a cost disadvantage. A pioneer strategy appears more successful in markets where the purchasing frequency is high, or distribution important (e.g. fast-moving consumer goods), but confer no advantage where there are frequent product changes or high advertising expenditure (e.g. consumer durables).

Therefore technological leadership in firms does not necessarily translate itself into economic benefits. The capacity of the firm to appropriate the benefits of its investment in technology depends on: its ability to translate its technological advantage into commercially viable products or processes, for example, through complementary assets or capabilities in marketing and distribution; and its capacity to defend its advantage against imitators, for example, through secrecy, standards or intellectual property rights. Some of the factors that enable a firm to benefit commercially from its own technological lead can be strongly shaped by its management: for example, the provision of complementary assets to exploit the lead. Other factors can be influenced only slightly by the firm's management, and depend much more on the general nature of the technology, the product market and the regime of intellectual property rights: for example, the strength of patent protection.

The early work on this was by economists who argued that under perfect market conditions there would be no incentive for individual entrepreneurs or firms to innovate, as ease of imitation would make it difficult to achieve returns from the risky investment in innovation.[1] Subsequently, the focus has been on creating the conditions necessary to encourage risk taking and innovation, but prevent monopoly positions emerging.

Innovation and Firm Performance

Most research on the relationships between innovation and firm performance uses econometric techniques to assess the impact of innovation inputs, specifically the expenditure on R&D, and on some measure of performance, typically productivity or patents. Research shows that *product* R&D is significantly less productive than *process* R&D.[2] Other studies using the SPRU significant innovations database found that the impact of the *use* of innovation was around four times that of their *generation*.[3] The same studies found that the productivity increases took 10–15 years to be fully effected. Using R&D as a proxy for *inputs* to the innovation process, and patents as an indicator of *outputs*, at the national level, patents and R&D are correlated and, also, to some extent at the sectoral level, but the extent of unexplained variation is high at the level of cross-company analysis. Part of the difficulty in obtaining stable relationships between patents and R&D lies in the fact that firms have different propensities to patent their discoveries. This partly reflects the ease of protecting the gains from innovation in other ways, such as secrecy and first-mover advantages. Furthermore, the effectiveness of patents varies across industries, for example, being strong in pharmaceuticals but weak in consumer electronics.

INNOVATION IN ACTION

R&D and Innovation Strategy

Since 2005 the international management consultants Booz Allen Hamilton have conducted a survey of the spending on and performance of innovation in the world's 1000 largest firms. The most recent survey found that there remain significant differences between spending on innovation across different sectors and regions. For example, the R&D intensity (R&D spending divided by sales, expressed as a percentage) was an average of 13% in the software and healthcare industries, 7% in electronics, but only 1–2% in more mature sectors. Of the 1000 companies studied, representing annual R&D expenditure of US$447 billion, 95% of this spending was in the USA, Europe and Japan.

(continued)

However, like most studies of innovation and performance, they find no correlation between R&D spending, growth and financial or market performance. They argue that it is how the R&D is managed and translated into successful new processes, products and services which counts more. Overall they identify two factors that are common to those companies which consistently leverage their R&D spending: strong alignment between innovation and corporate strategies; and close attention to customer and market needs. This is not to suggest that there is any single optimum strategy for innovation, and instead they argue that three distinct clusters of good practice are observable:

- *Technology drivers*, which focus on scouting and developing new technologies and matching these to unmet needs, with strong project- and risk-management capabilities.
- *Need seekers*, which aim to be first to market, by identifying emerging customer needs, with strong design and product development capabilities.
- *Market readers*, which aim to be fast followers, and conduct detailed competitor analysis, with strong process innovation.

They conclude that: 'Is there a best innovation strategy? No . . . Is there a best innovation strategy for any given company? Yes . . . the key to innovation success has nothing to do with how much money you spend. It is directly related to the effort expended to align innovation with strategy and your customers, and to manage the entire process with discipline and transparency' (p. 16).

Source: Jaruzelski, B. and K. Dehoff (2008) Booz Allen Hamilton Annual Innovation Survey, *Strategy and Business*, issue 49.

The most likely explanatory factors are *scale, technological opportunity* and *management*.[4] The evidence on scale is mixed. There are two linked hypotheses – that the size of the R&D effort counts, and that the size of the firm makes R&D more effective, say, because of economies of scope between projects. Studies suggest that the scale of R&D effort is important only in chemicals and pharmaceuticals. Firm size is a more difficult issue to study because the interpretation of R&D and patents differs between class sizes of firms. One study compared over 600 manufacturing firms between 1972 and 1982 in the UK, matched to the SPRU database of significant technical innovations.[5] It suggests that large firms tend to innovate more because they have a higher incentive to do so: a doubling of market share from the mean of 2.5% will increase the probability of innovation in the next period by 0.6%. This result is qualified by noting that less competitive firms (higher concentration and lower import ratios) innovate less. Technological opportunity also exists at the firm level via the spillover effects from other firms, but this is not automatic, and demands explicit attention to technology transfer and search for external sources of innovation. A major problem with measuring inputs and outputs is: how do we take account of the 'spillover' of innovation benefits or information to other firms or industries? A particular form of spillover occurs when the economy, as a whole, benefits more from an innovation than is appropriated as profits. A difference, then, occurs between the private rate of return and the social rate of return, and in general the social benefits of innovation far exceed the private returns to individual firms.[6]

The classic study of the managerial efficiency of R&D inputs is the SPRU project SAP-PHO, best summarised in Freeman, which found that commitment to the project by senior management and good communications are crucial to success.[7]

Analysis of the SPRU database of innovations and company accounts shows that the profit margin of innovators is higher than non-innovators, controlling for other influences, although the effect is rather small. The relationship between profitability and lagged indicators of capital input, marketing expenses and R&D reveals that the rate of return to R&D is about 33%, with an average lag of about five years. Process innovation has four times the rate of return as product innovation, but is more risky with more variable returns.[8] Moving to the outputs of innovation, product announcements have a positive effect on the share price of the originating firm.[9] The impact of the announcement on share price depends on two factors: first, an assessment of the probability of success of the new product; second, an evaluation of the level of future earnings from the product. The study found that firms introducing new products accrue around 0.75% excess market return over three days, beginning one day before the formal announcement. The average value of each new product announcement was found to be $26 million (in 1972 dollars). Of course, the precise return and value of each product announcement depends on the industry sectors: the highest returns were found to be in food, printing, chemicals and pharmaceuticals, computers, photographic equipment and durable goods. Excess returns due to new product announcements suggest that past and current accounting data have little predictive value. The P/E (price/earnings) ratio may be a better indicator of (future) innovation performance. The average P/E ratio of the firms making new product announcements is almost twice that of the firms which make no new product announcements. This implies that the stock market is valuing the long-term stream of future earnings generated by the innovative firms at a much higher rate than the non-innovators.

INNOVATION IN ACTION

Diversity of Strategic Games for Innovation

The MINE (Managing Innovation in the New Economy) research programme at Ecole Polytechnique in Montreal, Canada, together with SPRU, University of Sussex, UK, conducted qualitative and quantitative studies to gain an understanding of the diversity of strategies for innovation. Almost 925 chief technology officers (CTOs) and senior managers of R&D (from Asia, North and South America, and Europe) across all industrial sectors of the economy responded to a global survey. The survey tool is available at www.minesurvey.polymtl.ca. Respondents come from firms such as Intel, Synopsys, Motorola, IBM Global Services, Novartis and Boeing. Executives were

(continued)

asked what competitive forces impact on innovation, what value-creation and -capture activities are pursued in innovating, and what strategies and practices are used.

Games of innovation involve many interdependent players, persist over time, and are strategically complex. Games are distinct, coherent scenarios of value creation and capture involving activities of collaboration and rivalry:

- Each involves a distinct logic of innovative activities that is largely contingent on product architectures and market lifecycle stage.
- They follow persistent trajectories, bound by some basic economic and technical forces and thus tend to fall into a small number of natural trajectories.
- They result in differing levels of performance. Market-creation games involve radical innovations, grow fast, and display high variations in profitability. By contrast, market-evolution games are characterised by process innovations, a slower pace of growth, but good profitability.
- However, games are not fully determined by their contexts, but allow degrees of strategic freedom to interact with members of relevant ecosystems and to adopt collaborative and competitive moves to expand markets.

Clustering analyses led to the identification of seven distinct and stable groups each containing at least 100 firms that create and capture value in similar ways. Each game is characterised by statistically different value-creation and -capture activities:

- patent-driven discovery;
- cost-based competition;
- systems integration;
- systems engineering and consulting;
- platform orchestration;
- customised mass-production;
- innovation support and services.

Source: Miller, R. and S. Floricel (2007) Special Issue, *International Journal of Innovation Management*, **11** (1).

Market differentiation measures the degree to which all competitors differ from one another across a market. Therefore, market differentiation is related to market segmentation and is a measure of market attractiveness. Customers in different market segments will value different product attributes. The joint effect of relative quality and market differentiation is significant. Markets in which there is little differentiation and no significant difference in the relative quality of competitors are characterised by low returns. High relative quality is a strong predictor of high profitability in any market conditions. Nevertheless, a niche business may achieve high returns in a market with high differentiation without high relative quality. A combination of both high market differentiation and high perceived relative quality yields very high ROI, typically in excess of 30%. The importance of market share varies with industry. Intuition would suggest that share would be most important in capital-intensive manufacturing and production industries, where economies of scale are required. However, PIMS suggests that market share has a much stronger impact on profitability in innovative sectors, that is, those industries characterised by high R&D and/or marketing expenditure. For the R&D and marketing-intensive businesses, the ROI of the market leader is on average 26 points higher than the average small share business. In the manufacturing-intensive businesses, the corresponding difference is only 12 points. This suggests that scale effects are more important in R&D and marketing than in manufacturing.

Our own study of the relationship between innovation and performance examined 40 companies, representing five different sectors.[10] We chose companies to provide a range of R&D intensity in each of the five sectors. Analysis of the data confirms that expenditure on R&D, as a proportion of sales, has a significant positive effect on value-added, but also the number of new product announcements made. This suggests that R&D contributes both to increasing the number of new products introduced as well as their value. The introduction of a term to represent the interaction of research and development with sales indicates diminishing efficiency of innovation with firm size; in other words, larger firms introduce more new products, but not in proportion to their size. The results suggest that the financial markets do value expenditure on research and development. The coefficient of about 0.3 on R&D/sales may be used to estimate an elasticity of the dependent variable at the mean value of R&D/sales of 2.9. A 1% rise in R&D/sales would translate into a 0.08% rise in the market-to-book value. This suggests that the financial markets may somewhat undervalue R&D expenditure. If we use ratio of new products introduced/absolute R&D as a proxy for research efficiency, we find that the efficiency of research also has a significant positive effect on the market-to-book value. This suggests that the market values the past efficiency of R&D (that is, track record), as well as the expenditure on R&D.

 Go online to find how Value Analysis can help to identify how to create value from innovation.

www.iande.info

Choosing a Business Model

The term 'business model' is perhaps inappropriate as all organisations, private, public and social, seek to create and to some extent capture value, broadly defined, so perhaps the term 'value model' is more generic. The value model of a venture is simply how value is to be created and captured. The distinction between the creation and capture of value is central, as some ventures are better at one aspect than the other. Moreover, some ventures create value that is captured by others in their network: for example, customers or users of an innovation may benefit more than those that generated it. Typically the development of a value model will include consideration of the value proposition, mechanisms for revenue generation, capabilities and processes, and position in the value network or ecosystem:[11]

- *Value proposition* – How does the innovation or venture create value and for whom? The value created will be specific to target market segments and customer groups, and different types of innovation will contribute in different ways.
- *Revenue generation* – How does the enterprise capture and appropriate the benefits (or 'rents' as *The Economist* calls them)? In the case of public and social ventures, capture and revenues are less important than demonstrating value, and ensuring that resources, human and financial, are sustainable.
- *Capabilities and processes* – How can the innovation or venture deliver? This is much more than access to financial and other resources. It requires a (rare) combination of resources, knowledge and capabilities. A common mistake entrepreneurs make is to focus too much on the initial creation of value and not to pay sufficient attention to how value will be captured in the longer term.
- *Position in the network* – How are risks, responsibilities and rewards distributed? Suppliers, customers and collaborators will all play a role in the creation and capture of value, but often there are big disparities between shares of value creation and capture. This can be the result of positional advantages, for example, due to size or power, ownership of IP, brands or standards, and access to distribution channels and customers.

ENTREPRENEURSHIP IN ACTION

(Old) New Business Models

The concept of novel 'business models' is not new. Contrary to popular belief, architect of the Industrial Revolution, James Watt, did not invent the Steam Engine, which had been patented in 1698, almost 40 years before his birth. However, Watt did make significant technical improvements to existing steam engines by introducing a separate condenser to reduce waste energy and hence increase significantly their efficiency and effectiveness. Although he had developed a working model by 1765, and received the key patent in 1769, Watt did little subsequently to develop the engine into a commercial innovation, and he worked as a surveyor and civil engineer for the next decade.

It was not until 1775 when he entered a partnership with Matthew Boulton that the business began to grow. Watt had the technical ingenuity, but Boulton had the capital and commercial knowledge. Together they formed a new venture, Boulton and Watt, to exclusively manufacture steam engines, and by 1800 had installed almost 1500 engines.

However, this was not simply a case of technological innovation. The firm represented an early example of a 'systems integrator' with an innovative business model. The firm of Boulton and Watt did not manufacture steam engines, but instead required their customers to purchase

(continued)

parts from a number of suppliers which were then assembled on site. This reduced the need for working capital and inventory costs. Moreover, Boulton and Watt did not make their profits from selling the engines. The company made its profit by comparing the amount of coal used by the machine with that used by the previous, less efficient engine, and required payments of one-third of the savings annually for the next 25 years. This innovative business model made the company and its two founders phenomenally wealthy and influential, and created the basis for the Industrial Revolution. Boulton used to brag that the company didn't sell steam engines but provided *power*, although it was Watt's moniker that was later adopted as the SI unit of power.

Table 12.1 illustrates a typical range of value-added by sector. Value-added is commonly used by economists as a proxy measure for the productivity of organisations. Note that there are large variations in value-added in the same sector and across different sectors (column 2).

TABLE 12.1   Variation in value-creation within and across sectors

Sector	Value-added/ sales (%)	Capex/ sales ratio	R&D mil/ new products
(1) Services			
Company A	58.9	12.8	na
Company B	50.9	9.7	na
Company C	39.3	na	na
Company D	11.1	na	na
Company E	4.1	na	na
(2) Food and drink			
Company F	30.1	5.2	5.9
Company G	29.4	5.7	2.4
Company H	22.6	4.5	25.6
Company I	12.1	1.5	13.4
Company J	9.9	1.7	na
(3) Electronics			
Company K	61.0	2.9	4.4
Company L	47.8	2.9	3.4
Company M	39.8	3.3	2.7
Company N	35.9	4.6	6.2
Company O	28.2	10.2	1.1
(4) Engineering			
Company P	48.0	4.1	4.9
Company Q	42.3	3.2	12.8
Company R	39.7	5.4	9.3
Company S	34.1	3.6	12.0
Company T	30.8	1.5	0.8

Source: Derived from Tidd, J. (2006) *From Knowledge Management to Strategic Competence.* Imperial College Press, London, second edition pp. 119–120.

The same wide range of performance is evident for almost all measures, such as the utilisation of capital investment (column 3), which measures the relative investment in plant and equipment, and the efficiency of the new product development process (column 4). This wide variation of performance within and across sectors does suggest there is significant scope to create and capture value in most contexts, and that the ability to do so is not evenly distributed.

Both process and product improvement contribute to value creation, but contribute in different ways. Improving the quality of processes and products can affect performance in two ways:

- It can reduce costs by helping to eliminate defects, scrap and rework, and lowering inspection and warranty costs. Typically these may represent up to a quarter of the cost of manufacturing, so the impact on productivity can be significant.
- Differences in the relative quality of products and services (the outputs) can increase sales and market share. Moreover, firms with higher quality relative to their competitors are able to demand higher prices.

Therefore improving the quality of both processes (to reduce costs) and products and service (to increase sales or prices, or sometimes both!) can boost profitability.

In addition, where product and service improvement leads to greater differentiation (i.e. being different, rather than better than competitors' offerings), this can also enhance market and financial performance. For example, according to research based on the PIMS (profit impact of market strategy) database of companies, both quality and differentiation are positively associated with financial performance. Figure 12.1 illustrates this relationship. The horizontal axis is a measure of how highly differentiated a product or service is: that is, how different it is compared with competitors' products or services. The vertical axis is a measure of quality relative to competitors' products or services. In both cases assessment is made on the basis of

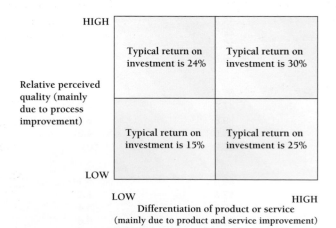

FIGURE 12.1 Effects of process and product performance on value creation.
Source: Derived from the PIMS database.

> ## INNOVATION IN ACTION
>
> ### Low-Cost Airlines
>
> Ryanair and the other low-cost airlines are based on a business model first developed by Southwest Airlines in the USA. The model demands the management of a number of key aspects of operations, including:
>
> - fast turnaround times at airports, which increases plane utilisation and punctuality;
> - use of a common fleet of planes to reduce pilot and maintenance costs;
> - automation of bookings, and ticketless booking, to reduce overhead costs;
> - flexible working practices, and continuous improvement;
> - outsourcing or contracting out of non-core services, e.g. baggage handling;
> - use of cheaper secondary airports to reduce overhead costs.
>
> As a result, low-cost airlines typically have superior load factors and higher utilisation of their aircraft than traditional carriers. This is partly the result of difference in the length of journeys (e.g. Europe versus USA), but also due to shorter turnaround times. These airlines also compete on the basis of relatively low and declining operating and staff costs compared to the industry norms.

customers' perceptions. Each quadrant shows the average return on investment (ROI) for the product or service. Higher relative quality or differentiation is strongly associated with higher returns. In the extreme case, the ROI for products which are both high quality and highly differentiated is double that of the base cases.

Value-added is a generically useful measure of performance, applicable to almost all types of enterprise. John Kay (1993) places great emphasis on the value-added by a firm as a measure of corporate performance (Table 12.2). He argues that there can be no long-term rationale for a firm that does not add value. However, the measurement of value-added is not only

TABLE 12.2 Added-value statement

Relationship with:		Financial flow:
Customers		Revenue
	less	
Labour		Wages and salaries
Investors		Capital costs
Suppliers		Materials
	equals	
		Added value

Source: Kay, J. (1993) *Foundations of Corporate Success*, Oxford University Press.

useful at the corporate level; it is arguably even more meaningful and useful at the operational level. There is no single definition of value-added, but essentially it is simply the difference between the market value of outputs and the cost of inputs. The most straightforward definition of value-added is revenue or income less materials and services purchases. This definition has the advantage that it is simple to calculate and interpret; it enables comparison to be made between very different activities and cannot be manipulated to the same extent as accounting profit. The assessment of value-added can also take into account the cost of capital inputs, depreciation and a provision for a reasonable return on the capital invested. In this case there is a trade-off between simplicity and completeness.

The PIMS database is a useful framework which attempts to identify, through operational measures, the most important drivers of performance. PIMS was established in 1972 by General Electric in the USA, which in 1975 established the Strategic Planning Institute with a number of other leading firms. Today around 3000 business units representing 450 companies have contributed data. For each business unit PIMS collects 200 items of information including data on market conditions, competitive position and financial and operating performance. The measures of performance used in each case are profit as a percentage of sales (i.e. profit margin or return on sales – ROS), and profit as a percentage of investment (return on investment – ROI). Of the two measures, ROI is superior to ROS as it relates results to the resources used to achieve them. By analysing such data, using cross-tabulation and multiple regression, PIMS attempts to identify the measures of operations that most affect performance. The indicators listed in Table 12.3 account for the majority of the differences in the performance between businesses, irrespective of sector.

A more complete statistical model, which includes market conditions, can explain over 70% of the difference in performance. Value-added, capacity utilisation and productivity are all strongly positively related to performance. High relative quality is a strong predictor of high

---

TABLE 12.3   The impact of process and product innovation on performance

Aspect of operations	Measure	Impact on performance
Processes	Capacity utilisation	Positive
	Labour productivity	Positive
	Inventory % sales	Negative
Investment	Plant % sales	Strongly negative
	Newness of plant	Positive
Product policy	Relative quality	Strongly positive
	Value-added % sales	Positive
	Standardisation	Negative
Innovation	R&D as % of sales	Negative/positive*
	Patents	Positive

*Negative for low market share businesses; positive for high market share
Source: Derived from PIMS database.

TABLE 12.4   Factors associated with high market growth

	Real annual growth rate (%)		
Percentage	0–5	5–10	10+
Gross margin sales	26.9	25.7	29.7
Change in value-added per employee	9.8	10.3	13.0
Change in investment	9.7	11.6	17.8

Source: Derived from PIMS database.

profitability in any market conditions. The data also suggest that a business with higher perceived relative quality can demand higher relative prices and achieves increased market share. Interestingly, there appears to be no significant relationship between quality (as measured) and relative cost. This suggests that higher quality is not necessarily the result of higher costs. As we can see from Table 12.4, increased gross margins, value-added and investment are all associated with high rates of market growth. This suggests that such measures are useful for assessing and tracking the health of an organisation.

INNOVATION IN ACTION

The Disruptive Business Model of Skype

Skype successfully combined two emerging technologies to create a new service and business model for telecommunications. The two technologies were Voice over Internet Protocol (VoIP) and peer-to-peer (P2P) file sharing. The first allowed the transfer of voice over the Internet, rather than conventional telecommunications networks, and the other exploited the distributed computing power of users' computers to avoid the need for a dedicated centralised server or infrastructure.

Skype was created in 2003 by the Swedish serial entrepreneur Niklas Zennström. Zennström was previously (in)famous for his pioneering web company Kazaa, which provided a P2P service, mainly used for the (illegal) exchange of MP3 music files. He sold Kazaa to the US company Sharman Networks to concentrate on the development of Skype. He teamed up with the Dane Janus Friis and together they built Skype. Unlike other VoIP firms like Vonage, which charges a subscription for use and is based on proprietary hardware, Skype was available for free download and use for free voice communication between computers. Additional premium pay services were subsequently added, such as Skype-Out to connect to conventional telephones, and Skype-In, to receive conventional calls. The service was made available in 15 different languages which covered 165 countries, and partnerships were made with Plantronics to provide headsets, and Siemens and Motorola for handsets. Happy users quickly recruited family and friends to the service which grew rapidly.

(continued)

Given the provision of free software and free calls between computers, the business model had to be innovative. There were several ways in which revenues were generated. The premium services like Skype-In and Skype-Out proved to be very popular with small and medium-sized firms for business and conference calls, and the licensing of the software to specialist providers and the hardware partnership deals were also lucrative. Later, the large user base also attracted web advertising.

By 2005, there were 70 million users registered, but despite this rapid growth the core model of providing a free service meant that revenues were a rather more modest US$7 million, equivalent to only 10 cents per user. In 2008, Skype had around 310 million registered users, 12 million of which were online at any time. Its revenues were estimated to be US$126 million, equivalent to 40 cents per user. This does represent an improvement in financial performance, especially as costs remain low, but the business model remains unproven, except for the founders of Skype. They sold the company to eBay Inc. in October 2005 for US$2.6 billion, with further performance-based bonuses of $1.5 billion by 2009. For eBay, the plan is to use Skype to increase trading turnover by introducing voice bargaining and pay-per-call advertising, and exploit its previous acquisition PayPal to provide improved billing for Skype customers.

Source: Derived from Rao, B., B. Angelov and O. Nov (2006) Fusion of disruptive technologies: lessons from the Skype case, *European Management Journal*, **24** (2 & 3), 174–188.

INNOVATION IN ACTION

Business Model Innovation

For many years, Costas Markides at London Business School has been researching the links between strategy, innovation and firm performance. In recent work he argues for the need to make a clearer distinction between the technological and market aspects of disruptive innovations, and to pay greater attention to business model innovation.

By definition, business model innovation enlarges the existing value of a market, either by attracting new customers or by encouraging existing customers to consume more. Business model innovation does not require the discovery of new products or services, or new technology, but rather the redefinition of existing products and services and how these are used to create value.

For example, Amazon did not invent book selling, and low-cost airlines such as Southwest and EasyJet are not pioneers of air travel. Such innovators tend to offer different product or service attributes to existing firms, which emphasize different value propositions. As a result, business model innovation typically requires different and often conflicting systems, structures, processes and value chains to existing offerings.

However, unlike the claims made for disruptive innovations, new business models can co-exist with more mainstream approaches. For example, Internet banking and low-cost airlines have

(continued)

not displaced the more mainstream approaches, but have captured around 20% of the total demand for these services. Also, while many business model innovations are introduced by new entrants, which have none of the legacy systems and products of incumbent firms, the more mainstream firms may simply choose not to adopt the new business models as they make little sense for them. Alternatively, they may make other innovations to create or recapture customers.

Sources: C. Markides (2006) Disruptive innovation: in need of a better theory, *Journal of Product Innovation Management*, 23, 19–25; (2004) *Fast Second: How Smart Companies Bypass Radical Innovation to Enter and Dominate New Markets*, Jossey-Bass, San Francisco.

Go online to find the interactive Flash tool we have developed to help identify the scope for innovation and the way in which value is created, the 4Ps.

www.iande.info

Growing the Venture

In most developed economies, around 10% of the economically active of any nation's population engage in new venture creation each year, a slightly higher proportion, 15% or so, in the USA and Asia, and a little lower, 6%, in Europe (excluding the UK). However, the rate of churn – new ventures closed versus those created – is high. For example, in the UK there are around 425,000 start-ups each year, but almost 500,000 closures. Closure does not necessarily indicate failure, as founders may choose to change business or seek alternative employment. Survival rates are quite high: in the UK after 2 years 80% survive, and 54% after 4 years (Barclays Capital, 2008). In the USA there are more short-term failures, probably due to the ease of establishing a business there, but similar rates of longer-term survival: 66% survive 2 years, 50% four years, 40% more than six years.[12]

Go online to listen to Simon Murdoch describe the development, growth and sale of his business BookPages.

www.iande.info

Despite these relatively high rates of survival, very few firms grow significantly or consistently, the so-called 'gazelles', perhaps only 5%.[13] However, although these high growth ventures are atypical, they account for a disproportionate proportion of new employment: between 12 and 33% in Europe. The founding conditions appear to have a very significant and

---

TABLE 12.5   Initial conditions influencing the success of new ventures

---

Most significant (5% level):
Size of target market
Industrial experience of founders
Strength of social networks
Business management skills

Significant (10% level):
Product attractiveness to target market
Ownership structure and governance

Not found to be significant:
Profit potential
Entrepreneurial attitude
Leadership skills
R&D and production planning
Market development
Financial forecast

Based on 95 new ventures, 1999–2007.

Source: Adapted from Gao, J., Li, J., Cheng, Y. and Shi, S. (2010) Impact of initial conditions on New Venture Success, *International Journal of Innovation Management*, 14(1), 41–56.

persistent effect on the subsequent success and growth of a new venture, but it is difficult to separate the effects of business planning, strategy and context (Table 12.5). Most, but not all, studies suggest that formal business planning contributes to success.[14] We discussed the role of business plans in detail in Chapter 7.

The most significant controllable factors shown in Table 12.5 all help to build credibility for a new venture, what our colleague Sue Birley refers to as the 'credibility carousel': factors which help to recruit and convince other stakeholders of the viability of a venture.[15] This can be a slow, painful process, but is essential in order attract the necessary talent, resources and initial customers.

Studies consistently find that the age, educational level, number of founders and starting capital all have a positive effect on venture success. The effects of age on the success and growth of a new venture are probably the best understood, and shown to be significant in almost every research study. The consensus is that the most common age of successful founders is between 35 and 50 years old.[16] The explanation for this clustering is that younger founders tend to lack the experience, resources and credibility, whereas older founders may lack the drive and have too much to lose. Of course there are many examples of successful entrepreneurs younger or older than this age range, but the association between age of founders and success is very significant.

To understand the influence of education, one study tracked 118,070 new start-up firms over 10 years, and found that human capital at foundation, measured by university degree, had a strong and persistent positive effect on subsequent success. In addition, four structural factors at the time of foundation were predictors of success: firm size at foundation (positive), rate of firm entry into the same sector (negative), concentration of the sector (positive) and GDP growth (positive).[17] Other research examined 622 young or new small firms over 5 years, and found human and financial capital available at start-up was found to be a strong predictor of survival and growth, specifically the founder's education (degree or above) and access to bank finance.[18] As with age, there are many examples of successful entrepreneurs who chose not to go to college or dropped out early, but the research does consistently demonstrate a strong association between level of education and venture success and growth, especially in more knowledge- or technology-intensive businesses.

Access to sufficient capital is another widely cited founding condition for success and growth. However, the evidence is more mixed than for the effects of age and education. Some studies suggest that access to external capital is associated with higher growth, especially in the case of more high-technology ventures,[19] but others find no such effect or even the exact opposite relationship, that higher growth is associated with maintaining internal funding and ownership.[20] The conflicting evidence and advice may be due to methodological differences, such as definition of high growth, time period studied and so on, but may also reflect the influence of more fundamental moderating factors, for example, the type of venture and market or the roles and control needs of founders.

These founder effects are even stronger for new technology-based firms (NTBF). NTBFs are actually lower risk than many other types of new venture, with higher survival and growth rates. This is partly because of the human capital necessary, especially the higher education of founders:[21]

- 85% have a degree, almost half a PhD;
- 12 or more years' experience in large private-sector firm;
- Founders' ages cluster mid-30s; two-thirds between age of 30 and 50.

Table 12.6 shows some of the common characteristics of high-growth technology ventures in the UK. Two factors are apparent form this; the age of the founders clusters around the mid-30s, and the timing of the creation of these successful Internet ventures was around 1998, just before the Internet Bubble burst in 2000. This means that they would have had access at the early stages to finance, at least for the first few crucial years.

Finally, companies competing on price, rather than by differentiation, are much less likely to survive. Contrary to the popular folklore of the poorly educated, disadvantaged entrepreneur, this study confirms that the more typical profile of a successful new venture is a rare combination of human capital in the form of the university education of founders, availability of sufficient bank finance, and a strategy of growth by product or service differentiation. Figure 12.2 shows how gross margins of new ventures change following external capital investment. First this declines, as the venture builds capability, and then these margins recover but at a much higher level of output. Figure 12.3 identifies the sector-distribution of high-growth ventures in the UK and confirms that whilst the finance and property sectors dominate, gazelles are possible in almost every part of the economy.

TABLE 12.6 Common characteristics of UK high growth internet ventures

Peter Cruddas	CMC Markets	Founded 1989, aged 35	£1,000 m
Russell de Leon	Party Gaming	Founded, 1998, aged 32	£700 m
Michael Mortiz	Sequoia Capital (Google, YouTube)	Founded 1986, aged 32	£651 m
Peter Coates	Bet365	Founded 2000, aged 32	£400 m
Peter Wilkinson	Freeserve	Founded 1998, aged 43	£301 m
Michael Birch	Bebo	Founded 2005, aged 33	£250 m
Tihan Presbie	Miniclip	Founded 2001, aged 36	£196 m
Simon Nixon	Money Supermarket	Founded 1998, aged 30	£140 m
Richard Goulding	Play.com	Founded 1998, aged 28	£80 m
Rory Sweet	MessageLabs	Founded 1999, aged 32	£74 m

Personal fortunes at 2009, not company valuations.
Source: Sunday Times, Rich List, April 26th, 2009

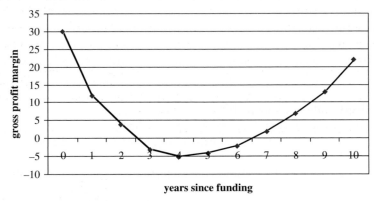

FIGURE 12.2 Changes in gross margin following investment.
Source: NESTA/BVCA (2009) *From Funding Gaps to Thin Markets: UK Government support for early-stage venture capital*. NESTA/BVCA, London.

INNOVATION IN ACTION

Blue Ocean Innovation Strategies

For the past decade INSEAD professors W. Chan Kim and Renée Mauborgne have researched innovation strategies, including work on new market spaces and value innovation. Their most recent contribution is the idea of Blue Ocean Strategies.

(continued)

By definition, Blue Ocean represents all potential markets which currently do not exist and must be created. In a few cases whole new industries are created, such as those spawned by the Internet, but in most cases they are created by challenging the boundaries of existing industries and markets. Therefore both incumbents and new entrants can play a role.

They distinguish Blue Ocean strategies by comparing them to traditional strategic thinking, which they refer to as Red Ocean strategies:

1. Create uncontested market space, rather than compete in existing market space.
2. Make the competition irrelevant, rather than beat competitors.
3. Create and capture new demand, rather than fight for existing markets and customers.
4. Break the traditional value/cost trade-off: align the whole system of a company's activities in pursuit of both differentiation *and* low cost.

In many cases a Blue Ocean is created where a company creates value by simultaneously reducing costs and offering something new or different. In their study of 108 company strategies they found that only 14% of innovations created new markets, whereas 86% were incremental line extensions. However, the 14% of Blue Ocean innovations accounted for 38% of revenues and 61% of profits.

The key to creating successful Blue Oceans is to identify and serve uncontested markets, and therefore benchmarking or imitating competitors is counter-productive. It often involves a radically different business model, offering a different value proposition at lower cost. It may be facilitated by technological or other radical innovations, but in most cases this is not the driver.

Sources: W. Chan Kim and R. Mauborgne (2005) Blue Ocean strategy: from theory to practice. *California Management Review*, **47** (3), Spring, 105–21; (2005) *Blue Ocean Strategy: How to Create Uncontested Market Space and Make the Competition Irrelevant*, Harvard Business School, Boston, MA; (2004) Blue Ocean strategy, *Harvard Business Review*, **82** (10), October, 76–84.

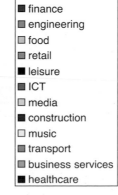

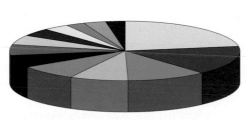

Top 1000 UK entrepreneurs ranked by personal
fortunes at 2009, not company valuations.

FIGURE 12.3   High growth UK ventures by sector.
Source: Sunday Times, Rich List, April 26th, 2009

However, lack of credibility and managerial experience of founders is a major barrier to funding new ventures. In the early stage, developing relationships with potential customers and suppliers is the most critical, but as the venture grows the relationship and role of partners in the network of a new venture will change. Later, external sources of funding need to be cultivated, which can result in changes of ownership and the dissolution of some of the initial relationships and substitution for more mature partners in more stable networks. Over time, the roles of different actors in the venture network become more specialised and professional.[22] Individual skills are essential in building and developing such relationships and networks. These skills include:[23]

- social and interpersonal communication – to build credibility and promote knowledge sharing;
- negotiating and balancing skills – to balance co-operation and competition, and to develop awareness, trust and commitment;
- influencing and visioning skills to establish roles, and shares of responsibilities and rewards.

Therefore the challenge is to simultaneously manage the more mature firm and its relations, but to maintain the early focus on innovation.

Go online to find the case study of Solid Works, which demonstrates many of the challenges of raising funds for growth.

www.iande.info

ENTREPRENEURSHIP IN ACTION

Factors Influencing Venture Success

A study of 11,259 new technology-based ventures in the USA over a period of five years found that 36% survived after four years, and 22% after five years. To try to explain the success and failure of these ventures, the researchers reviewed 31 other key studies of technology ventures, and found only eight factors that were consistently found to influence success:

1. *Value chain management* – co-operation with suppliers, distribution, agents and customers.
2. *Market scope* – variety of customers and market segments, and geographic reach.
3. *Firm age* – number of years in existence.
4. *Size of founding team* – likely to bring additional and more diverse expertise to the ventures, and better decision making.
5. *Financial resources* – venture assets and access to funding.

(continued)

6. *Founders' marketing experience* – but not technical experience, or prior experience of start-ups (see below).
7. *Founders' industry experience* – in related markets or sectors.
8. *Existence of patent rights* – in product or process technology, but R&D investment was not found to be significant.

The first three factors were by far the most significant predictors of success. However, clearly there is also some interaction between these effects, for example, the founders' marketing and industry experience is likely to influence the attention to market scope and the value chain, and patent rights make raising finance easier, and vice versa.

In addition, they found that some commonly cited factors had no effect, including founders' experience of R&D or prior start-ups. The importance of other factors depended on the precise context of the venture, for example, for independent start-ups R&D alliances and product innovation both had a negative effect on performance, but for ventures of mixed origins R&D alliances and product innovation both had a positive effect on performance.

Source: Song, M., K. Podoynitsyna, H. van der Bij and J.I.M. Halman (2008) Success factors in new ventures: a meta-analysis, *Journal of Product Innovation Management*, **25**, 7–27.

STRATEGIC AND SOCIAL IMPACT

Measuring the Contribution of Innovation

Traditionally, R&D expenditure has been used as proxy for innovation investment. This measurement bias has shaped innovation policy. After several decades of measurement of R&D, many countries have formulated policies to encourage more of it. For example, the Lisbon European Council set a target that EU member states should spend the equivalent of 3% of GDP on R&D, and have introduced R&D tax credits as a means of increasing it.

However, R&D represents only 11% of the investment in innovation measured by the Index, which includes a range of complementary investments needed to commercialise ideas, including product design, training in new skills, organisational innovation, developing new customer offering and brands, and copyright. The Index includes a number of investments that relate to important aspects of 'hidden innovation', such as organisational innovation, the investment in skills needed to provide new services, investment in product design, and investment in branding necessary to take an innovative product or service to market. Many of these, such as training and skills development and organisational improvement, are particularly relevant for innovative services businesses, and constitute the bulk of their investment in innovative offerings.

(*continued*)

Two-thirds of UK private sector productivity growth between 2000 and 2007 (1.8 percentage points of productivity growth per year) was a result of innovation. Innovative firms enjoyed a much faster growth rate than non-innovative ones in a wide range of sectors, for example, in innovative software 13% average revenue growth per year compared with just above zero, and even in traditional conservative sectors like legal services, where innovative firms enjoyed average revenue growth of over 10%, while non-innovative firms' revenues shrank on average.

Source: NESTA (2009) The Innovation Index. National Endowment for Science, Technology and Arts. www.nesta.org.uk/assets/documents/innovation_index

Chapter Summary

In this chapter we have reviewed how innovation and entrepreneurship contribute to personal, economic and social success. Traditional measures of technological innovation such as R&D spending and number of patents granted are associated with economic growth at the national level and in some sectors, but are not predictive across most sectors and are not good indicators at the firm or individual level. Broader indicators of innovation, such as proportion of earnings from new products and degree of differentiation are more general and stronger drivers of economic success. More fundamentally, process, organisational and managerial innovations are more likely to result in economic and social benefits. Moreover, the adoption of innovations can have a far greater impact than the generation of innovations. Innovation can occur in all elements of a business model to create and capture value. High growth new ventures contribute disproportionately to economic growth and employment, but these 'gazelles' are rare. The growth of a new venture is very sensitive to the founding conditions, and the combination of a small number of factors is a very strong predictor of success: the age, number, experience and education of founders; access to adequate capital; and an explicit strategy of differentiation and intent to grow.

Discussion Questions

1. What are the relationships between R&D spending, patents and economic performance?

2. How does product and service differentiation contribute to value-added?

3. Why is value-added a good general measures of the benefits of innovation?

4. What are the main components of a Business Model?

5. What are the differences between a Blue Ocean Strategy and a more conventional Red Ocean Strategy?

6. What are the main founding conditions which influence the success of a new venture?

7. How are high-growth 'gazelles' different from other new ventures?

Key Terms Defined

Blue Ocean Strategy   aims to avoid direct competition by identifying or creating uncontested markets, often challenging accepted cost–value propositions. It is essentially an extreme type of differentiation.

Business model   is the mechanism used to create and capture value. Typically this includes the value proposition, mechanisms for revenue generation, capabilities and processes, and position in the value network or ecosystem. The term is perhaps inappropriate as all organisations, private, public and social, seek to create and to some extent capture value, broadly defined, so perhaps the term 'value model' is more generic.

Gazelles   are new ventures with consistently high rates of growth. They are rare, but contribute disproportionately to economic growth and employment.

Value-added   is a generically useful measure of performance, applicable to almost all types of enterprise, private and social. There is no single definition of value-added, but essentially it is simply the difference between the market value of outputs and the cost of inputs. The most straightforward definition of value-added is revenue or income less materials and services purchases, but can also take into account the cost of capital inputs, depreciation and a provision for a reasonable return on the capital invested. In this case there is a trade-off between simplicity and completeness.

Further Reading and Resources

Discussions of how innovation and entrepreneurship contribute to performance tend to be very narrow and technical, using econometrics to identify relationships. However, for more accessible and general treatments, see John Kay's *Foundations of Corporate Success: How business strategies add value* (1995, Oxford University Press) and Paul A. Geroski's *Market Structure, Corporate Performance and Innovative Activity* (1995, Oxford University Press). If you prefer a more quantitative approach, try Angelo Dringoli (2009) *Creating Value Through Innovation* (Edward Elgar).

There are many articles on business models, but most are based on single company case studies rather than systematic review or research. Recent useful papers include: Johnson, M.J., Christensen, C.M. and Kagermann, H. (2008) Reinventing your business model, *Harvard Business Review*, 86(12), December, 51–59; Chesbrough, H. (2007) Business model innovation: it's not just about technology', *Strategy & Leadership*, 35(6), 12–17; Giesen, E., Berman, S.J., Bell, R. and Blitz (2007) Three ways to successfully innovate your business model', *Strategy & Leadership*, 35(6), 27–33; and Morris, M., Schindehutte, M. and Allen, J. (2005) The entrepreneur's business model; toward a unified perspective', *Journal of Business Research*, 58, 726–735.

Most texts on Entrepreneurship and New Business fail to cover the factors which influence the success and growth of new ventures, but the worthy exception is the work by our colleagues David Storey and Francis Green (2010) *Small Business and Entrepreneurship* (Financial Times Prentice Hall) which provides a thorough review of the research on venture growth. For more succinct but excellent recent reviews of the research on the initial conditions which influence subsequent success and growth, see Gao, Li, Cheng and Shi (2010) 'Impact of initial conditions on New Venture Success, *International Journal of Innovation Management*, 14(1), 41–56, and Geroski, Mata and Portugal (2010) 'Founding conditions and the survival of new firms', *Strategic Management Journal*, 31, 510–529.

References

1. Arrow, K. (1962) Economic welfare and the allocation of resources for invention. In R. Nelson (ed.) *The Rate and Direction of Inventive Activity*, Princeton University Press, Princeton, NJ.

2. Tidd, J. (2006) *From Knowledge Management to Strategic Competence*, second edition, Imperial College Press, London; Tidd, J., C. Driver and P. Saunders (1996) Linking technological, market and financial indicators of innovation, *Economics of Innovation and New Technology*, 4, 155–72; Griliches, Z. and A. Pakes (1984) *Patents R&D and Productivity*, University of Chicago Press, Chicago; Stoneman, P. (1983) *The Economic Analysis of Technological Change*, Oxford University Press, Oxford.

3. Geroski, P. (1991) Innovation and the sectoral sources of UK productivity growth, *Economic Journal*, **101**, 1438–1451; Geroski, P. (1994) *Market Structure, Corporate Performance and Innovative Activity*, Oxford University Press, Oxford.

4. Hay, D.A. and D.J. Morris (1991) *Industrial Economics and Organisation*, Oxford University Press, Oxford.

5. Blundell, R., R. Griffith and S. Van Reenen (1993) Knowledge stocks, persistent innovation and market dominance. Paper given to SPES Discussion Group, Brussels, September.

6. Mansfield, E. (1990) *Managerial Economics: Theory, Application and Cases*, sixth edition, W.W. Norton.

7. Freeman, C. (1982) *The Economics of Industrial Innovation*, Pinter, London.

8. Scherer, F. (1965), Firm size, market structure, opportunity and the output of patented inventions, *American Economic Review*, 55, 1097–1125; (1983) The propensity to patent, *International Journal of Industrial Organisation*, 50(1), 107–128.

9. Chaney, R., T. Devinney and R. Winer (1992) The impact of new product introductions on the market value of firms, *Journal of Business*, 64(4), 573–610; Griliches, Z., B.H. Hall and A. Pakes (1991) R&D, patents and market value revisited, *Economics of Innovation and New Technology Journal*, 1(3), 183–202.

10. Tidd, J. (2006) *From Knowledge Management to Strategic Competence*, second edition, Imperial College Press, London; Tidd, J., C. Driver and P. Saunders (1996) Linking technological, market and financial indicators of innovation, *Economics of Innovation and New Technology*, 4, 155–172.

11. Johnson, M.J., Christensen, C.M. and Kagermann, H. (2008) Reinventing your business model, *Harvard Business Review*, 86(12), December, 51–59; Chesbrough, H. (2007) Business model innovation: it's not just about technology', *Strategy & Leadership*, 35(6), 12–17; Giesen, E., Berman, S.J., Bell, R. and Blitz, A. (2007) Three ways to successfully innovate your business model', *Strategy & Leadership*, 35(6), 27–33.

12. Head, B. (2003) Redefining business success: distinguishing between closure and failure, *Small Business Economics*, 21(1), 51–59.

13. Storey, D. and Green, F. (2010) *Small Business and Entrepreneurship*. Financial Times Prentice Hall; Storey, D. (1994) *Understanding the Small Business Sector*. Thomson Learning.

14. Barr, S.H., Baker, T., Markham, S.K. and Kingon, A.I. (2009) Bridging the Valley of Death: Lessons Learned From 14 Years of Commercialization of Technology Education, *Academy of Management Learning and Education*, 8(3), 370–388; Beaver, G. (2007) The strategy payoff for smaller enterprises, *The Journal of Business Strategy*, 28(1), 9–23; Lyles, M.A., Baird, I.S., Orris, B. and Kuratko, K. (1993) Formalised planning in business: increasing strategic choice, *Journal of Small Business Management*, 31(2), 38–51.

15. Birley, S. (2002) Universities, Academics and Spin-Out Compnaies: Lessons from Imperial, *International Journal of Entrepreneurship Education*, 1(1), 133–154.

16. Capelleras, J.L. and Greene, F.J. (2008) The determinants and growth implications of venture creation speed, *Entrepreneurship and Regional Development*, 20(4), 317–343; Koeller, C.T. and Lechler, T.G. (2006) Employment growth in high-tech new ventures, *Journal of Labor Research*, 27(2), 135–147; Persson, H. (2004) The survival and growth of new establishments in Sweden, *Small Business Economics*, 23(5), 423–440.

17. Geroski, P.A., Mata, J. and Portugal, P. (2010) Founding conditions and the survival of new firms, *Strategic Management Journal*, 31, 510–529; Gao, J., Li, J., Cheng, Y. and Shi, S. (2010) 'Impact of initial conditions on New Venture Success, *International Journal of Innovation Management*, 14(1), 41–56.

18. Saridakis, G., Mole, K. and Storey, D.J. (2008) New small firm survival in England, *Empirica*, 35, 25–39.

19. Birley, S. and Westhead, P. (1994) A taxonomy of business start-up reasons and their impact on firm growth and size, *Journal of Business Venturing*, 9(1), 7–31; Davila, A., Foster, G. and Gupta, M. (2003) Venture capital financing and the growth of start-up firms, *Journal of Business Venturing*, 18(6), 689–708.

20. Cosh, A., Hughes, A., Bullock, A. and Milner, I. (2009) *SME Finance and Innovation in the Current Economic Crisis*, Centre for Business Research, University of Cambridge.

21. Storey, D. and Tether, B. (1998) New technology-based firms in the European Union, *Research Policy* 26, 933–946; Tether, B. and Storey, D. (1998) Smaller firms and Europe's high technology sectors: a framework for analysis and some statistical evidence, *Research Policy* 26, 947–971.

22. Oberg, C. and Grundstrom, C. (2009) Challenges and opportunities in innovative firms' network development, *International Journal of Innovation Management*, 13(4), 593–614.

23. Ritala, P., Armila, L. and Blomqvist, K. (2009) Innovation orchestration capability, *International Journal of Innovation Management*, 13(4), 569–591.

CASE STUDY 12

Creating Value through Reputation and Relationships

The interaction of reputation and relationships can help to create value, and in this case we examine the case of Technology and Engineering Consultancies (TECs). These companies work closely with clients on projects. We develop and illustrate the notion of *generative interaction* where a series of mechanisms produce a self-reinforcing ecology that favours innovation and profitability. We also observe the opposite dynamic of self-reinforcing *degenerative interaction* which may produce a cycle of declining innovation and profitability. In the specific context of project-based firms, we show that user and open innovation can negatively affect performance and provide insights into the consequences (positive and negative) of different patterns of interaction with clients.

Introduction to TECs

TECs provide services to support the design, development, maintenance and renewal of almost all the physical infrastructure of modern economies (e.g. buildings, transport, utilities) over their entire life cycle. As such they provide a very wide range of technical services, ranging from conceptual design, project development, environmental assessment, site selection, investment and acquisition appraisal, warranty management to decommissioning and rehabilitation.

Examples of a large multidisciplinary consulting firm would include employee-owned firms such as Mott MacDonald or publicly listed companies such as Atkins Plc. However there are numerous much smaller firms focusing on fewer or even single markets. TECs operate in many distinct sectors of the economy nationally and internationally, providing facilities and systems (e.g. for water/energy utilities, industrial and commercial assets, transport infrastructure, hospitals and schools), although many of the roles they play in these sectors are broadly similar. The top ten clients for UK civil engineers in 2005 tendered for contracts worth between £286m and £1.9bn each. These included both UK government departments (Transport, Health, Defence) as well as private firms (Asda, National Grid Transco, Land Securities, News Corporation).

Characteristics of TECs

TEC firms	Age (years)	Group structure	Employees	Group revenues	Profit margins
A	20+	Single sector consultancy	>100	>£10M	14%
B	100+	Single sector consultancy	>1000	>£100M	6%
C	100+	Multidisciplinary consultancy	>5000	>£100M	3%
D	30+	Multidisciplinary consultancy	>5000	~£500M	4%
E	100+	Conglomerate offering diverse services, including engineering	>1000	>£1000M	5%
F	50+	Multidisciplinary consultancy	>10,000	>£1000M	8%
G	50+	Multidisciplinary consultancy	>25,000	>£5000M	3%

The ecosystem around infrastructure projects is composed of a web of specialised consultants and contractors, typically connected to a central systems integrator. TECs play important roles within this ecosystem by helping to define problems and solutions. Over recent years the number of contractual roles open to TECs appears to have increased. For example, TECs may work with the client to design an asset, but also can work in consortia with other contractors to provide an integrated 'design and build' package for the client, handing over the asset when complete. Alternatively, Private Finance Initiatives (PFIs) allow consortia to design, build, own and run assets, whereby they deliver to the client not the power station, for example, but electricity at a pre-arranged price per kilowatt hour. Therefore TECs' role can vary. They can provide services to design assets, or to design the competition that awards contracts to build the assets, or indeed to provide technical advice to the client or financiers of such projects. TECs capture value by building experience and accumulating knowledge through partnerships with operators, strategy consultants, and vendors. This builds reputation, technological and project management capabilities, network connections and leads to further assignments. We suggest that the main drivers of innovation in this category are selecting experienced consultants to jointly envision new solutions with clients; structuring the governance of projects for distributed problem-solving between clients and specialised consulting and engineering firms; and developing project management competencies that enable firms to cope with critical changes. TECs often access external knowledge in a systematic manner and therefore operate in a classic open innovation system. The quote below, from an engineer in Transport TEC, discusses development of data-capture methods from work sites that bring university research into use, and ultimately new safety standards and wider practice in the professional community:

> I know certainly with this work on [Tube Train Line] there is quite a good link with [University X] . . . they are actually instrumenting some of the sites that we are working on with monitoring instrumentation and their knowledge . . . they've gained, is then sent back to us so that we can actually see exactly what is going on during a certain remedial process or whatever, and it is that type of stuff that then gets published and is then slowly filtered through and becomes sort of more recognised, and it's when an updated standard is written that the findings raise the level . . . really, that's the cycle.

The Managing Director (MD) of a TEC discusses the development of a novel system developed for an application in the highly regulated nuclear sector:

> you get all the expertise from [Client nuclear plant], from [a Blue Chip engineering firm], from [Name of Engineering Procurement Contractor], from [name of another Nuclear Client], all of these experts and the nuclear inspectorate . . . and we claimed the credit but the truth is it's an industry developed design . . . So you can feel a lot more confident with it because I've had all the bloody experts of the industry crawling all over it and changing it.

These two quotes illustrate how knowledge accumulation takes place through networks, links to universities, other contractors, suppliers and regulators. Much of the knowledge is formalised into decision methodologies that help retain past learning and experience, including professional guidelines and building regulations.

Project-Based Innovation

TECs are Project-Based Organisations (PBOs), which tend to be inherently more open and user-centric than conventional product development. Such organisational forms are used to realise specific one-off projects (such as construction of a major facility like an airport or a hospital) or for managing the design and fabrication of complex systems like aero engines, flight simulators or communications networks.

Project organisations bring together many different elements into an integrated whole, often involving different types of firms, long time-scales and high levels of technological risk. PBOs can create and re-create new organisational structures around the demands of each new project and client, and can more easily integrate diverse types of knowledge than functional organisations. However, the PBO also has the inherent weakness in the co-ordination of resources across projects and capture of innovation and learning. Despite these problems PBOs have been associated with major innovations in project management and organisation in areas such as project financing, regulation and risk-sharing in sectors as diverse as pharmaceuticals and civil engineering. Although such projects may appear very different from the core innovation process associated with conventional new product development, the underlying process is still one of careful understanding of user needs and meeting those. The involvement of users throughout the development process, and the close integration of different perspectives will be of particular importance.

Research suggests the dynamics of network connections are important influences on success and failure of PBOs. Networks shape the flow and sharing of information and generate power and control imbalances among actors. As a result, the position an organisation occupies in a network is a matter of great strategic importance that reflects its power and influence. Sources of power include resources (technology, expertise, economic strength), processes (decision making) and legitimacy (trust). In particular, successful innovative collaborations result from situations where two organisations with different perspectives and capabilities share commitment to a common direction, interact in a recurring manner and value, monitor and nurture their relationship. These generative relationships and interactions can create positive effects that may extend from project to project, with the same client or with new clients, as reputation develops.

Dynamics of Generative Interaction

Getting to a position where TECs, their clients and other stakeholders, such as contractors and suppliers, can innovate together is a multi-stage process that can, under certain conditions, generate a positive feedback cycle or *generative interaction*, producing benefits for both the TECs and their clients. During generative interaction TECs use both external knowledge networks and more conventional internal capability- and reputation-building. Together these (internal) micro- and (external) meso-level mechanisms account for the generative development of stocks of expertise that can flow in the project network between TECs and their clients and partners.

Figure 12.4 begins with the proposition that innovation delivers added value for the client's business. Value for clients is generated in a number of ways, for example, through *enhanced prestige* (e.g. being associated with a striking buildings such as the London's 30 St. Mary Axe ('the Gherkin') or the Burj-al-arab hotel

1. [Quote relates to car maker clients] The other aspect of making profit if you can't sell more, [is to] cut your costs ... that's been a real big focus and shift change in the last five years ... If you look at the amount of money they've spent on warranty bills and the damage that that does to the brand image the car industry really needs to crack that nut and that's what we're helping them do [Automotive – Managing Director]

2. Our efforts there are obviously to deliver what the customer needs ... helping to define what those needs might be, more specifically, for a given project and also to create innovations that enhance the achievement of those and those enhancements would be risk reduction and adding value [Transport Director 1]

3. There are some areas where we have the experts...the best expertise in the country and that differentiates us ... there's nobody else who can really do it or if they try to go somewhere else they have to come back to us ... the majority of what we do is based on our ability to come up with innovative solutions and to be able to think through the problem ... we don't try to shoehorn solutions into problems simply because we have already got that solution and the company is recognised. That means they [the client] will get something which is geared directly to their particular problem. [Water R&D Head]

(i) Innovation adds value to the client's business

4. We leave our customer as happy as possible ... trying to listen and make sure the customer is happy is very important to us, it is fundamental to our survival, If we can get that right then obviously we can enhance the reputation and we get repeat business and improve our market share [Industrial Prcesses A - Managing Director]

5. Success for [Emerty TEC] Is making money and keeping the client happy. If they are happy then they will come back for more business ... This means they come back and the cost of sales is lower [ˇEnerty Director 1]

6. Let's say we get 85% of our business as repeat business okay? And that's really how we operate, how we get a client on board, and take good care of them and they just stay with us ... *They added later.* It costs us much more when you've got to bid for everything instead of stuff just walkin in the door [Industrial Process B – VP sales]

(ii) Adding value for the client benefits the TEC through reputation and repeat business

7. One of the key roles [of business development] is to make sure that [that staff member] develops that relationship and there are a number of instances now, they will come directly to [Water TEC] because they know we have that particular skill or they know we can develop that type of approach [Water – R&D Head]

8. In terms of, you know, reputation within the market place and the brand, it's very well throught of and we generate a lot of work from that [Water – Innovation Head]

9. So there are not that many consultants who have the expertise but we are world renowned at our expertise in jack tunnels now [Transport Director 1]

10. The skills that we pick up, the power industry have sort of led, the private power industries led ... now being used by other industries, so we had skills that people could take and participate in other projects [Energy TEC – project manager]

(iii) Reputation, repeat business and the accumulation of expertise feed each other

11. I make a substantial profit on the jobs that I try to do but that's small jobs and the reason I make a profit is that ... I've done them so many times before, its a bit like one client saying "if you've done it for everybody else why do [they] have to pay for it at all!" [Public amenities – Innovation Leader]

12. In this business to survive you have to have something better than that to offer and the more you have to offer the more margin you can get away with in negotiation [Automotive – Managing Direcrot]

13. I've got to be at the front where the margins are, where it has not been done before, that's what we are always looking for [Industrial Process A – Managing Director]

14. Our investment has paid for itself more than ten times over a very short period. You know on a lot of research we do get a ten times payback but it takes ten years to get there. But with [this project] we got there in less than five [R&D Head]

(iv) The cycle in (iii) benefits the TECs through increased profitability

FIGURE 12.4   A chain of mechanisms that support generative interaction.

Source: Derived from Michael M. Hopkins, Joe Tidd and Paul Nightingale (2011) Generative and degenerative interactions: Positive and negative dynamics of open, user-centric innovation in technology and engineering consultancies, *R&D Management*.

('the Sail') in Dubai); through *improved functionality* of assets (e.g. improved acoustics in a concert hall, reduced infection rates in a hospital); and *cost savings* (e.g. designs with faster build times through the use of prefabricated components such as for railway station platforms and railway embankment renewals); or *less disruption* (e.g. through the use of tunnel jacking and ground freezing to slide a prefabricated road tunnel under operational railway lines during Boston's 'big dig') or improved safety during a project (e.g. using movement monitoring systems to reduce the risk of collapse during underground excavations).

Furthermore, when TECs generate client added value this may produce on-going benefits for the TEC. Important mechanisms through which this is achieved include an improved ability to win repeat business and boosted reputation. This in turn may help TECs win competitive tenders. As one Project Manager stated:

> we were in a competitive situation on the [Nuclear plant] project which made a big difference . . . I suppose [to] how much profit at the end of the day, how much profit we can make. When you are in a competitive situation it's, you know, you get beaten up a lot more commercially at the start. But I am sure that one of the things that went in our favour was our track record at the [name of prior client] project because all of the people within the nuclear industry know each other and they are interconnected and I am sure they talk to each other. So I am sure the [previous] project helped us actually win the [Nuclear plant] project.

Generating repeat business or developing a reputation that increases chances of success in tender competitions is an important competency because it lowers the cost of sales by spreading the fixed costs involved in running a TEC and bidding for contracts. There is a reinforcing dynamic between reputation, repeat business and the accumulation of expertise as these feed into each other. Finally, this cycle generates increased profit margin for TECs. As we have seen already this may be due to reduced cost of sales, but it may also be because innovation and scarcity of a particular resource allow premium pricing. This supports previous research which suggests firms can use 'magnet' projects to enhance their reputation for design or problem solving in order to attract future customers.

In projects the TEC has to innovate with the client, and other contractors in the project's innovation network also have to be brought into agreement. This is important because generative interaction can only occur when the gap between the project participants undertaking design and its implementation is bridged, particularly in civil engineering, where Design Consultants and Engineering Procurement Consultants are distinct types of business. TECs emphasised that this required incentive systems to be harmonised, and Transport, Public Amenities, Health, and Industrial Process B TECs each mentioned the importance of methods such as so-called 'open-book accounting' in projects whereby contractors and clients could work together with a mutually shared understanding of each other's incentive structures. Such approaches were one way in which innovation could be introduced into a project:

> . . . commercial risk, health and safety, technical risk . . . there are lots of different types of risk but the way to manage this area is to actually get the parties together in a different procurement way and have a workshop on risk where everybody in a non-confrontational way . . . can raise it, it gets owned, examined and proportioned and then you can show that the risk of being conventional is actually higher in all sorts of ways. All those factors where the risk hits you can demonstrate and then you can move forward to introduce . . . which is effectively innovation.

Health TEC had found an alternative way to introduce innovation and facilitate generative interactions. They choose to forgo joining the consortia bidding for larger but higher risk contracts to design and build hospitals in favour of taking and adapting the traditional role of the client's technical adviser (who helps the client to develop the tender documentation and run the competition). The Health TEC Project Manager explained, 'you sacrifice a much bigger fee for the right to be more innovative in the business . . . technical advisor role isn't new but the way we approach it . . . is quite new.' The concept is based on persuading the client to send out a much more detailed tender than is usual, with particular advantages (including increased fees): 'If the brief is very well defined and the design is well defined then . . . not only is the programme time shortened, but the cost of bidding is a lot less'. Health TEC claimed that by showing clients how to create a space in the bidding process for innovative design, they had begun to win a new stream of stimulating work internationally, as well as introducing clients to the one-stop-shop for additional design features that their multidisciplinary consultancy hosted. The Health Project Manager concluded 'all this can be looked at outside of, if you like, the red hot competitive bidding stage . . . it's [a] more rational integrated holistic engaging approach with the client so that you get buy-in.'

The soft skills and status of the TEC's project manager may also play an important role in influencing the client's receptiveness to innovative solutions. This may, in turn, allow the TEC to work in ways that create value for their clients. The following quote, by a leading engineer in his field, illustrates these points:

> . . . so understanding of customers' needs and identifying solutions that will satisfy them is a particular strength. It's obviously grounded in technical expertise, but it's also dependent on advocacy, mentoring, learning from experience and conveying that understanding to the customers through precedent and reputation . . . I mean our competitors obviously do that to a certain extent as well.

If the TEC staff can indeed convey the benefits of an innovative approach, and actually deliver the added value, then the cycle is complete and further benefits may accumulate to TEC and client as outlined in the figure, and opening the way for future cycles, and more generative interaction.

Summary of Web Resources

Cases

- Solid Works

Media

- Simon Murdoch on BookPages

Tools

- 4Ps Flash
- Value Analysis

Chapter 13

Learning to Manage Innovation

Go online to find additional . . .

Cases

Tools

Media

www.iande.info

Introduction

Let's take stock of where we've been going in this book and the key themes we've tried to introduce.

In Chapter 1 we introduced the idea of innovation not as some luxury to be thought about occasionally but as a business and social imperative. Unless established organisations change what they offer the world and the ways they create and deliver that offering they are likely to fall behind their competitors and even disappear. On a more positive side creating new business through coming up with and deploying ideas is well-established as a powerful source of economic growth – not to mention a great way to make the successful entrepreneurs behind those ideas very wealthy!

This process works right across the economy – whether we are talking about cars, clothes or silicon chips. It isn't confined to manufacturing – it works just as powerfully for the services which make up the majority of most economies – banks, insurance companies, shops and airlines all have to look hard and often at the innovation challenge if they are to stay ahead.

For public services the same is true – but here we begin to see that it isn't always money which drives the entrepreneurial wheels. Innovation here is targeted at improving education, saving lives, making people more secure and addressing other basic needs. And whilst some innovation is about taking costs and waste out of established service delivery processes, much is about coming up with new and better ways of improving the quality of human life. Whether in a start-up or across a large public sector department there is a strong thread of social entrepreneurship running through driven less by a desire for profits than literally wanting to change the world.

But whatever drives innovation and wherever it happens – big firm, small firm, start-up business, public sector department – one thing is clear: successful innovation won't happen simply by wishing for it. This complex and risky process of transforming ideas into something which makes a mark needs organising and managing in strategic fashion. Passion and energy aren't enough – if we are to do more than just gamble enthusiastically then we need to organise and focus the process. And we need to be able to repeat the trick – anyone might get lucky once but being able to deliver a steady stream of innovations requires something a bit more structured and robust.

Innovation is a generic process, running from ideas through to their implementation. Despite the many different ways in which we see it playing out in manufacturing or services, at heart the process is about weaving knowledge and resources together. And it's this creative tapestry that we have to organise and manage as we move through finding opportunities, mobilising resources, developing the venture and capturing the value.

We know that this process is influenced along the way by several things which can help or hinder it – for example, having a clear sense of direction (an innovation strategy) or working within a creative network of players. We looked particularly at some of the levers we could use as architects and managers of the process. For example, how can an entrepreneur channel his or her energy, passion and ideas in such a way that it motivates others and gets them to 'buy into' the vision? How can we construct innovative organisations which allow creative ideas to come through, let people build on and share knowledge and feel motivated and

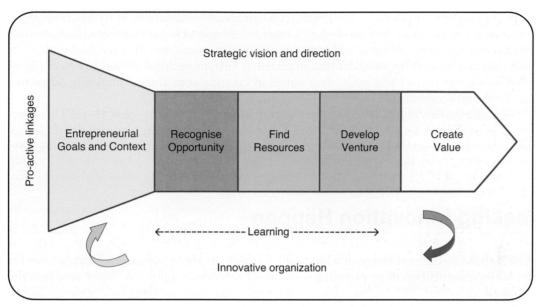

FIGURE 13.1   Simplified model for innovation management.

rewarded for doing so? How can we harness the power of networks, making rich and extensive connections to deliver a stream of innovations? Figure 13.1 illustrates the complete model.

Entrepreneurship as the Engine for Innovation

The energy and passion which drives through the process is *entrepreneurship* – the seeing and making real of opportunities. It is clearly involved in a start-up where a new business requires an individual/small group to channel their creative energy and drive to make something new. But it's also needed in an established company where renewal comes through stimulating and enabling the same drive and creativity to deliver both a stream of improvement innovations and also the occasional inspired leap which helps reinvent the business. And increasingly such drive, energy and enthusiasm is being harnessed to more than economic growth – in start-ups and established organisations where the challenges of sustainability are being picked up. Social entrepreneurship is literally about changing the world – but it uses the same basic engine.

Of course the context for innovation and entrepreneurship varies hugely. The particular pattern of threats and opportunities from which ideas emerge and are selected isn't a case of 'one size fits all' but an incredibly rich and diverse environment including manufacturing and service sectors and small to giant firm players. It's happening on a global stage which is placing increasing emphasis on networks and extended and often virtual connections. Innovation takes place against a backdrop of increasing concern about sustainability in terms of energy, resources and meeting basic human needs in a more balanced and better-distributed fashion – and this has brought many different and sometimes opposing actors into the play. And there is the long-standing tension between innovation aimed at sustaining what we already have (doing what we do but better) and innovation aimed at creating something completely different – *discontinuous* innovation.

But despite this richly varied context we still have to make it happen. How? This chapter looks at the key lessons learned about organising and managing the process of innovation and entrepreneurship – and how we might use those lessons to review and strengthen our capability.

Making Innovation Happen

Rather than the cartoon image of a light bulb flashing on above someone's head, we need to think about innovation as an extended sequence of activities – a *process.* We've seen that this involves:

- recognising the opportunity;
- finding the resources;
- developing the idea;
- capturing the value.

The key question is how can we best organise to make these activities happen?

It's interesting to look at success stories. Whether we are talking about individual entrepreneurs or giant transnational corporations, a common theme is that success isn't a lucky accident. Rather they reflect on what worked when things succeed – and crucially also on why they failed. Learning how to manage innovation and entrepreneurship is a key theme – and it doesn't happen automatically. It requires time, space, courage to recognise mistakes, structure to help focus reflection on those mistakes etc.

The lack of such capability can explain many failures, even amongst large and well-established organisations. For example, the:

- failure to recognise or capitalise on new ideas which conflict with an established knowledge set – the 'not invented here' problem;
- problem of being too close to existing customers and meeting their needs too well – and not being able to move into new technological fields early enough;
- problem of adopting new technology – following technological fashions – without an underlying strategic rationale.

The costs of not managing learning – of lacking the dynamic capability – can be high. At the least it implies a blunting of competitive edge, a slipping against previously strong performance. (For example, 3M was for many years in the top three of *Business Week*'s list of innovative

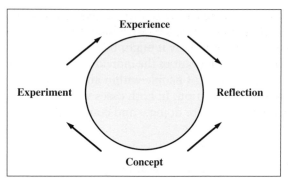

FIGURE 13.2   Simple model of the learning cycle.

companies. But following a change in CEO and a shift in emphasis away from breakthrough innovation and towards incremental improvement linked to a 'Six Sigma' programme, their position fell to 7th in 2006 and 22nd in 2007. This prompted significant debate both within the company and in its wider stakeholder community and a refocusing of efforts around developing their core innovation capabilities further). In some cases the fall accelerates and eventually leads to terminal decline – as illustrated by the fate of companies like Digital, Polaroid or Swissair, once feted for their innovative prowess.

The psychologist David Kolb developed a simple model of learning which is worth bringing in here – he used it to talk about how adults learn but we can adapt it to think of entrepreneurs and organisations. Figure 13.2 gives a simple illustration.

The model suggests that learning is not simply about acquiring new knowledge – it is a cycle with a number of stages. It doesn't matter where we enter but only when the whole cycle is complete does learning take place. So to enable effective learning about how to manage innovation better we need to:

- Capture and reflect on our experiences, trying to distil patterns from them about what works and doesn't work.
- Create models of how the world works – concepts – and link these to those we already have.
- Using our revised models engage again in innovation – trying new things out.

There are many ways we can help this process – for example:

- Rather than simply stepping back for a reflective pause we could employ some structured question frameworks. And we could ask others to help us in the process, acting as critical and challenging partners to help us learn.
- We can develop our own concepts – but we can also use, adapt and try out new ideas developed elsewhere. The 'theory' of innovation has emerged from many experiences codified into a rich body of knowledge and this is available to draw upon – we don't have to reinvent the wheel.
- Similarly we don't have to make all the mistakes ourselves – we can learn from other's experiences.

In the book we have tried to distil some of the accumulated learning about innovation and entrepreneurship and in the following sections we'll look at some simple aids to structured and critical reflection to help think about how it might be managed better. We'll take two 'lenses' in doing so – looking from the standpoint of the individual entrepreneur looking to create and grow a new venture – and from that of people within an established organisation, looking to renew and sustain it through innovation. In both cases we will develop a simple set of reflective questions around how well we are doing – and could we do it better?

Recognising the Opportunity

Ideas – as we've seen – can come from anywhere. Some boffin in a lab may have a 'Eureka!' moment. Or someone talking with customer may see a need which hasn't been met. A competitor might start offering a service we haven't got in our repertoire. A civil servant may change the rules of the particular game our business is playing and force us to rethink what we do. Or a newcomer from a different industry might spot a way to reframe the game and bring in a completely new way of looking at it – as we see every day on the Internet. And social entrepreneurship often arises from individuals looking at the world and seeing ways in which public services could be delivered better, or disadvantaged groups could be enabled, or resources more equitably distributed.

Wherever the ideas come from the challenge for us is to make sure we pick them up and harness them to provide the fuel of the innovation process. Entrepreneurship may give us the drive but without ideas the engine will be running on empty. So how could we organise and manage this search process? Needless to say there isn't a standard recipe but – as we saw in Chapter 6 – we need to spread the net widely and make sure we cover the spectrum from 'exploit – do what we do better' through to 'explore – do something different'.

ADVICE FOR FUTURE ENTREPRENEURS

Ask Yourself – Reflection Questions

. . . for start-up entrepreneurs

When looking for triggers for innovation, smart players try to cover as many bases as possible. So in reviewing your approach, how far do you:

- Explore the technology space – find opportunities but also check who else is doing it?
- Explore market space – find out if there is a market and how big, how fast it's growing, etc.? And how do you find out about competitors, real and potential, and about barriers to entry, etc.?

(continued)

- Explore what others are doing – who else is or could be playing, and could we learn from them?
- Explore future space – do you look ahead at how threats and opportunities might develop and affect both technical and market space?
- Exploring with others – do you bring in different stakeholders into the process, using their perspectives and ideas to enrich the variety and generate new directions?

. . . and for established organisations – how well do we do it?

There are many approaches an organisation could take to managing the challenge of finding opportunities to trigger the innovation process. How well it does so is another matter, but one way we could tell might be to listen to the things people said in describing 'the way we do things around here' – in other words, the pattern of behaviour and beliefs which creates the climate for innovation. And if we walked around the organisation we'd expect to hear people talking about the methods they actually use. We should hear things like:

Around here . . .

- We have good 'win-win' relationships with our suppliers and we pick up a steady stream of ideas from them.
- We are good at understanding the needs of our customers/end-users.
- We work well with universities and other research centres to help us develop our knowledge.
- Our people are involved in suggesting ideas for improvements to products or processes.
- We look ahead in a structured way (using forecasting tools and techniques) to try to imagine future threats and opportunities.
- We systematically compare our products and processes with other firms.
- We collaborate with other firms to develop new products or processes.
- We try to develop external networks of people who can help us - for example, with specialist knowledge.
- We work closely with 'lead users' to develop innovative new products and services.

Dealing with the unexpected

Of course, part of the search question is about picking up rather weak signals about emerging – and sometimes radically different – triggers for innovation. So people in smart firms might also say things like:

Around here . . .

- We deploy 'probe and learn' approaches to explore new directions in technologies and markets.
- We make connections across industry to provide us with different perspectives.
- We have mechanisms to bring in fresh perspectives – for example, recruiting from outside the industry.

(continued)

- We make regular use of formal tools and techniques to help us think 'outside the box'.
- We focus on 'next practices' as well as 'best practices'.
- We use some form of technology scanning/intelligence gathering – we have well-developed technology antennae.
- We work with 'fringe' users and very early adopters to develop our new products and services.
- We use technologies like the Web to help us become more agile and quick to pick up on and respond to emerging threats and opportunities on the periphery.
- We deploy 'targeted hunting' around our periphery to open up new strategic opportunities.
- We are organised to deal with 'off-purpose' signals (not directly relevant to our current business) and don't simply ignore them.
- We have active links into the long-term research and technology community – we can list a wide range of contacts.
- We recognise users as a source of new ideas and try to 'co-evolve' new products and services with them.

Finding the Resources

The trouble with ideas is that you can have too much of a good thing. A well-developed search process will throw up all sorts of possible opportunities – interesting ideas which are all waiting to take flight if only they had the resources to help them get off the ground. But no organisation – and certainly no individual entrepreneur – has infinite resources so the next stage in the process involves making some tough decisions about which ideas to back – and why. Inevitably this is a risky process – we have to take decisions about ideas which are in their earliest stages and which could become the best thing since sliced bread, but which could equally crash into oblivion and take us down with them!

For the entrepreneur the challenge is daunting – like taking part in a high-stakes competition. The test is one of how to put across your wonderful idea to a panel of judges who seem determined to find fault with everything. Passion and energy are all very well but they are looking for the impossible – guarantees that the idea will work, that people will want to buy and use it when it is developed and, most important, that they will get a return on their investment in you and your idea. Whether you are trying to convince a venture capitalist, a group of business angles or some close friends who might be interested in backing you, the same problem will emerge – is your pitch good enough to persuade them that they are taking a well-calculated risk rather than a wild gamble? Putting the business plan together is critical – and it doesn't hurt to have a sense of the kind of questions they might be thinking of asking you.

Which brings us to the other side of the fence. How do those responsible for judging ideas and selecting the best for further investment actually think? What are their concerns and how do they go about building an effective and balanced portfolio of ideas? The judges may be venture capitalists specialised in examining and taking risks with innovative ideas. But they could also be the management board reviewing the company's portfolio of new products or services, or a department manager considering a new process to implement across her group, or a hospital administrator looking for new ways to reduce costs or increase quality of service being delivered.

As with the previous stage we have learned quite a bit about the ways in which this task of selection can be organised and managed – a 'good practice' model which we can learn from and adapt. Smart organisations don't simply gamble – they make choices on the basis of some clear round rules – does the idea have promise? Is it a good fit with where we are trying to go in our wider business strategy? Does it build on things that we know and can take advantage of – or, if not, can we get hold of this knowledge to make it work? They make use of techniques and structures to help them in the selection process – and make sure these are flexible enough to help monitor and adapt projects over time as ideas move towards more concrete innovations. And if they aren't going as well as expected – because of unexpected developments on the technological or market front – they have mechanisms in place to stop the process and either go back to the drawing board or kill it altogether. (Chapter 9 described many of these approaches in more detail and there are a variety of tools to help on the website.)

ADVICE FOR FUTURE ENTREPRENEURS

Ask Yourself – Reflection Questions

. . . for start-up entrepreneurs

How far do you:

- Know what resources you will need to take your opportunity forward?
- Plan ahead to identify the resources which you will need – and work out where and how you will get those you don't have?
- Build rich networks to give you to access wider resources?
- Build contingency plans – what if I can't get access to these key resources? What other routes can I take to exploit this opportunity?
- Learn from how others have obtained resources?

. . . and for established organisations – how well are we doing it?

If we visited a smart organisation we'd expect to find evidence that these ways of helping the selection and resource-finding process were widely used. People we approached would tell us things like:

(continued)

> Around here . . .
>
> - We have a clear system for choosing innovation projects and everyone understands the rules of the game in making proposals.
> - When someone has a good idea they know how to take it forward.
> - We have a selection system which tries to build a balanced portfolio of low- and high-risk projects.
> - We focus on a mixture of product, process, market and business model innovation.
> - We balance projects for 'do better' innovation with some efforts on the radical 'do different' side.
> - We recognise the need to work 'outside the box' and there are mechanisms for handling 'off message' but interesting ideas.
> - We have structures for corporate venturing.

Developing the Venture

Having decided on which ideas to back, the organisation has one small problem left – how to actually make them happen. Moving from a gleam in some entrepreneur's eye to a product or service people use and value, or a business process which employees buy into and work with, can be a somewhat difficult journey! It isn't usually a simple matter of project management, balancing resources against a budget of time and money – the big difference with innovation is that we don't know whether or not things will work until we start doing them. So it's a case of developing something against a background of uncertainty. The only way we reduce the uncertainty is by trying things out and learning, even if what we learn is that it isn't going to work after all!

We're also weaving together different strands of knowledge about the innovation – the 'technological' (will it work as an idea?) and the 'market' (is there a need for this idea and do we understand and meet that need?). So a key aspect of implementation is making sure the threads come together and intertwine successfully – which in practice means making sure the right people get to talk with each other at the right time and for long enough to make something happen.

Innovation is often described in terms of the metaphor of a journey – and this helps us particularly to think about the implementation phase. What stages does our idea need to go through before it becomes a successful innovation as a product/service in the marketplace or a process in everyday use within the business? And what structures and techniques do smart entrepreneurs and firms use to help their innovation along this journey – and to check its progress? Chapter 9 explored this theme in detail and highlighted the kind of learning that experienced entrepreneurs and organisations bring into play when dealing with this challenge.

For example, it would be foolish to throw good money after bad so most organisations make use of some kind of risk management as they implement innovation projects. By installing a series of 'gates' as the project moves from a gleam in the eye to an expensive commitment of time and money it becomes possible to review – and if necessary redirect or even stop something which is going off the rails. And they employ a variety of project management structures to help balance flexibility, spread of different knowledge inputs and engagement of key stakeholders against the demands of time and budget.

INNOVATION IN ACTION

What Makes for Success in Product/Service Innovation?

These are some examples of the mechanisms, tools and structures which smart firms and entrepreneurs use.

Key needs/issues on the journey	Key mechanisms
Systematic process for progressing new products/services	Stage-gate model Close monitoring and evaluation at each stage
Early involvement of all relevant functions	Bringing key perspectives into the process early enough to influence design and prepare for downstream problems Early detection of problems leads to less rework
Overlapping/parallel working	Concurrent or simultaneous engineering to aid faster development whilst retaining cross-functional involvement
Appropriate project management structures	Choice of structure – e.g. matrix/line/project/heavyweight project management – to suit conditions and task
Cross-functional team-working	Involvement of different perspectives, use of team-building approaches to ensure effective team-working and develop capabilities in flexible problem-solving
Advanced support tools	Use of tools – such as CAD, rapid prototyping, computer-supported co-operative work aids – to assist with quality and speed of development
Learning and continuous improvement	Carrying forward lessons learned – via post-project audits, etc. Development of continuous improvement culture

---

Managing innovation projects is more than simply scheduling resources against time and budget. Dealing with unexpected and unpredictable events and gradually bringing projects into being requires high levels of flexibility and creativity – and in particular it involves integrating knowledge sets from across organisation, functional and disciplinary boundaries. And we've learned a lot about how to do this – for example, through using cross-boundary teams, through various forms of parallel or concurrent working, and through the use of simulation and other exploration technologies to anticipate downstream problems and reduce time and resource costs whilst enhancing innovation quality.

ADVICE FOR FUTURE ENTREPRENEURS

Ask Yourself – Reflection Questions

. . . for start-up entrepreneurs

How well have you thought through:

- How you will manage the project from your idea to full-scale launch?
- Who will you need to involve – and how will their involvement be timed?
- Is there a clear project plan with a timeline and plans for resources – especially cash flow – throughout the life of the project?
- Do you have criteria for stopping the project if it is going seriously off-track?
- How will you know how well you are doing in terms of project progress? When and how will you review?
- Do you have contingency plans – what if something goes unexpectedly wrong or late?

. . . and for established organisations – how well are we doing it?

We can compare ourselves against the 'good practice' model in the box above to identify where and how we could improve the ways we manage the implementation of innovation. If we visited a smart organisation we'd find many of these structures and techniques in use to help make the process happen well – and if we asked people we'd find evidence that they were using them. We'd hear things like:

Around here . . .

- We have clear and well-understood formal processes in place to help us manage new product development effectively from idea to launch.
- Our innovation projects are usually completed on time and within budget.
- We have effective mechanisms for managing process change from idea through to successful implementation.
- We have mechanisms in place to ensure early involvement of all departments in developing new products/processes.

(continued)

- There is sufficient flexibility in our system for product development to allow small 'fast track' projects to happen.
- Our project teams for taking innovation forward involve people from all the relevant parts of the organisation.
- We involve everyone with relevant knowledge from the beginning of the process.

    We'd also expect them to have some provision for the wilder and more radical kind of project, which might need to go on a rather different route in making its journey. People involved might say things like:
    Around here . . .

- We have alternative and parallel mechanisms for implementing and developing radical innovation projects which sit outside the 'normal' rules and procedures.
- We have mechanisms for managing ideas that don't fit our current business – for example, we license them out or spin them off.
- We make use of simulation, rapid prototyping tools etc. to explore different options and delay commitment to one particular course.
- We have strategic decision-making and project selection mechanisms which can deal with more radical proposals outside of the mainstream.
- There is sufficient flexibility in our system for product development to allow small 'fast track' projects to happen.

Innovation Strategy – Having a Clear Sense of Direction

Innovation doesn't take place in a vacuum – it's subject to a range of internal and external influences which shape what is possible and what actually emerges. In particular it needs clear strategic leadership and direction, plus the commitment of resources to make this happen. Innovation is about taking risks, about going into new and sometimes completely unexplored spaces. We don't want to gamble – simply changing things for their own sake or because the fancy takes us. And passion, drive and energy are critical entrepreneurial characteristics but they carry the risk that we might point them in the wrong direction. No organisation has resources to waste in that scattergun fashion – innovation needs a strategy. But equally we need to have a degree of courage and leadership, steering the organisation away from what everyone else is doing or what we've always done and into new spaces.

Again we've learned that successful entrepreneurs and innovating organisations use a range of structures, tools and techniques to help them create, articulate, communicate and deploy a clear strategy. For example, many organisations take time – often off-site and away from the day-to-day pressures of their 'normal' operations – to reflect and develop a shared strategic framework for innovation. Start-up entrepreneurs may not have this luxury – but they certainly need to 'look before they leap' and be sure that they have a coherent and clear strategic plan for their venture. Two key questions underpin this:

- does the innovation we are considering help us reach the strategic goals (for growth, market share, profit margin – or changing the world in some way through creating social value, etc.) we have set ourselves?
- do we know enough about this to pull it off (or if not do we have a clear idea of how we would get hold of and integrate such knowledge)?

Much can be gained through taking a systematic approach to answering these questions – a typical approach might be to carry out some form of competitive analysis which looks at the positioning of the organisation in terms of its environment and the key forces acting upon competition. Within this picture questions can then be asked about how a proposed innovation might help shift the competitive positioning favourably – by lowering or raising entry barriers, by introducing substitutes to rewrite the rules of the game, etc.

In carrying out such a systematic analysis it is important to build on multiple perspectives. This can be done in a variety of ways: for example, using tools for competitor and market analysis or looking for ways of deploying competencies – things the individual or organisation knows about and is good at. It can build on explorations of the future or use techniques like 'technology road mapping' to help identify courses of action. It's important in all of this to remember that strategy is not an exact science – it's the process of building a shared framework which matters.

For the start-up entrepreneur the challenge will be to share his/her vision with others and get them excited and engaged with it. And unless people within an established organisation understand and commit to the strategy it has developed it will be hard for them to use it to frame their actions. The issue of strategy *deployment* – communicating and enabling people to use the framework – is essential if the organisation is to avoid the risk of having 'know how' but not 'know why' in its innovation process.

Stretching Leadership

As we've seen, challenging the way the organisation sees things – the corporate mindset – can sometimes be accomplished by bringing in external perspectives. IBM's recovery was due in no small measure to the role played by Lou Gerstner who succeeded at least in part *because* he was a newcomer to the computer industry, and was able to ask the awkward questions that insiders were oblivious to. And when Intel was facing strong competition from Far Eastern producers senior managers like Andy Grove and Bill Noyce reported on the need to 'think the unthinkable', i.e. get out of memory production (the business on which Intel had grown up) and to contemplate moving into other product niches. They trace their subsequent success to the point where they found themselves 'entering the void' and creating a new vision for the business.

Doing this may need mechanisms for legitimating challenge to the dominant vision. This may come from the top – such as Jack Welch's challenge to 'destroy your business' memo within General Electric. Perhaps building on their earlier experiences Intel now has a process called 'constructive confrontation', which essentially encourages a degree of dissent. The company has learned to value the critical insights which come from those closest to the action rather than assume senior managers have the 'right' answers every time.

The same pattern holds for the start-up entrepreneur. Unless he or she has the sense of compelling vision – and the ability to communicate this passion to others – then getting the early stage support for their idea is unlikely to happen. Equally it is precisely because of their willingness to push the frontiers that major and exciting changes get to happen. George Bernard Shaw, the famous playwright, got pretty close to it when he observed that :

'The reasonable man adapts himself to the conditions that surround him . . . The unreasonable man adapts surrounding conditions to himself . . . All progress therefore depends on the unreasonable man. (*Mrs. Warren's Profession*, 1893)

ADVICE FOR FUTURE ENTREPRENEURS

Ask Yourself – Reflection Questions

. . . for start-up entrepreneurs

- Do you have a clear and concise 'story' which you can share with others about your idea?
- Where will you be in a year's time – and how will you know whether or not you have succeeded?
- What comes next if things go well – what will you do to grow or develop the venture further?
- Can you 'paint a picture' – make your idea come alive for others to see and share what excites you about what you are trying to do?
- Is there a clear road map for how you will get from your idea and exciting vision today to making that dream a reality next year?

. . . and for established organisations – how well are we doing it?

Statements we'd expect to hear around such a strategically focused and led organisation might include:

- People in this organisation have a clear idea of how innovation can help us compete.
- There is a clear link between the innovation projects we carry out and the overall strategy of the business.

(continued)

- We have processes in place to review new technological or market developments and what they mean for our firm's strategy.
- There is top management commitment and support for innovation.
- Our top team have a shared vision of how the company will develop through innovation.
- We look ahead in a structured way (using forecasting tools and techniques) to try to imagine future threats and opportunities.
- People in the organisation know what our distinctive competence is – what gives us a competitive edge.
- Our innovation strategy is clearly communicated so everyone knows the targets for improvement.

And we'd also expect some stretching strategic leadership, getting the organisation to think well outside its box and anticipate very different challenges for the future – expressed in statements like:

- Management create 'stretch goals' that provide the direction but not the route for innovation.
- We actively explore the future, making use of tools and techniques like scenarios and foresight.
- We have capacity in our strategic thinking process to challenge our current position – we think about 'how to destroy the business'!
- We have strategic decision-making and project selection mechanisms which can deal with more radical proposals outside of the mainstream.
- We are not afraid to 'cannibalise' things we already do to make space for new options.

Building an Innovative Organisation

The key to innovation and entrepreneurship is, of course, people. And the simple challenge is how to enable them to deploy their creativity and share their knowledge to bring about change. For small start-ups the structures may be very loose and informal, and the sense of trust and co-operation high. But, as we saw earlier, being small has limits in terms of resources and so entrepreneurs here need to work hard at building and maintaining rich creative networks.

It's easy to find prescriptions for innovative organisations which highlight the need to eliminate stifling bureaucracy, unhelpful structures, brick walls blocking communication and other factors stopping good ideas getting through. But we must be careful not to fall into the chaos trap – not all innovation works in organic, loose, informal environments or 'skunk works', and these types of organisation can sometimes act against the interests of successful innovation. We need to determine *appropriate* organisation: that is, the most suitable organisation given the operating contingencies. Too little order and structure may be as bad as too much.

Successful entrepreneurs and innovative organisations recognise this – and make use of a range of structures, tools and techniques to help them achieve this balance. Table 13.1 gives a list of key components in building an innovative organisation.

TABLE 13.1   Components of the innovative organisation

Component	Key features
Shared vision, leadership and the will to innovate	Clearly articulated and shared sense of purpose Stretching strategic intent 'Top management commitment'
Appropriate structure	Organisation design which enables creativity, learning and interaction. Not always a loose 'skunk works' model; key issue is finding appropriate balance between 'organic and mechanistic' options for particular contingencies
Key individuals	Promoters, champions, gatekeepers and other roles which energise or facilitate innovation
Effective team working	Appropriate use of teams (at local, cross-functional and interorganisational level) to solve problems. Requires investment in team selection and building
Continuing and stretching individual development	Long-term commitment to education and training to ensure high levels of competence and the skills to learn effectively
Extensive communication	Within and between the organisation and outside. Internally in three directions – upwards, downwards and laterally
High involvement in innovation	Participation in organisation-wide continuous improvement activity
External focus	Internal and external customer orientation Extensive networking
Creative climate	Positive approach to creative ideas, supported by relevant motivation systems
Learning organisation	High levels of involvement within and outside the firm in pro-active experimentation, finding and solving problems, communication and sharing of experiences and knowledge capture and dissemination

ADVICE FOR FUTURE ENTREPRENEURS

Ask Yourself – Reflection Questions

. . . for start-up entrepreneurs

- Have you got the key skills and resources which you need to make the venture succeed?
- Have you identified the key people who will help you achieve your vision?

(continued)

- How will you motivate them – how will you get them to 'buy-in' to what you are trying to do?
- How will you handle conflicts and disagreements?
- How will you take decisions – and make sure everyone sticks to what is decided even if they don't agree?
- How will you communicate and keep everyone in the loop?
- How will you make sure teams perform as greater than the sum of the individual parts – rather than less?

. . . and for established organisations – how well are we doing it?

If we visited such an organisation we'd find evidence of these approaches being used widely and people would say things like:

Around here . . .

- Our organisation structure does not stifle innovation but helps it to happen.
- People work well together across departmental boundaries.
- There is a strong commitment to training and development of people.
- People are involved in suggesting ideas for improvements to products or processes.
- Our structure helps us to take decisions rapidly.
- Communication is effective and works top-down, bottom-up and across the organisation.
- Our reward and recognition system supports innovation.
- We have a supportive climate for new ideas – people don't have to leave the organisation to make them happen.
- We work well in teams.

We'd also find a recognition that one size doesn't fit all and that innovative organisations need the capacity – and the supporting structures and mechanisms – to think and do very different things from time to time. So we'd also expect to find people saying things like:

- Our organisation allows some space and time for people to explore 'wild' ideas.
- We have mechanisms to identify and encourage 'intrapreneurship' – if people have a good idea they don't have to leave the company to make it happen.
- We allocate a specific resource for exploring options at the edge of what we currently do – we don't load everyone up 100%.
- We value people who are prepared to break the rules.
- We have high involvement from everyone in the innovation process.
- Peer pressure creates a positive tension and creates an atmosphere in which to be creative.
- Experimentation is encouraged.

Networking for Innovation

We've always known that innovation is not a solo act: successful players work hard to build links across boundaries inside the organisation and to the many external agencies who can play a part in the innovation process – suppliers, customers, sources of finance, skilled resources and of knowledge, etc. Twenty-first century innovation is increasingly about 'open innovation', a multi-player game where connections and the ability to find, form and deploy creative relationships is of the essence.

As we saw in Chapter 8, making this happen requires skills in finding network partners, building relationships with them and finally linking their contributions with others so that the whole becomes greater than the sum of the parts.

The challenges include:

- how to manage something we don't own or control;
- how to see system-level effects not narrow self-interests;
- how to build trust and shared risk taking without tying the process up in contractual red tape;
- how to avoid 'free riders' and information 'spillovers'.

ADVICE FOR FUTURE ENTREPRENEURS

Ask Yourself – Reflection Questions

. . . for start-up entrepreneurs

- Have you identified who you will need to help you in taking your venture forward?
- How will you engage and motivate them to 'buy in' to the project?
- How will you manage conflicts and tensions within the network?
- How will you share information and communicate?
- How will you take decisions – and see that people stick to them?
- How will you find partners for your network and with these people build a sense of shared identity and commitment?

. . . and for established organisations – how well are we doing it?

If we were to visit a successful innovative player we'd get a sense of how far they had developed these capabilities for networking by asking around. People would typically say things like:

- We have good 'win-win' relationships with our suppliers.
- We are good at understanding the needs of our customers/end-users.
- We work well with universities and other research centres to help us develop our knowledge .

(continued)

- We work closely with our customers in exploring and developing new concepts.
- We collaborate with other firms to develop new products or processes.
- We try to develop external networks of people who can help us – for example, with specialist knowledge.
- We work closely with the local and national education system to communicate our needs for skills.
- We work closely with 'lead users' to develop innovative new products and services.

And there would be some evidence of their increasing efforts to create wide-ranging 'open innovation' type links – with statements like:

- We make connections across industry to provide us with different perspectives.
- We have mechanisms to bring in fresh perspectives – for example, recruiting from outside the industry.
- We have extensive links with a wide range of outside sources of knowledge – universities, research centres, specialised agencies – and we actually set them up even if not for specific projects.
- We use technology to help us become more agile and quick to pick up on and respond to emerging threats and opportunities on the periphery.
- We have 'alert' systems to feed early warning about new trends into the strategic decision-making process.
- We practice 'open innovation' – rich and widespread networks of contacts from whom we get a constant flow of challenging ideas.
- We have an approach to supplier management which is open to strategic 'dalliances'.
- We have active links into long-term research and technology community – we can list a wide range of contacts.
- We recognise users as a source of new ideas and try to 'co-evolve' new products and services with them.

Learning to Manage Innovation

No individual or organisation is born with the perfect set of capabilities to make innovation happen. Instead they learn and develop these over time and through trial and error. In this chapter we've looked at a range of 'good practices' which are commonly found across very different entrepreneurial organisations – and some reflection questions to help us think about how well we are doing. But one last set of questions we should ask refer to whether we are good at learning itself – whether we take the time out, use challenging reflection, bring in new concepts and develop our own models for how we will manage innovation in the future. So we should finish with some reflection questions around this theme – and remember that a common characteristic shared by successful serial entrepreneurs and long-running businesses is that they do have an awareness of what it is they do and how they can use their insight to continue to succeed.

Ask Yourself – Reflection Questions

. . . for start-up entrepreneurs

Looking back on the project (whether it succeeded or failed):

- What could I do more of (because it helped)?
- What could I do less of or even stop doing (because it didn't work or slowed things down or in some other way blocked the project)?
- What new/different things might I try?
- What advice would I give to someone else about to start a new venture, based on what I have learned?
- What three key 'do's' and three key 'don'ts' would I take away from this venture and apply to my next one?
- What have I learned?

. . . and for established organisations – how well are we doing it?

Smart firms actively manage their learning – and the kinds of thing people might say in such organisations would be that: around here . . .

- We take time to review our projects to improve our performance next time.
- We learn from our mistakes.
- We systematically compare our products and processes with other firms.
- We meet and share experiences with other firms to help us learn.
- We are good at capturing what we have learned so that others in the organisation can make use of it.
- We use measurement to help identify where and when we can improve our innovation management.
- We learn from our periphery – we look beyond our organisational and geographical boundaries.
- Experimentation is encouraged.

Innovation Auditing in Practice

Learning isn't easy – individuals and organisations are usually too busy getting on with building and running their ventures to find time to stop and think about how they might do things better. But assuming they did manage to get offline and reflect on how they might improve their innovation management they would probably find some structured framework for thinking about the process helpful. We can use the idea of comparing against what we've learned about good practice to develop simple audit frameworks which could be used for diagnosis. How well do we do things compared with what the 'good practice' is? How far would we agree with the kinds of statements we've listed in the chapter associated with good innovators? Where are our strengths? And where would we want to focus our efforts to improve the organisation? This kind of audit and review process doesn't come with any prizes but it can help with making the organisation more effective in the ways it deals with the innovation challenge. And that might lead to some pretty important outcomes – like survival or growth!

INNOVATION IN ACTION

Measuring Innovation Performance

In reviewing innovative performance we can look at a number of possible measures and indicators:

- Measures of specific outputs of various kinds – for example, patents and scientific papers as indicators of knowledge produced, or number of new products introduced (and percentage of sales and/or profits derived from them) as indicators of product innovation success.
- Output measures of operational or process elements, such as customer satisfaction surveys to measure and track improvements in quality or flexibility.
- Output measures which can be compared across sectors or enterprises – for example, cost of product, market share, quality performance, etc.
- Output measures of strategic success, where the overall business performance is improved in some way and where at least some of the benefit can be attributed directly or indirectly to innovation – for example, growth in revenue or market share, improved profitability, higher value-added.

We could also consider a number of more specific measures of the internal workings of the innovation process or particular elements within it. For example:

- Number of new ideas (product/service/process) generated at start of innovation system.
- Failure rates – in the development process, in the marketplace.
- Number or percentage of overruns on development time and cost budgets.
- Customer satisfaction measures – was it what the customer wanted?
- Time to market (average, compared with industry norms).
- Development man-hours per completed innovation.
- Process innovation average lead time for introduction.
- Measures of continuous improvement – suggestions/employee, number of problem-solving teams, savings accruing per worker, cumulative savings, etc.

There is also scope for measuring some of the influential conditions supporting or inhibiting the process – for example, the 'creative climate' of the organisation or the extent to which strategy is clearly deployed and communicated. And there is value in considering inputs to the process – for example, percentage of sales committed to R&D, investments in training and recruitment of skilled staff, etc.

There is no single framework for doing an innovation audit – and no 'right' answer at the end of the process. But using such frameworks can be helpful and we have included some in the website accompanying this book. There are audits which look in general terms, those which focus on capabilities to manage the more radical end of innovation, those which deal with sector differences like how to manage innovation in services. And there are those which focus on aspects of the organisation – like how well it is able to engage its whole workforce in the innovation process? Audits can be targeted at the individual – for example, on the website there is a framework for reflecting on 'how creative are you?'

 Go online to find various audit tools, including those for exploring how well the organisation manages innovation and how well it handles search, service innovation, high involvement innovation and discontinuous innovation.

www.iande.info

There are also an increasing number of online audit resources available, and a growing consultancy industry built around providing this kind of 'mirror' on how well an organisation is doing at innovation together with some advice on how it might do it better. But it's not the audits so much as using them in the *process* of questioning and developing innovation capability which matters. As the quality guru, W. Edwards Deming, pointed out, 'If you don't measure it you can't improve it!'

Managing Innovation and Entrepreneurship

We began the book by talking about innovation as a survival imperative. Quite simply, if organisations don't change what they offer the world, and the ways they create and deliver those offerings, then they may not be around in the long term. But simply saying 'we believe in innovation' isn't likely to get us very far – it's going to need a considerable amount of action to make it happen. Getting a good idea into widespread and successful use is hard enough – but growing and sustaining a business requires the ability to repeat the trick. Even serial entrepreneurs, whose philosophy is to make this happen and then make their (hopefully wealthy) exit, only do so in order to repeat the process with another good idea.

Success isn't about luck – although there is probably some truth to the old saying attributed to various famous sportsmen and women that 'the more I practice the luckier I get!' Innovation is about managing a structured and focused process, engaging and deploying creativity throughout but also balancing this with an appropriate degree of control. No organisation or individual starts out with this – it's essentially something they learn and develop over time. This learning can come through trial and error – but it can also come through learning from others and building on their hard-won experience. And it can come through using tools and models to help understand and engage with managing innovation more effectively. We hope that the lessons we've tried to capture in the book provide some helpful input to this process.

Chapter Summary

1 Wherever innovation happens – big firm, small firm, start-up business, social enterprise – one thing is clear. Successful innovation won't happen simply by wishing for it. This complex and risky process of transforming ideas into something which makes a mark needs organising and managing in strategic fashion.

2 Entrepreneurship provides the drive, the motive power behind innovation. But force alone won't make effective change – and many entrepreneurs fail. Those who succeed – and especially those who do so repeatedly – understand that innovation is a process to be understood and managed.

3 It's a generic process, running through four core stages – recognising opportunities, finding resources, developing the venture and creating value.

4 We know that this process is influenced along the way by several things which can help or hinder it. Is there clear strategic leadership and direction? How can we construct innovative organisations which allow creative ideas to come through, let people build on and share knowledge and feel motivated and rewarded for doing so? How can we harness the power of networks, making rich and extensive connections to deliver a stream of innovations?

5 A wide range of structures, tools and techniques exist for helping think about and manage these elements of the innovation process. The challenge is to adapt and use them in a particular context – essentially a learning process.

6 Developing innovative capability needs to begin with an audit of where we are now – and there are many ways of asking and exploring the core questions:

- Do we have a clear process for making innovation happen and effective enabling mechanisms to support it?
- Do we have a clear sense of shared strategic purpose and do we use this to guide our innovative activities?
- Do we have a supportive organisation whose structures and systems enable people to be creative and share and build on each other's creative ideas?
- Do we build and extend our networks for innovation into a rich open innovation system?

DEVELOPING PERSONAL CAPABILITIES

'Those who don't learn from history are condemned to repeat it.' That quote, attributed to various writers, throws down an important challenge in innovation and entrepreneurship. If we don't learn from our mistakes, we're likely to repeat them and get increasingly frustrated in the

(continued)

process. Of course we don't have to learn by our own mistakes – another option is to learn from others, whether their mistakes or their successes. And we can learn from trying things out – designing experiments to see if something works or not, rather than assuming there is one 'best' way to do things.

If we are to learn effectively we will need:

Structured and challenging reflection on the process – what happened, what worked well, what went wrong, etc.

Conceptualising – capturing and codifying the lessons learned into frameworks and eventually procedures to build on lessons learned.

Experimentation – the willingness to try to manage things differently next time, to see if the lessons learned are valid.

Honest capture of experience (even if this has been a costly failure) so we have raw material on which to reflect.

In fact the key to effective learning is to use a variety of approaches – but at the centre, to ensure we reflect on what we or others have learned and use this to drive different approaches in the future. Amongst the ways in which we might improve our learning capabilities are:

Reflection	Conceptualise	Experiment	Experience
Post-project reviews	Theories and models	Pilot projects	Capture experience – on video, via diaries, project records, photo- graphs, etc.
Benchmarking	New structures and process designs	Testing and prototyping	
Structured audits		R&D activities	
Project evaluation	Formal planning reviews	Designed experiments and simulations	Sharing experience – via display, direct exchange, etc.
Measurement	Training and develop- ment		
			Documentation and display
			Measurement

Key Terms Defined

Innovation audit   structured review of innovation capability across an organisation.

Innovation strategy   statement of how innovation is going to take the business forward – and why.

Innovation strategy deployment   communicating and enabling people to use the framework.

Further Reading and Resources

A number of books offer more detailed discussion of managing innovation and entrepreneurship – see for example:

Allen, T. (1977). *Managing the Flow of Technology*. Cambridge, Mass., MIT Press.

Burgelman, R., C. Christensen, et al., Eds. (2004). *Strategic Management of Technology and Innovation*. Boston, McGraw-Hill Irwin.

Cooper, R. (2001). *Winning at New Products* (3rd edition). London, Kogan Page.

Dodgson, M., Gann , D. and Salter, A. (2008). *The Management of Technological Innovation*. Oxford, Oxford University Press.

Goffin, K. and Mitchell, R. (2009). *Innovation Management*. Palgrave Macmillan, London.

Griffin, A. (1998). Overview of PDMA survey on best practices, *PDMA Visions*, January.

Jones, T. (2002). *Innovating at the Edge*. London, Butterworth-Heinemann.

Kolb, D. and Fry, R, (1975) Towards an applied theory of learning, in C. Cooper et al, Eds. *Theories of Group Processes*. John Wiley & Sons Ltd, Chichester.

Schilling, M. (2005). *Strategic Management of Technological Innovation*. New York, McGraw-Hill.

Tidd, J., J. Bessant, et al. (2008). *Managing Innovation: Integrating technological, market and organizational change* (4th edition). Chichester, John Wiley & Sons Ltd.

Tidd, J. and F. Hull, Eds. (2003). *Service Innovation: Organizational responses to technological opportunities and market imperatives*. London, Imperial College Press.

Trott, P. (2004). *Innovation Management and New Product Development*. London, Prentice Hall.

Van de Ven, A. (1999). *The Innovation Journey*. Oxford, Oxford University Press.

Von Stamm, B. (2003). *Managing Innovation, Design and Creativity*. Chichester, John Wiley & Sons Ltd.

There are plenty of sites which look at aspects of managing innovation so just typing the phrase into a search engine should get you started! But these are some useful links which offer research and related support:

Advanced Institute of Management Research http://www.aimresearch.org/
Academy of Management (which has a TIM special interest group) http://www.aomtim.org/
SPRU http://www.sussex.ac.uk/spru/
CENTRIM http://centrim.mis.brighton.ac.uk/
Imperial College Innovation Studies Centre http://www3.imperial.ac.uk/portal
McMaster University (they run an excellent newsletter) http://mint.mcmaster.ca/mint/mint.htm
International Association for the Management of Technology (IAMOT) http://www.iamot.org/

Innovation auditing is increasingly popular and a number of websites offer frameworks for carrying this out – see, for example,

www.innovationdoctor.htm, www.thinksmart.htm, www.jpb.com/services/audit.php, www.innovation-triz.com/innovation/, www.cambridgestrategy.com/page_c5_summary.htm, and www.innovationwave.com/

Discussion Questions

1. Is innovation manageable – or just a random, gambling process? If it is manageable, what factors are important?

2. What lessons can we derive from studies of innovation success and failure about key principles on which to focus management attention?

3. If you were trying to ensure an innovation project had no hope of succeeding, what would you recommend?

4. How can innovation be measured?

5. The Managing Director of your company has asked you to give her some clear guidance on what they should measure to ensure their investment in innovation is worthwhile. What would you suggest as possible measurement targets, and why?

Team Exercise

1. Using one of the innovation audits on the website (www.managing-innovation.com), review a case of an organisation and develop a perspective on how well you think they manage innovation? Why? And where do they need to concentrate their development efforts to enhance their capability for the future?

   (There are several cases to choose from available on the website – for example, Corning, Marshalls, Coloplast.)

Assignment Questions

1 Although innovation is a generic process we need to configure the ways we organise and manage it for different circumstances. How might such an innovation process look for:
   a. A fast food restaurant chain?
   b. An electronic test equipment maker?

c. A hospital?

d. An insurance company?

e. A new entrant biotechnology firm?

2 Fred Bloggs was a bright young PhD scientist with a patent on a new algorithm for monitoring brainwave activity and predicting the early onset of a stroke. He was convinced of the value of his idea and took it to market having sold his car, borrowed money from family and friends and taken out a large loan. He went bankrupt despite having a demonstration version which doctors he showed it to were impressed by. Why might his failure be linked to having a partial model of how the innovation works – and how could he avoid making the same mistake in the future?

3 All organisations have their own particular approach to managing innovation – even those which don't formally try to manage it at all! It's a bit like having a particular personality – even firms in the same sector often approach innovation in very different ways. These represent the results of their own learning processes and the way they manage things accumulates by trial and error.

Think about an organisation with which you are familiar and try to map its 'innovation personality' – its particular approach – on to our generic framework model. How do they search, select, implement, etc?

4 Think about an innovation success story with which you are familiar – or from a case study example. Try to identify what factors helped that to happen? What key influences made for success – and if you were trying to repeat the trick, what would you take from that experience and apply again?

Now do the same with a failure story – what factors are associated with negative outcomes? What would you try to do if you were determined to stop an innovation succeeding?

List these two sets of factors alongside each other – there will be many that are mirror images of each other. But this exercise will often begin to highlight some of the key success/failure factors which have also emerged consistently in the literature.

CASE STUDY 13

Exploring Innovation in Action: Innovation at 3M

3M began life just over 100 years ago as the Minnesota Mining and Manufacturing Corporation. Its beginnings weren't entirely auspicious – the original idea was to make sandpapers to supply the growing automobile industry of the time. But the property which they had bought to mine for carborundum (the key abrasive in sandpaper) turned out not to contain any, so they had to go back to the drawing board! Despite this setback they grew a business based on supplying abrasives and made an important breakthrough early on when they introduced the first wet and dry papers – which meant that the problems of dust associated with dry papers could be avoided. Perhaps the first key breakthrough – which took them beyond the abrasives product and into many other markets – was the innovation of masking tape in 1925.

Since those days as an abrasives producer they have grown into a global business with around 70,000 employees, operations in over 200 countries and a turnover around $15bn. Their product range has also expanded – currently running at around 50,000 items across the range. Significantly there is still a competence around key fields like coatings which goes back to their days as a sandpaper maker – the difference is that they have deployed their skills in surface coatings in fields like magnetic oxides (for recording tape, computer drives, etc.), adhesives (with the famous Post-it range) and optical coatings for lenses.

Innovation 'Claim to Fame'

During its lifetime 3M has established a clear reputation as a major innovator. Their technical competence has been built up by a long-term commitment to R&D on which they currently spend around $1bn p.a.; this has yielded them a regular position amongst the top 10 in US patents granted. They have launched a number of breakthrough products which have established completely new markets and they have set themselves a consistent stretch target of getting 30% of sales turnover from products launched during the past four years. Their success can be measured in the many household-name breakthrough products they have introduced – Scotch tape, Scotch-Guard carpet protection, Post-its are all well-known examples – but also in their regular presence as award winners. For example they were in the top 3 of *Business Week*'s most innovative companies in the world in 2005 and 2006.

How Do they Manage Innovation?

The company presents a consistent picture in interviews and in publications – innovation success is a consequence of creating the culture in which it can take place; it becomes 'the way we do things around here' in a very real sense. This philosophy is borne out in many anecdotes and case histories – the key to their success has been to create the conditions in which innovation can arise from any one of a number of directions, including lucky accidents, and there is a deliberate attempt to avoid putting too much structure in place since this would constrain innovation.

Innovation Strategy and Leadership

3M has always valued innovation and this has been a consistent and key theme since the company's inception; their 'hero' figures amongst previous CEOs have been strongly associated with enacting and supporting the innovation culture which characterises the firm. (In particular, William McKnight, who ran the firm from

1929 until 1966, laid down many of the core principles by which the firm still operates.) Their overall innovation strategy is focused on two core themes – deep technological competence and strong product development capabilities. They combine these to enable them to offer a steady stream of breakthrough products and line extensions/product improvements. A great strength is the integrated input from the technical and marketing side, which enables 'creative association', coming up with new and often powerful combinations of needs and means.

A number of key strategic enablers are worth flagging:

- Setting stretch targets – such as 'x% of sales from products introduced during the past y years' – provides a clear and consistent message and a focus for the whole organisation.
- Investing in R&D to support this – typical spend is $1bn p.a., or around 6% of sales, which is high for their type of business.
- Allocating resources as 'slack' – space and time in which staff can explore and play with ideas, build on chance events or combinations, etc.
- Encouragement of 'bootlegging' employees working on innovation projects in their own time and often accessing resources in a non-formal way – the 'benevolent blind eye' effect.
- Provision of staged resource support for innovators who want to take an idea forward – effectively, different levels of internal venture capital for which people can bid (against increasingly high hurdles). This encourages 'intrapreneurship' – internal entrepreneurial behaviour – rather than people feeling they have to leave the firm to take their good ideas forward.

In recent years they have seen their momentum falter, in part because of the sheer scale of the operation and the range of competition. Their response has been to identify a series of 'Pacing Plus' programmes which attempt to focus and prioritise around 30 key areas for development across the business – essentially an innovation strategy.

Enabling the Process

The high spend on R&D gives them a strong position in their field – they claim to have deep knowledge of 42 diverse technologies, for example. Much of their philosophy involves making sure there is cross-linkage across the firm – so, for example, technology originally developed for layered plastic lenses is also applied in reflective road signs, durable abrasives and golf gloves which allow tighter grip without having to squeeze harder.

Having been working on innovation for so long they have developed a set of structures and polices to guide innovative activity from picking up signals through to implementation. Importantly they allow for parallel routes through their system so that innovations can come from close market interactions or from deep technology research in their labs or from various forms of collaboration, or from serendipitous discovery by their staff. As they put it, 'we don't have a skunk-works – round here everyone is a skunk!' Their skill in enabling *association* is particularly relevant; many of their breakthrough products have come because staff with technical knowledge have worked alongside those with awareness of real or latent market needs and the result has been a creative combination.

There is a formal stage-gate system for innovations and extensions based on established products but in addition there is a clear progress route for more radical ideas, moving from an incubator stage where they are encouraged and where development funds are available against loose targets through to much more rigorous business plan appraisal for projects further down the line. The 'trial by fire' approach is well-known but carries with it a strong element of encouraging innovation champions to take non-linear ideas through the system. Effectively they run parallel systems which all involve funnels and clear gateways through which ideas pass into narrower parts of the funnel and which also commit more extensive resources – but although the mechanisms differ, the intent is the same.

Building an Innovative Organisation

McKnight's strong legacy can particularly be felt in the underlying values which drive the organisation. He is famous for summarising his philosophy for success as being 'Hire good people and let them do their job in their own ways'. And tolerate mistakes.

- Recognition and reward – throughout the company there are various schemes which acknowledge innovative activity (for example, their Innovator's Award which recognises effort rather than achievement).
- Reinforcement of core values – innovation is respected (for example, there is a 'hall of fame' whose members are elected on the basis of their innovative achievements).
- Sustaining 'circulation' – movement and combination of people from different perspectives to allow for creative combinations, a key issue in such a large and dispersed organisation.
- Allocating 'slack' and permission to play – allowing employees to spend a proportion of their time (typically 15%) in curiosity-driven activities which may lead nowhere but which have sometime given them breakthrough products.
- Patience – acceptance of the need for 'stumbling in motion' as innovative ideas evolve and take shape. Breakthroughs like Post-its and ScotchGuard were not overnight successes but took two to three years to 'cook' before they emerged as viable prospects to put into the formal system.
- Acceptance of mistakes and encouragement of risk-taking – another famous quote from McKnight is often cited in this connection: ' Mistakes will be made, but if a

person is essentially right, the mistakes he or she makes are not as serious, in the long run, as the mistakes management will make if it's dictatorial and undertakes to tell those under its authority exactly how they must do their job . . . Management that is destructively critical when mistakes are made kills initiative, and it is essential that we have many people with initiative if we are to continue to grow.'

- Encouraging 'bootlegging' – giving employees a sense of empowerment and turning a blind eye to creative ways which staff come up with to get around the system – acts as a counter to rigid bureaucratic procedures.
- Policy of hiring innovators – recruitment approach is looking for people with innovator tendencies and characteristics.
- Operate a dual career ladder so that technically skilled people can progress to the highest levels rather than get diverted into management roles in order to gain promotion.

Linkages and Networking

- Recognition of the power of association – deliberate attempts not to separate out different functions but to bring them together in teams and other groupings.
- Encouraging broad perspectives – for example, in developing their overhead projector business it was close links with users made by getting technical development staff to make sales calls that made the product so user-friendly and therefore successful.
- Strong culture dating back to 1951 of encouraging informal meetings and workshops in a series of groups, committees, etc., under the structural heading of the Technology Forum – established 'to encourage free and active interchange of information and cross-fertilisation of ideas'. The model persists and every year the 9700 staff meet to share and explore ideas. This is a voluntary activity although the company commits support resources – it enables a company-wide 'college' with fluid interchange of perspectives and ideas. Smaller scale versions run across different labs and make extensive use of webcasts and intranets to consolidate links. Larry Wendling, Vice-President for corporate research calls networking '3M's *secret weapon*' and formal and informal linkages are encouraged.
- Recruiting volunteers – particularly in trying to open up new fields, involvement of customers and other outsiders as part of a development team is encouraged since it mixes perspectives.
- Linking research closely with customers, with many staff spending time out of the labs working with users to understand their needs. Post-it Photo Paper was a typical result of this – a product which emerged from understanding what people do with digital photos. Typically they take many photos but fail to print them or else put the batch in a drawer. Making the photos easy to print and then stick up – on walls, fridge doors, car dashboards, etc. – opens up a new market space to use a well-established 3M technology.

Questions

1 Carry out a critical review of the ways in which the 3M organisation manages innovation. Some frameworks for this have been developed throughout the book, and the 'innovation audit' frameworks on the website provide a structured aid. Use this review to argue whether or not you think 3M will still be around for another hundred years.

   This can be an individual reflection or a group review and presentation.

Summary of Web Resources

Tools

- Innovation management audit
- Search strategies
- Service innovation audit
- High involvement innovation audit
- Discontinuous innovation audit

Index

'100 club' 15
3D Agenda 135
3M 251, 272, 348, 350, 542, 566–70

Abernathy, William 232
absorptive capacity 284–5, 286
acceptance 168–9, 569
accidents 230–1
accumulated tacit knowledge 105
Ace Trucks 211
acquisitions 462–3
action plans 168–9
adaptors 159
Adidas 224
Adobe Flash 501–2
adoption 233–4
    growth and sustainability 106, 111, 126, 130
    new socio-technical systems 126
Advanced Institute of Management Research
        (AIM) 357
advergaming 278
advertising 129, 335–6
after-sales service 105
agnostic marketing 127
Ahold 61
Airbus 277
Albert, Michel 99
Allen, Thomas 271
ALNAP 209–10
Alternative Investment Market (AIM) 439,
        440–1, 451
alternative technologies 116, 117–18
Altshuller, Genrich 483, 498
Amazon 9, 288, 351, 502, 518
American Apparel 278
Anglo-Saxon model 99
antecedent influences 427
antilock braking systems (ABS) 226
Appelbaum, Hylton 77

Apple
    i-Pad 214, 501
    i-Phone 356, 501
    iPod 48, 307, 380, 500–2
    iTunes 505
Aravind Eye Care System 54, 55
architectural innovations 117, 477–8
architectures 251
ARM Holdings 489–90
artefacts 174
Arup 386–7, 469
Asda 531
Ashoka Foundation 55
Aspa 132
assembly customisation 219
association, creative 568, 569
assumptions 168, 173
Atkins PLC 531
attribute gaps 311
audit framework 560–1
Autonomy 418

B&Q 60–1
BAA 280
Balon, Adam 171–2
bandwagons 125, 137, 326
Bang & Olufsen 281
Bangalore 93
Baumol, William 6
Baylis, Trevor 76–82
BBC i-Player 505
behavioural factor 475–6
beliefs 173
Bell, Alexander Graham 8, 13
benchmarking 227, 237
Benetton 277
Berkhout, Frans 115
Besser, Mitch 56–7
best practice clubs 353

Best, Michael 344
bias 319
blockbuster products 381–3
Blue Ocean strategy 214–15, 523, 527
blue sky activities 35, 270
Blu-ray 504
BMW 278
Boisot, Max 466–7
Bookham Technology 438
bootlegging 272, 287, 568, 570
Bottom of the Pyramid 215–17,
    237, 256
Boulton, Matthew 512–13
boundary objects/practices 472
Bower, Joseph 316
brainstorming
    internal analysis 308
    networking 339
    spider diagrams 191–2
branding 380
Branson, Richard 17
BRIC nations 88, 91–4, 100–2, 113–14,
    141–5, 215
bridge strategy 475
British Broadcasting Corporation (BBC) 348,
    349, 388
British Gas Trading (BGT) 387
brokering 287
brokers 282
Browns, Carlo 7
Browns Industries 7
BT 60
Buffett, Warren 57
building acceptance 168–9
bundling 126
business
    angels 434, 441, 451
    markets 121–3
    model innovation 517–19, 528
    models 198
        value 511–18
    plans 169–72, 188–9
        development 300–5
        new ventures 433–4
        social entrepreneurship 72
business process re-engineering (BPR) 190, 210
buy-in 312
buying behaviours 118

C-space 466–8
Cable and Wireless Global Markets
    (CWGM) 387
capabilities
    cultural 148–50
    dynamic 17, 18, 109, 270
    entrepreneurship 447–8
    functional 148
    globalisation 84, 91–4, 107–10, 113–14,
        148–50
    innovation management 18, 30, 36, 562–3
    knowledge 491–3
    networking 359
    organising innovation 187–8
    personal 36, 235–6, 288–9
    positional 146, 148
    product development 400
    regulatory 146, 148
    resource 146
    service development 400
    social entrepreneurship 72
    upgrading 108
capitalisation 440–1
Capitalism against Capitalism 99
Carft, Tim 222, 223
Carlsen, Chester 252
Carroll, Darrel 278
Castaldo, Gennaro 46, 49
cause and effect diagrams 165–6, 193
Celltech 488
CEMEX 66–7
challenge 178–80
Charcol On-Line 384
Chesborough, Henry 265, 267, 268, 365
chip design 107
Chiroscience 443–4
Christensen, Clayton 119, 128–9, 324, 354
Churchill Potteries 208
churn, rate of 519
circulation 569
CITER 344
cites per patent 483
Citicorp 216–17
claim to fame 567
clear
    and complete disclosure 482
    product definition 378
    and stable vision 381

client-project orientation 386
Clifford, Robert 6
climate for innovation 172–87, 193
clockwork radios 76–82
clusters
    spatial 345, 360
    strategic 395
co-creation 267
co-evolution 257, 287
    sustainability 115
co-laboratories 353
coaching 437
codified
    knowledge 464–8, 496
    technology 142
cognitive maps 166–7, 193
collaboration under pressure 382–4
collective efficiency 355, 359, 360
Coloplast 223
combination 466
commercialisation 392–3, 427–8
commitment 171
commodified knowledge 465
communication, innovation 7–8, 13
communities of practice 271, 287
    intellectual property 471–2, 497
    networking 345, 361
companies 449
compatibility 189, 311
competencies *see* core competencies
competition 384
competitive
    advantage 145–8
    analysis 394
    factors 28, 31
    rivalry 98
complementary assets 105
complex networks 341
complexity 22, 31, 189, 287, 312
complexity theory 257
component innovation 21–2, 40
computer-aided design and manufacture
    (CAD/CAM) 396
computer-aided radio therapy (CART)
    455–7
concept models 277
concept generation 392, 394
conceptualisation 563

confidentiality agreements 493–4
conflicts
    entrepreneurship 182–4
    knowledge-sharing 472
Connect and Develop 363–7
consortiums 345
constructive confrontation 183–4
consultants 394
consumer markets 120–1
context transferrals 32
controllable factors 170, 433
coolness 380
Cooper, R. G. 391
'copy and develop' strategy 226
copyright 485, 486, 497
core competencies
    entrepreneurship 425
    globalisation 87, 94, 108–2
    innovation 13
    knowledge 468–70
    sustaining 112–13, 149–50
core rigidities 112, 424
corporate
    governance 99–101, 137, 143, 144
    social responsibility 57, 61–2
corporate entrepreneurship 287
corporate venturing 281–2
Cosworth 342
creating value 504–7
creative association 568, 569
creativity
    definition 156, 193
    environmental factors 157, 159,
        172–87
    innovation management 26
    networking 342
    organizing innovation 156–72, 193
    personal 160–1
    personalities 157, 158–63
    processes 157, 164–72
    supporting 554
crisis 209–10
cross functional teams
    entrepreneurship 184–5, 185
    innovative organisations 555
    knowledge 472–3
    product and service development 375, 382,
        385, 388, 389, 399

crowd sourcing approaches 224
culture
    capabilities 148–50
    climate 172–3, 193
    culture-space 466–8
    entrepreneurship 428
    environmental factors 174–6,
        193
current impact index (CII) 483, 484
customer
    contact 374
    services 60–1
    surveys 307–8
customer-developers 394
customisation
    mechanistic 386–7
    options 219–20
    service development 373, 375

Daksh 93
Dansk Plastic Emballage 223
data, definition 464
DAWN Programme 63–4
De Bono, Edward 167–8
debate 182–4
'deep diving' 279–80, 287
deeply held assumptions 173
degenerative interaction 531
delighters 120, 432
Delphi method 91, 309, 326
Democratizing Innovation 127
demographic trends 431
deployment 552, 563
deregulation 229
design
    customisation 220
    for manufacture 395–6
    rights 486
Design Council 281
Design Works 228
developers 400
development
    consortiums 345
    funnels 391, 392–3, 405
    globalisation and 84
    solutions 168
    see also product development; service
        development

Diabetes Attitudes, Wishes and Needs (DAWN)
        Programme 63–4
diffusion 233–4, 327
    scales 466–8
digital media 506–7
disability 60–1
disclosure 482
discontinuity 258–62
discontinuous innovation 287
    knowledge 478
    management 34–6, 40
    networking 354
discounted cash flow (DCF) 321, 324
discovery phase 478–80
disruptive innovation 213–14, 237
    social entrepreneurship 66
    sustainability 119
distortion 168
distribution
    customisation 219
    knowledge 470–5
diversification
    globalisation 110–11
    networking 357
dominant designs 504
dotcom bubble 257
double bottom line 73
Drayton, Bill 55
Drucker, Peter 10, 156
dynamic capabilities
    globalisation 84, 109
    innovation 17
dynamic capability 270
Dyson, James 206–7

eBay 9
e-choupals 67
economic factors
    entrepreneurship 431
    globalisation 88, 94, 98
edge
    of chaos complex 256–7
    market 212–14
Edison, Thomas 228, 241, 346–7
education 160, 162–3, 417
    influence on venture creation 520–1
effectiveness 177, 188–9, 484
efficiency

globalisation 110
intellectual property 484
sustainability 116
Eka Nobel 132
electric cars 123–5
electronic data interchange (EDI) 474–5
Electronic Frontier Foundation (EFF) 502
electronic gaming 196–8
Eli Lilly 278
embedded
knowledge 464–5
strategies 474–5
embodied
knowledge 464–6
technology 142
embrained knowledge 464–6
emergent
networks 134
properties 339, 341–2, 361
empowerment 80
Encarta 225
encoded knowledge 464–5
encultured knowledge 464–5
Encyclopaedia Britannica 225
engineered networks 134
enhancement 149
Enron 20–1
enterprise resource planning (ERP) 190
entrepreneurial commitment 171, 430
entrepreneurship 6, 414–19
capabilities 447–8
case study 455–7
context 419–25
environmental factors 157, 159, 172–87
exercises 450–1
growth entrepreneurs 414
incubator organisations 419–21, 425–8, 451
innovative entrepreneurs 414
innovative organisations 541–2
knowledge 463, 476
learning 431
lifestyle entrepreneurs 414
management 15–17, 17–19, 561
networking 345–6
opportunism 430–2, 447–8
organizing innovation 155–201
personal 160–1
personalities 157, 158–63

processes of creativity 157, 164–72
quality function development 432
resources 452–3
science parks 421
size of organisation 422–5
strategic leadership 552–3
see also new ventures; social entrepreneurship
environmental factors
challenge and involvement 178–80
conflict and debate 182–4
culture 174–6, 193
entrepreneurship 427
freedom 186–7
organizing innovation 57, 59, 172–87
risk-taking 185–6
rituals and heroes 173
support and space for ideas 180–2, 186
sustainability 116, 130
symbols and artefacts 174
trust and openness 176–8
values, beliefs and deeply held assumptions 173
Eon 160–1
ethnicity 160, 161
ethnography 280, 287
European Community innovation 264
Evans, Chris 425, 443–4, 484
exaggeration 168
exit strategies, entrepreneurship 435, 442–7
expeditionary marketing 127, 137
experience
creativity 160, 162–3
curves 105
innovation management 563
experimentation 563
experts 394, 398
explicit knowledge 464, 466, 497–8
exploitation 150, 252–3, 254, 287
exploration 255, 287
explorers 252–3, 400
exploring data 165
external
links 445–6
networking 348–51
externalisation 466
externalities 312, 137
extrapolating trends 394, 398
extreme users 226, 237, 256

fabrication customisation 220
Facebook 278
fads 475–6
failure mode and effects analysis
        (FMEA) 315
Fair Trade products 61, 70
family backgrounds 160, 161, 417
Fanning, Sean 48
fashion statements 475–6
fault tree analysis (FTA) 315
feedback 177, 382, 487
file-sharing 32, 48
FilmOn 505
financial leverage 357
finding relationships 359
firm age 524
fish bone diagrams 165–6, 193
FITEC 114
five generations of innovation models 341
flexibility, globalisation 110
flow approach 474
fluency 338
fluid phase 257, 287
focus groups 394, 398
followership 505–6
Ford Model T 8–9, 218
Ford, Henry 20, 231, 233, 234–5
forecasting 229
    innovation 306–15
    limits 307
    tools 306–10
foreign direct investment (FDI) 101, 142, 143
forming relationships 359
Fortune at the Bottom of the Pyramid, The
        (Prahalad) 65
founder effects 521
founding team, size of 524
frames 248–51
    multiple 276
framing 165, 287
free riders 357, 360
freedom 186–7
Freeman, Chris 19, 231, 509
Freeplay Energy 78
Freeplay Foundation 80–1
Friedman, Thomas 84
Fuji Film 256
functional

    capabilities 146, 148
    performance 112
    teams 385
fuzzy front end 302–5, 327

games 509–10
Gardiner, Paul 19
gatekeepers 121, 357, 129, 133, 271, 287
Gates, Bill 4, 57, 59
'gazelles' 519, 528
General Electric 88, 348, 516, 553
General Motors 218
General Public Licenses (GPL) 487
generating ideas *see* idea generation
generative interaction 531, 534
Genpact 94
Gerstner, Lou 182, 552
globalisation 83–153
    BRIC nations 88, 91–4, 100–2, 113–14
    capabilities 84, 91–4, 107–10, 113–14
    competitive rivalry 97–8
    core competencies 95, 107–25
    creating value 504–7
    development and 84
    exercises 137, 357
    innovation 84–94
    institutions 94, 96, 99–100
    intellectual property 106–7
    international value chains 84, 102–7
    learning from foreign systems 89–94
    management 115
    national demand 96–8
    national systems of innovation 84, 94–107
    networking 339, 348
    resources 138–9
    social impact 135
    translating technology 105
Globetronics Bhd. 104
Goldcorp 224
good enough solutions 213
Google 9, 272, 501
Goonj 56
government funding 434, 435, 441–2
Grameen Bank 55, 58–9
Green, Ken 115
Grossman, Dave 182
Grove, Andy 5, 15, 200, 52
growth

adoption 126, 130
entrepreneurs 414
forecasting tools 306–10
globalisation 144
imperatives 4, 5–6, 7, 11–12
open systems of innovation 130–5
service development 372
strategies 442–5
see also sustainability
GSK 270
Guilford, J. P. 338
Gupta, Anshu 56

Hall, Richard 470, 112
Hamel, Gary 108–9
Hargadon, Andrew 228
heavyweight project manager structures 385
Helx AB 455–7
heroes 173–4
hidden innovation gazelles 527
hierarchical process model 478–80
high-growth ventures 444, 446–7
high innovators 382–4
high involvement innovation (HII) 238, 267,
    272, 287
high involvement jams 272
high-value innovation networks 357
Hoover 23
horizontal collaboration 353
Howe, Elias 23
Hoy, Patrimonio 67
human capital 113
Huston, Larry 366–7
hybrid
    cars 123–5
    knowledge-sharing 387
Hyve 280

IBM 13, 213, 274, 481, 484, 552
idea generation
    innovation management 17, 26
    organizing innovation 167–8, 180–1, 196–8
    scouting for 275–6
ideejager 275
IDEO 282, 431
IKEA 131–2
Immelt, J. 4
implementation

creativity 158
    enabling 568–9
    innovation management 16, 23–4, 26
    organizing innovation 158, 188–9
    product development 390
    service development 390
    social entrepreneurship 70, 71
implicit knowledge 464, 466
importance of innovation 4–10
improvisation 382
incremental innovation 21, 22, 40, 232, 248,
    249–50
incrementalism 324
incubator organisations 419–21, 425–8, 451
individual talent 196–8
industrial applications 482
industry experts 394, 398
influencers 129
informal working 185
information
    definition 464
    exchange 382
    spillovers 360
    see also knowledge
Infosys 93–4
INFU programme 288
Innocent 171–2
InnoCentive 366
Innocentive.com 278
innovation adoption, pre-launch decisions
    329–31
innovation capability 29–30
innovation, definition 19
Innovation Exchange 350
innovation followership 103, 505–6
innovation leadership 103, 505
innovation life cycle 232–3, 238
innovation management 3–37
    audit framework 563
    blue sky research 35
    capabilities 18, 30, 36, 562–3
    case study 46–9, 566–70
    creativity 26
    discontinuous innovation 34–5, 40
    dynamic capability 17
    entrepreneurship 10–12, 561
    exercises 43–4, 565–6
    globalisation 89–99

innovation management (*Continued*)
  hierarchical process model 478–80
  how to manage 15–17, 17–19
  idea generation 16, 17, 26
  implementation 16, 26, 568–9
  innovation spaces 28, 33
  innovative organisations 554–6, 569–70
  integrated management 28
  knowledge 26–7, 469, 475–81, 493–4
  learning 27, 89–92, 558–9
  model for 24–30
  networking 358–9, 557–8, 570
  proactive linkages 28–9, 39
  process 19–22
  product development 377–9, 381, 401
  resources 16, 25, 35–6, 546–7
  service development 377–9, 381, 401
  social entrepreneurship 68–71
  social impact 35–6
  strategic
    advantages 30–2
    choice 16–17, 26–7
    leadership 567–8
  sustainability 115–17
  types of innovation 19–22
innovation spaces 28, 33, 252–3
innovation strategy deployment 552, 554,
    561, 563
innovation technologies 281
innovative entrepreneurs 414
  see also social entrepreneurship
innovative organisations 27–8, 554–6, 569–70
Innovator's Solution, The 128–9
innovators 159
input prices 97
Institute of Development Studies (IDS) 135
institutions 94, 96, 99–100
intangible
  product advantage 380
  resources 145–9
integrated
  innovative organisations 388
  management 28
integration 474
Intel 104, 199–200, 552
intellectual property (IP) 350, 461–502, 506
  copyright 485, 486, 497
  costs 490–1

definition 498
design rights 486
entrepreneurship 425, 426, 430
exploiting 462, 470, 481–8
globalisation 104, 106–7, 112, 141, 144
licensing strategies 488–91
networking 357
open source software 486–7
patents 482–5, 489, 498
product and service development
    377–8
intellectual stimulation 179
interaction 395
interconnected group networks 341
inter-firm relationships 331–2
internal
  analysis 308
  innovation 186–7
  networking 347
  project teams 345
internalisation 466
international value chains 84, 102–7
internationalisation *see* globalisation
Internet 9, 277–8
  Bubble 521
  music industry 47–9
  networking 339, 366
inter-sectoral upgrading 108
intranet 271
intrapreneurship 272, 287, 556, 568
inventive steps 482
Investors in People awards 179
involvement 179–80
Ishikawa diagrams 165–6, 193
IT, globalisation 86, 88
ITC 67

Jaipur foot 8
Jobs, Steve 4, 48, 200, 212–13, 307

kaizen 238, 254
Kanter, R. M. 172
Karolinska Hospital, Stockholm
    10, 227
Kay, John 515
keiretsu 134
Kelly, Tom 431
key attributes 145–50

Khosa, Veronica 57
Kirton Adapter-Innovator (KAI) scale 158–9,
     194
knowledge 461–502
  acquisition 462–3
  architectures of innovation 477–8
  brokers 472, 498
  capabilities 491–3
  case study 500–2
  codified 464–8, 497
  communities of practice 471–2, 497
  definition 464
  diffusion scales 466–8
  distribution 470–5
  economy 110
  exercises 497
  flows
     networking 339, 349
     sustainability 127
  generation 462–3
  globalisation 105, 110
  hierarchical process model 478–80
  identification 464–8
  innovation 462, 475–81
  knowledge-sharing 387, 462, 470–5
  learning 462
  management 26–7, 469, 475–81, 484, 493–4
  networking 85–6, 466, 557–8
  resources 498–9
  retrieval 468–70
  social impact 494–5
  storage 468–70
  translators 472
  types 463, 464–6
  see also intellectual property
knowledge production 266
knowledge pull 207–8
knowledge push 204–7, 238
knowledge spaghetti 265
Koska, Marc 416

Lafley, A. G. 364
Lambert Review of Business–University
     Collaboration 429, 495
Land Securities 531
Lane, Robert 4
latent needs analysis 394
lateral thinking 167–8, 193

lead times 105
lead-users 218, 287
  networking 558
  product and service development
     394, 399
  sustainability 128–9, 138
leadership 505
  globalisation 103–4
  strategic 567–8
lean thinking 210, 211, 227
learning
  curves 105
  evaluation 321–3
  entrepreneurship 431
  from foreign systems 89–93
  innovation management 27, 28, 30,
     558–9
  knowledge 462
  networks 352–3, 361
  supply-chain 343, 346, 361
learning as you go 280–1
legal profession 376–7
Lego 224, 281, 356
Leicester Royal Infirmary 10
Leonard, Dorothy 112
Levitt, Theodore 128
liberalisation 113
Liberty Life Foundation 77
Lifeline Energy 81
lifestyle
  entrepreneurs 414
  segmentation 129
light bulb 240–3
light emitting diode (LED) 242–3
lightweight project manager structures 385
linkages *see* proactive linkages
Linus 356
Linux 487
local
  factors 97
  markets 67
  norms 428
location 374
loss aversion 319
Lucent 114
Lucozade 20
Lynch, Mike 418
Lynn, Gary 381

Machiavelli, Niccolo 37
Malaysian Technology Development
        Corporation (MTDC) 104
Malcolm, Jamie 161
management buy-outs/buy-ins (MBO/MBI) 439
management *see* innovation management
Mansfield, Edwin 316
manufacturing
   globalisation 90–1
   networking 343
market
   capitalisation 440–1
   differentiation 510–11
   experimentation 394, 398
   fragmentation 266
   knowledge 378
   readers 508
   scope 524
   surveys 307–8
   virtualisation 266
Marx, Karl 58
mass customisation (MC) 217–21, 238, 267
mass production 217
Massachusetts Institute of Technology (MIT)
        419–20
matrix organisations 385
Matsushita 488
McKnight, William 567, 569
mechanistic customisation 388
mental models *see* paradigm innovation
metaphors 168
Metcalf, Ben 349
micro finance 55, 58–9, 69, 70
Microsoft 4, 5
   Windows 488
   Xbox 505
Mindlab 212
MINE research program 509–10
Moore's Law 205, 255, 288
motivation 555
Mott MacDonald 531
MovieFlix 505
moving frontier problem 270
MP3 protocol 47–8, 481
multinational corporations (MNCs) 113–14, 143
multi-technology firms 111
Mumpuni, Tri 57
music industry 46–9, 481

must-be's 432
must-haves 120
Myers–Briggs type indicators (MBTI) 162
MySpace 278

n-Ach *see* need for achievement
n-Aff *see* need for affiliation
Napster.com 48
national demand 96–8
National Diabetes Programmes (NDPs) 64–5
National Grid Transco 531
National Health Service (NHS) 253, 281, 283,
        375, 402
national systems of innovation 84, 94–107
   competitive rivalry 96
   institutions 99–100
   learning from foreign systems 89–94
   national demand 96–8
natural resources 98
need for achievement (n-Ach) 161–2, 301
need for affiliation (n-Aff) 162
need pull 238
need seekers 508
neon lamp 242
net present value (NPV) 321
Netflix 351
network externalities 134, 137
networking
   capabilities 359
   case study 363–7
   design 197, 356–7
   discontinuous change 257
   emergent properties 339, 341–2, 361
   exercises 362
   for exploration 354–5
   external 348–51
   five generations of innovation models 341
   globalisation 340, 348
   innovation management 358–9, 557–8, 570
   internal 347
   Internet 340, 366
   knowledge 466
   knowledge flows 339, 349
   learning networks 343, 361
   resources 361
   social entrepreneurship 69, 71, 72
   social impact 359
   spaghetti model of innovation 340–1, 347

start-ups 346–7
sustainability 130–5
types 341–6
new
markets 215–17
technology development consortiums 346
services 116
socio-technical systems 125–9
technologies 245, 346
see also emerging markets
New Delhi Television (NDT) 94
new emerging economies 88, 94, 102–3
markets 215–17
standards 346
New Product Pre-announcements (NPPAs) 336
new technology-based firms (NTBFs) 424–5,
451, 521
new ventures
Alternative Investment Market 440–1, 451
business angels 434, 441, 451
business plans 425, 433–4
capabilities 447–8
case study 455–7
design 445
exercises 450–1
exit strategies 435, 442–5
external links 445–6
funding 434–7
government funding 434, 435, 441–2
growth strategies 442–5
high-growth ventures 444, 446–7
innovation 445
networking 346–7
opportunism 430–2, 447–8
quality function development 432
resources 452–3
types 414–19
venture capital 421, 437–41
News Corporation 531
new-science-based technologies 87–8
Nike Foundation 57
Nintendo Wii 214–15
Nippon–Rhineland model 100
Nokia 14, 30, 216, 281–2
non-disclosure agreements (NDAs) 493–4
not invented here effect 13, 24
novel niches 119–25
novel products 120

novelty 21, 31, 482
Novo Nordisk 62–5, 217, 276–7
Noyce, Bill 552
Noyce, Bob 199–200
nurture phase 478–81

O2 276
Oakley, Alex 160–1
objectives 168
observability 189, 310, 311, 312–13
one-dimensionals 120, 432
open innovation 225, 238, 265, 267–9,
282, 287
networking 348, 349, 355–6, 557, 558,
562
sustainability 130–5
open search 272–83
open source software (OSS) 486–7
openness 176–8
opportunism
case study 291–5
construction 165
knowledge 463
networking 349, 350
new ventures 430–2, 447–8
recognition 171
resources 289–90
social entrepreneurship 69
social impact 234–5, 288
understanding 165–7
order-winners 120
organisational
memory 469
slack 181–2
structure 129
see also culture
organisational characteristics 155–201
capabilities 187–8
case study 199–201
climate for innovation 172–87, 193
creativity 155–94, 193
entrepreneurship 155–94
environmental factors 157, 159, 172–87
exercises 191–2
personalities 157, 158–63
processes of creativity 157, 164–72
resources 194
social impact 190

orientation to change 400
original equipment manufacture (OEM) 90, 102, 142
outsourcing 93–4
overconfidence 319
own brand manufacture (OBM) 90
own design and manufacture (ODM) 90

Palo Alto Research Center (PARC) 42
paradigm innovation 19, 256
    social entrepreneurship 54, 66
    strategy 19, 20–1, 34, 39, 40
Pareto analysis 165, 194
partnerships 449
Partnerships UK (PUK) 494–5
patent citations 92
patents 506, 507, 525
    globalisation 94
    intellectual property 481–5, 489, 498
    social entrepreneurship 78
patience 569
peer-to-peer (P2P) file sharing 517
performance
    measuring 507–11
    perceptions 374–5
    product and service development 388–9
performing capabilities 359
Perini, Fernando 113
perpetual beta 224, 279
personal capabilities see capabilities
personal creativity 160–1
Personal Digital Assistants (PDAs) 490
personal entrepreneurship 160–1
personalities
    backgrounds 160, 161
    education and experience 160, 162–3
    organizing innovation 157, 158–63
    psychological profile 160, 161–2
Pfizer 230
philanthropy 55–6
Philips 85, 407–12
    Atmosphere Provider program 410–11
    Think the Lighting Future (TTLF) project 408–10
planning for action 168–9
platform innovation 196
Porter, M. 103
position innovation 19

social entrepreneurship 55
    strategy 20, 33, 34, 38, 39, 40
positional capabilities 146, 148
positioning 334
Post-Its 567, 569, 570
potential problem analysis (PPA) 315
poverty trap 59
Prahalad, C. K. 65, 71, 108–9, 216, 217
pre-qualifiers 120
price factors, product development 380
price/earnings (P/E) ratio 509
Private Finance Initiatives (PFIs) 532
private investment 97
privatisation 424
proactive linkages
    social entrepreneurship 69, 71
    strategy 28–9, 38, 570
proactive management 357
problem-solving style 400, 405
process
    development consortiums 345
    interactions 133
    upgrading 107
process improvement 211–12
process innovation 19, 211
    social entrepreneurship 55
    strategy 19, 20, 33, 34, 38, 39, 40
    value and 509
processes of creativity
    business plans 169–72
    idea generation 167–8
    organizing innovation 157, 164–72
    planning for action 168–9
    understanding opportunities 164–7
Procter and Gamble 61, 216, 268, 269, 271, 348, 350, 363–7
product 335
    advantage 377, 380
    complexity 106
    interactions 133
    upgrading 108
product cycle 86
product development 184
    capabilities 400
    case study 407–12
    commercialisation 392, 393
    concept generation 392, 394
    development strategies 377–84

exercises 404
high innovators 382–4
innovation management 377–9, 381, 401
organisation 385–9
processes 390–3
product advantage 377, 380
quality function deployment 386, 396–9, 405
resources 405–6
social impact 401–2
state-gate approach 390–1, 405
tools and technology 393–9
versus service development 372–7
product innovation 19
social entrepreneurship 55
strategy 19, 20, 38, 40
value and 509
productivity paradox 372
proficiency of execution 379
profit impact of market strategy (PIMS) 103,
382, 506, 511, 514, 516
project
execution teams 385
management structures 385
organisation 378
resources 379
selection 392–3, 395
Project Based Organisations (PBO) 533–4
prototyping 280–1
psychographic segmentation 129
psychological profile 160, 161–2, 417
public
investment 98
opinion 260
pull innovation 207–9, 231
push innovation 231

quality function deployment (QFD) 271
entrepreneurship 432
product and service development 386,
396–9, 405

radical innovation 21, 22, 36, 39, 40, 232,
248, 249–50
Railtrack 402
random inputs 168
ranking 395
rapid prototyping 396, 398
rapid, reiterative redevelopment (RRR) 375

Raynor, Michael 128–9
Raytheon 262
RCA 252
realisation phase 478–80
recognition 171, 569
recombinant innovation 228, 238
reconfigurations 32
RedHat Software 487
reduced instruction set computing (RISC) 118, 490
Reed, Richard 171–2
reflection 563
reframing 255–6, 287
regression analysis 306
regulation 228–9, 238
regulatory
capabilities 146, 148
changes 431
Reilly, Richard 381
relative advantage 188–9, 310, 311
research and development (R&D) 205, 507–8
globalisation 85–7
innovation measurement using 525–6
product 507
process 507
resources
anticipation of 320–5
capabilities 146, 147–8
innovation management 16, 17–18, 25–6, 40–2
results orientation 55, 56
retrieval of knowledge 468–70
return on investment (ROI) 510, 511, 515, 516
return on sales (ROS) 516
Reuters 436–7
reverse engineering 506
reward 569
rewriting the rules 6, 9, 11, 32
Rickman, Andrew 438
ring-fencing 127
ripple strategy 474
risk 327
assessment 317–20, 378
as probability 316–18
perceptions of 319–20
-taking 185–6, 569
rituals 173–4
Roberts, Ed 300, 433
Rogers, Everett 188–9
Roper, Andrew 208

Rothwell, Roy 19, 341
Route 128 419–20
routines 269
Ryanair 515

Sadangi, Amitabha 56
safety credibility 313
SAP 282
SAPPHO project (SPRU) 509
scale 508
scenarios 327
  building 394
Schein, E. H. 172–4
Schumpeter, Joseph 58, 71, 421–2
Schwab, Charles 281
Schwab Foundation 57
Science and Technology Research Unit
    (SPRU) 135, 509
science linkage (SL) 483, 484
science parks 419–20
science strength (SS) 483
Scotch 272
scouting for ideas 275–6, 287, 437
S-curve analysis 91
search strategies 253–64
  implementation 264–9
Second Life 278
secrecy 105–6
sectoral
  forums 346
  networks 345
segmentation
  business markets 121–3
  consumer markets 120–1
  product and service development 399
  sustainability 121–3, 128
sensitivity analysis 325
service development
  capabilities 400
  case study 407–12
  characteristics 373–4
  commercialisation 392, 393
  concept generation 392, 394
  customisation 373, 375
  development strategies 377–84
  exercises 404
  high innovators 382–4
  innovation 376–7

innovation management 401
organisation 385–9
processes 390–3
quality function deployment 386, 396–9, 405
resources 405–6
social impact 401–2
state-gate approach 390–1, 405
tools and technology 393–9
versus product development 372–7
Shaw, George Bernard 553
Shell 229, 276
Siemens Mercosur 85, 102, 114, 348
Silicon Valley 419, 421
simulated outcomes 395
simultaneity 374
Singer 23
skills development 180
Skoll Foundation 57
Skovlund, Soren 63
skunk works 554
Skype 9, 517–18
slack 181–2, 568, 569
small and medium-sized enterprises (SMEs)
  entrepreneurship 422–5, 445–6
  failure 13
social capital 113
social entrepreneurship 53–82, 283
  assumptions 65–6
  capabilities 72
  case study 76–81
  challenge 59
  characteristics 54–7
  corporate social responsibility 57, 60–1
  definition 73
  exercises 75
  funding 55, 58–9
  implementation 70
  innovation 54–7
  innovative organisation 71
  management 68–71
  networking 69, 71
  new ventures 414–16, 450, 451
  opportunism 69
  principles 58–9
  proactive linkages 69, 71
  resources 69–70
  size of organisation 63–4
  social impact 70–1

triple bottom line 57, 62, 73, 74
see also sustainability
social enterprise 73, 74
social impact
  globalisation 135
  knowledge 494–5
  networking 359
  organizing innovation 190
  product development 401–2
  service development 401–2
  social entrepreneurship 70–1
  socialisation 466
social interactions 133
Social, Technological and Environmental
    Pathways to Sustainability (STEPS)
    Centre 135
social venture funds 450
Society of Motor Manufacturers and Traders 343
socio-technical systems 125–9
solar energy 77–9, 81
sole proprietorship 448
Sony 488
  PlayStation 504
Sorensen, Lars Rebien 64, 277
Southwest Airlines 227, 515
space
  innovation 180–2, 283–4
  search, navigating 262–3
spaghetti model of innovation 340–1, 347
spatial clusters 345, 360
specialised supplier firms 425
Spengler, J. Murray 23
spider diagrams 191–2
spillovers 138, 142
spin-off/spin-out companies 421, 426–7, 429
'squeaking wheels' 210
stage-gate model 569
Staines, Christopher 77
stakeholder participation 267
stakeholders, social entrepreneurship 62–5
standards 106
Star Syringe 416
Starbucks 60
state-gate approach 390–1, 405
Stear, Rory 77
Stora 14
storage
  knowledge 468–70

service development 374
strategic
  advantages 30–2
  choice 16–17, 26
  clusters 395
  leadership 567–8
  style 87
strength of intellectual property 106–7
stretch goals 554
suggestion boxes 235
superstars 423–4, 451
supplier firms 425
supply-chain learning 343, 346, 361
support 180–2, 192
surrogate entrepreneurs 430
surveys 394
survival imperatives 4–6, 9, 16, 38
Sussex Manifesto 135
sustainability 36
  adoptio 106, 111, 126, 129
  alternative technologies 116, 117–18
  case study 141–5
  competitive advantage 145
  exercises 138
  forecasting tools 306–10
  globalisation 145, 147
  innovation 115–17
  networking 130–5
  new socio-technical systems 126–31
  novel niches 121–5
  open systems of innovation 130–5
  resources 138–9
  segmenting markets 121–3, 128
  users 123, 126–8, 138, 313–14
sustaining competencies 112–13, 149–50
Svenska Cellulosa Aktiebolaget (SCA) 132
symbiosis 255
symbols 174
system networks 341
systems innovation
  management 21–2
  sustainability 116, 126

tacit (implicit) knowledge 86, 464, 466,
    468, 498
tanda network 67
tangibility 373
targeting 334

Tata Consultancy Services (TCS) 88
Tata Corporation 215–16
Taylor–Nelson classification 121
technical entrepreneurship 162–3
technological opportunity 508
technology
    fusion 475, 478
    road mapping 552
    strength (TS) 483
    trajectory 87
    maturity 87
Technology and Engineering Consultancies
    (TECs) 531–7
technology cycle time (TCT) 483
technology drivers 508
Technology Forum 570
Technopreneur Promotion Programme
    (TePP) 6
timing 232, 332–4
Tokugawa, Yoshimune 235
Tomorrow's World 77
top management support 379, 381
Toshiba 488
total productive maintenance (TPM) 211
total quality management (TQM) 210
totally chlorine–free (TCF) products 132
Toyota 124–5, 210, 277
trade liberalisation 93, 113–14
Trade Related Intellectual Property System
    (TRIPS) 141, 482
Tranfield, David 478
transfer strategy 475
translating technology 105
transnational corporations (TNCs) 90
trends 394, 398
trialability 189, 310, 311, 312
triple bottom line 57, 62, 63, 74
TRIZ system 483, 498
trust 176–8
TUI 14

U-boat projects 272
uncertainty 327
    recognition of 315–17
uncontrollable factors 170, 433
understanding opportunities 164–7
university incubator 419–21, 425–9, 451
UnLtd 449

upgrading 107–8
user-centred design 267
user-led innovation 238
users 123, 126–8, 138, 266, 312–13
    active 278–9
    extreme 226, 256
    as innovators 222–6
    lead 287
Utterback, James 232

value, creating economic and social
    504–7
value-added 515–16
    within and across sectors 513, 528
value chains 138
    international 84, 102–7
    management 524
    product and service development 384
value model 511–18
value network 251
valued attributes 146–8
values 173
Venkataswamy, Dr G. 54, 55
venture
    capital 95, 421, 437–41
    capitalism 301
    credibility 171, 430, 520
    creation 519–26
vertical cooperation 353
Viagra 251
vicarious learning 313
viral marketing 72
visibility 313
vision 381
Vodafone 216
Voice over Internet Protocol (VoIP) 517
volunteers 570
Volvo 117
von Hippel, Eric 127, 222
Vonage 517
vulnerability 434

Wal-Mart 505
Watt, James 512–13
Web2.0 355
Webasto 279
Welch, Jack 183, 553
Wendling, Larry 272, 350, 570

Western Union 13
Whatif! 282
Wikipedia 55
Williamson, Audley 230–1
win–win
  combinations 71, 73
  relationships 557
Wipro Technologies 93
World is Flat, The: The Globalized World in the
    21st Century 84
Wright, Jon 171–2

Xerox 230, 252, 420, 424

Yahoo 436–7
YET2.com 283
Young Foundation 57, 350
YouTube 348
Yunus, Muhammad 55, 58

zaibatsu 97, 134
Zara 277, 294–5
ZML 505